he Hidden Psychiatr y
f the Old Testament

What has been is what will be,
and what has been done, is what will be done;
there is nothing new under the sun.
(*Eccles.* 1⁹)


He asks us to understand those who are sick in mind, for who among us knows reality? Hold no man insignificant and nothing improbable, for there is no man that has not his hour and no thing that not its place.
(*Sayings of the Fathers, cited in the RSGB Prayer Book*)


Banish anxiety from your mind and pain from your body.
(*Eccles.* 11¹⁰)

# Contents

# Foreword

Every reader of the Old Testament recognises that some of the characters who appear in its pages are psychologically odd. King Saul has periods of deep gloom, soothed only by music played by his servant David, but also behaves homicidally towards David when he offends him, and even throws a spear at his own son, Jonathan. The prophet Ezekiel sees strange, complex visions involving peculiar creatures, and engages in odd behaviour – lying on his side for weeks on end, and throwing cuttings from his hair and beard to the four winds as a symbol of the coming exile of his countrymen to Babylonia. And Job is surely deeply depressed. All this has long been known.

But no one has ever undertaken an exhaustive study of psychiatric conditions in the Bible, or tried to be more specific about them from a modern diagnostic point of view. The reason is obvious: most biblical scholars are not psychiatrists, and most psychiatrists are not interested in the Old Testament. George Stein, however, combines knowledge in both spheres. As an experienced consultant general psychiatrist, he is alert to hints of psychiatric conditions not only in the cases where even a layperson can see that characters are disturbed in mind, but also in many other places in the Old Testament. So he deals also with Jeremiah, who suffered from panic attacks, and with the portrayals of 'fools' in Proverbs, many of which, he believes, represent early descriptions of individuals with personality disorders. The Psalms yield a rich harvest of depressive symptoms, and the Old Testament includes several cases of suicide.

Two things are *not* on offer in this absorbing study. One is psychoanalysis. There have been many psychoanalytically driven studies of the Old Testament, but this is not one of them. Psychiatry is not psychoanalysis, but is the study and treatment of gross mental illnesses that cause crippling life problems. It is part of medicine, and is not the same as analysis, counselling or psychotherapy. Dr Stein's work on the Old Testament is not an attempt to look beneath the surface for underlying 'complexes', but a recognition of descriptions of symptoms that would be identified, if encountered today, as signs of mental illness. The descriptions of symptoms can be compared with the standard modern handbooks of psychiatric conditions, and often match remarkably closely.

The second thing that this book is not, is a guide to using the Bible as an aid in time of mental distress. There are, again, many such works, mostly from a Christian perspective, but Dr Stein's work is not religiously motivated: it is a historical study of psychiatric symptoms as described in an ancient document. For the most part the literature of the Old Testament is older than the Greek sources that are usually seen as the beginnings of an interest in abnormal psychology, and it describes a remarkably broad range of conditions. Of course it is not being suggested that the writers of the Old

Testament knew about such conditions as schizophrenia or bipolar disorder, but they did carefully describe symptoms that we would now attribute to those illnesses. Some of the writers may have suffered from such conditions themselves – the psalmists, for example, may in some cases have been depressed – or they may have known those who did: either way, they often show remarkable insight into how it feels to be afflicted in these ways. Where personality disorders are concerned, they tend to explain the behaviour they produce as the result of moral wickedness, especially in the book of Proverbs and the other 'Wisdom' literature, whereas we should probably refrain from ethical criticism; but they do recognise the signs in question.

Some may accuse this book of anachronism: surely we cannot find in such ancient literature descriptions of psychiatric conditions only identified in the twentieth century? The 'strong' form of this objection is a relativistic belief that there is absolutely nothing in common between ancient and modern societies, so that any interpretation of ancient people in modern psychological terms is bound to be anachronistic. This is a philosophical question, and 'hard' relativists of this persuasion cannot be convinced by any amount of empirical evidence. But there is also a 'soft' version of the objection that simply says we do not have any evidence of psychiatric insights in ancient literature such as the Old Testament. That version is surely demolished by the material presented here.

Showing that there are descriptions in the Old Testament of symptoms that match those in current psychiatric manuals is not 'reading in' modern ideas of psychiatric diagnosis; it is simply recognising empirical evidence where it can be shown to exist. I think that one reason why many have been unwilling to see psychiatry in the Bible, whereas there is less resistance to finding its beginnings in Greek and Latin literature, is a sense that the ancient Israelites were more unlike us than were people in the classical world. Dr Stein's work helps to call that very assumption in question, by demonstrating that mental illnesses we recognise today occurred in ancient Hebrew culture just as they did in other ancient societies, and just as they do, cross-culturally, today. People who think mental illness is just a social construction will not be convinced by this; but most of those who have encountered mental illness, as doctors, patients or patients' family members, are likely to find that the Old Testament describes, sharply and illuminatingly, symptoms that can still be recognised today.

John Barton, FBA

*Emeritus Oriel and Laing Professor of the Interpretation
of Holy Scripture, University of Oxford*

# Chapter 1

# Introduction

This book is about the psychiatry to be found in the Old Testament. More so than the religious literature of all the nations that came before Israel, or all of those that came after it, the Hebrew Bible contains a veritable treasure trove of psychiatric case histories, psychiatric insights and references to all variety of matters related to mental disorder. Without knowing exactly what they were writing about, the Old Testament scribes and their editors were sufficiently compassionate and sensitive to a wide range of psychiatric issues to record them in their main religious text, the Hebrew Bible. We do not know why this should be and much of this psychiatry comes to us hidden within the sublime verse of the Bible, hence the title *The Hidden Psychiatry of the Old Testament*.

Work on this book started many years ago, at around the time of my son's bar mitzvah, a confirmation ceremony which usually takes place at the age of 13; my son is now in his late thirties. Our rabbi, knowing I was a psychiatrist, asked me to 'take a look at Saul' and do talk on the topic to my fellow congregants. Saul did indeed turn out to have a mental illness, as explored in Chapter 6.

But there was another reason for pursuing this enquiry, concerning suffering as a result of mental disorder. The Bible is about religion, but it is also about the human condition and most importantly this includes the problem of suffering. What had become perplexing in my day-to-day work as a community psychiatrist was that I was bearing witness to a truly enormous amount of human suffering resulting from the common mental disorders. But it struck me that all this terrible suffering I had seen was rarely if ever mentioned during religious services or indeed in any of the biblical passages we read. Might it be that the ancient Israelites were somehow immune from mental disorder? Or was it that without modern medical knowledge it was simply not recognised? A third possibility might have been that mental illness was in fact obscurely alluded to within the text, but for the most part was concealed.

What this book seeks to address is the question of whether the ancient Israelites suffered from psychiatric disorder, and whether this was the same psychiatric disorder as is seen today, and if so how it appears in their religious text, the Hebrew Bible. Today, we can describe the main symptoms of mental illness, and thereby diagnose its presence, and we also have some effective treatments, even though the cause for the most part remains elusive. The ancient Israelites had virtually no knowledge of any mental disorder apart from a suggestion that sometimes a person's soul was troubled or not in harmony with itself or with God. Although they sometimes described a person as mad, they did not know that such an entity as mental illness existed, and so perhaps we should forgive them for omitting to mention the problem.

The preparation of the talk on King Saul involved reading the whole book of Samuel. It became apparent that Saul was not the only depressive in 1 Samuel: Hannah, the mother of Samuel, had also been depressed about her infertility. Further searching revealed that a great deal of mental disorder is actually present in the Old Testament, but lies buried beneath many layers of myth, history and religion, making it almost invisible to any but the psychiatrically trained eye. Uncovering this confusion was in some ways similar to the work of the archaeologist sifting through thousands of shards of ancient pottery to find a few inscriptions, in order to be able to make intelligent guesses as to what life was like in the ancient world, what foods people ate, where they traded and what their rules were, and so gradually build up a picture of life in the ancient world. Instead of sifting through shards of ancient pottery, the task here was to examine ancient biblical verses, remove their history, and any fictional elements, and to see whether there was any evidence of psychiatric disorder.

Once such verses had been uncovered, the next task was to ascertain the era from which they dated, what they might have meant to the people of the day and, finally, whether they showed any link to our modern concepts of mental illness. Gradually, as the story unfolded, it seemed as if quite a large chunk of modern psychiatry, at least in the form of a thumbnail sketch, was actually buried within this ancient text, but this was far from obvious. However, given the chaotic way in which the Bible was put together over many centuries, it is hardly surprising that the psychiatry it contains should also appear in a jumbled and confusing manner.

Deviant human behaviour comes mainly in two forms: crime and mental disorder. Crime is well described and was also well understood in the ancient world. The Bible contains a vast catalogue of all sorts of crimes that human beings perpetrate against one another other, and many are described in lurid detail. To complement its description of crime, the Bible elaborates on a complicated scheme of crime management, in the form of a huge number of laws which help to regulate the way society works. The Torah itself has a total of 613 commandments covering every aspect of life, from the most serious crimes of murder to the most trivial episodes of cross-dressing. In later generations, these were further elaborated in the Talmud and the Halachic law of the Middle Ages, to the extent that a modern glossary of Jewish law extends to no fewer than four massive volumes (Elon, 1994).

Crime has always been newsworthy. By contrast, mental health has never held much sway, and does not seem to have attracted the interest of the scribes of yesteryear or those of today, but the suffering resulting from poor mental health can be just as great as that caused by crime, often more so. Schizophrenia will destroy the fabric of a young person's personality. The parents will be distraught and will remain so for the rest of their lives. Manic depressive illness often destroys careers, marriages and relationships and sometimes lead to suicide. The wife of the alcoholic psychopath comes to the clinic with a black eye and bruised arms. The depressive weeps uncontrollably in the public space of the clinic. The statistics also speak of the huge toll imposed on society by mental disorder, with depression carrying the second greatest burden of disease in the world today. In modern

Western societies suicide is now the foremost cause of premature death in people aged between 18 and 45. Many families will have a member with a serious mental illness or know of someone with such a condition.

Crime does not have the same continuous draining effect as mental illness has on those who are affected by it, directly or indirectly. Thus, although some of the adverse consequences of insanity became recognised from the Middle Ages onwards, it is only in the last two centuries that the massive scale of the human suffering due to mental illness came to be recognised. Psychiatry started as a medical specialty in the late 18th century. Even in the 19th and 20th centuries, mental disorder was stigmatised and psychiatry regarded as a Cinderella medical specialty. Perhaps we should be more forgiving of the ancient world for not paying much attention to these conditions because in those times whole populations might be decimated by epidemics of infectious disease, wars and famines; common medical disorders lacked any treatment and so had a high mortality. Even in Greek or Roman society, there is little evidence of schizophrenia being mentioned (Evans et al., 2003). The earlier Egyptian and Sumerian religious literatures also make little or no mention of these conditions. Psychiatry of course did not exist in the two great empires of Egypt and Sumeria. Strictly speaking, then, there is no psychiatry in the literatures of these nations or in the Bible, but mental disorders, and mental symptoms probably did exist at the time as they probably always have done. So how, then, did psychiatry, albeit in a concealed form, enter into the biblical text?

## The Old Testament

Ancient Israelite history starts with the story of God commanding Abraham to leave the ancient Mesopotamian city of Ur and travel to Canaan, where he is to take up residence and become the founding patriarch of the Hebrew nation. Sometime later Moses leads the Hebrew slaves out of Egypt and back into the land of Canaan.

Thus religious tradition tells us that Israelite civilisation found its origin in the earlier civilisations of Egypt and Mesopotamia. No doubt geographical proximity, trade and law also helped to foment cultural links with these two much larger nations. Another important and more local contribution, which is often overlooked, came from Canaan itself and the small Kingdom of Ugarit, which lay to the north of Canaan and flourished from 1600 to 1300 BCE, before it passed into oblivion. It gave the world its first alphabetic language, Ugaritic, from which the later Greek and Hebrew alphabets stemmed. Alphabetic language enabled these two small nations to write in a far more simplified and repeatable way than the hieroglyphic and cuneiform scripts of ancient Egypt and Mesopotamia permitted, and it also allowed more complex topics to be discussed.

Ancient Hebrew texts were generally written on papyrus, which deteriorates after a while and so there was a need for repeated copying. This sometimes led to copying errors, but it had the advantage of letting the scribes who did the copying tinker with text, make small alterations here and there, and in effect edit the text. This repeated copying helped to retain the more worthy passages as well as censor out material they thought was poorly written, or of poor quality or thought to be irrelevant. In contrast, the cuneiform religious scripts of Mesopotamia were etched into clay and then fired, and so were set in stone right from the start; because the tablets did not deteriorate there was little need for rewriting, and so the early canonical texts of these ancient religions did not undergo a process of redaction as was the case for the Hebrew Bible. The bulk of this redaction was done in the early post-exilic period, between 586 and 400 BCE, and no doubt greatly enhanced both the literary quality and the religious meaning of the work. The text was edited and re-edited over hundreds of years. It seems some but not all of these editors (redactors) were sympathetic to psychiatric material.

The first part of the Old Testament, the Torah (the five Books of Moses), describes the creation and the early history of the Hebrew nation, its patriarchs, the exodus from Egypt and the sojourn in Canaan, and takes us up to around the 12th century BCE. It has very little psychiatric content. The religion of this period, like that in all ancient Near Eastern cultures, was very much a religion of the cult. Scribes were few and far between, and they worked for the priests and kings, who were the government of the day. In effect, the scribes were their civil servants. Indeed, their writings reflect the orientation of a good civil servant, being largely impersonal, factual and supporting the establishment of the day. Personal feelings were either never mentioned or were later redacted. Also, there was little or no psychiatric material in the religious writings of the other ancient Near Eastern cults. The polytheistic religions of the region were similarly largely based on mainly cultic preoccupations and lacked any significant personal information. Thus, while some of the gods of Egypt or Mesopotamia might have had human or animal-like characteristics, the human beings of these societies were depicted very much as pastiches and rarely had much character or individuality, and certainly it was rare for personal feelings or any mental symptoms to be included in these texts.

Very gradually, particularly with the writings of the prophets, individual feelings and emotions began to appear, morals and ethics began to replace laws and crimes, and religious literature became a little more personal. Such a transition had already started in pre-exilic times and can be seen in the Psalms: some (the royal psalms) concern the king and the royal court but others, such as the psalms of lament, and especially those of individual lament, are about the trials and tribulations of ordinary people, which we can readily identify with.

But the critical change from a cultic religion to a more personal one only came with the exile, where the cult could no longer exist as a state with a government, and this followed from the siege of Jerusalem and the deportation in 586 BCE. In his monumental tome *The History of Israelite Religion* Yehezkel Kaufmann, Professor of Religion at the Hebrew University, writes:

> The fall of Jerusalem is the great watershed in the history of Israelite religion. The life of the people of Israel came to an end; the history of Judaism began. To be sure, the people lived on and were creative after the fall, but the form of their life and the condition of their existence and creativity were radically transformed. Israel ceased to be a normal nation and became a religious community.

This development was rooted in the ideas of the pre-exilic religion, both priestly and prophetic. Its manifestations are the crystallization of the Torah book and the transformation of Israel into a witness to the nations, the bearers of a universal religious mission.

The goal of the religious ferment that arose in the age of the fall was to found the life of the nation on the basis of the word of God alone. Earlier the word of God was but one of several manifestations of Yahweh's presence in Israel: its land, its sanctuaries, its monarchy, its prophecy were also all vehicles of the divine grace: Israel's history and life as a whole were the expression of the divine will. With the fall and the exile, however, the simple faith of the people in the working of the divine in their own lives and the indwelling of God's presence among them was shattered. Yahweh had turned his back on them. The life of Israel was no longer the arena of his mighty acts. With land, Temple and King gone only one contact with the holy was left. The divine word. (Kaufmann, 1961, p. 447)

All that remained of the ancient Hebrew religion were its written texts and it no longer served the power structure of a state. This led to a transformation from a religion of the cult to a much more personal religion; the individual, his feelings, oddities, his personal foibles, moods and any strange behaviours and all matters we now consider to be psychiatric gradually assumed much greater importance. They were no longer edited out of the text by a civil service of scribes.

One editor, the Deuteronomist(s), who was responsible for the major historical books of the Hebrew Bible, known as the Deuteronomic history, may also be important, as commentators note that the Deuteronomist had a much more humanistic and compassionate approach, and this meant that any personal feelings recorded in an original story were not censored out but were retained in the text. Such personal feelings played only a very small part in the polytheistic religions of Israel's neighbours, but this new and much more personal and compassionate religion seems to have facilitated the inclusion of psychiatric material in the text.

## Psychiatry

Psychiatry was a much later creation and did not exist in the empires of the ancient Near East and so strictly speaking there is no psychiatry in the Bible. But mental disorders, and mental symptoms probably did exist in the ancient world, as they probably have always done. In their monumental tome on the history of psychiatry, Wallach and Gach (2008) define the period before psychiatry properly took off in the 18th century as *proto-psychiatry* and this broadly covers the classical period, the early Middle Ages and the Renaissance. They include ancient Greek psychiatry within their proto-psychiatry but nothing earlier, so presumably the psychiatry in the Bible would count as the very earliest phase of proto-psychiatry. So how, then, did psychiatry, albeit in an almost concealed form, enter the biblical text?

A tradition of religious prophecy starting at around 1800 BCE existed in the ancient Mesopotamian city state of Mari. Prophecy had probably always existed throughout the ancient Near East and the prophets were prone to bouts of ecstasy. Towards the end of the 7th century BCE, two of the great literary prophets, Ezekiel and Jeremiah, began to criticise the wisdom of their political leaders, as well as the ethical and moral standards of the citizenry. Both these prophets also wrote in detail about their own personal feelings, their joys and their sadness, and as both seem to have a mental disorder their books provide splendid autobiographical accounts of their conditions, bringing a whole catalogue of mental symptoms into their texts.

The greater bulk of the Bible was written, or at least finalised, during the early post-exilic period, a time of great intellectual fervour, from 586 BC to 400 BCE, and it was during this period that psychiatric symptoms began to enter numerous books of the Bible. The biblical writers sensitively recorded their observations on suffering in their fellow man as well as the stranger behaviours of some of the great biblical heroes; they seemed to have some concept of mental symptoms, but no concept of mental disorders as we understand them today.

Ancient Greek civilisation (dated from around 600 BCE to 600 CE) in its later period began to make a separation between medicine and religion. Simon (2009) provides an overview of the Greek perception of mental disorder and suggests there were three ways the Greeks recorded insanity: first, there is a lengthy poetic tradition of madness and tragedy appearing in the Greek epics and dramas; second, the great philosophers Plato, Aristotle and others conceived of good mental health as being due to a balance of forces within the soul; and finally, the more secular and medical model begins to emerge around 400 BCE with the medical writings of Hippocrates and others. Some of the early biblical accounts of mental disorder such as the insanity of King Saul seem to follow in the tradition of a Homerian epic, while the later Wisdom literature of Sirach has rather more in common with the secular Hippocratic tradition in its treatment of mental disorder.

A notion common to both the Hebrew and Greek writings is the idea of a life force or breath which figures prominently in the way mental turmoil is described in both traditions. Thus the Greek word *psyche* originally denoted breath, or the force that kept human beings alive but persisted in the spirit of the dead. This is similar to the Hebrew word *ruah*, also meaning breath, and both words gradually came to signify spirit, mind or even soul.

The classical period saw some advances in medicine, particularly the development of the occupation of the physician, as well as the comprehensive writings of anatomical scholars such as Galen. There were even descriptions of a few psychiatric disorders, such as manic depression, by Arateus of Cappadocia in around 150 CE. However, there was little advance in psychiatric knowledge. Despite a huge increase in literacy and written material from such times, Evans *et al.* (2003) could find no description of schizophrenia in the whole Greco-Roman classical literature.

Psychiatry as a medical specialty began to emerge only towards the end of the 18th century and the early 19th century, and was born out of the chaos and misery of the Industrial Revolution. Prior to the 18th century, the feudal economy was mainly agricultural and most people lived in villages or small towns, where there might have been one or two village idiots, but there was little point in housing them in an institution offering neither cure nor any hope of escape. For the wealthy, the private mad-houses had already developed in the 17th and 18th centuries, providing a lucrative trade for their owners. However, with rapidly increasing urbanisation and industrialisation large numbers of impoverished and insane people flocked to the new cities. Any who were mentally unwell would be unlikely to be able to feed or care for themselves and sometimes in their more insane moments might commit dangerous or bizarre acts. If they were arrested, they had to be contained; and so asylums specifically for the insane were founded all over Europe.

In France, hospitals such as the Salpêtrière and the Bicêtre were founded and assumed the role of the care of the insane. Because they were said to suffer from 'mental alienation from society', their doctors became known as 'alienists'. In England Parliament passed a series of laws requiring each county to build a mental asylum to house insane people and by law the super-intendent of these asylums had to be a medical doctor. Thus the alienists of France and the medical superintendents of the asylums in England were doctors and became the first true practising clinical psychiatrists.

However, it was in Germany that academic psychiatry took off. The term 'psychiatry' (Greek *psyche* = mind; *iatros* = doctor) was first coined by J. C. Reil in 1808. It indicated that the physician should be able to use his own mind as an agent of healing (Marx, 1990). The first professor of psychiatry, appointed to the first chair at the University of Leipzig in 1827, was J. C. A. Heinroth, who wrote extensively about paranoid disorders. But it was the genius of the great German psychiatrist Emil Kraepelin (1856–1926) that made psychiatry the academic discipline it is today. He kept meticulous records on all his patients and in the fifth edition of his textbook, published in 1896, he was able to devise a diagnostic classification scheme that has more or less held up to this day.

He classified mental disorders into three groups: (1) organic psychoses such as the dementing illnesses and delirium, which all affected the brain; (2) the endogenous psychoses, which included both *dementia praecox*, a dementing illness of the young, now known as schizophrenia, and manic depression, now known as bipolar disorder; and (3) deviations of personality and various reactive states, such as anxiety, depression, hysteria and so forth.

For the next 60 years the Kraepelinian model held sway in asylum psychiatry. Precise diagnosis mattered little, as most patients never got better and the few who seemed to recover did so on their own accord – the diagnostic and therapeutic efforts (apart from the offer of asylum) of those caring for them played little part in their recovery. But in the 1950s a revolution swept through psychiatry: drugs were discovered which seemed to confer major therapeutic benefits. Antidepressants were developed for the treatment of depression and antipsychotics for the treatment of schizo-phrenia. Now for the first time diagnostic accuracy became a necessity, to ensure that patients received the correct drug. Flaws in the then current system for diagnosis soon showed up; thus, in America schizophrenia was diagnosed twice as often as in Europe but studies showed this was explained entirely by the different diagnostic criteria used by American and British psychiatrists (Cooper *et al.*, 1972). Some sort of standardisation in the way a diagnosis was made was now urgently required.

How was this achieved? This story starts with an American psychiatrist John Feighner, a professor at the University of Iowa, who introduced the first set of operational criteria to define a particular psychiatric disorder. His method was very simple – little more than a check-list of symptoms or behaviours for each mental disorder. All the psychiatrist had to do was tick off which symptoms the patient had, and if a sufficient number met the definition of the disorder then it could be diagnosed. His scheme was taken up and refined by the American Psychiatric Association in its *Diagnostic and Statistical Manual of Psychiatric Disorders* (DSM). The third edition of that work, published in 1980, represented a complete catalogue of all psychiatric conditions. The most recent refinement of the scheme is DSM-5 (2013) but it differs little from the fourth edition, published in 1994, indicating that the definitions have probably now reached their optimum in the light of current psychiatric knowledge. A similar scheme is set out in the *International Classification of Diseases* (ICD), published by the World Health Organization. Both schemes are reliable and good but the American scheme is easier to use and because it is based on check-lists it can more readily be applied to pieces of literature or historical writings such as those found in the Bible.

But there should be a note of caution. Psychiatric illness is very dependent on the culture within which it finds itself and it can change dramatically over time and between cultures. The DSM system is useful for American psychiatrists treating their clientele in modern New York or Chicago but this society is very different to ancient Rome or the small city states of ancient Israel such as Jerusalem, Bethel or Shiloh. There is a massive distance in both time and culture, and what applies in one culture may not in another.

However, when it comes to comparing the individual symptoms there is very much less confusion. Thus the grief of yesteryear is the same as the grief of today and perhaps in both instances sometimes this is a depression. A racing heart suggests tachycardia; waking up weeping in the night is insomnia, possibly depressive insomnia. An impulse to hang one's self possibly represents a suicidal thought. Thus, the cross-cultural problems of the DSM system apply to a much greater extent to a completed diagnosis of mental disorder rather than to its constituent individual symptoms and behaviours.

Making a psychiatric diagnosis in the modern clinical world is not a simple exercise: it requires a trained psychiatrist to conduct a thorough clinical interview. This is because only a person with suitable training will know what to look for and will be able to exclude the irrelevant and yet maintain therapeutic contact throughout the interview. Even so, the initial diagnosis is sometimes wrong, but repeated meetings with the patient, taking into account the views of close relatives, the medical records, the effects of various treatments as well as observing the patient's condition over time will ensure that the diagnosis gradually becomes more robust and validated and therefore useful.

Obviously, none of these secondary validations can be applied to the diagnosis of a character in the Old Testament. However, it is possible to make a reasonable diagnostic guess on the basis of a patient's case records. Such paper-based diagnoses have often been made on the biographies of great musicians, artists and writers in recent years and are best described as 'literary diagnoses'. They are far less robust than a diagnosis based on a clinical interview; thus, for example, it would be unwise to institute any sort of treatment based on a purely literary diagnosis. All the diagnoses made on passages and characters in the Bible in this book are of a literary type and therefore hold a considerable degree of uncertainty but it will be for readers themselves to decide on the 'goodness of fit' between the biblical text and the respective diagnostic criteria as laid out in the DSM scheme.

## Methodology and scope of this book

This is a book about the very early history of psychiatry, which, as noted on page 5, is sometimes known as proto-psychiatry; it is not about religion but because its source is a major religious text, it is of course closely linked to religion. It seeks to understand all the references to mental disorder in one of the greatest of the sacred texts, the Old Testament (OT). The historical period covered is approximately from 1100 to 200 BCE; it includes the apocrypha but not the New Testament. There are occasional references to the psychiatric literature of the ancient Greeks, the Talmud, the Dead Sea Scrolls and other later Jewish sacred writings, but only in the context of their relevance to the OT. Similarly, there are some references to ancient Egyptian and Mesopotamian psychiatry but this is not a comprehensive examination of the psychiatry of these ancient cultures.

The approach is mainly secular but it is impossible to ignore the religious meaning or the sublime quality of the writing in the Old Testament. Fortunately most of the passages which carry a psychiatric content have little religious significance, and so are not controversial. They relate to the day-to-day life of the ancient Israelites and for the most part these passages are very rarely used in either the Jewish or Christian liturgy.

The scope of the psychiatry adopted here is that of a community practitioner of general psychiatry but some topics which occur in the psychiatric literature have been included, as well as tasks that psychiatrists sometimes undertake. Psychoanalytic interpretations have largely been eschewed, mainly because I am not a psychoanalyst, but also because this is a highly culture-bound discipline of the 20th century and the text does not really lend itself to any sort of psychoanalytic examination. Indeed, I was surprised to find so few psychoanalytic articles on the Old Testament, with the possible exception of Job and his suffering.

Once a verse is identified as having psychiatric content, some associated biblical literature (highly selected) on the verse has been added for context. Another author might have selected a different piece of biblical commentary but without some sort of selection the work would have ended up as a multivolume unreadable tome. I have also added in the psychiatry relevant to the verse. Neither the psychiatry nor the Old Testament scholarship is original, nor is it at a particularly high level. All that is novel is the linking together of the biblical verse with its proposed psychiatry.

These verses and the symptoms they describe form the core of this book. In certain places groups of symptoms cluster together in a way suggestive of a particular psychiatric disorder and in these cases diagnostic schemes such as DSM-5 have been applied. In appropriate places biblical verses are paired with the individual diagnostic criteria as laid out in DSM-5. Surprisingly, despite the huge cultural gulf and the 2,500-year time gap and misgivings that the DSM system would not work, the biblical authors write so sensitively and accurately about the mentally ill that most of the DSM-5 definitions seem to fit the Old Testament very well. Rather than label an Old Testament character with a particular diagnosis it may be to safer to think in terms of what sort of diagnosis would be given today to someone presenting with the behaviour and symptoms described in the biblical text, as this avoids the possibility of any sort of derogatory or stigmatising labelling. At the end of some chapters there is an appendix which includes a description of the psychiatric disorder written for the benefit of the lay reader. This is written at a level of knowledge no greater than that required of a medical student.

## The plan of the book

When I started to put the book together it seemed logical to place the chapters and topics in the order of the books of the Bible, that is, starting with Genesis and ending with Malachi, but it soon became clear that the distribution of the psychiatry bore no relationship to this sequence. Thus the Torah (the five books of Moses) has almost no psychiatry in its bounds. But the Prophets (*nebi'im*) and the Writings (*Ketubim*) abound in psychiatry and so a grouping by psychiatric topic became more logical. Also, a few major characters in the Bible sometimes had a particular condition and so merited a whole chapter to themselves. Thus, the final order is a compromise mainly based on psychiatric conditions but also including some chapters on particular important characters. A limited amount of similar literature derived from neighbouring ancient Near Eastern cultures, known as the para-biblical literature, has also been included, because this gives the historical and geographical context of where the biblical literature came from. It also has an independent significance in the history of psychiatry as these descriptions probably represent the first descriptions of many different mental disorders.

It starts with the Book of Job, a somewhat obscure text, but it is obscure precisely because it contains a huge treasure trove of psychiatry in Job's autobiographical account of his depression. This is followed by other biblical books containing affective disorder, including Jeremiah, Lamentations, Psalms and Saul in the Books of Samuel. There is a chapter here on suicide. Next comes a section related to schizophrenia, in particular the autobiographical account of schizophrenia that Ezekiel gives us . This is followed by a much shorter chapter considering any evidence for chronic mental illness and other references to psychotic disorders. A third section describes personality disorders in both men and women. This is followed by a group of topics that are difficult to classify but individually do not merit a whole chapter and have been placed in a chapter on psychosomatic and miscellaneous affective disorders; there is then a chapter on children. The ancient Israelites liked their drink and so there is a chapter on alcoholism. The book ends with a chapter on the Book of Sirach (*circa* 200 BCE) because he seems to have written about a wide variety of psychiatric symptoms/syndromes, albeit at a rather superficial level, and his compendium makes his work a sort of mini-textbook of psychiatry. Appendix 1 at the end of the book lists all the psychiatric symptoms and disorders in the OT together with their biblical references. Appendix 2 describes all the translations of the Bible referred to in this book.

In all cases the biblical verses themselves are quoted, in order to give readers the opportunity to make up their own mind as to whether the particular verse is truly describing psychiatric material, or whether the link is too tenuous to be meaningful. Working with the sacred texts has been a profoundly elevating experience and I hope that readers will also derive a similar pleasure from this enquiry, even those who disagree with my findings.

## Acknowledgements

Many people have helped me in this work, but above all I must acknowledge the assistance and wisdom of Professor John Barton, of Oriel College, Oxford, who corrected some of my more outlandish ideas, and directed my reading to the best of modern biblical scholarship, gave me numerous cups of tea, and helped to ensure the completed text at least made some sense. My colleague at work of more than 30 years, Dr Morris Bernadt, served in a similar role with regard to the psychiatry, correcting most of the more obvious errors, but some errors certainly remain in this large work and these are wholly my responsibility and I hope readers will forgive me for them. The assistance of Professor Nicholas Wyatt for translating the Ugaritic passages, and of Dr Walid Abdul-Hamid for highlighting the Surpu, a Mesopotamian prayer, is gratefully acknowledged. Ralph Footring helped to convert an untidy manuscript into the splendid text of this book, and I was grateful for the support of my publisher, Holly Buchanan of Hamilton Books. Finally, I need to thank my wife Suzanna and both my sons Benjamin and Joseph for their patience and support while I went off to delve into some huge books about the Old Testament as well enjoy many hours of contented sleep in the Maughan Library of King's College London.

## References

American Psychiatric Association (1980) *Diagnostic and Statistical Manual of Mental Disorders* 3rd edition (DSM-III). Washington, DC: American Psychiatric Association.

American Psychiatric Association (1994) *Diagnostic and Statistical Manual of Mental Disorders* 4th edition (DSM-IV). Washington, DC: American Psychiatric Association.

American Psychiatric Association (2013) *Diagnostic and Statistical Manual of Mental Disorders* 5th edition (DSM-5). Washington, DC: American Psychiatric Publishing.

Cooper, J. E., Kendall, R., Gurland, B., *et al.* (1972) *Psychiatric Diagnoses in London and New York*. London: Oxford University Press.

Elon, M. (1994) *Jewish Law: History, Sources, Principles Volumes I–IV*. Translated from the Hebrew by Bernard Auerbach and Melvin Sykes. Philadelphia: Jewish Publication Society.

Evans, K., McGrath, J. and Milns, R. (2003) Searching for schizophrenia in ancient Greek and Roman literature: a systematic review. *Acta Psychiatrica Scandanavica* 107 (5): 323.

Feighner, J. P., Robins, E., Guze, S. B., *et al.* (1973) Diagnostic Criteria for use in Psychiatric Research. *Archives of General Psychiatry* 26: 57–67.

Kaufmann, Y. (1961) *The History of Israelite Religion.* Original Hebrew published 1937. Translated and abridged by Moshe Greenberg. London: George Allen and Unwin.

Marx, O. M. (1990) German Romantic Psychiatry. *History of Psychiatry* I: 351–381.

Simon, B. (1978) *Mind and Madness in Ancient Greece: Classical Roots of Modern Psychiatry.* New York: Cornell University Press.

Wallach, E. R. and Gach, J. (2008) *History of Psychiatry and Medical Psychology.* New York: Springer.

World Health Organization (1992) *Tenth Revision of the International Classification of Diseases and Related Health Problems* (ICD-10). Geneva: WHO.

# Chapter 2

# Job: a man with severe depression

## Introduction

The book of Job has been hailed as one of the great literacy masterpieces of the Old Testament. Apart from the prologue and the epilogue, it is written entirely in biblical verse and so is the longest single piece of poetry in the Old Testament. The book is about suffering and faith, the suffering of the innocent, and the struggle Job has in maintaining his faith in the face of great torment. The popular view of Job is of a man of great stoic patience who endured everything that God and Satan threw at him, without complaint. He is mentioned in the New Testament in the Epistle of James – 'Behold we count them happy which can endure. You have heard of the patience of Job' ($5^{11}$) – and the phrase 'the patience of Job' remains in popular usage to describe the ability to endure great suffering without complaint.

According to Gordis (1965) this popular image of Job has survived because few readers get beyond the prologue and into the main part of the book, the dialogues, where a very different Job emerges, one who is far from patient, and is angry with his comforters and angry with God. He repeatedly asserts how unfairly God has treated him, because he has done nothing wrong, yet is punished by great mental torment. He wants to prove his innocence in court and take out a lawsuit against God, with some kind of an independent umpire to judge the case. Sometimes, in his critique of God his language is quite intemperate, not falling far short of blasphemy. These dialogues contain his debates with his three comforters, Eliphaz, Bildad and Zophar, on topics such as punishment, sin, the suffering of the innocent, whether God is helpful or not, the doctrine of reward and retribution – all in sublime biblical verse.

The psychiatry in the Book of Job is fairly obvious and there is nothing new in saying Job was depressed. However, a detailed scrutiny of the book reveals a comprehensive catalogue of most of the common symptoms of depression; indeed, the verse is so clinically accurate that modern diagnostic criteria for depression can be applied to his illness and this exercise forms the main part of the present chapter.

## Authorship, place and date

No one knows who wrote the Book of Job, nor the land where it is placed, nor the era when it was written. Most of the books of the Old Testament are probably composite products, having several authors and editors. The book starts with a prologue and ends with an epilogue, both of which are fairly short. These have the familiar style of a biblical narrative, similar to that found in the tales of the great patriarchs, having an almost fairy-tale-like quality. Some have likened the writing in these sections to that found in Genesis. In between the prologue and the epilogue are the dialogues (chs 3–27), all written in verse. They speak with one passionate voice and tell a story of depression and suffering. There is some speculation that another person wrote the prologue and epilogue because the style and content are so very different to the dialogues.

With regard to the name 'Job', Gordis writes:

> Ewald has suggested that it is derived from the Arabic Awab meaning 'he who turns to God'. The name has an analogue in A-ja-ab, the King of Pella mentioned in the Tel-el Amarna letters. Meyer identifies Job with Jobab, a name found in the genealogy of Esau and Jobab is used in the apocryphal Testament of Job. The most likely explanation is that iyyob is a Hebrew folk etymology of a previously existing Semitic name, being a passive participial noun from the verb ayob 'to hate hence the hated, persecuted one'. (Gordis, p. 67)

Most biblical scholars have suspected the writer must have suffered from some sort of personal agony. Thus for example Pope writes:

> The author himself has probably experienced physical and mental agony since it is hard to understand how one could have written such material without a personal knowledge of suffering ... although Job's biblical outcry resembles some of the bitter outcry of the psalms of lamentation. Lamentation however was a common literary genre of the ancient near East.

Pope recognises the writer himself as the true sufferer, as do most biblical commentators, but lacking any medical knowledge makes no sort of guess as to what Job was suffering from. In this chapter we look at what precisely Job's condition was, and consider the extent to which it corresponds to depression as we understood it today.

Unusually for a piece of Old Testament literature, the book lacks any reference to the Hebrew Patriarchs or indeed any of the other early heroes of the Bible. As Pope suggests, there is no certainty that the author was an Israelite, or that the original language was Hebrew. The book has numerous Aramaisms, and on linguistic grounds alone Tur-Sinai suggests that the original language was the Aramaic of 7th-century Babylon. The French scholar Guilliuame proposes that it was Arabic. An Egyptian origin was proposed by Humbert because of its description of the *Leviathan*, which may resemble a hippopotamus, and the *Behemoth*, which may be similar to a crocodile, both creatures of the River Nile. Most scholars seem to favour biblical Hebrew as the initial language, but this was not the Hebrew of the Jerusalem Temple.

The location of the story is also obscure. The book starts with the line 'There once was a man in the land of *Uz* whose name was Job'. Such a place is actually named in the Book of Lamentations ($4^{21}$) in a parallel with Edom. Quite possibly the writer wished to convey the notion of an obscure place, somewhere in the east, to give the tale a sense of mystery.

Of the early versions presently available to us, that in the Greek LXX (the Septuagint) is considerably shorter than that in the MT (Masoretic Text), with the Hebrew version having around 2200 poetic stichs and the LXX one around 1850 stichs, although there is general agreement that the Hebrew version was the original. There are also some minor differences in the expressions of religious belief. Thus Job had little belief in the afterlife and was sceptical about resurrection, and so in the Hebrew version Job asks 'If a man dies, can he live again?' By contrast, in the Greek version the question is changed into a statement of fact: 'If a man dies, he will live again'. Similarly, in the Greek version the final verse confirms the afterlife: 'And Job died, an old man and full of days; *and it is written that he will rise up with those whom the Lord raises up*' (42$^{17}$). The italicised section is only in the LXX, not in the Hebrew version. Possibly at the time of the earlier Hebrew versions (?7th–5th centuries BCE) the notion of an afterlife was poorly formed, but by the time of the LXX (3rd century BCE) it would have been almost heretical not to believe in an afterlife and this may explain the discrepancies. Other differences include a rather longer section devoted to Job's wife, who complains about how much she has suffered bearing her children while witnessing Job's agitation and misery. These small differences do not affect the psychiatry of the book, as the verses reporting his depression are broadly the same in both versions.

The Book of Job is discussed in the Talmud in a typical Talmudic debate. Thus a certain well known Rabbi said Job never existed but he is only a typical figure and a parable. In response to this assertion R. Samuel ben Nachmai disapproved of calling Job a parable. R. Joshua ben Hyracanus maintained that Job served God purely out of love. R. Shemon ben Lakesh taught that Job never existed and is not destined to exist either. But this does not contradict opinion cited by Bar Ka'pra that Job lived in the days of Abraham. Say therefore that Job did exist but his trials never existed. So then why were the trials attributed to him in the text? He answered 'to teach that, had such trials befallen him, he would have been able to withstand them' (Jerusalem Talmud: Sotah 5:6, quoted in Spero, 2009).

The time of composition also is uncertain. Job-like stories go back to the second millennium BCE in the earlier Mesopotamian literature (see Appendix 1). There is no mention of the national catastrophe of the exile anywhere in the Book of Job, and because this event dominated many of the biblical books of this period, an early post-exilic period is probably excluded. The prominent place of Satan in the prologue was probably a Persian influence, and because of this Gordis suggests composition during the Persian period (i.e. between the 6th and 4th centuries BCE). He explains that Satan was not originally a Hebrew concept, because it was incompatible with Israelite monotheism, where a single God was responsible for both the good and evil. During the Persian period, Jews came into contact with Zoroastrianism and its doctrine of 'two forces' in the universe. Thus Ahriman was the God of darkness and evil, and Ahura-Mazda the God of light and righteousness. This dualism offered a simple answer to the problem of evil, and so freed God from being responsible for evil and malevolence. Such dualism was in conflict with the by then all-powerful Hebrew monotheism and so Satan never became an independent deity in Hebrew theology. Satan first appears in the Hebrew literature in the Book of Job, gradually assuming increasing prominence in later Hebrew and early Christian theology as a quasi-independent symbol of the forces of evil. The Hebrew word *Ha-satan* as the prosecuting attorney in the heavenly court probably dates from this period (Gordis, p. 71).

Late composition is also unlikely, as Job is mentioned in the works of Ben Sira (3rd century BCE) and also large tracts from the Book of Job were found in the Dead Sea scrolls (Qumran literature, 1st and 2nd century BCE).

## The story

The book is in three sections: the prologue, which is a short introduction describing Job's catastrophic losses; followed by the dialogues, which are debates between Job and his three comforters, covering a wide range of theological and philosophical issues, followed by the speeches of Elihu; and the epilogue, written in the same style and probably by the same person as the prologue.

The prologue introduces us to all the main characters of the book. We discover Job, a man of great integrity and virtue, who lives in the land of Uz. He is an upright and pious man who fears God and leads a blameless existence. He is very wealthy and has many thousands of farm animals and has seven sons and three daughters, and always makes his sacrifices to God.

The second scene opens up in heaven; God is with his sons and Satan is said to be one of them. Satan walks up and down the earth looking for people who have disobeyed God's laws. He is like a celestial intelligence officer who must report to God in the heavenly council. One day God says to Satan, 'Have you considered my servant Job, there is no one like him, he is a blameless and upright man'. Satan replies that maybe he is like that because you (God) have given him so much wealth, but if you test him and touch all he has, he will curse you to your face. God accepts the wager and says to Satan 'You may go out and test him, but the only condition is that he is not to be damaged'.

The prologue continues to describe the testing of Job. Four messengers bring Job successive tales of catastrophes. The first messenger arrives and tells him the Sabeans have killed all his oxen, donkeys and servants; a second messenger brings news that a fire has burnt all his sheep and servants; the third messenger reports the Chaldeans have killed all his camels; and finally the fourth messenger reports that a great wind has destroyed his house where his sons and daughters were dining and they too are now all dead. Job accepts all these tragic losses with dignity and utters his timeless verse ($1^{21}$):

> Naked I came from my mother's womb
> and naked shall I return there;
> the Lord gave, and the Lord has taken away;
> blessed be the name of the Lord.

Job holds on to his faith and to test him further Satan inflicts a skin disease on him which gives him sores all over his body. His wife, seeing his terrible distress and that there is no end to his suffering, says to him 'Curse

God and die' – believing that if he curses God, then God will surely kill him and end the whole terrible saga. Also his three friends Eliphaz, Bildad and Zophar are so shocked to see his state of misery that they sit with him in silence for seven days.

## The dialogues

A good man who has done nothing wrong is afflicted by a set of terrible disasters. Why should such a terrible injustice occur? The prologue sets the scene for the next section of the book – the dialogues between Job and his three friends. After each of Job's speeches, one of his 'comforters' replies, and there are three such cycles. Job cannot understand why he is made to suffer so much and declares repeatedly he has not committed any sin. His three comforters explain that he must have sinned a very great deal, and the proof of this is in the severity of his illness and the terrible suffering he has to endure. This can all be explained in terms of the dogma of the day, the divine laws of retribution, and his friends do so repeatedly throughout the dialogues. Job brings to the debate the issues that trouble him, and depression and mental torment are among them. Although Job is seeking to prove his innocence, his comforters fiercely reject his questioning of God, and bring further charges against him, making him feel even worse. Job believes that it is God who has made him feel so poorly.

Thus a severe illness was nothing less than a punishment from God – and this was because of one's sins. But Job feels he has done no wrong; he is certain of this and protests his innocence throughout the book. He has an overwhelming wish to clear his name and is prepared to take God to a court of law to prove his innocence, but in the end he is so intimidated by God's awesome majesty and so fearful of his terrors that he withdraws his suit against God.

Unable to prove his innocence he ends with a tragic soliloquy (ch. 29) with his final appeal to God to answer him directly (ch. 31) At the end of the dialogues another character appears, Elihu, who is much younger than Job's three friends, and he intervenes because he thinks the three comforters have not explained their case of conventional religious dogma properly, and Elihu delivers a further six speeches in answer to Job (chs 33–77).

It is within these debates that the great religious and philosophical themes that have so fascinated readers of the book are to be found. Habel lists some of the topics thrown up in the dialogues. These include the concepts of knowledge, of suffering, particularly the suffering of the innocent, of the human condition itself, of the mystery of evil and why the wicked prosper, of the rule of God, of the nature of divine justice (theodicy) and of the natural order, as well as some less weighty themes, such as the role of friends and relationships between man and animals and parallels between man's behaviours and those of some animals. Throughout there are small sections of biblical wisdom, similar to those found in Proverbs. A whole chapter is devoted to the search for wisdom, which concludes that it can never be found. These topics are all extensively dealt with in the huge religious literature on Job and so will not be elaborated on here.

The book ends with the epilogue, written in the same almost fairy-tale style as the prologue, probably by the same person. God accepts Job's story and his innocence, and castigates his three friends for having 'not spoken of me what is right as my servant Job has done'. Job's farm animals are not only all restored to him but he is given twice the number he had before. He acquires seven new sons and three new daughters – all more beautiful than his first family of children and the book ends on a happy note ($42^{16}$):

> After this Job lived for one hundred and forty years and saw his children and children's children four generations and Job died old and full of days.

## The description of depression in the Book of Job

The Book of Job provides one of the most magnificent and comprehensive description of depression in world literature, all written in exquisite biblical verse. However, the depression is far from obvious from a superficial read with an untrained eye. Depressive symptoms are dropped like asides from a Shakespearian play, almost randomly throughout the text. Job's depression can best be seen by breaking down the depression into its constituent parts, namely the individual depressive symptoms. They appear as metaphors for all variety of stories, but when examined in detail they reveal the sensitive perceptions of the poet and his wish to communicate his depression to the world. When all the verses suggestive of any depressive symptom are collected together and placed under a single roof, the comprehensive nature of his description of depression becomes obvious. Although Job himself is the main sufferer, depressive symptoms sometimes flow from the mouths of his three friends, suggesting the true sufferer must have been the writer himself. In the process of writing about his own depression and suffering, the author throws the door open to a wide range of theological and philo-sophical questions, most of which will touch every generation and even today mostly remain unanswered.

In the following sections the verses describing his depressive symptoms have been grouped together and placed in the order as found in DSM-5. This is accompanied by a brief description of the surrounding religious text. These comments have in the main been taken from the erudite com-mentaries of biblical scholars, mostly from the work of Hartley (1988) but also Cohen (1946), Gordis (1965), Habel (1985) and Pope (1965). A detailed account of the phenomenology of depression as it is understood today, mainly for the benefit of non-psychiatric readers, taken from Lee (2007), is given in Appendix 2. The order of symptoms of major depressive disorder in the Book of Job is:

(1) General depression, sadness, misery, weeping
(2) Anhedonia (loss of a sense of pleasure)
(3) Weight and appetite disturbance
(4) Sleep disturbance
(5) Agitation and retardation
(6) Fatigue or loss of energy

(7) Feelings of worthlessness, excessive or inappropriate guilt
(8) Diminished ability to think or concentrate
(9) Recurrent thoughts of death or suicidal ideation, planning or suicidal attempts
Other depressive symptoms
(10) Psychic pain
(11) Paranoid symptoms
(12) Psychotic symptoms
(13) Panic disorder

## (1) General depression

Job has many complaints against God because he feels he has been very unfairly treated and is so miserable that he wants to take God to court. Chapters 29–31 comprise his formal court testimony, which will be brought to a pubic assembly and addressed to God. However, one section of his plea ($30^{15-31}$) contains a large concentration of depressive thoughts and symptoms and most probably would have been written while the writer of Job was in a state of acute depression. Biblical text is on the left-hand side of the page and comments are on the right.

| | Biblical text | Comments |
|---|---|---|
| $30^{15}$ | Terrors are turned upon me; | Heb. Terrors=*ballahot* ?panics |
| | my honour is pursued by the wind, and my prosperity has passed away like a cloud. | Great losses have occurred; I am nothing now |
| 16 | And now my soul is passed out within me; | Weak in body and mind |
| | days of affliction have taken hold of me. | My suffering will continue |
| 17 | The night racks my bones and the pain that gnaws me takes no rest. | Sleep disturbance, unremitting pain ?physical or ?psychic pain, or both; no respite from the pain |
| 18 | With violence he seizes my garment; he grasps me by the collar of my tunic. | Unpleasant sensations in his neck ?choking for breath as in a panic attack |
| 19 | He has cast me into the mire and I have become like dust and ashes. | I am of little worth; low self-esteem |
| 20 | I cry to you and you do not answer me; I stand, and you merely look at me. | My pleas fall on deaf ears I stand= as a lawyer, pleading in court |
| 21 | You have turned cruel to me; with the might of your hand you persecute me. | Heb *Akzar*= cruel, used to describe the cruel ferocious leviathan paranoia, feeling persecuted by God |
| 22 | You lift me up on the wind, you | I am lifted up ?Up in mood or in my fortunes – but your ulterior motive is to cause a great fall (Habel, p. 421) |
| | make me ride on it, and you toss me about in the roar of the storm. | Tossed about ?Up and down in mood |
| 23 | I know you will bring me to death and to the house appointed for all living. | Thoughts of death Everyone is going to die |

| 24 | Surely one does not turn against the needy, when in disaster they cry for help. | Job accuses God of a lack of compassion for the needy when they are in a crisis and seek help |
|---|---|---|
| 25 | Did I not weep for those whose day was hard? | By contrast I wept for the needy |
| | Was not my soul grieved for the poor? | empathy for the poor |
| 26 | But when I looked for good, evil came; and when I waited for light, darkness came. | pessimism<br>Heb (*le-or*)=light or good fortune<br>Heb *Opel*=darkness, sinister |
| 27 | My inward parts are in turmoil, and are never still; | Stomach churning?<br>?gastric anxiety in depression and panic |
| | days of affliction come to meet me. | more suffering ahead |
| | I go about in sunless gloom; | Heb *qdr* means blackened |
| 28 | I stand up in the assembly and cry for help. | My legal plea to the assembly<br>Distressed and seeking help |
| 29 | I am a brother of jackals | I wail like the jackal, but like the jackal no one listens to me; |
| | and a companion of ostriches. | likewise no one listens to the ostrich |
| 30 | My skin turns black and falls from me, and my bones burn with heat. | Physical sickness. Job's skin disease<br>?Fever as well (Hartley, p. 406) |
| 31 | My lyre is turned to mourning, And my pipe to those who weep. | Mourning, but no bereavement<br>lyre=*kinnor*, pipe=*ugub* |

This passage is replete with depressive symptomatology; thus depressed mood has several mentions, sunless gloom (28), mourning (31), grieving for the poor (25), weeping for those whose day was hard (25), the voice of those who weep (31). Biological symptoms of depression are also present: sleep disturbance, 'the night racks my bones' (17); also anergy and weakness, 'my soul is poured out within me' (16); and several different types of depressive thoughts, including feelings of rejection, 'cast me into the mire' (19) as well as some nihilistic thoughts, 'become like dust and ashes' (19).

There are thoughts of death, 'you bring me to death' (23), paranoid feelings about God, 'with your hand you persecute me' (21); and this sorry state will continue, as 'days of affliction come to meet me' (27) and 'days of affliction have taken hold of me' (16).

As well as depression, there is a suggestion of anxiety/panic disorder. There is a sensation of choking: 'he grasps me by the collar' (18); gastric anxiety, 'my inward parts are in turmoil' (27); as well as emotional lability, 'you toss me about' (22).

It is barely conceivable that a person in a normal frame of mind could have composed verse with such a wealth of depressive symptoms and the writer would have had to have been in a state of deep depression to have composed such poetry. Perhaps, like the writers of some of the psalms of lament (e.g. Psalm 88) he was writing while in the midst of an episode of depression.

### Weeping
Weeping is mentioned in ch. 16, when Job describes how God 'has gnashed his teeth against me' and 'has slashed open my kidneys and shown no mercy', and all this has made him miserable and weep (16[16]).

My face is red with weeping,
and deep darkness is on my eyelids...

The King James Version for 16 has the much more poignant 'And on my
eyelids is the shadow of death', which Cohen suggests means that he feels
that the approach of death is so close that it casts a shadow over his eyes.
Verse 16[20] goes on:

My friends scorn me;
My eye pours out tears to God.

Cohen has 'even though my friends have deserted me, and even deride me,
my streaming eyes are turned to God'. Weeping, particularly in men, for any
prolonged period, usually signifies severe depression.

### Putting on a front

Sadness is also mentioned in the context of Job's legal case against God
when he wonders whether he should drop his case against God, forget about
his depression and just display a cheerful front (9[27]):

| | |
|---|---|
| If I say, I will forget my complaint; | forget the court case |
| I will put off my sad countenance | drop my usual sad face |
| and be of good cheer. | put on a cheerful front. |

For short periods many quite severely depressed patients can cover over their
depression and put on a cheerful front. Some may conceal their depression
from their loved ones, displaying a happy mien for longer periods, but later
may be found dead (having killed themselves) by shocked relatives. Perhaps
Job is alluding in this verse to this ability of some depressives to put on a
cheerful facade and hide their agony.

### Morning depression and diurnal mood variation

Depression is often very bad in the morning and improves as the day goes
on. This is known as 'diurnal mood variation'. It usually signifies fairly severe
depression. There are two possible references to this (7[17,18]):

What are human beings, that you make so much of them,
that you set your mind on them [human beings],
*visit them every morning,*
test them every moment?

Hartley writes 'Job experiences God's vigilance as unremitting oppression.
Instead of praising God, Job uses this as a complaint against God's continual
effort to find and punish his every flaw. God's testing becomes too heavy
for him, a mere mortal, to bear'. These theologian's comments are quite
compatible with the psychiatry, where the only interest lies in the *time of the
day*. Thus the visits and oppressive testing by God all seem to take place *in
the morning*.

In ch. 24 Job is explaining the nefarious ways in which criminals carry out
their crimes. They seem to prefer to operate at night as it is dark and so there
is less chance of being caught (King James Version, 24[16,17]):

In the dark they dig through houses, which they marked for themselves in the daytime: they know not the light.

*For the morning* is to them as the shadow of death: if one know them, they are in the terrors of the shadow of death.

Hartley explains:

They [the criminals] do not want to have any risk of discovery, so they avoid the light. Their day is reversed. Morning fills most people with joy or expectation but it is for them a deep darkness (*salmawet*) because of the risk of discovery.

The shadow of death is not a good place to be, and it seems to appear in the morning. The text is about the fears of common criminals being caught in the act, but the writer seems to have drawn on his own experience of morning depression to empathise with the fears of the common criminal being caught in the morning in the aftermath of their night of crime.

God's oppressive testing also occurs in the morning, and so both verses point to the morning with a bad feeling, and so perhaps it was the writer himself who had the morning depression.

## (2) Anhedonia

This is a subtle symptom, but it denotes a loss of any sense of pleasure and is described in Appendix 2. Job compares himself to the plight of a labourer who is not being paid.

| | |
|---|---|
| 7²     Like a slave who longs for the shadow | |
| and like labourers who look for their wages | |
| ³     So I am allotted months of emptiness | emptiness = ?anhedonia |
| and nights of misery are apportioned to me. | misery = depression; |
| | ?depressive insomnia |

'Months of emptiness' suggests his episodes last for periods of months, which is the approximate duration of untreated depression (usually around 6 months). The paid labourer can at least enjoy his wages but Job likens his fate to the unpaid labourer who has no reward or pleasure in his existence.

A further reference to possible anhedonia appears in $9^{25a,b}$, when Job compares the swiftness of the passing of his day to that of a runner, that 'his days are not good'. Much depends on the translation of the Hebrew *tova*, meaning 'good'.

    [a] My days are swifter than a runner
    [b] They flee away they see no good

Other translations for line 25b point to 'loss of joy', which is more obviously anhedonic. Thus some alternative translations for 25b are:

•    They fly away without a glimpse of Joy (New Interlinear Version – NIV)
•    Seeing no happiness in their flight (Jerusalem Bible)

- They fly without one happy ray (Moffat translation)
- They flee without experiencing pleasure (Hartley)

All the latter translations convey a meaning of a lack of joy or any sense of pleasure, suggestive of anhedonia.

## (3) *Weight and appetite changes*

Disturbances of appetite, usually loss of weight and loss of appetite, are common in severe depression, and there are two possible references to this:

| 6⁶ | Can that which is tasteless be eaten without salt, or is there any flavour in the juice of the mallows? | food is tasteless, or altered sense of taste unpleasant taste |
|---|---|---|
| 7 | My appetite refuses to touch them; they are like food that is loathsome to me. | loss of appetite the food tastes unpleasant I hate the food |

Two different depressive symptoms are reported here: first, an altered sense of taste, so that the food tastes unpleasant, or bitter, or has no taste at all; and secondly, a loss of appetite altogether. Several different translations of the Hebrew *halamot* (mallows) are given; Hartley (p. 131) gives as alternative translations 'slime of purslane, a weed'; the Targum has 'the white of an egg'; Tur-sinai has 'saliva of dreams'; and Pope has 'Slimy cream cheese'. However, all meanings point to an unpleasant taste. The altered sense of taste reported here is important as this is sometimes associated with hallucinations of smell which Job also seems to sometimes suffer from.

A second reference to loss of appetite suggests a physical illness rather than simple depression, as the weight loss appears to be greater than normally encountered in depression.

| 33¹⁹ | They are also chastened with pain upon their beds, and with continual strife in their bones, | Heb. *Hukah* = chastened, or indicted as in a legal case |
|---|---|---|
| 20 | so that their lives loathe bread, and their appetites dainty food. | They cannot eat bread No appetite even for nice food |
| 21 | Their flesh is so wasted away that it cannot be seen; and their bones, once visible, now stick out. | Severe weight loss |

The anorexia here seems to be profound: not even dainty food can be eaten, and there is severe weight loss. The speaker here is Elihu and he is describing how God will treat a man who sins to make the sinner change his ways. The anorexia and bone pain are not with Job, but they are God's punishment for the sinner.

## (4) *Sleep disturbance*

There are several references to sleepless nights and three specifically to nocturnal panic, and also to depressive sleep disorder:

| $7^3$ | So I am allotted months of emptiness, and nights of misery are appointed to me. When I lie down I say, 'When shall I rise?' | Anhedonia (see page 67) depression in the night anxiety about the insomnia and the passage of time in the night passes all too slowly (see page 165) |
| 4 | But the night is long, and I am full of tossing until dawn. | tossing and agitation in the early hours suggest early morning wakening |

In $7^3$ the subject is already in a state of misery (depression); the night is long and there is insomnia, and before dawn he wakes up in an agitated state and is tossing about. Such a pattern is known to occur in depression and is known as 'early morning awakening', making it likely that Job is complaining of depressive insomnia (see Appendix 2, page 71).

## (5) Agitation and retardation

Agitation refers to a sense of inner restlessness and Job seems to describe this well ($3^{26}$):

> I am not at ease, nor am I quiet;
> I have no rest, but trouble comes.

Hartley (p. 100) explains:

> Job concludes his lament with the assertion 'I have no ease' and he is despondent over his lack of rest. Dhorme (1984) distinguishes the Hebrew words *salak* = mental rest; *saquat* = quiet; and *nuag* = rest in general. The rest Job seeks is one of both repose and tranquillity, and in such a state of deep serenity he may be able to enjoy life to the full. Conversely a person lacking in repose is filled with deep agitation encompassing physical torment, agony of mind and social discomfort. Job exclaims 'trouble comes', the Hebrew word *rogez* is used, denoting emotional turmoil and thus he reports his agitated state which is due to a complete lack of peace.

Hartley is a theologian not a psychiatrist. He bases his description of agitation on this verse, and it appears to be similar to the modern concept of agitation, as for example in an agitated depression.

A second possible reference appears in one of Zophar's speeches, when Job accuses his 'so called friends' of being unhelpful. Zophar is stung by this criticism ($20^1$):

> Then Zophar the Naamathite answered:
> 'Pay attention! My thoughts urge me to
> answer because of the agitation within me.

The Hebrew for agitation here is *Husi bi*, which the MT translates as 'my haste in me'. Beer, Fohrer and others read *rahas libbi* as 'my heart is agitated'. Note that it is not Job who is the agitated person here, but Zophar, one of his comforters. The writer of the Book of Job, like that of Tobit, likes to distribute his depression widely among the cast of his drama.

*Retardation or psycho-motor slowing*

Psycho-motor retardation is the obverse of agitation. Instead of pacing up and down as an agitated person might do, patients slow down and may just sit still for long periods, speak very slowly, or in extreme cases do not speak at all and become mute. The text gives three possible examples. Thus at the end of the prologue, Job rejects the counsel of his three friends, who are so shocked to see the abject state he is in that they all sit together in silence for seven days.

| | | |
|---|---|---|
| $2^{12}$ | When they saw him from a distance, they did not recognise him, | they = his comforters, |
| | and they raised their voices and wept aloud; | Eliphaz, Bildad and Zophar weeping |
| | they tore their robes and threw dust in the air, upon their heads. | Traditional mourning rituals |
| $^{13}$ | They sat with him on the ground for seven days and seven nights, | Job and his friends are mute for 7 days |
| | and no one spoke a word to him, for they saw his suffering was very great. | |
| $3^1$ | After this Job opened his mouth and cursed the day of his birth.... | His first words are depressive, suggesting this is depressive mutism |

A period of seven days for muteness and for mourning runs through the OT. Thus Joseph mourns for his father Jacob 'and he observed a time of mourning for his father for seven days' (Gen $50^{10}$). Ezekiel was mute for 7 days as he sat with the exiles: 'And I sat there among them stunned, for seven days' (Ez. $3^{15}$). The seven days of mourning has been institutionalised into Jewish burial rituals, when the bereaved will sit together with friends and relatives for seven days after the death of a loved one, in a mourning ritual known as sitting *shiva*.

A second reference to muteness comes in one of Elihu's speeches. By this time Job's three comforters are fed up with him and are no longer able to argue against Job, but Elihu still has a lot to say.

| | | |
|---|---|---|
| $32^{15}$ | 'They are dismayed, they answer no more; | Heb. *Hatat* = dismayed |
| | they have not a word to say.' | They = Eliphaz, Bildad and Zophar |
| | | Silent = ?muteness |

The King James Version has 'They left off speaking' and the MT 'his words are departed from them'. The sense is they cannot get it together or think of what to say and so cannot speak. Such transitory loss of speech is common in depression and if prolonged is called mutism.

The Hebrew *Hatat* means be dismayed, but also be shattered or broken. It implies the fear, shame and confusion that arise from defeat. Here the friends are daunted from further debate with Job but now Elihu takes the stand (Hartley, p. 435). There is no mention of how long the silence lasts, and the passage continues with Elihu declaring that he is full of words and will give his opinion.

In ch. 29 Job is the speaker and is describing his many good deeds. He tells us that he cares for the blind and the lame, the orphan and the widow. Everyone will be so utterly amazed by this that they will be unable to speak.

| 29⁹ | the nobles refrained from talking, | silent and ?mute |
| | and laid their hands on their mouths; | |
| 10 | the voices of the princes were hushed, | |
| | and their tongues stuck to the roof of their mouths. | ?mute |

The writer would have been familiar with the inhibition of speech and muteness sometimes associated with a low mood as he mentions this three times. Only Ezekiel reports states of muteness more often.

### (6) Fatigue or loss of energy

This is criterion 6 in the DSM-5 scheme and is described in Appendix 2, page 69. The Book of Job has four possible references to weakness and weariness. Chapter 6 is a lament where Job hopes that God will deliver the final blow against him and let him die, but he also alludes to his weakness.

| 6¹² | Is my strength the strength of stones, or is my flesh bronze? | strong hard material extremely strong material |
| | In truth I have no help in me, | No. I am weak |
| | and any resource is driven from me. | My strength has been taken away (?by the depression) |

Job asks a rhetorical question as to whether he has the strength of stones or bronze. The answer is no, his affliction has taken his strength. His complaint is about the loss of strength or weakness (Hartley).

A second reference to weariness comes in 3¹⁷,¹⁸, when Job is talking about how everything comes to rest in Sheol, where there will be a relief from weariness.

> There the wicked cease from troubling,
> and there the weary are at rest.
> There the prisoners are at ease together,
> they do not hear the voice of the taskmaster.

Hartley explains:

> There is complete rest for the weary in Sheol. Even the wicked (*Rasah*) are quiet and no longer stir up trouble, whereas usually the life of the wicked is full of turbulence. Prisoners are also at ease and no longer hear the terrifying shouts of the task master.

Sheol seems to be a sort of rest home and a 'low-energy place' but the rest there has a pleasant quality of a relief as well.

A third possible reference to low energy appears in 17⁷ᵇ,

| 17⁷ᵃ | My eye has grown dim from grief, | Heb *me'ka'as* = grief |
| ᵇ | and all my members are like a shadow. | |

The Hebrew *yetsura*, = members, also means 'frame of me' and refers to his limbs, and Hartley interprets 7b to signify general weakness. Whether this is a physical weakness or mental weakness or a bit of both is unclear.

A fourth possible reference to weariness comes in Eliphaz's third speech in his critique of Job's harsh attitude to the poor.

22⁷    You have given no water to the weary to drink,    Thirst combined weariness
       and you have withheld bread from the hungry.     Not eating

Eliphaz lists all of Job's sins and argues that Job lacks compassion for the thirsty and the hungry. Thirst is combined here with weariness, which presumably signifies exhaustion. Thirst, and not eating or not drinking can occur in severe depression and patients in this state are usually very ill and totally exhausted. This may be a life-threatening symptom, particularly among the elderly, and can lead rapidly to severe dehydration and is one of the few indications for emergency ECT. Has this writer been through phases of not eating, not drinking and exhaustion, during one of his episodes of depression? We shall never know, but he seems to be able to write about it.

These four references to weariness and weakness may signify 'the low energy' or 'anergy' of depression as described in Appendix 2.

## (7) Feelings of worthlessness, excessive or inappropriate guilt

These are central to the psychopathology of depression. Depressive thoughts include a sense of worthlessness, low self-image, a sense of guilt or guilty pre-occupations over minor past failings, as well as ubiquitous feelings of despair and hopelessness, all of which are well represented in the Book of Job.

### Guilt

Guilt is an integral part of depression and depressive guilt is described in Appendix 2. Guilt is also integral to the religions of most of the Abrahamic faiths and so its meaning within the sacred texts is difficult to fathom. Thus on the Day of Atonement, all religious Jews are meant to express their guilt and to atone for their sins and there are similar passages in the Christian liturgy at Lent – but none of this is in the context of depression.

In the ancient world the situation is even more confusing because almost any serious illness was held to be a punishment from God because of a person's sins. If a person was sick then they must have sinned, and so should expect to feel guilt, and the path to a cure was to repent for one's sins. Job feels very ill but he does not think he has committed any sin.

Guilt in ancient Israel was recognised only in the context of a court case, when a person received a verdict of being guilty, or not guilty. The word *rasah* used as a verb meaning 'be wicked' came to denote guilt, as in the court case in the Book of Job. *Rasah* can also be an adjective and applied to a noun, as in 'the wicked criminal'. Themes of guilt and innocence pervade the Book of Job and a simple numerical analysis may be helpful.

Thus the adjective *Rasah* is widely and evenly distributed in the different books of the OT. By contrast, when *Rasah* is used as a verb, 'be wicked', it appears 11 times in the Book of Job, in Daniel 3 times and 2 times in Deuteronomy. This suggests some sort of pre-occupation with 'being wicked' in the Book of Job.

Job also frequently protests his innocence. The phrase 'I am innocent' appears no fewer than six times ($9^{15}$, $9^{20}$, $27^6$, $31^5$, $33^9$, $34^5$). The narrator in the prologue also supports this position and says 'Job did not sin' ($1^{22}$). However, on occasion, Job does admit that he sins: 'How many are my iniquities and my sins' ($13^{23}$).

There is a pre-occupation with the themes of both guilt and innocence (being not guilty) and, taken together with the numerous uses of *rasah* as a verb meaning 'to be guilty', it is reasonable to conclude that Job was very much pre-occupied by *feelings of guilt*.

Others, such as God, also think he may have sinned. Thus for example, ' If I sin, you watch me, and do not acquit me of my iniquity' ($10^{14}$). Zophar believes that Job must have been a really big sinner: 'Know then that God exacts from you less than your guilt deserves' ($11^6$). Eliphaz makes a similar remark: 'Is not your wickedness great? There is no end to your iniquities' ($22^5$). In both these verses the accuser is someone else, and this is compatible with the way guilt may appear in the more serious depressions, especially in psychotic depressions, as *guilty ideas of reference* (see Appendix 2, page 71). Job's comforters are probably no more than the creation of the writer and it is the writer who is the true sufferer of the depression. He sometimes admits to guilt, and at other times it is outsiders who accuse him of guilt and sin, and in these instances the phenomenology seems to correspond to guilty ideas of reference.

A further difficulty which no doubt puzzled Job and his comforters is that the entity of depression was unrecognised at the time and so there would have been no concept of guilt being a *symptom* of depression rather than a *cause* of depression. During biblical times the link between guilt and illness was one of causation. Thus, sin caused illness, guilt arose because of the sin, and prayer for forgiveness would lead on to redemption and cure.

The modern concept is quite the opposite. The illness (depression) causes the guilt, which is only a symptom of the depression and not its cause. The guilt in depression is usually inappropriate and excessive. Sin does not come into it at all. Neither Job nor his comforters would have had any idea about this more modern formulation.

What sense can we make of this? Job is clearly pre-occupied by themes of guilt and innocence. He is also obviously quite depressed as well, and so he probably did suffer from depressive guilt. But he cannot make any sense of it. The knowledge at the time does not permit the concept of 'psychiatric or depressive guilt'; nor does the language of the day have any word for guilty feelings. Guilt meant a conviction in the court and of committing some wrongdoing. Job knew that he did not have the guilt of having committed many crimes or sins – and he repeatedly points this out. He was not a criminal. His comforters just cannot accept this and they argue against him repeatedly on this point. In a less than subtle way, the writer explodes the whole doctrine of retribution and rewards and the then current theory that sin was the cause of illness.

Because guilt meant guilty purely in a judicial sense, the only way to redress this matter was to go to a 'court of appeal' and try to reverse the verdict that he sinned – and a cure would follow if he was vindicated. Taking

God to court would not be easy, but this is precisely what Job tries to do. What seems to have driven him to take this unprecedented step seems to have been his overwhelming feelings of guilt, completely unexplained by the theology of his day, but most likely the result of his depression.

## Self-loathing

Low self-esteem and poor self-image are common in depression and are usually associated with a lack of self-confidence. In more severe cases it may present as self-loathing. Direct expressions of self-loathing appear three times in the book. First (10[1]):

> I loathe my life;
> I will give free utterance to my complaint;
> I will speak in the bitterness of my soul.

Job hates his life, and he seems to attribute this to the 'bitterness' of his 'soul'. Unknowingly, but perhaps correctly, he is seemingly suggesting that his inner torment, namely his depression, is the cause of his self-loathing.
Second (7[16]):

> I loathe my life; I would not live for ever.
> Let me alone, for my days are a breath.

Pope explains that in the Hebrew, the verb *ma'asti*, meaning 'I loathe', has no verb following and so translators have added in 'my life' to make better sense of this verse. The word for breath, *hebel*, also means vapour. Job sometimes uses this word to convey a sense of futility caused by his sorrow (Hartley, p. 150) (9[21-23]):

> I am blameless; I do not know myself;
> I loathe my life.
> It is all one; therefore I say,
> he destroys both the blameless and the wicked.
> When disaster brings sudden death,
> he mocks at the calamity of the innocent.

Hartley explains 'I am blameless' refers to his defence against feelings of guilt and his feeling that God accuses him of wrongdoing. Paul (Bib 1958, 79, 545–7) argues that the phrase 'I do not know myself' is an expression denoting some insight into this mental disorder – he is quite beside himself. The self-loathing is also quite explicit here.
   The succeeding verse (22) contains the fundamental theological dilemma of the Book of Job. God punishes *both* the wicked and the innocent. Punishing the wicked makes sense – but why the innocent? In Job's mind God seems to 'mock' the innocent in their tragedies. Does he truly care for them? And why should the innocent deserve any punishment at all? This is one of the key questions thrown up by the Book of Job and one which theologians of every generation seek to answer – only to discover that no answer can be found.

*Low self-image*

Bildad's third speech starts with him singing the praises of God. He makes peace, he has any number of armies, the stars are impure compared to him, so how can man possibly match him:

| 25⁶ | How much less a mortal, who is a maggot, | Heb. *Rimma* =maggot |
|---|---|---|
| | and a human being, who is a worm! | Heb. *Tolea*= worm |

The worm is a creature of very lowly status in the animal kingdom. Hartley writes:

> A human being is but a worm which symbolises a wretched lowly existence, and having the smell of death about them. Illness and loss make his life so wretched that he feels like a maggot and he can look forward only to the grave where he will be consumed by worms. Bildad is seeking to show Job that his hope of defending his own integrity is absurd in the light of God's holiness.

Likening a human being to a worm is suggestive of a very low self-image for mankind.

*Hopelessness and despair*

A feeling of hopelessness is a common feeling for those facing great adversity and is also important in depression and is a known predictor for suicide. Chapter 17 is a painful lament where Job complains about his suffering and how he feels rejected by God. The lament begins and ends with expressions of his despair.

| 17¹ | My spirit is broken, | Heb. Spirit, *ruah*; broken=*Hebel* |
|---|---|---|
| | my days are extinct, | Life is fading away |
| | the grave is ready for me. | Death awaits |

Hartley explains:

> Job expresses the depth of his despair in three short lines. His spirit (*ruah*) and desire for life is broken (*Hebel*), a word which also means ruin, destroy. Depression is robbing his inner resources so that only the graveyard awaits him.

The chapter ends in a similar vein. There are also thoughts of death, another key depressive symptom, but these are not suicidal thoughts.

| 19¹⁰ | He breaks me down on every side, | He (God) has caused my breakdown |
|---|---|---|
| | and I am gone | I'm a goner |
| | he has uprooted my hope like a tree. | He has ripped my hope away |

Hartley writes:

> *He has broken me down*, Job charges God with stamping out his life. God has pounded him as though he was a fortified wall. The metaphor then changes to horticulture, *You have uprooted my hope like a tree*. When a tree is cut down, there is still hope that new growth can occur again – but once the roots are torn up and they die, all hope of any regrowth is extinguished forever.

The last four verses of ch. 17 also give an explicit reference to a disappearing hope which others cannot even see, and his hope and his person (life) will perish together.

| | | |
|---|---|---|
| 17¹³ | I look for Sheol as my house, | In Sheol the dead lived in houses. |
| | If I spread my couch in darkness, | |
| ¹⁴ | if I say to the Pit, 'You are my father', | |
| | and to the worm, 'My mother', or | |
| | 'My sister', | |
| ¹⁵ | where then is my hope? | I have no hope |
| | Who will see my hope? | no one can locate it |
| ¹⁶ | Will it go down to the bars of Sheol? | |
| | Shall we descend together | Both my life and my hope perish |
| | into the dust? | together |

Hartley explains: Job feels so abandoned by God and by his own relatives that he appoints the graveyard as his father, and its chief inhabitant, the worm, as his mother, a superficially comic yet also a deeply tragic image. He asks where his hope is, but no one answers and none is to be seen. His hope and his life will perish together.

In one of his most famous metaphors, Job also applies the workings of the weaver's loom to his life and how hopeless it all is (7⁷):

My days are swifter than a weaver's shuttle
and come to their end without hope.

The meaning of this verse is not immediately obvious from the English translation. It hinges on a wordplay for the Hebrew word *Tiqwa*, which can mean both 'hope' and 'thread' in the original Hebrew. Hartley explains:

Job feels his life is passing very quickly and this is similar to the rapid movement of the weaver's shuttle. His days whizz past, just like the flying shuttle of the loom. This means the weaving will end quite soon, and when the cloth is finished, the completed cloth will be cut from the thread (*Tiqwa*). The sense seems to be that while a slender hope (also *tiqwa*) of life persists, human beings can cling to their hope, but with death, both hope and life will be extinguished together. Job will have no more *tikwa* (hope and thread) and an ability to enjoy life. (After Habel, and Hartley)

A loss of hope also can also strike others in society, and as part of God's punishment for the wicked. Eliphaz describes how God will inflict terrifying sounds upon them, which will lead them to despair. The writer distributes his depressive symptoms to all and sundry in his book.

| | | |
|---|---|---|
| 15²¹ | Terrifying sounds are in their ears; | The wicked will hear unpleasant |
| | in prosperity the destroyer | sounds of destruction |
| | will come upon them. | |
| ²² | They despair of returning from darkness, | They lose hope |
| | and they are destined for the sword. | and will be killed |
| ²³ | They wander abroad for bread, saying | and end up destitute |
| | 'Where is it?' | |
| | They know a day of darkness is at hand. | |

The wicked will be destroyed but once they realise this is their fate they 'despair'. Their fall from having great wealth to a state of destitution is so great that now they must scavenge for their food. This theme of a fall from grace into a state of poverty is frequently mentioned by Job and is further discussed below.

Job often mentions the theme of the wicked or the wealthy losing all their riches and becoming poor, indeed this is one of the trials Satan inflicts on him in the prologue. There may however be other reasons for the emergence of this theme; *delusions of poverty* are a common type of delusion found in psychotic depression (which Job probably has: see below). People with delusions of poverty believe all their money has been stolen or lost and mutter such thoughts repeatedly and that they will be doomed to eternal poverty. An alternative explanation for his constant pre-occupation with poverty might have been his own state of penury. Thus in a country without any welfare benefits, an illness such as a severe depression which Job suffered from would probably result in a rapid descent into poverty. It is the writer who truly suffers from the depression, and perhaps it was the writer who became destitute once his depression overwhelmed him.

### Paranoid thoughts: persecuted by God

Although for most of the time Job is rational about his relationship with God, and keeps his faith and sings God's praises, on a few occasions he believes God is attacking him, spying on him and poisoning him – all typical paranoid thoughts, at times even bordering on paranoid delusions.

| 6[4] | For the arrows of the Almighty are in me; my spirit drinks their poison; | Almighty = *Shaddai* God is shooting arrows into him God is poisoning him |

A little further on he believes that God is spying on him (7[20]):

> If I sin, what do I do to you, you watcher of humanity?

Although the paranoia here is fairly clear, most commentators give this verse a literal interpretation. Thus Cohen writes for *watcher of men*, 'Here a bitter phrase is used in reproach of God's hostile espionage and his relentless scrutiny of man's most innocent conduct'.

Job describes how God is hunting him down and brings his troops against him:

| 10[16] | Bold as a lion you hunt me; you repeat your exploits against me | God hunts me down Heb. *hitpalla* = your skills |
| 17 | You renew your witnesses against me; and increase your vexation towards me; you bring fresh troops against me. | Others are used against me making things worse for me More troops to hunt me down |

These verses convey how frightened Job is of God's persecution; he is like a hunted animal and God's soldiers are out to get him. In most of the OT, God is held to be a protector but here Job seems to experiences him as a persecutor.

Job also says that God hates him.

16⁹ He has torn me in his wrath, and
hated me; he has gnashed his teeth          Heb: *satam* = hated
at me; my adversary sharpens his            Heb: *satan* = adversary, prosecutor
eyes against me.

Hartley (p. 260) writes:

> The word for hated (*satam*) and for adversary (*satan*) though different in
> meaning, rhyme in the Hebrew. Job is unable to fathom out God's role in his
> affliction, and fears that God has become his enemy rather than his advocate. It
> is the ultimate test. Job portrays God as a wild animal, voraciously tearing up
> its prey, its eyes fixed in a glassy stare snarling at its prey. Like this wild animal,
> God enjoys terrorizing his victim wearing down any resistance his victim can
> muster.

In ch. 19 Job repeats the thought of God's army attacking him as in a
military campaign (19¹¹,¹²).

> He has kindled his wrath against me,
> and counts me as his adversary.
> His troops have come on together;
> they have thrown up siege-works against me,
> and encamp around my tent.

Hartley writes:

> Job feels the full brunt of God's hostility as he regards Job as one of his
> enemies. The analogy of a military siege is used to describe his feelings. The
> tent (in a real military siege it would be a city) is surrounded; its weakest point
> identified and that is where the siege ramparts are built to breach the walls.
> Job highlights the brutality of the attack. With this hyperbole Job expresses his
> utter astonishment at God treating him so roughly.

The battlefield metaphor and its violence is repeated (16¹³):

> His archers surround me.
> He slashes open my kidneys, and shows no mercy;
> he pours out my gall onto the ground.

Habel also points out that uniquely for a book in the Canon, at times Job
writes about a very dark side of God. He sees him as an enemy, a spy rather
than a protector, a hunter and not a healer, a wild animal, and sometimes as
one who destroys rather than mends.

Being spied on, hunted, cut open, having God's armies against him
cannot be real but must be a reflection of Job's experience of a persecutory God. In severe depression, paranoid ideation, similar to this, is very
common, including paranoid thoughts about God. His paranoid thoughts
may even represent paranoid delusions, although without a clinical interview
this must remain speculative. An explanation in terms of depressive paranoia
makes sense today, but would not have been available either to Job or to
his readers in ancient Israel, since there was no concept of depression or
paranoia as we understand them today.

What is truly puzzling is how he could accuse God of all these horrendous actions and in effect commit blasphemy – yet his book still found its way into the canon. The traditional explanation is that God himself did nothing bad to Job: all this was inflicted on him by Satan as a part of Satan's wager with God as a test of Job's faith, as set out in the prologue. Job is quite unaware that it is Satan who has caused his suffering, but the reader will have been well briefed in advance about this secret wager so artfully placed in the prologue, and conveniently before the reader encounters these horrific anti-God diatribes. This will protect the reader from thinking as badly of God as Job seems to. Could it be that the whole story of Satan and his wager with God was a later addition by another scribe to neutralise Job's paranoia, and his powerful and near agnostic doubts about God? Who knows?

*Psychotic thoughts. Does Job have psychotic depression?*
Chapter 19 is a diatribe against God. Job writes that God has done horrible things to him. Far from being a compassionate God, he has tormented and humiliated Job, thrust him into the darkness and alienated his family from him. The language is passionate and against God that it might have been considered to be blasphemous. In the middle of this chapter are five verses ($19^{15-20}$) suggesting he may have been psychotic at the time of composition, indicating the possibility of a psychotic depression, a particularly malignant type of depression.

| | |
|---|---|
| $19^{15}$ My serving-girls count me as a stranger; I have become an alien in their eyes. | Feelings of alienation from the servants Their perception of me has changed *Not* my perception of them. |
| 16 I call to my servant but he gives me no answer; I must plead with him. | I have lost my authority. The servants hold me in contempt |
| 17 My breath is repulsive to my wife; I am loathsome to my own family. | ?olfactory hallucination. See note 1 thinks his own family hates him |
| 18 Even young children despise me; when I rise, they talk against me. | He thinks children have turned against him |
| 19 All my intimate friends abhor me, and those whom I loved have turned against me. | Similarly friends and family hate me ?ideas of reference |
| 20 My bones cling to my skin and to my flesh, and I have escaped by the skin of my teeth. | weight loss ?due to severe depression Origin of the English proverb |

All the biblical scholars who comment on these verses place a literal meaning on them, namely that it is quite true that the servants have turned against him, that friends and family also hate him, and that the little children are saying bad things about him and that his breath gives off a bad smell. By contrast almost any psychiatrist encountering a patient who says that little children are saying bad things about him, and that he gives off an offensive odour which his wife finds repulsive, will immediately wonder whether these are delusions and hallucinations and make a tentative diagnosis of psychotic depression.

Hartley provides the traditional explanation for the key phrase 'my breath is repulsive to my wife'. His breath was strange (*ruah* = spirit; *zarah* = strange). His foul-smelling breath makes him repulsive to his wife. Pope argues this is halitosis. No wonder the little children laugh at this smelly old man. However, no one actually complains of his smell and it is only Job who believes that he is giving off a bad smell, and this is known as an olfactory hallucination. Sims (p. 73) explains the phenomenology:

> Olfactory hallucinations occur in epilepsy, schizophrenia and organic states. The patient has an hallucination of smell. The smell may or may not be unpleasant but it usually has a special and personal significance, for example it may be associated with a belief that people are pumping a poisonous gas into the house. One patient said 'I smell repulsive, unbearable like a corpse, like faeces'. This particular patient killed himself. He felt that he would be intolerable in any reasonable society. In general those who report they can smell a strange smell usually have schizophrenia, while those who believe that they smell, or that they are giving off a strange repulsive odour have depression, usually psychotic depression and this appears to be the case with Job.

In verse 18, Job believes that even young children are saying bad things about him. The Hebrew *dibber be* means 'they jeer'. Those with psychotic depression commonly complain that they know or can even hear other people talking about them, usually saying something bad, or mocking them, or conspiring against them, and these are classed as paranoid ideas of reference. When such beliefs are held with delusional intensity this becomes paranoid delusions of reference. Job's beliefs are not delusional, but he seems to have ideas of reference about the young children who make malicious remarks about him. When combined with his possible olfactory hallucinations, this suggests psychotic depression. Psychotic depression should not be diagnosed lightly, and to do so without a clinical interview would today be considered a step in the dark, but the text seems to support this possibility.

Verse 20 features the phrase *escaped with the skin of my teeth*. Traditional explanations focus on his illness. Rashi writes 'All my flesh has been smitten with leprosy and worms except the gums of my teeth'. Ibn Ezra comments 'I escape only as teeth through the skin'. Cohen (p. 98) writes that the probable interpretation is that his entire body is ravaged by disease, so that even his teeth have fallen out and he is left with just his bare gums. Whatever the original meaning might have been, Job has enriched the English language with this well known saying, which has come to mean a very lucky escape.

### (9) Recurrent thoughts of death or suicidal ideation, planning or suicide attempts

The final criterion for major depressive disorder in DSM-5 relates to thoughts of death and suicide: 'recurrent thoughts of death (not just fear of dying) recurrent suicidal ideation with or without a specific plan for committing suicide'.

Job appears to have frequent thoughts of death, and death wishes, a wish never to have been born, but there are no direct suicidal thoughts or suicide plans, or attempts.

| $3^{20}$ | 'Why is life given to one in misery, | misery/depression |
| | and life to the bitter in soul, | my bitter soul ? my depression |
| | who long for death but it does not come.... | wishes for death |
| $3^{22}$ | .... and are glad when they find the grave? | Death as a relief, and a way out |

Related to his death wishes is the regret that he ever saw life in the first place, and he regrets the day of his birth

| $3^1$ | After this Job opened his mouth | His muteness ends with a |
| | and cursed the day of his birth. | depressive thought |
| 2 | Job said: | |
| 3 | 'Let the day perish on which I was | The day of my birth should disappear |
| | born, and the night that said, | forever |
| | "A man child is conceived." | |
| 3 | Let that day be darkness! | |
| | May God above not seek it, | |
| | or light shine on it. | |

Hartley explains Job's curse of the day of his birth in terms of the cosmology of the ancient world. The ancients believed that God created each day anew, much in the same way as God created the world, but between each day lay chaos, and an unorganised lifeless mass of water overshadowed by total darkness. This is the night.

Job is reminded of his day of birth every year on his birthday, and the only way he will be able to forget his day of birth is to have it removed from the calendar. To do this he must invoke a 'counter-cosmic incantation', a special type of spell which will overturn the cosmic order and this will expunge the day of his birth from the calendar. Once this is done he will no longer be reminded of his day of birth or his birthdays – it will all be replaced by total darkness as in the night.

The same thought of death at birth appears a little further on in the chapter ($3^{11,16}$):

> Why did I not die at birth,
> come forth from the womb and expire? ...
> or why was I not buried like a stillborn child...?

Until the 20th century perinatal and infant mortality rates were very high, and so a stillbirth was a common and distressing event, familiar to all. Job identifies with the dashing of hope that birth a brings as it turns into the tragedy of a stillbirth. Jeremiah expresses a similar thought, but there are two important differences.

Job curses away the day itself and somehow by magic wants the day itself to be removed altogether; Jeremiah is perhaps more realistic in knowing that a day cannot be wished out of existence and so he saves his curses for the messenger who brings the news of his birth to his father. A second difference relates to the medical cause of death, Job identifies the cause of death as a stillbirth, a relatively common event, whereas Jeramiah describes an intra-uterine death, a rare and sinister cause of death because it almost always kills the mother as well (see page 119). Although Job himself never expresses a suicidal thought, Job's wife, who witnesses his torment and probably has to endure his morbid paranoid ravings, does tell him 'to curse God and die', because she knows that if he offends God by cursing him he will certainly die.

Job's trials continue when Satan inflicts some awful skin disease on him and he responds by cutting himself with a piece of broken potsherd – the ancient equivalent of a razor or a piece of broken glass.

| | | |
|---|---|---|
| 2⁷ | So Satan went out from the presence of the Lord, and inflicted loathsome sores on Job from the sole of his foot to the crown of his head. | Satan gives Job his skin disease. See Appendix 2 |
| | | Skin disease. See below |
| 8 | Job took a potsherd with which to scrape himself and sat among the ashes. | Cutting ?self-mutilation superficial cutting to relieve itching |
| 9 | Then his wife said to him, 'Do you still persist in your integrity? 'Curse God and die'. | Do you still have faith? Get God to make you die |
| 10 | But he said to her, 'You speak as any foolish woman would speak. Shall we receive the good at the hand of God, and not receive the bad?' In all this Job did not sin with his lips. | Accept whatever life throws at us both the good and the bad His faith is maintained |

Hartley explains: 'Job is in desperate state and sits in the ash heap, one of the ways the ancients express their deepest grief. He scratches his skin with a potsherd.' Many depressives superficially scratch their skin with a razor or a piece of glass to relieve their tension and agitation, and so this may be an act of self-mutilation, due to his depression. Alternatively, it may be an attempt to relieve the itching due to his skin disease. This episode is the only place in the whole book where his wife appears. She urges him to offend God so that God is provoked into making Job die. Job calls her a foolish woman, and argues that if we accept the good from God we must also accept the bad, and so at least in the prologue Job defends God from any criticism and upholds his faith.

### (10) Psychic pain
Some patients with depression experience bodily pain as well as or instead of depressed moods.

| | | |
|---|---|---|
| 6⁹ | That it would please God to crush me, that he would let loose his hand and cut me off! | He wishes that God would kill him |
| 10 | This would be my consolation; I would even exult in unrelenting pain; for I have not denied the words of the Holy One. | I may even enjoy the pain I still have my faith in God |

In his wish for death, he hopes that God will take his life away, but there is no question of him committing suicide. In verse 10, he reports feeling exulted – a feeling of joy (Heb: *ve'asalda*) – and this is linked to his unre-mitting pain (*belehah*), together with a declaration of faith, giving a sense of martyrdom. This linkage of pain with some pleasure is suggestive of a sado-masochism but this is not what is intended here. However, some depressives appear to wallow in their symptoms and seem to derive an almost perverse pleasure in describing their depression – or, as Robert Burton (1621, p. 69) put it:

> All my joys to this are folly,
> Naught so sweet as melancholy.

Chapter 14 is about the human mortality. It opens with a famous verse on the transitory nature of life and needs no elaboration ($14^1$):

> A mortal, born of women, few of days
> and full of trouble,
> comes up like a flower and withers,
> flees like a shadow and does not last.

The chapter continues to describe the human condition in generalities, and ends with a description of their death, but even after this mortals will continue to feel pain.

| $14^{20}$ | You prevail forever against them, and they pass away; | All will eventually die |
| 21 | you change their countenance, and send them away. | |
| 22 | Their children come to honour, and they do not know it; they are brought low, and it goes unnoticed. | Their children's success will be not be recognised because you will be dead nor will you know about their failures |
| 23 | They feel the pain of their own bodies, and mourn only for themselves. | even after death, pain is felt and misery (?depression) |

Habel explains: 'Even in Sheol, they (mortals) are not totally extinguished at death, but reduced to the shades, who continue to have a capacity for pain and self-pity.' The pain in this verse is linked to mourning (?depression).

Other characters of the book are sometimes used to describe psychic pains. Thus in Eliphaz's second speech he describes the punishments that will befall the wicked ($15^{20}$):

> The wicked writhe in pain all their days,
> through all the years that are
> laid up for the ruthless. (NRSV translation)

The translation offered by Hartley has a slightly different sense:

> All his days the wicked person is racked with pain
> even throughout the years stored up for the tyrant.

Hartley writes:

Eliphaz turns to his main theme, a detailed description of the fate of the wicked. The wicked person (*Rasah*) is the tyrant (*aris*) and one who defies God. He will be racked with pain all his days. Eliphaz uses such forceful language to counter Job's assertion that the doctrine of retribution has been unfairly applied – the wicked are spared. This is a bone of contention as Job says 'the tents of the marauders are safe', as God seems to let the wicked off. The word for pain used here is the pain of labour (*hitholel*) and this word is often used in the psalms as well to describe the pain of childbirth.

## Cause, treatment and outcome of Job's depression

As well as assessing the symptoms of depression, a comprehensive psychiatric assessment usually aims to try to find out how the patient understands the cause of their illness, the effects of any treatments, as well as its outcome. Job comments on all three of these areas.

Job vehemently rejects the traditional cultic explanation that he must have sinned to be so terribly ill and all this is a punishment from God. Thus he frequently protests his innocence. The book itself is sometimes seen as an attack on the doctrine of retribution, which in Job's eye seems to be both cruel and untrue. But if not caused by sin, then how did his illness arise? The text offers three alternative causal explanations. Firstly, humans are just born that way: it is an inevitable part of the human condition to be miserable.

| $5^6$ | For misery does not come from the earth, | Heb. *awen*= misery |
| | nor does trouble sprout from the ground; | Heb. *amal*= trouble |
| 7 | but human beings are born to trouble | Heb. trouble – *amal* |
| | just as sparks fly upward. | Heb. sparks – *sons of Rephesh* |

Habel explains this verse as follows:

> The dust (earth) from which humans originate is not only a mark of their fragility, but also a mark of their chthonic connections (chthonic deities are Gods of the underworld). Dust (*apar*) and ground (*dama*) are the source of evil (*awen*) and trouble (*amal*). Dust also has connections to death and the underworld. The earth is thus the source from which all mortals come, but also the cause of their continued suffering, and trouble (*amal*) is an integral part of the human experience. The Hebrew for sparks in this passage is *bene Rephesh*, or the sons of *Rephesh*, a Canaanite God associated with the underworld. The sons of *Rephesh* appear to be the various diseases and illnesses which fly forth from the underworld to plague human beings.

By modern standards, such an explanation for disease might seem a little far-fetched, but at least it makes a change from the omnipresent doctrine of sin and retribution, and frees the sufferer from the guilt of its causation.

The second cause Job cites for his illness is that 'the hand of God is upon him' ($19^{21}$):

> Have pity on me, have pity on me,
> for the hand of God has touched me.

The same thought is repeated a little further on ($23^2$):

> Today also my complaint is bitter,
> his hand is heavy despite my groaning.

In other books of the Bible 'the hand of God' inflicts terrible diseases. Thus in the earlier wars against Philistines (I Sam $5^6$): 'The hand of the Lord was heavy upon the people of Ashdod, and he terrified and struck them with tumours, both in Ashdod and in its territory...'.

Ezekiel also experiences the hand of God on him and *Rashi* says this usually signifies an episode of madness (see page 330). The 'hand of God' was seen as the cause of many physical and mental ailments in the ancient Near East and such beliefs were not confined to the Israelites (see page 333). Many centuries previously in the Babylonian epic *Ludlul bel Nemeqi*, the hero says 'His hand was heavy upon me; I was not able to bear it' (see Appendix 1).

A third way in which God may make a person ill is that God takes out a lawsuit against them. Elihu explains how God will punish the wicked:

$33^{19}$   They are also chastened with pain      Heb. *Hukah*=chastened, indicted
         upon their beds,
         and with continual strife in their bones.

Habel (p. 469) explains the word *Hukah*, translated in the NRSV as chastened, but really meaning 'indicted' or 'charged', as in a lawsuit. Elihu explains that such a serious illness as Job has is evidence that God has taken out a lawsuit against him. This is experienced in the bones, hence the phrase 'strife in their bones', which refers to such a lawsuit.

It is of some interest that in the dialogues Job offers no secular cause for his misery, only theological explanations – it is the product of sin, as in the doctrine of retribution; the hand of God that has touched him; or God has taken a lawsuit against him; or that God has turned against him in other ways, However, the prologue presents a conventional and much more plausible *set of quite different reasons* for the terrible depression that afflicts Job. He has lost all his farm animals, which in those days meant all his wealth; he has lost his position in society; and, most tragically, all his ten children have been all killed by a storm. This tells us that there must have been some understanding at the time that depression might be caused by loss. Such losses would be enough to make anyone depressed – but in the dialogues (chs 3–27) quite mysteriously he never mentions these losses again, and this puzzle suggests separate authorship for the prologue and the dialogues, as discussed above.

The text offers little in the way of treatment. In biblical times there was none, and indeed it was not until 1938 that an effective treatment for depression appeared, in the form of ECT (electroconvulsive therapy), and shortly afterwards the antidepressant drugs appeared. Job's three friends, Eliphaz, Bildad and Zophar, try to comfort him in his depression, but they lecture him, blame him for his misfortunes and seem to make matters worse. The victim is responsible for his condition and Job complains about the uselessness of his comforters:

16¹    Then Job answered:

²    'I have heard many such things;
miserable comforters are you all.    Heb. *Amal*=miserable, trouble

³    Have windy words no limit?
Or what provokes you
that you keep on talking?

Cohen writes that 'miserable comforters' are in fact, more literally, 'comforters of trouble', but whose attempts at bringing solace only adds salt to the wound. The thought is repeated further on:

13⁴    As for you, you whitewash with lies;    Heb. *tapal* =whitewash
all of you are worthless physicians.

Hartley explains:

> Job accuses his comforters of doing a whitewash in order to make the established religion look flawless. Because of their inability to face the hard facts, the friends prove to be 'worthless physicians' (Heb. *Rope'im*). These charlatans are seen as vainly daubing a sore with a useless salve and are of no help.

Thus little consolation is to be gleaned from the words of his comforters, and it seems that Job fails to obtain any cathartic relief either when he, himself speaks (16⁶): 'If I speak my pain is not assuaged'.

Cohen writes that 'my pain' is his physical suffering and his mental anguish, and quotes Ibn Ezra: 'My pain does not go away'.

Thus the two arms of psychotherapy, listening and talking to a therapist and hearing his kind words, seem to offer Job no relief. However, even in biblical times there seems to have been an understanding that sometimes a talking treatment (psychotherapy) can help depression. Thus in the Book of Tobit, when Raguel gives his daughter Sarah away to Tobias, his parting words to his future son-in-law are 'and you shall cheer up my daughter, who has been depressed' (Tob 8²⁰).

Job presumably did try to talk to his friends and others about his depression. We will never know why Job's depression was not helped by his comforters or why a psychotherapeutic approach failed, but we do know that some of the more severe types of depression, especially psychotic depression and depression with melancholic features (which Job seems to have had), rarely respond to psychotherapy and sometimes not even to the standard physical treatments of medication and ECT.

Job does get better in the end, and his fortunes are restored to him in the epilogue, giving the reader an uplifting feeling. After all of Job's losses and his terrible depressions, the good are rewarded and everything comes right in the end – except that this happy outcome, with its purpose of confirming the doctrine of rewards and retribution, lacks any genuine feel to it, but instead serves only as a fairy-tale complement to the prologue.

However, within the dialogues there are passages which signify more genuine types of improvement. Thus Job's friends describe what it will be like when he emerges from his misery. These passages, very much more than the epilogue, show that the writer did have familiarity with how a person feels when their depression finally lifts. Thus Bildad explains how God eventually rewards good people during their life:

| | | |
|---|---|---|
| 8$^{20}$ | See God will not reject a blameless person nor take the hand of evildoers. | Doctrine of rewards/retribution<br>Job is a good person |
| 21 | He will yet fill your mouth with laughter, and your lips with shouts of joy. | God will return your sense of pleasure and laughter to you again and give you a happy mood |

Hartley draws a parallel with this verse and psalm 126$^{5-6}$:

| | | |
|---|---|---|
| 5 | May those who sow in tears reap with shouts of joy. | Weeping = depression<br>no more anhedonia |
| 6 | Those who go out weeping, bearing the seed for sowing, | Weeping/depression |
| | shall come home with shouts of joy, carrying their sheaves. | Switching to happiness able to carry on work |

Zophar also explains to Job that even though he had sinned, if he were 'to repent', or, as he puts it, 'redirect his heart away from iniquity and turn to God he will be pleasantly surprised'.

| | | |
|---|---|---|
| 11$^{15}$ | Surely then you will lift up your face, without blemish; | His skin disease is now cured |
| | you will be secure, and will not fear. | No more anxiety |
| 16 | You will forget your misery; | Depression all gone |
| | you will remember it as waters that have passed away. | Even the memory of depression will be quite fleeting, and difficult to recall |
| 17 | And your life will be brighter than the noonday; | An almost 'high' feeling described here |
| | its darkness will be like the morning. | Even the bad moments will not seem so black |
| 18 | And you will have confidence, because there is hope; you will be protected and take your rest in safety. | Return of hope and confidence |
| 19 | You will lie down, and no one will make you afraid; | Sleep will be undisturbed<br>No more panics, especially at night |
| | many will entreat your favour. | Friends and family no longer alienated |

The writers of both Job and Psalm 126 are probably drawing on their personal experience of when their depressions lifted. Some depressions can even end in a brief high (without necessarily signifying bipolar disorder) and it seems as if Job is reporting such transient elation in the second of these passages.

The writer captures with great accuracy the mood as an episode of depression lifts. There is now a good feeling that the low moods and anxiety have finally gone. All memory of the depression and its painfulness seem to be obliterated and they even become difficult to recall. The previous black thoughts now become quite trivial. There is relief that the truly frightening symptoms such as nocturnal panic are no more.

These subtle mood changes when a depression lifts are not described in most other autobiographical accounts, nor in standard textbook descriptions of depression, where the focus is almost exclusively on the severe and disabling symptoms. To describe his relief as the mood lifts with such accuracy indicates the poet's great familiarity with such moments. It points to him having been there many times before, suggestive of a history of repeated episodes of depression all resolving spontaneously, and this is all points to the natural history of a recurrent depressive disorder.

In my own clinical work, I recall the long winter outpatient clinics when patients would talk at length about their terrible depression, despairing of ever seeing an end to it all, only to return in the spring when some would happily report 'it's all gone now', bringing the consultation quickly to a close. There was no need to say any more. There are few more magical moments in the practice of psychiatry for either patients or their physicians than sharing the delight of a person emerging from a lengthy painful depression. Job captures this moment well, all in sublime biblical verse.

## Making the diagnosis of Job's depression and panic using modern diagnostic criteria

The Book of Job has almost a 'full house' of depressive symptomatology and because it is written so clearly there is little doubt as to the meaning. Whilst the composition is more than 2,500 years old, the symptoms and depressive thoughts Job reports are unmistakable and even though expressed in a religious terminology there is no great 'trans-cultural' issue which might serve as a source of confusion. This makes comparisons with modern definitions of depression a relatively straightforward exercise.

Most of the symptoms are with Job himself, but the writer was not averse to placing some of them in the mouths of his comforters. The writer would have been a man of great insight, almost certainly with a personal experience of depression. Modern psychiatric diagnoses depend on identifying the patient's psychiatric symptoms and then matching them to agreed symptom definitions, and summating them to ensure there are more than the minimum number of symptoms required for diagnosis as laid out in standardised and internationally recognised glossaries. These are the Diagnostic and Statistical Manual of the American Psychiatric Association (DSM-5; APP, 2013) and the International Classification of Diseases (ICD-10; WHO, 1992). This is usually a straightforward and reliable process which forms the basis for all diagnostic work today. Whilst it is possible to criticise applying such a modern methodology to an ancient text such as the OT, there is no other alternative which would have any degree of acceptability to the profession today.

In Table 2.1, the criteria for major depressive disorder as it is defined in the American DSM-5 scheme is on the left hand column whilst matching verses from the Book of Job are placed on the right.

Job meets eight out of the nine criteria for DSM-5 major depression. There is no evidence in the text that he has any cognitive impairment (poor concentration and inability to think or indecisiveness). Also, even

**Table 2.1** DSM criteria for major depression and the Book of Job

| *DSM major depression* | *Book of Job* |
|---|---|
| The DSM system requires at least five of the following nine symptoms within a two-week period, and at least one of the five has to be depressed mood or diminished interest/pleasure (anhedonia) | |
| (1) Depressed mood (feels sad or empty, is tearful) | $7^{31}$ I go about in a sunless gloom<br>$7^3$ I am allotted months of emptiness<br>$7^{15}$ where then is my hope<br>$17^7$ My face is red with weeping |
| (2) Diminished interest/pleasure | $9^{25}$ My days are swifter than a runner; they flee away, they see no good |
| (3) Weight loss | $33^{21}$ their bones, once visible, stick out<br>$33^{20}$ Their lives loathe bread |
| (4) Insomnia or hypersomnia | $7^4$ I am full of tossing till dawn |
| (5) Psychomotor agitation or retardation | $20^1$ Because of the agitation within me<br>$21^3$ Seven days and seven nights no one spoke |
| (6) Fatigue/loss of energy | $3^{17}$ There, the weary are at rest |
| (7) Feelings of worthlessness or guilt | $30^{14}$ Become like dust and ashes<br>$13^{23}$ How many are my iniquities and my sins |
| (8) Trouble concentrating | Not present |
| (9) Recurrent thoughts of death or suicide | $17^1$ the grave is ready for me |
| The condition is not a mixed episode | No evidence of mania or hypomania or a mixed episode |
| Impaired social functioning | Wife turns against him |
| The condition is not the result of drug use or a general medical condition | Job has skin disease, but it appears be coincidental, rather than causal |
| The condition cannot be attributed to bereavement | Bereavement appears only in the prologue, not in the dialogue (see page 56) |

though he has many thoughts about death, there is no evidence of suicidal ideation. Otherwise, the Book of Job has most of the key symptoms of major depressive disorder as defined in DSM-5.

## Job's depression and DSM-5 melancholia

Job's masterly account of his own depression is so detailed that it permits the application of more sophisticated sub-typing of his depression in accordance with the DSM-5 scheme.

Thus DSM-5 has nine separate 'specifiers' for depression and two of these, 'with melancholic features' and 'with mood congruent psychotic features', may apply to Job.

For many years in the first part of the 20th century the classification of depression was beset with controversy. A popular scheme in the 1950s was to subdivide depression into an 'endogenous type' characterised by the biological symptoms of depression, namely appetite, body weight, sleep disturbance, agitation and retardation and morning depression, which seemed to have a biological cause, and 'reactive depression', which had mood lability and was reactive to the environment and had an obvious social or environmental cause. However, studies showed that although this appeared to be a neat division, no such division occurred in clinical populations. It was all one disorder, but some cases were severe and others were less severe. The old term 'endogenous depression' was abandoned but a melancholic subtype was substituted instead, which had all the biological symptoms of depression. It seems as if Job had this type of depression and the DSM-5 text gives a brief account of the melancholic sub-type:

> there is a near-complete absence of the capacity for pleasure. The 'distinct quality' of mood that is characteristic of the 'with melancholic features' specifier is experienced as qualitatively different from that during a non-melancholic episode, not only as more severe or longer lasting. Psychomotor changes are nearly always present. This type is more frequent amongst in-patients as opposed to out-patients and more likely to occur amongst those with psychotic features. (APP, 2013)

In Table 2.2, verses from the book of Job are compared to the features of DSM-5 melancholia.

Job's depression fulfils criteria for 'depression with melancholic features'. This is more than a minor technical detail. Thus the DSM-5 classes depression into three grades of severity, mild, moderate and severe, and melancholic depressions are always classed as severe. Such depressions are far more severe than non-melancholic depressions and more often associated with psychotic features.

## Does Job have psychotic depression?

This signifies the presence of delusions and hallucinations in the depression, and these are with 'mood-congruent psychotic features'. The DSM-5 text explains:

**Table 2.2** Criteria for depression with melancholic features and verses from the Book of Job

| (A) *Either one of the following:* | |
| --- | --- |
| Loss of pleasure in all, or almost all activities | 9²⁵ My days flee away without a glimpse of joy (NIV translation) |
| Lack of reactivity to usually pleasurable stimuli | |
| **(B) *Three or more of the following*** | |
| A distinct quality of depressed mood characterised by profound despair and/or moroseness, or by so-called empty mood | 3²⁰ Why is life given to one in misery; 17¹ My spirit is broken; Job morose throughout the whole text; 7³ I am allotted months of emptiness |
| Depression that is regularly worse in the morning | 7¹⁸ You [God] visit them every morning and you test them every moment |
| Early morning waking | 7⁴ I am full of tossing till dawn |
| Marked agitation | 20² Because of the agitation within me |
| Psychomotor retardation | 2¹³ mute for 7 days |
| Significant anorexia or weight loss | 3²¹ Their bones once visible now stick out |
| Excessive or inappropriate guilt | 13²³ How many are my iniquities |

> The content of all the delusions/and or hallucinations is consistent with typical depressions and is depressive or negative in type. Depressive themes of personal inadequacy, guilt, disease, death, or deserved punishment are said to be mood congruent.

Such themes pervade the Book of Job but his actual psychotic symptoms (as described on pages 34–35) comprise olfactory hallucinations and that he is giving off a bad smell (19¹⁷, 'My breath is repulsive to my wife') and he believes small children say bad things about him (19¹⁸, 'Even young children despise me, When I rise they talk against me'). Nowadays to make the more subtle diagnosis of a psychotic depression, a face-to-face interview with the patient would be required, and so although Job's diagnosis of 'Depression with melancholic features' appears to be quite solid, there is rather less certainty about giving Job a diagnosis of psychotic depression.

Psychotic depression is not common but neither is it rare. It is a dangerous disease. A survey of 19,000 subjects in five European countries found 20% of those with depression had psychotic features, and unipolar depression with psychotic features affected around 1–4 per 1000 individuals in the population, but the type is also commonly associated with the depressed phases of bipolar disorder. Among those hospitalised for depression around 25% have psychotic depression as indicated by the presence of some psychotic symptoms. By and large, psychotic depression will be encountered only by psychiatrists working in hospital settings and so is largely unfamiliar to GPs, priests, rabbis and biblical scholars today. It would have been unknown in the ancient world. Compared with non-psychotic depression, those with psychotic depression have more commonly associated melancholic features: loss of appetite, weight loss, loss of interest, or sense of pleasure, terminal insomnia, rumination, more feelings of worthlessness and guilt and feeling deserving of punishment, and more suicidal ideation, and psychomotor retardation.

Psychotic depressives have more severe symptoms. Treatment is more difficult and cases do not respond well to a single antidepressant but may sometimes respond to a combination of antidepressants and/or combinations of antidepressants with antipsychotics but the response rates to ECT are generally good (86%). In drug trials, the placebo response rate from non-psychotic depression is 13% but for psychotic depression it is 0%. There is virtually no response to psychotherapy, which is often helpful for those with non-psychotic depression. The lifetime risk for suicide attempts is 42% compared with 20% for non-psychotic depression.

Whilst modern textbook accounts of the delusions that occur in psychotic depression offer some clues to understanding Job's illness, a better comparison would be with accounts of depression in the pre-treatment era, that is prior to 1938, when electroconvulsive therapy came in. There are very few such studies, but a detailed account of a study of 67 inpatient cases in an article entitled 'The Prognosis of Involutional Melancholia' (Hoch and MacCurdy, 1922), based on a group of inpatients in a New York Asylum, is helpful, as the depressive delusions recorded in this study are very similar to those described by Job. Table 2.3 compares a few of those cases with Job's condition.

**Table 2.3** Cases of involutional melancholia and the case of Job

| *Hoch and MacCurdy, 1922* | *Job* |
|---|---|
| Case 17. Depressed, listless, says she is going to die, also will infect everybody by her unclean breath, will be thrown on the dump naked. | Job has: he sat among the ashes (2[8]); My breath is repulsive to my wife (19[17]) |
| Case 20. Why was I born? Am I to blame? | Job has: Why did I not die at birth (3[11]) |
| Case 47. Says the police are coming to take her, the food is poisoned. Giving off an odour from her flesh. | Job has: My breath is repulsive to my wife (19[17]) |
| Case 52. Almost mute and fearful, says she is wicked, and responsible for all the wickedness in the world and has lost her soul. There is no life in me, seems as if my limbs were dead | Job has: All my members are a shadow (17[7]); mute for seven days and seven nights (2[13]) |

Hoch and MacCurdy (1922) comment on delusions of poverty:

> Probably related psychologically to loss of life, is the delusion of poverty. In
> its mildest forms this is merely a worry about expenses, in the most exagger-
> ated types the patient is convinced that the family home is dissipated and his
> relatives are all in the poorhouse. *Three-quarters of all patients have them.*

Possibly this explains the very frequent reference to bankruptcy and poverty
in the Book of Job. It seems that the content of the delusions found in Job's
depression is similar to that found in recent cases and has changed little over
the last 2000 years.

In terms of duration of episodes in this study, the average duration for all
episodes was 22 months; the average period before improvement was seen
was 9.5 months; 33 patients improved during the first year of their psychosis,
5 during the second, but thereafter improvements were sporadic although
one patient improved after 8 years. Kraepelin (1907) also reported on the
very poor prognosis for melancholic patients and found 32% were chronic
and 19% died within two years of the onset. With a prognosis for melancholia
as poor as this in the 20th century CE, one can only wonder in amazement
at how Job survived at all in the 6th century BCE, let alone being able to
muster the strength to write his amazing book. Perhaps it was his great faith
and supreme intellect which helped him through his terrible depression
which he describes so well.

## The severity of Job's depression

Job's depression is undoubtedly severe, and is by far the most severe of
all the depressions recorded in the Bible. The reader of the Psalms will be
comforted by the psalms of lamentation, particularly as God brings about
healing. Not so with Job's depression. Thus even for a depressed person, the
writing delivers little comfort; the depression is far too punitive and Job has
a particular harshness in his imagery.

Thus in writing about the punishment for a betrayal for money he says
($17^5$): 'Those who denounce friends for rewards-the eyes of their children
will fail'.

When describing the profession of debt collection, a common problem in
all societies, he explains ($24^9$): 'There are those who snatch the orphan child
from the breast / and take as a pledge the infant of the poor'.

As for the punishment of the wicked ($20^{16}$): 'They will suck the poisons of
Asps / The tongue of the viper will kill them'.

Finally the punishment he and his wife will get is truly strange, if he
should ever have an adulterous thought about the wife of his next door
neighbour ($31^{30}$): 'then let my wife grind for another / and let other men
kneel over her'.

Psychoanalysts write of an overly harsh super-ego in depression, and
these verses surely fit such a pattern, affording little comfort to the reader.
More significantly, it would be very difficult, even if one were a depressive,
to identify with such punitive sentiments, and so it is not surprising that the
Book of Job was not widely read. Although canonical and in places truly

brilliant, its punitive quality, its lack of a comforting quality, as well as his paranoid attacks on God may also explain why it does not play a major role in either the present-day Jewish or Christian liturgies.

## Panic disorder

Job suffers from depression, but like Jeremiah he seems to have panics as well. In Jeremiah's case the panic and terrors are the main condition, with some depression accompanying his panic. With Job, the depression appears to be far more dominant and the panic disorder is less obvious and can only be inferred from his frequent mention of 'the terrors'.

Habel usefully links $13^{21}$, $30^{15}$ and $31^{23}$, which, he says, show that Job suffers from 'debilitating fear'. Thus Job is anxious about appearing before God in the forthcoming court case when he is going to challenge God, but is frightened that God will inflict his terror on him.

$13^{21}$ Withdraw your hand from me,
and do not let dread of you terrify me.    ?fear of panic

Job is also bewildered by God's great power and sovereignty. Even thinking about God brings on a panic:

$23^{15}$ Therefore I am terrified at his presence;     Heb. *Bahal* =terrified
when I consider, I am in dread of him.     Heb. *pachad* = terror
$^{16}$ God has made my heart faint;     faintness ?dizziness
and the Almighty has terrified me;

In this verse the 'terror' is accompanied by faintness – which is one of the somatic symptoms of panic. The word *pachad* is often used by Jeremiah to denote terrors, which in his case are more definitely panic attacks.

Elihu is also awestruck by the presence of God and he tells Job about the effect his "crashing' (? loud noises) has on him.

$36^{33}$ Its crashing tells about him;     Heb. *Re'eyv* ?crashing, ?thunder
he is jealous with anger against iniquity.
$37^{1}$ At this also my heart trembles,     ?increased awareness of heart beat
and leaps out of its place.     Heb. *yittar* = leap
$^{2}$ Listen, listen to the thunder of his voice     Heb. *Rogez* = turmoil, thunder
and the rumbling that comes from
his mouth.

This is the familiar God of the Old Testament, who thunders at any and all iniquity, a mantle later happily assumed by pastors of the church almost everywhere and down through the ages. The RSV states the word 'crashing' (Heb. *Re'eyv*) is of uncertain meaning, but Hartley gives 'shouting, roar' and by extension 'thunder' and the NIV also has 'thunder' and so some kind of powerful shock is suggested. From a psychiatric perspective, Elihu reports 'my heart trembles', that his heart leaps out of his chest (?increased awareness of his heartbeat), a common physical accompaniment of a panic attack. This combination of anxiety and an increased awareness of their own heartbeat is also reported by Jeremiah ($4^{19}$) and it heightens anxiety levels to such a degree that many panic-disordered subjects believe they are having a heart attack and so take themselves off to the A&E department. Perhaps Elihu is reporting similar extremely high anxiety levels here.

Job is the recipient of the terrors inflicted by God. Thus:

| $30^{15}$ | Terrors are turned upon me;<br>my honour is pursued as by the wind,<br>and my prosperity has passed away<br>like a cloud. | Heb. *ballahot* = Terrors<br><br>Loss of all my wealth |
|---|---|---|

Hartley (p. 401) writes: 'the terrors are turned on him. The wording suggests the hand of death is behind these attacks. All prosperity and dignity is lost'.

In the next quote, Job describes how he used to sit in judgement over his fellow man, but was always terrified of making a mistake – and if he does '*El*' (God) will visit him and inflict a calamity on him.

| $31^{23}$ | For I was in terror of calamity<br>from God,<br>for I could not have faced his majesty. | Heb. *pahad* = terror;<br>a word also used by Jeremiah |
|---|---|---|

Sometimes it is not Job who is the recipient of God's terrors (panic attacks?) but they fall on other characters in his drama. Bildad explains to Job the punishments that lie in store for the wicked:

| $18^{11}$ | Terrors frighten them on every side,<br>and chase them at their heels... | Heb. *Ballahot* = terrors |
|---|---|---|
| $18^{14}$ | they are torn from the tent in which<br>they trusted and are brought to the<br>king of terrors. | They will experience much terror |

Sarna (1963) suggested that *ballahot*, or terrors, was an epithet for Sheol, and *Melek Ballahot*, the King of Terrors, was the God Mot, king of the underworld, as in Ugaritic mythology. The first-born son of Mot was a demon who brings misfortunes and the destruction of people to satisfy the great cravings of Sheol. This demon attacks the body and makes the person deathly ill. Such a sudden loss of vigour and health reduces the person to one haunted by nightmares and stricken with terror (Hartley, p. 279).

Zophar repeats similar thoughts concerning the fate of the wicked in his second speech as well:

| $20^{24}$ | They will flee from an iron weapon;<br>a bronze arrow will strike them through. | An arrow pierces them |
|---|---|---|
| 25 | It is drawn forth and comes out of their<br>body, and the glittering point comes out<br>of their gall; terrors come upon them. | ?an unbearable gastric sensation<br>(Heb. *ayeme's* = Terrors ?panics) |
| 26 | Utter darkness is laid up for their treasures. | ?catastrophic losses of wealth |

Hartley writes: 'God's arrows will tear up his insides and so no wonder he is afflicted by God's terrors'. The pain of an arrow going through one's stomach is unthinkable, and points to some horrible sensation in the stomach. Perhaps these are the waves of panic that sweep through his body. Cohen explains '*all darkness laid up for his treasures* is figurative for the calamity. That which he acquired and hoarded will end in ruin'. Note the terrors are once more associated with material/financial losses.

Eliphaz also describes how the wicked will be at the receiving end of harsh punishment, in the form of terror and anxiety.

| | | |
|---|---|---|
| 15²¹ | Terrifying sounds are in their ears; | Terrors ?hyperacusis |
| | in prosperity the destroyer will come among them.... | Catastrophic thinking |
| (15²²⁻²³ omitted) | | |
| 15²⁴ | distress and anguish terrify them; | High anxiety levels ?panics |
| | They prevail against them, like a king prepared for battle. | A frightening situation: if the king loses, he and all his men will be killed |

Loud noises are experienced accompanied by feelings of terror (? waves of panic) and there is increased sensitivity to noise (hyperacusis) as occurs in a panic attack. Cohen writes he is in a state of constant dread that his ill-gotten gains will be taken from him by another unscrupulous person.

Cohen explains:

> The Hebrew noun *kidor* = battle, occurs nowhere else and is connected with an Arabic root meaning 'the onrush of an attacking army'. The sense is therefore that distress and anguish will overwhelm the wicked man as the flames of destruction lay waste to the city attacked by the king's armies.

An alternative and literal explanation might be that a king before a battle would be extremely anxious because if he lost the battle then both he and his soldiers might all be killed.

## Nocturnal panic attacks

Some people with panic disorder wake up in the night with a panic attack. They wake up abruptly in a state of fear, believe that the worst has happened, think they are about to die, or have lost everything or are having a heart attack. Nocturnal panic is not a separate disorder but is thought to be a particularly distressing symptom of panic disorder, and there are three possible examples of episodes of nocturnal panic, although night terrors is a possible alternative diagnosis.

Eliphaz is explaining the doctrine of rewards and retribution to Job in the following passage:

| | | |
|---|---|---|
| 4¹² | Now a word came stealing to me, | ?Auditory hallucination |
| | my ear received the whisper of it. | ?Hypnopompic hallucination |
| 13 | Amid thoughts from visions of the night, | Dreams or nightmares |
| | when deep sleep falls on mortals, | Heb. *Tardema* = deep sleep |
| 14 | dread came upon me, and trembling, | Acute fear (?panic) with tremor. |
| | which made all my bones shake. | Severe tremor |
| 15 | A spirit glided past my face; | Visual experience? ?dream |
| | the hair of my flesh bristled. | ?Goose pimples |

| 16 | It stood still, | The LXX has 'I stood still' |
|----|----------------|---------------------------|

but I could not discern its appearance.
A form was before my eyes;
There was silence, then I heard a voice.

Eliphaz passes from the waking state and into sleep and as he does so he sees a vague spirit and hears whispering in his ears. Both auditory and visual hallucinations are suggested here, but as these occur during the process of entering into the sleeping state they are considered to be 'hypnopompic hallucinations' and are a normal phenomenon, not thought to be pathological. The term 'hypnogogic' is used when the change is from sleep to waking, and 'hypnopompic' when it is from the waking state to sleep.

At this point his mood seems to be full of dread. This may represent waves of panic and it is accompanied by tremor (trembling, bones shaking). He sees a spirit and the NRSV has 'it stood still', presumably referring to the spirit, but the LXX has 'I stood still'. Hartley (p. 109, footnote 6) states 'The LXX reads the first person form (Greek '*a'amod* ) meaning 'I stopped''. This suggests that Eliphaz reports he cannot move and so maybe his inability to move is a paralysis.

In terms of the differential diagnosis of sleep disorders this distinction is very important. If Job truly 'stopped' at this point in time, and that is in the change from a phase of waking to entering sleep, then he might be might be describing a state of sleep paralysis, but an interview with Eliphaz would be needed to confirm this.

A recently recognised but rare sleep disorder called *hypnogogic terrors* is associated with terrifying visual and auditory experiences on waking, and this is also associated with a brief state of hypnogogic sleep paralysis and this seem to be exactly what Eliphaz is describing here, although in Elphaz's case this is an hypnopompic phenomenon.

A second episode of nocturnal panic occurs when Job is explaining how those who are wealthy and wicked will be punished by God:

| 27¹⁹ | They got to bed with wealth, | ?go to sleep |
|------|------------------------------|--------------|
|      | but will do so no more; | It's the last time they have wealth |
|      | they open their eyes, | open eyes = wake up? |
|      | and it is gone. | wealth all gone |
| 20   | Terrors overtake them like a flood; | Heb. *ballahot* terrors = ?waves of panic drowning feeling |
|      | in the night a whirlwind carries | the terrors occur at night |
|      | them off. | death occurs |

The nocturnal panic is not obvious, however; the wicked go to bed with all their wealth, and in the night they experience the terrors (? waves of panic). When they wake up, the ultimate catastrophe for the rich, has happened – all their wealth has gone, and this is accompanied by thoughts of death. Terrors on waking in the night combined with thinking about catastrophes is suggestive of a panic attack – but as it all occurs at night, this is nocturnal panic.

Habel (p. 387) provides an exposition in terms of the mythology of ancient Canaan. The terrors refers to the terrors of death, and the demonic forces of the underworld. The *supa* (whirlwind) is also a symbol of divine judgement and destruction and it strikes at night – a time when the wicked supposedly feel safe. The psychiatric and mythological explanations use different paradigms to give quite different meanings to this verse, but they are not incompatible. The genius of the writer lies in how he weaves his own personal experience of nocturnal panic (or hypnopompic terrors) into a moral punishment that God will inflict upon the wealthy.

In the third episode Elihu is speaking, and is giving a lesson on the dangers of pride, again through the vehicle of his nocturnal panic:

| | | |
|---|---|---|
| 33[15] | In a dream, in a vision of the night, | nocturnal event |
| | when deep sleep falls on mortals, | deep sleep = *tardema* |
| | While they slumber in their beds, | |
| [16] | then he opens their ears | They wake up hearing things |
| | and terrifies them with warnings, | Terror = waves of panic ? loud noises |
| [17] | that he may turn them aside from their deeds, | |
| | and keep them from pride, | pride is the great sin |
| | to spare their souls from the Pit, | thoughts of death implied |
| | their lives from traversing the River. | Heb. *selah* channel, river |

In this stanza, Elihu is having a nightmare; he is in a deep sleep, then he wakes up with terrors and hears loud noises, which frighten him and he has thoughts about death (the pit). The river refers to the subterranean channel that leads from the grave to Sheol. In Greek mythology this is the River Styx; in Mesopotamian mythology this channel is called the *hubur*.

The symptom sequence is similar to the previous episode: a sudden awakening from a deep sleep, accompanied by loud noises, terrifying warnings and then thoughts of death.

Only Jeremiah and Job report the experience of terrors from God, although it is also mentioned in some of the psalms. In Jeremiah there is clear evidence of the waves of terror being accompanied by the somatic symptoms of panic (see page 127), making the diagnosis of panic disorder rather more definite. With Job there is some evidence of autonomic symptoms accompanying the nocturnal panic: gastric anxiety (30[27]), choking sensations (30[18]), tremor(4[14]), goose pimples (4[15]), faintness (23[15]) and cardiac symptoms (37[1]). It seems likely that Job also suffers from panic disorder – but the picture of panic in Job is far less definite than with Jeremiah. Interestingly, the ultimate catastrophe for Job was the loss of all his wealth, whereas for Jeremiah it was a more general catastrophe (*seber*) and ruination (*suddadanu*); perhaps Job was more money minded.

## Job's skin disease

Apart from his depression, Job suffers from a non-fatal skin condition. Portraits of Job usually show him covered in blotches and his skin disease has been a source of fascination for both artists and scholars alike. Verses describing his skin lesions are given below:

2⁷      So Satan went out from the presence of the Lord, and inflicted loathsome
        sores on Job from the sole of his foot to the crown of his head. Job took a
        potsherd with which to scrape himself, and sat among the ashes.

7⁵      My flesh is clothed with worms and dirt;
        my skin hardens, then breaks out again.

30³⁰    My skin turns black and falls from me, and my bones burn with heat.

Job seems to suffer from inflamed eruptions, intense itching, ulceration and
blackening of the skin. There is no unanimity in the literature as to what
skin disease this might be. Mclintlock and Strong's *Encyclopaedia* (2000)
offers either elephantiasis or black leprosy as possible diagnoses. An article
by three Belgian rheumatologists suggests it was scabies (Applebaum *et
al.*, 2007). However, neither of these opinions is from a dermatologist.
A fellow congregant, Dr L. Shall, is a consultant dermatologist in the
NHS and his opinion (Shall, 2016) is that none of the above is tenable
but the most likely condition is leishmaniasis. This is a tropical infection
caused by the Leishmania parasite, of which there are about 20 different
species. It is spread by the sandfly, which is endemic in Africa, India and
the Middle East. Today, there are about 4–12 million cases distributed in
98 countries. Cases have been reported from Sinai but not from Israel in
recent times. Cutaneous leishmaniasis is the most common form, which
causes an open sore at the bite sites, which heals in a few months to a year
and half, leaving an unpleasant-looking scar. Diffuse cutaneous leishmaniasis
produces widespread skin lesions which resemble leprosy, and may not heal
on its own. In the early 20th century, cases were common in the near East
and came to be known as 'Jericho's button', as there was a cluster around
Jericho (Wikepedia, 2017). There is no reason to believe that this common
disorder of the Middle East would have been any less common in biblical
times and the skin lesions give a reasonable fit to the biblical description of
Job's skin disease.

## The suffering of others

Job, like the other Old Testament prophets, was a man with a huge social
conscience and was acutely aware of the suffering of others in society.
Perhaps this empathy was related to his own personal suffering as a result of
his depression. As with the chapter on Jeremiah I have listed in Table 2.4
all the other categories of suffering that Job mentions and these are given
below and can be compared with the categories of suffering that Jeremiah
felt an empathy for (see page 121).

Both Job and Jeremiah record a broadly similar range of social problems.
The most important difference is that Jeremiah is troubled by the destructive
effects of alcoholism and, to a lesser extent, the problems of the insane. Job
seems not to be bothered by alcoholism and even though he has psychotic
symptoms their presence in others is not an issue for him.

However, Job is clearly disturbed by seeing people in states of abject
poverty, starvation, having no clothes to wear, the predatory behaviours of

**Table 2.4** Harms and suffering of others in the Book of Job

| Harm | Verse |
|---|---|
| Social harms, poverty-related harm | |
| Hunger and Famine | $5^4$, $5^{20}$+ |
| Needy | $5^{15}$, $29^{12}$, $30^{24}$+ |
| Slavery and economic exploitation | $7^2$, $31^{33}$+ |
| No clothing | $22^6$, $30^{20}$+ |
| Debt collection | $20^{19}$, $22^6$, $24^6$, $24^9$+ |
| Widows | $23^{21}$, $29^{12}$, $31^{16}$+ |
| Orphans | $22^9$, $2^{43}$, $29^{12}$, $31^{17}$+ |
| Infertility | $23^{21}$ |
| War | $5^{20}$ |
| *Medically related harms* | |
| Stillborn | $3^{16}$ |
| Stumbling lame | $4^9$, $29^{12}$ |
| Sudden death | $9^{23}$ |
| Senile dementia ? | $12^{20}$ |
| Learning difficulties ? | $11^2$ |
| Depression in others ? | $5^6$ |
| Dying | $24^{12}$ |

The + symbol denotes a poverty-related harm.

the debt collector, and the exploitation of the poor. An empathy with the poor is not unique to Job and is a topic raised by most of the prophets. But quite uniquely, Job writes frequently about sudden financial catastrophe: the abrupt loss of all one's wealth he mentions no fewer than six times in the dialogues ($30^{15}$, my prosperity has passed away like a cloud; $20^{26}$, utter darkness is laid up for their treasure; $27^{19}$, their wealth is all gone; $15^{21}$, in prosperity the destroyer will come upon them; $20^{21}$, their prosperity will not endure; $15^{23}$, they scavenge for bread – where is it?).

Why should this be? The obvious answer is that this is the tale of terrible losses afflicted on him by Satan as laid out in the prologue. Assuming the prologue and dialogue are a unity, written by the same author, this makes good sense. However, if the prologue and the dialogues have different authors or were written during different historical periods, then the pre-occupation with poverty and his repeated mentions of a fall from grace and a loss of all wealth may have other explanations.

One possibility is that it was the writer's depression itself that plunged him into a state of penury, as he was no longer able to carry on with his 'day job', although we have no idea what this was. Another possibility is that the repeated thoughts of financial ruin relate to one of the common symptoms of his psychotic depression, namely delusions of poverty. As stated above, in the pre-treatment era around 75% of those with 'melancholia' suffered from delusions of poverty (Hoch and Macurdy, 1922). Job had melancholia, which therefore made it quite likely that he did harbour such delusions. Those afflicted by delusions of poverty go around repeatedly uttering how poor they are, how they have lost everything, and that financial ruin stares them in the face. Might this explain Job's pre-occupation with the theme of financial ruination? We shall never truly know.

## Authorship and the distribution of depressive symptoms within the Book of Job

The vast majority of the verses containing psychiatric symptomatology are confined to the dialogues between Job and his comforters, as are all the references to suffering amongst other people. The prologue, the epilogue and the speeches of Elihu have almost no mention of psychopathology, no record of social harms; nor do they contain any of the paranoid ideation about God. There is much speculation in the Old Testament scholarship on Job based mainly on purely literary considerations about which parts of the book may have had a separate authorship. Thus the prologue and the epilogue are both in prose and are said to adopt a rather naive fairy-tale style similar to Genesis. The dialogues are all in verse. The word for God in the prologue is *Yahweh*, whereas in the dialogues the words used are *El*, *Eloah*, *Elohim* and *Shaddai* (the Almighty) and *Yahweh* is rarely mentioned; some scholars have argued on this basis for a different authorship between these two sections of the book.

Only the dialogues contain the bulk of the psychopathology and their writer almost certainly suffered from severe depression, and so the psychiatric evidence seems to support separate authorship.

A second difficulty for assigning single authorship to the book is that the prologue tells the story of a good man who has suffered from a series of tragic losses and the reader is prepared for an illness due to loss – a bereavement depression. However, the depression described in the dialogues has nothing to do with bereavement. Clinically, it is a classic endogenous melancholic illness. There are no pangs of grief, no visits to the graves of loved ones, no hearing the voices of departed relatives and, above all, even though the protagonist has lost 10 children there is only a single mention of his dead children (29[5]). He never calls out any of his children's names, never says how he loves them and misses them, and this would be very unusual for a depression due to bereavement, especially one involving the death of his children.

The only losses the writer repeatedly mentions in the dialogues is the loss of all wealth and prosperity, sometimes ending up as states of destitution. A religious explanation is given: thus Job's losses are the work of Satan, and the consequence of Satan's wager with God as outlined in the prologue – but a psychiatric explanation that these are based on his delusions of poverty is also possible.

In her book *Mr and Mrs Job* the Dutch biblical scholar Ellen Van Wolde argues that the prologue was a later addition to make some sense of debates in the dialogues and also to offset the negative remarks made about God in the dialogues and so ensure that the whole work would be accepted into the canon. If this is the case, the book of Job started its life with the dialogues alone. Israelite priests and redactors of the time realised immediately this was a piece of religious writing of extraordinary quality and great import. However, in a few places it was fiercely anti-pathetic to the existing dogmas of the day, it had many unacceptable passages about God, some even bordering on blasphemy, and there was no obvious reason for the terrible depression and suffering described in this poetic masterpiece. The story of the prologue and epilogue was then either taken from other Job-like legends of the period, of which there were many, or was an original creation by another scribe and adapted to include a story of loss and bereavement. It also included the wager with Satan, a literary creation to ensure the reader would believe that Job's suffering was caused by Satan and not by God. Thus because the epilogue had a good ending, this 'proved' that the 'good' will always be ultimately rewarded and so the tale upheld the doctrine of reward and retribution. The speeches of Elihu (chs 32–37) were also possibly later insertions with a similar aim. Although written in verse, the Elihu speeches do not have the same sort of content as the dialogues. In these speeches there is no doubting the doctrine of reward and retribution. God is never portrayed as being persecutory or harmful. Some of the words used for God, particularly the repeated use of *El*, come from an older stratum of Hebrew literature. They probably do not add greatly to the overall message of the book and indeed Pope Gregory the Great (540–604 CE) dismissed the Elihu speeches as being of little value, and more recent scholars have also suggested they may be a later insertion and have a different authorship (Gordis, p. 157).

The purpose of these additions was to ensure the attacks on conventional religion, and the paranoia directed at God in the book, would not lead to this masterpiece being discarded and rejected from the canon. Gordis suggests that it proved to be acceptable to the canon because the story in the prologue was charming in its own right and was very popular amongst the Jews of the diaspora and also because in any case very few people read beyond this section, into the dialogues. This was because the dialogues were largely incomprehensible. We have no idea whether any of these speculations are true or not, because there is no existing literature on the canonisation of Job – but happily it seems to have got through without any objection.

## The medical and psychiatric literature on Job

Job has fascinated theologians and philosophers through the ages and has inspired a vast literature and it would be quite beyond the scope of the present chapter to review this. However, Job is one of the few books of the Bible to attract the interest of the medical profession and three aspects stand out. First, there is a theme of suffering, especially the suffering of the innocent. A second theme is the parallel between the story of Job's comforters and their failure to bring any healing to him. Therapeutic failure is common in medicine and psychoanalysts have an interest in this situation and draw parallels between Job's comforters, and the overly defensive and dogmatic physicians of today. Thirdly, there is the diagnostic issue, namely what illness was Job actually suffering from. This third question has attracted very little interest, and despite numerous psychological and psychoanalytic studies on Job, in the last 50 years there is only one other psychiatric report, apart from the present study, which addresses the issue of diagnosis (Kapusta and Frank, 1977).

The first physician to write extensively about Job was Robert Burton (1577–1639), who wrote a truly massive tome, *The Anatomy of Melancholy* (1621). Burton was the Dean of Divinity at the University of Oxford and was himself a depressive. The book is not a summary of depression but rather more of a gigantic compendium of anything written or said appertaining to depression that Burton had ever encountered and his book has more than 1000 references. Most of his quotes were derived from ancient classical sources and later European literature, but some were also taken from the Bible. Burton thought that depression could be a force for creativity and could explain some of the prophetic writings:

> Melancholy men of all others, are most witty and their melancholy causes many times divine ravishment, and a kind of enthusiasmus ... which stirreth them up to be excellent philosophers, poets, prophets etc.

Not surprisingly Job figures quite prominently in this book and some examples are given below. A verse of Job's that Burton repeats several times is how depression seems to be an inevitability for mankind ($14^1$, King James Version):

> Man, that is born of women, is of few
> days and full of trouble.

In his chapter on treatment entitled 'Remedies of All Manner of discontents', he writes about the use of 'good counsel and comfortable speeches' but also quotes many who say that speeches are of little use:

> Words add no courage which Catalina once said to his soldiers 'A captain's oration does not make a coward into a valiant man and as Job feelingly says to his friends 'you are but miserable comforters'....

Burton devotes a whole chapter to the topic of 'Religious melancholy', which perhaps was a common problem in his day, citing passages from the Psalms and the Book of Job. In one passage he pairs the suffering of Christ to that of Job: 'Christ in his garden cried out 'My God my God why hast thou forsaken me?', while Job in his anguish says 'the arrows of the Almighty God were in him' ($4^4$). Burton then quotes a further five verses from the Book of Job before moving on to the depression of King David and then on to the boils that afflict Lazarus (p. 658). In his chapter on the 'Prognostics of Melancholy' Burton writes:

they [depressives] are perpetually tormented, a burden to themselves as Job was, they can neither eat, drink, or sleep ... they curse their stars with Job and the day of their birth and wish for death; for as Pineda and most interpreters hold, Job was even melancholy to despair and almost madness itself. (p. 261)

The next 'heavyweight' psychiatrist to tackle Job was C. J. Jung in his book *An Answer to Job*. Although the book is readable, only one-tenth of it is about Job and there is little psychiatry or even psychoanalysis in it. The book is more about theology, Yahweh and Christ. Jung argues that because Yahweh and Satan inflict their tests and torment on Job, which he successfully withstands, and maintains his faith throughout, he proves himself to be morally superior to Yahweh. Two psychoanalysts (Spero and Reid) both describe the work as 'strange', although they do not criticise it.

William Blake (probably a manic depressive himself) was fascinated by Job and produced 21 steel engravings surrounded by various verses from the Book of Job. Marion Milner, a psychoanalyst from the British Kleinian school, commented that in Blake's engravings the face of God is identical to that of Job. She saw the work as a denial of human destructiveness, and called this 'a manic defence', a much favoured theme of the Kleinian school.

Probably the most readable of the psychoanalytic studies is that of Reid, which is at least comprehensible. Reid draws heavily on the work of Freud and the relationship between the ego and super-ego. It is based ultimately on the proposition in chapter 8 of Freud's book *Civilisation and Its Discontents*:

that the sense of guilt is the most important problem in the development of civilisation.... This is the price we pay for our advancing civilisation and is the loss of happiness through the heightened sense of guilt ... it is the internalisation of man's aggressive impulses occasioned by the conditions of civilisation that has resulted in an intolerable burden of guilt.... In the allegory Job is the ego and God and 'the voice of whirlwind' is the super-ego and the three friends represent the ineffectual voice of reason in its attempts to mitigate between the two warring factions.

An overly harsh super-ego (conscience/parental representative/religious authority/ God) attacking the ego is the traditional psychoanalytic explanation for depression and understanding the source of this guilt is a key to therapy in the reliving of this earlier parent–child relationship through the transference and is central to the understanding of depression in psychoanalysis. Such a view is not too far from ordinary general psychiatry, where guilt is also seen as integral to depression, although not explained in terms of persecution of the ego by the super-ego. The story of Job is replete with, guilt, sin and the denial of sin, and shows much resemblance to the way guilt-ridden depressives report their condition today.

A lengthy recent review by Spero tries to marry up orthodox halachic Judaism with a psychoanalytic perspective on Job and although such a union is far from satisfactory, his review includes a comprehensive set of references and footnotes on the rabbinic tradition and psychoanalytic literature on Job, but he makes no attempt at diagnosis.

Kahn, a child psychiatrist and psychotherapist, wrote a book entitled *Job's Illness: Loss Grief and Integration,* in which he identifies Job's dilemma as being illustrative basic human problems. He assigns three common psychiatric diagnoses to Job: obsessional neurosis, depression, and paranoia, with the depression being the most important. He tries to integrate the biblical tale with psychiatric explanations of depression current in the 1960s and 1970s, giving the work a slightly dated feel. Kahn likens the trials of Job to the therapeutic processes that patients need to negotiate as they try to integrate their experience of loss and illness, to help them to survive on an emotional level as well as to mature through their depression.

Ilan Kutz, an Israeli liaison psychiatrist, in a mildly humorous article entitled 'Job's illness: bedside wisdom in the Book of Job', describes Job as a thriving livestock rancher of the Middle East (as opposed to the American Mid-west) and highlights the failure and defensiveness of Job's three friends and their need to adhere rigidly to the dogma of the day, namely the doctrine of divine retribution which Job repeatedly questions. He draws parallels with the defensiveness and occasional anger of the physicians of today in the face of therapeutic failure. He also describes an agnostic patient who had no knowledge of the Bible or Job, suffering from acute leukaemia, who became depressed after a course of chemotherapy, and who asked 'What have I done to deserve this?' and then added 'There is someone up there testing me'. Many patients who cannot comprehend their suffering ask their physicians 'Why me?', a question for which there is never a satisfactory answer. Like Kahn, Kutz understands the book as an early description of how patients and their helpers struggle through the processes of loss and illness to attain a state of healing.

The only other study, apart from the present account, to focus on the diagnostic issue is that of Kapusta and Frank (1977). They also highlight ch. 30 as an almost complete compendium of depression, and quote most of the verses highlighted in the present study. Like the present author, they were very impressed with the clinical accuracy with which Job describes his depression and call it a 'timeless medical masterpiece' which still has much to offer the psychiatrist of today.

## Concluding remarks

There is much psychiatry in the Book of Job, some that is obvious even to the naked eye of the untrained reader, but some that is hidden within the theology. The finding that Job was a man with the severe depression is neither new nor original. However, the verse-by-verse account of his depression reveals just how severely he suffered from a very wide panoply of depressive symptoms and the way the depression penetrates deeply into the religious fabric of the book. The description is sufficiently detailed to permit a comparison with modern diagnostic criteria for depression and its subtypes. He emerges with a diagnosis of major depressive disorder, having the 'with melancholic features' and 'with psychotic features' specifiers.

Does making a modern diagnosis of depression matter? The answer to this question is both 'Yes' and 'No'. It tells us that depression some 2500 years ago was virtually identical to that found in the clinics of today. The suffering that Job complains of is specifically the suffering of a man with severe depression. The guilt of the writer, which was probably due to his depression, becomes transformed into the religious guilt of his creation, Job, and his pre-occupation with sin. The reason why the answer may also be 'No' to whether a diagnosis matters is that it is already well known that Job had depression and so the precise labelling of his illness in 21st-century terms makes little or no difference to the great philosophical issues and unanswerable questions thrown up by the Book of Job, namely the suffering of the innocent, or why there is evil in the world, and the significance of faith in the presence of terrible adversity.

The Book of Job is by far the most detailed account of depression in the Bible. The writers and redactors of this piece of literature were aware they were working with a text of importance, defining a fundamental aspect of human nature – but they had no idea of exactly what this was, or any concept of depression. Psychiatric writing of this quality and depth is not to be found in any of the literature or religions of other ancient civilisations and indicates a unique depth of understanding and tolerance in the Israel of the 7th century BCE. The later inclusion of this work in the Hebrew canon ensured that for all generations thereafter its account of severe depression and the philosophical problems surrounding the themes of the suffering of the innocents would forever be woven into the fabric Judaeo-Christian ethics and religion.

The analysis also adds some understanding to the Book of Job itself. A distinction should be made between the writer and his creation, Job. The agony of depression can seem to be unbearable; indeed, anyone who has sat with a person deep in the throes of severe depression will attest to the mental torment the illness inflicts upon its victims. The suffering of the writer's creation 'Job' is far more extensive and complicated than that due to depression alone, as he brings in many other groups who also suffer, including the poor, the exploited, the widow, the orphan, but above all there is a repeated and powerful identification with the suffering of the innocent – and this remains a burning issue today just as it was in biblical times.

Job suffers, and not only does he complain to God about his suffering but he blames him for it. Many patients with depression today do likewise, despairing of themselves and of their God, although few attack God with quite such a fierce anger as Job does. Throughout it all, Job holds onto his faith, but only just. Thus Job never gives up his belief completely or assumes the position of an atheist, but at times he has grave doubts about God's compassion and in this expression of his doubts about God perhaps he was the first true agnostic.

Job maintains his faith and many scholars interpret his rebellion not so much as an attack on God or religion, but more as a specific attack on the laws of divine justice and theodicy promulgated at the time. Job cannot square up his inner feelings of depression and guilt to an act of divine retribution but neither does he have any idea where they came from. It makes no sense to him as he has committed no sin.

The writer of the Book of Job has severe depression of an endogenous type, for which there was no treatment at all prior to the advent of ECT in 1938, but the picture of melancholia at the turn of the last century gives a reasonably good fit to Job's illness. Job has psychotic depression and even today the treatment of this particular subtype is difficult. Suicide, destitution and poor self-care can be a consequence of severe untreated depression today, but how a sufferer would have survived such a condition in the 6th century BCE cannot be imagined.

The Book of Job, more so than any other book of the Bible, has attracted the interest of the medical profession and his questions 'Why me?' and 'What have I done to deserve this?' are the daily diet of many physicians in certain medical specialties the world over. People continue to look within themselves to try to explain their illnesses, in terms of some wrongdoing earlier in their lives, or that God has somehow unfairly picked on them, and such thought processes are just as prevalent today as in Job's time – and all this in spite of the very much greater knowledge of disease causation we possess today.

Job does not take well to the 'therapy' offered by his comforters, and it has to be conceded that they were mostly unhelpful and even hostile to him. Indeed, at the end of the book God comes down on Job's side and says that he was right all along and his comforters should apologise to him. Job openly states that talking about his problem has not helped: 'If I speak, my pain is not assuaged'($16^6$). The only thing he wants to do is write a book: 'Oh that my words were written down! Oh that they were inscribed in a book' ($19^{23}$). His desire to write is usually understood as his wish to set out his legal case against God for posterity. But perhaps, like the other great depressive poets in history, his wish to write stems from no more than the relief from depression that the act of writing bestows on him.

Perhaps we have much to thank his comforters for their abject failure to afford him any sort of comfort, as this may be what drove him to seek consolation elsewhere, namely by taking up his pen and gain healing through the act of writing, giving the world a literary and medical masterpiece – the Book of Job.

## References

Appelboom, T., Cogan, E. and Klastersky, J. (2007) Job of the Bible: leprosy or scabies? *Mount Sinai Journal of Medicine* 74: 36–39.

Burton, R. (1621) *The Anatomy of Melancholy* (5th edition, published by J. W. Moore, Philadelphia, 1853). Oxford: Cripps.

Cohen, A. (1946) *Job: The Soncino Books of the Bible*. London: Soncino Press.

Dhorme, E. (1984) *A Commentary on the Book of Job*. Translated by H. Knight. Nashville: Nelson.

Gordis, R. (1965) *The Book of God and Man: A Study of Job*. Chicago: University of Chicago Press.

Guilliaume, A. (1968) *Studies in the Book of Job, with a New Translation*. Leiden: E. J. Brill.

Habel, N. C. (1985) *The Book of Job: A Commentary*. London: SCM Press.

Hartley, J. E. (1988) *The Book of Job*. Grand Rapids, MI: William B. Eerdmans.

Hoch, A. and McCurdy, J. T. (1922) The prognosis of involutional melancholia. *Archives of Neurology and Psychiatry*, 7: 1–17.

Jung, C. J. (1952) *Answer to Job.* London: Routledge (1987).

Kahn, J. (1986) *Job's Illness, Loss, Grief and Integration: A Psychological Interpretation.* London: Gaskell.

Kallen, H. (1918) *The Book of Job as a Greek Tragedy.* New York: Moffat Yard and Co.

Kaputas and Frank (1977) The Book of Job and the modern view of depression. *Annals of Internal Medicine,* 86: 667–672.

Kramer, S. N. (1981) *History Begins at Sumer* (3rd edition). Philadelphia: University of Philadelphia Press.

Kutz, I. (2000) Job and his doctors' bedside wisdom in the Book of Job. *British Medical Journal,* 321: 1613–1615.

Lambert, W. G. (1960) *Babylonian Wisdom Literature.* Oxford: Clarendon.

Lee, A. (2007) Clinical features of depressive disorders. In *Seminars in General Psychiatry* (pp. 1–21), eds G. Stein and G. Wilkinson. London: Gaskell.

Mclintlock and Strong (2000) Job's skin disease. *Encyclopaedia* (CD-ROM). Seattle: Biblesoft.

Milner, M. (1956) The sense in nonsense (Freud and Blake's Job). In *The Suppressed Madness of Sane Men* (pp. 169–191). London: Routledge, 1987.

Pope, M. H. (1965) *The Anchor Bible: Job, Introduction, Translation and Notes.* Garden City, NY: Doubleday.

Reid, S. A. (1983) The Book of Job, *Psychoanalytic Review* 60, 373–391.

Sarna, N. M.(1963) The mythological background of Job 18. *Journal of Biblical Literature* 82, 315–318.

Shall, L. (2016) Personal communication.

Spero, M. H. (2007) The Hidden Subject of Job. Chapter 18 pp. 213–266, in *Hearing Visions and Seeing Voices* Eds. Gerrit G., Moshe Halevi Spero, Peter Verhagen and Hermann M. Van Praag. Dordrecht: Springer.

Stein, D. A., Kupfer, D. J. and Schatzberg, A. F. (2006) *Textbook of Mood Disorders.* Washington, DC: American Psychiatric Press.

Tur-Sinai, N. H.(1957) *The Book of Job.* Kiryath Sepher: Jerusalem.

Van Wolde, E. (2009) *Mr and Mrs Job.* London: SCM Press.

Wikepedia (2017) Leishmaniasis. 1 November.

# Appendix 1. Job stories in the Sumerian literature

## *The poem of the righteous sufferer Ludlul bel Nemeqi*

This is the best-known of the Babylonian Job stories. It is a lengthy monologue of a wealthy nobleman who encounters almost every type of calamity and illness but is eventually restored back to good health by the God Marduk. The poem was written on four tablets, of which the first three are reasonably well preserved but the fourth is not and missing sections have been inferred from other fragments found at Assur and at Sultantepe. The library of Ashurbanipal is dated to the 7th century BCE and it had nine manuscripts of this story, but the original story is much earlier; and it is also mentioned in the catalogue tablet which lists all the works of this great library. Because all the names quoted in this text are from the Cassite period it is presumed that the piece was first written during the Cassite period of Babylonia (1600–1150 BCE) and so it precedes the Book of Job by several centuries

The story is an account by the narrator of how Subsi-Mesre-Sakkan, a wealthy farmer who occupied high office in Babylonia, has been forsaken by his Gods, following which every kind of disease afflicts him. His fellow men, from the King right down to his slaves, turn against him. He then has a series of three dreams in which his deliverance is promised and finally he is freed from all diseases. Parallels with Job are fairly obvious but the tone of the piece is very different. Thus Job believes he suffers because God is attacking him and he is being punished for his sins. In *Ludlul* the narrator is far more forgiving of his God: he believes there has been an administrative mix-up and that his case has been confused with that of a wrongdoer. There are stories of demons and incantation priests – the *Asipu* – giving some notion of Babylonian medicine in this period (the second millennium BCE). It represents one of the very earliest accounts of depression.

The poem has around 500 lines and each tablet is about 120 lines in length and the whole poem can be found in *Babylonian Wisdom Literature* by W.C. Lambert. In the very limited quotation below, taken mainly from the first tablet, only those lines, which are numbered, with a suggestion of depression have been included here but the full version in cuneiform script and its translation are given in Lambert (1960).

## *Depression in Ludlul Bel Nemeqi*

### *Tablet I*

| | | |
|---|---|---|
| 1 | I will praise the Lord of wisdom | (Title of the piece) |
| 47 | My strength is gone, my appearance has become gloomy. | Anergy; depressive facies |
| 48 | my dignity has flown away, my protection made off. | I feel vulnerable |
| 49 | fearful omens beset me. | ?anxiety |
| 50 | I am got out of my house and wander outside | On the move ?agitation |
| 51 | The omen organs are confused and are inflamed for me every day. | ??gastric anxiety |
| 52 | The omen of the diviner and the interpreter cannot diagnose me | Neither the diviner nor the dream priest can explain my condition |
| 53 | What is said in the street portends ill for me | ??ideas of reference |
| 54 | When I lie down at night my dream is terrifying | ??nightmares ?nocturnal panic |
| 55 | The King, the flesh of Gods and the sun of his peoples is angry | The cause of my sickness is the anger of the King, a part-God |
| 56 | His heart is enraged with me and cannot be appeased... | God's anger is the cause |
| 71 | So that I whose lips used to prate have become like a mute | Muteness |
| 72 | My sonorous shout is reduced to silence | I can't talk, |
| 73 | My lofty head is bound down to the ground | I look down ?depressed |
| 74 | Dread has enfeebled my robust heart... | Anxiety is crippling me |
| 79 | To my many relations I am like a recluse | I am isolating myself |
| 92 | My family treat me as an alien | Estrangement from my family |
| 93 | The pit awaits anyone who speaks well of me.... | everyone speaking ill of me |

| 105 | By day, there is sighing, by night lamentation, | by day exhaustion; by night |
|---|---|---|
| 106 | Monthly, wailing; each year, gloom | depression, for months on end |
| 107 | I moan like a dove all my days | |
| 108 | For the song I emit groans | Wailing, complaining |
| 109 | My eyes.... through constant weeping | Profuse crying |
| 110 | My lower lids are distended [through abundance] of tears | |
| 111 | ... fears of my heart | ?anxiety |
| 112 | .... panic ... | ?panic |

*Tablet II*

| 39 | He who was alive yesterday is dead today | Life is transient and fickle |
|---|---|---|
| 40 | For one minute he was dejected suddenly is exuberant | Mood lability/or switching |
| 41 | one moment people are singing in exaltation | Going high then switching |
| 42 | another they groan like professional mourners | into severe depression |
| 43 | Their condition changes like opening and shutting [the legs] | |
| 48 | I am appalled at these things I do not understand their significance | No knowledge of mental symptoms or ?depression |
| 49 | As for me the exhausted one, Tempest is driving me! | Exhaustion, agitation |
| 50 | debilitating disease is let loose upon me | It is a chronic illness |
| 60 | my face is gloomy my eyes are in a flood | Depression, weeping |
| 61 | they have wrenched my neck muscles and taken strength from my neck | Weakness ?choking |

*Tablet III*

| 1 | His hand was heavy upon me I could not bear it | Hand of God is the cause |
|---|---|---|
| 2 | my dread of him was alarming it ... | Panics causing anxiety |
| 3 | his fierce ... was a tornado | ?anger of God |
| 4 | you stride was ... it ... | |
| 5 | the severe illness does not .... my person | |
| 6 | I forget makes .... my mind strays. | Poor Memory, concentration |
| 7 | day and night alike I groan | Bad days, and bad nights |
| 8 | In dream and waking moments I am equally wretched | |

The story mentions numerous physical symptoms as well but it is quite difficult to make any sort of diagnosis on his physical ailments. However, there is a catalogue of mental symptoms, including weeping, depressed mood, muteness, panic, exhaustion, low energy and anxiety, mood switching, sleep disorder and memory and concentration difficulties confirming a diagnosis of depression. The description lacks the richness of Job's poetry but the writer is conveying the idea of a fairly severe state of depression, possibly of a melancholic type. It is all caused by 'the hand of God' and the 'anger of the King', who in this culture was thought to be a part God, and no obvious triggering event is mentioned.

There are also other earlier Babylonian Job-like stories, including *Man and his God* (Kramer) and the *Counsels of the Pessimist* (Lambert, 1960), which also have verses with depressive symptoms, but for reasons of space are not included here. The significance of both Ludlul and the Sumerian poem *Man and His God* lies in the fact that they represent man's first recorded attempt to deal with the age-old problem of human suffering and yet antedate the book of Job by more than 1000 years. An Egyptian poem, 'The man who was weary of life', is also sometimes taken as a parallel, and has an excellent account of depression and suicidal thoughts. It is briefly covered in the appendix in Chapter 7, page 285. With their dates in the 2nd millennium BCE, these accounts would be the very earliest written records of depression.

## Appendix 2. Depression: clinical aspects and modern phenomenology

Job has more references to depression than any other book of the Bible and so it is fitting that the description of depression should be placed here but this account applies to all the other references to depression in the Bible. The emphasis in this account is more or less exclusively on the description of the actual depressive symptoms or its phenomenology as this is the only evidence for depression presented in the ancient texts such as the Bible. Symptom identification also forms the kernel of correct diagnosis today.

Depression is one of the most common disorders treated by GPs while severe depression, as in Job's case, falls into the domain of the psychiatric services. An earlier historical preoccupation with causation, psychodynamics, and the role of stress, and so forth led to frequent misdiagnosis and so cases were often missed, resulting in occasional tragedies. Understanding and recognising depressive symptoms and then summating their total number forms the core of the modern diagnostic systems such as the ICD-10 (WHO, 1992) and DSM-5 (American Psychiatric Association, 2013).

Making a diagnosis for any disorder in psychiatry usually hinges on recognising a particular pattern or constellation of symptoms. When only one or two symptoms are present there may be no disorder at all, because most psychiatric symptoms are non-specific and quite common in the community. Thus the presence of a single symptom such as a low mood or a queasy stomach may have little significance on its own. However, as the number and intensity of the symptoms increases and the whole picture unfolds, the likelihood of a clinically significant disorder being present also rises. Modern definitions of psychiatric disorders hinge on three elements:

(1)   specifying which particular symptoms need to be present

(2) quantifying the minimum number of symptoms as well as their minimum duration that are required

(3) a requirement that this accumulation of symptoms has caused a significant amount of distress and impairment of function for it to be considered a 'clinical disorder'.

The American Psychiatric Association has published a manual (DSM-5) incorporating these three principles, and gives easily understood definitions for all significant psychiatric disorders, and this is both simple to understand and easy to use. In the section that follows a more detailed description of individual depressive symptoms is given and most of these symptoms seem to have been observed in biblical times as well. The list of the main symptoms of depression as in DSM-5 is given in Table 2.1 on page 44 and the account below of depressive symptoms is drawn from Lee (2007).

## Depressed mood

Depressed mood is the commonest symptom found in depressive disorders and it includes feelings of sadness, misery and dejection. The mood is painful and oppressive and often without apparent cause. It is distinguished from normal feelings of sadness by its greater intensity, duration and pervasiveness. Sufferers feel heavy hearted and weighed down by their misery, tears come easily and unexpectedly and for no reason. Those with very severe depression sometimes cannot cry and are in a state of frozen misery. Some patients can successfully conceal their depressed mood and put on a cheerful face. It is unusual for a patient to open a consultation with a complaint of depression and more often they will speak of some current life difficulty. Some will present their depression in culture-specific ways as for example with pain or other bodily symptoms. The symptom must have been present more or less continuously for at least 2 weeks to qualify for it being due to depression. The 2-week clause applies to all the other symptoms described below, and is used because when the symptoms have lasted for 2 or more weeks they are likely to persist for several months unless treated, whereas depressive symptoms of briefer duration will frequently resolve spontaneously and may not signify the presence of a true depressive episode.

## The symptom of anhedonia

Anhedonia refers to a loss of any sense of pleasure or joy and is a key symptom of depression. The word 'anhedonia' itself was coined by the French psychologist Ribot to refer to 'an insensibility relating to pleasure alone', which was to contrast with 'analgesia' or the absence of pain. Anhedonia is the second most common symptom in depressive disorders. Whereas painful sadness is the psychological opposite of pleasure, anhedonia refers to its absence. In depressive anhedonia, the subject cannot enjoy anything and their whole sense of pleasure has gone. Anhedonia is part of a wider phenomenon and, as Jaspers describes, 'the feeling of having lost feelings and is associated with a terrible emptiness – a subjectively felt void'. It is closely linked to feelings of dulled perception and depersonalisation and also to feelings of insufficiency and lack of vitality. Those with anhedonia do not experience pleasure even if something good happens. They are not cheered by fine weather, receiving a compliment, winning a game, or even a surprise windfall. They cannot enjoy the company of friends and are not happy spending time at their previous hobbies and interests. Those living in the countryside with depression and anhedonia are no longer able to enjoy the sight of the fields, the sky, the trees and the flowers.

Klein considered it to be a marker for classic depressive states and the first criterion for DSM-5 depression is that the person has *either* a depressed mood *or* the symptom of anhedonia lasting for at least two weeks. Thus anhedonia is central to the diagnosis of a depressive episode.

## Anxiety

Anxiety is also common in depressive disorders, while more severe cases present with full-blown panic attacks. Usually anxiety is experienced as a sense of apprehensive foreboding as if something terrible is about to happen. Sometimes the autonomic accompaniments of panic, which include a dry mouth, palpitations, tremulousness, sweating, flushing, butterflies in the stomach, choking, and difficulties in getting breath and dizziness, are present but in the absence of a full-blown panic. Panic disorder itself is commonly associated with depression but is today diagnosed as a separate condition. A state of depression with anxious thoughts often appears on waking amongst those with morning depression. The feeling of anxiety is often coloured by cognitive distortions, in particular pessimistic thinking, low self-esteem and preoccupations with death. Danger is felt to be imminent, as are feelings of loss and disgrace. Everyone encountered is a potential thief or is out to pick a quarrel. Friends or relatives will die. There is fear of collapse, of madness, or death or eternal damnation.

## Agitation

This is the combination of marked anxiety accompanied by excessive motor activity. Sufferers feel anxious and restless and complain they cannot keep still. They continually wring their hands, or fidget with some object. They may constantly shift position, cannot remain seated, pace up and down, and feverishly pick at their clothes. In more severe states they may have a staring gaze with wide open eyes and a half open mouth. The sufferer cannot escape from a round of painful thoughts. One woman in a state of agitation said 'I know that something has to be done but I don't know what it is'. In severe agitation there may sometimes be gross excitement, having an explosive and aggressive quality, and some of the episodes of violence due to depression may occur as a result of severe agitation.

## Retardation

This is the obverse of agitation but is equally unpleasant. Subjects feel their movement is slowed; speech may be slow, hesitant and laboured, with sentences seldom having more than 10 words. There may be long pauses before replying and also pauses between each word. In extreme cases the subject sits in a chair motionless and not speaking and becomes mute.

## Irritability

This is experienced as a decreased threshold to anger and annoyance in the face of frustration. Sometimes sufferers are able to contain the emotion but in other cases they may exhibit increased argumentativeness, quarrelling and outbursts of temper which seem to be out of character for the individual concerned. In extreme cases they may break things, punch the wall, or even be violent to others.

## Changes in mood, mood lability

Fluctuation in mood is common and can be abrupt and dangerous. Some depressives are very reactive to small changes in their circumstances (e.g. a visit from a friend might cheer them up, but then they might collapse on a piece of bad news). There is a temptation to regard mood lability as a sign of a less serious depression because on one day the patient appears to be quite cheerful, only to hang themselves on the next day.

Around 50% subjects with depression have a fixed pattern of mood lability called 'diurnal mood variation'. They wake up with severe depression in the morning, which gradually improves as the day goes on, often attaining a state of euthymia (normal mood) by the evening. This pattern is said to be characteristic of the melancholic subtype of depression. As their depression gradually improves, the time of day when their mood switches to normal becomes increasingly earlier on in the day and eventually the morning depression disappears altogether.

## Anergy: loss of energy

Loss of energy is usually framed in terms of unpleasant or inappropriate tiredness, listlessness and exhaustion. Sufferers complain of sluggishness, or of feeling sapped or drained, or lacking strength. Their limbs feel like lead. They lack vitality; they describe themselves as worn out, or too exhausted even to move. Kraepelin writes:

> He drags himself with difficulty from one day to another lacking any spirit or will power. He cannot work any longer.... The smallest piece of work costs him an unheard of effort. Even the most simple everyday tasks such as house work, getting up in the morning, washing and dressing are only achieved with the greatest effort, and are often left undone. Work, important business letters, grow like a mountain in front of the patient and are just left undone.... Sometimes a veritable passion for lying in bed develops. (Kraepelin 1921, p. 78, reference in Lee)

Informants report the neglect of children, of cooking meals, housework tasks, personal cleanliness and tidiness. Depressed people are sent home or even suspended from their work because of their inefficiency. The combination of daytime exhaustion together with the inability to sleep at night may be particularly hard to bear.

## Apathy and loss of interest

The enthusiast gives up his hobbies, the gardener leaves the weeds alone, and the golfer lets his clubs rust. There is a marked diminution in both domestic and leisure activities, and this is accompanied by apathy and associated with the sense of helpless futility. This symptom is probably due to a combination of anhedonia together with depressive anergy. However, the change in participation in these once pleasurable activities is something that patients and their relatives will notice early on and will frequently voice amongst their complaints.

## Inefficient thinking, poor concentration and indecisiveness

There are several components to the difficulties in thinking found in depression. These include an inability to concentrate, indecisiveness, a tendency to ruminate and some memory impairment. Patients with poor concentration complain their thoughts just tend to drift off; they cannot follow a TV programme, or can follow only a few lines in a book or a newspaper. They have difficulty following a conversation and cannot put their thoughts together; their head feels heavy and they feel stupid and confused. Sometimes they may forget where they put things as a result of an impaired memory. Indecisiveness may show itself in inconstancy, with sufferers frequently changing their minds or considering at great length the simplest of matters and/or being completely paralysed by the challenge of coming to a decision. Others complain of too many thoughts coming into their heads and feeling confused.

## Disturbances of appetite and weight

In most cases there is little appetite for food and drink and in more severe cases the food lacks any flavour. In some cases there is no more than a disinclination to eat due to loss of appetite but sometimes there is outright refusal. Carers may need to use persuasion and cajolery to make the subject eat. Reluctance to eat can stem directly from a delusional belief that their food has been poisoned. Weight loss as a result of loss of appetite in depression is common and ICD-10 diagnostic criteria specify more than 5% of body weight is lost in a month. However, weight loss usually stabilises at around 6–7 kg (1 stone), unlike the continuing decline seen in anorexia nervosa and amongst those with undiagnosed malignant disease.

In around 10% of subjects there is weight gain and this is sometimes associated with hypersomnia and/or comfort eating.

Loss of thirst is less common but when it occurs amongst elderly depressives it can rapidly become life-threatening as it causes dehydration.

## Depressive sleep disorder

Kraepelin's patients lay in bed, sleepless, for hours on end, tormented by painful ideas. If they did sleep they had confused and anxious dreams and then woke up feeling worn out and weary.

Three patterns of sleep in depression are described. In initial insomnia there is a delay in sleep onset; more than one hour's delay in getting off to sleep is required for diagnosis and a two-hour delay marks a more severe disturbance. Middle insomnia refers to a pattern of frequent awakenings in the night or a prolonged period of being unable to return to sleep. People with depression sometimes fall into a deep sleep before they are due to wake up. The third pattern, which is traditionally associated with the melancholic subtype of depression, is early-morning wakening. This is defined as waking at least one hour earlier than normal, while waking more than two hours earlier than normal marks are very much more severe disturbance and this is required to satisfy ICD-10 criterion for the somatic syndrome (the melancholic subtype in DSM-5). During early-morning wakening, the depression and agitation may be very severe and this is the time when the risk for suicidal behaviour is at its highest. Occasionally there is increased duration of sleep (hypersomnia) associated with depression and sometimes there is inverted pattern with poor sleep during the night and long periods of sleep during the day.

## Disorders of thought: depressive cognitions

Cognitive distortions can relate to the past, present or future, or to the self, or the outside world. Thinking about the past is dominated by self-reproach and guilt. In the present, the self is often viewed as worthless and helpless. Hypochondriacal ideas may occur as well. The outside world is seen as useless, meaningless and sometimes persecutory; the future is viewed with apprehension, pessimism and hopelessness, and nihilistic thoughts and thoughts of death are common. Suicidal ideation may follow in the setting of acute hopelessness and despair but sometimes can arise independently.

## Guilt

Guilt is one of the most striking features of depression and is present in 75% of cases. Three separate phenomena are recognised:

(1) *Pathological guilt.* Those affected blame themselves for some trivial action that others would not take seriously; they may even recognise this to be out of proportion but dwell on it repeatedly and cannot help but feel self-blame. They blame themselves for duties they have ignored, unwise decisions, stealing sweets as a child, letting friends down, and a host of other trivia. Characteristically sufferers also feel blame for bringing an illness onto themselves. Ideas of worthlessness and self-depreciation are strongly associated with guilt.

(2) *Guilty ideas of reference.* Those affected feel that others are blaming them; in a more severe form they feel accused by others. This might

count as 'ideas of reference' Insight is preserved and so sufferers recognise the feelings as their own. Intense forms can shade into persecutory delusions. Job probably has this and the text does describe guilty ideas of reference.

(3) *Delusions of guilt.* As the depression deepens, ideas of guilt become less realistic and insight is lost. Patients magnify their own role in events and give an entirely false account of some serious misdemeanour, as in a delusional memory. Patients may believe they have committed adultery or incest, that they have killed their families or caused a train crash or some other disaster. Patients with delusional guilt may repeatedly give themselves up to the police. It may also involve feelings of responsibility for others. Thus one patient became convinced that she was making other patients in the ward mentally ill.

## Thoughts of worthlessness and self-deprecation

In depressive states any premorbid tendency to feelings of inferiority and low self-worth may be amplified. Patients often regard themselves as worthless and total failures; sometimes there are delusions of poverty or that they are bankrupt. They feel themselves to be unwanted or unloved and not worthy of having any friends and feel discontented with themselves and lack confidence; they may feel that they will lose their jobs and face ruin. In severe cases there may be feelings that border on self-loathing and self-hatred. Some people have a low opinion of themselves all the time and the identification of depressive low self-esteem depends on the way it fluctuates with the mood. Thus it should be absent prior to the depression and should go once the depression has resolved.

## Depressive delusions

These only occur as an endpoint to severe cognitive distortion and where the content is depressive. These are said to be *mood congruent* and include delusions of guilt, of poverty, of catastrophe, of hypochondriasis and nihilistic delusions. Cotard (1882) described a syndrome of nihilistic delusions associated with hypochondriasis where patients believe they have no brain or no bowels, or that their bowels are not working, and are completely blocked up or that their bowels have ceased to exist.

*Non-mood congruent delusions* include persecutory delusions, delusions of jealousy, delusions of bodily change. These may occur in depression as well as in other psychotic disorders. Persecutory delusions in depression commonly take the form that the patient is under surveillance, or that there is a plot, an organisation such as the CIA is pursuing them, or other patients are detectives or secret agents, food is poisoned and so forth. The persecution is usually felt to be just and deserved and derives from guilty ideas of reference but some patients show resentment at its unjust nature, and may even loudly proclaim their innocence, as Job does.

Other symptoms of depression are described elsewhere in this book. *Suicidal thoughts* are described in the chapter on suicide, *depersonalisation and derealisation* in the chapter on Jeremiah, and *stupor* in the chapter on Ezekiel.

### Prevalence, causation and outlook

Only the briefest account of issues of prevalence and causation will be given here, as such information is widely available in standard textbooks of psychiatry. The very large American 'Epidemiological Catchment Area Study' gave a one-year prevalence of 2.7% and a lifetime prevalence of 4.9% for major depression. The mean age of onset for depression was 27 years. In pre-pubescent children there is little difference between the rates of depression in boys and girls, but after puberty depression becomes twice as common in females compared with males. There is wide variation in the sex ratio for depression, probably related to socio-cultural factors such as the position of women in society; for example, in India the sex ratio is over 3:1.

Rates are lower among those who are married than among those who are divorced, separated or never married. Lower socio-economic status and unemployment are both associated with higher rates of depression. Long-term follow-up shows that in most cases the depression will recur and 10-year follow-up studies show that around 75% of cases become recurrent depression, a figure which increases to 90% when the follow-up period is extended to 20 years. Thus, a single episode of major depression which does not recur is unusual. Depression often occurs together with other psychiatric disorders. A study in Holland found that 46% of depressed men also had a comorbid anxiety disorder and 43% had substance abuse. A small number of those with severe depression experience their depressions as a part of their bipolar disorder.

Depression is a common and debilitating disorder. Over the last 30 years there has been an interest in the concept of 'burden of disease', which refers to the economic and social cost of an illness, and depression has the second highest burden of disease, after diabetes. Depression has huge economic costs, partly due to the loss of work and associated benefit expenses, but also because there is high consumption of medical resources as a result of the depression itself and also as a result of associated medical disorders.

Depression can be a life-threatening disorder and some 60% of all suicides are associated with depression, and for those between 18 and 50 suicide has recently become the most common cause of death.

Causation is only partially understood; depression can run in families, and twin studies point to a substantial genetic contribution. This is greater in the more severe types of depression, such as the depressions of bipolar disorder, where up to 90% of its causation is thought to be genetic. Stress, life events, in particular losses or negative life events, also play a role. Normal bereavement, which may resemble depression, is usually excluded; however, many cases of bereavement go on for a very long time and are much more severe than usual and in these cases the bereavement is said to be pathological and has developed into an episode of major depression.

Neuro-imaging brain studies have shown decreased metabolism in certain areas of the brain. The fact that antidepressants act on certain specific brain chemicals, such as serotonin and noradrenaline, has led to a huge upsurge in studies of brain chemistry in depression. So far no single chemical cause has been identified but these studies have paved the way for new antidepressants and provided a basis for understanding the condition in biochemical terms.

Today, treatment is usually a combination of an antidepressant with some sort of counselling or cognitive behavioural therapy and is usually effective. Treatment-resistant cases are encountered in around 15–20% of subjects and are more frequent in psychotic depression, the category that Job seems to have. The treatment of resistant depression is more difficult and requires complicated combinations of drugs and/or ECT. Even with the modern armoury of medication, not all cases respond and for those that do, later recurrence rates may be high. Further details on the modern management of depression is given in modern textbooks of psychiatry such as *The Oxford Textbook of Psychiatry*.

# Chapter 3

# Jeremiah: the nature of his woe

Jeremiah was truly the genius of torment and discord, the Euripides, the Pascal, or the Dostoyevsky of the Old Testament.
(Jean Steinman, 1952)

## Introduction

The Book of Jeremiah contains the legacy and sayings of the prophet Jeremiah, who lived in the seventh century BCE in ancient Judah. His book is the largest of the three great literary prophetic works in the Hebrew scriptures. According to Bright (1965), an Old Testament scholar, Jeremiah was one of the seminal figures of Israel's history:

> He was a man of great spiritual insight and depth, a man of driving eloquence who possessed unusual poetic gifts; he was, moreover, in the profoundest sense of the word a brave person, a passionate and exceedingly human man, who captures our sympathies as few figures from ancient times do.

His writings reveal that he was often a troubled soul, and indeed his name is synonymous with that of a pessimist, while the word 'jeremiad' has come into the English language to signify a long and mournful complaint.

Throughout his life Jeremiah was acutely sensitive to the suffering of his nation, the suffering of his fellow man, but also to his own inner turmoil. What was the nature of this angst, and can it be understood through the lens of modern psychiatry? The sentiments of an ancient biblical prophet of the 7th century BCE are distant in both time and culture to modern Western psychiatry, perhaps making our understanding of his psychic pain difficult, yet his writings are so lucid and precise that the reader can readily recognise the mental symptoms he writes about.

In this chapter all the verses which contain possible mental symptoms have been highlighted. This is accompanied by a brief discourse on their historical-cultic significance as determined by Old Testament scholars, so as to place the psychiatric interpretation in its proper social context. However, before embarking on this, it may be helpful to set out the life and times of Jeremiah, and how the book which bears his name came to be written and became the text we have today.

## The life and times of Jeremiah

We know remarkably little about Jeremiah's personal life; the few details we have come mainly from the book which bears his name. We are told that he began his prophetic career in the thirteenth year of the reign of King Josiah, which corresponds to 627 BCE, suggesting that he would have been born around 645 BCE. He was born in the town of Ananoth, in the ancient tribal territory of Benjamin, which lies about three miles north-east of Jerusalem and near the present-day village of 'Anata. Jeremiah came from a priestly family, the son of Hilkiah, who himself was said to be a descendent of Abiathar, a priest of David. However, this was not the Hilkiah (the son of Shallum) who was the high priest involved in the Josianic reforms. We know nothing about his childhood, but Bright speculates that his upbringing at the hands of his priestly father may have been strict, perhaps accounting for his later bitterness towards the clergy. Jeremiah never married or had a family and so may have led quite a lonely life. One passage states that he was in fact commanded not to marry, although this may have been a later insertion, possibly added during post-exilic times, when his single status would already have been known (Bright, 1965).

Jeremiah lived at a time of great historical turbulence, a period of political instability in his own land of Judah, with frequent wars between the neighbouring states. The three powerful surrounding empires, Egypt, Assyria and Babylon, jostled for supremacy and the minor statelets in the region such as Judah had to constantly switch their political allegiances to ensure their survival. The lands of Judah and Samaria lay on the trade routes between these empires and imperial armies would pass through these two small Hebrew states to wage their wars. Judah was therefore very much caught up in the vortex of these ancient power struggles. News of the size of the armies, the weaponry, the bloodshed, the victories and defeats as well as the suffering of civilians would have been known in Jerusalem. More so than for any other Old Testament prophet, the events and politics of the day became the focus of Jeremiah's writings. He was an educated man and would have been all too aware of these seismic historical events, which no doubt influenced his profound anti-war rhetoric.

Judah was then reigned by King Manasseh. Judah had been a vassal state of Assyria for more than a century and so had come to assume the cultic practices of its Assyrian masters; the worship of Assyrian gods such as Baal and the paying of tribute should be understood in this light. The much maligned Manasseh, who gets a very bad press in the Bible, probably did no more than make essential political compromises and his submission to the Assyrians kept the peace for 50 years.

Once Assyria had been decisively defeated in 616 BCE by the Babylonians, Judah was briefly able to reassert itself. With Manasseh dead and Assyria no longer in control, there was a renaissance of nationalism accompanied by a wish to return to the older Yahwistic ways of worship. The former northern kingdom (Israel), now known as Samaria, once more came under the hegemony of Jerusalem, at least for the purposes of cultic and religious practice. In 622 BCE some workmen while making repairs to the walls of the Jerusalem Temple found a small scroll which contained an 'Old Book of the Law', now thought to be an early version of the book of Deuteronomy. It was shown to King Josiah, who gave it his approval and used it to usher in a series of religious and cultic innovations, the so-called 'Josianic reforms'. These reforms were aimed at reversing the nation's moral decline.

The essence of the Josianic reform was to purge the nation of all non-Yahwistic cults and practices, which included Baal worship, practices of magic and divination, as well as practices such as child sacrifice, all of which were abolished. Also, certain key personnel such as the eunuch priests and sacred Temple prostitutes of both sexes were put to death. The second arm to these reforms was more administrative, leading to the abolition of regional shrines, such as those at Bethel and Shiloh, resulting in the centralisation of all public worship to the Jerusalem Temple. Bright (1965) reminds us of the dominant role the priesthood had in the ancient world: 'In ancient Israel, religious life, political life, church and state were never separate'. Although Jeremiah did not play a major role in these reforms, he was very much opposed to the worship of foreign gods, personal immorality and practices such as child sacrifice.

In this world of shifting alliances, the Egyptians had become alarmed at the seemingly unstoppable rise of Babylonian power in the east. They tried to assist Assyria in its attempts to retake the city of Harran. The Egyptian king, Neco II (610–594 BCE), marched north, but Josiah, in a vain attempt to support the Assyrians, tried to stop him and interposed his forces and lost his life at the battle of Megiddo. This brought to an end Judah's brief flirtation with independence and relative freedom. For the next four years (609–605 BCE) Judah and Samaria came under Egyptian hegemony. One of Josiah's sons, Jehoahaz, was placed on the throne, but his tenure lasted for only three months, and he was replaced by Jehoaichin, another son of Josiah, who then became the Egyptian vassal king.

Jeremiah began his ministry with the belief that his country was coming under judgement, perhaps to be destroyed by some monstrous enemy from the north (now thought to be Babylon), as punishment for the apostasy of its people. Jeremiah appears to have had a good relationship with King Josiah, but Jehoaichin was a wilful petty tyrant, contemptuous of religion.

In his 'Temple sermon' (Jeremiah $7^{1-15}$) Jeremiah criticises the nation for widespread social injustice, the oppression of foreigners, widows and orphans, the increasing violence and the decline in the nation's moral standards, which had all accompanied the return to Baal worship. Not surprisingly, Jeremiah soon found himself to be a very unpopular figure, *contra munde*, falling out of favour with the royal establishment, the clergy, as well as the people. The crowd repeatedly jeered him and there were calls for the death penalty for unpopular prophets. Things got so bad that at one stage Jeremiah was arrested by an officer of the Temple called Pashur, who placed him on trial.

During this period, Jeremiah's writings reveal considerable emotional turmoil. Bright (1965), a theologian with no real psychiatric knowledge, writes as follows:

> his spirits almost broke.... He gave way to fits of angry recriminations, depression and even suicidal despair. Thus we can see him lashing out at those who abused him. His language is most violent and he calls on his God to join his cause and judge them without mercy.

Bright seems to be implying that Jeremiah was teetering on some sort of a nervous breakdown during this period, which corresponds to the early part of King Jehoaichin's reign.

Judah was under Egyptian tutelage only briefly, but a seismic shift in power was to about take place. Following the defeat of the Egyptians at the hands of the Babylonians in the battle of Carchemish in 605 BCE, the Babylonian armies advanced over the Philistine plains, seizing and deporting the people of Ashkelon, an important Canaanite seaport, a defeat which caused great consternation in Jerusalem.

Judah's fortunes went full circle in a 20-year period, from being a vassal state of the Assyrian empire, then coming under Egyptian hegemony for a period, followed by a relatively brief period of independence, before finally coming under the rule of the Babylonians. Jeremiah lived through these dangerous times and his writings gave religious meaning to these events. He was convinced that the Babylonians had been appointed to serve as Yahweh's agents of destruction and they were tasked to punish Judah and its people for their crimes and their apostasy. This made it pointless to fight the Babylonians, as this would be the same as fighting against Yahweh. Later, Jeremiah's ambivalent attitude to the Babylonians came to haunt him, particularly during the siege of Jerusalem, as such utterances were perceived as treasonable and he was punished, nearly losing his life, because his preaching at the time was thought to be seditious.

Matters began to move to a climax in Judah when Jehoaichin rebelled against Nebuchadnezzar in 601 BCE. Jeremiah viewed this to be an act of folly, as it was to precipitate Nebuchadnezzar's return, and the defeat of Jerusalem and the first deportation in 598/597 BCE. Thereafter Zedekiah (one of Jehoiachin's sons) was placed on the throne as the Babylonian vassal king. A few years later, prompted by disturbances in Babylon itself, Zedekiah toyed with the idea of rebelling against his Babylonian tutelage and met with the kings of the neighbouring states of Edom, Moab, Ammon, Tyre and Sidon. Together they hatched a plot to overthrow their Babylonian masters. Jeremiah warned against the folly of such a conspiracy and to demonstrate his point he appeared before the kings of the neighbouring states wearing the yoke of an ox. He told the kings to submit to the will of Nebuchadnezzar – in the same way as he had submitted to the yoke of an ox – if they were to stand any chance of avoiding total annihilation. Such symbolic 'sign actions' were said to be characteristic of the great prophets.

Jeremiah then briefly left Jerusalem to visit his hometown of Ananoth on family business, possibly to buy land, but by this time even the people of Ananoth hated him so much that they denounced him and sought to kill him. Jeremiah tried to leave the city, but was arrested at the city gate of Jerusalem and charged with desertion. After a summary trial before a panel of princes he was thrown into a water cistern which had thick mud at the bottom. He would almost certainly have died there had he not been rescued by an Ethiopian eunuch called Ebed-Melech. Jeremiah was freed but was confined to the court of the guard until the final surrender of Jerusalem.

The siege of Jerusalem is described in graphic detail in the book of Lamentations, which is traditionally held also to have been written by Jeremiah. Probably by this time he was a much venerated figure, and he came under the care of the new governor, a man called Gedaliah. Exactly how he came under the care of the governor is uncertain, but one version suggests he was found by one of Nebuchadnezzar's bodyguards among a group of prisoners in Ramah who had been assembled for deportation. He was offered the choice of whether to go to Babylon or stay in Jerusalem under the care of Gedaliah. Jeremiah initially chose to remain in Jerusalem. Unfortunately, Gedaliah was soon to be assassinated, and those in the royal court associated with this crime duly took off for Egypt, taking Jeremiah and his friend Baruch with them. Jeremiah must have been over 60 years of age by this time, and the group took refuge in the town of Taphanes, just inside the Egyptian border, which corresponds to present-day Tel-Defnah. After this we hear nothing more about Jeremiah, who seemingly died in Egypt.

Jeremiah was far more than an observer and recorder of the historical destiny of his nation. He was an active participant in its religious and political life as well as its struggle for survival. Sometimes he found favour with the establishment of the day, but for much of his life he assumed the role of a dissident and a prophet. His writings reflect his own personal struggles, as well as the fate of his people and of his nation. His writings form a complicated mélange of religious rhetoric and politics. Carrol (1985) uses the term 'theo-politics' to describe his theology because in the ancient world religion and politics were virtually one and the same. Suffering is also a central theme to his life: the suffering of his nation, his own personal suffering, as well as the pain and suffering of many unnamed ordinary individuals he encountered. However, it is within his report of the suffering of the people and his own suffering that we find an eloquent account of his psychiatric disorder – all written in exquisite religious poetry.

## The Book of Jeremiah and its composition

His book, like most of the larger prophetic works, is a collection of separate writings, or, as Bright suggests, 'an anthology of anthologies'. It is difficult to read, in part because it is written in alien tongue and in part because of its subject matter – it concerns an ancient people, whose history is largely unknown and whose wars with neighbours seem now to be irrelevant.

We have two versions of the Book of Jeremiah: the Septuaguint (LXX), which is dated around 200 BCE and written in Greek; and the Masoretic text, written in Hebrew, known as the official Jewish text, of which the earliest authentic version is the Codex Leningradiensis, dated around 1010 AD. The texts of the Book of Jeremiah in these two versions differ considerably, perhaps more so than for any other book of the Old Testament. The LXX version is one-eighth shorter and after ch. 25 assumes a different order. These differences, though, do not impinge on the psychiatric material.

We do not know for certain who wrote the Book of Jeremiah, as much of it is now known to have been edited and rewritten during the post-exilic period, 586–400 BCE. Literary analysis initially by Duhm (1901) and later by Mowinckel (1914), a Swedish Old Testament scholar, has identified three different types of material in the book, known as Mowinckel types A, B and C, with each type probably having separate authorship.

Type A material is mainly in verse and found in Jeremiah chs 1–25. It is thought to be pre-exilic and probably composed by Jeremiah himself.

Type B material is mainly in prose. In these passages Jeremiah is referred to in the third person. The material is mainly biographical and often in a chronological order. Baruch the scribe and friend of Jeremiah is thought to be the author of much of the type B material.

Type C material is less easily classified but consists of sermons or discourses, often in the style of Deuteronomy, as well as debates between God and Jeremiah, and between God and the people; moralising passages about sin and judgement; and promises of future restoration and renewed covenants. Mostly written in prose, these sections are thought to be mainly post-exilic compositions recorded by unknown editors.

Perhaps the most important of these editors was the Deuteronomist(s) or the Deuteronomist school of writers, sometimes abbreviated as 'D'. There may have been other post-exilic contributions as well. Hyatt (1984) suggests that D operated after the exile in Babylon, around 550 BCE, and he provides an extensive review of the Deuteronomist's contribution to the Book of Jeremiah. The ideas of D are distinctive and persuasive and his writings can be recognised by the use of certain phrases (for details see Weinstein, 1972; Hyatt, 1984). The main thrust of D's ideas were as follows: Yahweh alone was to be worshiped and idolatry was one of the greatest sins. D had a great interest in the theology of history, with special emphasis on the doctrine of divine retribution:

Hyatt provides a list of all the passages in the Book of Jeremiah thought to be Deuteronomistic later insertions, but none of these contain mental symptoms, suggesting that for the greater part the verses describing mental phenomena were probably authentic Jeremiah material, rather than being post-exilic additions. The Deuteronomist(s) believed that Yahweh always punishes the wicked and rewards the righteous. 'A high social morality is demanded, with social justice for all, with humanitarianism directed towards the less fortunate members of society' (Hyatt, 1984).

The humanitarianism and compassion of the Deuteronomists were values which Jeremiah also aspired to. More significantly, they may have also been the key to permitting the account of Jeremiah's own personal suffering to remain in the text and so become a part of later scripture. Crucially, D did not censor out such obviously highly personal material from the book and this included details of his psychiatric symptoms. This was unusual for a religious text of the ancient world, as well as for the rest of the OT, where the focus is far more exclusively on cultic preoccupations. Jeremiah was the first great anti-hero, replete with misery, terror and depression, and such characters are few and far between in both the Bible and the literature of the ancient world, which tends to be much more dominated by myths, legends and heroes who triumph in the fields of war, marriage and procreation, rather than nervous and depressed solitary individuals such as Jeremiah.

The vast majority of the text with psychiatric significance is in chs 1–25, written in verse, and probably Mowinckel's type A material. Almost all the verses which describe significant mental phenomena are to be found within his confessions. It is sensible to make inferences about any possible mental disorder only if the verses containing mental symptoms were written by Jeremiah himself, but this, then, appears to be the case.

## The prophetic literature

The Israelite prophetic books form a unique genre in the literature of the world which is central to the three great spiritual faiths which sprang from it. The prophets are conventionally thought of in two groups: the 'ecstatic prophets' and the 'great literary prophets'. The writings of the great literary prophets commences in the 8th century BCE; it starts with Amos and extends down to the exile in 586 BCE. There are three great literary prophets, Isaiah, Ezekiel and Jeremiah, and 12 more minor prophets, whose works are collectively known as the 'Book of 12'. Abraham Heschel, a Chasidic rabbi but also a professor of theology, explains prophecy from a religious perspective:

> The prophet's task is to convey a divine view, yet as a person he has a point of view. The prophet deals with relations between God and man, where contradiction is inevitable. Escape from God and return to him are inextricable parts of man's existence.... He speaks from the perspective of God as perceived from his own situation ... as well as being a prophet, he is also a poet, preacher, statesman, social critic and moralist ... the prophet seldom tells a story but casts events. He rarely sings but he often castigates.... He does more than translate reality into a poetic key: he is the preacher whose purpose is not self-expression or the 'purgative of emotions' but of communication. His images must not shine, they must burn.... The prophet is intent on intensifying responsibility, he is impatient of excuse and contemptuous of any pretense and self-pity. His tone is rarely sweet and caressing but is frequently consoling and disburdening: his words are often slashing, even horrid, designed to shock rather than edify.... Above all the prophets remind us of the moral state of a people: few are guilty, but all are responsible. If we admit that the individual is in some measure conditioned or affected by the spirit of society, an individual's crime discloses society's corruption.... (From Heschel, 1962, *The Prophets*)

## The religious importance of Jeremiah

Fishbane (2002, pp. 540–545) explains that Jeremiah provides a mixture of repeated prophecies, mainly of doom but also of new hope. His doom prophecies relate to breaches of the covenant, both cultic – in his repeated attacks on idolatry, as well as moral, in his condemnation of the people's sinful behaviour. As a consequence, Yahweh will bring retribution to the nation. This is the explanation for the wars and famines that beset the nation. Not all his prophecies are doom laden, because he is also commanded 'to build and to plant' and to allow the people to take comfort. He urges the exiles in Babylon not to pine away in a vain messianic hope, but instead to build homes and take wives and, in short, to get on with their lives. Jeremiah's prophecies of rebuilding and planting are the leitmotif of hope and he foresees national restoration. Themes of restoration have assumed great importance in both Christian and Jewish theology. The Book of Jeremiah also plays a direct part in the liturgy of the Jewish religion. Thus passages from the prophets (the *haftarot*) are read in the Sabbath service throughout the year, and six of these are derived from the Book of Jeremiah.

Sections from two of these *haftarot* are included here because they also include some psychiatry.

Jeremiah writes with compassion and suffers together with his people, but as well as the 'national suffering', he suffers much personal anguish as well. What was the nature of his suffering? Can we understand his anguish in the language of modern psychiatry? And if so, is this going to be a worthwhile exercise? The underlying thesis of this chapter is that Jeremiah suffered from two common conditions, namely panic disorder and depression. Panic disorder is common in the community; waves of fear sweep over subjects who report sudden overwhelming feelings of terror, often starting abruptly and appearing out of the blue. The condition is described in the appendix at the end of the present chapter. Jeremiah wrote freely about his feelings of terror and panic – as well as the many somatic symptoms that accompanied these feelings. Few readers will be surprised to learn that Jeremiah also suffered from depression as well – the word Jeremiah being almost synonymous with pessimism and depression. To make better sense of these passages and place them in their historical and religious context, commentary has been taken from the writings of Old Testament scholars, particularly the works of Lundbom (1994, 1999), Holladay (1985), Bright (1965) and Carroll (1985). In addition, the relevant psychiatric literature has also been highlighted.

The chapter proceeds with Jeremiah's description of panic disorder and its main symptoms, while in the latter part of the chapter the evidence for his depression is discussed. Jeremiah's account is entirely autobiographical, and while he knew he was suffering, he had no idea that this might be a medical disorder as we construe it today.

## Panic disorder

### The foe from the north: Jeremiah 4$^{19-31}$

Chapter 4 of the Book of Jeremiah concerns the terrible disaster about to be befall the nation at the hands of the 'foe from the north' and is one of Jeremiah's prophecies of doom. The poem has an overall feel of alarm (best appreciated by reading it in one go), suggesting he wrote it either while in the midst of a panic attack or shortly afterwards, when he was recovering from his feelings of terror. The chapter opens with a plea from Yahweh to his people Israel to return to him and relinquish their apostasy and other sinful ways. Truth, justice and uprightness should be pursued if the people are to receive forgiveness and redemption. But there is also a big stick if the people should fail to change their ways: Yahweh will bring a terrible 'foe from the north', who will lay siege and destroy their land. Jeremiah is personally much troubled by the forthcoming disaster, and his personal lament starts at verse 19 and is replete with the symptoms of panic. The whole passage (Jeremiah 4$^{19-31}$) is quoted below on the left, accompanied by commentary highlighting the psychiatric symptoms on the right.

| | |
|---|---|
| 19  My anguish, my anguish! I writhe in pain! | Severe anxiety; distress |
| Oh, the walls of my heart! | ?Pain in the chest wall |

| | |
|---|---|
| My heart is beating wildly;<br>I cannot keep silent;<br>I hear the sound of the trumpet,<br>the alarm of war. | Tachycardia; increased awareness<br>of his own heartbeat<br>unpleasant noises |
| 20 Disaster overtakes disaster, the whole<br>land is laid waste.<br>Suddenly my tents are destroyed,<br>my curtains in a moment. | anxiety about future catastrophes<br><br>an abrupt onset to the destruction |
| 21 How long must I see the standard,<br>and hear the unpleasant noises of war<br>sound of the trumpet? | |
| 22 For my people are foolish, they do not<br>know me; they are stupid children,<br>they have no understanding.<br>They are skilled in doing evil,<br>but do not know how to do good. | It is the fault of the people |
| 23 I looked on the earth, and lo it was<br>waste and void; and to the heavens,<br>and they had no light. | Devastation following invasion |
| 24 I looked on the mountains, and lo,<br>they were quaking, and all the hills<br>moved to and fro. | Shaking and quaking?<br>?allusion to tremor |
| 25 I looked, and lo, there was no one at all,<br>and all the birds of the air had fled. | Devastation so great that even<br>the birds have fled |
| 26 I looked, and lo, the fruitful land was<br>a desert, and all its cities were laid in<br>ruins before the LORD, before his<br>fierce anger. | total destruction |
| 27 For thus says the LORD:<br>The whole land shall be a desolation;<br>yet I will not make a full end. | |
| 28 Because of this the earth shall mourn,<br>and the heavens above grow black;<br>for I have spoken, I have purposed;<br>I have not relented nor will I turn back. | ?famine; mourning ?depression<br>Black heavens ?depression |
| 29 At the noise of horseman and archer<br>every town takes to flight<br>killers are coming they enter thickets;<br>they climb among rocks;<br>All the towns are forsaken,<br>and no one lives in them. | Thoughts of imminent death |
| 30 And you, O desolate one, what do you<br>mean that you dress in crimson, that you<br>deck yourself with ornaments of gold,<br>that you enlarge your eyes with paint?<br>In vain you beautify yourself.<br>Your lovers despise you; they seek your life. | Jerusalem ignores the danger and<br>its people continue in their sinful<br>ways, like a common prostitute |
| 31 For I heard a cry as of a woman in labour,<br>anguish as of one bringing forth her first<br>child, the cry of daughter Zion gasping<br>for breath, stretching out her hands,<br>'Woe is me! I am fainting before killers!' | Extreme anxiety/distress<br>Gasping?<br>Over-breathing; fainting;<br>thoughts of imminent death |

Regarding verse 19, 'My anguish, my anguish', Craigie *et al.* (1991) write:

> the passage begins with the language in the form of a lament. The language is
> very physical but its roots lie in the mind that has grasped the oncoming terror.
> The Hebrew word for anguish used here is *me'ay*, which literally means 'my
> bowels', and Jeremiah repeats this twice. It seems as if he is sick to the stomach
> as he envisages the judgment that has now fallen upon the nation.

The allusion to stomach discomfort is relevant because a panic attack
will often start with a peculiar and unpleasant non-specific gastric upset,
sometimes called 'butterflies in the stomach'. Such sensations are characteristic of panic attacks, particularly in the lead-up to the attack, as well as
during the episode itself. It is possible that Jeremiah is reporting on his own
uncomfortable gastric feelings here as well as his more obvious psychological
distress. The verse then continues to describe some of the cardiac symptoms
of anxiety/panic.

- *Oh the walls of my heart.* Holladay translates the Hebrew *key-rot libbi*
  as the walls of my heart and he explains 'the word *key-rot* is used as an
  expression to describe architectural walls or the like. H. Wolff thinks of
  this as angina pectoris but surely this is too medical. Jeremiah's heart is
  in uproar as are his viscera' (Holladay, 1986, p. 161). Holladay is right to
  dismiss angina pectoris as an explanation for the chest pain. The walls
  of the heart may refer to the chest wall and people with panic attacks
  often report central chest pain and retro-sternal discomfort, which can
  sometimes be confused with true cardiac pain.
- *My heart is beating wildly.* One of the key somatic symptoms of panic is
  tachycardia (a rapid heartbeat) and this is sometimes accompanied by an
  increased and unpleasant awareness of the subject's own heartbeat. When
  this is combined with central chest pain, sufferers often become frightened
  that they are having a heart attack and will phone for an ambulance and
  get taken to their local A&E department, but on arrival the attack will
  usually subside quickly. Tests are carried out, true cardiac problems
  are generally excluded and the patient is sent home. In Jeremiah's time
  there was no knowledge of panic disorder so it was no wonder that these
  powerful and unpleasant chest sensations, especially when combined with
  rapid heartbeat, would have truly terrified him.
- *I cannot keep silent.* The biblical meaning is that Jeremiah cannot keep
  silent about the terrible fate about to befall Judah; he feels compelled to
  forewarn the people of this forthcoming danger. However in composing
  this phrase he may have drawn on his experiences of one of the more
  embarrassing fears associated with panic attacks. Patients are sometimes
  overwhelmed by a fear or compulsion that they will scream out and
  then say something quite crazy or lose control of themselves while at the
  height of their panic, hence the phrase *I cannot keep silent.*
- *I hear the sound of the trumpet.* The battle has not yet begun, but
  Jeremiah (presumably in his imagination) can already hear the sounds of
  the trumpet (*shofar*). These are the sounds of war – by definition a sound
  with horrific implications. Sometimes subjects with panic attacks or other

anxiety disorders report hearing unpleasant noises or that normal sounds have acquired a loud and distressing quality. This symptom is called *hyperacusis* and Jeremiah sometimes seems to report being distressed by unpleasant sounds (see page 101), although we can never know precisely what Jeremiah actually heard.

- *Disaster overtakes disaster.* Lundbom writes that 'the Hebrew word for disaster used here *seber* is translated as crash, shattering or collapse and the translation of this phrase is "crash upon crash resound". This particular phrase occurs 15 times the book of Jeremiah but the sense here is of one loud crash after another which will be understood by anybody who has experienced the sounds of war' (Lundbom, 1999, p. 353). The possible link of this phrase to catastrophic thinking is discussed further on page 106.
- *Suddenly my tents are destroyed.* This refers to their destruction in battle at the hands of the invaders. A sudden onset is characteristic for panic attacks, especially for those episodes which seem to come out of the blue, perhaps adding to their frightening quality. The use of the word 'sudden' in the OT is discussed on page 108.
- *Verse 24, The mountains were quaking.* Yahweh makes the mountains shake and this is a common biblical metaphor used both in the Psalms (e.g. 18[7]) and the prophetic literature, but it is also found in the older Sumerian literature as well. Jeremiah may have drawn on his own feelings of shaking or tremor, as might occur during a panic episode, because he often uses this metaphor. Similarly the phrase *the hills were moving to and fro* also implies a personification of bodily shaking or instability.

Verses 22–29 describe the terrible destruction that the 'foe from the north' will wreak upon the land; it will be rendered desolate. These verses do not record any psychiatric symptoms. There will be no people about; cities will be in ruins and even the birds will disappear from the skies as the earth mourns. Ellie Wiesel, an Auschwitz survivor, when writing about his time in Auschwitz, recalled that the destruction in the camp was so terrible that even the sounds of birds disappeared from the sky and he recalls the comfort he took from this particular poem by Jeremiah (see Carrol, 1985).

Verse 30 describes a woman who symbolises Jerusalem but who will continue to dress up and paint her face and behave like a whore. She blithely ignores all the destruction going on around her. Jeremiah is critical of the people of Jerusalem who are oblivious to the forthcoming disaster and so continue in their immoral ways. Craigie *et al.* (1991) explain versus 30 and 31 in the following terms:

> The language of childbirth is introduced in verse 31. The prostitute of verse 30 is also pregnant; Jerusalem's demise would be like that of a prostitute giving birth to her first son who is a bastard. Jeremiah's language here is certainly not pretty, but it was designed to catch attention and so to evoke a reaction in those to whom it is addressed. In verse 31 the Prophet implies not merely death during childbirth (in the metaphorical sense) but also a quite real death at the hands of the ruthless soldiers, a practice that was not uncommon in the wars of the ancient near east.

The final verse of this poem (31) includes four more features of panic, and this serves to heighten the emotional intensity of the passage.

- *The birth of the first born.* A woman's labour, especially with her firstborn, is often much more prolonged and painful than her subsequent labours. Perhaps Jeremiah selected this metaphor to highlight the enormity of the pain that Israel will experience.
- *Gasping for breath.* Gasping for breath occurs in childbirth but is also a key symptom of a panic attack. Sometimes there is only a subjective feeling of shortness of breath, but quite often patients with panic begin to gasp and then go on to over-breathe (this is known as hyperventilation) to the extent they make themselves dizzy and may even end up fainting.
- *Woe is me.* Feelings of despair and a low mood are usually the dominant mood of a panic attack.
- *I am fainting.* Fainting and going dizzy due to the hyperventilation are common during an episode of panic. Fainting can also occur as a result of the extreme levels of anxiety, even in the absence of hyperventilation.
- *I am fainting before killers.* Earlier in this passage Jeremiah describes the invading soldiers from the north, who through their archery are killing the people. This is the literal meaning of this phrase. However, subjects experiencing a panic attack often experience distressing thoughts of imminent death, or think they are having a heart attack, or that they are going crazy. Jeremiah's expression that the archers are killing people and that he is fainting before killers suggest thoughts of imminent death, which are characteristic of panic attacks.

## The diagnosis of panic in 4$^{19}$ and 4$^{31}$

Jeremiah's prophetic purpose in this poem was to warn Judah about the forthcoming disaster coming from the north. He drew on his own feelings of distress to give his personal reaction to this catastrophe, especially in the two verses 19 and 31. Verse 19 has four symptoms of panic (extreme anxiety, chest pain, tachycardia, stomach distress) and verse 31 has a further five symptoms (distress, gasping, dysphoric mood, fainting, thoughts of imminent death) giving a total of eight key symptoms of panic. In fact, only four key symptoms are required to qualify for a DSM-5 diagnosis of panic (see page 108 for the diagnostic criteria for panic).

The intervening verses also have alarming content: there are archers who are going to kill people, the mountains are shaking, there is destruction, the agony of childbirth, etc., and it is as if the writer is in a state of high arousal throughout its composition. One might speculate that Jeremiah wrote these verses very quickly, perhaps while in the midst of a panic attack, or in its immediate aftermath when he recorded his thoughts while they were still fresh in his mind.

His description is also remarkably succinct. DSM-5 represents the best efforts of 20th-century psychiatry to produce an accurate yet brief definition of this disorder and this consists of only 89 words. Jeremiah's version is very different; it is autobiographical, unintended, and appears as religious verse.

However, it includes most of the main features of a panic attack and in its English version is actually shorter than DSM-5, having only 76 words (verse 19 has 36 words; verse 31 has 40 words) but the original Hebrew version is even more succinct, having only 34 words, and yet still describes the main features of a panic attack. In this brief poem, composed around 2,600 years ago, Jeremiah provides a razor sharp and clinically accurate account of his panics – although this was never his intention.

## *The direct use of the word 'panic' in Jeremiah*

The word 'panic' itself appears in three separate places in the NRSV translation. In each instance the biblical text uses a different Hebrew word for panic, each having a different shade of meaning, suggesting that panic and its varieties was well known at the time. Panic is a common condition today, and it seems as if the ancients were familiar with sensations of overwhelming fear, and some of the physical symptoms which accompany these fears, but the modern construction of a panic attack, namely the combination of attacks of fear together with unpleasant bodily sensations (autonomic symptoms) occurring in the absence of a threatening situation is a more recent and 20th century construction.

## *A time of distress for Jacob: Jeremiah 30^{4–7}*

These verses report on the terror and panic the people will suffer on the 'Day of Yahweh', which is akin to the Day of Judgment. The mood of fear relates to the people, rather than to an individual.

| 30⁴ | These are the words that the LORD spoke concerning Israel and Judah: | |
|---|---|---|
| 5 | Thus says the LORD: We have heard a cry of panic, of terror, and no peace. | The word *harada* is used for panic |
| 6 | Ask now, and see, can a man bear a child? Why then do I see every man with his hands on his loins like a woman in labour? Why has every face turned pale? | Men behaving like women signifies weakness Change of facial colour due |
| 7 | Alas! that day is so great there is none like it; it is a time of distress for Jacob; yet he shall be rescued from it. | to fear |

Holladay (1989) considers this passage to be authentic Jeremiah material. Lundbom explains:

> In this poem of lament, Jeremiah articulates his own anguish and that of the people of Jerusalem, as the city teeters on the verge of destruction. Here is not a vision of what will happen at some future time but rather a report of something happening right now. The prophet hears together with everyone else a frightful sound, the sound of anguish and terror, and those listening enquire whether it is possible for a man to bear a child? The audience need not know the answer. Their faces have the look of death. (Lundbom, 1999, p. 386)

The actual Hebrew words used for distress and panic here may also be relevant. For panic the Hebrew word is *harada,* which translates as 'deep fright', but in some versions as 'tremble', while *pahad* means terror. In verse 7 the Hebrew for distress is *sara* and Jeremiah links this to the distress of childbearing. The image of men changing into women and giving birth also occurs in Isaiah 13[8] and is a common metaphor used in the ancient world to convey the notion of weakness in men. A similar thought is also expressed in Jeremiah's oracle against Babylon (51[30]): when the Babylonian soldiers are defeated 'their strength has failed, they have become women'.

## *The change of facial colour*

*Why has every face turned pale?* The last line of verse 6 describes a change in facial colour. Commenting on this phrase, Holladay (1989, p. 172) writes:

> the Hebrew word *leyerakon,* which means paleness, is used to describe the colour of the face in this verse. The word is not used anywhere else to describe any sort of human condition and is more usually associated with diseases of plants such as mildew or rust. The Hebrew root also gives rise to words for verdure or greens. In LXX versions, the Greek word which means jaundice is used, and so the reference here is to pallor, as when the blood leaves the face.

Fainting and facial pallor can occur in anyone experiencing sudden overwhelming fear, for example following a major disaster or during a panic attack, but as the attack subsides, facial colour will return to its more normal pinkish hue, and this is the most likely explanation for the change of facial colour described here. In support of this, Lundbom cites two further references in the OT to a change in facial colour associated with acute states of fear. Firstly, Nahum 2[10]:

> devastation desolation and destruction
> hearts faint and knees tremble
> all loins quake
> all faces grow pale.

Secondly, Joel 2[6]:

> Before them peoples are in anguish
> all faces grow pale.

It is common knowledge that intense fear can lead to facial pallor (e.g. the phrase 'white with fear' or 'hasn't she gone white?') and the OT citations given above suggest such a change in facial colour was also well known during biblical times. What is less well known, and would not have been appreciated in the ancient world, is that the vast majority of instances when facial pallor occurs are during episodes of panic rather than following some major disaster, as these events are relatively rare, whereas panic attacks are quite common.

## Panic of the fleeing Babylonian soldiers (50³²)

A further use of the word 'panic' appears in the oracle against Babylon in the section known as 'The oracles against the nations', which is towards the end of the Book of Jeremiah:

| | | |
|---|---|---|
| 51²⁹ | The land trembles and writhes, | The personified land has tremor |
| | for the Lord's purposes against Babylon | |
| | stand, to make the land of Babylon | |
| | a desolation, without inhabitant. | |
| 30 | The warriors of Babylon have given up | Weakness and despair, with fear |
| | fighting, they remain in their strongholds; | and paralysis, in the soldiers who |
| | their strength has failed, they have | become like women |
| | become women; her buildings are set on | |
| | fire, her bars are broken. | |
| 31 | One runner runs to meet another, | Catastrophe |
| | and one messenger to meet another, | |
| | to tell the king of Babylon that his | |
| | city is taken from end to end: | |
| 32 | the fords have been seized, the marshes | |
| | have been burned with fire, | |
| | and the soldiers are in panic. | Panic hits the soldiers |

The Hebrew word for panic here is *nevhalu*, which also means terror. Holladay also considers these verses to be authentic Jeremiah material. The oracle is a prediction of the fate that will befall the Babylonian soldiers sometime in the future, rather than a description of any current battle. In Jeremiah's poetic imagination he thinks that when soldiers are faced with defeat, they will suffer from panic attacks. History tells a very different story, because when Babylonian power eventually crumbled at the hands of King Cyrus of the Medes, the Persian army just walked into the city of Babylon; there was no fighting, no bloodshed nor any fleeing Babylonian soldiers.

## Concerning Damascus (Jeremiah 49²³⁻²⁴)

In these verses panic is associated with the overthrow of Damascus by some unknown enemy. The whole passage has the feel of alarm and panic and includes several symptoms of panic.

| | | |
|---|---|---|
| 49²³ | Hamath and Arpad are confounded, | |
| | for they have heard bad news; | |
| | they melt in fear, they are troubled | Overwhelming fear, |
| | like the sea that cannot be quiet. | emotional turmoil, |
| 24 | Damascus has become feeble | weakened through fear, |
| | she turned to flee, and panic seized | seized by panic; urges to escape; |
| | her, anguish and sorrows have taken | anxiety and depression |
| | hold of her, as of a woman in labour. | |

Carrol (1986) explains:

> Damascus was the capital city of the Aramaens, and Hamath was a nearby city state on the River Orontes, while in modern times Arpad has been identified as an excavation site near Aleppo in northern Syria. The text depicts Damascus

as panic stricken and routed – a famous city now abandoned. The report of the catastrophe makes the people of Hamath and Arpad very anxious. No specific historical situation can be discerned in this poem nor is a cause given for the panic. Rather, it is Yahweh who has destroyed Damascus. Stereotypical phrases identify Yahweh as the opponent of the foreign nations and it is possible to detect here a hint of an apocalyptic orientation in the writing.

The Hebrew word for panic used here is *retet* and this is the only appearance of that word in the Old Testament. The word *retet* is related to the Aramaic *reret*, which means to tremble (Holladay, 1989). The phrase *we-retet heheziqah* translates as 'and she seized panic' or 'and panic has seized her', which is an apt description for the onset of a panic attack: as if the person has been seized by the panic.

## Terror all around

The well known American biblical scholar James Muilenberg (1970) draws attention to Jeremiah's frequent use of the phrase 'terror all around' (Heb. *Magur-missabib*). Carrol (1986, p. 203) calls this phrase 'almost the leitmotif of the Jeremiah tradition'. This unusual phrase appears six times in the book of Jeremiah and in four of these instances it is linked to other features of a panic attack The best known of these episodes is Jeremiah's imprisonment in the stocks by Pashur, who was a priest of the Temple. The phrase is used in Jeremiah's complaint to Yahweh about the difficulty of the prophet task ($20^7$); in his description of 'the foe from the north' ($6^{22-26}$); and finally in his report on the fears of the people in the cities of Kedar and Hazor ($49^{29}$).

## The Pashur episode: Jeremiah is imprisoned in the stocks (Jeremiah $20^{1-6}$)

This is short passage has some historical significance as it provides information on the way political and religious dissidents were treated at the time (late 7th century BCE) in Judah shortly before its demise.

Jeremiah is placed in the stocks for one night because he is openly critical of the corruption among the priests and the elders and the general state of immorality in the nation. Baal worship has become widespread, the people kill each other and they indulge in child sacrifice. Jeremiah admonishes them for their sins and says they are 'too stiff necked' to listen or change their ways. He goes on to prophesy that as a result of their wickedness a terrible destruction will descend upon Judah at the hands of the Babylonians. The people will be irrevocably broken, just like a potter's jar, which once broken can never be mended. Jeremiah's denunciation of the priesthood and his prophecy of doom for the nation do not go down well with the people or the authorities of the day, so he is arrested and placed in the stocks – but this is just for one night.

$20^1$ Now the priest Pashhur, son of Immer, who was chief officer in the house of the LORD, heard Jeremiah prophesying these things. $^2$Then Pashur struck the prophet Jeremiah, and put him in the stocks that were in the upper Benjamin Gate of the house of the LORD.

³The next morning when Pashur released Jeremiah from the stocks, Jeremiah said to him, The LORD has named you not Pashhur but 'Terror all around'. ⁴For thus says the LORD: I am making you a terror to yourself and to all your friends; and they shall fall by the sword of their enemies while you look on. And I will give all Judah into the hand of the king of Babylon; he shall carry them captive to Babylon, and shall kill them with the sword.

Holladay (1986) gives this episode a modern perspective, and explains that Pashur was, effectively, the 'chief of the Temple police'. The first part of this passage reports on Jeremiah's arrest, his imprisonment in the stocks and his anger towards his jailer, Pashur, but the passage then goes on to describe the deportation of the nation to Babylon. Subtly Jeremiah joins these two themes together through his invective against Pashur. Carroll (1985) explains:

> The beating and restraining of Jeremiah overnight signify a rejection of his prophetic message against Jerusalem. This will warrant a response from the Prophet when he is released. The first part of the oracle, which describes a change in name to *magur-missabib* (terror-all-around), personalises the second part of the judgment against Jerusalem, which is to be destroyed and Judah (whose people are to be deported) and so the change of name comes to symbolise both Pashur's fate as well as the fate of Judah. (Carroll, 1985, p. 394)

Lundbom (1999) provides a similar explanation but points out that the LXX translation has a rather different text. Thus the LXX omits the phrase 'on every side' (*heb missabib*), probably as a result of haplography (a copying error), and the Hebrew word *magur* is assumed to be derived from the root *gur*, meaning 'to sojourn'. Thus in the LXX, Pashur acquires a new Greek name, *e metoikin* (Mr Exile).

The writing here is both complex and subtle. Although it is Jeremiah who suffers from the waves of terror, in his writings he takes revenge for his beatings and in his poetic imagination inflicts this same terror on his jailer, Pashur, who now becomes the victim and is called 'terror all around'. Through this transformation Pashur comes to symbolise the forthcoming destruction of Judah at the hands of the Babylonians.

The fact that Jeremiah is placed in the stocks for only one night indicates the degree of tolerance afforded to a dissident at the time. Most nations throughout history have had little tolerance for their critics, typically having them either killed or incarcerated for long periods. It seems that for a brief period when Judah had freed itself from Assyrian and Egyptian domination, but immediately before its destruction by Babylon, there was a modest degree of religious and political freedom, enabling Jeremiah to speak out, and receive what seems to have been only a token punishment – no more than one night in the stocks.

## Jeremiah complains about how hard it is to be a prophet (20⁷⁻¹⁰)

Jeremiah complains to Yahweh vociferously about the difficulties of his duties as a prophet. It is hard work: the people dislike his moralising, his constant criticisms and the pessimism of his prophecies. He says that he would rather stay silent but he is impelled to speak his mind or, as Lundbom puts it, 'he

is damned if he speaks out, dammed if he doesn't'. There is no solution and
no way to achieve any sort of peace. This section describes how he is torn
between the need to speak out and the pain this gives him; the people mock
him and as a consequence he reports he is feeling 'terror all around'.

20[7]    O Lord, you have enticed me, and I was
         enticed; you have overpowered me,
         and you have prevailed. I have become
         a laughing-stock all day long;
         everyone mocks me.

[8]      For whenever I speak, I must cry out,
         I must shout 'Violence and destruction!'          compulsion to scream out
         For the word of the LORD has become
         for me a reproach and derision all day long.

[9]      If I say, 'I will not mention him,
         or speak any more in his name',
         then within me there is something like
         a burning fire shut up in my bones;               compulsion to scream out, he
         I am weary with holding it in,                    cannot contain this compulsion
         and I cannot.

[10]     For I hear many whispering:                       Ubiquitous feelings of terror
         '*Terror is all around*! Denounce him!
         Let us denounce him!' All my close                Feeling of being watched
         friends are watching for me to stumble            fear of failure

The phrase 'terror all around' is an apt description for the *subjective
experience of a panic attack*. As the feelings of anxiety and terror sweep over
subjects, they often feel very isolated; the terror is everywhere, so the sufferer
thinks that even those around may be experiencing the same waves of terror.
In trying to make sense of Jeremiah's frequent use of the phrase 'terror all
around', Bright suggests that this may have been a nickname applied to
Jeremiah during his lifetime:

> apparently Jeremiah used the expression so often that it became like a
> nickname. One can imagine one man in the crowd nudging another and saying
> 'there goes old *Magur-Missabib*'. (Bright, 1965, p. 132)

Muilenburg (1970) concurs with this view:

> Jeremiah was destined to be a messenger of judgment, so much so, that his
> enemies taunt him with the name '*terror on every side*', a sentence he employs
> in his poem about the foe from the North as well is in the title he assigns to
> Pashur. It is revealing that he should refer to this nickname in his confessional
> disclosures.

This passage also mentions twice Jeremiah's 'compulsion to speak out'
in 'I must cry out, I must shout'. He struggles to contain this impulse ('I
am weary with holding it in, I cannot'). The scriptural meaning refers to
the urge to broadcast the prophetic message, but a feeling of having uncontrollable urges to scream out is also characteristic of how some people
feel during a panic attack, although they very rarely do actually scream out.

*Terror all around: the enemy from the north ($6^{22-26}$)*

Chapter 6 comprises five separate short poems, possibly with each having a different author, all conveying notions of judgement and doom (Bright, 1965). Only the fourth of these poems is relevant, because it contains Jeremiah's phrase 'terror all around' and this poem also includes other features of panic.

| 22 | Thus says the Lord: | |
| | See, a people is coming from the land | |
| | The foe from the north a great nation is | |
| | stirring from the farthest parts of the earth. | |
| 23 | They grasp the bow and the javelin, | |
| | they are cruel and have no mercy, their | Thoughts of death |
| | sound is like the roaring sea; they ride on | unpleasant sounds |
| | horses, equipped like a warrior for battle, | |
| | against you, O daughter Zion! | |
| 24 | 'We have heard news of them, | |
| | our hands fall helpless; | Paralysis through fear |
| | anguish has taken hold of us, | |
| | pain as of a woman in labour. | Severe anxiety |
| 25 | Do not go out into the field, or walk on | |
| | the road; for the enemy has a sword, | |
| | *terror is on every side.'* | Terror ?panic |
| 26 | O my poor people, put on sackcloth, | |
| | and roll in ashes; | Mourning, depression |
| | make mourning as for an only child, | |
| | most bitter lamentation: for suddenly | |
| | the destroyer will come upon us | sudden onset |

The enemy from the north is about to attack Zion. Since Judah was eventually attacked by the Babylonians there is a presumption that the mysterious enemy from the north may have been the Babylonians. In later apocalyptic writings the language of these battles is retained but now refers to purely mythical events and the foe from the north becomes the mythical north (Craigie *et al.*, 1991).

## Rabbinical commentary

- *We have heard the news.* R. Kimhi says that the prophet includes himself among those in Israel who listen to his words and the people are helpless and there is *magur-missabib* or 'terror on every side'. Once more the image of the woman in labour is used to describe this distress. Because the whole episode will end in a most terrible destruction of the land, daughter Zion is instructed to dress in mourning.
- *A for an only child.* Rashi points out that the grief at the loss of a son is intense and for an only son even more so (from Rosenberg, 1995). A similar comment about the intensity of the grief following the loss of an only child is given in Amos $8^{10}$.

*Psychiatric aspects*

The passage mentions some features of panic; the formulaic expression of pain, 'as of a woman in labour', points to states of severe distress whether physical or mental and Jeremiah's personal signature 'terror all around' is used here. All these events will occur suddenly; perhaps this is an allusion to the way a panic strikes a person suddenly.

- *Our hands fall helpless.* A state of paralysis through fear is suggested here; during a panic attack subjects often sit motionless in a limp position.

The doom predicted in this poem has not yet occurred – no one has been killed; the foe from the north has not yet turned up – yet there is a tremendous sense of an impending disaster. Thinking of this type, namely anxiety about some future event, is said to be characteristic of the anxiety disorders, but thinking about disasters is more especially associated with panic disorder and today this is called catastrophising. Although, almost by definition, an 'oracle of doom' will be about some future disaster and the Book of Jeremiah is replete with oracles of doom, only this particular oracle of doom mentions other features of panic disorder (thoughts of death, unpleasant sounds, anguish, paralysis through fear, grief, etc.).

## Other individual symptoms of panic in the Book of Jeremiah

A group of sensations or symptoms that Jeremiah writes about are also features of panic disorder. These include depersonalisation, abruptness of onset or suddenness, sensations of tingling, tremor, sensitivity to noise, disgust and disgust sensitivity and catastrophising. Taken individually it is difficult to be sure whether their references in the Bible correspond to modern parallels of anxiety symptoms. However, if considered together as a *group of symptoms* it is difficult to provide any other coherent explanation for their inclusion in a single text, other than that the author was drawing on his own experiences of panic.

*Drunk without the drink: is this depersonalisation-derealisation ($23^{9-10}$)*

This passage has attracted considerable interest among the rabbinical scholars of the Middle Ages as well as from modern Old Testament exegetes but none seem to have been able to comprehend Jeremiah's strange mood described here.

$23^9$   Concerning the prophets:
My heart is crushed within me, all my          ?chest pain,
bones shake; I have become like a               tremor;
drunkard, like one overcome by wine,
because of the Lord and because of his         drunken feeling of unreality
holy words.
$^{10}$      For the land is full of adulterers because
of the curse  the land mourns and the
pastures of the wilderness are dried up....

Here Jeremiah indicates he is writing about 'the prophets' who are the so-called 'false prophets'. They are his enemies and they upset him, but then the passage then goes on to allude to three key symptoms of panic:

- *My heart is crushed within me.* This is possibly a reference to the unpleasant retro-sternal chest sensations found in people with panic and anxiety disorders.
- *All my bones shake.* This is a suggestion of tremor.
- *Drunk without the drink.* The real mystery of this passage is the meaning of the phrase *'I have become like a drunkard like one overcome with wine'.* The line has the implication that he is feeling drunk and is in a state of feeling disorientated, yet without having consumed any drink.

### Rabbinical explanations

Rosenberg cites the views of the rabbinical commentators who focus more on the content of these verses rather than his mood at the time. They suggest that this is Jeremiah's diatribe against the false prophets.

Redak says the prophets mentioned here are the false prophets – they mislead Israel; they are overly optimistic and wrongly preach that no harm will befall Israel, whereas Jeremiah knows this is not true and is pessimistic about the future.

Rashi says that Jeremiah's heart is broken by the false prophets. Rashi translates the Hebrew word *rachafu* into the old French as *tremblant*, 'to tremble', which suggests an anxiety state, and he translates the whole phrase as 'like a madman the wine has overcome'.

Redak explains this as meaning: 'I was like this because of the Lord who was profaned by these prophets (i.e. the false prophets)'.

Arbabanel understands this as follows:

> Jeremiah was very upset by the loss of control of his facilities when the spirit of prophecy comes upon him and ... this must be the experience of prophetic ecstasy. The false prophets will experience nothing of the sort; they will not experience prophetic ecstasy but they will just continue to prophesy their false prophecies but at the same time engage in physical pleasures such as adultery, hence the mention of adultery at the end of verse 10. (After Rosenberg, 1985)

More recent biblical scholarship has also attempted to grapple with Jeremiah's strange mental state as described in this passage. Bright (1965) writes:

> the poem in verses 9–12 consists of a brief soliloquy of Jeremiah expressing shock at the moral corruption he observes around him. The first line *my heart is crushed within me* is actually translated literally as my heart is broken but this gives the wrong impression. Jeremiah is not heartbroken but he is very disturbed in his mind, both upset and shocked.

Both Lundbom (2004) and Holladay (1989) follow Lindbom's earlier view that Jeremiah's mood is abnormal here and is most likely one of prophetic ecstasy.

Holladay writes:

> the image here is one of weakness and instability and a drunk individual cannot hold a cup in their hand or maintain their balance while walking.

He then quotes Calvin, who explains the phrase 'I have become like a drunkard and like a mighty man that wine has overcome' by saying Jeremiah was stunned and all his senses had been taken from him. It is doubtful that Jeremiah is reporting the divine word while he is in such a state of ecstasy (Lundbom, 2004, pp. 181–182; Holladay, 1989, pp. 624–626).

### A possible psychiatric explanation: is this depersonalisation?

A peculiar stunned and almost dissociated mental state is described here. The rabbis of the middle ages as well more recent biblical scholars are at a loss to define his mood here, either in religious or even in more conventional terminology. Jeremiah writes in an extremely accurate and sensitive way about his mood and inner feelings. He is distressed by his peculiar mood state, which he likens to a drunken feeling, yet there is no report of him consuming any alcohol; the phrase conveys a sense of unreality, poor concentration and being 'out of it'. Such feelings of unreality are common among those who suffer from panic attacks and are even included as one of the core diagnostic features of a panic attack in DSM-5. Around 35% of subjects report such feelings of unreality during their panics and nowadays these are diagnosed as two related symptoms, called depersonalisation and derealisation. In the 1950s in the UK these feelings of unreality or depersonalisation were held to be central to the whole syndrome of panic, to the extent that one prominent formulation of the disorder at the time was known as 'the phobic-anxiety depersonalisation syndrome' (Roth, 1959) but depersonalisation may also occur in other disorders, such as depression.

Lee (2007) provides a lucid explanation:

> Depersonalisation is not a common symptom of depression but when present is striking. Sufferers feel unreal as if they were acting a part, or as if they were a robot. Insight into the abnormality of this phenomenon is retained. The feeling is highly unpleasant, but difficult to describe, and hence metaphor is often used. One patient said 'I've got this dreadful feeling as if I am unreal, a sort of dead feeling, inside. I'm changed; I do things mechanically'. Jaspers analysed depersonalisation as resulting from loss of (1) the sense of awareness; (2) the self as an active agent self; (3) the temporal continuity of the self; (4) and the distinction between the self and the outside world.
>
> Only about half of those presenting with depersonalisation are depressed and the symptom sometimes occurs in healthy persons under stress or in association with intense anxiety or following sensory deprivation…. It may have a protective effect in acute anxiety.

A note of caution should be mentioned here. Diagnosing a state of depersonalisation is sometimes difficult and depends on having a good clinical interview to elicit the key features, and so making such diagnostic inferences about rather more obscure psychiatric symptoms solely on the basis of a single phrase in a biblical verse may be stretching the data a little too far, but this may be one possible explanation for this puzzling verse.

## Tremor and shaking due to anxiety

Both tremor and shaking are well recognised features of fear, hence the phrase 'shaking with fear'. In a panic attack there is often a fine tremor, but sometimes rather more gross shaking. In ancient times there would have been no knowledge that the shaking associated with fear might be due to a 'clinical disorder' such as panic, even when there was no obvious external threat.

Metaphors involving the earth shaking or shaking mountains occur throughout the OT as well as in the older Babylonian literature, but when the shaking is reported together with a state of fear, it suggests the tremor of anxiety. In the Book of Jeremiah there are three instances where the shaking is linked to anxiety and its symptoms, while in a fourth instance it is associated with the emotion of anger:

| | | |
|---|---|---|
| 23$^9$ | my heart is crushed within me<br>all my bones shake | Tremor and chest pain |
| 4$^{24}$ | I looked on the mountains<br>and lo they were quaking<br>and all the hills moved to and fro. | Mountains shaking |

In 4$^{24}$ the mountains are described as shaking, but as this verse follows almost immediately after a comprehensive description of a panic attack in 4$^{19}$. It suggests the tremor of a panic attack, with the mountains and hills being imbued with the qualities of motion.

In relation to anger and trembling, in one of his tirades against the idolatrous practices of the people, Jeremiah asks whether the people have any fear for Yahweh – they should all be trembling before him.

> 5$^{21}$ Hear this, O foolish and senseless people
> who have eyes, but do not see
> who have ears but do not hear.
> $^{22}$ Do you not fear me, says the Lord
> Do you not tremble before me
> I placed sand as a boundary for the sea
> A perpetual barrier that it cannot pass .....

The New English Bible is even more explicit and has 'shivering' instead of 'trembling':

> $^{22}$have you no fear of me? Says the Lord
> will you not shiver the before me,
> who made the shivering sands to bound the sea.
> (New English Bible, 1970, p. 915)

Lundbom explains:

> The people do not wish to listen to Yahweh, and do not fear him, but they should fear him and they should tremble before him. A sea wall cannot control the sea and the waves, and likewise Yahweh has no control over his people, because they are a stubborn and rebellious lot. The people should shiver

before the Lord, the sands are also shivering. The suggestion is that Jeremiah believes the people should be shaking with the fear that they should have of Yahweh.

In another verse the shaking earth is linked to the emotion of rage

$10^{10}$ At his wrath the earth quakes: and nations
cannot endure his indignation.

## Suddenness and abruptness of onset

An abrupt onset to the episode of fear is characteristic of panic attacks, and indeed is incorporated into the modern definition as one of its key diagnostic criteria. Daube (1964) in his treatise *The Sudden in the Scriptures* traced the use of the word *pith'om* and *petha* (sudden) in the OT and found that this was almost always associated with some sort of evil, such as a military defeat, a punishment or some other disaster. However, its use in the later Hebrew literature was rather less strongly linked to disaster. He wrote:

> during insecure times, among which for the present purpose we may include the entire Old Testament period, the distrust of unforeseen events is bound to be greater than in times of comparative security. This is behind the gradual relaxation of the meaning of *pith'om* and *petha* in post-biblical Hebrew, where we shall see these words are no longer tied to misfortune.

There are three references to the use of the word sudden *(pith'om)* in the Book of Jeremiah, where it is specifically linked to destruction. Two of these have already been discussed: 'suddenly my tents are destroyed' ($4^{20}$); 'for suddenly the destroyer will come upon us' ($6^{26}$). The third reference to sudden destruction appears in Jeremiah's anti-war rhetoric of $15^{7-8}$: Jeremiah hated war and his sympathies lay with the civilian populations, especially the families of the bereaved. Jeremiah even took pity on the soldiers of Israel's enemies killed in war. In this passage he uses the word 'sudden' to describe the onset of terror, although in this case the terror is due to sudden bereavement.

| | | |
|---|---|---|
| $15^7$ | I have winnowed them for a winnowing-fork in the gates of the land; I have | Massacres during wars |
| | bereaved them, I have destroyed my people; they did not turn | Family bereavement |
| | from their ways. | Wars are a punishment |
| 8 | Their widows became more numerous than the sand of the seas; | Compassion for the |
| | I have brought against the mothers of youths a destroyer at noonday; | many widows of war |
| | I have made anguish and terror | terror |
| | fall upon her suddenly. | sudden onset of terror |

The meaning of the passage is clear; there has been a war and many are dead. The war was brought upon the people by Yahweh as a punishment for their apostasy and their failure to change their ways. However, there is compassion for the suffering of the widows; they have lost their husbands and sons. Anguish and terror will descend suddenly on the bereaved mothers whose sons were killed in battle. Jeremiah may have drawn on his own experiences of panic, thus in a panic the onset of feelings of terror is sudden.

Two types of panic attacks are recognised. Situational panic occurs in a particular place or situation, as in agoraphobia, and to some extent these attacks are predictable. The second type of panic attack is more frightening; it is non-situational and may arise without warning. The waves of terror suddenly appear as if out of nowhere and without rhyme or reason. They strike the sufferer abruptly, who then becomes very frightened; it seems as if this may have been Jeremiah's experience.

### Hissing, disgust and disgust sensitivity

Jeremiah uses the unusual word the *seriqot* five times, which is more than in any other book of the OT; it means 'hissing'. In most instances it is used to describe the reaction of passers-by to a vanquished and desolate city which they shake their heads at, and hiss at the city in contempt.

In a moralising passage where Jeremiah complains how the people have deserted his teaching, Jeremiah describes how they have gone down 'by-paths' and so ruined their lives and made their land a horror – and so others will hiss at them.

$18^{15}$ But my people have forgotten me,
they burn offerings to a delusion;
they have stumbled in their ways,
in the ancient roads,
and have gone into by-paths,
not the highway,
$16$ making their land of horror,
a thing *to be hissed* at forever.
All who pass by are horrified
and shake their heads.

Likewise he writes about a city that is about to be destroyed:

$19^8$ And I will make this city a horror
a thing *to be hissed* at;
everyone who passes by it will be horrified
and *will hiss* because of all of the plagues thereof.

The next two citations of the word hissing come towards the end of the book in 'the oracle against the nations', in particular against Edom and Babylon. It should be noted there is some question as to whether some of the verses towards the end of the book are later, post-exilic insertions and so possibly may not represent authentic Jeremiah material.

$49^{17}$ Edom shall become an object of horror;
everyone who passes it will be horrified
and *will hiss* at it because of all its disasters.

50[13]   because of the wrath of the Lord
        She will not be inhabited
        but shall be an utter desolation
        everyone who passes by Babylon
        shall be appalled
        *and hiss* because of all her wounds.

Hillers suggests that the shuddering of passers-by at a ruined city or land was a standard curse of ancient times (Hillers, 1964, pp. 66–67). A ruined city may have many dead and decomposing human and animal bodies and other decaying materials and may give off bad smells. It is tentatively suggested that Jeremiah's pre-occupation with hissing, which is unique to him in the prophetic literature, may reflect a trait now known as 'disgust sensitivity' – a part of the anxiety spectrum of disorders.

*Disgust sensitivity*
Recent studies have shown that 'disgust sensitivity' may be important in the anxiety disorders. Traditionally, fear has been held to be the dominant emotion underlying the anxiety disorders. People who have 'fear sensitivity' when they find themselves in a worrying situation may quickly become hyper-anxious and panicky, whereas a person lacking such a predisposition would only sense a mild increase in anxiety levels. Similarly, a person with disgust sensitivity might become very perturbed at the sight or smell of rotting food, whereas a normal person might just remove it, with little emotion.

Darwin (1872/1965) described disgust as something offensive to the taste and that its expression consists of expelling movements around the mouth. The notion of oral incorporation stems from the familiar facial expression of disgust which centres around the mouth, with the opening of the mouth and the closing of the upper part of the nares. Such a facial expression will prevent the import of a noxious odour as well as reject food that is already in the mouth (Rozin and Fallon, 1987).

Fear and disgust are two discrete emotional states but both play an important role in the anxiety disorders. They have differing facial expressions: fear is associated with closure of the mouth, furrowing of the brow and tensing of the facial muscles; disgust focuses around the mouth, with opening of the mouth and closure of the upper part of the nares, and these are identical to the facial movements involved in the act of hissing.

Researchers have devised ways of measuring a person's sensitivity to the emotion of disgust, by for example asking subjects to rate their feelings on seeing rotting food, body products or unpleasant smells. Thus in the 'contaminated cookie test', subjects are asked to rate how they feel about eating a cookie, and then eating another cookie which a worm has just crawled across. It seems as if some people are more sensitive to feelings of disgust than others and will use words that express disgust more often. People with certain anxiety disorders, namely blood injury phobia (needle phobia) and small animal phobia, have been shown to be very highly 'disgust sensitive'.

Fear and disgust elicit different states of physiological arousal. Fear involves the sympathetic nervous system and leads to tachycardia, sweating and tremor; disgust involves the parasympathetic system and results in nausea, dizziness and fainting. Both sets of symptoms are frequently mentioned by Jeremiah. The traits commonly occur together and some have questioned whether there is any advantage in separating them, at least in clinical disorders (Thorpe and Salkovkis, 1998).

Jeremiah writes directly about the emotion of disgust in one of his oracles against Jerusalem:

6⁸ Take warning O Jerusalem
or I shall turn from you *in disgust*
and make you a desolation
an uninhabited land.

Disgust sensitivity forms a part of the anxiety disorder spectrum and may explain Jeremiah's frequent use of the word 'hissing' – no other explanation is given in the huge Jeremiah literature but it should be noted that this is speculative.

## Hyperacusis

Jeremiah hears loud trumpet-like noises during at least one of his panics:

4¹⁹ My anguish! my anguish!
I writhe in pain!
Oh the walls of my heart;
my heart is beating wildly;
I cannot keep silent,
For *I hear the sound of the trumpet*
the alarm of war.

This verse has been discussed in greater detail on page 85 and the setting is clearly during a panic attack and there are the harsh noises of the trumpet (the *shofar*). The *shofar* is actually a ram's horn and not a trumpet, and it continues to be used in Jewish religious services, particularly the New Year service. It has shrill and jarring tone but is not unpleasant. A second reference to the unpleasant sounds of war comes later on

6²³ They grasp the bow and the javelin
They are cruel and have no mercy,
*Their sound is like the roaring sea*
They ride on horses....

Again, Jeremiah gives this sound a bad connotation – it is the sound of war. He was not actually present at the scene of the battle during either of these instances and heard these noises only in his imagination, but he may have been in a state of panic at the time of composition, as suggested by the rest of the verse. There is no comment in either the older rabbinic or the more recent Old Testament literature on these sounds or their significance.

The symptom of *hyperacusis* (an unpleasant experience of noise) sometimes occurs during a panic attack and this may be one explanation.

## Tingling in the ears

Sensations of tingling are unusual, but they can occur during a panic attack. Patients sometimes hyperventilate during an episode of panic and exhale excessive amounts of carbon dioxide (an acidic substance). This renders their blood chemistry alkalotic, which in turn stimulates nerve endings, particularly in the arms and legs, resulting in unpleasant tingling sensation known as paraesthesia.

19³   Thus says the Lord of hosts, the God of Israel;
      I am going to bring such disaster upon this place
      that the ears of everyone who hears it *will tingle*      Heb. *tissenay* = Tingle

The word *tissenay* occurs only once in the Book of Jeremiah but translations of *tissenay* have 'tingle' or 'ring'. Carroll (1999, p. 839) has tingle or quiver.

Because the phrase used is 'tingling in the ears' it is unclear whether this refers to a ringing noise in the ears which the subject hears, or to a physical sensation of tingling which is felt; this is not clarified further in the OT literature on Jeremiah. Although this is an uncommon symptom of panic, Ingham (1993, p. 23) in her book written for the general public about the symptoms of a panic attack writes:

> My body froze like a statue. My pulse would race very, very fast. My sense of reasoning would become completely muddled and confused. A *ringing in my ears* would occur and my body temperature dropped.

## Self-reference to panic

The Book of Jeremiah has numerous references to feelings of fear, panic and terror. For the most part the fear and terror are the fate that will befall someone else – soldiers in the face of defeat, the people of Judah because of their sins, or some foreign nation – but just occasionally the writing is explicit and the feelings of terror refer to Jeremiah himself and he uses 'I' in the first person to report his suffering.

### A personal confession

Chapter 17¹⁴⁻¹⁸ is a personal confession written in the style of one of the Psalms of Lament where the prophet prays for healing from Yahweh. Specifically he asks for Yahweh not to be a terror for him, suggesting that he may be seeking relief from his own feelings of terror (?panics). Although the critical line is to be found in verse 17, the passage makes sense only when it is placed in context.

17¹⁴   Heal me, O Lord, and I shall be healed;      A plea for healing, as if from some
       Save me, and I shall be saved; for you        sickness
       are my praise.                                The plea is for 'I' to be saved
15     See how they say to me,
       Where is the word of the Lord?
       Let it come!
16     But I have not run away from being a         I have been a good servant
       shepherd in your service, nor have I

| | desired the fatal day, You know what came from my lips; it was before your face. | I have been a good prophet |
|---|---|---|
| 17 | *Do not become a terror to me*; you are my refuge on the day of disaster | Please do not give me the terror any more |
| 18 | Let my persecutors be shamed, but do not let me be shamed; let them be dismayed, but do not let me be dismayed; bring on them the day of disaster; destroy them with double destruction! | My persecutors should get the terror instead of me |

Most scholars accept this passage as authentic Jeremiah material and class it as Mowinckel type A material. This is of critical importance if one is to make any sort of inference about 'Jeremiah the person' as opposed to some later reconstructed 'historical Jeremiah figure'. The lament starts with a plea to the Lord for healing. Lundbom (1994) writes 'the poetry in this passage is confessional in nature. Jeremiah pours his heart out to Yahweh and receives a divine answer promising deliverance. In verse 14 he seeks "healing".' Craigie *et al.* (1991) explain the Hebrew word *refa'ayne* (healing) can imply healing from an illness but it also can mean to repair or make whole. The petition in this verse is for wholeness within and liberation from external troubles.

What were these external troubles? Who was against Jeremiah? Those who opposed him were the so-called 'false prophets' and these verses are thought to be an invective against them. The false prophets take an overly optimistic view of the affairs of state, whereas Jeremiah assumes a more pessimistic position on Judah's future. In verse 17 Jeremiah pleads with Yahweh to spare him from what he hates most, namely the terror. In the NRSV translation the word 'dismay' is used for the Hebrew word *mehitta,* which usually means terror, and its translation as 'dismay' gives the verse an insipid feel. It is the terror that he hates and in this verse he implies it comes from God or at least God can stop it. He experiences it as a punishment. Please give it to my enemies instead of me. The translation by Craigie *et al.* (1991) restores the full force of the original Hebrew word *mehitta* as terrors and this is the punishment Jeremiah wishes to inflict upon his enemies.

| 18b | Let them for their part be *terrorised* Bring upon them an evil day, and with double destruction destroy them. | Heb. *mehitta* = terrorised |
|---|---|---|

These authors write:

> terror is a favourite word of Jeremiah, whether referring to the actions of others directed against him, or to God's judgment on others for their sins.... Verse 17 contains a petition to Yahweh not terrorize him; verse 18 asks Yahweh to inflict these same feelings of terror and shame upon his enemies. The sentiments expressed here are similar to his feelings towards Pashur onto whom he also wishes to inflict the feelings of terror. (Craigie *et al.*, 1991, p. 234)

The anxiety and panic disorders are 20th-century constructions to describe states of overwhelming fear and as such would not have been known in biblical times. Yet in this passage Jeremiah shows a degree of insight into his condition. He prays to Yahweh for healing, as if from some sickness, which he says is the terror. A psychiatric insight may be helpful in trying to link the thoughts expressed by Jeremiah here to the way patients with panic disorder talk about their panics. These patients both hate and fear the waves of terror that sweep over them mercilessly during their panics and are desperate for a cure. Often this is associated with a sense of deep shame because they have become so incapacitated. Patients with panic disorder usually want immediate relief and will often say 'If only you knew how awful I felt. It is so bad, that I wouldn't even wish it on my worst enemy' – but in Jeremiah's case it seems as if he did wish it on his worst enemies!

## Other possible symptoms of anxiety

### Fears about speaking in public

The first chapter in the book of Jeremiah describes his call to become a prophet. The prophetic life usually starts with a call from God and 'the call' for Jeremiah follows a similar pattern to that described for other prophets. Not surprisingly Jeremiah is worried about the prophetic path that Yahweh has chosen for him. However, the final three verses of his call (Jeremiah $1^{16-18}$) describe a much more specific worry he has.

> [16] And I will utter my judgements against them, for all their wickedness in forsaking me; they have made offerings to other gods, and worshipped the works of their own hands. [17] But you, gird up your loins; stand up and tell them everything that I command you. *Do not break down before them, or I will break you before them.* [18] And I for my part have made you today a fortified city, an iron pillar, and a bronze wall, against the whole land – against the Kings of Judah, its princes, its priests and the people of the land.

It is suggested that verse 17 represents Jeremiah's fear of speaking out in public. Much hinges on the precise translation of the last part of verse 17 and specifically on the word *al-taychat*, variously translated as breakdown, fear or panic. Below are two other translations of this verse.

> [17]Don't lose your nerve because of them
> lest I shatter your nerve because of them. (Bright, 1965)

> [17]Never be scared at them lest I scare you
> at the sight of them. (Moffat, 1926)

Holladay paraphrases and explains the meaning:

> Jeremiah is told to 'gird up his loins'. The phrase denotes tying a belt or something similar around one's waist, so as to confine the tunic or the long garment, and so to tuck up the extremities to free the legs for running, physical work, doing battle and the like; a modern expression with a similar meaning is 'roll up your sleeves'.... The command 'do not be panicked' (*al-taychat*) is a variant of 'do not be afraid' (*al-tayrah*) and the two verbs are found often in parallelism together in the OT. The traditional translation 'be dismayed' is too weak and the verb here refers to physical shattering and it appears *to be used to convey psychological paralysis or an inability to function at all....*'

Yahweh tells Jeremiah not to be paralysed by the threat of his enemies, or in more modern terminology 'do not be paralysed by one of your panic attacks'. Psychological paralysis is a feature of severe anxiety and usually occurs at the height of a panic attack, where patients sit weak and motionless, quite unable to do anything at all.

Both Holladay and Hyatt consider verses 16, 18 and 19, to be Deuteronomistic insertions but 17 (which contains all the psychiatry about his fears of speaking out in public) to be authentic Jeremiah material. It is fascinating to see how the Deuteronomist wraps his theology around the psychiatry. Thus 16 contains the moral strictures against the idolatry of the people, a typical Deuteronomistic theme, while 17 describes Jeremiah's fears of public speaking. The two verses which follow (18 and 19) describe how Yahweh will give Jeremiah strength and support and are also thought to be Deuteronomist insertions, but the verse describing Jeremiah's fears of breaking down while he is speaking in public is thought to be authentic Jeremiah material.

Jeremiah will have a difficult job as a prophet, but subsumed within this more general complaint he tersely captures his own fears of speaking out:

(1) His fear that he will break down if he is asked to speak in public.
(2) He has not spoken out yet in public; his worry is that he might panic in the future (today this would be classed as an anticipatory anxiety).
(3) If he does have a breakdown or panic while speaking, his audience will witness this, and this will add to his sense of shame and the resulting distress will rebound back onto him, and cause him to have even more breakdowns or panics. He attributes these further panics to Yahweh rather than to any condition that he might have.

These are the core features of 'fears of public speaking', which is one of the most common types of anxiety disorder and is described below.

Fears of speaking in public are classed as one of the performance anxieties, which constitute the social anxiety disorders (social phobia), and they are often accompanied by high levels of autonomic arousal. Some consider public speaking phobia as a distinct and separate type of social anxiety disorder, but the consensus now is that it represents one of the many fears that social phobics experience. Surveys have shown that around one in five people will report some anxiety about speaking in public, but only 2% of subjects reporting being really distressed by their fear.

Patients with a fear of public speaking may have various underlying fears: they may be afraid that others can see their embarrassment, their blushing, shortness of breath or that they are under scrutiny by others. They are also particularly concerned about their performance and fear they will make a mistake or say 'stupid' things, or do something embarrassing during their talk. The end result is an expectation that they will be humiliated or ridiculed because of their poor performance (Starcevic, 2010, p. 210).

## Claustrophobia – feelings of entrapment: the oracle against Moab

In the latter part of the book, in the 'oracle against the nations', there is a diatribe against the people of Moab, a small state lying to the east of Judah around the Dead Sea. Little is known about its people or their history, but there are several references to the Moabite people in the Bible. Ruth was a Moabite but otherwise the Hebrew Bible has few kind words for the people of Moab, who were rivals to Judah. The discovery of the Moabite stone (also known as the Mesha stele), in 1868 in the Jordanian village of Dhiban, by the Reverend Augustus Klein, a German missionary, was a major archaeological find. The stone is dated circa 840 BCE and records the defeat of King Ahab of Israel by the Moabite King Mesha, an event that might have been known to Jeremiah, and is one of the very few external records of any biblical person or event.

The oracle against Moab reads as follows:

| | | |
|---|---|---|
| 48⁴² | Moab shall be destroyed as a people, because he magnified himself against the Lord. | Pride; hubris |
| ⁴³ | Terror, pit, and trap are before you, O inhabitants of Moab! says the Lord. | Feelings of terror (panic) linked to feelings of entrapment |
| ⁴⁴ | Everyone who flees from the terror shall fall into the pit, and everyone who climbs out of the pit shall be caught in the trap. | Escape will be impossible; there is no escape from being trapped |

In this oracle Jeremiah describes how the people of Moab will try and flee but they will be trapped in a pit from which they cannot escape and this will terrify them. The association of feelings of panic with a sense of entrapment, together with powerful urges to escape, is a central feature of panic disorder as well as one of the core features of the agoraphobia–claustrophobia syndrome, which is itself also strongly associated with panic disorder.

The words for terror, pit and trap in their Hebrew offer a very strong assonance, *pahad wapahat wapah*. The onomatopoeia in this cadence adds greatly to the dramatic effect of the piece. There is no actual record of whether these poor people of Moab were actually trapped or not; rather the verse reflects how Jeremiah imagined they might have felt – and this would be in a state of panic.

## Catastrophic thinking: the words suddadanu (ruined) and seber (crash)

Jeremiah writes about the history, famines and wars which faced his nation, as well as the many personal tragedies he witnessed around him. In this context, it is quite appropriate for him to write about disasters – because these were the reality of everyday life in biblical times. However, more so than for any other prophet, he seems to be preoccupied with catastrophes and it is suggested here that this preoccupation may represent the so-called 'catastrophising' characteristic of the thinking of those who suffer from panic and other anxiety disorders. Thus, for example, in a judgement against the people of Jerusalem he writes:

4¹²ᵇ  Now it is I who speak in judgment against them,

13    Look! he comes up like clouds
      his chariots like the whirlwind;
      his horses are swifter than eagles –
      *woe to us, for we are ruined.*                    Heb. *suddadanu*

The critical line in this passage is the last one, and differing translations give a slightly different meaning – for instance:

- *woe betide us, we are undone* (Moffat, 1926)
- *alas we are overwhelmed* (New English Bible, NEB 1970)
- *woe to us, for we are devastated* (Lundbom, 1994).

The meaning in all translations is that some kind of a disaster will occur. The Hebrew word *šuddādănŭ* is used here and means 'ruined, devastated, overwhelmed'. There is nothing exceptional about its use in a judgement oracle – except that Jeremiah uses the word a total of 26 times (it also appears a further 24 times throughout the rest of the OT).

### The word *sēbēr* ( *crash* )

In his poem about the foe from the north, Jeremiah ($4^{20}$) includes the phrase 'Disaster overtakes disaster...' ('the whole land is laid waste'). Another translation (NEB, 1970) has 'crash upon crash...' ('the whole land goes down in ruin').

Lundbom (1994) explains that the term *sēbēr* can denote physical damage done to or sustained by a person, as in a break or fracture, or it may refer to a psychological condition indicating brokenness, shattering or collapse. The word *sēbēr* appears 16 times in the Book of Jeremiah, on nine occasions on its own; on the other seven occasions it is combined with the adjective *gadol*, meaning big, *seber gādol*, meaning 'big crash', or 'great destruction' as in $4^6$, 'for I am bringing evil from the north and a *great destruction*'.

Taking the words *šaddādănŭ* and *sēbēr* together, which seem to have a similar meaning, namely some sort of disaster or catastrophe, they occur a total of 42 times in the Book of Jeremiah. This is far more than for any other book of the Bible, and far too frequent to be mere chance. The only group of subjects today who are so preoccupied with disasters are those who suffer from panic disorder and they are said to suffer from 'catastrophising' or 'catastrophic thinking'. Jeremiah, in his frequent reference to disasters, seems to fit this pattern well.

### Making the diagnosis of panic disorder

The earlier DSM-III-R (APA, 1987) stipulated that there should be a minimum of four panic attacks over a four-week period, but in DSM-5 (APA, 2013) this was changed to having persistent concerns over having panic attacks. The main features of the DSM-5 definition of panic disorder are given in Table 3.1 and biblical citations corresponding to each relevant item are given in the right-hand column.

**Table 3.1** The main features of panic disorder according to the DSM system and verses from the Book of Jeremiah

| DSM | Book of Jeremiah |
| --- | --- |
| A surge of intense fear or discomfort is experienced within minutes, with four (or more) of the following: | 4²⁰; Suddenly my tents are destroyed. Also 6²⁶ and 15⁸ |
| 1. Palpitations | 4¹⁹ My heart is beating wildly |
| 2. Sweating | Not present |
| 3. Trembling/shaking | 5²² Do you not tremble before me |
| 4. Shortness of breath | 4³¹ daughter Zion gasping for breath |
| 5. Feelings of choking | Not present |
| 6. Chest pain/discomfort | 23⁹ My heart is crushed within me |
| 7. Nausea/abdominal discomfort | 4¹⁹ My anguish; Heb. *me'av* = my bowels |
| 8. Dizziness/feeling faint | 4³¹ I am fainting before killers |
| 9. Chills or hot flushes | Not present |
| 10. Paraesthesias (tingling sensations) | 19³ The ears of everyone who hears it will tingle |
| 11. Derealisation/depersonalisation | 23⁹ I have become like a drunkard |
| 12. Fear of losing control or going crazy | ?20⁸ I must cry out 'violence' |
| 13. Fear of dying | 6²⁵ For the enemy has a sword |

Jeremiah reports at least nine (six definite and three possible) out of the 13 key symptoms of panic disorder whereas only four are required for a diagnosis. When all the relevant verses are taken together, the conclusion that Jeremiah himself most likely suffered from panic disorder seems to be quite likely.

## The weeping prophet: depression in the Book of Jeremiah

Mourning, gloom and despair appear frequently in the Book of Jeremiah and given his reputation as a pessimist we should not be surprised to find evidence of depressive disorder. In fact, detailed examination of his depression, at least in his writings, shows that it is rather less prominent than the panic disorder, and probably represents a depression of only moderate severity – there is no evidence of any psychotic features or acute suicidal thoughts. Depressive thoughts appear in a variety of settings, but especially in Jeremiah's laments, with frequent mentions of woe, weeping, lack of joy and the wish that he had never been born.

## *Jeremiah's grief (8¹⁸–9¹)*

This is one of Jeremiah's best-known laments; Bright (1965) calls it 'Jeremiah's Passionate Grief'. The poetry of this passage has great beauty and the German composer Felix Mendelssohn used these verses in his last great oratorio, *Elijah* (Lundbom, 1994). This passage also has great liturgical significance in Jewish religious services, traditionally being read on the morning of Tisha B'Av, a service that commemorates the destruction of the Jerusalem temple.

| | | |
|---|---|---|
| 8¹⁸ | My joy is gone, grief is upon me, my heart is sick. | Loss of joy, so possibly anhedonia; grief which makes him think he is sick |
| ¹⁹ | Hark, the cry of my poor people from far and wide in the land: | Jeremiah is the speaker here |
| | 'Is the Lord not in Zion? Is her King not in her?' | |
| | 'Why have they provoked me to anger with their images, with their foreign idols?' | Yahweh is now the speaker, Anger because of the idolatry |
| ²⁰ | 'The harvest is past, the summer is ended, and we are not saved.' | The harvest has gone: the people face starvation |
| ²¹ | For the hurt of my poor people I am hurt, | |
| | I mourn, and dismay has taken hold of me. | A mixture of mourning (?depression) and dismay (?anxiety/fear) |
| ²² | Is there no balm in Gilead? Is there no physician there? | A search for healing |
| | Why then has the health of my poor people not been restored? | Why is there no help? |
| | | |
| 9¹ | O that my head were a spring of water, and my eyes a fountain of tears, | |
| | so that *I might weep day and night* for the slain of my poor people! | Weeping, day and night |

In the final verse (9¹) Jeremiah reports profuse crying and he is weeping day and night; this has led to one of Jeremiah's nicknames, 'The weeping prophet'. The psychiatry of this lament is relatively straightforward, but the historical and cultic references in this passage are complex.

- *My joy is gone, grief is upon me.* Lundbom translates this verse as 'My joy has flown away, grief floods in upon me'. His loss of joy may represent the psychiatric symptom of anhedonia (see page 67); even more explicit grief is also present and so the anhedonia is within a depressive setting.
- *My heart is sick.* It all feels like a sickness. Like the depressive of today, Jeremiah regards his affliction as so severe that he calls it a 'sickness' and so it merits 'healing' by a physician but none can be found.
- *The cry of my poor people.* Carroll writes that there is some uncertainty as to who is the speaker here – whether it is the people in the city who cry out, or the whole nation, or Jeremiah himself, or even Yahweh. However, Yahweh is not there to save them. Fishbane (2002) suggests

that Jeremiah and God are alternate speakers in this verse. All this has come about because of the apostasy of the people.

- *The harvest is past.* Carroll (p. 237) explains 'the harvest is over, the summer has ended: the time when the fruits and grains should be gathered in is now over, and there is nothing in the granaries. The prospect ahead is for a winter without food, and starvation looms, so we are lost'.

- *For the hurt of my poor people, I am hurt.* Lundbom (p. 533) writes: 'Driver imagines Jeremiah to be broken mentally. The word *seber* (translated here as hurt) means, wound, collapse, brokenness, shattering ... here it is seen as clearly as anywhere how the 'I' can be a personal 'I' and Jeremiah in a most profound way may be identifying with the hurt of his people'. Both Lundbom (1994) and Bright (1965) seem to infer that when Jeremiah composed this lament he was going through some sort of a breakdown, but as both are theologians rather than physicians they were unable to elaborate on the nature of this breakdown. It is suggested these feelings of hurt may have been part of Jeremiah's depression.

- *I mourn.* The Hebrew *qadarti* literally means 'I am dark' and is a reference to the dark attire of mourning.

- *Is there no balm in Gilead.* This is a famous phrase, probably referring to a medicinal product of the time. Balm was a resin, taken from trees in much the same way as sugar is taken from sugar maples. It was thought to have come from balsam, mastic or storax resin, and was used for body oils, perfumes or medicine. Gilead was a highland region of the Trans-Jordan, and balm taken from the trees of this area was particularly highly thought of.

- *Is there no healer there?* Lundbom explains that during pre-exilic times, there were no physicians or healers. In Israel, any referral to the healer would signify Yahweh, and the writer of this lament asks 'Why is Yahweh absent from the scene?'

- *My head a spring of water.* This phrase may have been taken from the much older Ugaritic literature, from the legend of King Keret, where a similar phrase appears (Gervitz, 1961).

Crying at night is repeated twice in the Book of Jeremiah and crying of this severity especially at night is unusual. Today, crying in men almost always signifies a depression of at least moderate severity. This particular passage also has great liturgical significance in Jewish religious services, traditionally being read on the morning of Tisha B'Av, a service that commemorates the destruction of the Jerusalem Temple. Because of its religious significance an abstract from Fishbane's commentary on this particular *haftorah* is given below:

> The intense symbiosis between Jeremiah and God in this passage is also a theme in the Rabbinic Midrash. In one late formulation dealing with the exile and destruction, *Rabbi Aha* has God usurp Jeremiah's own words in 9[1] when he says 'Israel cries during the night and Jeremiah cries during the day but I shall cry day and night, as it is said "I would weep day and night for the slain of

my people'". This relationship between the prophet and God is also expressed in an early sermon introducing the book of Lamentations, where *Resh Lakish* explains 16[17] as God's invitation to the dirge singers to join him in lamenting his people, because of his own lack of strength to do so alone.

'I and you', God says, 'shall lament, weep and cry over the sorrow of Israel. By way of a parable the sage goes on to hint that the whole book of Lamentations may itself be God's lament for his city, and people. (For Talmudic references see Fishbane, 2002, p. 452)

Thus this lament is far more complex than purely being about Jeremiah's depression and it covers a multiplicity of themes. There is a plea for salvation, prayers for healing in general, a plea for protection from invaders, concerns about the harvest, condemnation of the sin of apostasy, and so forth. From a psychiatric perspective it matters little whether it is regarded as a 'communal lament' or an 'individual lament', but only that there is an accumulation of depressive symptoms: loss of joy (?anhedonia); grief and mourning (depressed mood); uncontrollable weeping both night and day (?depressive insomnia); feelings of brokenness; dismay (?anxiety); and a general feeling that this is a sickness – all associated with hopeless despair that there is no available healer. These are all features of depression.

## Weeping in secret

In this brief poem, Jeremiah is upset because of the people's pride. The people are told if they do not listen to him, he will weep in secret. Psychiatric interest lies in the fact that the weeping of the depressive is often also in secret, because it is usually accompanied by a sense of shame.

| | | |
|---|---|---|
| 13[15] | Hear and give ear; do not be haughty for the Lord has spoken. | Do not show pride |
| 16 | Give glory to the Lord your God before he brings darkness, and before your feet stumble on the mountains at twilight; While you look for light, he turns it into gloom and makes it deep darkness. | Switch into darkness? ?dark mood Allusion to the shepherd's stumbling as darkness falls<br><br>depressed mood |
| 17 | But if you will not listen, my soul will weep in secret for your pride; my eyes will weep bitterly and run down with tears, because the Lord's flock has been taken captive. | weeping in secret profuse weeping Judah taken captive The national catastrophe |

Lundbom (1994) writes:

the poem starts with a judgment; the people should listen and not be haughty. Yahweh will cause the light to turn to darkness, and then the poem gives way to lamentation – Jeremiah will have to weep because his people do not listen. Darkness in the Bible usually signifies some forthcoming calamity.

Nicholson (1993) suggests the image of feet stumbling on the mountains at twilight and oncoming darkness reflects the anxiety and plight of shepherds caught high up in the mountains as night falls. Metaphors based on shepherds are frequent in the OT as for example in Psalm 23. Jeremiah is speaking but it is God who is weeping, and this is about the national calamity of the exile and the deportation.

Psychiatric interest in this passage lies in four aspects. First, the weeping is profuse. Secondly, it is done in secret, and this a feature of depressive crying. Young women with depression, perhaps at work, flee to the toilet to have their cry in secret. Men should never cry in public: this would signify weakness and shame. Thirdly, the weeping arises from a state of gloom, indicating that it is probably related to the depression. Finally, the weeping is bitter because of the people's pride. The actual emotion associated with the secretive weeping of the depressive is one of shame. The admixture of themes of gloom, secretive weeping and feelings of shame could only really have been conjured up by someone with a repeated personal experience of depressive weeping and all its associated emotions.

## Tears flowing night and day

Chapter 14 is a lament about famine and war, the two major disasters to afflict the peoples of the ancient world. Jeremiah cries night and day for the terrible scenes of war he has witnessed but there is no help to be found. The passage forms a part of his powerful anti-war rhetoric.

| 14[17] | You shall say to them this word: | |
|---|---|---|
| | Let my eyes run down with tears | Profuse crying both night and day |
| | night and day, and let them not cease, | |
| | for the virgin daughter – my people – | |
| | is struck down with crushing blow, | |
| | with a very grievous wound. | |
| 18 | If I go out into the field, | |
| | look – those killed by the sword! | massacres in war |
| | And if I enter the city, | |
| | look – those sick with famine! | famine |
| | For both prophet and priest ply their | They have no clue as to |
| | trade throughout the land and have | the people's plight |
| | no knowledge. | |
| 19 | Have you completely rejected Judah? | Yahweh has let this happen |
| | Does your heart loathe Zion? | |
| | Why have you struck us down | |
| | so that there is no healing for us? | |
| | We look for peace, but find no good; | |
| | for a time of healing, but there is | |
| | terror instead. | terror; is this panic? |

The passage opens with Jeremiah weeping uncontrollably, both night and day. Depressive weeping is known to occur both day and night and can go on for several hours at a time. It continues remorselessly for the whole duration of the depression and so can persist for months on end. Simple situational weeping after some personal crisis is very different and usually over in a day or two, and will settle once its cause has resolved.

Lundbom (pp. 712–714) explains these verses:

> In this very personal lament Jeremiah calls for his own tears to flow night and day because his dear people have sustained an unimaginable blow. The reference to the virgin daughter is perhaps meant to represent the city of Jerusalem which hitherto, like a virgin, has not been violated. The grievous wound according to *Rashi* is a sickness whilst *Kimhi* interprets 'the crushing blow' as a severe illness. The whole nation is mortally wounded or nearly so. If Jeremiah were to go out into the field, there would be dead bodies everywhere; if he were to enter the city, disease would meet him at every turn. Some scholars have thus placed this lament at 597 BCE when the Babylonian conquered Jerusalem.... The prophet knows who has brought this tragedy about, but he does not blame Yahweh, but merely pleads whether he has rejected Judah and Jerusalem as he asks why is there no healing.

Historians since the dawn of civilisation have written about wars and have tried to understand their causes, and such themes forms a major part of the historian's agenda for almost any generation. While it may seem strange to us today that Yahweh should be held responsible for wars that occur between men, Yahweh was held to be responsible for all of history, wars included, and this lay at the core of the Deuteronomistic theory of history.

While the drama of these verses plays out on the national stage, and this a communal lament, Jeremiah was depressed and crying seemingly at the national plight, but people in such states of turmoil will also seek out 'healing' at a more personal level as well. Yet all he receives is 'the terror' (panic?). This passage is one of the few that mentions a depressive symptom at the beginning (crying both day and night) and a symptom of panic (the terror) at the end, suggesting that he might have been experiencing symptoms of both depression and panic during its composition.

The writing here concerns a subtle admixture of his own weeping (depression) and terror, and a plea for healing at a personal level, all intertwined with the national angst about the forthcoming disaster. In addition there is a Deuteronomistic explanation for the cause of this war and this is enjoined to a plea for national salvation. Perhaps the richness of his quality of thought and his ability to meld together so many diverse themes all point to Jeremiah's huge intellect, but the simplicity of the writing also attests to his literary genius.

## Anhedonia in the Book of Jeremiah

The Book of Jeremiah provides three probable references to anhedonia, which refers to a loss of the sense of pleasure, a key depressive symptom, as described on page 67. These are: Jeremiah's banishment from feasts; Yahweh's indictment of Judah, to be followed by its destruction by King Nebuchadnezzar; and the destruction of the vineyards of Moab.

### The ban on feasting

According to Bright (1965) ch. 16 is autobiographical and authentic Jeremiah material, whereas Hyatt (1984) suggests it is a late Deuteronomistic insertion written in the post-exilic period and not composed by Jeremiah. It describes three symbolic actions which Jeremiah tells us he is forbidden to take part in. He cannot marry – because any children born from such a union will die of disease; he cannot comfort his people in their sorrows during a mourning service; and thirdly there is a ban on feasting (described below). The passage stresses the loneliness of Jeremiah's life.

| | | |
|---|---|---|
| 16[8] | You shall not go into the house of feasting to sit with them, to eat or drink. | self-imposed ban on eating ?loss of appetite |
| 9 | For thus says the Lord of Hosts, the God of Israel: I am going to banish from this place, in your days and before your eyes, the voice of mirth and the voice of gladness, the voice of the bridegroom and the voice of the bride. | loss of joy ?anhedonia a symbol of happiness |

Lundbom (1994, p. 761) explains the passage:

> the third command prohibits Jeremiah from entering houses of feasting, which strikes at the heart of community well-being – again *Shalom* (Hebrew: peace). The message is that Yahweh will bring an end to all joyful sounds – not least of which are the sounds of the bride and groom. The word is addressed to the people directly. At the end the audience is brought back to Jeremiah and the wife denied him. No joyful wedding sounds for him either.

Jeremiah's banishment from feasting may also reflect the symptom of anorexia or loss of appetite. Depressed subjects not only complain that they have lost their appetite but also find that the food they eat is tasteless and that eating gives them no pleasure. This can be profound during a severe depression, and if Jeremiah found he was unable to eat, or enjoy the food of a feast, he would have had no other explanation for it – other than that Yahweh had inflicted it on him. Loss of appetite, as such, is not mentioned elsewhere but Yahweh also imposes a ban on him taking part in mourning ceremonies. In ancient times, this would have involved sharing a meal with the mourners as happens for example in the traditional Irish wake. His explanation for his apparent inability to experience any sense of joy, or any pleasure in eating, is that Yahweh has banished these feelings from him; in Jeremiah's eyes, it is God who is to blame for both the anorexia and the anhedonia, two key depressive symptoms.

### *The indictment of Judah and its punishment by King Nebuchadnezzar*
An almost identical verse describing 'loss of joy', or anhedonia, to that discussed above is found in ch. 25, but the setting here is quite different. Here the loss of joy is the punishment for Judah's disobedience, and it will be the result of the forthcoming national destruction, at the hands of King Nebuchadnezzar.

| | | |
|---|---|---|
| 25[8] | Therefore, thus says the Lord of Hosts: because you have not obeyed my words, | Disobedience |
| 9 | I am going to send for all the | Yahweh will punish the people |

tribes of the North, says the Lord
even for King Nebuchadnezzar of Babylon,
my servant, and I will bring them against      Nebuchednezzar will destroy
this land and against all the nations           the land
around; I will utterly destroy them and
make them an object of horror and
of *hissing*, and an everlasting disgrace       For hissing see page 100
10   *And I will banish from them the sound*
*of mirth and the sound of gladness*, the       loss of joy, anhedonia
voice of the bridegroom and the voice
of the bride, the sound of the millstone        sounds of activity
and the light of the lamp.                      no light, so darkness

The people have disobeyed Yahweh's word and so Jeremiah warns
them that Yahweh will send the tribes from the north, together with King
Nebuchadnezzar, who will invade and destroy the land. This will not be a
direct action of Yahweh, but will be through his servant Nebuchadnezzar.
His invasion will end the sound of mirth and the sound of gladness, or in
modern terminology kill all joy – hence anhedonia. Jeremiah blames Yahweh
both for destruction of the land by the Babylonians as well as for its consequence – the anhedonia. The ban on the voice of the bride and bridegroom
further emphasises the feeling of anhedonia as these are said to be among
the most joyful sounds and symbols of human activity.

The final phrase of this passage ($25^{10}$) is also of psychiatric significance: 'the
sound of the millstone and the light of the lamp' are also banished. Holladay
explains the line 'the sound of the millstone' as signifying the beginning of
the day, when the day would start with millstone grinding the flour, but this
is now silenced. The banishing of the 'light of the lamp' represents the end
of the day, when the light of lamp would indicate darkness at night. Cornill
(1905) writes:

> Since the supply of bread must be baked daily, the noise of the grinding of
> the handmill was heard wherever people dwelt, and this symbolises the typical
> work and activity of daily life. Dead silence during the day, uninterrupted by
> any human sound, together with an unearthly darkness at night which is not
> illumed by any gleam from a lamp – is quite a unique depiction of complete
> barrenness which could only be achieved by a poet of God's grace. (Cornill,
> 1905, quoted in Holladay, 1989, p. 289)

Such a picture of darkness, silence and inactivity will be familiar to most
adult psychiatrists who treat depression. Often I have had requests from
spouses who are alarmed by their partner, who in the midst of a severe
depression will just sit in an armchair in their house in a state of utter silence
and total inactivity, in a darkened room with the curtains drawn. They sit
silently, staring vacantly into space, sometimes motionless for hours on end,
and at night do not turn the lights on. Whoever wrote the last line of verse
10, which seems to depict such states of silent inactivity throughout the day
and darkness in the night, probably had some personal experience of such
moods, and might have composed this verse while in the midst of a severe
depression.

## Older Akkadian parallels

Lundbom (1999, pp. 248–249) draws attention to similar compositions which mention loss of joy in the earlier Akkadian literature. This is of interest to the study of the history of psychiatry since the ancient Akkadian literature is much older (circa 1500–2000 BCE) than the Old Testament and there seems to be some knowledge concerning the symptom of anhedonia. These are described by Cohen (1988), and appear in the form of 'Treaty Curses'. Thus an Esarhaddon inscription contains the curse 'No joyful man enters its streets, no musician is met.' In one of the older Balag city laments of ancient Mesopotamia these lines appear:

> The city, where its young girls are no longer happy
> The city where its young men do not rejoice....
> The dancing places are filled with ghosts
> The street is not sated with joy.
> (Cohen, 1988, pp. 245, 336)

The Balag laments are all communal laments, mainly dated to around the 2nd millennium BCE, and others to the 1st millennium. Perhaps the symptom of anhedonia and the loss of joy and loss of the sensation of pleasure is a symptom which sensitive poets have written about from the very earliest days.

## Wailing for Moab

Towards the end of Jeremiah's diatribe against Moab in ch. 48, his lament describes the ending of wine production in the fertile vineyards of Sibnah at the hands of the destroyer, presumably some foreign invader.

| | | |
|---|---|---|
| 48[31] | Therefore I wail for Moab; | wailing; weeping |
| | I cry out for all Moab; | |
| | for the people of Kir-heres I mourn. | mourning? depression |
| [32] | More than for Jazer I weep for you, | crying |
| | O vine of Sibnah! | |
| | Your branches crossed over the sea, | |
| | reached as far as Jazer; | |
| | upon your summer fruits and your vintage | |
| | the destroyer has fallen. | |
| [33] | *Gladness and joy have been taken away* | Anhedonia |
| | from the fruitful land of Moab; | |
| | I have stopped the wine from the wine | |
| | presses; *no one treads them with shouts of* | loss of joy ?anhedonia |
| | *joy; the shouting is not the shout of joy.* | |

Because this poem appears in an almost identical form in Isaiah 16[9-10], there is controversy surrounding its authorship. Some have argued that because Isaiah preceded Jeremiah by more than half a century, Jeremiah took it from Isaiah. On the other hand, Jeremiah writes frequently about loss of joy or anhedonia and is known to be a depressive, whereas there is no suggestion of depression for Isaiah. Kaiser (1975) cites seven diverse scholastic opinions, some of which favour Isaiah, some favouring Jeremiah, but some who suggest the putative author was neither Isaiah or Jeremiah, but rather some later but unknown post-exilic writer.

Carroll (1985, p. 792) explains the meaning of the poem: 'It is the speaker who wails for Moab, rather than Moab or its peoples. The focus of the mourning is the destruction of the land, in particular the vineyards of Sibnah. In the late summer the vintage will be at its best, but the destroyer will take away all the pleasure of the harvest.' The threefold use of the word shout (Heb: *haydad*) in the final verse is another good example of biblical onomatopoeia. This is not so obvious in the English translation but is dramatic in the original Hebrew, where the verse reads '*lo yederech haydad haydad lo haydad*', the assonance of the repetition adding drama and force to the piece. The repetition 'that the shouting is not of joy' emphasises the anhedonic quality of the passage. Immediately preceding these verses, crying and wailing are mentioned, suggesting this is depressive anhedonia.

## Mourning

Mourning appears frequently in the OT and the Hebrew word for mourning, *avla*, occurs six times in the Book of Jeremiah, loosely referring to states of misery, grief or sadness. When linked to the death of an individual it reflects a bereavement process, but in the Book of Jeremiah it is almost always linked to the land, a land destroyed either by either drought or wars.

12[4]   How long will the land mourn,
        and the grass of every field wither?
        for the wickedness of those who live in it....

This is a reference to drought as there are no rains. In the ancient world rain was a gift of God and a drought was taken as a sign of his disfavour – and here the cause is the wickedness of the people. A similar thought is expressed in 14[1-3].

[1]     The word of the Lord came to Jeremiah
        concerning the drought:
[2]     Judah mourns and her gates languish;
        and the cry of Jerusalem goes up.
[3]     Her nobles send their servants for water....

'Gates languish' gives the verse a depressive timbre. Lundbom (1994) explains that the writer is using indirect metaphors, which he calls *abusios*. It is the people who mourn, not the inanimate land. Gates do not languish, but people do, especially if they have depression. Languishing usually results from the combination of a lack of energy and a lack of motivation, the so-called depressive anergia, which is a key depressive symptom.

A land destroyed by invaders or rendered infertile through drought or destruction would be unable to grow any food and hence would result in a famine. This was the ultimate nightmare for the peoples of the ancient world and it would certainly lead to the people 'mourning' as well. The earth mourning is also described following its destruction by the invaders from the north:

4²⁸     Because of this, the earth shall mourn
        and the heavens grow black;

## The lament of Baruch

Baruch was the scribe who recorded the words that Jeremiah dictated to him and the two were friends for more than 20 years. The lament is that of Baruch but the words are those of Yahweh as spoken to Jeremiah. The passage is dated to around 605 BCE. Bright (1965) thought that Jeremiah was going through a period of emotional turmoil at this time.

45¹    The word that the prophet Jeremiah spoke
       to Baruch son of Neriah, when he wrote
       these words in a scroll at the dictation of
       Jeremiah, in the fourth year of
       King Jehoiakin son of Josiah of Judah.
2      Thus says the Lord, the God of Israel to
       you, O Baruch:
3      You said, 'Woe is me! The Lord              low mood
       has added sorrow to my pain; I am weary     painful sorrow; exhaustion
       with my groaning, and I find no rest'.       complaining, agitation
4      Thus you shall say to him, 'Thus says
       the Lord: I am going to break down what
       I have built, and pluck up what I have
       planted – that is the whole land.'

Opinion is divided on the authenticity of this piece and how much of it represents a later Deuteronomistic insertion. Both Mowinckel and Hyatt, for differing reasons, regard this chapter, particularly verse 4, as the work of the Deuteronomist whereas Bright (1984) and Holladay (1989) regard the whole chapter as being authentic to Jeremiah. For the purposes of this discourse, this discrepancy probably does not matter as the authorship of verse 3, which contains all the relevant psychiatry, is not in question. Here Jeremiah writes about his sorrow, which is painful and this quality of painfulness is typical of the low mood of the depressive. He also mentions how weary he is (low energy, exhaustion) and that he can find no rest (agitation).

## Cursed on the day of my birth

An essential component of the routine assessment of all patients with depression is the issue of suicide and particularly the presence of suicidal thoughts or any active plans. Some people will go on to describe such thoughts, but when the suicidal intent is of a lesser degree some depressives will report that they just wish they were dead, or regret their life and their very existence. Although Jeremiah suffers much despair, nowhere in the book is there any mention of suicidal thoughts or plans, but in the lament of ch. 20 he has regrets about ever being born.

20[14] Cursed be the day          Regrets about being alive
on which I was born!        and having been born
The day my mother bore me,
Let it not be blessed!

[15] Cursed be the man who brought
the news to my father, saying,
A child is born to you, a son',
making him very glad.

[16] Let that man be like the cities
that the Lord overthrew without pity;
let him hear a cry in the morning
and an alarm at noon,

[17] because he did not kill me in the womb;    intra-uterine death
so my mother would have been my grave,    ?mother's death as well
and her womb forever great.        Pregnancy which is prolonged

[18] Why did I come forth from the womb
to see toil and sorrow,          Regrets about being alive
and spend my days in shame?     Shame and sorrow

Bright is sensitive to Jeremiah's complaint of despair in these verses:

> In this passage there is another confession which indicates how little Jeremiah knew of permanent peace, which shows us Jeremiah at the end of his resources plunged into well nigh suicidal despair. One can neither exaggerate the agony of spirit revealed here, nor improve on the words which Jeremiah found to express it.... There is little in all of literature which compares with this piece and nothing in the Bible except perhaps the third chapter of Job to which it is similar. (Bright, 1965, p. 134)

A comparison with Job ch. 3 is helpful, as Bright suggests. Job also expresses the wish that he had never been born – but there is an important difference between Job's curse for the day of his birth and that of Jeremiah. This relates not to scripture but to obstetrics, yet it tells us something very important about Jeremiah's powers of observation and his compassion with those afflicted by terrible medical tragedies.

Job writes 'Why did I not die at birth' (3[11]) and repeats this sentiment with 'or why was I not buried like a stillborn child' (3[16]). In both these verses Job refers to the sad event of a stillbirth which in the ancient world must have been fairly common. Most women generally recover from this and many will go on to have children who survive. However, in verse 17, Jeremiah is writing about a less common but much more sinister medical condition, namely a death occurring in the womb in late pregnancy; in modern obstetrics this is called an intra-uterine death. In such cases unless labour supervenes very quickly, the pregnancy itself will continue seemingly indefinitely ('her womb forever great'). Today, if following an intra-uterine death, labour does not start quickly and of its own accord, obstetricians will induce labour artificially by administering drugs intravenously. In the ancient world, intra-uterine death would have led to a prolonged pregnancy that would end only when the dead foetus became infected, but this would result in maternal septicaemia and the inevitable death of the mother ('my mother would have been my grave').

The scenario of an intra-uterine death as described here is unique to Jeremiah, indicating he most probably was the author of this passage. Possibly Jeremiah had personally witnessed such a tragedy. One can only speculate that Jeremiah may have been so struck by witnessing such a tragedy that he later recalled the image while he contemplated the despair of his own existence. The passage ends (verse 18) with Jeremiah giving his reasons for wishing that he was dead and these are *amal*, which means hard times or mischief, and *yāgōn*, meaning sorrow, perhaps the nearest the lexicon of the Old Testament gets to our modern concept of depression.

### Suffering in the Book of Jeremiah

There is much suffering in the Book of Jeremiah. Much of this concerns the suffering of the nation and this is central to the theology of the book and its place in the scriptures. A second type of suffering relates to his own personal anguish, which is the focus of this chapter, and it is suggested that at least in part this relates to his panics and depressions. However, in addition we find a third type of suffering – mainly that of his fellow man in a variety of social and medical settings. Most of these tragedies are only briefly mentioned, perhaps as an elaboration on some other theme or as a metaphor, and are not explained, but taken together give an insight into some of the human quandaries which seemed to have greatly troubled Jeremiah. These problems are placed into the categories of social, medical and psychiatric problems in Table 3.2, which shows that Jeremiah had both an awareness and empathy for the wide range of suffering. Like most of the other great prophets, he seems to have been troubled by aspects of human nature, notably the tendency for some people to exploit their weaker brethren. He had great concern for the vulnerable of society: widows, orphans, foreigners and slaves. He was especially compassionate towards women, in labour, bringing up children or in states of bereavement or widowhood as a result of war. He also seems to have been perturbed by medical tragedies, particularly when they affected the young or during labour.

Of particular interest to psychiatrists is his occasional mention of mental difficulties in others. Thus he mentions madmen, delusions, hallucinations and self-mutilation; he also expresses a marked antipathy to alcohol and its adverse effects. Taken together with the extensive description of his own panics and depression he seems to have had some kind of a special empathy to matters we now call 'psychiatric'. Most of the other great prophets who came before him, such as Amos or the '12', who shared an equally powerful social conscience, do not mention any symptoms of mental disorder in their writings: the special sympathy and insight Jeremiah had into psychiatric difficulties seem to have been unique to him within the prophetic genre.

## Concluding remarks

Jeremiah was one of the great literary prophets of the Old Testament. His writings are replete with notions of suffering; he describes his personal suffering at the hands of the King and the Temple authorities. He was

**Table 3.2** Human suffering other than 'the national suffering' or Jeremiah's own depression or panic mentioned in the Book of Jeremiah

| Type of harm | Reference in the Book of Jeremiah |
| --- | --- |
| _Social harms_ | |
| Slavery | $2^{14}$ |
| Divorce | $3^1$ |
| Exploitation and violence to aliens | $7^6$, $22^3$ |
| Exploitation, violence to widows and orphans | $7^6$, $22^3$ |
| Exploitation of the poor | $2^{34}$ |
| Rights of the needy | $5^{29}$ |
| Care for orphans and widows | $5^{28}$, $49^1$ |
| Bereavement of war widows, bereaving women | $15^8$, $31^{15}$ |
| Mothers | $31^8$ |
| _Medical problems_ | |
| Children dying, fatal diseases of children | $2^{30}$, $16^4$ |
| Sickness and wounds | $6^7$ |
| Women in labour | $13^{21}$, $31^8$ |
| Infertility | $18^{30}$ |
| Intra-uterine death | $20^{17}$ |
| Maternal obstetric death | $20^{17}$ |
| Handicap: the lame and the blind | $31^8$ |
| _Psychiatric symptoms (excluding panic and depression)_ | |
| Delusions | $3^{23}$, $11^{15}$, $51^8$ |
| Visions | $23^{16}$, $38^1$ |
| Antisocial personality disorder | $4^{26}$ |
| Arresting the insane | $25^{26}$ |
| Transgender problem | $31^{22}$ |
| Self-mutilation | $10^6$, $47^5$, $48^{37}$, $49^3$ |
| _Alcohol-related problems_ | |
| Alcoholic anger | $7^{18}$, $25^{15}$ |
| Within-family alcoholic violence | $13^{14}$ |
| Alcoholic vomiting | $25^{27}$, $48^{22}$ |
| Being teetotal | $35^{22}$ |
| Fatal alcoholic coma | $51^{39,57}$ |

arrested and placed in the stocks, put on trial and imprisoned, where he nearly died; he was forced to watch the destruction of his nation, which he had previously foretold, but then found himself trapped in the siege of Jerusalem only to witness the starvation of its citizenry and their descent into cannibalism, culminating in their eventual deportation. Most significantly, he reports on his own personal inner turmoil and this can be recognised in the idiom of modern psychiatry as two common conditions, panic disorder and depression.

The main features of both disorders are well described in his book, but do not appear as a single sequential text as might be found in a modern textbook of psychiatry, and so are all the more difficult to untangle. The many different somatic symptoms of panic disorder are widely distributed throughout his book in a seemingly random fashion. Only in a few places are groups of somatic symptoms clustered together with the terrors, for example in the poem about the 'foe from the north' ($4^{19-31}$). His depression is confined for the most part to his confessions. Almost all the psychiatric material is to be found in the first part of the book (chs 1–25), which most authorities seem to accept as authentic Jeremiah material, rather than being the later embellishment of post-exilic writers. The Book of Jeremiah is over 2,600 years old, and these writings almost certainly represent the first detailed autobiographical account of panic disorder.

One critical issue needs to be addressed: what is the significance of the 'I' in the Book of Jeremiah. Does the 'I' relate to a real person who may have suffered or experienced the events described within the text, or does the 'I' refer to the whole nation of Israel? This question is relevant to understanding the psychiatry because if 'I' refers to the suffering of Jeremiah the man, then this is an autobiographical account of his panic disorder. However, most religious authorities interpret the 'I' as representing the cult and Jeremiah's pain as spiritual pain, which they link it to the troubles of his nation.

Perhaps the main protagonist of the view that the 'I' represents the whole nation was Reventlow (1963). His treatise *Liturgy and Prophecy: The 'I' in Jeremiah* has been translated from the German by Jobling (1984), who writes:

> Reventlow wrote that Jeremiah was a cultic functionary, and as the title suggests the use of the first person singular in the book directs us not to the prophetic personality but to cultic situations in the temple as described in the Book of Psalms where the use of 'I' was formally required.... Personal testimony is not to be found in the book of Jeremiah at least not in the area where one usually seeks them, not even in his confessions which rank as the main source from which such statements arise. In his confessions he probably expresses not his own, but the people's prayers. The 'I' that appears there has passed over completely into the 'we', it is nothing other than a representative and embodiment of the community. (Jobling, 1984)

A contrasting position is taken by Bright (1965), who views the confessions as authentic Jeremiah material. He states:

> there is no real parallel to these little self-revelations in which Jeremiah lays before us his most intimate feelings. Within this classification one should

properly place not only these matchless passages, telling of the prophet's inner struggle, which are usually labeled as his confessions, but also those numerous other passages where Jeremiah is speaking in the first person and gives vent to his anguish, and reports of his thoughts. Characteristic of such passages is the fact that Jeremiah speaks in his own name: the 'I' is not the Yahweh as in the oracles, but the Prophet himself.

Bright (1965) is dismissive of Reventlow's cultic formulation, and adds:

> I can only say that I am not convinced by Reventlow's cultic interpretation and continue to regard the confessions and the passages in the book as authentic reflections of the actual experiences of the prophet's life.

These contrasting positions on the meaning of the 'I' in the confessions of Jeremiah have been debated since Talmudic times and the interested reader is referred to reviews by Polk (1984) and Jobling (1984) for a more detailed discussion.

Does making a modern diagnosis of panic disorder and depression in the prophet Jeremiah make any sense, or have any meaning or validity? The biblical texts are distant in time, being more than 2,600 years old, as well as in culture – an ancient Middle Eastern rural society as opposed to the modern industrial West. For some the distance may be too great to assign any useful meaning to the possible symptom parallels. Others may perceive the attempt to assign a diagnostic label to a great religious icon as a far too reductionist exercise which goes against the very spirit of the scriptures. Heschel (2001), a modern Jewish theologian, is critical of psychological approaches which have sought to deduce prophecy entirely from the inner life of the prophet and reduce it to a subjective personal phenomenon. Such an approach, he argues, fails to separate the person from the content of his writings and the meaning of prophecy. Many also still fear and dislike the thought of any sort of psychiatric disorder, regarding its sufferers as being different from so-called 'normal' people – the stigma against psychiatric illness, still widely prevalent today, as it always has been.

Yet these disorders, which Jeremiah so clearly suffers from, are all part of the human condition, and their inclusion in the text of the OT greatly enhances its overall truth, compassion and appeal to all readers, believers and non-believers alike. Purdue in his comments on the debate about the meaning of the 'I' in Jeremiah, and on Jeremiah's suffering, writes:

> Jeremiah comes to be viewed as the father of a personal religion, characterized by internal spiritual and ethical qualities which reject the ethical formalism of the cultic religion, including traditions, sacrifice, festival and temple. It is a personal relationship but loving father God, and not the communal experience of formal worship that characterizes the apex of Jeremiah's and thus Israel's religion. (Purdue, 1984)

Jeremiah's suffering is central to his writings and his personal religion. Much of his suffering takes the form of mental disorder, albeit presented in his book in a concealed and disorganised fashion, and in this chapter an attempt has been made to unscramble the pattern of his distress and reformulate it in the language of modern psychiatry. Jeremiah is a person we are all familiar with. He is the great worrier. Certainly he was no hero, and history would almost certainly have consigned him to oblivion – had it not been for his literary genius. The admixture of theology and history, combined with the raw yet poetic account of his panic attacks and depression, will resonate with readers, today as well as down through the ages – because many will have suffered in similar ways.

Writing of this type is in marked contrast to the dry historical accounts of the dynasties of ancient Egypt or the wars of the Assyrian empire. His ideas on the meaning of history, the destructiveness of man and the misery that man inflicts on his fellow man, through exploitation, war and ignorance, have been much enhanced by the inclusion in the text of his own personal suffering. One has only to think of the horrific man-made tragedies of the 20th century, such as the Holocaust, the genocides in Cambodia and Rwanda, or the famines of modern China, to appreciate Jeremiah's pessimistic view of human nature. In his writings on the catastrophes of his day, he applies a subtle mélange of history, theology, images of daily living, together with his own mental symptoms, all expressed in sublime biblical verse. This brings a personal immediacy to his writings. Many readers will themselves have experienced the terrors of a panic attack or the despair of a depression, and so will readily appreciate his writings at a more deeply personal level and perhaps this underlies the universality and continued appeal of his work.

Jeremiah was not always a misery and pessimist and just occasionally the sun shines brightly through his writings, giving us a message of hope. In a sub-section of the book known as 'The book of consolations' he gives an address to the exiles in Babylon saying Yahweh will enable them to return to Zion. The passage has great liturgical significance in the Jewish religious calendar and is traditionally read as the Haftorah on the second day of the Jewish New Year (Rosh Hashanah), normally seen as a joyful festival. These verses have both warmth and much beauty, and later gave comfort to countless generations of Jews exiled in the Diaspora; the same verses also assume importance in Christian theology because of their message of hope and restoration. A feeling of hope and joy, accompanied by the deliberate banishment of all thoughts depressive, are to be found in this piece of sublime biblical poetry (Jeremiah 31[8–9; 12–14]) – and so make a fitting end to this chapter.

31[8]   See, I am going to bring them from the land of the north,
      and gather them from the farthest parts of the earth,
      among them the blind and the lame,
      those with child and those in labour, together;
      a great company, they shall return here.
[9]   With weeping they shall come,
      and with consolations I will lead them back,
      I will let them walk by brooks of water,
      in a straight path in which they shall not stumble;
      for I have become a father to Israel,
      and Ephraim is my first born.

...

12     They shall come and sing aloud on the height of Zion,
    and they shall be radiant over the goodness of the Lord,
    over the grain, the wine, and the oil,
    and over the young of the flock and the herd;
    their life shall become like a watered garden,
    and they shall never languish again.
13     Then shall the young women rejoice in the dance,
    and the young men and the old shall be merry.
    I will return their mourning into joy,
    I will comfort them, and give them gladness for sorrow.
14     I will give the priests their fill of fatness,
    and my people shall be satisfied with my bounty.

## Appendix. Panic disorder today

Panic disorder is an important common psychiatric disorder and an excellent guide is given by Barlow (2002), a leading authority on the subject, from which the account below is taken.

The roots of the experience of panic are deeply embedded in our cultural myths. It is named after the Greek god Pan, the god of nature, who lived in the countryside, presiding over rivers, woods and streams and the grazing animals. But Pan did not fit the popular image of a handsome god. He was very short, had legs resembling those of a goat, and was ugly. Pan had a habit of napping in a small cave or thicket near the road. When disturbed from his nap by a passer-by, he would let out a scream that was said to make one's hair stand on end. Pan's scream was so intense that he made many a terrified traveller die. This sudden, overwhelming terror or fright came to be known as 'panic' and on occasion Pan would use his unique talent to vanquish his foes. Even other Gods were subject to his terror or his mercy (after Barlow, p. 605).

Given that Jeremiah's description of panic is largely autobiographical it may be helpful to place it in context by quoting some more recent autobiographical accounts of panic. One of Barlow's patients describes her experience of panic thus:

> I was 25 when I had my first panic attack. It was a few weeks after I'd come home from the hospital. I had had my appendix out. The surgery had gone well, and I wasn't in any danger, which is why I don't understand what happened. But one night I went to sleep and I woke up a few hours later – I'm not sure how long – but I woke up with this vague feeling of apprehension. Mostly I remember how my heart started pounding. And my chest hurt; it felt like someone was standing on my chest. I was so scared. I was sure that I was dying – that I was having a heart attack. And I felt kind of queer, as if I were detached from the experience. It seemed like my bedroom was covered with a haze. I ran to my sister's room, but I felt like I was a puppet or a robot who was under the control of somebody else while I was running. I think I scared her almost as much as I was frightened myself. She called an ambulance.

'Medical' descriptions of the anxiety disorders, which include panic, probably go back to the American Civil War, when an American physician, Da Costa (1871), wrote about a condition of severe chest pain and anxiety in otherwise healthy young men who suffered from a condition he called irritable heart and this was caused by 'quick long marches ... or even slight exertion in those whose constitution had been impaired by insufficient or indigestible food ... it seems to me most likely the heart has become irritable from its overactive and frequent excitement, and disordered innervation keeps it so'.

During World War I, Da Costa's syndrome once more assumed importance and an official category, 'Disordered action of the heart', was diagnosed in 60,000 soldiers by doctors in the British army. The condition was also diagnosed in peacetime and was renamed as 'the effort syndrome' by the London cardiologist Sir Thomas Lewis. At around the same time, but in civilian settings, a similar syndrome which combined symptoms of anxiety with chest pain, known as neuro-circulatory asthenia, became a fashionable diagnosis and most of these cases would today be diagnosed as panic disorder. There are numerous other formulations in the literature. Thus Roth *et al.* (1959) identified a separate syndrome they called 'phobic anxiety depersonalisation syndrome', which emphasised the combination of anxiety with feelings of unreality or depersonalisation. In this syndrome cardiac symptoms such as tachycardia, vasomotor neurosis and nervous exhaustion and feelings of unreality were highlighted, and it is noteworthy that Jeremiah shows many of these features.

Up until 1960, no distinction was made between generalised feelings of anxiety and those who had more severe and abrupt episodes of anxiety which we now consider to be panic attacks (nowadays classed as a separate disorder). Klein separated panic disorder from the other anxiety disorders because they were highly responsive to the then new tricyclic antidepressants (Klein and Fink, 1962; Klein, 1964). The dominant emotion that underlies *all* the anxiety disorders is fear. The American physiologist W. B. Cannon called this the 'fight or flight' response, and key to its success was its high state of cognitive and emotional arousal so that the organism can react both strongly and speedily. Acute fear of any cause will lead immediately to such states of high arousal, combined with urges to escape. Fear is also the dominant emotion in people with panic disorder, but the main difference between fear and panic is that in panic disorder the 'fight or flight' reaction has become redundant, because there is no external threat. More detailed consideration of the relationship between fear and panic is given in Barlow (2002) and other textbooks on psychology.

## Clinical presentation of panic

In essence, a panic attack comprises an acute attack of fear or terror which is accompanied by a number of physical symptoms. The first formal definitions emphasise the sudden onset, where panic is defined as 'The sudden onset of intense apprehension, fear or terror often associated with feelings of impending doom'. Sudden onset is defined as a period of 10 minutes or less during which the panic will reach its peak, and this temporal criterion remains in the latest official definition, in DSM-5 (APP, 2013). When panics have been observed in the laboratory, the abrupt surge in the intensity of the symptoms appears in the first 1–4 minutes. In Jeremiah's account he emphasises the sudden onset to the terror, adding weight to the notion that he is indeed describing panic attacks.

A typical panic attack is relatively brief, usually no more than 10–20 minutes. Panics are self-limiting, but subjects frequently feel quite unwell for several hours afterwards, with a residue of anxiety. During the attack subjects may experience a rapid heartbeat; physiological studies conducted during a panic attack show there may be a rise of around 40 beats per minute. An accumulation of 'cardiac' symptoms, including central chest pain, rapid heartbeat and shortness of breath, leads sufferers to believe they are suffering from a heart attack, and so they often call an ambulance and make an emergency visit to the A&E department or the cardiac clinic. Those who experience feelings of unreality often express the thought they are going crazy or that they will scream out and there is a suggestion that Jeremiah may have also suffered from this feature. Dizziness, light-headedness, a fainting feeling, loss of balance and a feeling of walking on water are also symptoms of panic, especially among those who have agoraphobia as well.

In a typical attack several of these bodily sensations will cascade together, gradually becoming more intense as the attack develops. This crescendo will block calm and rational thinking and patients go on to report a feeling of being trapped, often accompanied by powerful urges to escape. Although some people experience only an occasional panic, those with clinical panic disorder have repeated attacks and eventually come to develop a fear of further panics, fear of losing their self-control, and of social embarrassment, and generally become frightened individuals.

There is a characteristic type of thinking in panic and Barlow (p. 109) writes 'The prominence of cognitive symptoms, fear of dying, fear of losing control or going crazy are common and *catastrophic cognitions* associated with panic are found in 95% patients with panic disorder'. Jeremiah was no exception and he certainly seems to have shown catastrophising in his thinking, frequently using the words *seber* and *saddedanu*, meaning disaster. As a consequence of the ubiquity of such cognitions a stipulation of the DSM-5 criteria for panic disorder is that 'at least one of the attacks has been followed by one month or more of worry about the implications of that attack or its consequence (e.g. losing control, having a heart attack or going crazy)'.

Salkofkis and Clark(1996) emphasise the role of catastrophic thinking and proposed that panic attacks were the consequence of catastrophic mis-interpretation of benign physical sensations. Their explanation for panic was that certain ordinary bodily sensations or mild symptoms which most people take for granted or ignore can give rise to panic when they are mis-interpreted in a catastrophic fashion. According to this model, these physical sensations are experienced as dangerous because the subject views them as inevitably leading to some catastrophic outcome; for instance, a person with a headache jumps to the conclusion that they have a brain tumour, or those with palpitations assume they are going to have a heart attack. The abrupt onset of symptoms induces a fear of imminent death. Eventually those with panic disorder come to believe that the experience of anxiety itself is very dangerous, whereas a normal individual will take such minor fluctuations in bodily sensations in their stride. Cognitive behaviour therapy focuses on these cognitive distortions by teaching sufferers to detach these essentially normal feelings from their catastrophic misinterpretations – an approach that has been very useful in the treatment of panic.

## Basic epidemiology of panic disorder

The large American epidemiological study, the Epidemiological Catchment Area Study (ECA), gave a lifetime prevalence of 1.7% for the population having panic disorder, and a one-month prevalence of 0.5%. The female-to-male ratio is 3:1. The initial onset of panic disorder is commonly associated with a significant life stressor such as a serious medical condition, either in the subject, or in a close relative. However, subsequent episodes usually occur without any particular life stressor or an obvious trigger.

Family studies have revealed a fivefold increased rate of panic disorder among first-degree relatives of panic sufferers as compared with general population rates. Panic disorder is also more common in the widowed, divorced and separated than among married individuals. Patients with panic disorder display more help-seeking behaviour than those with any other psychiatric condition and tend to present for treatment rapidly. They also appear more frequently in cardiac clinics (16–23%), presenting mainly with atypical non-cardiac chest pain. Because they are often troubled by other bodily symptoms they are sometimes encountered in gastroenterology clinic (stomach unease), neurology (dizziness and fainting) and ENT clinics (dizziness) (Pollack *et al.*, 2010).

Panic disorder may occur in isolation, but often it occurs together with other psychiatric disorders and this is known as co-morbidity. The strongest association with other psychiatric disorders is with agoraphobia. Thus among those with panic disorder somewhere between 22% and 58% will also have agoraphobia (Weissman *et al.*, 1997). In the Book of Jeremiah there is one reference to feelings of being trapped, a core feature of agoraphobia, in his description of the fleeing Moabite soldiers (page 116).

Rather less strong is the association with social anxiety disorder (social phobia). Here the central fear is having a panic on exposure to a particular social situation and being embarrassed or humiliated. Jeremiah expresses his fear of speaking in public (see page 104). We cannot know whether Jeremiah also suffered from either agoraphobia or social phobia, but we do know he was not a great socialiser; he seems to have avoided contact, never married and probably led a rather lonely life. Panic subjects have an impaired quality of life with high rates of occupational failure, financial dependence, excessive use of medical services, and more frequent problems in the realms of marital and family function. Often they feel that no one understands them, including family and close friends, and so sometimes withdraw socially and find themselves isolated.

Treatment today is with antidepressants, mainly of the SSRI group, and, if available, cognitive psychotherapy. The reader is referred to standard texts (e.g. Barlow, 2002) for further details.

The long-term outlook for panic disorder in the pre-treatment era was certainly bleak. Marks and Lader (1973) concluded that only 40–50% ever improved. A study by Anderson and Herta (2003) conducted when treatment was widely available found around that one-third of subjects went into remission, but at 15-year follow-up 51% still reported recurrent panic attacks. However, as people get older they report being less troubled by their panic episodes.

Jeremiah had no knowledge of panic attacks or that he might be experiencing such a clinical condition but he writes freely about his thoughts and fears. He also sought help and prayed to Yahweh for relief from his terrors. Bright suggests that the people of Jerusalem might have known about his anguish, as his phrase 'terror all around' might have been a nickname for him as he used the term so often. Within his writings he mentions most of the key symptoms of panic to a sufficient extent that diagnostic criteria can be applied to the text. To some extent his active complaining and the frequent mention of his symptoms are characteristic of panic disorder subjects, as they are usually very active in their complaining and in seeking help.

# References

American Psychiatric Association (1987) *Diagnostic and Statistical Manual of Mental Disorders*, 3rd edition, revised (DSM-III-R). Washington, DC: American Psychiatric Publishing.

American Psychiatric Association (2013) *Diagnostic and Statistical Manual of Mental Disorders*, 5th edition (DSM-5). Washington, DC: American Psychiatric Publishing.

Andersh, S. and Hertla,A.(2003) A 15 year follow up study of patients with panic disorder. *European Psychiatry* 18: 401–408.

Barlow, D.H. (2002) *Anxiety and its disorders, the nature and treatment of anxiety and panic.* Chapter 4, pp. 105–138. New York: Guildford.

Bright, J. (1965) *The Anchor Bible Jeremiah: Introduction, translation and notes.* Garden City, New York: Doubleday and Company Inc.

Budde, K. (1882) Das Hebräische Klagelied. *Zeitschrift fur die Alftestamente Wissenshaft* 2: 1–52

Carroll, R.P. (1985) *Jeremiah, A commentary.* SCM Press Ltd. London.

Cohen, M. (1988) *The Canonical lamentations of Ancient Mesopotamia I–II.* Potomac MD: Capital Decisions Limited.

Cornill (1905) *Das Buch Jeremia.* Leipzig: Tauchnitz.

Craigie, P.C., Kelley, P.H. and Drinkard, J.F. (1991) *Word Biblical Commentary. Vol. 26, Jeremiah 1–25.* Dallas Texas: Word Books.

Da Costa, J.M. (1871) On irritable heart; A clinical study of a form of functional cardiac disorder and its consequence. *American Journal of Medical Science,* 61, 17–52.

Darwin, C. (1965) *The expression of emotions in man and animals.* Chicago. University of Chicago Press (originally published in 1872).

Daube (1964) *The Sudden in the Scriptures.* Leiden: E. J. Brill.

Diodorus Siculus (1954; originally 3rd century BCE) The Library of History, Vol. XIX, para. 94.1. Loeb Classical Library. Boston: Harvard University Press.

Duhm (1901) *Das Buch Jeremia* HKATII: Tübingen: J. C. B. Mohr.

Fishbane, M. (2002) *The Jewish Publication Society Bible Commentary: Haftarot.* Philadelphia: Jewish Publication Society.

Gervitz, S. (1961) The Ugaritic parallel to Jeremiah 8:23. *Journal of Near Eastern Studies* 20: 41–46.

Heschel A. J. (1962) *The Prophets.* Philadelphia: Jewish Publication Society.

Hillers, D. R. (1965) A convention in Hebrew literature. The reaction to bad news. *Zeitschrift für die altesttametliche Wissenschaft,* 77: 86–90.

Holladay, W.L. (1985) *Jeremiah I: A Commentary on the Book of the Prophet Jeremiah.* Chapters 1–25. Philadelphia: Fortrus Press.

Holladay, W.L. (1989) *Jeremiah 2: A Commentary on the book of the Prophet Jeremiah.* Chapters 26–52. Minneapolis: Fortrus Press.

Hyatt, J.P. (1984) 'The Deuteronomic Edition of Jeremiah', in *A Prophet to the Nations: Essays in Jeremiah Studies,* pp. 247–260. Eds L.G. Perdue and B. W. Kovacs. Winona Lake, Indiana: Eisenbrauns.

Ingham, C. (1993) *Panic Attacks: What They Are, Why They Happen and What You Can Do About Them.* London: Thorsons.

Jobling, D. (1984) The quest of the historical Jeremiah: Hermeneutical implications of recent literature, pp. 285–298 in *A Prophet to the Nations: Essays in Jeremiah Studies,* eds L. G. Perdue and B. W. Kovacs. Winona Lake, Indiana: Eisenbrauns.

Kaiser, O. (1975) *Isaiah 13–39: A Commentary.* London: SCM Press Ltd.

Klein, D.F. and Fink, M. (1962) Psychiatric reaction patterns to imipramine. *American Journal of Psychiatry,* 119, 432–438.

Lee, A. (2007) Clinical features of depressive disorders. In *Seminars in General Psychiatry* (pp. 1–21), eds G. Stein and G. Wilkinson. London: Gaskell.

Lundbom, J. (1994) *Jeremiah 1–20: A new translation with introduction and commentary. Volume 21A Anchor Bible.* New York: Double Day.

Lundbom, J. (1999) *Jeremiah 21–36: A new translation with introduction and commentary. Volume 21B Anchor Bible.* New York: Double Day.

Lundbom, J. (2004) *Jeremiah 21–36: The Anchor Yale Commentaries.* Boston: Yale University Press.

Marks, I.M. and Lader, M. (1973) Anxiety states (anxiety neurosis): A review. *Journal of Nervous and Mental Disease,* 156, 3–18.

Mowinkel, S. (1914) *Zur compositon des buches Jeremia:* Kristiana: Dubward

Muilenberg, J. (1970) 'The terminology of adversity in Jeremiah' pp. 42–70 in *Translating and Understanding the Old Testament.* Essays in Honor of Herbert Gordon May. Eds H. T. Frank and W. L. Reed, Nashville and New York: Abingdon Press.

New English Bible with the Apocrypha (1970) Oxford: Oxford University Press.

Nicholson, E. W. (1975) *The Book of the Prophet Jeremiah.* Cambridge Biblical Commentary. Cambridge: Cambridge University Press.

Polk, T. (1984) The prophetic persona: Jeremiah and the language of the self. *Journal for the Study of the Old Testament,* supplement series 32.

Pollack, M. H., Smother, J. W., Otto, M. W., *et al.* (2010) The phenomenology of panic disorder. Chapter 21, pp. 367–80 in *Textbook of anxiety disorders* 2nd edition. Eds. D. J. Stein, E. Hollander and B. O. Rothbaum. Washington: American Psychiatric Publishing Inc.

Purdue, L.G. (1984) Jeremiah in Modern Research: Approaches and Issues. pp. 1–33 in *A prophet to the Nations: Essays in Jeremiah Studies.* Eds L. G. Purdue and B. Kovacs Winona Lake, Indiana: Eisenbrauns.

Reventlow, H.G. (1963) *Liturgie und prophetisches 'Ich' bei Jeremia Gütersloh,* Gerd Mohn

Rosenberg, A.J. (1985) *The Book of Jeremiah. Vol. 1.* A New English Translation. New York: Judaica Press Inc.

Rosin, P., and Fallon, A.E. (1987) A perspective in disgust. *Psychological Review,* 94, 23–31.

Roth M. (1959) The phobic anxiety-depresonalization syndrome. *Proceedings of the Royal Society of Medicine;* 52: 587–95.

Salkovskis, P. M., Clark, D. M. and Gelder, M. G. (1996) Cognition–behaviour links in the persistence of panic. *Behavior Research and Therapy* 34(5–6): 453–458.

Starcevic, V. (2010) *Anxiety disorders in Adults,* 2nd edition. Oxford: Oxford University Press.

Steinman, J. (1952) Le prophète Jérémie: Sa vie, son oevre et son temps. *Lectis divina* 9, 296 Editions du cerf.

Thorpe, S.J. and Salkovskis, P.M. (1998) Studies on the role of disgust in the acquisition and maintenance of specific phobias. *Behaviour Research and Therapy,* 36, 877–893.

Von Rad (1984) The confessions of Jeremiah. In *A Prophet to the Nations. Essays in Jeremiah Studies,* eds L.G. Purdue and B.W. Kovacs, pp. 339–340. Winona Lake, Indiana: Eisenbrauns.

Weinfeld, M. (1972) *Deuteronomy and the Deuteronomic School.* Oxford: Clarendon.

Weissman, M.M., Bland, R.C., Canino, C.J., *et al* (1997) The cross-national epidemiology of panic disorder. *Archives of General Psychiatry,* 54: 305–309.

# Chapter 4

# Lamentations

## Introduction

The greatest tragedy in the history of ancient Israel was the siege of Jerusalem, the destruction of its Temple, and the deportation of its peoples. The bare facts of this history are set out in 2 Kings 25, which tells us its date, why it happened and the names of its key perpetrators.

It is recorded in 2 Kings 25[1-4, 8-12] how Zedekiah rebelled against the King of Babylon:

> [1] And in the ninth year of his reign on the tenth day of the tenth month King Nebuchadnezzar of Babylon came with all his army against Jerusalem and laid siege to it; they built siege-works all around it. [2] So the city was besieged until the eleventh year of King Zedekiah. [3] On the ninth day of the fourth month the famine became so severe in the city that there was no food for the people of the land. [4] Then a breach was made in the city wall; the king with all his soldiers fled.... [8] Nebuzaradan, the captain of the guard, a servant of the king of Babylon, came to Jerusalem. [9] He burned the house of the Lord, the king's house, and all the houses in Jerusalem; every great house he burned down.... [11] Nebuzaradan carried into exile the rest of the people who were left in the city and the deserters who had defected to the king of Babylon – all the rest of the population. [12] But the captain of the guard left some of the poorest people to be vine-dressers and tillers of the soil.

Zedekiah's rebellion triggered the fury of King Nebuchadnezzar and made him march on the city and lay siege to it. His captain, Nebuzaradan, then burnt down the city and the first Temple and then deported most of the population to Babylon in 586 BCE. By contrast to this historical account in 2 Kings, Lamentations supplies the human meaning to these facts. It is a recital of the horrors, atrocities, starvation and physical suffering the people endured during the siege of Jerusalem. In the modern era an even greater calamity befell the Jewish people – the Holocaust, in which more than six million Jews were gassed or murdered. The meaning of this suffering is almost impossible to imagine. It required accounts of individual victims to bring home the magnitude of this tragedy. A striking example is the *Diary of Anne Frank*, a book which chronicles the trials and suffering of a 15-year-old Dutch girl hiding from her Nazi persecutors; her diary provides an intimate detail of how the national persecution caused pain, suffering and starvation to a single family during this historical calamity. The Book of Lamentations has a similar purpose – it describes the pain and suffering of one or possibly two poets as well as the terrible conditions prevailing during the siege, giving flesh to the bones of the story as set out in 2 Kings.

While most of the suffering is due to the horrific circumstances of the siege, and the five poems of Lamentations are replete destruction, doom and gloom, some of the sadness appears in the form of psychological pain and a catalogue of depressive symptoms appears in Lamentations 1 and 3, indicating that their writer had personal knowledge of depression and was most likely a sufferer himself.

The book is not only an expression of grief. There are big questions, such as 'Where was God in this tragedy?' and 'Why did God inflict such great suffering on his people?' Job asks similar questions, but in contrast to Job, who maintains throughout that he is innocent of all sin, and so is undeserving of any punishment, the writer(s) of lamentations openly ascribe blame for this tragedy to the people of Jerusalem. It is because of their sins. Such an explanation for a national catastrophe first appears in Deuteronomy and was later espoused by the Deuteronomist(s), and is a central part of Deuteronomic theory of history. Although it is the Babylonians who actually inflict the suffering on the Israelites, the poet lays the blame squarely on to God, implying that the Babylonians were merely acting as his agents.

## Name and authorship

In the Hebrew Bible, Lamentations has the title *'echah* ('How'), which is a question and the first word of the book. In the Babylonian Talmud (*Baba Bathra* 14b) and other early Jewish writings it is called *qinot*, or Lamentations. The Septuagint has *Threnoi* and the Vulgate *threni*. Its place in the Hebrew Bible is within the *Ketubim* ('the writings') and it is one of the five scrolls or *Megillot* and each scroll is read at a different festival. Lamentations is read at the Festival of *Tisha b'av*, which is the ninth day of the month of *Av* and this usually falls in July or August. It commemorates the destruction of both the first Temple in 586 BCE by the Babylonians and the second Temple in 70 CE by the Romans. In Christian liturgies portions of Lamentations are read in services on Maundy Thursday, Good Friday and Holy Saturday. There are eloquent musical settings to these texts and in modern times Leonard Bernstein used texts from Lamentations for his *Jeremiah* symphony (1942) as did Stravinsky for his choral and orchestral work *Threni* (1958).

Religious tradition holds that the work was originally written by Jeremiah, and the Septuagint opens with 'And it came to pass after Israel had gone into captivity, and Jerusalem was laid waste that Jeremiah sat weeping and composed this lament over Jerusalem and said...'. The Syriac version of the Bible (the *Peshitta*) titles the work 'The Book of Lamentations of Jeremiah the Prophet'. The Book of Lamentations describes the conditions of siege warfare in cities of the ancient world. Thus warfare with sieges was frequent in ancient Mesopotamia and this generated many siege laments, the most famous being that in response to the siege of Ur, but this has no references to depression. These siege laments are known as the *Balag* laments, some of which are much older than Lamentations and very lengthy; a comprehensive account of 38 such siege laments is given in Cohen (1988). Only four of these have any suggestion of depression, and in all cases the depression is objectively rather than subjectively expressed and so its detail is relatively thin in comparison with Lamentations. The *Balag* laments in Cohen with some depression are: 'The City is Sighing' (p. 70); 'Fashioning Man and Woman' (pp. 243–244); 'The City which has been Pillaged' (p. 587); and 'My House' (pp. 640–642).

Jeremiah's authorship was first questioned by H. von der Hardt in 1712, who proposed that the five chapters were written by another set of biblical characters, namely by Daniel, Shadrach, Meschach, Abednego and King Jehoiachin. While this seems to be just as improbable as an authorship by Jeremiah, the true writer(s) of these poems remains elusive. Salters (2014) suggests the authors were unknown poet-priest(s) working in the Temple. He cites one scholar, Lohr (1904), who makes a distinction between Lamentations 2 and 4, which have 'an eyewitness character', while Lamentations 1 and 3 assume a more subjective approach. The psychiatric evidence is consistent with this distinction, in that chs 1 and 3 are autobiographical accounts of depression, although some depression is mentioned in the other chapters as well. The historical background to the siege of Jerusalem is given on pages 76–79.

## Outline of the book

A brief outline of the five poems of Lamentations is given below. Chapters 1 and 3 have been quoted in full since, as stated above, it is mainly these chapters that record depressive symptomatology.

In ch. 1 the author laments the desolation of the City of Jerusalem, which is personified as a widow who is in agony. But at the same time the writer makes it clear that it is Yahweh who has caused this – it is a just punishment for her transgressions.

Chapter 2 concentrates on the cause of the affliction and again the blame is placed directly with Yahweh. He has become the enemy of his people and caused the King and his people to go into exile, while those left behind are starving and in mourning.

Chapter 3 has the character of an individual lament and describes the subjective suffering of one individual. He calls on others to repent, but still maintains that it is Yahweh who has caused the suffering. The final verses however are given over to an appeal to Yahweh for vengeance against the enemy.

Chapter 4 describes the horror, destitution and cannibalism in the streets of Jerusalem, contrasting the present state with a happier past. The lucky ones were those killed by the sword. The priests and prophets are to blame because they failed to steer the people on the right course. There is an allusion to an expectation of help from Egypt but this ends in disappointment.

Chapter 5 calls on Yahweh to consider the tragedy. The land and homes of the peoples are now in the hands of aliens. There is a breakdown of law and order, women are being raped. Occupied Judah is a lawless and dangerous place to live.

Chapters 1–4 are written as acrostics: each new verse starts with a word whose first letter starts with the next letter in the Hebrew alphabet. Some chapters have two lines following each letter. To find sets of words which complied with such a strict set of rules and had appropriate meaning must have placed quite a demand on its writer(s), who must have been quite sophisticated poets. There is also an extensive literature on the technical aspects of the poetry of Lamentations.

In the sections which follow, Lamentations 1 and 3 are considered first and in detail, as they contain good accounts of depression, and then chs 2, 4 and 5 are given a brief overview. Biblical commentary is taken from Hillers (1972) and Salters (2014). As elsewhere in this volume, commentary is placed to the right of the biblical text.

## Lamentations 1

1   How lonely sits the city
    that once was full of people!
    How like a widow she has become,
    She that was great among the nations!
    She that was a princess among
    the provinces has become a vassal.

The first word *echah* means 'how' or 'alas!'
The city is a woman and here is personified as a widow.
The author, prone to hyperbole, writes that she was great among the nations (Salters)

2   She weeps bitterly in the night,
    with tears on her cheeks;
    among all her lovers
    She has no one to comfort her;
    all her friends have dealt
    treacherously with her,
    They have become her enemies.

weeping at night ?insomnia
Copious weeping (*Rashi*)

feelings of rejection/lack of support, both personal and political, as previous allies have deserted her

3   Judah has gone into exile with
    suffering and hard servitude;
    she lives now among the nations,
    and finds no resting-place;
    her pursuers have all overtaken her
    in the midst of her distress.

The exile: suffering and punishment

No fixed home now
No rest; ?a state of agitation
Heb *maytzar* also used in Ps 116[3] and 118[5] denoting severe anguish

4   The roads to Zion mourn,
    for no one comes to festivals;
    all her gates are desolate,
    her priests groan;
    her young girls grieve,
    and her lot is bitter

Even the roads are mourning
?lack of joy; ?anhedonia
where the elders congregate
Priests and even young girls are miserable now
depressive thoughts

5   Her foes have become the masters,
    her enemies prosper,
    because the Lord made her suffer for
    the multitude of her transgressions;
    her children have gone away,
    captives before the foe.

The Babylonians are the masters now; they live well
The covenant was broken because of Jerusalem's sins

The deportees

6   From daughter Zion has departed
    all her majesty.
    Her princes have become like stags
    that find no pasture;

Sense of humiliation

no food

they fled without strength          Weakness; no energy
before the pursuer.

7    Jerusalem remembers, in the days
     of her affliction and wandering,
     all the precious things
     that were hers in days of old.
     When her people fell into the
     hand of the foe,
     and there was no one to help her,
     the foe looked on mocking
     over her downfall.

8    Jerusalem sinned grievously,       It is the people's fault
     so she has become a mockery;       These are a woman's sins
     all who honoured her despise her,
     for they have seen her nakedness;  Female nakedness
     she herself groans,
     and turns her face away.           feelings of shame

9    Her uncleanness was in her skirts;    ?Sexual immorality has brought
     she took no thought to her future;    on this tragedy. The disgraced city
     her downfall was appalling,           is a harlot ( J. Kara)
     with no one to comfort her.           no comfort; isolation
     'O Lord, Look at my affliction,
     for the enemy has triumphed!'

10   Enemies have stretched out their    The Babylonians are looting
     hands over all her precious things;  the city of Jerusalem
     she has even seen the nations       Babylonians have entered the Temple
     invade her sanctuary,
     those whom you forbade
     to enter your congregation.         *your* (i.e. God's) congregation

11   All her people groan                Misery with desperation
     As they search for bread;          starvation
     they trade their treasures for food  selling their children for food
     to revive their strength.
     Look, O Lord, and see
     how worthless I have become.       low self-image

12   Is it nothing to you, all you
     who pass by?                       Feelings of neglect
     Look and see
     if there is any sorrow like my sorrow,  my depression is extreme
     which has brought upon me,
     which the Lord inflicted           assertions that God has caused
     on the day of his fierce anger.    all this in his anger.

13   From on high he sent fire;         The bones were thought to be
     it went deep into my bones;        the site of severe pain
     he spread a net for my feet;       God is a hunter; similar
     he turned me back;                 imagery in Job

he has left me stunned,                    ?mute ?shocked
faint all day long.                        ?exhausted, lack of energy

14    My transgressions were bound into      It is the totality of my sins
      a yoke;                              that has caused this
      by his hand they were fastened       Hand of God causing this
      together;                            see page 333
      they weigh on my neck,               feelings of heaviness ?guilt
      sapping my strength;                 causing weakness, no energy
      the Lord handed me over
      to those whom I cannot withstand.    No fight left in me

15    The Lord has rejected                Yahweh's rejection has taken
      all my warriors in the midst of me;  all the fight out of me.
      he proclaimed a time against me
      to crush my young men;               young men, and young women
      the Lord has trodden                 crushed as in the wine press
      as in a wine press
      the virgin daughter Judah.

16    For these things I weep;             uncontrollable crying
      my eyes flow with tears;
      for a comforter is far from me,      no one can help; terrible isolation
      one to revive my courage;
      my children are desolate,            my children are also miserable
      for the enemy has prevailed.

17    Zion stretches out her hands         Pleas for sympathy and help
      but there is no one to comfort her;
      the Lord has commanded against       Because it is God's command
      Jacob that his neighbours should     that no one should help
      become his foes;
      Jerusalem has become a filthy        Heb. *Nidah* = filthy, menstrual, hence
      thing among them.                    to be avoided

18    The Lord is in the right,
      for I have rebelled against his word; I rebelled and so I am in the wrong
      but hear, all you peoples,
      and behold my suffering;             My suffering= the national suffering
      my young women and young men
      have gone into captivity.            the deportation

19    I called to my lovers                reference to other allies and
      but they deceived me;                neighbouring nations (?Egypt)
      my priests and elders                Heb: *remunee* = deceived but also
      perished in the city                 means abandoned, a common
      while seeking food                   feeling in depressives
      to revive their strength

20    See, O Lord, how distressed I am;    Low mood/anxiety
      my stomach churns,                   ?anxiety in the stomach
      my heart is wrung within me,         ?anxiety in the chest
      because I have been very rebellious. Guilt: it's my fault

| In the street the sword bereaves; | killing going on |
| and in the house it is like death. | thoughts of death |

21  They heard how I was groaning,          distress
    with no one to comfort me.             isolation; no help
    All my enemies heard of my trouble;
    they are glad you have done it.
    Bring in the day you have announced,
    and let them be as I am.

22  Let all their evil doing come           ?vengeful feelings.
    before you;
    and deal with them                      They should be punished
    as you have dealt with me               like me (us – the nation)
    because of all my transgressions;       guilt
    for my groans are many                  distress
    and my heart is faint.                  weakness no energy

The explanation given below is taken mainly from Hillers (1972). Lamentations I is an impressive poetic depiction of the desolation of Jerusalem or Zion – the city of God. The destroyed city is personified as a widow, enabling the poet to describe the national catastrophe in more personal terms and giving the suffering of its citizens a more universal meaning than the factual historical account in 2 Kings permits. The poem contains a mixture of third-person objective description from the poet himself, who seems to have been a witness to the tragedy, as well as subjective first-person views, from the perspective of 'the widow Jerusalem'.

The personification of Zion heightens the expression of anguish and this may help intensify the emotional experience of the worshipper when the poem is used in the liturgy, and it seems as if the poem was used in worship from very early on. Thus fragments of Lamentations were found among the Qumran (Dead Sea) scrolls. Hillers (1972) suggests that the parallel between the fallen city of Jerusalem and a widow was chosen because widows and orphans were among the most defenceless people in ancient society. In support of this he cites numerous references, particularly in Isaiah, to asking those in authority to care for the widows and orphans in their communities.

In verse 2, however, the personification of Zion as a woman changes direction – it is now Zion who has become a faithless women whose friends have betrayed her and became hostile to her. Rejection by friends and family is also described in the depressive poetry of both Job (page 34) and Psalm 88[8,18] (see page 153), where this feeling is more clearly related to the writer's depression. A similar thought appears in the Babylonian literature in the 'Poem of the Righteous Sufferer' (*Ludlul bel nemeqi*) which has the line 'My friend has become my foe' (Lambert, 1960; see also page 64).

But the betrayal also has a political meaning, and the lovers of Israel represent neighbouring states and allies, most likely Egypt, who were either unwilling or unable to help defend Israel against the Babylonian onslaught. The emptiness and desolation lead to mourning – the roads are empty (these are the roads to Jerusalem and not the roads in the city) because now no one travels to Jerusalem for the festivals and the priests have no worshippers.

The destruction is a punishment – the result of Israel being rebellious – 'For Yahweh afflicted her for her many rebellions'.[5] Hillers indicates that this is a direct consequence of the curses associated with the covenant. It was Israel who broke the covenant with Yahweh and this led to the destruction and was the main cause of the siege and the exile. 'Her children have gone away, captives before the foe'.[5]

There is then a possible suggestion of paranoia. 'Her enemies saw her and laugh at her collapse'[7] and 'people shake their heads at her';[8] all who once respected her despise her for having seen her naked. The Hebrew word *nidah* (literally, 'object of scorn', but also 'nodding') may have been a pun on a similar sounding word *niddah*, meaning 'menstrual' or 'unclean'. Portraying Jerusalem as a woman offers the writer a chance to highlight themes of female sexuality, 'for they have seen her nakedness'[8] and 'her uncleanness was in her skirts'[9]. Male religious leaders throughout history have often taken a very harsh line on any sort of female sexual deviancy or infidelity and the writer here tries to include this as among the sinful behaviours that led to her (i.e. Jerusalem's) downfall.

The horror of the destruction of Jerusalem is then described. The starvation was extreme: 'They trade their treasures for food'[13] to revive their strength, meaning that they had to sell their own children to survive to buy food. A later verse in Lamentations ($5^{10}$) describes frank cannibalism of the children: 'The hands of compassionate women have boiled their own children; they became their food'. Conditions under the siege were appalling. Such conditions are also described in other famines in the Ancient Near East. Thus in the *Atra-hasis* epic, in connection with a great famine occur the lines 'the daughter watched the scales at the sale of the mother. The mother watched the scales at the sale of the daughter' (Lambert and Millard, 1969).

The hopelessness of the siege is described: 'In the street the sword bereaves and in the house it is like death'. Similar images occur elsewhere in the OT: 'The sword outside, and pestilence and famine inside: he who is in the field shall die by the sword and he who is in the city pestilence and famine shall devour him' (Ez. $7^{15}$). They also occur in the Mesopotamian literature, for instance in the Lamentation over the destruction of Ur: 'Ur ... inside it was to die of famine/outside we are killed by the weapons of the Elamites' (Pritchard, 1955, p. 618, lines 403–4). The final coda of Lamentations 1 could hardly be more depressive: 'For my groans are many and my heart is faint'.[22]

## Psychiatric aspects

The psychiatry is relatively straightforward. The poet draws on his own experience of depression but he places the emotions within the mourning widow of Jerusalem:

- *distress, sadness, low mood* – in the midst of her distress;[3] if there is any sorrow like my sorrow;[12] see Lord how distressed I am;[20] how I was groaning[21]
- *anhedonia* may possibly be present – no one comes to festivals[4]

- *feelings of rejection and isolation*;no one comes to comfort her (a phrase that is repeated five times)[2,7,9,17,21]
- *low self-image* – how worthless have I become[11]
- *feelings of shame* – she herself groans and turns her face away[11]
- *bitterness* – and her lot is bitter[4]
- there are also suggestions of *depressive insomnia* – she weeps bitterly in the night[2]
- psychomotor retardation or *mutism* – he has left me stunned[13]
- *lack of energy* – faint all day long;[13] and my heart is faint;[22] sapping my strength[14]
- *presumed guilt* appears indirectly – my heart is wrong within me because I have been very rebellious[22] and (in the same verse) you have dealt with me because of my transgressions[22]
- *somatic anxiety* is also present – my stomach churns;[20] my heart is wrong within me[20]
- *morbid feelings of death* – and in the house it is like death.[20]

Although many would question whether it is culturally appropriate to apply 21st-century diagnostic criteria to such an ancient text, this is the only way to assess whether this ancient poem represents a depressive episode in the same way as we understand it today. Thus in Table 4.1 the symptoms

**Table 4.1** DSM criteria for major depression and verses from Lamentations 1

| *DSM major depression* | *Lamentations 1* |
| --- | --- |
| The DSM system requires at least five of the following nine symptoms within a two-week period, and at least one of the five has to be depressed mood or diminished interest/pleasure (anhedonia) | |
| (1) Depressed mood (feels sad or empty, is tearful) | If there is any sorrow like my sorrow;[12] see Lord, how distressed I am[20] |
| (2) Diminished interest/pleasure | No one comes to the festivals[4] |
| (3) Weight loss | Not present |
| (4) Insomnia or hypersomnia | She weeps bitterly in the night[2] |
| (5) Psychomotor agitation or retardation | ?My stomach churns; my heart is wrong within me[20] |
| (6) Fatigue/loss of energy | faint all day long[13]; sapping my strength[14] |
| (7) Feelings of worthlessness or guilt | How worthless I have become;[11] You have dealt with me because of my transgressions[22] |
| (8) Trouble concentrating | He has left me stunned[13] |
| (9) Recurrent thoughts of death or suicide | And in the house it is like death[20] |

identified in this poem are compared with the diagnostic criteria of major depression as defined in DSM-5 (APP, 2013).

Lamentations 1 has a tapestry rich in depressive content, having eight out of the nine key symptoms required for a diagnosis of major depressive disorder. The only item not included is anorexia, although this is mentioned in verse 11 as an allusion to searching for food to revive strength, but this is clearly in the context of starvation. Even if the somewhat dubious assertion that 'anhedonia' or 'lack of pleasure' can be equated with 'no one comes to the festivals' is removed, seven key depressive symptoms remain while the DSM-5 diagnostic criteria require only five symptoms. As noted in the discussion of Psalm 88, the poet must have been clinically depressed or recently emerging from a depression to put together this particular combination of thoughts, feelings and symptoms. The description of depression in Lamentations 1 is far more vivid and powerful than the insipid catalogue of DSM-5 symptoms of the modern glossaries. Part of the appeal of Lamentations I and its use in the liturgy of mourning ceremonies lies in its ability to echo more or less exactly what the mourner is going through. The features of normal mourning are identical to those of depression. In ancient times these two conditions were not distinguished and that is why its use in mourning ceremonies even today is so apt.

## Lamentations 3

Lamentations 3 stands apart from the other chapters in the book of Lamentations in both its form and its content. Hillers writes that the despair described in Lamentation 3 is applicable to 'Everyman' – any person whose life is in crisis. It is independent of its historical origin in the siege of Jerusalem, has no references to any geographical places, and has only one reference to 'the destruction of a nation', but it gives no names of conquering armies, nor even makes explicit reference to Jerusalem, but rather is simply a piece of timeless poetry. A cursory psychiatric examination reveals that it is nothing less than the poet's account of his own depression in the form of an individual lament.

It is set out as an alphabetic acrostic poem, as are Lam. 1, 2 and 4. However, each letter of the alphabet is given three lines; thus verse 1 has three lines starting with *aleph*, verse 2 has three lines starting with *beth* and so on. Because there is no reference to the fall of Jerusalem or the tragedy that followed, there is even a suggestion by Budde (1882) and more recently by Westerman (1981) that it has nothing to do with the siege of Jerusalem and may have been written at a much later date. The poem takes the form of a statement of personal suffering and starts with the line 'I am the one who has seen the affliction' and so resembles other psalms of lament. Many of the images and metaphors of misery are formulaic and can also be found in other psalms and especially also in the Book of Job, which this lament resembles. As an autobiographical account of depression in the OT, it is second only to Job in its detail, but the writer of Lamentations 3 achieves a state of healing and delivers a prayer of thanks for his cure, whereas Job has a much more unremitting and severe depression, with melancholic features and little evidence of remission. The central portion of the lament (21–43) is a prayer of hope and does not record depression and for reasons of space is omitted, but the rest of the poem is quoted in full. Biblical commentary is taken from Hillers (1972) and Salters (2010).

| | | |
|---|---|---|
| 1 | I am the one who has seen affliction under the rod of God's wrath; | Is the 'I' Jeremiah?, God has caused 'this' |
| 2 | he has driven and brought me into darkness without any light; | Personal description of depression to a dark place ??no hope. |
| 3 | against me alone he turns his hand, again and again, all day long. | Yahweh is attacking me, pervasive bad feeling |
| 4 | He has made my flesh and my skin waste away, and broken my bones; | Yahweh has made me ill Weight loss ?physical illness |
| 5 | he has besieged and enveloped me with bitterness and tribulation; | No escape from unpleasant depressive thoughts and anxiety |
| 6 | he has made me sit in darkness like the dead of long ago. | ?dark moods thoughts of death |
| 7 | He has walled me about so that I cannot escape; He has put heavy chains on me; | No escape ?from this mood or ? the imprisonment of the siege feelings of heaviness |
| 8 | though I call and cry for help, he shuts out my prayer; | Seeking help from the distress My prayers seem futile |
| 9 | he has blocked my ways with hewn stones, he has made my paths crooked. | Yahweh is deliberately frustrating my attempts to progress |
| 10 | He is a bear lying in wait for me, a lion in hiding; | Yahweh attacking me (as in Job) |
| 11 | he led me off my way and tore me to pieces; he has made me desolate; | God destroying me (as in Job) Heb: *semaam* despair, wretched occurs often in Lamentations |
| 12 | he bent his bow and set me as a mark for his arrow. | |
| 13 | He shot into my vitals the arrows of his quiver; | God shooting his arrows in to me (as in Job) ??somatic pains |
| 14 | I have become the laughing-stock of all my people, the object of their taunt songs all day long. | ?a reality or ?ideas of reference ?paranoia; as in Job |
| 15 | He has filled me with bitterness, he has glutted me with wormwood. | Heb: *Maroreem* Bitterness the bitter herbs of Passover; |
| 16 | He has made my teeth grind on gravel, and made me cower in ashes; | ?teeth grinding; (?bruxism) |
| 17 | my soul is bereft of peace; I have forgotten what happiness is; | Constant anxiety, agitation no happiness, ?anhedonia |
| 18 | so I say, 'Gone is my glory, and all that I had hoped for from the Lord'. | ?humiliation |
| 19 | The thought of my affliction and my homelessness is wormwood and gall! | ?real homelessness due to exile or isolation; bitterness |
| 20 | My soul continually thinks of it and is bowed down within me. | unremitting anxiety depressed mood |
| 21 | But this I call to mind and therefore I have hope… | Not everything is hopeless |

As stated above, verses 22–41 (a prayer of hope and faith) are omitted.

42   We have transgressed and rebelled,      ?guilt. It was our fault
     and you have not forgiven.
43   You have wrapped yourself with anger   God's anger has caused this
     and pursued us, killing without pity;
44   you have wrapped yourself with a cloud
     so that no prayer can pass through.
45   You have made us filth and rubbish      ?low personal self-esteem
     among the peoples.                      or ?degradation of the nation
46   All our enemies have opened             surrounding nations have
     their mouths against us;                ?attacked and devoured us
47   panic and pitfall have come upon us,    panic
     devastation and destruction.
48   My eyes flow with rivers of tears       weeping because of the
     because of the destruction of           the national disaster
     my people.                              (Only mention of the nation)
49   My eyes flow without ceasing,           uncontrolled weeping
     without respite,
50   until the Lord from heaven
     looks down and sees.
51   My eyes cause me grief at the fate of   the depression
     all the young women in my city.        ?the rape of women by soldiers
52   Those who were my enemies              ?real enemies ??paranoia
     without cause have hunted               as they have no cause
     me like a bird;
53   they flung me alive into a pit          thoughts of death
     and hurled stones on me;
54   water closed over my head;              drowning feelings
     I said 'I am lost'.
55   I call on your name, O Lord,
     from the depths of the pit;             ?cistern ?grave ?prison (*Rashi*)
56   you heard my plea, 'Do not close        feelings of isolation
     your ear to my cry for help,            plea for support
     but give me relief!'
57   You came near when I called on you;
     you said 'Do not fear!'                 Fear/anxiety
58   You have taken up my cause, O Lord,     Heb: *reyav* legal pleading
     you have redeemed my life.
59   You have seen the wrong done to me,
     O Lord; judge my cause.
60   You have seen all their malice,         ?real persecution or paranoid thoughts
     all their plots against me.             with conspiracy feelings
61   You have heard their taunts, O Lord,    ?real plots or paranoia
     all their plots against me.
62   The whispers and murmurs of my          God has heard the gossip
     assailants are against me               or ?paranoid auditory experiences
     all day long.                           I hear this all the time
63   Whether they sit or rise – see,
     I am the object of their taunt-songs.   ideas of persecution
64   Pay them back for their deeds,          feelings of anger, revenge
     O Lord, according to the work of
     their hands!

| | | |
|---|---|---|
| 65 | Give them anguish of heart; Your curse be on them! | agitation; anxiety Inflict anxiety on them |
| 66 | Pursue them in anger and destroy them from under the Lord's heavens. | vengeance: Inflict anxiety on them and destroy them |

## Psychiatric aspects of Lamentations 3

Salters (2014, p. 187) writes:

> In verses 1–25 ... the poet seems bent on describing his distress and misery in every conceivable way, pulling metaphor and imagery from every walk in life, giving the impression that he is trying to convey, albeit in poetic language, that Yahweh's onslaught was as complete and multi-faceted as could be. The fact that he attributes his misery to Yahweh suggests that he was a believer in Yahweh; that he still believed that Yahweh was in control; but he indicates that the physical and mental violence which he has experienced has led him to abandon hope in his God. The figure of Job comes to mind.

A little further in his comments on 3[20], Salters adds: 'The speaker continues to reflect on his own terrible circumstances and *is depressed* as a result' (p. 221, emphasis added).

Although one might understand how the original poet of Lamentations 3 would have no knowledge concerning depression, Salters was writing in the 21st century and his summary above captivates all the essence of a depression, yet he is still somehow is unable to identify depression as an illness as the underlying theme for the whole lament.

The poem is itself a powerful description of misery yet the central portion contains a pledge of trust in God and a prayer of hope. The deity is all-powerful in being both the ultimate cause of the misery as well as the only agent capable of healing it. 'Although he causes grief, he will have compassion'.[32] It is likely that the 'grief' here refers directly to depression of the sufferer, but equally it may represent any form of human misery or tragedy. At other times the poet writes in terms of 'We', but only once does the phrase 'the destruction of the nation'[48] appear, placing it in the context of some national catastrophe – but the poem has no references to either Jerusalem or the Babylonians.

The main allusions to depressive disorder are:

* *depressed mood* – made me desolate;[11] my soul is bowed down within me;[20] I am lost[54]
* *depressive thoughts* – enveloped me with bitterness and tribulation;[5] filled me with bitterness[15]
* *weeping* – my eyes flow without ceasing;[49] my eyes flow with rivers of tears[48]
* *low self-esteem* – you have made us filth and rubbish [45]
* *anhedonia* – I have forgotten what happiness is[17]
* *anxiety/agitation* – 'my soul is bereft of peace;[17] give them anguish of heart[65]

- *guilt* – we have transgressed[42]
- *weight loss* – my flesh and my skin waste away[4]
- *panic* – panic and pitfall have come upon us[47]
- *ideas of reference* – I have become the laughing stock of all my people;[14] the object of their taunt songs all day long[63]
- *auditory hallucinations* – the whispers and murmurs of my assailants are against me all day long[62]
- *paranoia and conspiracy* – those who were my enemies without cause have hunted me like a bird;[52] you have seen all their malice, all their plots against me;[60] you have heard their taunts Oh Lord, all their plots against me[61]
- *thoughts of death* – he has made me sit in darkness like the dead of long ago.[6]

The lament contains many more metaphors of misery but only those occurring in DSM-5 are highlighted here. In Table 4.2 the diagnostic criteria from DSM-5 are matched against particular verses of Lamentations 3.

**Table 4.2** DSM major depression and verses from Lamentations 3

| *DSM major depression* | *Lamentations 3* |
| --- | --- |
| The DSM system requires at least five of the following nine symptoms within a two-week period, and at least one of the five has to be depressed mood or diminished interest/pleasure (anhedonia) | |
| (1) Depressed mood (feels sad or empty, is tearful) | [5]made me desolate; [20]my soul is bowed down within me; [48] my eyes flowed with rivers of tears |
| (2) Diminished interest/pleasure | [48]I have forgotten what happiness is |
| (3) Weight loss | [4]My flesh and my skin waste away |
| (4) Insomnia or hypersomnia | Not mentioned |
| (5) Psychomotor agitation or retardation | [17]My soul is bereft of peace; [65]Give them anguish of heart; [7]He has walked me about so that I cannot escape |
| (6) Fatigue/loss of energy | [45]You have made us filth and rubbish; [42]We have transgressed and rebelled |
| (7) Feelings of worthlessness or guilt | ?[7]He has put heavy chains on me |
| (8) Trouble concentrating | Not mentioned |
| (9) Recurrent thoughts of death or suicide | [6]He has made me sit in darkness like the dead of long ago |

The table shows that Lamentations 3 refers to seven out of nine symptoms of major depression. It is uncertain whether 'he has put heavy chains on my heart'[7] refers to a feeling of heaviness in the chest – which is common in depression – or to the symptom of low energy and inactivity or possibly both. Since only five symptoms are required for a diagnosis, the required diagnostic criteria are still met. It is noteworthy that in both Lam. 1 and Lam. 3 there is no mention of sleep disorder, loss of appetite, morning depression or weight loss and the reference to fatigue is doubtful, all suggesting that this writer did *not* suffer with the more severe sub-type of 'depression with melancholic features', whereas Job did have this more severe sub-type (see page 45 for explanation). However, mild psychotic symptomatology in the form of paranoia, ideas of reference and auditory hallucinations are seemingly present and repeated, suggesting the poet may have experienced such symptoms.

It is through the depression, a common and universal condition, that the writer is able to greatly widen the appeal of these verses, making it into a highly evocative poem within the religious liturgy, or, as Hillers puts it, making it applicable to an 'Everyman'.

## Lamentations 2

Lamentations 2 continues to elaborate on the devastation of the siege, but only a few symptoms of depression are mentioned. Thus there is an objective comment on how mourning has increased during the siege: 'The Lord has become like an enemy, he has destroyed Israel ... and multiplied in daughter Judah mourning and Lamentation' ($2^5$).

There are several references to the poet's personal suffering 'My eyes are spent with weeping, my stomach churns' ($2^{11}$). The walls also express the depression: 'he caused rampart and wall to lament; they languished together' ($2^8$). In verse 10, perhaps there is muteness: 'the elders of daughter Zion sit in silence'. The Hebrew word used in this lament is *daman*, which means 'be silent', but in other passages the same word is taken to mean 'to wail, mourn'.

The description of the elders throwing dust on their heads ($2^{10}$) is symbolic of lowliness (Hillers). In this position a man is in direct contact with dirt – a reminder of the mourning tradition of the bereaved putting dust on their heads which appears frequently in the OT. The poet describes his own grief: 'My eyes are spent with weeping; my stomach churns'[11] – perhaps suggestive of some sort of gastric anxiety. As elsewhere in the OT, the bowels or liver (my bile) are thought to be the physical organ involved with emotion and the author describes how 'my bile is poured out onto the ground because of the destruction of my people'.[11]

The sufferer is almost commanded to weep 'Give yourself no rest, Your eyes no respite' ($2^{18}$), indicating the crying is ceaseless. The crying is 'day and night' and 'at the beginning of watches', which would have been in the early morning and so suggestive of early morning wakening and morning depression as well as depressive insomnia. The phrase 'pour out your heart like water' ($2^{19}$) is probably similar in meaning to the English phrase 'to cry out from the heart'.

There are several depressive symptoms in Lamentations 2, including of sadness, uncontrolled crying, muteness, gastric anxiety, extreme tension, insomnia and morning dysphoria, are all quite suggestive of depression but the picture is incomplete and less certain than the portrayal of depression offered in Lamentations 1 and 3.

## Lamentations 4

Lamentations 4 has no mention of any mental symptoms. Like ch. 2 it contains a catalogue of the effects of starvation on the civilian population. Thus infants are thirsty because their mothers cannot give them milk, older children beg for food, but there is none, and some are even boiled to become food for their starving mothers. The punishment is even worse than that meted out to the sinful city of Sodom. Although it is God's anger that has done this, blame is placed on the prophets and the corrupt priests who failed to guide the people away from their sins and so permitted this terrible punishment to befall them. Such an explanation for the national catastrophe, which might seeming strange to the modern reader, is typical of the deuteronomistic theory of history, widely held by the priesthood and scribes of the day. The account of the starvation and siege conditions is very similar to other historical accounts of sieges and the accompanying human degradation, such as in the siege of Calais in the 13th century, or that of Leningrad in World War II. Although there is some anger directed at the enemy, at God and at the corrupt priesthood, the tone is not emotional but matter of fact in its observation of the events and the suffering.

## Lamentation 5

Lamentation 5 falls into the genre of the communal laments. These poems were probably composed and used at times of great national distress. Other commonly cited communal laments include Psalms 44, 60, 74, 79, 80, 83 and 89. Although this lament has 22 verses, it is not an acrostic poem and uses the plural 'we' or 'our' to describe the suffering of the vanquished nation. There is also a suggestion that the poem was written fairly soon after the fall of Jerusalem in 586 BCE because the conditions described seem to be consistent with the immediate aftermath of a battle, before a civilian administration is installed, where the conquering soldiers might have run amok among the defeated population. Thus the lament complains about strangers taking over our homes, being ruled by foreigners, food being difficult to obtain; even water must now be paid for. Conditions in the street are so dangerous that getting food is hazardous and young women who venture out run the risk of being raped. There is exploitation of the young while the elders no longer meet at the city gates. These are the hard facts of a foreign occupation in any era.

Psychiatry is minimal. Perhaps there is a suggestion of anhedonia (loss of happiness) in 'The joy of our hearts has ceased; our dancing has been turned to mourning' ($5^{15}$) but otherwise there is little evidence of depressive thinking. The poem ends with a famous verse sometimes used in the synagogue liturgy ($5^{21}$):

> Restore us to yourself, O Lord, that we may be restored; Renew our days as of old.

## Concluding remarks

Lamentations is a short but powerful book about the suffering of the civilian population during warfare. Siege is a terrifying form of warfare that continues to this day. Lamentations tells us about the pain and suffering of such sieges and through its verse and its subtle incorporation of depression makes it into a highly evocative piece of biblical liturgy which continues to be read in religious services today. Lamentations 3 is second only to the Book of Job in respect to the detail of the depression it describes.

## References

Budde, K. (1882) Das Hebraishes Klagelied. *Zeitschrift fur die alttestamentliche Wissenschaft* 1–52.

Cohen, M. E. (1988) *The Canonical Lamentations of Ancient Mesopotamia*. Potomac, MA: Capital Decisions.

Hardt, H., van der (1712) *Threnos quos vulgus jeremiae tribuites*. Helmstadii.

Hillers, D. R. (1972) *Lamentations*, Anchor Bible Series. Garden City, NY: Doubleday.

Lambert, W. (1960) *Babylonian Wisdom Literature*. Oxford: Clarendon Press.

Lambert, W. and Millard, H. R. (1969) *Atra-Hasis: The Babylonian Story of the Flood*. Oxford: Clarendon.

Lohr, M. (1904) Threni III und die Jeremianische Autorschaft des Buches Der Klagelieder *Zeitschrift fur die alttestamentliche Wissenschaft* 24, 1–16.

Porteus, N. (1961) 'Jerusalem–Zion: The growth of a symbol. In *Verbannung und Heimkehr, Rudolf Festschrift*, pp. 244–245. Tubingen.

Salters, R. B. (2014) *A Critical and Exegetical Commentary on Lamentations*. London: Bloomsbury.

Westerman, C. (1981) *Praise and Lament in the Psalms*. Edinburgh: T&T Clark.

# The Hebrew Psalms and affective disorder

## Introduction

No book in the Hebrew Bible has been read more widely than the Psalms and it forms an essential part of both the Jewish and Christian liturgy as well as being the most commonly used book for private prayer. The English word 'psalm' is derived from the Greek *psalmos*, which denotes the twanging of a musical instrument, while the earlier Hebrew word *mizmor*, which means 'song', may have its root in the ancient Akkadian word *zamaru,* meaning 'to sing the word', while *zammeru* means 'singer'. In the Hebrew Bible, the Book of Psalms is also known as the 'Sefer Tehillim' and forms a part of the Ketubim or 'the writings'. In the Hebrew canon it is placed immediately before the Book of Job, but in the Christian canon it comes after Job.

Modern study of the psalms starts with the monumental contributions of the German scholar H. Gunkel and his Swedish pupil S. Mowinckel, both of whom published large treatises on them. A wide variety of different topics are covered in the 150 psalms comprising the book, and to make sense of this diversity Gunkel proposed a classification based on the role that each psalm might have had in the cultic life of the ancient Israelites. Some psalms were used for prayer; some were hymns of praise to God or for the monarchy and were for collective use; others were more specifically for individual use and sought forgiveness, justice or relief from suffering. Most were sung in the Temple or in later synagogue worship as a part of the daily liturgy. Gunkel's classification, which is based on the '*sitz im Leben*' or 'their place in life', has been generally accepted as the best categorisation. He grouped psalms together on the basis that: they shared the same place in cultic worship; they shared a common treasury of thought and feeling; and they had a shared diction or literary style (Seybold, 1990). Six major groups were recognised:

(1) *Hymns.* These psalms combine song with professions of faith and prayer. They might extol God for his acts of creation or for his role in the great acts of history. They usually had a fixed place in temple liturgy and were used in worship in both the first and second Temples.
(2) *Royal psalms.* These relate to the royal cult at the state sanctuary. They describe the kings, the coronation, his battles and marriages, and many relate to David, but others to Solomon or later Kings. Because the monarchy ceased with the exile, the royal psalms must have had a pre-exilic origin, even though they probably reached their final form only after the exile.

(3) *Communal laments.* These are psalms in which the nation laments some communal disaster such as the destruction of the Jerusalem Temple. They are generally acts of worship dedicated to either lamentation or atonement. Sometimes they assume the form of a debate with God, for example by recalling promises of the past. Their aim is to obtain God's intervention in the nation's affairs, as for example in dealing with neighbouring peoples or in seeking deliverance from some communal disaster.

(4) *Individual laments.* Just as the communal lament bemoans the fate of the nation, the individual lament bemoans the fate of the individual who utters them (Day, 1990). This is the largest of Gunkel's groupings. These psalms usually start with an invocation to God, followed by the lament itself, which usually comprises a description of a particular type of misery, perhaps a sickness or an injustice, and then follows up with a plea for intervention by God. They usually end with a prayer of thanksgiving and a short hymn of praise, which the whole congregation will join in. Two broad groups are recognised. First, there are 'the prayers of the accused', where an accused person perhaps awaiting judgement in the court of the Temple seeks mercy or relief from his accusers, who are deemed to be unjust. Secondly, there are the psalms of ill health or the 'sickness psalms'. It is only within this group that descriptions of psychiatric disorder, generally depression, can be found. The actual content of these psalms and how the text implies psychiatric symptoms is most likely a reflection of the feelings of the psalmist/composer and these psalms provide the core of this chapter. The sickness psalms include the seven penitential psalms (6, 32, 38, 51, 102, 130 and 145), which are traditionally sung in the Christian Church on Ash Wednesday. Psalms 6, 13, 22, 31, 38, 69 and 88 all appear to contain a degree of depression and are examined in this chapter. In addition, certain verses from Psalms 48 and 55, not normally considered as sickness psalms, include descriptions of panic disorder, while Psalm 30 describes mood switches. A few other isolated verses from other psalms which suggest psychiatric symptomatology will also be discussed.

(5) *The songs of Yahweh's enthronement.* These are sometimes considered to be a sub-group of the hymns.

(6) *Prayers of individual thanksgiving.* Their purpose was to express thanks for deliverance from some personal distress.

In addition there are miscellaneous or minor groupings, such as the prophetic psalms, songs of the ascent, songs of victory, psalms of confidence, psalms of praise (the Hebrew *Hallel*) as well as many mixed types which do not fall readily into any one category.

## Authorship and the place of the psalms in their cultic setting

How did the psalms come to be written? The history of the psalms is the history of 150 separate texts, but their true authors were probably some unknown poet-priests who worked in the first Temple. The Book of Psalms itself ascribes the authorship of 73 psalms to David; 11 to Asaph, a Levite musician whose descendants continued the family tradition of music; 12 to the sons of Korah, who were also Levites, descended from Kohath, and they were also involved in the music at the Temple. Of separate and probably much later authorship are the two groups of the *Hallel* psalms and the psalms of the ascent. The Book of Psalms is itself divided into five separate books, taking this model from the Pentateuch .

Craigie points out that while the Book of Psalms comprises one of the largest sections of poetry in the Old Testament but there are many examples of more ancient poetry, such as the Song of the Sea (Exodus $15^{1-18}$) and the song of Deborah (Judges 5). These very early poems are thought to have Canaanite origins and are almost certainly pre-monarchic (i.e. they antedate the reign of Saul, which was around 1040 BCE).

Westerman suggests the many of the psalms started as part of the Temple liturgy and were composed by musicians involved in the rituals of sacrifice. The royal psalms all assume a monarchy and hence are ascribed to David. Even if they were not written by David himself, many may have been composed during his reign or during the reign of Solomon or the later kings. Nevertheless, most scholars agree that the bulk of the psalms reached their final form only after the exile while some were probably first written during this era. None could be more explicit than Psalm 137, with its famous opening line 'By the rivers of Babylon – there we sat down and there we wept when we remembered Zion'. A further subdivision for the psalms relates to which word is used to describe God: either *elohim* or *adonai* (Yahweh). In Psalms 1–41 mentions of *Yahweh* outnumber the *elohim* by a ratio of 18 to 1, whereas in Psalms 42–83 the word *elohim* outnumbers the word *Yahweh* by about 5 to 1. Scholars have taken this to signify that there is an elohistic psalter compiled by a text redactor, in the same way as the J and E texts of the first four books of the Pentateuch were edited. Seybold suggests that the *elohistic* psalter represents a collection of psalms that were employed for the theological education of the laity. Further redaction and selection of the most poetic and relevant psalms continued long after the exile, but it is thought that this process was probably completed by around 300 BCE. Support for this date derives from the Septuagint, which can be accurately dated to around 300 BCE, because this version of the Book of Psalms differs very little from the Qumran scrolls, which are also dated 300–100 BCE, and both these texts closely resemble the final Masoretic text (the official Jewish Bible – see Appendix 2 to the book, page 583).

E. S. Gerstenberger has suggested that most of the psalms were used in small-group community worship rather than originating from the Jerusalem Temple. Others have suggested that the psalms comprised the hymn book of the second Temple or the small synagogues that grew up after the return from the Babylonian exile.

## Poetic style – parallelism

The form of the poetry in the psalms was first described by Robert Lowth, who in 1753 published his study *De Sacra Poesi Hebraeorum Praelectiones*

*Academicae*, in which he identified the form of parallelism which is characteristic of the Hebrew poetry in the psalms and elsewhere. Parallelism may have had its origins in the way the psalms were sung or chanted and this form is shared by the even older Akkadian psalms and Ugaritic hymns. Cohen suggests that in early temple or synagogue worship the psalms were either sung or chanted with two groups sharing in the recital. One party chanted the first line, to which the other group responded. Such a procedure inevitably gave rise to a particular form of verse known as parallelism, where the second line repeats, or reflects or adds to the sentiments of the first line. In synonymous parallelism the same thought is reproduced using different words. Psalm 15[1] provides an example:

> Lord who shall sojourn in thy tabernacle.
> Who shall dwell upon thy holy mountain.

In antithetic parallelism a thought is reinforced by the method of contrasts. An example is provided by Psalm I[6]:

> The Lord regardeth the way of the righteous.
> But the way of the wicked shall perish.

In a third type of parallelism the thought continues from line to line, to build up a cumulative effect, and this is known as synthetic parallelism. Again, Psalm I provides an example:

> [1]Happy is the man that
> hath not walked in the counsel of the wicked
> nor stood in the way of sinners
> nor sat in the seat of the scornful.

Although other ancient Near Eastern peoples also wrote verse with parallelism, the poetry of the ancient Hebrew priests excelled in its beauty and quality of thought. With parallelism, the basis of the poetic 'rhyme' lies solely in the repetition of the meaning rather than in repetition of the sounds of the words or syllables. The 'rhyme' is therefore not language specific and so the poetry of the psalms can be translated into many different languages without any loss of poetic force. It is this characteristic that has enabled ancient Hebrew religious poetry not only to survive, but sometimes even to improve in translation, making the psalms into the universal prayers of so many diverse peoples for more than two millennia.

## Emotional impact and emotional disorder

The intense emotional impact of the psalms has also been the focus of some attention. Mumford (1992), in his study entitled *Emotional Distress in the Hebrew Bible: Somatic or Psychological,* writes:

> The richest variety of emotional states is found in the Psalms. The breadth of human emotions represented there explains why the Psalms have come to occupy such an important place in both private and congregational worship of Jews and Christians.

Craigie (1983) contrasts the use of prose to poetry in religious writings, and suggests prose is used only for communicating factual material while poetry has a more transcendental quality, being better suited to communicate moods, an effect further heightened by the accompaniment of music. He cautions against subjecting the poetry of the psalms to too much critical analysis, because poetry, like music, must be experienced and enjoyed rather than criticised and analysed. Nevertheless, some analysis is necessary for the purposes of this chapter. Certain well recognised common psychiatric symptoms and disorders must have been present in the minds of the authors at the time of writing. The psalms which have some depression in them are presented in the order of those with the most depression to those with the least: Psalms 88, 38, 31, 6, 13, 22, 69 and 30.

## Psalm 88

All commentators are agreed on the extreme gloominess of this psalm. Kirkpatrick (1902, p. 523) considers it to be the saddest in the whole psalter while Cohen (1985), a Jewish commentator, writes that the psalm is shrouded in gloom. In contrast to the other sickness psalms, there is no glimmer of hope breaking through to the supplicant. The Targum relates this gloom to the misery of Israel in captivity and Rashi provides a similar interpretation. Cohen questions such a purely historical interpretation, 'as the intense personal note is too evident to be missed'. Most commentators are unclear as to exactly what the psalmist is suffering from. The psalm describes a strong sense of rejection and alienation, which commences in the author's youth. It has been suggested that the illness described in the psalm is leprosy, a common ailment of those times. However, as Kraus (1988) points out, there is no mention of any dermatological lesions or of other physical symptom. Even prominent biblical scholars such as Craigie and Kraus do not offer a formal diagnosis for the suffering but they compare Psalm 88 to similar passages in the Book of Job, where the depression of the principal actor is generally accepted. Below, on the left hand side of the page Psalm 88 is quoted while on the right psychiatric aspects are commented upon:

> Psalm 88. A song. A psalm of the Korahites. To the leader according to Mahaloth Leannoth. A maskil of Heman the Ezrahite

| | |
|---|---|
| 1  Lord, God of my salvation, when at night, I cry out in your presence, | nocturnal distress, depressive insomnia? |
| 2  let my prayer come before you; incline your ear to my cry. | general distress |
| 3  For my soul is full of troubles, and my life draws near to Sheol. | psychic anxiety |
| 4  I am counted among those who go down to the Pit; I am like those who have no help, like those forsaken among the dead, like the slain that lie in the grave, like those whom you remember no more, for they are cut off from your hand. | fears of death hopelessness<br><br>fears of death and abandonment |

| | |
|---|---|
| 6 You have put me in the depths of the Pit,<br>in the regions, dark and deep.<br>Your wrath lies heavy upon me, | guilt, fear |
| and you overwhelm me with all<br>your waves | anxiety ?panic |
| You have caused my companions<br>to shun me, | feelings of rejection and |
| you have made me a thing of horror<br>to them. | ?ideas of reference |
| I am shut in so that I cannot escape; | entrapment |
| 9 my eye grows dim through sorrow. | ?depressed facies |
| Every day I call on you, O LORD;<br>I spread out my hands to you.<br>Do you work wonders for the dead? | |
| Do the shades rise up to praise you?<br>Is your steadfast love declared in the grave,<br>or your faithfulness in Abaddon? | anhedonia (see text) |
| 12 Are your wonders known in the darkness,<br>or your savings help in the land<br>of forgetfulness? | ? memory loss |
| 13 But I, Oh LORD, cry out to you;<br>in the morning my prayer comes before<br>you. | ?morning distress |
| 14 Oh LORD, why do you cast me off? | rejection by God |
| Why do you hide your face from me? | more feelings of rejection |
| Wretched and close to death from<br>my youth up, | young onset of depression |
| I suffer your terrors; I am desperate. | panic attacks |
| Your wrath has swept over me; | guilt or fear |
| your dread assaults destroy me | ?panic attacks |
| They surround me like a flood all day long;<br>from all sides they close in on me. | claustrophobia |
| You have caused friend and neighbour<br>to shun me; | feelings of alienation |
| my companions are in darkness. | with ideas of reference |

## Psychiatric aspects

The psalm starts with a plea to God to listen 'when at night, I cry out in your presence'. The Septuagint version has 'I have cried by day and in the night before you'. The Masoretic text also reports day and night distress 'by day I cried into night before thee', which Cohen suggests can only mean 'I cried in the daytime and my crying continued into the night'. This 24-hour distress is typical of severe depressed states.

In verse 2 the subject's soul (Heb. *nefesh* = mind) is full of troubles and so places the suffering in the mental rather than the physical domain, perhaps describing psychic anxiety. An alternative religious interpretation might be that this is spiritual suffering.

Verses 3 and 4 allude to death by using such phrases as 'my life draws near to Sheol' like those who go down to the Pit or who are forsaken among the dead. A feeling of being almost dead or a feeling that certain body parts are dead may occur in the nihilistic delusions of a severe psychotic depression. Sheol is mentioned in association with physical symptoms in the other sickness psalms (22, 38 and 69) but in Psalm 88 there is no mention of any physical symptoms, which suggests all the suffering lies within the psychic realm.

Verse 7 describes how the wrath of God 'lies heavy upon me'. Among depressives today it is not uncommon to hear patients pose the same question: 'Why has God turned against me?' or 'What have I done that God should be so angry with me?' The phrase 'lies heavy upon me' may refer to feelings of heaviness in their chest, or a sense of being crushed, also common complaints among depressives.

Verse 8 describes social alienation: 'You have caused my companions to shun me' (very much like Job). Subjective feelings of rejection are common but in reality rejection by friends and family is rare. The depressed person is no longer good company because he can only talk of gloom and doom or in a self-centred fashion about his own misery. In his perception the psalmist gives distancing a paranoid flavour as he believes his friends now despise or hate him: 'you have made me a thing of horror to them'. Similar sentiments appear in Job 19[15-19] and are discussed in the previous chapter, on page 137. The verse goes on to describe feelings of entrapment: 'I am shut in so that I cannot escape'. This is also a common thought among those suffering from severe depression, who can see no way out from their torment.

Verse 13 describes how bad the psalmist feels in the morning: ' But I, O Lord, cry out to you; in the morning'. Depressives are generally at their worst in the morning and this symptom is known as diurnal mood variation. Alternatively, Ferguson suggests 'the morning' may refer to crying out during morning prayers. Further feelings of rejection by God are also described in verse 14: 'Why do you hide your face from me?'

Verse 15 describes an onset since youth, as the phrase 'Wretched and close to death from my youth up' suggests a state of severe depression where the subject is unable to remember a time when he was not depressed, believing he has been depressed forever. Perhaps he can never remember feeling well, which is also common in severe depression. Alternatively, he may be describing an early-onset illness starting at puberty; such illnesses are usually severe. The phrase 'I suffer your terrors; I am desperate' suggests panic attacks. The psalm ends with familiar themes of alienation: 'You have caused friend and neighbour to shun me'. The sufferers of psychotic depression also believe that their friends and close relatives must also be suffering like them. Unlike the other sickness psalms, this psalm ends on a depressive note; there is no prayer to God for healing, there is no relief from the suffering, but only never-ending misery.

In summary, therefore, the main depressive symptoms in Psalm 88 are: depressed mood (verses 4, 12); sleep disturbance (1); anxiety (3); morbid thoughts of death (3, 4); hopelessness (4); ideas of reference (8, 18); diurnal mood variation (15); and possibly forgetfulness (12). The difficulties in applying modern diagnostic criteria such as DSM are briefly discussed in the introduction (page 8, and again page 66), but there does not seem to be any other way of joining together these symptoms apart from the use some sort of a diagnostic schedule, of which DSM-5 is the latest. Diagnostic requirements for an episode of major depressive disorder are for a depressed mood together with four other key symptoms (see page 44). Although many of the individual verses may have an alternative cultic explanation, the only way the pervasive misery of the whole psalm can be understood is that this writer was suffering from a depressive illness at the time of composition. It would be almost impossible for anyone without depression to assemble this particular constellation of symptoms at random. This description of depression in verse form was composed more than two millennia before Burton (1621) provided the world with a more comprehensive medical description of the disorder.

Although some authors have wondered why such a poem of despair was included in the psalter, formulating the psalm as a prayer which includes most of the symptoms of major depressive disorder may explain why the psalm has retained its place in the liturgy for more than 2,000 years. Different redactors must have pondered carefully whether to retain this psalm in the liturgy, but the high prevalence of depressive disorder in all communities would have meant that at least some redactors and certainly many worshippers would have been familiar with the themes expressed in these verses. Today, a depressed subject will confide his symptoms to his doctor or therapist and so obtain cathartic relief. In the pre-medical world of ancient Israel the role of the doctor was assumed by the priest and so a depressed person, by singing or reciting the 18 verses of Psalm 88, could effectively communicate the torment of his inner world of depression to the priest and by inference to God as well, because the psalm captures almost all the salient features of depression. This would have had a similar cathartic effect for a depressed subject as visiting a doctor today.

## Religious and cultic aspects

The preface to this psalm has attracted considerable interest among biblical scholars. Mowinckel suggests that the word *mahaloth* means song or playing the reed pipes at Lamentation ceremonies, and cites Jeremiah 48[36-37], where a similar word is used to describe the playing of the reed pipes over the lamentation of Moab. The word *leannoth* denotes penance, and the psalm is therefore a song of penance. It may have been used by the ancient Israelites in rituals linked to purification from illness, a place it continued to hold in later Jewish and Christian liturgies. The psalm is attributed to Heman the Ezrahite, and a person with a similar name is mentioned as one of Korahite Levitical singers in I Chronicles 15[17-19]. Heman is also mentioned as the King's seer (I Chr. 25[5]) and also as possibly a wise man of Solomon's reign.

Authorship of the psalm is attributed to one of the sons of Korah and in his book *The Psalms of the Sons of Korah* Goulder (p. 203) suggests that the entire psalm was used as a communal lamentation before the annual autumn festival of atonement. In this ancient rite a human scapegoat would be banished from the kingdom for a day and a night, with the king being the representative for the nation. It is unlikely that important kings such as Solomon or Ahab themselves were banished but a priest would have been sent away to substitute for them. The priest was then left alone in the darkness of a pit or cave surrounded by water, to undergo an experience similar to inhabiting Sheol – the realm of the dead. While in the cave the ghosts of the dead would supposedly mill around; the priest would pray for himself and the people, perhaps by repeatedly chanting this psalm. Goulder also speculatively identifies a possible place where this ritual might have taken place: the sanctuary at Dan, because the river disappears under the ground for some distance at the south-west corner of the city of Dan.

Other scholars, such as Seybold, Mueller and Kraus, suggest the psalm and its reference to Sheol signify severe physical sickness or death and cite similar passages in Isa. 38$^{10-19}$ and Job 33$^{22-28}$. Thus:

> The sick person feels near to death or believes himself to be caught in the flow of those who are descending to the pit; indeed, he already feels he is leaning towards the underworld, towards Sheol, the collecting centre for all the living.

An alternative, though less widely accepted, is offered by P. K. McCarter in his article 'The river ordeal in Israelite literature'. He suggests the psalm alludes to 'going down to the pit' (v. 4) and later being surrounded by a flood (v. 17), and this may be a part of the ancient pit-river literature, which refers to judgement by water. In this primitive type of justice, the guilt or innocence of the accused was decided by throwing him into a river. If the subject survived he was innocent, but if he drowned he was guilty. Survival or death was assumed to be at the will of the deity. Although there is no direct reference to this practice in the Old Testament legal material, the practice was widespread in the ancient Near East and it is likely the psalmists of Israel would have been familiar with it.

The land of forgetfulness described in verses 11–13 refers to a land where the shades (*rephaim*) cannot rise up and praise God. This may be an oblique reference to the mental symptom of anhedonia. It was taken as a sign of life and pleasure to be able to praise God: 'He who is alive and well sings the Lords praises', 'while for the dead, as one who does not exist, thanksgiving has ceased' (Ecclus 17$^{29}$; also Psalms 115$^{17}$, 118$^{19}$, 119$^{7}$). Westermann describes the link between life and singing praises to God even more strongly: 'Where death is, there is no praise; where there is life there is praise'. This half-alive half-dead state of the *rephaim* (the shades) where there is no praise and therefore no joy may be the psalmist's way of describing the distressing mental symptom of anhedonia, which is characterised by a loss of the ability to experience any sense of pleasure (see also page 67). The references to Abaddon are probably to the names of gods of the underworld in the ancient Near East, perhaps corresponding to Hades in Greek mythology.

Many commentators draw parallels with Psalm 88 and to the Book of Job, where the depression is obvious, and the mood of the subject is worsened by the desertion of friends and companions, who seemingly turn against the sufferer without cause.

The authorship and dating of the psalm are unknown, but Albright (1968) suggests that because Psalms 88 and 89 'swarm with Canaanitisms' an early origin, at the time of David, is possible. Craigie suggests that the earliest origin might have been the monarchic period, prior to 722 BCE, when the

Northern Kingdom fell, because if the sanctuary at Dan is the origin of the pit river, alluded to in this psalm, and Dan was in the Northern Kingdom.

## Psalm 38

A psalm of David for the Memorial offering

| | | |
|---|---|---|
| 1 | O Lord, do not rebuke me in your anger, | God's anger ?guilt |
| | or discipline me in your wrath. | ?guilt |
| 2 | For your arrows have sunk into me, | |
| | and your hand has come down on me | |
| 3 | There is no soundness in my flesh because of your indignation; | ?physical illness |
| | there is no health in my bones because of my sin. | physical illness; guilt |
| 4 | For my iniquities have gone over my head; | guilt |
| | they weigh like a burden too heavy for me. | guilt |
| 5 | My wounds grow foul and fester because of my foolishness; | infected wounds, ulcers |
| 6 | I am utterly bowed down and prostate; | sense of humiliation |
| | all day long I go around mourning. | depression |
| 7 | For my loins are filled with burning, | ?fever |
| | and there is no soundness in my flesh. | |
| 8 | I am utterly spent and crushed; | depressive thoughts; hopelessness |
| | I groan because of the tumult of my heart. | ?tachycardia ?anxiety) |
| 9 | O Lord, all my longing is known to you; | languishing |
| | my sighing is not hidden from you. | anergy |
| 10 | My heart throbs, my strength fails me; as for the light of my eyes – | |
| | it also has gone from me. | ?tachycardia, weakness, |
| 11 | My friends and companions stand aloof from my affliction, | rejection and alienation ?due to illness |
| | and my neighbours stand far off. | (alienation) |
| 12 | Those who seek my life lay their snares; | ?real enemies, or ?paranoia |
| | those who seek to hurt me speak of ruin, | ?auditory hallucinations |
| | and meditate treachery all day long. | ?true conspiracy/or ?paranoia |
| 13 | But I am like the deaf, I do not hear; | ?sensory inattention |
| | like the mute, who cannot speak. | ?depressive mutism |
| 14 | Truly, I am like one who does not hear | sensory inattention |
| | and in whose mouth is no retort. | mutism |
| 15 | But it is for you, O Lord, that I wait; it is you, O Lord my God, who will answer. | |
| 16 | For I pray, 'Only do not let them rejoice over me, those who boast against me when my foot slips'. | |
| 17 | For I am ready to fall, | falling ?humiliation |
| | and my pain is ever with me. | I will never get better |
| 18 | I confess my iniquity; | guilt |
| | I am sorry for my sin. | guilt |
| 19 | Those who are my foes without cause | ?real enemies, or ?paranoia |
| | are mighty and many are those | |
| | who hate me wrongfully. | ?paranoid sentiments |

20  Those who render me evil for good are
    my adversaries because I follow after good.
21  Do not forsake me, O Lord;                          fears of abandonment
    O my God, do not be far from me
22  Make haste to help me
    O Lord my Salvation


## *Psychiatric aspects*

Psalm 38 provides a rich description of human suffering, or in modern terminology depressive symptoms. In its literary form it is classified as an acrostic because it has 22 verses each starting with a letter in the alphabet and in alphabetic order and this is similar to other acrostics (Psalms 33 and 46, as well as Lamentations 1, 2, 3 and 4).

Like Psalm 6, Psalm 38 starts with a reference to the wrath of God, a force that was greatly feared by the ancient Israelites and held to be responsible for many of their woes. The phrase 'your arrows have sunk into me' (2) may be a reference to the Canaanite god Rephesh, who was an archer and also the god of pestilence.

Verses 3–6 provide the moral explanation for sickness, as the result of sin. The chain of causation starts with an individual's sinful behaviour, which leads on to God's anger, which leads him to mete out punishment in the form of sickness. Verse 3 states 'There is no soundness in my flesh because of your indignation', where the subject's illness is directly attributed to God's anger, and a similar thought is repeated in the parallelism 'there is no health in my bones because of my sin'. Until recent times, the commonly held view was that sin and the anger of God were the most likely causes for both mental and physical illness. Scientific advances have replaced these primitive explanations for physical illness, although such ideas still persist in some quarters. The poet writes that his unsound flesh is the result of God's indignation, the weakness in his bones are due to his sin. His wounds and abscesses are the result of his folly and as a consequence he is doomed to be in a permanent state of mourning. No exposition of this ancient theory of illness causation could be more succinct.

The association between physical and mental suffering is again explicit in verses 5–8. Infected wounds and burning flesh are described in conjunction with mourning, feeling crushed and having a tumultuous heart, and all are regarded as part of the same sickness. Today, physical and mental disorders have largely been separated, each receiving a diagnosis; the physical illness in this psalm appears to be an infective condition, while the mental disorder is suggestive of depression.

Within this catalogue of troubles, verse 4 has an allusion to depressive guilt, 'my iniquities ... weigh like a burden too heavy for me', and guilt is mentioned in one form or another on five occasions. A picture of mental torment describing either severe anxiety or a state of agitation appears in verse 8: 'I groan because of the tumult of my heart'. The Hebrew word for heart (*leb*) signifies mind.

Verse 10 describes a throbbing heart and weakness. Is this the tachycardia and weakness of a physical disorder such as an infection or does it represent the tachycardia of an anxiety state? In verse 11, 'My friends and companions stand aloof' describes feelings of isolation which are common in depressed subjects. Verse 12 becomes more distinctly paranoid, with others, who are unnamed, laying snares and seeking the author's life. In the presence of a serious and potentially fatal illness transient paranoid thoughts of this type may occur, but the more pervasive paranoid delusions, described here, that people 'meditate treachery all day long' (12), is more consistent with the paranoia of either a delusional disorder or a paranoid depression.

Verse 13 describes some of the more severe cognitive symptoms of depression, 'I am like the deaf, I do not hear' suggesting sensory inattention and poor concentration. This thought is repeated in a parallelism in verse 14: 'Truly, I am like one who does not hear'. Depressives have a severe deficit in attention and this presents as complaints of poor concentration. In depressive illness, both attention and memory are selectively impaired and this topic is reviewed by Robbins *et al.* (1993).

During a depression negative and depressing events are recalled with ease, whereas positive and happy occasions can be recalled only with great difficulty. Gotlib (1981) found that depressed subjects inaccurately recall receiving more punishment and less positive reinforcement. They also recall more negatively self-rated words (Bradley and Mathews, 1983), while in depressed subjects there is a mood-dependent selective impairment for the memory of positive events (see also Robbins, p. 293). These observations may explain why certain psalms, particularly 38 and 88, have little or no positive or even neutral material – they were probably composed while the author was in a clinically depressed state, or at the very least trying to recall their depressed state. It is noteworthy that neither of these psalms has a happy ending or a switch into prayer, or into the praising God, which is the ending for most psalms.

The second line of verse 13, 'like the mute, who cannot speak', refers to another important but uncommon symptom of severe depression – mutism – and this is echoed in the parallelism of verse 14: 'and in whose mouth there is no retort'. Further references to depressive mutism are given in Psalm 39[9], 'I am silent; I do not open my mouth, for it is you who have done it', and Psalm 77[4], 'You keep my eyelids from closing. I am so troubled I cannot speak'. Mutism occurs in depression as a consequence of a slowing of the thought processes, known as psychomotor retardation. In its extreme form psychomotor retardation results in a condition where the patient cannot move and is mute, a state is known as stupor. Today, mutism and depressive stupor are uncommon because treatment with antidepressants and electro-convulsive therapy (ECT) can rapidly reverse these symptoms.

Verses 16–20 continue to describe more paranoid thoughts: others rejoice at his misfortunes, the author has foes without cause, people hate him wrongfully. Verse 17 describes the continuous quality of the pain: 'my pain is ever with me'; it suggests the reason for this is that he is a good person, giving the verse a sense of victimhood. Paranoia at this level may be just within the normal range or alternatively the passage may refer to some real enemies with whom the author is in dispute. The psalm ends with a plea to God to come to his aid quickly, suggesting a degree of desperation.

In summary, Psalm 38 is a catalogue of both mental and physical symptoms but the physical disorder is too non-specific to make any diagnosis. There is mention of festering wounds (?abscesses), serious weakness, throbbing heart and burning loins (?fever). H. J. Kraus tentatively suggests the sufferer may have had leprosy on the grounds that he has 'no soundness in my flesh' and 'my wounds grow foul and fester' and 'there is no health in my bones', but not all scholars agree with this. The mental symptoms provide evidence of despair and depression (verses 1, 6 and 8); guilt (4); weakness (6); anxiety (8); poor concentration and cognitive symptoms (13, 14); psychomotor retardation (13, 14); and paranoid ideation and possibly paranoid delusions (12). There are probably a sufficient number of symptoms to qualify for a diagnosis of major depression.

## Psalm 31

Psalm 31 has the standard structure of an individual lament: it commences with a prayer and a pledge of trust in God; there is then the lament itself (verses 9–13); and it ends with a prayer. Verses with possible psychiatric significance are in the lament and only this section is given below. The psalm is said to be rich in formulaic language, which means that many of the verses are repetitions of verses in other psalms or in other books of the Bible, particularly Jeremiah and Lamentations. There are almost no cultic references in this psalm so its place in the life of the ancient cult or worship is unclear.

| | |
|---|---|
| 9  Be gracious to me, O Lord, for I am in distress; | distress |
| my eye wastes away from grief, | weeping ?depressive facies |
| my soul and body also. | ?psychic and physical illness |
| 10  For my life is spent with sorrow, | depression |
| and my years with sighing; | ?depression |
| my strength fails me because of my misery, | weakness/anergy due to depression |
| All my bones waste away. | weight loss ? physical illness |
| 11  I am the scorn of my adversaries, | real despise, or ideas of reference |
| a horror to my neighbours, | ?ideas of reference |
| an object of dread to my acquaintances; | ?ideas of reference |
| those who see me in the street flee from me. | ?ideas of reference |
| 12  I am passed out of mind like one who is dead; | ?dazed; can't think ?nihilistic thoughts; ?anhedonia |
| I have become like a broken vessel. | low self-image |
| 13  For I hear the whispering of many – | ?auditory hallucinations |
| terror all around! – | ?anxiety ?panic |
| as they scheme together against me, | ?paranoia |
| as they plot to take my life. | ?conspiracy beliefs |
| 14  But I trust in you, O Lord; | abrupt switch out of lament |
| I say 'You are my God'. | |
| My times are in your hand'... | |

## *Psychiatric aspects*

Depression itself is probably mentioned in 'my life spent with sorrow' (10), while 'grief' and 'distress' appear in verse 9. The 'eyes waste away' may be due to physical disorder, but the psalmist attributes his sunken eyes to grief, suggesting the appearance of a depressive facies. Similarly, weakness is described: 'My strength fails me' (12). This might be a physical symptom but the psalmist attributes his failing strength to his misery, suggesting this is a reference to his depressive low energy. 'All my bones wasting away' is suggestive of a severe physical illness, although weight loss of up to one stone can occur in depression.

Verses 11–13 describe ideas of reference (see appendix to chapter on Job, page 71). While it is possible that the author's neighbours and acquaintances had genuinely rejected him, it is more likely that feelings such as being ' a horror to my neighbours' or 'an object of dread to my acquaintances' arose from his paranoia and ideas of reference. Low self-worth is reflected in the thoughts that others 'flee from me' (11) or that he is 'passed out of mind' (12) or that he has 'become like a broken vessel'. The feeling of being 'like one who is dead' (12) is also a frequent complaint of patients suffering from severe depression. In some cases this is an allusion to the symptom of anhedonia, where the subject describes feeling half dead and is unable to derive any pleasure and these patients complain 'they might as well be dead' (see page 67 for full explanation of anhedonia). In a minority of cases of severe psychotic depression there is a genuine belief that they are dead or that a part of their body does not exist – the so-called Cotard syndrome or nihilistic delusions.

The psalmist continues to describe other possible psychotic phenomena. For instance, 'For I hear the whispering of many' suggests the presence of auditory hallucinations. A psychiatrist assessing a new patient who complains of auditory hallucinations will always enquire as to: firstly, whether there is one voice (phenome) or several voices; secondly, what emotions are associated with the voice; and thirdly, the content of the hallucinations. All three questions are answered in verse 13. There is not one voice but 'the whispering of many'; the associated mood is described as 'terror all around' or one of fear or panic, while the content is clearly persecutory, in 'they scheme together against me' and 'they plot to take my life', which tends to suggest these are paranoid auditory hallucinations.

The combination of depression, depressive thoughts with low self-image, anergy, depressive facies, ideas of reference and auditory hallucinations with a persecutory content would signify the presence of an episode of psychotic depression. The psalm becomes much more positive in verse 21 (not quoted here) where thanks are given to God, suggesting a recovery, and a spontaneous recovery from depression is a common and happy event.

## Psalm 6

This psalm describes panic and anxiety in the sufferer. It is included as one of the sickness psalms, although the actual sickness is not specified. Sometimes it is the subject's 'iniquity' or 'sin' which explains the suffering but in Psalm 6 blame is attributed to the subject's enemies. Today, patients in the clinic will usually either attribute their depression to their own inadequacies or blame some external circumstance or someone else.

The lament section, which contains the possible depression, is in the middle portion of the psalm and, as with other psalms of lament, this is followed by a prayer seeking relief from the suffering. Theologians such as Craigie, while acknowledging that Psalm 6 concerns physical and mental suffering, suggest the suffering is mainly spiritual, concerning the psalmist's relationship with God, and so place a primarily religious rather than a medical meaning on this psalm.

*Psalm 6. For the Leader with stringed instruments according to the Sheminith. A Psalm of David.*

1   O Lord, do not rebuke me in your anger,          fear of punishment
    or discipline me in your wrath.                  ?guilt
2   Be gracious to me, O Lord, for I am              low energy
    languishing;
    O Lord, heal me, for my bones are
    shaking with terror.                             Shaking + terror = ?panic attacks
3   My soul is also struck with terror,              ?panic attacks
    While you O Lord – How long?                     ?distorted perception of time
4   Turn O Lord, save my life;
    deliver me for the sake of your steadfast love.
5   For in death there is no remembrance
    of you;                                          ?anhedonia
    in Sheol who can give you praise?                no praising God
6   I am weary with my moaning;                      constant moaning; weary
    every night I flood my bed with tears;           crying at night, depressive
    I drench my couch with weeping.                  sleep disorder
7   My eyes waste away because of grief;             complaint of tired eyes
    they grow weak because of all my foes.           or a depressed facies
8   Depart from me, all you workers of evil,
    for the Lord has heard the sound of
    my weeping.
9   The Lord has heard my supplication;              ?mood switch
    the Lord accepts my prayer.
10  All my enemies shall be ashamed and
    struck with terror;                              ?panics as punishment
    They shall turn back and in a moment
    and be put to shame.

## Psychiatric aspects

The writer of Psalm 6 is in great torment. He cannot explain his suffering except by assuming that God must be angry with him – 'do not rebuke me in your anger'. Some depressed patients today also think that God must be angry with them. In verse 2 the phrase 'I am languishing' suggests a feeling of mental exhaustion and perhaps this is the low energy of depression. Verse 2b, 'my bones are shaking with terror', suggests the tremor of anxiety or panic, and is one of the autonomic symptoms of panic disorder. Verse 3 adds to the notion of panic by describing psychic anxiety: 'My soul also is struck with terror'. Although the word 'soul' in English has a religious connotation, the Hebrew word *nefesh* refers to mind or life force and so a more accurate translation would be 'my mind is struck with terror'. The use of the word 'struck' implies an abrupt onset of the episode of fear and such abruptness is central to panic attacks (see also page 98). Verse 4 starts with the phrase 'Turn, O Lord' and biblical scholars interpret this as referring to the psalmist having feelings of abandonment by God. Fears of abandonment are also prominent in a wide variety of psychiatric disorders, particularly in depressed borderline subjects (see Masterson for review). However, here the fear is one of being abandoned by God, suggesting feelings of a more spiritual abandonment.

Sheol (verse 5) is the place people went after death. It was neither heaven nor hell but a station on the journey where the dead were thought to exist in a shadowy half-life. In this state they were unable to experience the joy of any relationship with God, through either prayer or praise. This half-living half-dead state may correspond to the picture of a subject in a state of severe depression, and is also discussed above in relation Psalm 88, which also describes a person who is unable to obtain any sort of pleasure and so may be suffering from the symptoms of anhedonia.

The phrase 'I am weary with my moaning' (verse 6) may describe the frustration that many depressives feel at their own tendency to complain about their symptoms repeatedly, yet most find they are quite unable to stop this self-centred whingeing, and so perhaps the psalmist had some insight into this behaviour, which is due to his depression.

Verse 6 describes classical nocturnal depressive symptomatology. 'Every night I flood my bed with tears.' Crying oneself to sleep, or crying during the night, implies depressive insomnia and crying on waking are features of severe depression. Women suffering from depression cry more than men, but when a man complains of tearfulness the depression is generally quite severe. The psalmist was almost certainly a man, but it is possible in ancient Israel that the taboos against crying in men were not as strong as they are today.

Verse 7, 'My eyes waste away because of grief', describes a link between sunken eyes and low mood (grief). The phrase also occurs in Psalm 31[9] as described on page 160. Such an appearance of sunken eyes which waste away may be a reference to the characteristic appearance of the severely depressed patient – the so-called 'depressed facies'. Another possibility is that the psalmist is describing the sunken eyes found in severe physical illness due to dehydration.

In verse 9, the mood of the psalm suddenly changes, because the psalmist says the Lord has heard his prayer. In verse 10 there is an abrupt switch in mood from severe depression into normality or a feeling of triumph (?elation). This sudden improvement in the mood and change in tone form part of the religious experience of the psalm. The message is that help is at hand and things will get better. Line 10b, 'All my enemies shall be ashamed and struck with terror', reflects his feeling that others (his enemies) should know just how badly he feels, as a punishment for them. The latter is also a commonly expressed sentiment of some depressives: 'If only you knew know how badly I feel'. Even depressives of a more generous disposition sometimes express a similar sentiment: 'It was so awful I would not wish the depression onto my worst enemy'. However, the author of Psalm 6 does wish to punish his worst enemy with depressive pain and terror.

## Religious and cultic aspects

Psalm 6 is an individual lament and is one of the sickness psalms. The early church used this as one of the penitential psalms (the others being 32, 38, 51, 102, 130 and 143) which are traditionally sung on Ash Wednesday. Kraus suggests that it was used for prayer in the Jerusalem Temple and so a pre-exilic composition is possible. He also suggests that the psalm found use as a general prayer for any serious illness because it has no mention of a specific illness. The word *Sheminith* used in the introduction is a musical term meaning octave.

The Midrash also highlights the painfulness of the passage of time during an illness by using a parable but suggests this refers to national rather than individual suffering. 'What is meant by the words "How long"?' (v. 3). Rabbi Kahana tells the parable of a sick man who was in need of a physician. The sick man kept asking 'When will the physician come? At the fourth hour, the six, or the seventh?' But the physician did not come. The eighth, ninth and tenth hours passed – still none came and only as the sun was setting was a physician seen approaching. The sick man said, 'If thou hadst delayed thy coming by another instant my soul would have left me'. So too David cried out when he saw the cruelty of the Kingdom continuing in the affliction of the people of Israel. He exclaimed: 'And thou, O Lord, how long?'

Psalm 6 starts with an appeal to God because the petitioner knows that he stands under the wrath of God. According to Kraus, in the Old Testament nothing can be more terrifying than to face the wrath of God. Mountains may collapse (Jer. 10[10]), humans can fade away (Ps. 90[7]; Job 17[1]) and if sickness is to be healed God's anger must be averted. Throughout the Old Testament and much of the ancient Near Eastern literature, there is a strong association between guilt and sickness, with the sickness being a punishment from God for sin. However, in Psalm 6, although there is sickness, there is no admission to any sin or guilt – which is similar to the position adopted by Job. It is thought that the enemy referred to in this psalm is death because of the reference to Sheol. The switch in mood which occurs in verses 8/9 indicates the Lord has heard the psalmist's plea (*Shema adonai*) and suggests the presence of an oracle who serves as an intermediary between the supplicant and God.

## Psalm 13

Psalm 13 has only six verses. It describes the painfulness of the experience of the slowed passage of time, which sometimes occurs in depression combined with the seemingly never-ending feelings of suffering.

[1]  How long, O Lord?
    Will you forget me for ever?                    distress, and feelings of rejection
    How long will you hide your face from me?       shame
[2]  How long must I bear pain in my soul,          the suffering seems
    and have sorrow in my heart all day long?       never ending
    How long shall my enemy be exalted over me?
[3]  Consider and answer me, O Lord my God!

| | |
|---|---|
| Give light to my eyes, or I will sleep the sleep of death, | ?severe physical illness or ?morbid thoughts of death |
| 4 and my enemy will say, 'I have prevailed'; my foes will rejoice because I am shaken. | |
| 5 But I trusted in your steadfast love; my heart shall rejoice in your salvation. | faith: with mood switch for the better |
| 6 I will sing to the Lord, because he has dealt bountifully with me. | prayer: joy and thanks |

## Psychiatric aspects

This short psalm describes physical and mental suffering of an unspecified type. The most striking feature of the psalm is the fourfold repetition of the phrase 'How long...'. In the first verse this refers to feelings of abandonment by God and therefore has a spiritual connotation, but in verse 2 the question is 'How long must I bear pain in my soul, and have sorrow in my heart all day long?' and this seems to be specifically suffering of a depressive type. It is a reference to the painfulness of the subject's sorrowful state and how its duration seems never ending. Time hangs heavily for the those with depression. In recent years the precise way affective disorder distorts the perception of time has been recognised. Thus time passes more slowly (and painfully) in depression, while in mania the experience of time is the opposite; it seems to pass very quickly. A good literary example of how time seems to pass slowly and painfully during depression can be found in the writings of Sylvia Plath (1963), who describes her own depressive breakdown in the *The Bell Jar*:

> My mother told me I must have slept, it was impossible not to sleep in all that time, but if I slept it was with my eyes wide open, for I had followed the green luminous course of the second hand and the minute hand and the hour hand of the bedside clock through their circles and semi-circles every night for seven nights without missing a second or a minute or an hour....

The Hebrew word for soul (*nefesh*) refers to emotions, while the word heart (*leb*) refers to mind, and this indicates the suffering is both mental and emotional. In the modern era such severe mental suffering would lie in the realm of psychiatry. The 'sleep of death' may have several different meanings. It might refer to death itself, because death is sometimes portrayed as sleep (Job 14[12]), or it may refer to some serious physical illness. The sleep of death might also refer to the depressive's wish to sleep forever, which is one presentation of suicidal thoughts; or it may allude to the unpleasant quality of sleep in depression. Some depressed subjects dread going to bed because of the nocturnal turmoil associated with depression. The lament of this psalm is expressed only in the first three verses whereas the final two verses describe a happy response to the psalmist's prayer and include a brief hymn of praise (verse 6).

## Religious and cultic aspects

The phrase 'how long will you hide your face from me' (verse 1) conveys the notion of a deliberate abandonment by God as well as a sense of displeasure.

As previously noted, to incur God's displeasure was the worst possible fate for a person in the ancient world, and would usually be accompanied with a plea to return to close fellowship with God. Kraus explains the line in verse 2 'How long must I bear pain in my soul?' as an expression of the suffering caused by separation from God and the experience of the wrath of God. He places a primary spiritual meaning on the suffering. H. Gunkel considers Psalm 13 to be one of the individual laments, but he also believes the suffering to be more spiritual than medical. Kraus comments also on the fourfold repetition of the lament 'How long...' and offers an explanation in terms the metre of the poem. He cites a section from 'The Lament of Nebuchadnazzar I', a Babylonian psalm, which also conveys the notion of the painfulness of suffering the passage of time:

> Yet how long with me
> Yet how long in my land
> Yet how long in my people
> Until when, Lord of Babylon
> The groaning and depression
> This weeping and grieving
> This lamenting and weeping
> Do you tarry in the camp of the enemy.

This Babylonian royal lament shows remarkable similarities to Psalm 13, indicating this genre of writing was perhaps quite widespread in the ancient Near East. It probably also refers to painfulness of the experience of the passage of time, although the mention of the camp of the enemy suggests composition during some military campaign.

The Midrash (a body of Jewish interpretation) interprets the pining expressed in this psalm in terms of the Israel's relationship with God. In typical Talmudic style of question and response, it asks why God is hiding from Israel. Rabbi Hanina answers the question asked in 13[1], 'How long O Lord, will you forget me for ever? How long will you hide your face from me?' by replying to God with another question: 'Master of the universe in generations past you fought our battles for us.... Also for future generations you will fight for us.... But for us, the generation in between, you do not go forth'. God replies to this challenge with yet another question: 'Is it I who have forgotten you? Is it not you who have forgotten me as it is written "they forgot God their saviour"' (Ps. 106[21]).

Sclater observes that the phrase 'How long?' appears more than 50 times in the Bible (OT and NT) and around 16 times in the Psalms alone. For the most part it refers to a request to be released from intolerable suffering. Prayers seeking relief from suffering have been central to all religions throughout the ages. In some instances the circumstances of the suffering have a basis in reality rather than being due to depression, but in many instances the low mood and psychic pain are quite explicit, as in this psalm.

## Psalm 22

Psalm 22 is not primarily a depressive psalm, and the latter part comprises a hymn of praise. However, this psalm contains a few verses which describe quite severe depressive symptoms and for reasons of space only these are quoted below.

*Psalm 22. To the Leader: according to the deer of the dawn. A Psalm of David*

| | | |
|---|---|---|
| 1 | My God, my God, why have you forsaken me? | plea for help |
| | Why are you so far from helping me, | |
| | from the words of my groaning? | general complaint of |
| 2 | O my God, I cry by day, but you do | daytime distress ?weeping |
| | not answer; | |
| | and by night, but find no rest. | and ?depressive insomnia |

...

| | | |
|---|---|---|
| 6 | But I am a worm, and not human; | low self-esteem |
| | scorned by others, and despised by the people. | feelings of self-hatred |
| 7 | All who see me mock at me; | |
| | they make mouths at me, | |
| | they shake their heads | ideas of reference |

...

| | | |
|---|---|---|
| 10 | On you I was cast from my birth, | ?feelings of rejection |
| | and since my mother bore me you have | |
| | been my God, | |
| | | but I am close to you |
| 11 | Do not be far from me, for trouble is near | |
| | and there is no one to help. | ?separation anxiety |
| 12 | Many bulls encircle me, strong bulls of Bashan | |
| | surround me; | |
| 13 | they open wide their mouths at me, | feelings of being attacked |
| | like a ravening and roaring lion | either real or imagined |
| 14 | I am poured out like water, and all my bones | ?nihilistic delusions |
| | are out of joint; | ?somatic symptoms |
| | my heart is like wax; | ?metaphor of weakness |
| | it is melted within my breast; | |
| 15 | my mouth is dried up like a potsherd, | dry mouth of anxiety, or |
| | and my tongue sticks to my jaws; | dry mouth of dehydration |
| | you lay me in the dust of death. | |
| 16 | For dogs are all around me; | |
| | a company of evildoers encircles me. | paranoia or ?real enemies |
| 17 | My hands and feet have shrivelled; | severe weight loss |
| | I can count all my bones. | ?cachexia ?suggesting cancer |
| | They stare and gloat over me; | |
| 18 | They divide my clothes among themselves, | |
| | and for my clothing they cast lots. | |
| 19 | But you, O Lord, do not be far away! | invocation and prayer for help |
| | O my help, come quickly to my aid! | |

The psalm continues for a further 12 verses as a hymn of praise.

## Psychiatric aspects

Psalm 22 has many non-specific symptoms but it uses powerful metaphors to describe both physical and mental suffering. Verse 2 starts with a suggestion that the distress pervades the whole 24-hour period: 'I cry by day, but you do not answer; and by night, but find no rest'. There is weeping by day and unrestful sleep by night – perhaps this is depressive insomnia.

Verse 7 implies that the psalmist believes other people are talking about him; perhaps true, but perhaps these are ideas of reference: 'All who see me mock me. They make mouths at me. They shake their heads.'

Separation anxiety is hinted at in verse 11, 'Do not be far from me, for there is no one to help', but this may also be a formulaic poetic metaphor expressing a spiritual need to stay close to God rather the separation anxiety of an anxiety disorder.

Verses 12 and 13 continue in a paranoid vein, describing feelings of being attacked 'Many bulls encircle me, strong bulls of Bashan surround me; they open wide their mouths at me like a ravening and roaring lion'. These feelings are thought to refer to real threats from important people in the town or they may reflect a subjective sense of paranoia. The strong bulls of Bashan refer to cattle from a particular area in East Transjordan where the pastures were known to be especially fertile and as a result cows from these pastures were very fat and the bulls were big and strong.

Verse 14 describes somatic depressive symptoms but the phrase 'I am poured out like water, and all my bones are out of joint' is also suggestive of somatic nihilistic delusions. Such sentiments are continued in the parallelism 'my heart is like wax, it is melted within my breast'. In a complete nihilistic delusion, the denial of existence is total: patients do not believe they have a heart or a brain, or intestines. Although it might be possible for an imaginative poet to invent such powerful metaphors, it is more likely that these images were drawn from the writer's own personal experience of depression, with delusions that parts of his body are disintegrating or have melted away.

Somatic symptoms appear again with the complaint of a dry mouth: 'for my mouth is dried up like a potsherd and my tongue sticks to my jaws' (15). Is this the dry mouth of anxiety or the dry mouth of a physical disorder such as fever or dehydration?

Verse 17 also describes possible cachexia: 'My hands and feet have shrivelled, I can count my bones'. Weight loss resulting in the visibility of the bones is too severe for simple depression, but is consistent with the weight loss of severe physical illnesses such as cancer. The remainder of the psalm (not quoted here) has a much happier tone, as a hymn of praise. Craigie (1983) points out that the sickness psalms were never intended to serve as diagnostic formularies, and their general metaphors of suffering cover a multitude of maladies so that they can be used in prayer by anyone who is ill, and then the worshipper can give thanks to God for relief.

## Religious and cultic aspects

Psalm 22 has two separate types of material. The first part is the lament (verses 1–22) and this is followed by prayer and thanksgiving (verses 23–32). Some of the thanksgiving verses are repeated in the New Testament (Matt. 27[46]; Mark 15[84]) and some Christian scholars have suggested because of the suffering and subsequent deliverance the psalm predicts the crucifixion. Possibly this is why the psalm is sometimes read on Good Friday services. Others, such as Martin-Achard (1963), have suggested that originally there may have been two psalms which were later fused into one.

The psalm starts with an invocation to God and the psalmist asks why he has been forsaken. Kraus (1988) writes a state of 'God forsaken-ness' represents the ultimate archetypal affliction, which here takes the form of a mortal illness. The lament section, quoted above, describes a state of profound human misery, possibly depression, with suggestions also of some physical illness as well and the subject's life seems to be in danger. Some have classed Psalm 22 as an individual lament, but it is also included as a psalm of communal lament because the congregation joins in at the end. Kraus suggests that originally the prayer was part of a cultic ritual for kings who had fallen ill rather than it referring to an ordinary citizen. The person who is abandoned and suffers in this psalm is the king and it is the king who is revived at the end of the psalm. The whole community then thanks God at the end for saving their king, even though no particular king is identified. The Akkadian psalms of lament offer some support for this because in these rather more ancient psalms the person who suffered was almost always identified as the king. In the ancient world, scribes were too few and far between for their talents to be squandered on the ordinary man in the street, and so their talents were preserved for royalty.

The phrase 'But I am a worm, and not human' (6) is an excellent metaphor for low self-image, but has been given a more political and historical meaning by later Jewish commentators. Thus Cohen, following on from Kimchi and the Talmud, states this refers to the humiliation of the Israelite people and cites a similar metaphor in Isaiah: 'Do not fear, you worm Jacob, you insect Israel' (Is. 41[14]). The Midrash offers another explanation: 'like a worm whose only resource is its mouth, so the children of Israel [then in exile in Babylon] have no resource other than the prayers of their mouths'. Like a worm which roots out a tree with its mouth, so the children of Israel with the prayers of their mouths root out the evil decrees which hostile nations of the earth devise against them (Braude, 1959).

As the psalm progresses, the sufferer comes closer to death's door: 'They stare and gloat over me, they divide my clothes among themselves and for my clothing they caste lots' (18). This refers to the somewhat unsavoury practice in the ancient world of giving away the clothes of a condemned prisoner or the dying man even before he is dead, with the distribution of his possessions usually being decided by the casting of lots. Kraus cites an ancient Mesopotamian poem in support of this:

> The coffin lay open and people already helped themselves to my valuables:
> Before I was even dead, the mourning was already done.
> (Ungned, 1921, p. 130)

## Psalm 69

Psalm 69 is a lengthy lament having a total of 36 verses and so for reasons of space the last 6 verses which do not contain any psychiatric references have been omitted. For the most part the rest of the psalm has some suggestion of depression or paranoia, and of interest particular interest is the inclusion of the rare psychotic symptom of gustatory hallucinations.

*Psalm 69. To the leader: according to Lilies. Of David.*

¹  Save me, O God,
   for the waters have come up to my neck.

²  I sink in deep mire,                              a sinking feeling
   where there is no foothold;
   I have come into deep waters,
   and the floods sweep over me.                     a feeling of being overwhelmed

³  I am weary with my crying;                        weeping, lack of energy
   my throat is parched.                             dry mouth ?of anxiety
   My eyes grow dim                                  ?depressed facies
   with waiting for my God.

⁴  More in number than the hairs of my head         many people hate me
   are those who hate me without cause;              ?true or ?paranoia
   many are those who would destroy me,              ?real enemies or ?paranoia
   my enemies who accuse me falsely.                 ?real court case or ?paranoia
   What I did not steal                              ?plea of innocence to a charge
   must I now restore?                               of stealing

⁵  O God, you know my folly;
   the wrongs I have done are not hidden
   from you.                                         ?guilt

⁶  Do not let those who hope in you
   be put to shame because of me,
   O Lord God of hosts;
   do not let those who seek you be dishonoured
   because of me. O God of Israel.

⁷  It is for your sake that I have borne reproach,
   that shame has covered my face.                   feelings of shame

⁸  I have become a stranger to my kindred,          feelings of alienation
   an alien to my mother's children.                 within the family

⁹  It is zeal for your house that has consumed me;
   the insults of those who insult you have
   fallen on me.                                     ?paranoia

¹⁰ When I humbled my soul with fasting,             ?anorexia ?ritual fasting
   they insulted me for doing so.

¹¹ When I made sackcloth my clothing,               ?mourning ?depression
   I became a byword to them.

¹² I am the subject of gossip                       ?paranoia ?ideas of reference
   for those who sit in the gate,
   the drunkards make songs about me.

[13–16 omitted]

¹⁷ Do not hide your face from your servant
   for I am in distress – make haste to answer me.   distress, cry for help

¹⁸ Draw near to me, redeem me,
   set me free because of my enemies.

¹⁹ You know the insults I receive,
   and my shame and dishonour;
   my foes are all known to you.

²⁰ Insults have broken my heart,
   so that I am in despair.                          depression
   I looked for pity, but there was none;

| | |
|---|---|
| and for comforters,<br>but I found none. | failure of comforters |
| 21  They gave me poison for food,<br>and for my thirst they gave me vinegar<br>to drink. | ?paranoid delusions of<br>poisoning<br>altered sense of taste |
| 22  Let their table be a trap for them,<br>a snare for their allies. | |
| 23  Let their eyes be darkened so that they<br>cannot see,<br>and make their loins tremble continually. | vengeful feelings<br>?tremor. |
| 24  Pour out your indignation upon them,<br>and let your burning anger overtake them. | ?psalmists bad feelings<br>projected onto an enemy |
| 25  May their camp be a desolation;<br>let no one live in their tents. | |
| 26  For they persecute those whom you have<br>struck down,<br>and those whom you have wounded,<br>they attack still more. | |
| 27  Add guilt to their guilt;<br>may they have no acquittal from you. | guilt feelings |
| 28  Let them be blotted out of the book of<br>the living;<br>let them not be enrolled among the righteous. | |
| 29  But I am lowly and in pain;<br>let your salvation, O God, protect me.... | depression/despair |

[30–36 omitted]

## Psychiatric aspects

This psalm contains some references to depressed mood and paranoia. However, there is also a clear description of a very rare symptom, an altered sense of taste, which occurs almost exclusively in psychotic depression. It would be impossible to just imagine or write about such a symptom without having either experienced it personally or observed it in someone else, perhaps within the family.

Verses 1 and 2 describe how the psalmist is sinking, 'deep waters and the floods sweep over me', suggesting a sense of drowning. Depressives sometimes complain that they are drowning in their bad moods and problems; William Styron (1991, p. 17), an American author, in his autobiographical account of his own depression in his book *Darkness Visible*, wrote about the sensation of drowning:

> there is a basic inability of healthy people to imagine a form of torment so alien to every day experience. For myself the pain is most closely connected to drowning or suffocation – but even these images are off the mark.

The psalm writer's mental anguish, 'I am weary with my crying' (verse 3), is linked to a suggestion of a depressed facies: 'my eyes grow dim'. There may have been real accusers, because of the stealing charge (verse 4). However, the exaggerated description of the total number of persecutors in this verse, 'more in number than the hairs of my head are those that hate me without cause', indicates that accusers are numerous and ubiquitous and perhaps the whole world is against him, giving a much more pervasive quality to the paranoia, similar to that found in delusional disorder or psychotic depression.

Shame, a normal emotion but often heightened in depression, is described: 'that shame has covered my face' (verse 7). Alienation from the family, 'an alien to my mother's children', perhaps alludes to a distancing from the writer's siblings (verse 8). In depression a genuine rejection by close family may occasionally occur but is unusual; a much more likely explanation is that the depressed person is writing about his subjective feelings of estrangement – that he has been rejected by his close family. Such feelings of estrangement may have their root in the paranoia which pervades this psalm. The psalmist dons sackcloth (verse 11), a ritual usually associated with mourning, although no recent death is mentioned, and so the mourning is not occurring in the context of a bereavement. 'I am the subject of gossip for those who sit in the gate' (verse 12) suggests he believes that other people are talking about him, and thinking of this type is known as ideas of reference, although if he has been charged before the court, this may be true rather than delusional. Such thoughts continue in the parallelism of the second line of verse 12: 'the drunkards make songs about me'. These verses are probably describing ideas of reference rather than delusions of reference as no certainty is placed on these assertions, nor are they bizarre .

A reiteration of the feelings of sinking into the mire and drowning (verses 14 and 15) that opened the psalm, together with distress, 'for I am in distress – make haste to answer me', as well as despair, 'I am in despair' (verse 20), all suggest depression (indeed, these are key depressive features).

From the psychiatric point of view, verses 20 and 21 are the most interesting. [21a] 'They gave me poison for my food' is one of the most common paranoid delusions, namely of being poisoned. While a true episode of poisoning is possible, it is unlikely as the writer lived on to complete his psalm. The next line describes the very rare psychiatric symptom of an altered sense of taste or gustatory hallucinations: [21b] 'and for my thirst they gave me vinegar to drink'. Here the subject has the experience of the taste of vinegar in his mouth. Again, it is possible someone put vinegar in his drink but a far more likely explanation is the experience of an altered sense of taste. Sims (1988), in his textbook on psychiatric phenomenology *Symptoms in the Mind*, writes:

> *Gustatory hallucinations* (of taste) occur in various conditions. In schizophrenia, they sometimes occur with delusions of being poisoned. There may be a persistent taste, for example of onions, metallic, or some other bizarre type of taste. In depression and in schizophrenia, the flavour of food may disappear altogether or become unpleasant. The sensation may also occur in temporal lobe epilepsy and can on occasion be drug induced. (Sims, p. 74)

Fish (1985) also comments on this unusual symptom and states that it is usually associated with delusions of being poisoned, as in this psalm, because sufferers have no other way of explaining their weird sensations. Because the delusions in verse 21 point to a psychotic condition such as psychotic depression or delusional disorder, the latter part of verse 20 can also be explained. <sup>20b</sup>'I looked for pity but there was none; and for comforters, but I found none.' A comforter in biblical times might have been someone who could soothe a troubled mind with his words. However, an illness such as psychotic depression usually fails to respond to psychotherapy and needs to be treated with medication. Job similarly complains that his comforters offer him no solace and he also has psychotic depression. Sufferers may even feel worse after talking about themselves, so it is hardly surprising that the writer of these verses in Psalm 69 could 'find no comforters'.

Verses 22–28 continue in a vengeful tone, where metaphors continue to express the wish that his enemies should also suffer: 'let your burning anger over take them', 'may their camp be a desolation' and 'let them be blotted out of the book of the living'. <sup>27</sup>'Add guilt to their guilt' possibly refers to the punishing quality of the morbid guilt of depression. <sup>23</sup>'... and make their loins tremble' may signify the tremors of anxiety, but as the plural 'loins' is used the shaking may refer to the tremors of some unspecified neurological disease.

Finally, in verse 29 the psalmist admits to his misery: 'But I am lowly and in pain'. In the absence of any mention of physical disease, is this an allusion to the psychic pain of depression? The author William Styron wrote:

> What I had begun to discover is that mysteriously and in ways that are totally remote from normal experience, the gray drizzle of horror induced by depression takes on the quality of physical pain. But it is not an immediately identifiable pain like that of a broken limb. (Styron, *Darkness Visible*, p. 50)

In summary, the first 30 verses of this psalm refer to a large number of depressive and paranoid symptoms. Depressed mood (1, 17, 20, 29); weeping (2); lack of energy (3); morbid guilt (5, 27); low self-esteem (7). These all point to a depression. Paranoid symptoms are also described (4, 9), including paranoid delusions associated with gustatory hallucinations (20,21). There are ideas of reference (12) and a general sense of alienation (8). The most likely psychiatric diagnoses to cover this combination of both depressive and paranoid psychotic symptoms is *psychotic depression*, or depression with paranoid features. It would not be possible to assemble such an array of symptoms which give a picture of psychotic depression without having some personal experience of the disorder, indicating that the writer was probably the sufferer.

## Religious and cultic aspects

The psalm starts with an appeal to God to save the writer from drowning – 'I sink into the deep mire', 'the flood sweeps over me' – and these water/drowning images are repeated in verse 15 – 'do not let the flood sweep over me'. There are suggestions that these are references to Sheol, the place of the dead: <sup>15</sup>'or the deep swallow me up or the pit close its mouth over me'.

The Midrash provides a historical-political rather than a personal meaning to the phrase 'I sink into the deep mire, where there is no standing, I am come into deep waters where the floods overflow me' (69<sup>2</sup>), linking this to the exile. Thus 'deep mire' alludes to the exile in Babylon, the phrase 'where there is no standing' represents the exile in Medea and Persia, and 'floods' to the exile in Edom. The next verse – 'I am weary with my crying, my throat is parched' – together with the remaining verses in this psalm allude to oppression during the exile. The later repetition in verse 15 of the plea 'do not let the flood sweep over me ... or the pit close its mouth over me' is taken as a plea to deliver the psalmist out of this punishment of hell.

In verse 4 the psalmist is accused of stealing so it is possible that he is before the court, and his accusers are the advocates of the court. He protests his innocence and cannot understand why, in the face of his suffering, everyone hates him. Commentators compare these protestations to the story of Job who also protests his innocence.

The psalm describes a person who has sunk into a state of great misery and he is surrounded by enemies supposedly because of his devotion to God. The German scholar Duhm suggests the statement 'It is for your sake that I have borne reproach' (verse 7) is meaningful in the context of the sectarian disputes in the post-exilic Jewish community. Thus, the conflict between the psalmist and his enemies may simply be religious dissent with the psalmist representing official orthodoxy and the 'enemies' some dissenting group.

The structure of the psalm is similar to that of Psalm 22, and both are sometimes used in Good Friday services. Tate (1990) suggests the psalm can probably be dated to the sixth century BCE. In support of this he cites verse 7, 'It is zeal for your house that has consumed me', because the house is the second Temple and the zeal is the enthusiasm for rebuilding it, and this event has been dated to around 539 BCE. Like Psalm 22, the psalm was originally used for kings before it became more widely used in small-community worship.

Verse 17 mentions the city gate: 'I am the subject of gossip for those who sit in the city gate'. The recesses of the city gates were commonly used as meeting places, because in these recesses there was shade from the fierce Middle Eastern sun. The courts were sometimes placed at the city gates. Hence it is not surprising that this was the favoured site for local gossip.

The reference to the face of God in verse 17, which also appears in Psalms 13[2] and 88[15] and elsewhere in the Old Testament, is of religious significance. The consequence of being hidden from the face of God would have been devastating for an individual in the ancient world as this would imply a divine refusal to recognise someone and hence a failure to respond to the pleas of the supplicant. A vestige of this ancient metaphor of God's face and its beneficence remains in present-day Jewish services for the Sabbath, which end with a prayer drawn from the Book of Numbers (6[25]):

> The Lord make his face to shine upon you and be gracious to you
> The Lord lift up his countenance upon you and give you peace.

## Psalm 30

Psalm 30 has two verses which suggest an abrupt change of mood, characteristic of cyclothymia.

*A Psalm. A song at the dedication of the temple. Of David*

| | |
|---|---|
| 1   I will extol you, O Lord, for you have<br>    drawn me up,<br>    and did not let my foes rejoice over me | |
| 2   O Lord my God, I cried to you for help<br>    and you have healed me. | distress |
| 3   O Lord, you brought up my soul from Sheol,<br>    restored me to life from among<br>    those gone down to the Pit. | rescue from illness<br>?near-death experience<br>?anhedonia |
| 4   Sing praises to the Lord,<br>    O you his faithful ones,<br>    and give thanks to his holy name. | |
| 5   For his anger is but for a moment;<br>    his favour is for a lifetime.<br>    *Weeping may linger for the night,*<br>    *but joy comes with the morning.* | ?abrupt mood switch<br>in the middle of the night |
| 6   As for me, I said in my prosperity,<br>    'I shall never be moved'. | |
| 7   By our favour, O Lord,<br>    you had established me as a strong mountain;<br>    you hid your face; I was dismayed. | more distress |
| 8   To you, O Lord, I cried,<br>    and to the Lord I made supplication; | |
| 9   'What profit is there in my death,<br>    if I go down to the Pit?<br>    Will the dust praise you?<br>    Will it tell of your faithfulness? | ?near fatal illness<br>death approaching ?anhedonia |
| 10   Hear, O Lord, and be gracious to me!<br>    O Lord, be my helper!' | |
| 11   *You have turned my mourning into dancing;*<br>    *you have taken off my sackcloth*<br>    *and clothed me with joy,* | abrupt mood switch again<br><br>mood switch |
| 12   so that my soul may praise you<br>    and not be silent.<br>    O Lord my God, I will give thanks<br>    to you for ever. | |

## Psychiatric aspects

Psalm 30 is a short psalm which appears to repeat itself in two sections. Thus verses 1–4 describe a state of dejection, followed by an abrupt switch into joy. Verses 7–10 again describe a state of dejection followed by a second switch into a state of great happiness. There is a milder condition called *cyclothymia,* where the subject switches from states of mild depression to states of elation with increased energy, which falls far short of the severity found in mania or bipolar disorder. In cyclothymia the subject continues to function while retaining full insight into both their *present and previous mood state* and they are usually aware that their mood has switched. Such abrupt switches of mood (e.g. overnight) can also occur in bipolar disorder but in these cases the switch is from states of severe melancholia to mania, or hypomania, but the subject has no awareness of his mood or that it has changed. Jamison quotes William Blake, a known manic depressive poet, on the closeness of 'joy and woe' in this context:

> Joy and woe are woven fine
> A clothing for the soul divine
> Under every grief and pine
> Runs a joy with silken twine'
> (William Blake cited in Jamison, 1993)

According to DSM-5, *cyclothymia* occurs in around 0.4% of the population, but up to 3–4% of those attending specialised depression clinics may be sufferers. Typically the subject experiences mild to moderate depression for several weeks on end and then abruptly switches to a state of being 'high' (but not fully hypomanic) and full of energy. Subjects are able to recall the switches from low to high states, but this is then followed by a gradual and more imperceptible slide back into depression, and the disorder may be lifelong. These switches in mood occur independently of external events. The mood changes the author of Psalm 30 reports seem to have this quality:

- The switch is preceded by a period of misery/distress which might be considered depressive/dysthymic.
- The subject has full insight into both his high state and his low state, and is able to write eloquently about it and so presumably has retained a good degree of insight and functioning.
- There is no obvious precipitant for the switch.
- The words used in both mood switches are strongly affect-laden. Thus in the first mood switch 'weeping may linger in the night' while 'joy comes in the morning'. In the second mood switch 'mourning' becomes 'dancing', and instead of wearing 'sackcloth' the psalmist dons the 'clothes of joy'.

## Religious and cultic aspects

The Hebrew dedication of this psalm bears the title 'A song at the dedication of the temple', and there is a Talmudic reference (*b.Sop.* 18b) describing the cleaning and dedication of the Temple under Judas Maccabeus after its desecration at the hands of Antiochus Ephiphanes in 167 BCE, and so this psalm came into liturgical use in the festival of Hanukkah. It is classed as one of the psalms of individual praise, which contain an invitation for those around the participant to join in with the singing and also give thanks (Kraus, p. 353). The psalm is important in both the Jewish and Christian traditions but each attaches a different theology and meaning to it. In the Hebrew liturgy it is a part of the Purim story, and the Midrash considers the psalm refers to the story of Mordecai and Esther. According to the Midrash, the phrase 'Weeping may linger for the night' alludes to the fate of Mordecai at the time when Zeresh said to Haman 'Let a gallows be made fifty cubits high for Mordecai and in the morning to be hanged thereon; and all Israel spent the night weeping and wailing' (Est. 5[14]). But 'joy comes in the morning' alludes to the verse 'So they hanged Haman on the gallows that he prepared for Mordecai' (Est. 7[10]).

The second switch in mood, 'You have turned my mourning into dancing' (30¹¹), is given a similar meaning. 'There was great mourning among the Jews and many lay in sackcloth and ashes' (Est. 4²) but finally there came 'a day of gladness and feasting and a good day'.

There are several non-specific references to the suffering of an illness, such as ²'though didst heal me', followed by references to Sheol and being 'restored to life'. The mood switch which occurs in verse 5 has also attracted comment from Christian theologians, who provide a religious rather than a historical explanation. Thus Airoldi (1973) suggests that the references to evening and dawn (or morning) in this context should be interpreted poetically, not literally. Evening and the coming of night symbolise the experience of anger; the breaking of dawn symbolises deliverance or salvation. H. J. Kraus offers a similar explanation and writes:

> The normal work of God' (*opus proprium dei*) determines the meaning of time. Distress and weeping turn out to be events of yesterday. With the new morning comes the time of Yahweh's intervention; jubilation breaks forth as the spirit determines the meaning of life henceforth. A person's relation to time in the OT is determined by his nearness to God.

Who knows what the psalm originally meant, but the sudden improved mood and being 'clothed in joy' transform this into a most happy psalm!

## Psalm 77

This psalm also describes some symptoms of depression. There appears to be a reference to depressive mutism, a severe but comparatively rare symptom, also mentioned by Job and Ezekiel, and discussed on pages 296–298.

| | |
|---|---|
| ¹ I cry aloud to God | |
| aloud to God, that he may hear me | an appeal for help |
| ² In the day of my trouble | Heb. *tzarati'i* = distress |
| I seek the Lord; | |
| In the night my hand | |
| is stretched out without wearying | |
| ³ I think of God and I moan | |
| I meditate and my spirit faints | ? Lack of energy |
| ⁴ You keep my eyelids from closing | cannot sleep ?depressive insomnia |
| I am so troubled I cannot speak | *?mutism* |

## Panic attacks in Psalms 48 and 55

Psalms 48 and 55 are not classed as sickness psalms but they contain verses which are suggestive of a panic attack. Panic is described in greater detail in the chapter on Jeremiah (page 125). Psalm 48 describes the stunned reaction of the kings when they saw Mount Zion and the citadel within it, which may be a reference to the Temple.

⁴ Then the kings assembled,
they came together.

5   As soon as they saw it,
    they were astounded.
    they were in panic,                      panic attack
    they took to flight                      feelings of escape
6   trembling took hold of them there        tremors
    pains as of a woman in labour            severe anxiety
7   As when an east wind shatters            terrifying destructive forces
    the ships of Tarshish

Although it is unlikely that the kings themselves had panic attacks when they saw Mount Zion, they may have expressed wonderment at the new building of the Temple. It seems as if the writer may have drawn on his own personal experiences to explain what he imagined they went through; he uses the word 'panic' and then mentions a key autonomic accompaniment (trembling) as well as the wish to escape, both features of a panic attack.

A second possible example of panic is given in Psalm 55. Again, an attack of fear, a feeling of being out of control, autonomic accompaniments and a wish to escape are described. In this case the psalmist wishes to escape from his enemy:

4   My heart is in anguish within me,          anxiety state
    the terrors of death have fallen upon me.  acute attacks of fear
5   Fear and trembling come upon me,           fear with tremor
    and horror overwhelms me.                  feeling of being out of control
6   And I say 'O that I had wings like a dove! urges to escape
    I would fly away and be at rest;

## Do the 'enemies' in the psalms represent paranoid thinking?

Many of the psalms contain references to a rather non-specific enemy who is only occasionally named. The enemy in the psalms is usually an object of hatred, fear and derision and the psalmist usually wishes for the destruction of the enemy – often applying quite vengeful language. For the deeply religious reader, such hateful thoughts appear to be almost inexplicable. Thus, C. S. Lewis the author of the children's Narnia stories and a devout Christian, wrote: 'It is monstrously simple minded to read the cursings in the psalms with no feeling except one of horror at the uncharity of the poets. They are indeed devilish.' Some of the enemies posed very real threats such as enemy states who fought against Israel, but in other cases the enemy is ill defined and the writing is suggestive of clinical paranoia.

The topic of who exactly the enemies in the psalms were has been the focus of extensive debate in the theological literature. The discussion below draws on reviews by Hobbs and Jackson (1991) and Tate (1990). H. Birkeland (1955) wrote a monograph entitled *The Evil Doers in the Book of the Psalms* and argued that in the royal psalms and in the psalms of lament the enemies were foreign nations aligned against Israel , who would periodically wage war, and oppress or kill the Israelites. Such wars were common in ancient times and fears of invasion and oppression were quite realistic. Birkeland argued that those psalms that were rich in enemy imagery were not written in a historical vacuum but that their authors were probably commissioned to write such material by the royal court with the political aim of rallying the nation. Thus the description of the enemies was stereotyped, often using animal imagery consistent with the cultic beliefs of the time. In Psalm 83, the enemies are listed as Edom, Moab, Amelak, Philistia and Assyria and other more minor neighbouring nations; in Psalm 137 the tormentors are the Babylonians, who have taken Israel into captivity. Duhm (1922) proposed as an alternative that the enemies were sects within the Jewish community in Babylon and the psalm alludes to feuds between different religious sects. In these psalms the author protests that he is being attacked because he is defending God, but in reality he is defending his own particular sect. It is well known that sectarian disputes within one religion (e.g. Catholic versus Protestant, or Reform versus Orthodox Judaism) can sometimes be particularly vituperative. In some cases the accuser may represent the court and its advocates as the supplicant has been accused of some misdemeanour. Below, however, we consider whether the enemies in the psalms represent paranoid thinking.

The term 'paranoia' is derived from the Greek *para* (beside) and *nous* (mind) and it was used in the Greek literature to denote being 'out of mind' or insane. Within the general grouping of 'the enemies' literature in the psalms, there are certain verses that would strike most clinical psychiatrists as expressing similar thought processes to those reported by paranoid subjects.

Delusions of persecution are perhaps the most common presentation of paranoia, and in these the subject believes that someone, or some force or power, or some organisation, is trying to harm him; to damage his reputation; to cause him bodily injury; to drive him mad or bring about his death. Patients with a paranoid psychosis may hear voices or the whispering of plots or other malign influences to cause harm. In a milder form, paranoia may present as ideas of reference, where the subject has a strong feeling that people are taking notice of him on buses, in restaurants or other public places and they observe things about him that he would prefer not to be seen. Delusions of reference represent a more extreme elaboration of these emotions, and the person does not recognise his beliefs as false. Everyone seems to be gossiping about the subject, or he may see references to himself on television or in the newspapers. The subject may hear someone on the radio say something on a completely unrelated topic which he then thinks is about himself; he may sense that he is being followed, his movements are being observed.

Examples of a suspicion of plotting and conspiracy are frequent in the psalms, particularly when 'the enemies' are described, but in a few instances they are described in association with a voice, or whispering, suggesting the possibility of auditory hallucinations. Psalm 31 provides an example:

[13] For I hear whispering threats from roundabout
   while they conspire against me
   They scheme to take my life

Similarly in Psalm 44[16-17], the subject is humiliated and there is a voice who maligns him

[16] All the day my humiliation is before me
And shame has covered my face
[17] From the voice who maligns and reviles
from the enemy and the avenger
(Translated by Craig Broyles, p. 108)

A paranoid feeling of being persecuted and being watched combined with threats to life is described in Psalm 56:

[5] All day long they seek to injure my cause
All their thoughts are against me for evil
[6] They stir up strife, they lurch
they watch my steps
As they hoped to have my life.
[7] So repay them for their crime;
in wrath cast down the peoples, O God
[8] You have kept count of my tossings
put my tears in your bottle
are they not in your record?

The persecution described here may be real, or may be true with a paranoid elaboration, or possibly just purely paranoid. It is impossible to tell. However, the line [8]'put my tears in your bottle' suggests this in the context of a depression.

Fears of conspiracy are also expressed in Psalm 64, but as with Psalm 56 it is quite possible that real persecution is ongoing at the time, and this is no more than a paranoid elaboration. We cannot tell.

64[2] Hide me from the secret plots of the wicked
from the scheming of evildoers...
[5] They hold fast to their evil purpose
they talk of laying snares secretly;
thinking who can see us.

Paranoid feelings of conspiracy combined with people speaking of ruination are described in Psalm 38:

[12] Those who seek my life lay their snares
Those who seek to hurt me speak of ruin
and meditate treachery all day long.

As in Psalm 56, the paranoid thoughts are expressed in the frame of a depression, as most of the rest of Psalm 38 is about depression (see page 157).

Paranoia is a non-specific symptom occurring in a variety of psychiatric disorders ranging from severe mental illness, such as organic states and paranoid schizophrenia, through to depression and delusional disorder. Most of the paranoia of the psalms has its origins in depression rather than schizophrenia, and there is evidence that some of the psalmists may have been sufferers of depression. The multiple different ways paranoia has appeared in the psalms is shown in Table 5.1 in the next section. As with depression, paranoid feelings are ubiquitous and writing about such emotions is therapeutic for the sufferer. Even if C. S. Lewis was 'shocked to find such devilish thoughts' in the psalms, paranoia, like depression, is an integral part of the human condition.

## The totality of affective symptoms in the Book of Psalms

Interpreting particular verses in the psalms as having their origin in mood disorders is only one way of explaining these passages and within the limitations of space I have attempted to provide some of the other explanations for these verses drawn from the enormous volume of Old Testament scholarship on these sacred poems. However, it is only when *all the references to affective symptomatology* are placed together within a single glossary that the full breadth and depth of affective disorder in this ancient poetry can be appreciated and this is shown in Table 5.1, on the following page. The table shows the extensive range of depressive symptoms described in the Book of Psalms. There is mention of 34 different symptoms, some of which appear on multiple occasions. A comparison with the symptoms listed in any modern scale for depression such as the Beck or Hamilton scale, or would show that almost all the subjective feelings of depression are included somewhere in the psalms. The presence of paranoid and psychotic symptoms in a few psalms points to the more severe syndrome of psychotic depression in a few instances. The depressive content of Psalms 88 and 38 is remarkably similar and there are suggestions by Old Testament scholars for single authorship for these psalms (Ridderbos, 1972).

## Concluding remarks

The inclusion of a detailed and extensive glossary of depression in the Book of Psalms has hitherto not been recognised but may provide some explanation for their universal appeal as well as their long-term survival in the liturgy. Why should this be ? Depressive symptoms as described in the psalms by the ancient Israelite poets can be readily recognised by any modern psychiatrist as being more or less identical to the symptoms which depressed patients will describe in the clinic today. Life in the ancient world was probably just as stressful as life today, if not more so, but the depression would have been unrecognised and untreated. In these early religious writings, the emphasis is on suffering and the mental torment the depression brings, while the cause was usually attributed to anger or rejection by God, or the sins of the sufferer. In a pre-medical era such a cultic-religious rationale was probably the only available explanation and it is known that other ancient Near Eastern civilisations also had similar lament prayer material.

The Akkadian psalms of lament, described by Widengreen (1936), may be the most ancient report of depression, and probably extend back to the time of King Sargon of Agade in 2400 BCE. Ancient Akkadian, which is the language of northern Sumeria (present-day northern Iraq), was probably the *lingua franca* of the Near East in the second millennium BCE. These psalms of lament are largely about the Akkadian kings, particularly King Sargon I,

**Table 5.1** Affective symptomatology in the Hebrew Psalms

| | *Psalm no. and verse* |
|---|---|
| *Symptoms of depressive mood and thought* | |
| Depressed mood | $31^{10}$; $42^{11}$ |
| Distress | $88^2$; $13^1$; $22^1$; $69^{17}$; $42^5$; $31^9$ |
| Depression as mourning | $38^6$; $69^{11}$; $42^9$ |
| Depression as pain | $38^7$; $13^2$ ; $69^{29}$ |
| Hopelessness | $8^3$; $38^8$ ; $69^{20}$; $13^2$ |
| Low self-esteem | $22^6$ |
| Guilt | $88^7$; ?$38^1$; $38^4$; $38^{18}$; $6^1$; $69^5$; $69^{27}$ |
| Feelings of rejection | $88^{14}$; $22^7$ |
| Feelings of shame | $13^1$;$30^5$; $30^{11}$ |
| Anhedonia | ?$88^{10}$; ?$6^5$ |
| Depressive distortion of the perception of time | $6^3$; $13^{1-2}$ |
| Alienation/social withdrawal | $88^8$; $88^{18}$; $38^{11}$; $69^8$; $31^{11}$ |
| Depressed facies | $88^9$ $38^{10}$; $6^8$; $69^3$; $31^9$ |
| *Bodily and biological symptoms of depression* | |
| Morning distress ?diurnal mood variation | ?$88^{13}$ |
| Tearfulness | $6^7$; $69^3$; $42^3$ |
| Insomnia (nocturnal distress) | $88^1$; $6^7$; $22^2$; $77^2$; $77^4$; $42^3$ |
| Anergy | $6^2$; $77^3$; $31^{10}$ |
| *Cognitive/psychomotor symptoms* | |
| Mutism | $38^{13}$; $38^{14}$; $77^4$ |
| Sensory inattention/poor concentration | $38^{14}$ |
| *Affective paranoid and psychotic symptoms* | |
| Gustatory hallucinations | $69^{21}$ |
| Delusions of being poisoned | $69^{21}$ |
| Nihilistic delusions | ??$22^{14}$ |
| Ideas of reference | $88^{18}$; $22^7$; $69^{12}$; $31^{11}$ |
| Persecutory beliefs (paranoia) | $38^{12}$; $22^{13}$; $22^{16}$ |
| Conspiracy beliefs | $38^{12}$; $38^{19}$; $69^4$; $31^{13}$; $56^6$ |
| Plots to kill | $31^{13}$ and many places |
| Auditory hallucinations and whispering | $44^{17}$, $31^{13}$ |
| Feelings of being watched | $56^7$ |
| Ideas of reference | $69^{12}$ |
| Feelings of hatred without cause | $69^4$ |
| *Anxiety* | |
| Generalised anxiety | $88^3$; $38^8$; $22^1$; $42^{11}$ |
| Fears of death | $88^4$; $13^3$ |
| Fears of abandonment/?separation anxiety | $88^2$; $38^{21}$ |
| Panic attacks | $88^{15}$; $88^{16}$; $6^2$; $6^3$; $55^{4-6}$; $48^{4-7}$ |
| Tremor | $69^{23}$ |
| Dry mouth | $22^{15}$; $69^3$ |
| *Other symptoms* | |
| Cyclothymic mood switch | $30^5$; $30^{11}$ |
| Non-pathological mood switch | $6^7$; $13^5$ |

but they describe prolonged periods of gloom and doom, weeping, misery and sleeplessness. Similar Babylonian psalms of lament are described by Langdon Thomas (1926). They are written in cuneiform script on tablets found in the desert towns of northern Iraq near the ancient town of Agade. They probably precede the Hebrew psalms by more than 1,000 years, but the description of depression in these psalms is very simplistic. Though depression is recognisable, the Akkadian psalms lack any of the psychiatric sophistication or beauty of the Hebrew psalms.

Those psalms which highlight depression may also have served a thera-peutic role in the ancient cult, further enhancing the power and status of the priesthood. There were no doctors at the time and so the priest assumed the role of the healer. A person suffering from depression is isolated and in psychic pain and if he can share the psalms of individual lament (e.g. 38 and 88) with the priest he will be reassured that an important figure in his community who is 'in touch with God' knows how he feels. His sense of isolation might lessen, he might identify with symptoms described in these depressive psalms, and as these are accompanied by numerous positive and healing statements the act of reciting these psalms together with the priest might confer some therapeutic benefits.

The psalms show an extraordinary variety of affective symptomatology. The depression, when present, is always autobiographical, indicating that it was the writers themselves who were the sufferers. Like other depressed poets, they write with great eloquence about their depression. However, it is important not to exaggerate the quantity of depression in this sacred literature. Only eight psalms seem to report any sort of depression, which is around 5.5% of the total, and of these only one (Psalm 88) leads to a clear-cut diagnosis of major depressive disorder. The others have useful collections of symptoms but are relatively non-specific, so it is difficult to know what the actual sickness is about. On the other hand, when all the depressive psalms are placed together in one chapter, the depth of understanding that the ancient Israelites had about depression becomes apparent. Even obscure symptoms such as gustatory hallucinations, mood switching, panic and depressive sleep disorder get a mention.

Although the format of the psalms of lament are similar, the content and types of their depressions varies. Some emphasise panic, others paranoia and a few express psychotic symptoms such as Psalms 38, 69 and 44. Similarly, Job expresses some psychotic thoughts and he is paranoid about God while Saul hears the voice of Samuel in his depressions and so there is some docu-mentation suggesting psychotic depression existed in ancient Israel – but there is no suggestion that its significance was understood at that time.

Jamison's (1989) observations as described in the Appendix to this chapter provide some understanding of the way depression is distributed in the OT. First, it is striking that almost all the detailed descriptions of depression are found in only a few books of the Bible, particularly in the Book of Psalms, Lamentations, Job and Jeremiah, all of which are in verse, and were therefore the work of poets. As shown in the Appendix, poets appear to have very high rates of bipolar disorder. Within these writings the depression appears to have an intractable quality – there are constant appeals to God to relieve the suffering, but these appeals are not heard, God turns his face away, or is deaf to the psalmists' pleadings. Friends and family turn against the sufferer, and there is frequent reference to the failure of comforters to help; the suffering will go on forever.... Such a resistant quality is characteristic of bipolar depressions and the more severe and psychotic depressions, which have only really proved amenable to treatment in recent times, with the advent of ECT and later with antidepressant drugs in the 20th century. Thus, it is possible that the psalmists of ancient Israel were using their own intractable depressions as source material to draw on and then went on to describe 'the more general types of suffering' such as those of the nation in both the individual and communal laments. Superimposed on this need to write for their own therapy, an individual psalm might have been commissioned by the political or religious authorities of the day to serve some particular purpose in the life of the cult.

Probably many hundreds of psalms were written but only a few were selected for inclusion in the final psalter, a task left to the later biblical redactors in Babylon and Jerusalem, who completed this book by around 300 BCE. By this time the original cultic purpose or *sitz im leben* of the psalm may have become irrelevant because of the changed circumstances and so different criteria would have determined the final selection by the redactors. Some psalms had great beauty, others had prayers or hymns of praise, but to qualify for entry into the psalter a psalm would have had to have had certain universal qualities which were independent of their earlier historical setting. Depression is a universal form of human suffering, quite independent of historical era or national setting, and so perhaps these later redactors, a few of whom may also have been depressives themselves, recognised this, and so perhaps this is why such eloquent descriptions of depression entered into the psalter and have remained there.

## Appendix. Affective disorder in poets

The psalms are poems and this one fact provides a vital clue as to the psychopathology of their authors. Recent studies have demonstrated a very high incidence of depression and bipolar disorder among poets. The authorship of the psalms will never be known and almost certainly there were multiple authors. The psalms of individual lament (6, 13, 31, 38, 69 and 88) represent only six psalms out of 150, and so represent only 4% of the total. It is, therefore, important not to exaggerate the role of psychiatric disorder in the psalms. Ridderbos (1972) was the first to postulate single authorship for the psalms of individual lament and this hypothesis is supported by Broyles (1972). Based on an analysis of psychiatric content alone, Psalms 38 and 88 were both probably composed while their author/authors were in a clinically depressed state and so single authorship for these psalms is possible. Psalms 22 and 69 also resemble each other in terms of describing a similar psychiatric content – a mixture of depression and paranoia – but they have not previously been considered to have been the same author.

The study of the psychopathology of poets commences with Juda (1949), who personally interviewed 5,000 famous people between 1927 and 1943.

Of these, there were 113 artists, which included 37 poets. He found that of all the professions studied, poets had the highest rates of psychopathology, at 48%, in contrast to architects, who had the lowest rate, at 16%. Martindale gave a figure of 45% for English poets and 40% for a sample of French poets. Jamison (1989) conducted a very much more detailed study of authors and poets and showed that almost all the psychiatric disorder found in poets was affective disorder. She examined a group of 30 English poets who lived between 1705 and 1805 and found that 40% suffered from serious bipolar affective disorder, 20% had cyclothymia and 5% committed suicide. Ludwig (1992) also reported that 18% of the poets in his series had committed suicide.

In her study Jamison (1989) examined a sample of 47 contemporary British writers and artists (18 poets; 8 playwrights; 5 biographers; 8 novelists; 8 artists); the psychopathology of the different sub-groups showed important differences. Overall, 38% of the group had been treated for depression, but it was only the poets who needed the more serious physical interventions such as ECT and lithium or hospitalisation to treat their depression. Almost all the poets in her study also described periods of intense creativity, characterised by increases in enthusiasm, energy, self-confidence, speed of mental association, fluency of thought and the strong sense of well-being of cyclothymia or hypomania. Only one of the five biographers described such experiences. These findings suggest that perhaps as many as between a third to a half of poets suffer from bipolar disorder.

If there is a strong association between bipolar disorder and the poets, how does the bipolar disorder influence the quality and type of their poetry? Subjects with affective disorder experience intense emotions and moods and many also have high energy levels – all necessary attributes to be creative and write poetry. A passionate emotional constitution is thought by many to be an integral part of the artistic temperament. The American essayist and poet George Edward Berryman wrote:

> The sign of the poet, then, is that by passion he enters into life more than other men. That is his gift – the power to live.... Poets have been singularly creatures of passion. They lived before they sang. Emotion is the condition of their existence; passion is the element of their being; and moreover the intensifying power of such a state of passion must also be remembered for emotion of itself naturally heightens all the faculties and genius burns the brighter in its own flames. (After Jamison, p. 43)

Much of the poetry of the psalms carries this intense passionate quality which Berryman describes. Depression – or melancholy as it was known until recent times – can serve as an inspiration for creativity provided it is not too severe and paralysing and this has been recognised by numerous poets. Shelley, the great English poet who suffered from manic depression, in his autobiographical poem *Julian and Maddalo*, described how depression drove him to write poetry.

> For the wild language of his grief was high
> Such as in measure were called poetry

> And I remember one remark which then
> Maddalo made. He said wretched men
> Are cradled into poetry by wrong
> They learn in suffering what they teach in song.

Many writers and artists use their art and creativity as a form of therapy. Painting and music are widely accepted in the occupational therapy department of any modern psychiatric unit. The ability to write verse is a much rarer talent and few patients have abilities of this type so the possible therapeutic potential of verse writing is not known. However, some poets have written poems which imply that the act of verse writing itself may have a beneficial effect on melancholy. Thus John Donne thought that his grief could be tamed by 'fettering it in verse':

> I thought, If I could drawe my paines
> Through rimes vexation, I should then allay
> Griefe brought to numbers cannot be so fierce
> For he tames it that fetters it in verse.

Depression may also influence poetry by giving it a starker, more truthful quality. Thus the American poet Robert Lowell, himself a severe depressive, wrote about 'seeing too much and feeling it/with one layer of skin missing' (Jamison, p. 49). Such a stark and truthful quality pervades the psalms – there are no introductions, no small talk; the verses are tightly written with raw and powerful affects almost always reflecting the important themes of life.

# References

Albright, W.F. (1969) *Yahweh and the Gods of Canaan*. Garden City, NY: Doubleday. Anchor Books.

American Psychiatric Association (2013) *Diagnostic and Statistical Manual*, 5th edition (DSM-5). Washington, DC: American Psychiatric Publishing.

Birkeland, H. (1955) *The Evil-doers in the Book of Psalms*. Oslo: J. Dybnad.

Bradley B. and Matthews A. (1983) Negative self schemata in clinical depression. *Journal of Abnormal Psychology* 22: 173–181.

Braude, W.G. (1959) *The Midrash on Psalms*. New Haven: Yale University Press.

Broyles, C.C. (1989) The conflict of faith and experience in the Psalms. *Journal for the Study of the Old Testament Supplement, Series 52*. Sheffield: JSOT Press.

Burton (1621)*The Anatomy of Melancholy*. Oxford: Cripps (5th edition). Philadelphia: J.W. Moore, 1853.

Cohen, A. (1985) *The Psalms: Hebrew Text, English Translation with an Introduction and Commentary*. London: Soncino Press.

Craigie, P.C. (1983) *Psalms 1–50. Word Biblical Commentary*. Vol. 19. Dallas, Texas: Word Books.

Dieckmann, H. (1984) The enemy image. *Quadrant: Journal of the C.J. Jung Foundation*, fall, 61–69.

Duhm, B. (1992) *Die Psalmen*. Tubingen: JCB, Mohr.

Fish, F. (1985) Edited by Hamilton M. *Fish's Clinical Psychopathology: Signs and Symptoms in Psychiatry* (2nd edition). J Wright.

Gerstenberger, E.S. (1988) Psalms, Part 1, with An introduction to cultic poetry. *Forms of Old Testament Literature* 14. Grand Rapids Michigan: Eerdmans.

Gotlib, I.W. (1981) Self-reinforcement and recall: differential effects in depressed and non-depressed subjects. *Journal of Abnormal Psychology* 90: 521–530.

Goulder, M. (1982) The Psalms of the Sons of Korah. *Journal for the Study of the Old Testament Supplement, Series 20.* Sheffield: JSOT Press.

Gunkel, H. (1926) *Die Psalmen ubersetzt underklart HKAT II/2* (4th edition). Gottingen: Vandenhoeck und Ruprecht.

Jamison, K.R. (1989) Mood disorders and patterns of creativity in British writers and artists. *Psychiatry*, 52, 125–134.

Jamison, K.R. (1993) *Touched with Fire.* New York: Free Press.

Hobbs, T.R. and Jackson, P.K. (1991) The enemy in the Psalms. *Biblical Theology Bulletin*, 21, 22–29.

Juda A. (1949) The relationship between high mental capacity and psychic abnormalities. *American Journal of Psychiatry* 106: 296–307.

Kirkpatrick, A.F. (1902). *The Book of Psalms with introduction and notes.* Cambridge: Cambridge University Press

Kraus, H.J. (1988) *Psalms 1–59. A commentary.* Translated by H.C. Oswald. Minneapolis: Augsburg Publishing House.

Kraus, H.J. (1988) *Psalms 60–150. A commentary.* Translated by H.C. Oswald. Minneapolis: Augsburg Publishing House.

Lewis, C.S. (1958) *Reflections on the Psalms.* London: Geoffrey Bles.

Lowth R. (1753) *De Sacra Poesi Haeobrorum Praelectiones,* Academicae Oxonii: Habitae.

Ludwig (1992) Creative achievement and psychopathology. A comparison among professions. *American Journal of Psychotherapy,* 46, 330–336

McCarter, P.K. (1973) The river ordeal in Israelite literature. *Harvard Theological Review* 403–412.

Martin-Achard, R. (1963) *Remarques sur le Psaume 22* v Caro 64, 78–87.

Mowinkel, S. (1967) *The Psalms in Israel's Worship.* Translated by D.R. Ap-Thomas. Nashville Abingdon Press.

Mumford, D.B. (1992) Emotional distress in the Hebrew Bible: Somatic or psychological. *British Journal of Psychiatry* 160, 92–97.

Plath, S. (1963) *The Bell Jar* (originally published under the Pseudonym Victoria Lucas) Heinneman.

Ridderbos, N.H. (1972) Die Psalmen: *Stilistische Verfahren und Aufban mit besonderer Berucksichtigung von Ps.1 – 41.* BZAW 117 Berlin:Walter de Gruyter.

Robbins T.W. Joyce E.M. and Sahakian B. (1993) Neuropsychology and Imaging. Chapter 18, pp. 289–323, in *Handbook of Affectve Disorders* Ed. Eugene Paykel. Edinburgh:Churchill-Livingstone.

Rogerson, J.W. and Mackay, J.W. (1977) *Psalms 1–50.* Cambridge Biblical Commentary. Cambridge: Cambridge University Press.

Sclater *et al* (1994)*The Interpreters Bible* Vol. IV, eds. Buttrick, G.A., Bowie, W.R. New York: Abingdon Press.

Seybold, K. (1990) *Introducing the Psalms.* Translated by R.Graeme Dunphy. Edinburgh: T & T Clarke.

Seybold, K. and Mueller, U.B. (1981) *Sickness and Healing.* Nashville: Abingdon Press.

Sims, A. (1988) *Symptoms in the Mind: An Introduction to Descriptive Psychopathology.* London: Bailliere Tyndall.

Styron, W. (1991) *Darkness Visible.* London: Jonathan Cape

Tate, M. (1990) Word Biblical commentary Vol. 20b. *Psalms 51–100.* Dallas, TX: Word Publishing.

Ungned, A. (1921) *Die Religion der Babylonier und Assyrer,* p. 130.

Westermann, C. (1980) *The Psalms Structure Content and Message.* Minneapolis: Augsburg Publishing House.

Widengren, G. (1936) *Accadian and Hebrew Psalms of Lamentation as Religious Documents.* Uppsala: Almqvist and Wiksells.

# Chapter 6

# King Saul: the nature of his insanity

I gave thee a King in mine anger,
and took him away in my wrath.
(Hosea 13[11])

## Introduction

Saul was the first King of Israel, and it was Israel's misfortune that his insanity came on during his rule, culminating in his suicide following a disastrous defeat at the hands of the Philistines. His anointment by the priest Samuel, his battles with the Philistines and his struggle to retain power in the face of the rising political ambition of David are all told to us in the first Book of Samuel. The description of Saul's decline into insanity appears almost as an incidental within this mainly historical book. Theology is ever present in its depiction of the powers of Yahweh to determine the fate of nations and the course of history. The latter part of the first Book of Samuel is considered by many scholars to be a mainly political document, with much pro-Davidic propaganda to justify the dynastic change from the family of Saul to the House of David, and it also includes a powerful polemic against the corruption inevitable in a monarchy. In Jewish tradition, Saul is regarded with some sympathy as a tragic hero, but in some early Christian circles there was less sympathy. Thus because David was an ancestor of Christ, some early Christian writers, such as Augustine (5th century CE), saw Saul in his hostility to David as representing the Jews who sought the death of Christ (after Gunn, 1980, p. 23). Saul also has a place in Islam and appears in the Koran, where he is given the name Talut. His rivalry with David and his attempts to kill him as well as his séance at Endor are all recorded in the post-Koranic literature. Talut died in a holy war after reigning for 40 years (Bayer, 2007).

The primary psychiatric interest in the story of King Saul rests in a limited number of passages which describe a few clear-cut episodes of his mental illness – probably mania and depression – even though these are quite brief. The analysis of these verses will form the core of the chapter. The authenticity of the text and authorship are also matters of importance because the description of Saul's illness is one of the earliest recorded psychiatric case histories, if not the first. His insanity also had profound political consequence at the time, as well as a later religious and cultural impact.

## The biblical sources

The only source material presently available to study the life of Saul is the first Book of Samuel. According to the Talmud, the author of this book was Samuel himself (Babylonian Talmud *baba bathra* 14a,15b). After ch. 25, from the death of Samuel onwards, the book was said to be composed by Gad the seer and Nathan the prophet. Saul's life and times are not recorded in the contemporary literature of Egypt or Assyria or any other Near Eastern states. It is generally accepted that the Books of Samuel and Kings are part of the Deuteronomic history, redacted in the post-exilic period but based on compilations of older materials. The book is not an unbiased version of history but is written with a primarily religious intention. It is therefore a work of historiography, a biased account with its own purpose – apology, polemic or legitimation – and it is important to discern the orientation of the narrator. It is now thought that one of the original purposes of the text was to justify David's ascendancy to the throne. Thus David is portrayed as the hero with his good deeds and great military prowess and these are juxtaposed against Saul's defeats and descent into madness.

The study of the psychology of a particular historical character has been termed pathography. Schioldann-Nielsen (1988), a Danish psychiatrist who wrote the biography of the manic depressive Danish prime minister D.G. Monrad, defines this:

> Pathography is historical biography written from a medical, psychological and psychiatric viewpoint.... It is a descriptive analytic method applied within the biographical framework and depends on specific enquiry into the available materials.

Schioldann-Nielsen advocates the use of 'lengthy quotations' from the available material to corroborate any evidence or justify any particular hypothesis. The amount of material available for the study of King Saul is confined to the biblical text of 1 Samuel. A further difficulty arises in that the Books of Samuel are part of the Deuteronomic history, which has a strong pro-Davidic slant. To infer psychiatry from such a biased record is therefore not without difficulty. However, in the analysis of Saul's illness the method suggested by Schioldann-Nielsen is followed below and all the passages which may have any psychiatric significance have been quoted in full, leaving it for readers to decide the extent to which they depict insanity, depression and the like.

## The text of 1 Samuel

The Masoretic text (MT) of Samuel, which represents the 'official' Hebrew version, contains a large number of scribal errors and it is thought to suffer from a great deal of haplography (these are scribal omission of letters from the beginning or end of words which might alter the meaning). In the days before the printing press, every word had to be copied by hand and once an error entered the text it would tend to be perpetuated.

Otto Thenius (1842) and later Julius Wellhausen (1871) attempted to correct much of this haplography using the Septuagint version (LXX) to clarify many of the puzzling errors in the text. However, in 1952, a revolution in the study of the Hebrew text of Samuel came with the discovery of the Dead Sea Scrolls at the Qumran Caves, among which three separate fragments of the Book of Samuel were identified:

- 4Q$^a$ Sam. A large fairly well preserved scroll dating to about 50 BCE and containing parts of both 1 and 2 Samuel
- 4Q$^b$ Sam. A poorly preserved manuscript dating from 200–300 BCE and containing small parts of 1 Samuel
- 4Q$^c$ Sam. A manuscript of the early part of 1 Samuel (the story of Nabal and Abigail, and parts of 2 Samuel.

These ancient scroll fragments are the earliest documents concerning Saul – but even they describe events that had occurred some 700 years previously, since it is generally estimated that Saul reigned around 1020 BCE.

The Qumran fragments are in better agreement with the Septuagint (LXX) than with the Masoretic text. Of the three versions of the Septuagint (Codex Vaticanus, LXX$_B$, Codex Alexandrinus, LXX$_A$, and the Lucianic Manuscripts, LXX$_L$), the Qumran fragments show greatest resemblance to the Codex Vaticanus (LXX$_B$), which itself has numerous haplographic errors but which is the text thought to be nearest to the original Greek version, which was the first translation from the original Hebrew manuscript. LXX$_A$ and LXX$_L$ were both re-edited and changed to bring them in line with a version of the Masoretic text that was current at around 300 CE, but this version probably also had numerous errors. Since then, biblical scholars have worked out more or less all the additions, omissions and errors in the biblical texts and these are listed in McCarter's extensive commentary on I Samuel (McCarter, 1980, pp. 16–17). Fortunately, none of these errors appears to involve the few specific verses which describe Saul's mental aberrations, although different translations show some minor variations.

While there can never be certainty concerning the dating or authorship of any biblical text, for a psychiatric examination it is important only to know whether the verses which describe Saul's mental aberrations were recorded *in writing* at the time they occurred or whether, like some other earlier portions of the Old Testament, such as the stories of Abraham or Noah, they were transmitted in an oral form for several generations before being written down on scrolls of papyrus.

The final redactions of the Books of Samuel probably did not take place until after exile – more than 500 years after the death of Saul – so we cannot expect clinical detail to survive in any meaningful or accurate way over more than 20 generations had the transmission been only in oral form. On the other hand, if details of King Saul's rather gross degree of insanity were recorded at the time they occurred, then, apart from the copying errors of haplography, the biblical text is likely to be reasonably accurate. The original authors would have been the scribes of David's court, and some of them would have been eyewitnesses to Saul's mental deterioration and the insane behaviour of a reigning monarch, which almost certainly would have been the talk of the town at the time, just as it would be today.

## Saul: his life story

Saul's life story is one of the most colourful, dramatic, yet tragic biographies to be found in the Bible. His immediate predecessor was Samuel and prior to Samuel in the 12th and 11th centuries BCE Israel was ruled by a series of judges. As Samuel grew old the problem of his succession appeared and his sons Joel and Abijah were the heirs apparent. Even though they were both judges in the city of Beersheba, they were corrupt and took bribes and so they were deemed unsuitable for such high office.

At that time Israel was surrounded by many hostile nations and there was a need for a strong military leader. The people turned to Samuel to ask for a King 'so that we too can be like other nations' and so 'that our King may govern us and go out before us and fight our battles'.

Nothing is told to us about Saul's childhood or his early family life; the text just tells us that he was a tall, good-looking man from the tribe of Benjamin and he was the son of a merchant called Kish. Then follows the quasi-fictional saga of his selection: a man was sent out to search for some lost donkeys but returns with a Kingdom instead. Saul is accompanied in this search by a young lad and after several days of trying to find the lost donkeys, the two of them are about to give up when the young lad tells Saul there is an elderly seer in the town who might be able to help. They approach an elderly man who 'quite by chance' was none other than Samuel and Saul asks him to direct him to the house of the seer. Samuel replies that he is the seer and invites Saul to go with him to the holy shrine to make a sacrifice and also tells him to forget about the lost donkeys because they have already been found. When they are at the shrine Samuel takes out a phial of oil and pours it out over Saul's forehead; he kisses his head and says (10[1]): 'The Lord has anointed you ruler over his people Israel. You shall reign over the people of the Lord and save them from the hand of their enemies all around'.

Almost immediately after his anointment another strange episode occurs, where Saul encounters a band of prophets who are in a state of ecstasy and as he meets them he too falls into a state of ecstasy. This is the beginning of his long psychiatric career, although neither the text nor most of the later biblical commentators make this link. As he is about to be presented to the people as their King, he mysteriously disappears and hides in some baggage. Perhaps he was too shy or maybe he had a panic attack; the episode is unexplained. Eventually Samuel does bring Saul before the people at Mizpah who exclaim 'Long live the King'. We have no idea of whether the stories of Saul searching for his uncle's lost donkeys, his strange encounter with the ecstatic prophets and his hiding in the baggage are true or not but they are certainly entertaining, which may be why these tales have been retained in the text.

The early part of Saul's reign was mainly taken up with battles against Israel's neighbours, especially the Philistines (chs 11–15). The Philistines were a real danger as they possessed superior weaponry made from iron, whereas Israel lacked people with blacksmithing skills. From a religious perspective only two events in these wars have any significance, both acts of hubris where Saul disobeys orders from Samuel and, by implication, commands from God. The first of these was his failure to wait for seven days before Samuel could join him at Gilgal in the battle of Michmash (circa 1030 BCE). Saul was under pressure to start fighting against the Philistines, because his troops were starting to desert in droves. Thus he commences the battle without waiting for Samuel, but when Samuel arrives he castigates Saul for disobeying this order. The second act of hubris came in the war against the Amalekites, an ancient enemy of Israel. Saul defeated the Amalekites and captured their king, Agag, but he shows Agag mercy and fails to kill him. Samuel is very angry at this act of disobedience and he orders Agag to be brought before him. 'And Samuel hewed Agag to pieces before the Lord' while uttering the spine-chilling words to Agag 'As your sword has made women childless, so your mother will be childless among women' ($15^{33-34}$).

These two acts of disobedience are given as a theological reason for Saul ultimately losing his kingdom and Yahweh switching his favour from Saul to David, who would eventually replace him as King of Israel. To the modern reader these do not seem to be major crimes or serious moral defects. Saul's insanity is never used to explain or justify the loss of his throne. From ch. 16 onwards, Saul's story becomes intertwined with David's and most of Saul's psychiatric episodes are to be found in this section, where David's position in the court gets stronger and stronger while Saul declines into a state of incompetence and insanity.

Leonhard Rost (1926) was the first to identify this section as an independent document, almost certainly written during the reign of David, possibly by one of his scribes. Here, Saul's decline into incapacity, insanity and military defeat is juxtaposed against David's increasing military prowess and political skill. With the exception of the description of Saul's first episode of mania, Saul's bipolar illness is contained within this document. Within the 'history of David's rise' (HDR) narrative, David is presented as Saul's favoured armour bearer, his therapist and musician, a valiant fighter against Goliath, as well as a wise military general and a charismatic leader.

This part of the narrative starts in ch. 16, when Samuel anoints David as the future King and simultaneously the 'spirit of the Lord' leaves Saul only to be replaced by 'an evil spirit from the Lord', which most likely signifies the first episode of Saul's melancholia. David is summoned to play his music to Saul and this seems to be the first of many occasions when David's musical talents are used to sooth Saul's depressions; it also gets him into the royal household. Gradually his position gets stronger; he marries Saul's daughter, Michal, he becomes best friend to Saul's son Jonathan, and becomes one of Israel's leading generals, while Saul seems to have had several episodes of depression during this period.

Eventually David becomes a more popular figure than Saul and so, not surprisingly, Saul becomes jealous of this upstart who seems to be trying to steal his kingdom. It is a tale of realpolitik and paranoia and Saul becomes increasingly disturbed. It is thought that this part of the text was written after Saul's death, by court scribes loyal to David, and this may explain its pro-Davidic stance. Saul is plunged once more into severe depression and so David is summoned to play on his harp but this time the music lacks any beneficial effect. In a jealous rage Saul hurls a spear at David and a little later even becomes suspicious of his own son Jonathan over his friendship with David, and hurls a javelin at him. These are the acts of a madman. Jonathan warns his friend David of his father's murderous intentions and so David flees. Saul becomes increasingly paranoid and starts to hunt David down all over Israel. One of the first places David flees to is the city of Nob and the high priest there offers him shelter. When Saul hears this, he kills the high priest and goes on to massacre the priests of Nob, no fewer than 85 of them. David then flees to caves at Horesh in the wilderness of Ziph, but some Ziphites betray his whereabouts to Saul. By chance, Saul enters a cave 'to relieve himself' but he is unaware that this is the cave where David and his troops are hiding. David's men capture Saul and threaten to kill him but David stops them because 'Saul is the Lord's anointed' and a similar scene is acted out later again in the desert at Ein Gedi.

The end of Saul's life comes at the hands of the Philistines, who defeat him at Mount Gilboa. However, on the night before the battle there is a curious séance with a medium who calls up the voice of the now dead Samuel. In this séance Samuel tells him that 'tomorrow he and his sons will join him', meaning that Saul and his sons will all be killed in the forthcoming battle. Saul is severely injured in the battle and asks his armour bearer to complete the job of killing him, but the armour bearer refuses and so Saul commits suicide by falling on his sword, and his armour bearer then does likewise and so the saga of King Saul ends.

Episodes of mental illness are distributed throughout the story; sometimes their place in the narrative seems to make sense and fits in with the storyline, but in other instances the psychiatric episodes seem to have no connection with the on-going story, and it is as if these episodes have been almost randomly just dropped in.

## The insanity of King Saul: a psychiatric appraisal

Saul was almost certainly deemed to be insane during his own reign and there has never been any denial that he was mentally ill; both the theological and psychiatric literature has focused rather more on exactly what was wrong with him. The earliest medical reference for studying medical disorders in the Old Testament is that of Preuss (1911, republished 2004) in his book *Biblical and Talmudic Medicine*, which includes a chapter on mental disorder in which Preuss diagnoses Saul as being both melancholic and epileptic because of the abrupt onset of his depressions. In the analysis below, each of these episodes is discussed, together with some of the associated Old Testament scholarship.

### *The spells of ecstasy: were these episodes of mania or hypomania?*

Saul suffered from two spells of what the text calls 'prophetic frenzy', traditionally held to be religious ecstasy. Both episodes seem to occur 'out of the blue', with little logical connection to the surrounding narrative. The first episode occurs almost immediately after Saul's anointment by Samuel, during the tale of the lost donkeys, a story which does not seem to have any sort of a link to either religion or mental disorder. The second episode occurs much later, when Saul is pursuing David across the desert at Ramah, when he abruptly succumbs to an episode of excited behaviour. Both episodes occur in the company of bands of prophets, who display similar excited behaviours. In the more detailed analysis below an attempt is made

to see to what extent these two episodes correspond to the concept of mania
as it is understood today.

## *The first episode of possible mania*

Immediately after anointing Saul, Samuel tells him that soon he will meet
two men at Rachel's tomb, who will tell him that his uncle's asses have been
found. He then predicts that Saul will meet a band of prophets and then the
spirit of Yahweh 'will rush in on him'. In due course all of Samuel's predic-
tions come true. The correct prediction of an important future event by a
prophet was a biblical literary device used to emphasise the importance of a
story, as well as to enhance the powers of the prophet. This story is related
in I Sam 10:

| | |
|---|---|
| 10⁵ After that you shall come to Gibeath – Elohim at the place where the Philistine garrison is; | Heb. *Gibeath Elohim* literally the Hill of God |
| there, as you come to the town, you will meet a band of prophets coming down from the shrine with harp, tambourine, flute and lyre playing in front of them; | Heb. *hevel* = band of; *ne've'em* = prophets they lived at the religious shrines. See below for 'bands of prophets' |
| They will be in a *prophetic frenzy*. | They are in a prophetic ecstasy |
| ⁶ Then the spirit of the Lord will possess you | Heb. *ruah Yahweh* = breath of Yahweh |
| and you will be in a prophetic frenzy along with them and be turned | Saul will also be in ecstasy |
| into a different person. | a change in personality |
| ⁷ Now when these signs meet you do whether you see fit to do, for God is with you. | |
| ⁸ And you shall go down to Gilgal ahead of me; then I will come down to you to present burnt offerings and sacrifices of well-being. | Sacrifices offered at sacred sites 'communion offerings' (McCarter) |
| For seven days you shall wait until I come to you and show you what you shall do. | command to wait 7 days |
| ⁹ As he turned away to leave Samuel, God gave him another heart and all these signs were fulfilled that day. | God changes Saul's character |
| ¹⁰ When they were going from there to Gibeah | Repeat of the predicted events |
| a band of prophets met him and the spirit of God possessed him and *he fell into a prophetic frenzy* along with them. | but now occurring in real time Saul now in a possession state described as prophetic frenzy |
| ¹¹ When all who knew him before saw how he prophesied with the prophets the people said to one another | Saul in a state of religious mania, a condition usually associated with the prophets |

| | | |
|---|---|---|
| | 'What has come over the son of Kish? Is Saul also among the prophets?' | External observers see a change in Saul's behaviour |
| 12 | A man of the place answered 'And who is their father?' Therefore it became a proverb 'Is Saul among the prophets?' | Prophetic groups often had a leader called 'their father' |
| 13 | When his prophetic frenzy had ended he went home. | Self-resolving brief episode of prophetic frenzy |

The story then immediately reverts back to the story of the lost donkeys. Saul's uncle asks him where he has been and Saul replies that he has been out looking for the missing donkeys but he completely fails to mention that he has recently been anointed king or his escapade with the band of prophets. A brief episode of mental disturbance seems to have been just dropped into the middle of an amusing episode about the lost donkeys and a very major political and personal event – his anointment as King by Samuel.

The phrase 'prophetic frenzy' occurs twice, at $10^5$ and $10^{10}$, and also in the description of second episode of possible mania ($19^{21}$ – see below). McCarter (p. 182) explains and translates the Hebrew *wesaleha aleka ruah Yahweh* as 'the spirit of Yahweh will rush upon you'. The spirit of Yahweh (*ruah Yahweh*), or more properly the breath of Yahweh, refers to the vital force of the deity, and is the invigorating power of God as experienced by a human being. In most of the passages where this phrase appears, the hero generally experiences the spirit as an explosive surge of strength. The present case, even though it shares the same formulaic language, is somewhat different, insofar as the onrush of spirit finds expression *not in the heroic animation of the warrior, but in prophetic ecstasy instead* (McCarter, p. 182, emphasis added). The phrase seems therefore to denote an excited mental state while in a group situation.

The word 'frenzy' used in the NRSV but in many other translations is defined as 'mental derangement, temporary insanity, the uncontrolled excitement of a paroxysm of mania' (*Shorter Oxford English Dictionary*, 2007), and the word 'prophetic' presumably refers to talking/preaching/religious content and predicting the future. This brief phrase captures the essence of a manic episode – over-talkativeness, non-stop talking with a religious content and possible grandiosity in predicting the future and this is sometimes called religious mania. It may occur in religious and non-religious people alike, and if this is the type of mania that afflicted Saul it may provide an answer to the ancient riddle 'Is Saul among the prophets?'

The first episode of mania is predicted in the text at $10^6$: Saul 'will be turned into a different person'. Later we read how the people around him commented 'What has come over the Son of Kish? Is Saul also among the prophets?' Both these phrases imply an observable change of behaviour and that Saul must have been behaving in a fashion that was quite out of the normal, which can occur during a manic episode. This change has puzzled scholars. Traditional Jewish commentary cites Abavranal, who says 'Kish never prophesied and Saul had never prophesied before' (Rosenberg, p. 78). Ackroyd (1971) admits that we do not know the original meaning, and suggests that the question means 'Is Saul, the man of great standing, likely

to have been connected with these lowly ill behaved bands of prophets?'
Wilson (1980) suggests that the saying originated in pro-Davidic circles and
was used to denigrate Saul by calling attention to his madness.

## The second episode of possible mania

Most scholars also link the proverb 'Is Saul among the prophets?' to the
second episode of 'ecstasy' (I Sam 19[19-25]), which also ends with the riddle 'Is
Saul among the prophets?', indicating that the two episodes may have been
quite similar, a known feature of bipolar disorder, where successive episodes
tend to repeat themselves more or less identically. Like the first episode,
the second episode also occurs in a group situation, suggestive of epidemic
hysteria, with the prophets seemingly 'infecting' Saul's messengers with their
ecstasy so that eventually Saul catches it as well.

| | | |
|---|---|---|
| 19[19] | Now David fled and escaped;<br>he came to Samuel at Ramah and<br>told him all that Saul had done to him.<br>He and Samuel went and settled at Naioth.<br>Saul was told 'David is at Naioth in Ramah'. | Ramah: Saul's home town |
| 20 | Then Saul sent messages to David.<br>When they saw the company of the<br>prophets in a frenzy with Samuel<br>standing in charge of them, the spirit of<br>God came upon the messengers of Saul,<br>and they also fell into a prophetic frenzy. | Group ecstasy, their leader,<br>Samuel, is present. The spirit of<br>of God infects Saul's messengers,<br>which suggests epidemic hysteria |
| 21 | When Saul was told he sent other<br>messengers and they also fell into a frenzy.<br>Saul sent messengers again a third time<br>and they also fell into a frenzy. | More evidence of contagion<br><br>Even more contagion! |
| 22 | Then he himself went to Ramah. He<br>came to the great well that is in Secu.<br>He asked 'Where are Samuel and David?'<br>and someone said 'They are at Naioth<br>in Ramah'. | |
| 23 | He went then towards Naioth in Ramah;<br>and the spirit of God came upon him.<br>As he was going he fell into a prophetic<br>frenzy until he came to Naioth in Ramah. | Onset of more strange behaviours<br>Abnormal overactive state<br>? Religious mania |
| 24 | He too stripped off his clothes and he<br>too fell into a frenzy before Samuel.<br>He lay naked all that day and all that<br>night. Therefore it is said,<br>'Is Saul also among the prophets?' | Stripping: sign of acute psychosis<br>Insane *in front of* Samuel<br>Heb. *arom* = naked; hence it is a<br>witnessed episode<br>Is Saul insane like the prophets? |

Both accounts of mania (the first and second episodes) describe a broadly
similar type of illness with common elements. In both there is a premonition
of the ecstasy. In the first episode it is prophesied that Saul will develop 'a
prophetic frenzy'. In the second episode, it is others – his messengers – who
fall into the ecstasy, before he does. As noted previously, biblical redactors
frequently used literary devices such as repetition or prediction to highlight

important or unusual events– and what could be more spectacular than the sight of the King going mad?

A second commonality is the use of the phrase 'The spirit of the Lord will possess you', with slightly different phrasing in the second episode, 'and the spirit of the Lord came upon him'. The phrase 'the spirit of the Lord was with him' is sometimes used in the Bible to describe how someone suddenly acquires great additional strength, particularly before battles, or in modern parlance 'he was full of adrenalin', although, as McCarter says, in this case it refers to the onset of a state of ecstasy.

One very early biblical commentator, Rabbi Jonathan Ben Uzziel (1st century CE), a disciple of the great Jewish teacher Hillel, appears to be the first to state that this is insanity. Thus Rosenberg (1976, p. 165) writes, 'Ben Uzziel explains this state by using the term "is insane or mad", comparing him to one who is mentally ill and is unaware of the things that surround him.'

Hertzberg (1964, p. 168), a German biblical scholar, placed a more religious interpretation on the second episode of ecstasy:

> The narrative is much more concerned to bring Saul in contact with the prophetic ecstasy and this gives basis to the proverb 'Is Saul among the prophets?' Saul is drawn more strongly into the workings of the spirit than are his messengers as he tears the clothes from his body and lies on the ground in a state like a paralytic.

P. K. McCarter (p. 330), following on from Welhausen, writes that there has been a school of thought that regarded the second episode of mania ($19^{19-24}$) on mainly literary grounds as a late secondary insertion, with its aim of answering the question 'Is Saul among the prophets?' The story of him meeting the band of prophets does not seem to have a logical fit with either the tale of the lost donkeys or the anointing of Saul yet it is placed immediately after the latter.

The burning issue for the people of ancient Israel at the time must have been 'Is our King mad, like some of the prophets?' The narrator does not know the answer but he was placed under an imperative to explain to the people why their newly chosen King had gone mad. Psychiatric knowledge at the time would have been extremely limited but it was known that there were prophetic groups who roamed around the land who on occasion lapsed into states of ecstasy, or group hysteria, sometimes behaving in a grossly disinhibited fashion, and that such behaviour appeared to be infectious. Such contagion is especially highlighted in the account of Saul's second episode of mania. Saul was observed to be crazy even by the prophet Samuel as he fell naked before him, surely a sign of madness, but the puzzle was how exactly did he 'catch' his insanity.

With the limited knowledge of excited states available at that time, the narrator seems to have postulated that the most likely source of Saul's excitement was contagion from some ecstatic prophets. But did Saul truly come into contact with them? Skilfully, the narrator crafts a prediction and then a story that Saul would meet a group of ecstatic prophets, and in this way would be in contact with them and so be in a position to 'catch' their

**Table 6.1** DSM criteria for mania and Saul's two episodes of mania/hypomania

| DSM mania | Verse from I Samuel |
|---|---|
| Elevated or expansive or irritable mood for at least a week. At the same time, at least three of the following: | The spirit of the Lord will possess you and you will be in a prophetic frenzy ($10^6$); in episode 2, He fell into a prophetic frenzy ($19^2$) |
| (1) Inflated self-esteem/grandiosity | ?Behaving like a prophet |
| (2) Less need of sleep | He lay naked all that day and all that night ($19^{24}$) |
| (3) More talkative than usual | |
| (4) Flight of ideas/racing thoughts | |
| (5) Distractibility | Prophetic frenzy $10^5$; $10^{10}$; $19^{23}$ |
| (6) Increase in goal-directed activity or psychomotor agitation | Frenzy = increased motor activity |
| (7) Excessive involvement in activities with potentially unpleasant consequence (e.g. sexual indiscretion, spending sprees, imprudent business investments) | |
| Symptoms do not meet criteria of a mixed episode | He stripped off his clothes ($19^{24}$) See note 1 below |
| The symptoms impair social and occupational function, social activities or in relationships with others or there are psychotic features | Is Saul also among the prophets ($10^{11}$ and $19^{24}$) See note 2 below Change in occupational function – from being a King to behaving like a prophet: 'You will be in a prophetic frenzy with them and be turned into a different person ($10^6$) |
| The disturbance is not due to the physiological effects of a substance (drug of abuse or medication) or physical illness | |

Note 1 There are two other episodes of depression with serious violence, when Saul hurls spears at David and Jonathan. During these episodes Saul seems to be overactive, disinhibited and impulsive, all of which are features of mania, especially during mixed affective episodes ($19^{6-10}$ and $20^{30-34}$), which are more fully explained on pp. 204–205.

Note 2 Criterion C 'The episode (for mania) is associated with an unequivocal change of functioning *that is uncharacteristic of the person when not symptomatic.'* The text of 1 Samuel gives numerous references to change of character, e.g. the switch from a king to a prophet. 'Is Saul among the prophets?' ($10^{11}$ and $19^{24}$). 'The spirit of the Lord will possess you and you will be in a prophetic frenzy along with them and be turned into a different person' ($10^6$).

insanity. Thus it is not impossible the narrator made up the whole story of Saul meeting the band of prophets as a way of explaining Saul's episodes of mania. The addition of a predictive element gives extra gravitas to his encounter with the prophets. In this sense the present author is in agreement with Welhausen and others, that this story may have been a later insertion—with the underlying purpose of explaining why their King had gone mad.

The biblical text provides just about sufficient detail to apply DSM-5 criteria of mania to Saul's two episodes of prophetic frenzy/mania. Table 6.1 presents the DSM-5 criteria for mania together with the relevant text. The two episodes of mania have been combined for this purpose.

The differential diagnosis of Saul's episodes lies between mania (bipolar I) and hypomania (bipolar II) and uncomplicated religious ecstasy. Differences between these conditions concern its severity, its duration and the presence of psychotic features. The second episode has a shorter duration (one day and one night), although he was in a prophetic frenzy immediately prior to this. Probably it is impossible to make a distinction between the modern categories of mania and hypomania as there is so little clinical information but bipolar II disorder (hypomania) is characterised by a great deal of depression as well, which clearly Saul also suffers from. Simple prophetic ecstasy is also possible but is unlikely because only a very severe condition would be recorded by court scribes. Also, against the diagnosis of simple prophetic ecstasy is that it fails to explain his depressive episodes, paranoid jealous rages and eventual suicide. Between episodes of prophetic ecstasy subjects are usually quite normal and do not show other psychopathology, but clearly this is not the case with Saul. A diagnosis of bipolar disorder readily explains the totality of his psychopathology under a single umbrella.

## Saul's depressive episodes

There are at least five separate episodes of depression, with what appears to be remission in between, but the text implies there may have been many more. Their phenomenology shifts from being straightforward melancholic spells responsive to 'music therapy' in the early part of his reign to paranoid aggressive depressions later on, with a gradual descent into a more full-blown paranoia. The saga ends with an episode of possible psychotic depression at Endor and culminates in Saul's dramatic suicide following his defeat at the hands of the Philistines at Mt Gilboa. Around 15% of all manic depressives commit suicide, and this usually occurs during a depression, particularly a psychotic depression, and it is likely that Saul's suicide took place during such an illness. Most of the descriptions of depression in other parts of the Bible are autobiographical accounts replete with florid descriptions of the sufferer's depressive symptoms. By contrast, the few objective accounts of depression in the text are extremely terse, and the presence of any depression can only be inferred from very limited information.

### *The first depression: the anointing of David*

The first suggestion of any depression comes when Yahweh switches his favour from Saul to David and has anointed David:

16<sup>13</sup> Then Samuel took the horn of oil and | The prophetic anointing of David
anointed him in the presence of his
brothers: and the spirit of the Lord | Switch of divine spirit to David
came mightily upon David from that day
forward. Samuel set out and went to Ramah.

14 Now the spirit of the Lord departed
from Saul and an evil spirit from the Lord | and the spirit left Saul
tormented him | Heb. *ruah ra'ah*, evil spirit

15 and Saul's servant said to him 'See now | The servant notices a change in
an evil spirit from God is tormenting you | Saul's demeanour

16 Let our Lord command the servants who
attend you to look for someone who is
skilled in playing the lyre and when the | Heb. *Kinnor* = lyre or harp
evil spirit of God is upon you, he will | ? the depression
play it and you will feel better. | Therapeutic effects of music

This passage represents one of the great thresholds in 1 Samuel, marking the point where Yahweh's favour switches away from Saul to David. The text is written in such a way as to imply that the onset of Saul's melancholia is causally linked to this change in God's favour and also to the forthcoming switch in royal power. The phrase 'the spirit of the Lord' is used in two senses: to describe political and religious authority initially invested with Saul, and now to be with David; and to describe an 'evil spirit of the Lord', which is the cause of his melancholia. Traditional Jewish commentary links 'the evil spirit' to his depressions. Thus Arbravanel (15th-century Spain) writes: 'this was not a divine visitation of evil, as may be thought, but a *melancholia* which came over Saul after the divine spirit had departed from him, and he was deeply concerned with his impending doom' (cited by Rosenberg, 1976, p. 135).

This passage also has the imprint of the Deuteronomist, the later Babylonian editor(s) who rewrote the history of Israel in the light of Israel's relationship with God, and in the process transformed the history of this small Middle Eastern tribe into a major religious text. These verses also imply the divine selection of Kings – it is God who selects and then later rejects the King. Hertzberg (1964, p. 141) emphasises this religious overtone:

> Saul's suffering is described theologically – not primarily in terms of psycho-pathology or psychology. And rightly so, for in an obscure way the hand of God invades the life of this man who, as can be seen, often exerts himself so much for Yahweh....

More episodes are described in the text, but one verse (16<sup>23</sup>) specifically implies that there were many episodes:

> And *whenever the evil spirit* from God came upon Saul, David took the lyre and played it in his hand, and Saul would be relieved and feel better and the evil spirit would depart from him.

Thus whenever the gloom descended over Saul his courtiers would summon David, his 'music therapist', to soothe him. Kimchi wrote: 'This was a divine gift bestowed upon David – the power of relieving Saul's melancholia'. The use of the term 'whenever' implies that there were at least several such occasions, but exactly how many episodes is not known. A pattern of many episodes of depression is consistent with bipolar affective disorder, particularly bipolar II, a condition in which patients spend the bulk of their lives in depressive phases (Perris, 1992).

## The Hebrew word 'ruah' or spirit

The clinical description of both the manic and the depressive episodes in the Bible hinges greatly on the use of the Hebrew word *ruah*, translated as 'spirit' but literally meaning 'breath'. Thus the spirit or breath of God is usually taken as a positive sign, when God gives a person supernatural strength. For example, when Samson encounters a young lion at Timnah the text (Judges 14[6]) reads 'The spirit of the Lord rushed on him, and he tore the lion apart with his bare hands as one might tear apart a kid'. Likewise, when Saul hears that Nahash, King of the Ammonites, will gouge out the eyes of the people of Jabesh he becomes angry, 'And the spirit of God came upon Saul in power when he heard these words and he was greatly kindled'. In both these situations the breath or spirit of God gives the Israelite hero a shot of supernatural strength. However, the same word, *ruah*, is also sometimes used in association with psychotic episodes. For example, Ezekiel 2[2] states: 'And when he spoke to me a spirit entered into me and set me on my feet and I heard him talking to me'. Similarly in Ezekiel 8[3]: 'the spirit lifted me up between earth and heaven and brought me in visions of God to Jerusalem'. In both these examples the spirit seems to make the person act in a particular way suggestive of a psychotic experience.

There are two references to the *ruah elohim*, spirit of God, in the description of Saul's mania: first, in 10[5] in the prediction of the episode of mania, 'Then the spirit of the Lord will possess you and you will be in a prophetic frenzy and be turned into a different person'; and this is repeated during the actual episode, 'and the spirit of God possessed him and he fell into a prophetic frenzy along with them' (10[9]).

No distinction is made in the Bible between a spirit resulting in great strength and one causing psychosis. This should not be a surprise, because at the time psychosis was not a recognised condition. Even today, making the clinical distinction between a patient in a state of great rage and one in an uncontrolled psychosis is very difficult. A person with severe mania may show increased motor activity, paranoia, aggression and irritability and will be difficult to distinguish from a much enraged but normal individual. Since acute psychosis is rare and intense anger is common, we cannot be surprised that the ancient Israelites and later biblical commentators failed to make this distinction, and the word *ruah* was often used to describe states of both heightened anger *as well as psychotic states*, with no distinction being made between the two.

The phrase *ruah raa*, or evil spirit, is the essence of the Old Testament's description of Saul's depression. It raises a theological problem: the fact that in this phrase God is described as doing evil. According to Vriezen (1967, p. 81) the fact that not only good but also evil comes from Yahweh indicates that he holds absolute authority over evil as well. R. P. Gordon (1986) asserts that the OT tends 'to trace both good and evil back to Yahweh'. Eichrodt (1967) also argues that the evil spirit from the Lord is a spiritual power which is under God's sovereignty, and this is in marked contrast to the more widespread pagan dualism. The Jews just don't do Satan and in places where he is to be found in the OT, such as in the Book of Job, he is very much under God's control, but the concept is thought to have been borrowed from Zoroastrianism.

## Music, the first recorded treatment of depression

King Saul's servants appear to know how to cure Saul's melancholy: 'He will play it and you will be well' (I Sam 16[16]). Music as therapy was already known to the Babylonians. The musical instrument used was the *kinnor* (lyre) and the text states 'David played it with his hand, so Saul was refreshed and the evil spirit departed from him'.

Music was one way of approaching the deity. Thus the introduction to many of the psalms contains references to different musical instruments as well as musical instructions. Music was also a branch of the mathematical sciences in the schools of Babylonia and Phoenicia. The harmony of the spheres, the theory of numbers and musical therapeutics were all ideas that the Pythagoreans took from the Babylonians and imported into Greek culture, and it may have been a part of many other ancient Near Eastern religions. However, following the destruction of the Jerusalem Temple, the rabbis forbade the use of music as it symbolised joy; an exception was made, however, for its use in curing depression. Maimonides in the 12th century CE in the Shemma Peraquoi wrote: 'One who suffers from melancholy may rid himself of this by listening to songs and all kinds of instrumental music'. Commenting on King David as a musician, Yehuda Halevi (circa 1141) wrote: 'Music was then in David's time a perfect art. It wielded that influence on the soul which we attribute to music, the moving of the soul from one mood to another'. The Dutch Jewish philosopher Spinoza wrote 'Music is good to the melancholy' (cited in McCarter, p. 281).

Today, music forms an important part of the religious experience in both synagogue and church services. Music with its mood changing effects was probably the first recorded treatment for depression, preceding all the other effective remedies for depression, such as antidepressant medication, by almost three millennia.

Its efficacy has been established in modern controlled trials. For example, Erkkilä *et al.* (2011) assessed the effect of a combination of playing an instrument, listening and singing in a choir for a total of 20 weekly sessions in 79 Finnish subjects with depression. The study found that those with music therapy did significantly better than a control group who had only 'treatment as usual', with an odds ratio of 2.96 (an odds ratio of 1 means no difference). The music group had better scores on depression rating scales, an effect that was greatest at three months but that was no longer apparent six months after the initiation of the trial.

## Saul's morbid jealousy and paranoia

The first onset of jealousy is described in ch. 18, where the narrator provides a rational explanation for this – David is a better soldier than Saul because he kills more Philistines. However, once Saul's jealousy of David is kindled it soon reaches a level of uncontrolled violence.

| | | |
|---|---|---|
| 18⁷ | And the women sang to one another as they made merry, 'Saul has killed his thousands, and David his tens of thousands'. | Saul kills the Philistines but David is an even more prolific killer |
| 8 | Saul was very angry, for this saying displeased him. He said, 'They have ascribed to David tens of thousands and to me they have ascribed thousands; what more can he have but the kingdom?' | Envy of David First suspicion that David wants |
| 9 | So Saul eyed David from that day on. | the throne |
| 10 | The next day an evil spirit from God rushed upon Saul and he raved within his house, while David played the lyre as he did day by day. | Suggests depression but also *veyatnabi'i* = prophesying raving; try music therapy |
| 11 | Saul had his spear in his hand and *Saul threw the spear*,for he thought, 'I will pin David to the wall'. But David eluded him twice. | Saul attempts to murder David David escapes |
| 12 | Saul was afraid of David because the Lord was with him but had departed from Saul. | God has switched his patronage from Saul to David |

Saul's jealousy and his attacks on David are placed in the context of the dynastic struggle and the gradual shift in political power from Saul to David. The story is written on at least two levels, with a suggestion that some sections were added at a later period. In the religious history David is portrayed as the braver and better soldier because he has killed more Philistines than Saul, and understandably this makes Saul jealous. He begins to fear David's political aspirations and attempts unsuccessfully to neutralise them by having him join the royal household through marrying his daughter, Michal. In spite of this David continues to be a political rival, and so Saul tries to kill him. Murder in the royal palace was a common tale in the ancient world. When this fails he orders his troops to hunt David down and kill him – another familiar story, of the power-crazed tyrant who seeks to kill or crush all his political rivals. Paranoia in this situation becomes understandable for the circumstances. Biblical commentators such as Ackroyd (1971) suggest that the compiler was also trying to draw together the tale of Saul's envy and hostility to David with some important religious themes such as the divine right of kings and the protection God gives to subjects who were 'with the Lord'.

But on another level, the question arises, was Saul in a normal frame of mind during this episode? It seems not, and perhaps he was seriously disturbed at this time. His anger starts when he hears that David is a more prolific killer of the Philistines than himself. The phrase 'Saul eyed David from that day on' (18⁹) implies this was the beginning of his jealousy. Saul may also be in another one of his great depressions because 'an evil spirit of the Lord has returned' and so David is once more playing the lyre to soothe Saul's depression.

However, it is not just 'the evil spirit' of a depression that afflicts Saul. Thus in 18[10] the Hebrew reads *ruah Elohim ra'aa el saul veytnabe'ee*, which translates as 'the evil spirit of God rushed in and he prophesied'. The NRSV and many other translations have *raving* instead of prophesying, indicating that he was is a state of great arousal. *Rashi* (11th-century France) recognises this as madness:

> When a prophet experiences a prophetic trance, his mind becomes detached from his earthly surroundings, and he utters words which have no meaning to those around him. So the madman does likewise. Hence the identical term is used for both. (Cited by Rosenberg, 1976, p. 154)

Hertzberg draws a parallel with 10[10], where 'the spirit comes mightily upon Saul' and while with the band of prophets he goes into a state of prophet ecstasy. However, the prophesying here was not the happy prophesying of the ecstatic – nor was it the simple low mood of a depression, because he was raving.

Such mood states where there are *mixtures* of overactivity, prophesying and raving – all suggesting mania but which are then also combined with depression, as evidenced by the phrase 'an evil spirit of the Lord' – are known in psychiatry as 'mixed affective episodes'. They comprise mixtures of both manic and depressive symptoms occurring at the same time and are frequent in bipolar affective disorder, and will be familiar to most psychiatrists but are not general knowledge outside psychiatry.

It is during this episode that Saul hurls a spear at David and tries to kill him. The attack is impulsive and Saul is mentally ill at the time. An attack of this type is very different from the more frequent planned assassinations of political rivals by psychopathic despots who kill their enemies in cold blood. The statement in the final verse states that the 'spirit of the Lord had departed from Saul' can be understood in two ways: first, the traditional religious meaning, that all political and moral authority had now left Saul and resided with David; and second, that his depression and mental illness had returned and were caused by the departure of the spirit of the Lord – implying that the narrator believed that Saul's fits of melancholy were all controlled by the deity.

The whole episode is repeated in the next chapter (19[8-10]):

| | | |
|---|---|---|
| 19[8] | Again there was war, and David went out to fight the Philistines. He launched a heavy attack on them, so they fled before him. | There are many Philistine wars |
| 9 | Then an evil spirit from the Lord came upon Saul, as he sat in his house with his spear in his hand while David was playing music. | Saul is depressed once more

David called to play music |
| 10 | Saul sought to pin David to the wall with the spear; but he eluded Saul so he struck the spear into the wall. David fled and escaped that night. | Attempted murder of David |

This second episode is almost identical to the previous episode. David returns from the war. Saul is once more in a disturbed frame of mind ('evil spirit from the Lord') and he attacks David with a spear but David escapes. P.K. McCarter (1980) suggests that this is merely repetition, a biblical literary device used to emphasise the importance of a story. However, the second version appears to be more definitely depressive rather than a mixed episode because there is no suggestion of any hyperactivity/prophesying or manic symptoms. Hertzberg (1964) does not postulate repetition but suggests this is another distinct episode and that this is Saul's second attack on David, from which David successfully escapes. Hertzberg goes on to suggest that although Saul is sick, the religious leit motif of this passage is David's escape – because 'the Lord is with him'. David has many other escapes from Saul – the first through his own dexterity, the second with the help of Michal and the third with the help of Samuel. The religious message is that no matter how many attacks Saul makes, David will always be protected because 'the Lord is with him', and the theological intention of the story is to highlight the protective power of the deity.

## Saul hurls a spear at his own son, Jonathan

The next episode of illness (probably a paranoid irritable depression) includes a homicidal attack on his son Jonathan. Jonathan dodged out of the way and the spear missed its target, but had it struck and killed Jonathan then Saul would have been guilty of the unusual crime of filicide. Anyone who throws a spear at his own son should really see a doctor. The incident occurs at a time when Saul was becoming increasingly paranoid about David's rising star, to the extent that he was interrogating his own son Jonathan and other members of the court about David's daily movements. David's absence from an important communal meal arouses Saul's suspicions. By this time David has actually fled, and Jonathan explains to Saul that David has gone to visit his family in Bethlehem, but this apparently innocent explanation makes Saul explode.

| | | |
|---|---|---|
| 20[30] | Then Saul's anger was kindled against Jonathan. He said to him, 'You son of a perverse rebellious woman! Do I not know that you have chosen the son of Jesse to your own shame, and to the shame of your mother's nakedness? | Great anger (see below)<br><br>Heb. *na'awat* = perverse woman the insult is directed at Jonathan Heb. *erwat* = nakedness refers to female genitalia. He is swearing, obscenities |
| [31] | For as long as the son of Jesse lives upon earth, neither you nor your kingdom shall be established. Now send and bring him to me, for he will surely die.' | Thoughts of murder of David |
| [32] | Then Jonathan answered his father Saul, 'Why should he be put to death? What has he done?' | Jonathan puzzled by Saul's fury A simple question but Saul is now highly irritable |
| [33] | But Saul threw his spear at him to strike him; so Jonathan knew that it was the decision of his father to put David to death. | Saul tries to kill his own son |

The story starts with Saul merely being suspicious of David because he has not attended an important communal meal and in a reasonably civilised fashion Saul questions Jonathan concerning David's whereabouts. On hearing that David has gone to visit his family in Bethlehem Saul becomes very angry. There is a suggestion that Saul is raving and out of control. He makes allusions to Jonathan's mother as a perverse rebellious woman and to her nakedness. McCarter (p. 343) states the Bible euphemistically uses this to refer to his mother's genitalia. Only people who are quite highly aroused will swear using words denoting the female genitalia, implying Saul was either very ill and psychotic, or just plain furious. But he certainly seems to have been very touchy. Jonathan immediately surmised that Saul has murderous intentions towards David, and so he somewhat innocently asks 'Why should David be put to death?' There is not time for Saul to answer the question because he is so aroused that within seconds he hurls the spear at Jonathan. There was never a premeditated plan to kill Jonathan but because Saul is so irritable and paranoid he takes immediate offence at anyone questioning him. It is in this hyper-aroused state that he impulsively hurls a spear at Jonathan.

Different versions of this critical passage exist in different translations and it is worth noting some of the variations, as described by McCarter (p. 339). Thus for 'Saul's anger was kindled' ([30]), in three earlier versions, the Masoretic text, the Septuagint and the Qumran scrolls (4QSam[6]), the word 'greatly' is inserted before 'kindled', indicating that this was no ordinary anger. In verse 31, McCarter, basing his version on the Septuagint, has 'You are in league with the son of Jesse', instead of the NRSV's 'You have chosen the son of Jesse', giving the passage an even more paranoid flavour. Finally, for 'to strike him' ([32]) both the LXX and MT have 'to kill him'. The King James version has 'to smite him', which also points to a more definite murderous intent. In summary, the various translations all point to a man who was irritable, disinhibited and paranoid– all features of an aggressive manic episode.

An alternative differential diagnosis might be that Saul was not mentally ill at the time but merely having a temper tantrum. He swears obscenely when Jonathan gives him some upsetting news and then is so upset that he throws a spear at him. Against this non-psychotic interpretation, it should be noted that Saul was highly regarded in the court; he dutifully observed all the religious festivals; and there are no other descriptions of him being bad tempered. All his other bizarre actions, such as throwing the spear at David, or stripping naked, seem to occur only during episodes of illness. Saul had never previously or subsequently been observed to utter obscenities and this must have struck the scribes of the day as strange and perhaps this is why they recorded it. Finally, even tyrants such as Hitler or Stalin usually confine their killing sprees to their political opponents and tend to protect their own families, whereas intra-familial violence and filicide are well recognised complications of psychotic disorder.

Saul made homicidal attacks on both David and Jonathan, although fortunately both escaped unharmed. Both attacks were impulsive, probably occurring while he was mentally unwell. Some years later, following his defeat at Mount Gilboa, Saul committed suicide. Some understanding of Saul's homicidal attacks on David and Jonathan can be gleaned in the light of the modern homicide-suicide literature.

In his book *Murder Followed by Suicide* D. J. West (1965) examined 156 cases of murder followed by suicide and compared them with two groups of subjects who had committed only homicide. The first group had committed criminal homicide and the second domestic homicide. In the homicide-suicide group the victim was almost always related to the subject (93%) and was usually a spouse or child, but in the group who committed homicide alone, only 44% were known to the victim. The mental state of those in the murder-suicide group was established by psychological autopsy (interviewing relatives soon after the suicide). A majority (59%) were thought to be suffering from psychotic depression at the time, a condition which Saul may also have suffered from. A previous psychiatric history was more common among the homicide-suicide group, whereas a previous criminal history was more common among the homicide-only group. The crime of killing a child, usually perpetrated by mentally ill mothers suffering from psychotic depression, had a particularly strong association with suicide. West cites a study by Siciliano of Danish child homicides by a parent, who found that 85% of those who killed their children subsequently committed suicide.

In almost all the reported homicide-suicides, both deaths occur in the same episode of illness, with the suicide following shortly after the homicide. In this respect Saul's attempted homicide of his beloved son Jonathan and the suicide occurring some years later is atypical. It should be remembered, however, that Saul was a monarch with absolute power. No one had the temerity to apprehend him after these murderous assaults and there was little or no concept of what comprised insane behaviour or what might pass for 'normal' in a despotic tyrant in the ancient world, who had the power to put anyone to death at his whim. Saul's attacks on Jonathan appears to partially fit the homicide-suicide picture as described in the literature. Thus he had an extensive previous psychiatric rather than a criminal history, and most of these homicides seem to occur in the context of domestic arguments, often concerning jealousy within the family, with the perpetrator suffering from psychotic depression, which can occur in bipolar disorder.

Those present must have been very frightened at Saul's behaviour. Small wonder that the courtiers and the priesthood would be looking at other candidates such as David to take over the leadership. Their failure to displace Saul at this point led to further tragedies, such as the massacre of the priests of Nob, which occurs while Saul is in a severely paranoid state. In the UK today, attacks of the type Saul perpetuated on Jonathan and David would be indications for immediate compulsory hospitalisation and treatment with medication and possibly even long-term detention in a secure institution.

## Paranoia and the massacre of the priests of Nob

In the latter part of his life Saul descends into a state of paranoia. Some of this may have a basis in the reality of the ongoing dynastic struggle, because David has in real life also become his political rival. Saul pursues David in the deserts of southern Israel and while doing this accuses his troops of conspiring against him for failing to reveal where David is hiding (1 Sam 22$^{6-13}$).

| | | |
|---|---|---|
| 22$^6$ | Saul heard that David and those with him had been located. Saul was sitting at Gibeah, under the tamarisk tree on the height with his spear in his hand and all his servants were standing around him. | Gibeah was Saul's home town Holding a spear; a symbol of kingly status, as if holding court |
| 7 | Hear now you Benjaminites; will the son of Jesse give everyone of you fields and vineyards, will he make you all commanders of hundreds. | Cynical accusation that his soldiers are only loyal to him because of material rewards and David will give them more |
| 8 | Is that why all of you have conspired against me? No one discloses to me when my son makes a league with the son of Jesse, none of you is sorry for me or discloses to me that my son has stirred up my servant against me to lie in wait, as he is doing today. | Thinks his soldiers are conspiring against him feeling isolated; suspicious of Jonathan taking David's side; feelings of victimhood, as in paranoid states. Also believes there are plots to kill him. |

Thinking that his political rival may be plotting against him may be realistic but when it comes to accusing his own soldiers of conspiring against him and that he is a 'victim' the paranoia moves into a more clinical dimension. None of Saul's soldiers will tell him where David is hiding; perhaps their loyalty has switched or this may be his paranoid imagination. Only Doeg an Edomite tells Saul that David has fled to the nearby holy sanctuary of Nob, where he is being given asylum by Ahimelech, the chief priest. Saul immediately proceeds to the city and addresses Ahimelech:

| | | |
|---|---|---|
| 22$^{13}$ | Why have you conspired against me, you and the son of Jesse, by giving him bread and a sword, and by inquiring of God for him so that he has risen against me to lie in wait as he is doing today?' | More conspiracy theories<br><br><br><br>repeat of the belief that David wants to kill him |

Saul then orders his soldiers to kill the priests of Nob, but only Doeg the Edomite carries out the order and massacres no fewer than 85 priests of Nob, as well as men, women, children and animals of the city of Nob. McCarter (1980, p. 364) writes:

> In his paranoia, the deluded king sees conspiracy everywhere.... Saul by now is totally possessed by his own fears and suspicions, and commands the massacre not only the entire priesthood of Nob but also a pogrom against the inhabitants of the sacred city itself. The demented king is again the villain of the piece.

Hertzberg (p. 188) comments on the extreme viciousness of the massacre, and also that in this bizarre act he alienated the priesthood as a source of possible support for his monarchy. One priest, Abiathazar, was spared and he later joined forces with David. According to Hertzberg, Abiathazar might have later been given the role of the scribe and historian in the royal court of King David. Could he have been the scribe who so accurately recorded the episodes of Saul's insanity? Having witnessed the massacre of his fellow priests he might have had good reason to do so.

## The seance at Endor – another episode of depression?

The final saga of Saul's reign was his defeat by the Philistines at Mt Gilboa. Immediately before this battle there is a curious episode (1 Sam 28[3–7]) where Saul visits a medium at a place called Endor (modern Khirbet Essafsafe), about 4.5 miles north-east of Shunem, where the Philistines were encamped but behind Philistine lines. The story is one of the embattled king consulting a banned medium before the battle.

| | | |
|---|---|---|
| 28[3] | Now Samuel had died, and all Israel mourned for him and buried him in Ramah. Saul had expelled the mediums and wizards from the land. | It is dangerous to be a medium |
| 4 | The Philistines assembled at Shunem. Saul gathered all Israel and they encamped at Gilboa. | |
| 5 | When Saul saw the army of the Philistines he was afraid and his heart trembled greatly. | A very big army<br><br>Anxiety, tachycardia? Panic |
| 6 | When Saul enquired of the Lord, the Lord did not answer him, not by dreams, nor by urim, nor by prophets | Saul unable to consult with God before the battle On 'urim', see below |
| 7 | Then Saul said to his servants, seek out a woman who is a medium so that I may go to her and enquire after her. His servants said to him there is a medium at Endor. | His only chance of getting a prediction of the battle outcome will be through a medium |

'Urim' is usually placed in conjunction with 'thumin'. Objects of unknown shape and used in divination, the urim and thumin were put inside a pouch attached to the breast plate. Considering the scholars' conclusion that urim essentially means guilty and thumin essentially means innocent, this would imply that the purpose of the urim and thumim was an ordeal to confirm or deny suspected guilt; if the urim was selected it meant guilt, while selection of the thumin would mean innocence.

In disguise, Saul visits the medium illicitly, at night. The medium was a woman and, as Rabbi Kimhi says, 'She was a necromanceress because this practice was more common among women than among men, since they are frivolous and are easily drawn into superstition' (Rosenberg, p. 228). The medium was also very worried about her own safety because Saul had previously banished all wizards, mediums and witches in accordance with a commandment given in Exodus. However, Saul reassures the medium that he will not kill her. Consulting with a medium before a battle was important because a medium was able to communicate with the ghosts of the dead and through necromancy bring them back into the world so that the dead could talk to the living.

In ancient times it was customary for military leaders to consult oracles before important battles to pray for a good outcome and even to discuss strategy. Samuel is roused and says 'Why have you disturbed me by bringing me up'. Spirits were supposed to inhabit the netherworld of Sheol and were thought to be in a sleepy state most of the time, but they could be roused from their torpor. The verb *regez*, which means 'disturbed', probably refers to him being disturbed from this sleeping state. The Phoenician equivalent of the verb *regez* frequently appears on Phoenician sepulchral tombs and McCarter (1980, p. 421) cites its presence on a 5th-century epitaph of King Tabrit of Sidon as evidence for a widespread belief in the ancient Near East that important leaders who had died could be brought back to communicate with the living.

The underlying assumption in the ancient world and for many centuries later was that the dead have knowledge of the future; thus the witches in Macbeth call up the dead Banquo to point to future kings (*Macbeth*, Act IV, Scene 1). Saul asked the medium to bring up Samuel, who had recently died, which she then does. The text goes on to describe how Saul hears the voice of Samuel and talks to him. Samuel criticises Saul and tells him that both he and his children are doomed to die in the forthcoming battle. The story in ch 28$^{15-25}$ is of the anxious King on the eve of the battle seeking guidance from the oracle but within this tale several key depressive symptoms are mentioned, perhaps sufficient to justify a diagnosis of major depression:

| | | |
|---|---|---|
| 28$^{15}$ | Then Samuel said to Saul, 'Why have you disturbed me by bringing me up?' | Samuel talks to Saul and Saul seems to answer him |
| | Saul answered, 'I am in great distress, for the Philistines are warring against me and God has turned away from me and answers me no more, either by prophets or by dream; so I have summoned you to tell me what to do'. | God seems to be unavailable |
| 16 | Samuel said, 'Why then do you ask me, since the Lord has turned from you and become your enemy? | Samuel talks to Saul again |
| 17 | The Lord has done to you just as he spoke to me; for the Lord has torn the Kingdom out of your hand and given it to your neighbour, David. | Samuel explains that God is punishing him by taking his Kingdom away |
| 18 | Because you did not obey the voice of the Lord and carry out his fierce wrath against Amelak. | |
| 19 | Moreover, the Lord will give Israel along with you into the hands of the Philistines; and tomorrow you and your sons shall be with me; the Lord will also give the army of Israel into the hands of the Philistines.' | Samuel predicts defeat by the Philistines; thoughts of death for Saul and his sons<br><br>Defeat is predicted |
| 20 | Immediately Saul fell full length on the ground, filled with fear because there was no strength in him for he had eaten nothing all that day and all night. | Hysterical collapse due to severe anxiety<br>Weakness; low energy levels<br>Anorexia |

| | | |
|---|---|---|
| 21 | The woman came to Saul and when she saw he was terrified she said to him 'Your servant has listened to you; I have taken my life in my hand and have listened to what you have said to me. | The medium is quite sympathetic to Saul |
| 22 | Now therefore you also listen to your servant. Let me set a morsel of bread before you. Eat that you may have strength when you go on your way. | She urges him to eat She wants to nurse him back to health |
| 24 | He refused and said 'I will not eat'. But his servants together with the woman urged him and he listened to their words. The women then slaughtered a fatted calf and fed this to Saul together with some cakes. | Food refusal; The medium and his soldiers try and make him eat Good food is the answer |

The medium in her initial encounter with Saul is very worried that Saul is an *agent provocateur* because being a medium was a crime carrying a punishment of death. However, biblical commentators such as Fokkelman (1986) and Gordon comment that she ends up assuming almost a nursing role for Saul by trying to get some food into him to revive his strength. Such a role implies that those courtiers around Saul at the time must have thought he was quite ill.

Saul's most critical mental symptoms appear in his discussions with the dead Samuel. The story of the medium being able to bring up Samuel from the dead may or may not be true, and Saul certainly seems to have been talking to someone. If this was truly Samuel, then this would have been a case of necromancy since Samuel was dead. However, by the time of the Talmud and the great rabbis of the Middle Ages, necromancy such as this began to be questioned; thus Rosenberg (p. 235) summarises their opinions:

> *Rav Hai Gaon* and *Rav Saadia Gaon* also deny the validity of necromancy, and adopt a more plausible explanation in the light of the scriptures. They claim that the almighty resurrected Samuel to convey to Saul notice of his impending doom. When the woman saw Samuel rising from the grave, she was actually startled for she had not expected this to occur. *Abravanel* adopts a strange system, that Samuel's body was occupied by a demon, who spoke for him but his soul could not be conjured to earth by witchcraft. *Maimonides,* one of the greatest Jewish thinkers, and also a physician to the King of Egypt, *explained that Saul was a victim of hallucinations,* rather than hearing Samuel via necromancy through the medium. His constant thoughts concerning his future caused him to imagine that Samuel was speaking to him and prophesying his fate.

The present author is happy to be in the company of Maimonides and also shares his view that Saul was the victim of auditory hallucinations. Similar thoughts have appeared in the more modern literature. Thus one commentator, Alexander Heidel (1945), suggested the whole episode may have been 'a demonic delusion' and although he discusses the possibility of it being an apparition, he appears to be one of the few OT scholars who, like the present author, suggest the episode was delusional, although Heidel did not imply that this was the result of any mental illness.

Today, if anyone with a known mental illness on a psychiatric ward is observed having a conversation with someone who is not physically present, then the immediate inference is of a person responding to voices (auditory hallucinations). The sight of patients muttering to themselves is a common scenario on any psychiatric ward. Might this be what is happening to Saul?

The voice of Samuel is punitive, saying 'the Lord has torn the Kingdom out of your hand' (28[17]) and a reason for this punishment is also given in terms of disobedience and sin. [18]'Because you did not obey the voice of the Lord and carry out his fierce wrath against Amelak'. There are also morbid thoughts of death: [19]'tomorrow you and your sons shall be with me', meaning that Saul and his sons will be killed in the forthcoming battle. Pessimistic voices of a punitive type and having thoughts of death are typical of psychotic depression. Thus DSM-5, in its description of psychotic depression, states 'The psychotic specifier indicates the presence of either delusions or hallucinations (typically auditory)'. Most commonly, the content of the delusions or hallucinations is consistent with depressive themes. Such 'mood-congruent' psychotic features include delusions of guilt (e.g. of being responsible for illness in a loved one), delusions of deserved punishment (e.g. of being punished because of a moral transgression or some personal inadequacy), and nihilistic delusions (e.g. of the world or personal destruction). The content of the message Samuel delivers is consistent with this.

In support of the suggestion that this is all in a severe depression, several other depressive symptoms are also mentioned in this passage. Thus Saul also shows:

- severe anxiety with tachycardia – [5]'afraid and his heart trembled greatly';
- negative thoughts – [19]'The Lord will give Israel along with you into the hands of the Philistines';
- a distressed/depressed state – [16]'I am in great distress';
- weakness – [20]'no strength in him';
- anorexia with food refusal – [24]'He refused and said I will not eat';
- hysterical collapse – [20]'Immediately Saul fell full length on the ground';
- severe anxiety – [20]'he was filled with fear'.

In Table 6.2 Saul's depressive symptoms at Endor are matched with the definition of depression given in DSM-5.

To summarise, Saul has seven out of nine key symptoms for major depression: depressed mood, decreased appetite, agitation, loss of energy, feelings of inappropriate guilt, indecisiveness and thoughts of death. The episode fulfils criteria for major depression. There are also his auditory hallucinations and so this also qualifies for the psychotic specifier and hence the condition is psychotic depression. Job also suffers from psychotic depression and this sub-type is described in Chapter 2, on Job, on pages 46–48.

With the aid of hindsight and our present-day knowledge of psychotic depression it may be possible to speculate on what might have actually happened at Endor. Thus Saul was observed by his soldiers to be disturbed and troubled on the eve of battle. He was not eating, was distressed and was throwing himself hysterically to the ground. He may have been observed

**Table 6.2** DSM major depression compared with Saul's symptoms at Endor

| DSM major depression | The séance at Endor, 1 Sam 28 |
| --- | --- |
| The DSM system requires at least five of the following nine symptoms within a two-week period, and at least one of the five has to be depressed mood or diminished interest/pleasure (anhedonia) | |
| (1) Depressed mood (feels sad or empty, is tearful) | [15]I am in great distress |
| (2) Diminished interest/pleasure | – |
| (3) Weight loss | [22] Eat that you may have strength when you go on your way. He refused and said, 'I will not eat'. |
| (4) Insomnia or hypersomnia | – |
| (5) Psychomotor agitation or retardation | [20] Immediately Saul fell full length to the ground filled with fear because of the words of Samuel |
| (6) Fatigue/loss of energy | [20] There was no strength in him |
| (7) Feelings of worthlessness or guilt | [18] Because you did not obey the voice of the Lord and did not carry out his fierce wrath against Amalek. Therefore the Lord has done this thing to you today |
| (8) Trouble concentrating | [15] God has turned away from me and answers me no more, either by prophets or by dreams; so I have summoned you to tell me what to do. [Indecisiveness] |
| (9) Recurrent thoughts of death or suicide | The voice of Samuel who is dead says in [19] 'Tomorrow you and your sons will be with me' |

talking to himself, but in reality was responding to his own depressive auditory hallucinations, as any person with psychotic depression might do. The soldiers around Saul were alarmed at his deteriorated mental condition. How could a King who was so disturbed lead them into battle? Initially he sought help from God but there was no response so his soldiers took him to the nearest available 'healer', who happened to be a medium.

Together with his soldiers she tried to get some food into him, in the hope that this would restore him to health, making him fit for the forthcoming battle. Perhaps this was the original story: a fit of anxiety and depression in a top military commander before the major battle – probably not an uncommon tale in the history of warfare. Thus some 3000 years later, in 1967, when the descendants of the ancient Israelites, the modern Israelis, were once more at war with their neighbours, the Arabs presumably descendants of the ancient Philistines, the Israeli chief of staff, General Yitzhak Rabin, was totally incapacitated, to the point of incoherence, immediately before the Six Day War. General Rabin, unlike King Saul, recovered just before the battle and went on to enjoy a victory that helped secure the survival of the modern state of Israel (Krauthammer, 2007).

## The death of Saul by suicide

Suicide is known complication of bipolar disorder: around 15% of those with the condition end their lives by suicide. Saul's suicide is important to the extent that it is described in three separate books of the Bible. In essence, he was injured by the Philistine archers and asked his armour bearer to kill him. When his armour bearer refused, Saul fell on his own sword. Soon afterwards his armour bearer also fell on his own sword. Both suicides are discussed at length in the suicide chapter, on pages 236–240.

## Summary of Saul's psychiatric episodes and the overall diagnosis

Saul was the first King of Israel and his life and mental disorder are set out in the first Book of Samuel. These events occurred more than 3000 years ago but there is good evidence that writing existed at the time and some records were made contemporaneously, although the versions we have today may not have reached their final redacted form until the Babylonian exile some 500 years later. Nevertheless, sufficient details of Saul's mental aberrations are preserved within the text to permit modern diagnostic criteria such as DSM-5 to be applied to reach a psychiatric diagnosis. Thus the biblical text records Saul having at least 10 separate episodes of illness and Figure 6.1 shows his life chart.

(1)  The first episode of mania: ecstasy with the prophets (1 Sam 10$^{5-15}$)
(2)  The first episode of depression: an evil spirit of the Lord (16$^{14}$)
(3)  Further episodes of depression: David plays his harp many times (16$^{23}$)
(4)  Mixed episode comprising severe jealousy (18$^{6-12}$) with depression – 'an evil Spirit from the Lord' (18$^{10}$) – and raving associated with the attempted murder of David
(5)  paranoid depression (evil spirit, 19$^9$) and another murderous attack on David (19$^{8-10}$)
(6)  The second episode of mania: Saul strips naked (19$^{19-25}$)
(7)  Irritable depression: Saul's attempted murder of Jonathan (20$^{30-33}$)
(8)  A further paranoid episode: the massacre of the priests of Nob (22$^{7-13}$)
(9)  The seance at Endor: psychotic depression (28$^{16-25}$)
(10) Suicide at Mt Gilboa.

Saul's illness probably starts with a first episode of mania and as mania is an uncommon disorder, it was probably unknown to the scribes of ancient Israel, who place it in the context of epidemic hysteria, a condition with which they may have had greater familiarity. Ambelas (1987) has demonstrated that most episodes of mania are triggered by life events – in Saul's case these life events would have been his anointment to the throne by Samuel, his promotion from peasant farmer to King and the accompanying house move from the farm to the palace.

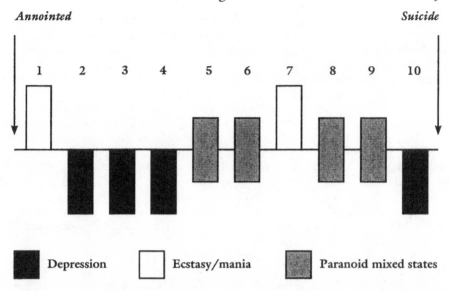

**Figure 6.1** Saul's episodes of mental disturbance, in the order given in I Samuel. 1, first episode of ecstasy ($10^{10}$); 2, first episode of depression ($16^{14}$); 3 and 4, further episodes of depression ($16^{23}$); 5, Saul throws a spear at David, mixed paranoid episodes ($18^{11}$); 6 ($19^{10}$); 7, second episode of ecstasy/mania ($19^{19}$); 8, Saul tries to kill Jonathan, paranoid mixed ($20^{30}$); 9, massacre at Nob, paranoid mixed episode ($22^7$); 10, depression at Endor ($28^{16}$); suicide on Mt Gilboa ($31^{1-5}$)

The second episode of mania (illness episode 6 above) occurs in the latter part of his reign, as Saul is pursuing David across the desert, and this was preceded almost immediately by a depressive episode. Like the first episode of mania, it is placed within the context of epidemic hysteria, with Saul's men also entering into trance-like states, so Saul's mania assumes the appearance of prophetic ecstasy. Some scholars suggest there were two separate episodes of 'ecstasy'; others that these are two descriptions of the same event but deriving from different documentary traditions. These episodes appear to fulfil DSM-5 criteria for mania.

Saul's depressions are all briefly described as him being possessed by an 'evil spirit of the Lord' (episodes 2, 3 and 4). As melancholia itself gradually became more widely recognised as a mental illness, later rabbis, scholars and physicians have equated the 'evil spirit' with his melancholic episodes. They were attributed to God and responded well to music therapy. Saul's depressions remit, but only to recur again, a pattern consistent with both recurrent depression and bipolar disorder.

The final episode of depression (episode 9) occurs when Saul consults the medium at Endor and hears the voice of Samuel. The content of this voice is both critical and punitive and contains thoughts of death. In modern psy-chiatric parlance these experiences would be called 'auditory hallucinations with mood-congruent psychotic features', because the themes expressed are consistent with his current mood, which was one of depression. Other features of depression such as weakness and anorexia with food refusal appear in this episode, which fulfils DSM-5 criteria for major depression.

More problematic from a diagnostic aspect are the two episodes where Saul hurls a spear first at David (episodes 4 and 5) and later at his own son Jonathan (episode 7). The attack on Jonathan seems to occur while Saul is paranoid, believing that Jonathan's loyalty has switched to David. However, both attacks are quite of character for Saul: they occur during times when he is said to be raving or prophesying; the violence is impulsive and not planned, and so probably occurs during episodes of illness. These may have been episodes of mixed affective states, dysphoric mania or paranoid irritable depressions and their dangerousness places Saul's illness at the more severe or forensic range of psychiatric disorder.

The jealousy and paranoia directed at David are understandable, as they occur in the context of intense political rivalry. However, the delusions of paranoid conspiracy directed at his own troops (episode 8) are less rational and suggest a more generalised paranoid state. Similarly, the massacre of the priests of Nob (also episode 8) seems to be out of character for a monarch who seemingly respects the priesthood and takes great care to observe even minor cultic festivals such as the new moon. While this murderous act may reflect no more than the whim of a blood-thirsty tyrant, the evidence points to a paranoid state at the time. Had he been mentally well, such a terrible crime would have been quite out of character. The change from depression to paranoia may be an age-related phenomenon. Thus with increasing age, paranoia features more prominently in many mental illnesses and it is possible that earlier possession by the 'evil spirit' or depressions responsive to music therapy later became paranoid depressive episodes – sometimes ac-companied by murderous rage. Saul's tragic end in suicide is characteristic of manic depression, with at least one in six sufferers taking their own life.

The detail provided in the Bible for most *individual episodes* is sparse and insufficient to be certain about diagnosis. Although a differential diagnosis (i.e. a set of alternative diagnoses) is possible for some of the individual episodes described above, only a diagnosis of bipolar affective disorder can explain *the totality* of his episodes under the umbrella of a single entity.

Saul's bizarre mental states have fascinated historians from the earliest times and many scholars, rabbis and psychiatrists have offered alternative diagnoses. Perhaps the first to throw his hat into the ring was the Roman Jewish historian Josephus, who proposed he was the victim of demoniacal possession – perhaps consistent with Roman theories of insanity at the time. Rabbi Jonathan Ben Uzziel (a disciple of Hillel in the 1st century CE) seems to have been the first to diagnose insanity and liken him to people with mental illness. Many later rabbis correctly identified his depressive spells as melancholia and these include Rashi and Maimonides, both of whom also recognised his insane spells but failed to make a link between the depression and the mania. In the modern era, Saul seems to have aroused the interest of several psychoanalysts, who have come up with a variety of different opinions. A few biblical scholars have taken interest and R. P. Gordon, a professor of Hebrew at Cambridge, thought he might have had meningitis, as well as insanity. He based his argument on the Arabic word *barsan*, meaning insanity (used instead of the Hebrew *arom*, nakedness in the MT), and he traces the possible origins of the English words 'sanity' and 'insanity'. Thus in the Babylonian Targum the word *Barsan* is similar to the ancient aramaic *senu* and the Syriac *sanya* meaning mad and to the Arab word *sana*, associated with insanity. These ancient terms are probably the origin of the Latin word *sana*, meaning mind, and the later English words 'sanity' and 'insanity'.

Littman (1981), a Canadian psychoanalyst, focused on Saul's paranoia in his article entitled 'King Saul: persecutor or persecuted?', and thought that his paranoia was fully justified given the politics of the royal palace at the time as well as the parlous position of ancient Israel, which he then likened to the dangerous position that modern Israel has with the same neighbours. Huisman (2007) thought that Saul's problem was one of depression as a result of 'occupational stress', as he had to face a huge and well armed Philistine army with very inadequate resources. Finally, A. Sims, a recent past President of the Royal College of Psychiatrists, suggested manic depression but equivocated in making a firm diagnosis, thinking the evidence in the text was insufficient to justify this. The present author concurs that this

**Table 6.3** Opinions on Saul's insanity through the ages

| *Name* | *Opinion* |
| --- | --- |
| Josephus (historian, 1st century CE) | Demoniacal possession |
| R. Ben Uzziel (disciple of Hillel, 1st century CE) | Insanity |
| Rashi (rabbinical scholar, 11th century, France) | Madness |
| Maimonides (physician/rabbi, 12th century, Spain) | Melancholia |
| Tanahum ha-Yerushalmi (rabbi, 13th century) | Depression, epilepsy |
| Preuss (physician, 20th century, Germany) | Melancholia, epilepsy |
| Zilboorg (psychoanalyst, 20th-century USA) | Melancholia |
| Rowley (OT scholar, 20th century, UK) | Mad fits |
| Littman (psychoanalyst, 1981) | Justifiable paranoia |
| Gordon (OT scholar, 1987) | ? Meningitis/insanity |
| Brasset (psychoanalyst, 1984) | Manic depression |
| Huisman (psychiatrist, 2007, Sweden) | Occupational stress |
| Sims (psychiatrist, 2010, UK) | ??Bipolar disorder |
| Stein (psychiatrist, present, UK) | Bipolar disorder |

References for Ben Uzziel, Rashi, and Maimonides and Tannahum ha Yerushalmi are in Rosenberg (1976) and other references are in the reference list.

is manic depression but argues it is too much to expect to find perfect, textbook accounts of psychiatric disorder in the literature of the ancient world. In Table 6.3, most of the published views on Saul's mental illness are summarised, but doubtless there are many more opinions in the religious and medical literature – after all, who can resist taking a guess at one of the great medical mysteries in the Bible?

Thus Israel's first King had bipolar disorder, the features of which are listed in Appendix 1 to this chapter. The combination of a monarch and bipolar disorder has occasionally repeated itself in history, usually with disastrous consequences for the individuals and the nations concerned, and in Appendix 2 some of the mad kings of history and their influence on their countries are considered. The consequences of Saul's illness on the nation of Israel and its history as well as its later influence on art, literature and music are described below.

## Saul, his illness and its influence on literature, art and music

Many famous authors and artists were drawn to Saul's tragic life and titles of their work suggest that his mental illness itself was the inspiration for their works. Unlike many other major figures of the Old Testament, Saul was accorded no particular significance in Christian Typology and thus his first appearance in the art and literature of the west starts after the Renaissance. A comprehensive list of all the artistic works about Saul is given in the *Encyclopaedia Judaica* (2007) and in the section below some of the more important works or those which allude to his mental illness are mentioned here. In Germany, the Meistersinger Hans Sachs wrote a play *Tragedia Koenig Sauls* (1557) while the French protestant dramatist captured his raving moods in the drama *Saul le Furieux* (1572). In England *The Tragedy of King Saul* (1703) was a verse play in five acts attributed to Joseph Trapp and Roger Boyle.

Later in the nineteenth century Lord Byron, himself a manic depressive, wrote three poems about Saul at Endor in his collection *Hebrew Melody* in 1815. These were later set to music by Isaac Nathan. Robert Browning also wrote a poem on Saul's visit to Endor. Other German tragedies include Gutzkow's *Koenig Saul* (1839) and Beck's *Saul* (1841). The more psychotic aspects of Saul's illness are described in Rainer Maria Rilke's poem *Saul unter der Propheten*. In the 1890's Andre Gide wrote a five act play entitled *Saul* which depicts Saul as an old man seeking to gratify his lust and Honegger added some incidental music to this drama. D. H. Lawrence also wrote a play *David*, originally entitled Saul in which the tragic king has a central role. Naum Isaakovich Shimkin, a Russian dramatist, wrote a drama called *Tsar Saul*. While the Dutch author, Israel Querido, wrote a tragedy *Saul en David* (1914), and there are numerous Yiddish books and plays on Saul listed in the Encyclopaedia Judaica.

In the World of Art, Rembrandt, himself a sufferer of very severe recurrent depressions, did two paintings of Saul, one in the Staedel Institute in Frankfurt and the other in the Hague Museum. In the latter work, the angry king is moved to tears and hides his face behind a curtain while David is absorbed in his music. The lives of David and Saul were also portrayed in a series of 41 lithographs by the Austrian artist Oskar Kokoschka. The front cover of this book has a picture of Saul and David painted by the Swedish artist Ernst Josephson, who later in life developed schizophrenia.

Musicians perhaps more than any other artists are sensitive to emotion, mood and depression, and so not surprisingly there are numerous musical works about Saul. An early keyboard work by Kuhnan *The Biblical Sonatas* (1700) alludes to his depressions as it is entitled *Der von David mittelst der musik curierte Saul*. Bononuni wrote *When Saul was King of Israel* (1722) as an anthem for the funeral of the Duke of Marlborough. Handel's oratorio *Saul* was first performed in London in 1739 and contains the *Death March of Saul* and this piece has entered the repertoire of standard funeral marches. Samuel Arnold composed an oratorio entitled the *Cure of Saul* in 1767 while Salieri left an unfinished oratorio called *Saulle*. Moussorgsky the famous Russian composer wrote a song for piano which was later orchestrated by Glazounov. Oratorios about Saul were also written by Hubert Parry and Rossini. Carl Nielson wrote an oratorio entitled *Saul og David*. Two more modern works include *The lamentation of Saul*, by Normal dello Joio (1954) based on D. H. Lawrence's play *David*, and Josef Tal's Concert opera *Saul at Endor*.

The fascination that Saul has held with the world of art and music must in part relate to his mental illness particularly his depression – probably because most of the writers and musicians who chose him as their subject were fellow sufferers. Themes such as his unexplained depressions, their relief through music, his therapeutic relationship with David which later turns sour through murderous political rivalry are of universal interest and provide motifs for many of these great works of art. Had Saul's illness been recognised at the time, or even worse had he been shunted off to some local mental hospital and silenced with medication, interest in his life story would have been minimal or non-existent. His illness was unrecognised at the time and so the full drama of his mysterious condition was allowed to play out on the Royal stage of ancient Israel, and so became a part of the Bible, a magnificent piece of literature. From a purely cultural perspective Saul may have been one of the most important manic depressives of all time.

## Appendix 1. Bipolar affective disorder

Arataeus of Cappadocia (2nd century CE) was probably the first to see mania and depression as different presentations of the same illness but this observation seems to have been lost to the medical profession for almost 2000 years. The more formal recognition that mania and depression were probably two sides of the same illness was not made until the 19th century, when Falret (1854) described *folie circulaire* and independently Baillerger (1854) wrote of *folie a double forme*. With such a late description of manic depression as a single entity it is not surprising that the post-exilic biblical redactors, the rabbis of the Talmud, and many later Old Testament scholars, failed to make any sort of link between Saul's phases of ecstasy together with his melancholia and his final suicide.

The DSM-5 criteria for bipolar I disorder represent the modern understanding of the classic manic-depressive disorder, differing from the classic description only to the extent that neither psychosis nor the lifetime experience of a major depressive episode is a requirement. However, the vast majority of individuals whose symptoms meet the criteria for a fully syndromal manic episode also experience major depressive episodes during the course of their lives.

Bipolar II disorder, requiring the lifetime experience of at least one episode of major depression and at least one hypomanic episode, is no longer thought to be a milder condition than bipolar I. This is because of the amount of time individuals spend in depression and because of the instability of mood, such that the disorder is typically accompanied by serious impairment in work and social functioning.

Bipolar disorder thus consists of two separate conditions, mania and depression, occurring in separate episodes in the same individual but at different times. Mixed affective states, which have features of both depression and mania, are common and may be severe. The presence of these illnesses was one of the lines of evidence used by Kraepelin to support his view that mania and depression are closely related illnesses, as they can seemingly occur together. A 'mixed affective episode' seems to have occurred when Saul hurls a spear at David, as he is both troubled by the 'evil spirit from the Lord' and is prophesying or raving at the same time. In the series of bipolar episodes studied by Perris, a predominantly manic colouring was present in 18%, a depressive picture in 26% but a mixed picture was most common, present in 54% of episodes (Perris, 1992). Depression is described in the appendix on Job (pages 66–74) and the syndrome of mania is described below.

## The features of mania

The main symptom of a manic illness is a change in mood, usually an elevation of mood, i.e. in the opposite direction to depression. Thus patients become elated, overly happy, excited and have an intense sense of 'well-being' which is quite out of keeping with personal circumstances. The elation may be accompanied by facetious joking, laughing, singing and a state of almost 'cheerful drunkenness'. It is distinguished from normal happiness by its intensity – it may last all day and night for several months on end without any break and the disinhibited behaviour and non-stop talk are inappropriate to the circumstances. If confronted, the patient may rapidly become irritable and bad tempered and occasionally even violent.

The predominant mood is not always elation, but may be aggressive or paranoid instead. In paranoid aggressive mania, patients may be quick to take offence and may react with outbursts of destructiveness, rage or even violence. Accompanying the mood changes there is increased motor activity, pacing, restlessness, increased energy, but all coherence and sense of the purposeful activity is lost. Sleep is poor or may be non-existent, with patients pacing up and down all night, much to the annoyance of their families.

Increased talkativeness (often to the point of being non-stop) is called 'pressure of speech', and this is characteristic of mania. Speech is not only profuse but also loud and any interruption may be met with irritability. Slang, rhymes and puns appear in the speech and these changes are known as clang associations. Characteristic of the speech disorder is 'flight of ideas', where the subject is talking non-stop and switches rapidly from one topic to another, albeit with some connection between the different topics.

In severe cases of mania there are also delusions of various types, with grandiose or religious themes predominating. The phrase 'prophetic frenzy', which occurs several times in the description of Saul's mania, conveys a picture of pressure of speech with flight of ideas accompanied by religious delusions. Such grandiose pictures accompanied by religiosity are found in mania today. Even though gross changes of behaviour are observed in manic subjects, the vast majority of those with mania have no insight into the fact that they are ill because in their state of elation they feel so happy that they cannot believe anything could possibly be wrong with them.

Manic patients also have marked degrees of disinhibition. They may spend their money with reckless abandon, which can result in financial catastrophe, and there is also increased sexual arousal in both male and female patients. Perhaps Saul's stripping naked in the desert is a manifestation of this feature. Patients may become overfamiliar, outspoken, abusive or even assaultive. When Saul hurls the spear at Jonathan he is abusive about Jonathan's mother and tries to assault Jonathan. Distractibility and poor concentration are also characteristic. Psychotic symptoms such as delusions and hallucinations occur in more than half the subjects but they are not as well formed as in schizophrenia. A change in personality during the acute episode is characteristic, but the personality usually reverts to normal between episodes. This character change is one possible explanation of the ancient riddle 'Is Saul also among the prophets?'

Hypomania is a milder condition; delusions and hallucinations are lacking and hospitalisation is not always necessary. The majority of patients with mania also suffer from depression and are said to be manic depressive but a small minority will only have repeated episodes of mania and are said to have unipolar mania. Saul, in common with most present-day sufferers, had many episodes of depression as well as his manic episodes and so qualifies for bipolar disorder. Because Saul's manic episodes seem to be fairly brief and he suffers frequently from depression, he fits best into the bipolar II group, but there is insufficient information to be certain of making the distinction between bipolar I and bipolar II in his case.

## Epidemiology, causation and treatment

Only the briefest account will be given here as such information is readily available in standard textbooks of psychiatry. The overall prevalence of bipolar I disorder is around 0.8% and for bipolar II disorder around 1.0%. The illness can start at any age but the peak age of onset for men is 18–25 years and is a little later for women. The majority of the psychoses starting after childbirth are bipolar in origin. Most cases have a relapsing and remitting course and on average patients will have around eight episodes in the 10 years following the initial episode. In Saul's case there are 10 documented episodes, but the text alludes to many more depressive phases because David is often called on to play music to soothe Saul's moods. There is a tendency for episodes to cluster around certain periods in the patient's life and in Saul's case such clustering seems to occur during the period when he is chasing David across the desert.

Both manic and depressive episodes will last some 3–6 months if untreated, but the illness usually resolves spontaneously with around 50% being better at 3 months and 93% by 2 years. Prophetic ecstasy alone, which results in a trance-like state, lasts for a few hours or a day at the most with reversion to normality the next day, and it is unlikely that the ancient scribes would have considered such a trivial episode as worth recording.

Bipolar disorder is a devastating condition and even with modern treatments takes a big toll on the lives of those who suffer from it, as well as their families. Wells *et al.* (1989) found that without adequate treatment a woman experiencing the onset of bipolar disorder in her mid-20s can expect, as a consequence of her bipolar disorder, to lose nine years of her life, 12 years of normal health, most of which would be in states of depression, and 14 years of major life activity, e.g. work, school or child raising. Thus even if Saul was only an 'average' case of bipolar II disorder, the effect of his illness on his ability to function as King would have been greatly impaired.

The cause of bipolar disorder is now thought to be mainly genetic and the condition often runs in families, with affected members appearing in successive generations. Modern treatments for mania include hospitalisation (usually on a compulsory basis), with the use of antipsychotic drugs to calm the patients down. Between episodes, drugs known as mood stabilisers (lithium, sodium valproate and others) are given to prevent relapses.

## Appendix 2. The other mad kings in history

A king holds a unique position in his nation, and so being both a king and a manic depressive is a rare but important historical coincidence. The king or the head of state wields a huge influence over his nation but just occasionally the manic depressive insanity of the ruler can change the course of a nation's history. There are only a few other examples in history where this unusual combination has occurred. Perhaps the best known of the mad kings was George III of England, but Philip V of Spain also seems to have had bipolar disorder. Another example of a manic depressive national leader was D.G. Monrad the 19th-century prime minister of Denmark, and each of these rulers and their illnesses will be briefly described below.

### King George III of England

The most famous of the mad kings of history must surely be George III of England and the account below is taken from the books on him by Ayling (1972) and Brooke (1972). That he developed serious mental illness in the latter part of his reign is not in question – but what is less well known is that when he was well he was a shrewd and astute politician, a patron of the arts and a founder of the Royal Academy of Arts, a patron of the Greenwich observatory and a supporter of the great astronomer Sir William Herschel. He took a great interest in the affairs of state and the decisions and personalities of all his ministers and wrote copious letters to all his ministers, civil servants and family all in his own hand. More is known about him than perhaps any other English monarch because his collected handwritten letters comprise 12 volumes which were edited by a contemporary historian Professor John Aspinall. In addition, his illnesses were treated by Dr James Willis, who kept a daily record of his moods and behaviour in a monumental work comprising of no fewer than 47 volumes.

Popular mythology has it that George III, in his insanity lost America but this is probably not true. The war against the American colonists was a popular one in England at the time because the Americans paid no taxes yet expected an administration and military protection and so this war was seen as a just cause in England. Many political and tactical errors were made by the British Government at the time but during the period 1766–1776 George III was sane and followed the advice (often unwisely) of his ministers. His mental illness had no part in the American debacle, and from the wider perspective of history the loss of America was probably inevitable.

George III was born on 4 June 1738 into the House of Hanover and when he was 23 years old George II, his grandfather, died on 25 October 1760, and so he assumed the throne. He was unmarried at the time, and as the Act of the Settlement forbade him from marrying a Catholic, a suitable Protestant princess had to be found.

This task was delegated to the Hanoverian representative in London, a certain Baron Gerlach Adolphe von Munchausen, who was the second cousin of the father of Karl Friedrich Hieronymus Baron von Munchausen of the eponymous 'Munchausen's syndrome' fame. Munchausen chose princesses from the province of Mecklenburg, which was next to Hanover, and from a short list of six German princesses the newly appointed George III selected Princess Charlotte of Mecklenburg-Strelitz to be his wife. In due course Princess Charlotte came to London and the two were married within a day of her arrival. The marriage appears to have been close and happy and blessed with no fewer than 15 children.

In 1765 at the age of 27 he developed his first episode of illness. There were bilious pains, a degree of paranoia, he complained of an 'ulcered mind, and indecisiveness'. He also had fever, sharp pains in the chest, hoarseness and coughing. Consumption (tuberculosis) was suspected but it was noted that the king's 'countenance and manner were a good deal estranged and he talked on several different subjects'. The king recovered but was alarmed by the episode and set in motion the Regency Act so that someone could take over from him in the event of illness or death.

He remained in good physical and mental health until the age of 50, when he developed what appears to have been a very severe episode of mania. The onset was in October 1788 again with a bilious attack and insomnia, but within five days he had 'agitation of spirits and delirium'. He went to a concert and one of his aides observed what today would be considered pressure of speech and flight of ideas. 'During the whole music he talked continually making frequent and sudden transitions from one subject to another: but I observed no incoherence in what he said, nor any mask of false perception...'. Sir George Baker, the president of the Royal College of Physicians, was called in to be his doctor and wrote that 'he had delirium, a hurry of spirits and incessant loquaciousness until he became hoarse'. Such symptoms are typical of mania.

At a family dinner he became positively delirious 'the queen could hardly contain herself and sobbed hysterically. The prince burst into tears and the princesses were in misery'. Baker was summoned once more and found the king 'under an entire alienation of mind'. The queen said 'the king's eyes were like black currant jelly, the veins in his face had swelled, the sound of his voice was dreadful and he spoke till he was exhausted – while the foam ran out of his mouth.' It was during this illness that the Prince of Wales, took over at Windsor, while Pitt who was the prime minister at the time, began to turn his thoughts towards carrying on the Government through a Regency appointment.

By the end of November seven doctors had been consulted but eventually the Reverend Francis Willis and his son were selected to care for the king. On meeting Dr Willis the King knew immediately that this meant he was deemed insane and said to Dr Willis 'Sir, your dress and appearance bespeaks you of the church, do you belong to it?' Dr Willis replied 'I did formerly but lately I have attended chiefly to Physic' The king replied with emotion and agitation ' I am sorry for this. You have quitted a profession I have always loved and you have embraced one I most heartedly detest'. Dr Willis then proceeded to treat the king with all the known remedies of the day – the straight waistcoat, the use of plasters of cantharides, and of mustard applied to cause blistering of his legs, and concoctions of various emetics and purgatives, which were quite sufficient to make anyone thoroughly ill.

Eventually, after 17 weeks, his illness resolved and he reverted to complete normality. However, there were at least four further attacks of severe mania – in 1801, 1804, 1811 and finally 1820 – but up until 1801 he had probably lost no more than six months in a state of severe mental illness. Around 50 years ago, Hunter and Macalpine (1969) proposed that King George III suffered from a rare metabolic disorder known as variegate porphyria however this hypothesis is no longer accepted on both psychiatric and bio-chemical grounds as porphyria is only associated with very mild disturbances of mental equilibrium whereas George III was grossly manic (Levy 1970).

The final years of George III were sad. He lived alone at Windsor and separate from his wife. He suffered from capricious moods, arranged imaginary concerts and at times was observed to talk with imaginary angels. At other times he would lie in a state of silent torpor for weeks on end. In 1817 he became deaf and by 1818 he could no longer walk and his wife died that year. Finally at the age of 81 he had another attack of delirious mania and talked incessantly for a period of 58 hours non-stop and then gradually faded away dying of old age and exhaustion.

As with Saul, the diagnosis was clear cut and the illness was undoubtedly manic depression. In his attacks, George III was probably very much more severely disturbed than Saul was. His manic episodes were prolonged and very severe and would certainly qualified as bipolar I disorder. Their effect on the kingdom, however, was very much less. Thus the illnesses of King George III were at least recognised as insanity at the time and by this stage the English Royal family had become a constitutional monarchy in contrast to the absolute monarchy of ancient Israel. An English king, even if sane, had only limited influence on a political decisions, and if insane could be removed from the political scene. The adoption of the Act of the Regency ensured a smooth handover to his son George IV, long before his death. Thus England was never exposed to the rulings of a mad King.

In Saul's case his illness was unrecognised at the time; he was thought to be a prophet. His replacement as head of state was a complicated and an almost sordid affair with David behaving like a usurper yet at the same time he was rescuing Israel from the whims of a madman. Much of the second half of the first Book of Samuel is concerned with justifying the removal of Saul from power, which must have been a national imperative at the time because Saul was insane, The reasons for his removal given in the Bible, are very different; he disobeys Yahweh but this is for two quite odd and minor offences – not waiting for Samuel for seven days and not killing King Agag – but the psychiatry suggests the real reason may have been his insanity .

## The Madness of Philip V of Spain

The Spanish royal family was plagued with insanity, perhaps more so than any other European monarchy. The grandfather of Philip V was Louis XIV and he told Philip 'You yourself are witness of the nervous disorder originating in the indolence of Kings your predecessors, and take warning by way of their example'. Philip's own son Ferdinand also later developed manic depression. Philip V was a somber hard working man who assumed the throne in 1700 and reigned until 1746 and the account below is taken from Kamen (2001) and Green (1993). He was very highly sexed and constantly at the side of his first wife Marie Louise of Savoy. Unfortunately she died at the age of 26 but Philip V did not wait long before remarrying an Italian princess called Elizabeth Farnese the daughter of the Duke of Parma.

His first serious illness came in 1717 when he complained of being consumed by a fierce internal fire and thought the sun was sending a piercing ray through his body. Nothing wrong was found and his physicians concluded he was delusional. The French ambassador thought he was making too great a sexual demand on his wife

'The King is wasting away through making excessive use of the queen. He is utterly worn out'. He developed hypochondriachal delusions, thought he would die immediately, summoned his confessor and drew up his will. He had many more episodes of melancholy and gradually his wife Elizabeth Farnese took over ruling the kingdom, a task which she greatly enjoyed. In 1723 he developed a bout of religious mania, and in 1724 he thought he was unfit to be a King and abdicated in favour of his son Prince Luis. However the abdication was to be short lived as Prince Luis died soon afterwards and so Philip V once more resumed the throne.

He became seriously ill in 1727, at times lethargic and depressed at other times excitable being violent towards his doctors and his confessor.

The queen tried to curb his religious devotions which she thought to be excessive, which he responded to by beating her. He suffered from delusions that he could not walk because his feet were of different sizes. He was obviously mentally ill with some sort of chronic psychotic condition and help was urgently needed (Green, 1993, pp. 168–171).

Elizabeth Farnese, the queen who was the wife of Philip V was of Italian origin. She invited the most a famous castrati singer of the day, Carlo Broschi later to be known as Farinelli to Madrid to sing for her husband In the middle of a hot summer afternoon in 1737 Philip V was in one of his profound depressions and he could not even get out of bed to listen to the concert. It is said that on that day as the clear tones of Farinelli's voice rose through the air they penetrated to the bedroom where the afflicted Philip lay. The divine voice of the famous castrati immediately resuscitated the King who snapped out of his depression and once more attended to his routine work as a King. Astonished by the therapeutic effects of Farinelli's singing the King and Queen demanded he sing for them every day.

Soon he was named as *Musico de Camara* of their majesties and given the Title *Familiar Cridao mio* (my personal assistant) and he entered the employ of the Royal household. He had to sing to the King every day thereafter but had to fit in with the King's strange daily routine Thus singing would start at midnight to the accompaniment of a trio of musicians. He was not released from singing duties until 5 a.m. when the King ate his supper. Usually it was the same five arias every single day for more than 11 years on end although Farinelli's diary revealed that he sang from a repertoire of a large number of songs. Sometimes when the singing was over 'the King threw himself into such freaks and howlings that all possible means were taken to prevent people from witnessing his follies' (after Green 1993, p. 173).

Farinelli's position in the royal court rose and he was given charge of all royal musical events, palace spectacles and entertainments for the Royal family and he became friends with the Royal children The strange story of Farinelli and King Philip V of Spain has recently been turned into a play 'Farinelli and the King'. The parallel between the manic depression of King Philip V of Spain and King Saul rests on the therapeutic effects that music brought to bear on their depressions. Both Saul and King Philip V were rich and powerful monarchs and they took their musician therapists into the Royal household almost to become members of the Royal family. At least initially, both these Kings seemed to have loved their musicians and did not let them go. No doubt this related to the therapeutic benefits that music bestowed on to these depressed monarchs. Both Farinelli and David rose in their positions in the Royal Household, although the relationship with David later soured as Saul became increasingly paranoid later in his life. The Bible tells us why Saul fell out with David, but tells us little of why David entered the Royal household in the first place and once installed assumed a much favoured position. Perhaps psychiatry can help here: it was Saul's depressions which give David the key to open the door of the royal household, and it is through the repeated beneficial therapy of music on Saul's depressions that the bond between Saul and David blossomed.

## The life of D. G. Monrad – the manic depressive prime minister of Denmark

D.G. Monrad was one of the most brilliant yet enigmatic prime ministers of Denmark. Like Saul he suffered from manic depression and like Saul his illness was florid even while he held high offices of state. Like ancient Israel, Denmark in the 19th century was engaged in a bitter territorial dispute with its more powerful neighbour Prussia, and the defeat of Denmark which occurred during Monrad's tenure as prime minister in the Schleswig Holstein War of 1864 at the hands of Bismarck led to a division of Denmark and a substantial loss of territory. Mental instability consequent on Monrad's manic depression played a major role in him making the wrong political and military decisions at the time. A detailed account of Monrad's life and the influence his illness had on the affairs of state is given by Johan Schioldann-Nielsen (1988) in his book *The Life of D.G. Monrad 1811 – 1887: Manic Depressive Disorder and Political Leadership*.

Monrad was born in Copenhagen in 1811, the son of a lawyer who himself had multiple hospital admissions for insanity, and his two sisters also suffered from melancholia. A sickly child but academically brilliant he studied theology, Hebrew, Arabic and Sanskrit. At the age of 18 he was hospitalised for 'hereditary delirium', and then again at 21 for 'furious delirium' and at 23 he was once more admitted for 'pervasive lassitude, headache, irritability and diminished appetite' and he wrote to a friend that he had 'total lack of strength'. During his student years he continued to suffer from melancholic bouts and was anxious he would become insane like his father. As a young man he wrote two plays on biblical themes 'The Doubt' which concerned Jephath and the tragic sacrifice of his daughter and the second entitled 'King Saul' which focused on Saul's suicide indicating that he may have likened his own mood swings to those of the biblical King.

Monrad recovered from these early illnesses, got married and became a county parson and later a Bishop. He then developed an interest in political journalism and soon became involved in the democracy movements sweeping through Europe at the time and eventually entered Parliament. A colleague at the time, A. Andrae, wrote that Monrad would 'become the absolute master and do the most crazy things'. Thus as soon as he was appointed foreign minister in a bout of elation he made the surprising decision to exile himself and his family to Paris for almost a year. It is likely that most of the time he was a minister and prime minister he was in a state of mild chronic hypomania. A fellow MP, S. Hogsbro, wrote 'He is a matchless workhorse, who instead of getting tired gets merrier under a workload which would rapidly overwhelm others'. During this period he delivered one-sixth of all the speeches to the Danish Parliament (820 out of a total of 5,000).

It was during his period as prime minister that Denmark was challenged by Prussia on the vexed issue of Schleswig Holstein as both these provinces had mixed Danish and German populations. Bismarck, the Prussian Chancellor was trying through both political and military means to unite all the German speaking statelets of Central Europe into a single nation. During political negotiations which preceded the 1864 War, Monrad assumed a very rigid stance being seriously over-optimistic about the strengths of the Danish position and army and so diplomacy soon gave over to war.

During the Danish Wars of 1864, Monrad made many errors of judgment – possibly due to his elated state. Thus the Prussian army had occupied Schleswig and Jutland and the Danish army of 30,000 men had retreated virtually intact to the fortified town of Dueppels. Monrad blandly insisted the fortress should be held at all costs defying all the expert advice of his Generals who foresaw rapid defeat. When the Germans attacked, there was a massacre of around 6,000 Danish soldiers being killed in the first hour and a further 3,000 being taken prisoner. Monrad was probably in a strange elated mood when he heard the news of the disaster, because he is said to have roared with laughter. In later years he regretted his decision to hold the fortress at Dueppels in the face of the superior German forces.

An armistice was offered at a conference in London, but despite the slaughter he did not make an agreement and wrote to a friend that 'he was still rather confident but cannot tell why'. Instead he wrote a grandiose letter in the name of the King of Denmark to King Carl of Sweden seeking a Nordic union 'In the annals of history this initiative shall encircle Your Majesties name with an eternal wreath.... It is the loss of Norway in 1814 which has created Schleswig Holsteinism. It is only the political unity of Scandinavia which will destroy it. It is with state bodies as with the celestial bodies. They exert a force of attraction relative.... To accomplish dynastic unity the two royal houses must be amalgamated. It could perhaps be arranged the following way. On behalf of my eldest son, Crown Prince Christian Frederick Wilhelm, I ask your Majesties daughter's Louise Josephine hand in marriage...'. The Swedish envoy D. Bjorstjern did not know whether the whole fantastic scheme was serious or in jest. Ministers at the time noted that Monrad was unwell and Vedel, one of his ministers, wrote 'Monrad is indiscrete, he is not safe, his position is appalling ... but furthermore he is seriously deteriorating and I believe no longer has the proper use of his faculties'. All this was going on while Denmark was about to lose one-third of its territory.

Meanwhile at the Armistice negotiations, Denmark had to accept a bitter and crushing defeat in which she had to relinquish not only the Duchies of Holstein and Lanenberg, but the whole of the old crownland of Schleswig, in all two-fifths of Danish Territory and one-third of her population - around one million people of whom around one-fifth were Danes. Holstein was permanently incorporated into Germany but the province of Schleswig was returned back to Denmark after the German defeat in World War I. Historians have speculated whether the war might have been avoided through negotiation, and whether if Monrad had been in a more sane frame of mind Denmark might not have lost half its territory and would have been a much bigger country today.

The parallel with King Saul lies in the deranged leadership which both Saul and Monrad showed at critical times in the history of their nations. Saul was probably psychotically depressed before the battle of Mt. Gilboa where he sustained a massive defeat and lost territory to the Philistines. Monrad lost half of Denmark and conducted the war and the peace negotiations following his defeat whilst in a state of hypomania. The bipolar illnesses of these rulers may have contributed to their disastrous military defeats, the heavy loss of life in these wars, and the loss of territory for both ancient Israel and nineteenth century Denmark.

# References

Ackroyd, P.R. (1971) *The First Book of Samuel*. Cambridge University Press, Cambridge.
Ambelas, A. (1987) Life events and mania. A special relationship? *British Journal of Psychiatry*. 150: 235–240.
American Psychiatric Association (2013) *Diagnostic and Statistical Manual*, 5th edition (DSM-5). Washington, DC: American Psychiatric Publishing.
Ayling, S. (1972) *George the Third*. London: Collins.
Baillerger, J.G.F. (1854) Folie à double forme, *Annales médico-psychologiques du système nerveux*.
Bayer, B. (2007) Saul. *Encyclopaedia Judaica* Vol. 18 pp. 78–83 Eds Skolnik F. and Berenbaum M. Keter Publishing House Jerusalem in association with MacMillan New York: Thomsen Gale.
Brooke J. (1972) *King George III*. London: Constable.
Eichrodt, W. (1967) *The theology of the Old testament Vol II p55* Philadelphia: Westminster.
Erkkilä, J., Punkanen, M., Fachner, J., *et al.* (2011) Individual music therapy for depression: randomised controlled trial *British Journal of Psychiatry* 199 (2) 132–139.
Falret, J. (1854) Mémoire sur la folie circulaire, forme de la maladie mentale caractérisée par la reproduction successive et régulière de l'état maniaque, de l'état mélancolique, et d'un intervalle lucide plus ou moins prolongé, *Bulletin de l'Académie impériale de médecine 19: 382–400*.
Fokkelman, J.P. (1986) *Narrative Art and Poetry in the Books of Samuel. Volume II. The Crossing Fates*, p.621. Maastricht, Netherlands: Van Gorcum Assen.
Green, V.H.H.,(1993) *The Madness of Kings: Personal Trauma and the Fate of Nations*. Strood Gloucestershire: Alan Sutton Publishing.
Gordon, R.P. (1986) *I and II Samuel: A Commentary*. Carlyle: Paternoster Press.
Gordon, R.P. (1987) Saul's meningitis according to Targum 1 Samuel 19²⁴, *Vetus Testamentum* 37, 39–49.
Gunn, D.M. (1980) *The fate of King Saul;* Sheffield: Journal for the Study of the Old Testament Press.
Heidel, A. (1946) *The Gilgamish Epic and Old Testament Parallels*, p. 189. Chicago: Chicago University Press.
Hertzberg, H.W. (1964) *I and II Samuel. A commentary*. Old Testament Library. Trans. J.S. Bowden from German. Philadelphia, Westminster.
Huisman, M. (2007) King Saul, work-related stress and depression. *Journal of Epidemiology and Community Health* 61(10):890.
Hunter, R. and Macalpine, I. (1969) *George III and the Mad Business*, Allen Lane, Penguin Press, London.
Josephus, F. (1987) *The Works of Josephus. Complete and unabridged*. Translated by William Whiston. Peabody Massachusets: Hendrickson Publishers.
Kamen, H. (2001) *Philip V of Spain. The King who Reigned Twice*. Newhaven. Yale University Press.
Krauthammer, C. (2007) Prelude to the six day war *Washinton Post*, 18 May.
Levy, R. (1970) Hanover's Complaint. *British Journal of Psychiatry*, 117, 106–107.
Littman, S.K. (1981) King Saul: Persecutor or Persecuted. *Canadian Journal of Psychiatry* 26:464–7.
McCarter, P. K. (1980) *I. Samuel. A new translation, Notes and Commentary. Anchor Bible Series, 8.* Garden City, New York: Doubleday and Co.
Mowat, R.R. (1966) *Morbid Jealousy and Murder*. London: Tavistock.
Noth (1960) *The History of Israel*. Translated by P.R. Ackroyd from the German New York: Harper and Row.
Perris, C. (1993) Bipolar–unipolar Distinction. Chapter 5 pp. 57–75 in *Handbook of Affective Disorders* Ed. E.S. Paykel. Cambridge: Cambridge University Press.

Preuss, J. (2004) *Biblical and Talmudic Medicine* Translated and edited by Fred Rosner from the Original *Biblisch und Talmudishes Medizin (1911)*. New York: Rowan and Littlewood and Jason Aronson.

Rosenberg, A.J. (1976) *The Book of Samuel I. A New English Translation of the Text, Rashi and a Commentary Digest.* New York: Judaica Press.

Rost, L. (1926) Die Uberlieferung von der Thronnachfolge Davids *Beitrage zur Wisenschaft von Attens und neuen Testament* 3/6. Stuttgart: Kolhammer Rost, pp. 119–253.

Rowley, H.H. (1963) in Peake's Commentary on the Bible. Eds. Black, M. and Rowley, H.H. p. 327. London: Thomas Nelson and Son.

Schioldann-Nielsen, J. (1988) *The Life of D.G. Monrad, 1811 – 1887. Manic depressive disorder and political leadership.* Odense Denmark: Odense University Press.

*Shorter Oxford English Dictionary* (2007). Volume I. New York: Oxford University Press.

Sims, A. (2010) Religion and psychopathology: psychosis and depression. Ch. 3.3, pp. 253–270, in *Religion and Psychiatry: Beyond Boundaries* (eds P. Vergan H. Von Praag, J. Lopez-Ibor, J. Cox and D. Moussaoui). Chichester: John Wiley.

Thenius, O. (1842) *Die Bucker Samuels Kurzgefasstes exegetisches* Handbuch zume alten Testament 4. Leipzig: Weidmann 2nd edition, 1964.

Vriezen C. (1967) *The Religion of Ancient Israel.* Philadelphia: Westminster.

Wellhausen, J. (1871) *Der Text der Bucher Samuel is untersucht.* Gottingen: Vandenhoech und Ruprecht.

Wells, K.B., Steward, K., Hayes, R.D., *et al.* (1989) The functioning and wellbeing of depressed patients; results from the medical outcomes studies. *Journal of the American Medical Association* 262:914–919.

West, D.J. (1965) *Murder Followed by Suicide. An Inquiry Carried Out for the Institute of Criminology,* Cambridge: Harvard University Press.

Wilson, R.R. (1980) *Prophecy and society in Ancient Israel.* Philadelphia: Fortress Press.

World Health Organization (1992) *International Classification of Diseases. Tenth edition.* Geneva: WHO.

# Chapter 7

# Suicide, suicidal thoughts and self-mutilation in the Bible

## Introduction

More than a million people commit suicide worldwide each year and the problem of suicide is central to psychiatry. The topic is also very old and there are descriptions in the Egyptian literature which predate the Old Testament (OT) by many centuries. However, the OT is unique in presenting a collection of several case histories of suicide, suicidal thoughts and self-harm, all within the confines of a single volume. The OT views the topic with equanimity; there is no law in the Torah banning it, nor is there any blame or moral condemnation for the act. It was duly recorded by the scribes of the day when it occurred in a person of some importance, such as a king. In this brief introduction an account is given of how our attitudes to suicide have changed over the last three millennia.

A rather more substantive account of suicide in the ancient world is to be found in the Graeco-Roman literature and this has been studied by Van Hooff (1990), who provides an insight into how suicide was viewed by the Greeks from between the 5th and 3rd centuries BCE, a time which approximates to the post-exilic period when much of the OT was finally redacted. In addition, the book *A Noble Death: Suicide and Martyrdom Amongst Christians and Jews in Antiquity* (Droges and Talbot, 1992) also provides a valuable resource, from which parts of this review are drawn.

Life in the ancient world was a much more of a chance affair than today and so attitudes to death were far more fatalistic. Today, most people can expect to reach old age. The average life expectancy in the UK is around 85 for a man and 88 for a woman. Life expectancy in the ancient world is unknown but parish records, which start in the Middle Ages, suggest a life expectancy of around 28–30 years; this is unlikely to have been any better in biblical times. A premature death lurked round the corner for all, as a result of wars, famine, epidemics or some untreatable medical condition, or death in childhood. In such a world, a self-killing might be a painless way out and so neither the Bible nor the much larger Greek literature on suicide gives any suggestion of blame or moral condemnation. It was nevertheless a disturbing event and became the focus of much philosophical and ethical debate, just as it does today.

Suicide is not criticised in the OT or in the early history of Judaism but the Talmudic literature, which comes somewhat later, in the 4th to 8th centuries CE, does condemn suicide. Talmudic comments are reviewed by Siegel (1979). The first Talmudic criticism comes from *Avodah Zarah 19a* and it tells the tragic story of Rabbi Haninah ben Teradyon, one of the great sages of the 2nd century CE. He was arrested by the Romans for the crime of teaching the sacred texts and was sentenced to be burnt alive at the stake. To make his death even more horrible the Romans placed pieces of wood on his heart in order to prolong the process of dying. When the disciples of Rabbi Haninah saw his agony they urged him to open his mouth to allow the fire to kill him more quickly. He answered, 'It is better that he who gave my soul to me should take it from me than I should injure myself', and this has been taken to imply that the Talmud forbade suicide in most cases.

The actual laws about mourning and suicide are laid out in *Semahot,* a late post-Talmudic tract of the 8th century CE. A verdict of suicide should not be given lightly because the consequences are dire. Rabbi Akiva said:

> What is accounted for a suicide: it is literally one who destroys himself? It is not one who climbs to the top of a tree or the top of the roof and falls to his death. Rather it is one who says 'Behold I am going to climb to the top of the tree or the top of the roof and then I will throw myself down to my death.' And thereupon others see him climb to the top of the tree or the top of the roof and see him fall to his death, such a one is presumed to be a suicide.

Thus the Talmud requires a very clear indication of *suicidal intent,* which a modern coroner's court also needs before a suicide verdict can be given. Rabbi Akiva continues 'therefore for such a person no rights whatsoever should be observed'. These rights would include the normal mourning rituals and in the Jewish religion these are having the comfort of sitting with friends and relatives for seven days (sitting *shiva*), tearing off the clothes and saying the prayer for the dead (the Kaddish) and a proper burial. In most Jewish sects today these strictures have been rescinded in parallel with changes in wider society. However, among Orthodox Jewry, suicide is still frowned upon for religious reasons. The Talmud proscribes suicide but it does make exceptions where the person was forced to commit incest, murder or idolatry; under these extreme instances a suicide is permissible.

In ancient Greece, suicide was viewed as a mainly stoic phenomenon. The most famous of the Greek suicides was that of Socrates, who, when already under a sentence of death, drank hemlock. Plato records his discussions with Socrates on the topic of suicide in his tract *Phaedo.* Socrates expresses his valuing of life, which he argues should not be taken away lightly:

> The Gods are our guardians and we humans are the possessions of the Gods. If one of your possessions should go on to kill itself when you had not intended that you wished it to die, would you not be angry with it and punish it? (Quoted by Van Hooff, 1990)

However, Socrates then went on to argue there were certain circumstances when the taking of one's life becomes permissible, as in his own case. 'It is not unreasonable to say that a person must not kill themselves until the Gods send some necessity (*anangke*) upon him – such as has now come upon me.' Socrates then came to view his forthcoming suicide positively and indeed urged every person 'with an interest in Philosophy to come after me as quickly as they can'. Many famous Greeks ended their lives by committing suicide and they did this not in a state of emotional turmoil but in a state of calm. Within this hall of fame were Pythagoras, aged 82, Anaxagoras, at 72, Epicurus, at 70, Diogenes, at 80, and, most ostentatiously, Empedocoles, at 71, who flung himself into the volcano Mt Etna. Elderly males are known to have a high suicide rate but there is no modern equivalent list of such intellectual heavyweights perishing at their own hands.

In the classical period of Rome, suicide was also sometimes viewed positively, particularly in the writings of Seneca, a philosopher of the 1st century CE who held that suicide was a liberating event. Thus in his 70th epistle he wrote:

> The wise man will live only as long as he ought, not as long as he can ... the wise man will consider the possibility of death long before he is under extreme *necessitas*.

Seneca believed the right to die at a time of one's choosing was one of the fundamental freedoms of man:

> In any kind of slavery the way lies open to freedom. If the soul is sick and because of its own imperfection and unhappy, a man may end his sorrows and at the same time himself.... Do not ask what is the path to freedom? Any vein in your body....

Such positive attitudes to suicide seemed to be more common in the ancient world than today, and probably led some people to seek martyrdom. Two sects in the early Christian Church, the Montanists of the 2nd century and the Donatists of the 4th century, seemed to view martyrdom by suicide almost too positively. In 185 CE the Roman proconsul to Asia, Arrius Antoninus, was confronted by a group of Montanist Christians who presented themselves to him wearing nooses around their necks demanding execution. Not quite knowing what to do, Antoninus simply sent them on their way, pointing out there were plenty of high cliffs and precipices in the neighbourhood from which they could jump should they choose to do so (Droges, 1992).

It was, however, the later florid suicidal behaviour of the Donatists, an extreme North African Christian sect of the 4th and 5th centuries CE, that turned the opinion of the Catholic Church under Augustine against the moral acceptability of suicide. Jacques Bels (1975), a French scholar, has shown that among the early Christians prior to Augustine, deaths due to martyrdom, suicide and murder in the context of religious persecution had a considerable overlap and the suicide deaths were most often linked to martyrdom. Almost as a reaction Augustine reversed this; he decreed suicide was to be separated from martyrdom and identified much more with murder, and this is set out in the Augustinian text *Against Gaudentius* (a Donatist bishop) as well as in his book *The City of God*. Augustine based his case against suicide on similar arguments that Socrates had expounded in *Phaedo*, namely that to sever the bonds between body and soul prematurely usurped a privilege belonging only to God. To do so would be an act of killing and so also violated the Sixth Commandment of the Decalogue

(Thou shalt not kill). Augustine even condemned those over-zealous virgins and martyrs who took their own life in order to save their virtue or bear witness to their faith in God and from that time on Christianity regarded suicide as a form of murder – an immoral act alongside other crimes such as apostasy and adultery.

A series of Church synods over the next few centuries gradually hardened the attitude to suicide. Thus in the council of Arles (452 CE), suicide was denounced as the work of the Devil. The synod of Braga (536 CE) decreed that full burial rites should be denied to those who committed suicide. Attempted suicide was punished at the synod of Toledo (693 CE) by exclusion from Church practice. In 1284 CE the synod of Nimes denied the rite of burial in consecrated ground to those who committed suicide. This led to the practice of suicide victims being buried just outside the walls of the churchyard.

Colt (1987) has described some of the past suicide rituals practised in more primitive societies. These include decapitation, burying the corpse outside the city limits and publicly burning the corpse of the suicide victim. Such rituals were gradually incorporated by the organised Church, ultimately leading to laws penalising suicide. Suicide was a crime against God; someone had to be punished for it, and since the deceased was gone the punishment was meted out to the surviving family, who were to be disinherited and sometimes even fined as well. Eventually it was decreed that the body of a suicide had to be buried outside the town, preferably at a crossroads, sometimes with a stake driven through the heart and a stone placed over the face. The logic of a burial at the crossroads was that the traffic going over two roads was heavier than that passing over only one, and this would make it much more difficult for the ghost of the suicide to escape and return to haunt the survivors. Driving a stake through the victim's heart gave added protection by preventing the ghost of the suicide victim from escaping.

How are we to understand these practices of the past? The answer lies in the effect that a suicide has on its survivors, the relatives, therapists or the whole community today. It can be a truly devastating event. Relatives always ask 'why?' Did the bereaved hate me? What had I done to deserve this? Those bereaved by a suicide have much higher levels of guilt, anger and anguish than those whose relative died through illness or accident. Many relatives, particularly the parents of teenagers or young adults, are particularly devastated. Shneidman (cited in Jobes *et al.*, 2000) estimates that for every one suicide there are six survivors. Shneidman writes:

> A person's death is not only an ending: it is also a beginning – for the survivors. Indeed in the case of a suicide, the largest public health problem is neither the prevention of suicide, nor the management of attempts, but the alleviation of stress in the survivor victims of suicidal deaths, whose lives have changed forever.

The reaction to a suicide death is also very strong among therapists and psychiatrists and this may be just as intense as among the relatives. Therapists may need their own special counselling from professional colleagues. Most psychiatrists will have to endure a death by suicide of at least one of their patients and my own personal reaction whenever a patient of mine committed suicide was of quite a severe depression, sometimes lasting two or three months.

The primitive exorcisms to banish the ghost of the suicide are no longer practised but instead exorcism is sought through the coroner's court. Was someone to blame? Might the death have been prevented? In suicides occurring in hospital there is also usually an internal inquiry – ostensibly to see if things could have been done any better – but in truth mainly to exorcise the suicide from the hospital itself and absolve the staff from any blame.

Because of the devastation that a suicide causes among the relatives, over the last 20 years survivor groups have emerged, of which there are over 300 in the USA (Jobes *et al.*, 2000). It is possible that this distress among those who have borne witness to the suicide is what gave the ancients the motivation to record these events as well as provide 'a meaningful story' to explain the act, and possibly this same distress is, at least in part, the driver for modern preventative programmes and the huge effort that goes into the modern study of suicide (suicidology).

The *Encyclopaedia Judaica* lists only four suicides in the Old Testament, those of Saul, Abimelech, Ahithopel and Zimri. However, Barraclough (1992), a psychiatrist with an interest in suicide, lists 11 biblical suicides and 15 descriptions of suicide in the whole Bible. An attempt has been made to try to draw parallels between the biblical suicides and the features of suicide as observed today, but the distance in both historical time and culture is very great, making such links somewhat uncertain. In the Bible itself the various suicides and episodes of self-harm are scattered throughout several different biblical books and so in order to structure this review the following have been grouped together:

- the deaths of the defeated kings of the Old Testament, Saul, Abimelech, Samson and Zimri, as well as the death of Saul's armour bearer
- the suicides of shame and betrayal, those of Ahithopel, Macron and Judas Iscariot
- the suicides of martyrdom – Razis, the mother, Hannah and the seventh son.

This is followed by a brief review of how suicide is viewed today, before the chapter returns to the Bible in its consideration of:

- suicidal thoughts (only the story of Tobit is included here)
- self-mutilation in the OT.

This is then similarly followed by a brief account of self-mutilation today.

The text is interspersed with modern psychiatric views on suicide, suicidal thoughts and self-harm and other aspects of psychiatry. Because suicide is such an important topic in psychiatry today, this chapter includes more discussion of modern psychiatry than other chapters of this book.

## The deaths of the defeated Kings: Saul, Saul's armour bearer, Abimelech, Samson and Zimri

### The death of King Saul (circa 1020 BCE)

Perhaps the best known of the Bible suicides is the death of King Saul, who fell upon his sword following his defeat at the hands of the Philistines at the battle of Mt Gilboa. His death was one of the great dramas in Jewish history and there are in fact three separate accounts in the OT of this momentous event. Although these versions share material, they differ in the meaning ascribed to the death of King Saul and their accounts of its aftermath.

### The account in I Sam 31[1-6]

> [1]Now the Philistines fought against Israel and the men of Israel fled before the Philistines, and many fell on Mt Gilboa. [2]The Philistines overtook Saul and his sons and the Philistines killed Jonathan and Abinadab and Malchishua, the sons of Saul. [3]The battle pressed hard upon Saul, the archers found him and he was badly wounded by them. [4]Then Saul said to his armour bearer draw your sword and thrust me through with it, so that these uncircumcised may not come and thrust me through and make sport of me. But his armour bearer was unwilling, for he was terrified, so Saul took his own sword and fell upon it. [5]When his armour bearer saw that Saul was dead, he also fell upon his sword and died with him.

The story continues to describe how the Philistine soldiers find the body of Saul and cut his head off. They place his armour in the temple of one of their female gods, Astarte, and fasten his body to the walls of the village of Beth-Shan. When the inhabitants of another nearby village, Jabesh-Gilead, hear about Saul's death they go out in the night to retrieve his body, bring it back to their village, cremate him and bury him with full mourning rites, including a fast of seven days. In the ancient world there could be no rite of passage to the afterlife without a proper burial. The citizens of Jabesh-Gilead later receive much praise from David for honouring Saul by giving him a proper burial.

Saul dies on the battlefield and the text portrays his suicide as both honourable and rational. Had he survived, the Philistines would have tortured him and so death was his only escape from the pain and the prospect of not having a proper burial and hence passage into the afterlife.

### The second account of Saul's death: killed by an Amalekite (2 Sam 1[4-10])

A rather different account is given in the second book of Samuel, which is much more concerned with the role of David and David's ascendancy to the throne than with Saul's demise. Thus after the battle at Mt Gilboa, David encounters an Amalekite, who had just come from the battlefield, and David asks him for an account of the battle and of how Saul died. 2 Sam: 1 records:

> [3]David said to him 'Where have you come from?' He said to him 'I have escaped from the camp of Israel. [4]David said to him 'How did things go? Tell me'. He answered 'The army fled the battle, but also many of the army had

fled and died and Saul and his son Jonathan also died. [5]Then David asked the young man who was reporting to him 'How do you know that Saul and his son Jonathan have died?' [6]'I happened to be on Mt Gilboa and there was Saul leaning on his spear, while the chariots and the horsemen drew close to him. [7]When he looked behind him, he saw me and called me to him. I answered 'Here Sir'. [8]And he said to me 'Who are you?' I answered him 'I am an Amalakite'. He said to me 'Come stand over me and kill me, for convulsions have seized me and yet my life carries on. [10]So I stood over him and killed him for I knew he could not live after he had fallen. I took the crown that was on his head and the armlet that was on his arm and I have brought them here to my lord. [11]Then David took all of his clothes and tore them and the men who were with him did the same. [12]They mourned and wept for Saul and his son Jonathan....

In both accounts Saul asks to be killed and so the suicidal intent is clear. In the first account he asks his armour bearer to kill him and the reason given is to escape from torture 'at the hands of the uncircumcised'. In the second account his death is at the hand of the Amalekite, but the reason is different; it is for relief from his injuries, which have given him convulsions from which he cannot recover. The second account goes to great lengths to proclaim David's loyalty to Saul and how he grieves for him. David also praises the people of Jabesh-Gilead for giving Saul a proper burial and he orders his men to kill the Amalekite because this man had killed Saul, who was 'the Lord's anointed'. He then sings a lamentation to King Saul and his son Jonathan, who had been his great friend.

> [19]Your glory, O Israel lies slain upon your high places, How the mighty have fallen!

'Your glory' refers to Saul and Jonathan, and 'high places' refers to Mt Gilboa. The phrase 'How the mighty are fallen' is now a well known English idiom, which originates from this biblical lament.

After the death of Saul, there remains the mystery of how David came into possession of the diadem and bracelet of the slain monarch. P. J. McCarter (1980, p. 62), drawing on a consensus of earlier German scholarship, suggests that the second account of Saul's death was all part of a propaganda exercise associated with the history of David's rise to power. David was the chief beneficiary of the fall of the house of Saul, but there was a need to exonerate David of any suspicion of blame for Saul's demise. David failed to fight with Saul at Mt Gilboa; instead, at the time he was fighting against the Amalekites in the south. Moreover, David had recently been a mercenary in the army of King Achish, one of the Philistine kings who fought against Saul on Mt Gilboa, and so his loyalty to Saul and the Israelite camp was questionable. McCarter writes:

> Moreover the diadem and the bracelet of the slain king turned up in David's possession and so we can hardly doubt that these things were publicly known in the reign of David, and taken collectively they cast a shadow over his kingship. The suggestion therefore that the diadem and bracelet of the slain King were brought to David by an Amalekite may therefore have been a convenient alibi.

Even while David was publicly lamenting the death of Saul, his principal lieutenant, a man called Joab, was hunting down Abner, who was Saul's general, and also plotting the murder of Ishbaal, Saul's one and only remaining live son. In the ancient world the extermination of all living relatives of the recently deposed King might happen after a change of dynasty. Perhaps this was a necessary precaution against retaliation from the previous regime. While mention of the death of Saul appears frequently in the second account, the mode of his death by suicide is of little interest to the narrator, who is pre-occupied with legitimising David's ascendancy to the throne.

*The third account of Saul's death (I Chronicles 10$^{r-13}$)*

The Book of Chronicles is a much later post-exilic work. In trying to date the book Klein (2006), in his massive commentary on it, highlights the mention of a Persian coin, the *daric*. 'They gave for the service of the house of God five thousand talents and ten thousand *darics* of gold' (I Chr. 29$^7$). The *daric* was a coin known to have been used during the reign of the Persian King Darius (527–486 BCE). Summarising several previous studies, Klein estimated that Chronicles was probably composed in the first half of the 4th century BCE, during the Persian period, but probably before the conquests of Alexander the Great, and so this version was written at least five centuries after the death of Saul.

The actual verses in I Chronicles are almost identical to the account in I Sam 31, with only two minor differences in detail. First, instead of Saul's head being taken to Beth-Shan, and placed in the temple of the female goddess Astarte, it is taken to the temple of a male god, Dagon. The main difference, however, is to be found in verses 10–13, which follow on from his death and concern theology.

> So Saul died for his unfaithfulness. He was unfaithful to the Lord in that he did not keep the command of the Lord, moreover he had consulted with a medium seeking guidance from the Lord. Therefore the Lord put him to death and turned the kingdom over to David, son of Jesse. (I Chr. 10$^{13}$)

This version suggests that it is Yahweh who has put Saul to death. Klein (2006) explains:

> The chronicler now mentions two specific misdeeds of Saul: he did not keep the word of Yahweh and he consulted the medium at Endor; instead he should have sought Yahweh – and not seeking Yahweh is a testament to his unfaithfulness. The Chronicler thus transforms Saul's defeat by the Philistines and his death into an act of Yahweh's divine judgement. The word *ma-al* (unfaithfulness) appears 35 times in the OT, 11 of which are in the Book of Chronicles.... Saul's unfaithfulness of course anticipates the unfaithfulness that will be practised by many other kings and the people as well.

Chronicles was written during the post-exilic period, a time of feverish intellectual and religious activity among the exiles, and so there should be no surprise that a theological meaning was applied to this ancient Israelite drama. It was to become a part of the doctrine of rewards and punishments and this took on a special form in the Book of Chronicles. Thus throughout the Bible, faithfulness is followed by reward and unfaithfulness by punishment. In Chronicles these rewards/punishments are more immediate and normally take place within a person's lifetime. For Saul the consequences of his unfaithfulness were his death and the loss of his kingdom.

In the first account of Saul's death following his defeat by the Philistines his suicide is to escape from torture and there is no criticism of this act. In the second account, the reason given is that Saul has serious injuries, causing convulsions from which he cannot recover, but in that account the narrator moves the focus of the story away from Saul and onto David, with the aim of showing that David has behaved with honour and so has the right to inherit the throne. Perhaps the second account was more of an essay in the real politik of the day and propaganda in support of David. Again, the mode of death – at his own request – invites little comment from the narrator.

The third account, in Chronicles, written several hundred years after the event, was little concerned with the honour of a fallen king, nor with the politics surrounding his succession; its purpose was to provide a religious meaning to the death of Saul. The Chronicler uses it as an example of the doctrine of divine retribution. It was Yahweh who has killed Saul 'because of his unfaithfulness'. The only feature these three accounts share is that Saul's death was by suicide but all three versions share the unspoken need to provide an explanation or meaning for such an unnatural death. Such a need to find an explanation for a person's suicide remains powerful today – a suicide verdict usually has to be made in the coroner's court following a detailed inquiry into the circumstances of the death.

There are also several modern formulations of King Saul's suicide and these incorporate psychiatric diagnoses as well. Littman (1981) viewed Saul's primary illness as paranoia, and when Saul believed that all of his main sources of support, namely God, Samuel and David had turned against him, as well as being defeated by the Philistines, he became depressed and killed himself. Huisman (2007) viewed his final depression as a case of occupational stress. The Israelite army had only 3,000 men but the Philistine army consisted of 'thirty thousand chariots and six thousand horsemen, and people as sand which is on the seashore in a multitude' (I Sam 13[5]). The Israelite soldiers were in panic at the overwhelming odds against them and the stress of the situation overcame Saul, who became depressed and then killed himself. Koch (2005) notes that Saul was frequently depressed, while the present author proposes that Saul was most probably in a state of psychotic depression on the eve of the battle when he visited the medium at Endor. His depression would have been worsened by the defeat at Mt Gilboa when he killed himself – but in the background he suffered from bipolar disorder, a condition associated with a high suicide rate (see page 262). Any or all of the biblical reasons or modern psychiatric formulations or combinations of them to explain Saul's suicide may be true. We shall never know what his thinking was on that final and fateful day on Mt Gilboa.

Suicide today is not the preserve of monarchs but occurs among ordinary people with little claim to fame. However, the events and circumstances which precede a suicide today often assume a similar character of humiliation or defeat, perhaps following a bankruptcy or a divorce, or following some other personal disaster. Few can claim anything as grand as a defeat by the Philistines at Mt Gilboa, but the experience of defeat and humiliation may be the same. Similarly, 'being made sport at the hands of the uncircumcised' would hardly be a likely outcome today, but the phrase conveys well the fear of an uncertain future, which to the subject seems to be a fate worse than death itself. Thinking along these lines sometimes plays a role in a suicide today.

## A double suicide: the death of Saul's armour bearer

> When his armour bearer saw that Saul was dead, he also fell upon his sword and died with him.... (I Sam 31[5])

There is no further comment in the Bible on the death of Saul's armour bearer, nor is there much mention of him in the large literature on King Saul. Van Hooff (1990) discusses such double suicides in the ancient world and classifies them as *devotees* and *Fides*. Two examples are given in late Jewish tradition in the Talmud. Thus the servant of Judah Ha Nasi killed himself on learning of his master's death, and the pagan executioner of Rabbi Hanina Ben Teradyon joined him in the flames which consumed him (*Avoda zara* 18a, cited in Cohn, 2007. The devotees were virtual slaves, women or other low-ranking friends, of their masters. In Japanese culture this type of suicide is called *Junshi*. Among the Celts, soldiers would pledge their life and soul to their leader to such a degree that they would share death with them.

Double suicides are sometimes the result of a suicide pact, although the actual relationship between the individual parties varies from case to case. Author Koestler, a prominent intellectual and philosopher and author of *Darkness at Noon*, an anti-Stalinist novel, was the Vice-President of the Voluntary Euthanasia Society of London. In old age he developed Parkinson's disease and leukaemia. However, his third wife, Cynthia, was in good health and she was only 55 when both of them overdosed on barbiturates and died. Some have suggested that such suicide pacts are patriarchal, where a dominant male coerces his wife to commit suicide. Fishbain *et al.* (1984) found the most common combination was one of a terminally ill partner and a dependent spouse. In a study of 5,895 suicides in Dade County, Florida, his group found 20 such pairs (40 suicides), giving an overall prevalence of 0.6% for suicide pacts among all suicides.

Soon after taking up my consultant position, on a cold winter's night, a suicidal patient with bipolar disorder was placed in a seclusion room for observation. The room had no heating and as the night wore on he complained of the cold and the nursing staff opened the door to permit some heat to enter the room. The bipolar patient had befriended a young man with a personality disorder a few days previously but the nature of their relationship was unclear. In the middle of the night both patients escaped from the ward, only to be found dead near a local lake the next day. Everyone was shocked. A huge enquiry ensued and nursing staff were blamed for opening the door to the seclusion room and then not observing the patient adequately. The whole episode cast a shadow over the unit for the next couple of years. Perhaps due to his lowly status, the death of Saul's armour bearer has not been given any religious meaning, but double suicides are deeply disturbing events and the death of Saul's armour bearer is an early example of such a double tragedy.

## *The death of Abimelech: the suicide of a psychopath (circa 1200 BCE)*

Abimelech died in battle after a woman injured him by throwing a heavy stone on his head. Knowing that he was severely injured, he, like Saul, asked his armour bearer to kill him 'so that people will not say about me a woman killed me'.

Abimelech lived during a period of considerable political violence and reigned for only three years. His life is described in the Book of Judges. It suggests he may have been an aggressive, violent and perhaps psychopathic individual. The account below draws on the commentaries of Butler (2009) and Boling (1975).The period of the Book of Judges relates to the very early history of Israel, long before it had become a viable state, some time during the 12th and 11th centuries BCE, and prior to the monarchy of King Saul, whose reign commenced in 1040 BCE. The book itself, however, is thought to have been edited at a much later date, possibly between the 9th and 7th century BCE and has a strong Deuteronomistic influence.

The Hebrew word *Sapat* (judges) actually means ruler, and the book is about the rule or rather the misrule of a series of judges of this period, their quarrels and their struggles for survival against internal enemies and their wars with their neighbours. The eminent archaeologist Sir Flinders Petrie wrote:

> the era of the judges was a terribly barbaric age, its fragmentary records speak of savage relations and fierce struggles amongst disorganised tribes. Judge after judge rises out of the mists of warfare, only to disappear and leave a confusion as black as before.

Abimelech was one of these judges, and perhaps the most blood-thirsty of all. He was the son of Jerubbaal (another name for Gideon), by one of Gideon's many concubines. In spite of being the son of a concubine, he still had a certain right to the leadership – but the manner in which he seized the throne shows what a ruthless individual he must have been, as described in Judges 9:

> [1]Now Ahimelech, son of Jerubbaal, went to Shechem to his mother's kinsfolk and said to them and to the whole clan of his mother's family. [2]Say in the hearing of all the lords of Shechem 'Which is better for you, that all seventy of the sons of Jerubbaal rule over you, or that one rule over you?' Remember also that I am your bone and your flesh. [3]So his mother's kinsfolk spoke all these words on his behalf in the hearing of the Lords of Shechem, and their hearts inclined to follow Abimelech for they said 'He is our brother'. [4]They gave him seventy pieces of silver out of the temple of Baal-Berith with which Abimelech

hired worthless and reckless followers who followed him. [5]He went to his father's house at Oprah and killed his brothers, the sons of Jerubbaal, seventy men on one stone; but Jotham, the youngest son of Jerrubbaal, survived for he hid himself.... [6]Then all the Lords of Shechem and all Beth-Millo came together and they went and made Abimelech king, by the Oak of the pillar at Shechem.

Shechem probably corresponds to the present-day Palestinian town of Nablus. According to the El-Armana letters, Shechem was the only sanctuary to have a substantial amount of territory surrounding it, and was one of the few city states to impose a tax on passing travellers. At one time it may have been the most important sanctuary in ancient Israel, but following its destruction by Abimelech, Bethel became more important and ultimately the role of the central sanctuary was taken over by the Temple in Jerusalem.

Abimelech seizes the throne through an appalling act of fratricide. Boling writes:

> The massacre of his siblings is financed by the Temple of Baal apparently at a price of one piece of silver per head. Funded in this way Abimelech hires 'Worthless and reckless men'.

Butler (p. 236) elaborates further on these bad characters:

> they are the rebellious have-nots, mercenaries, empty men, who operate beyond the bounds of filial honour, reckless and arrogant people not restrained by the usual conventions who arrogantly follow their own desires....

In more modern language, Abimelech's mercenaries seem to have been a bunch of rogues, criminals and psychopaths.

Even though Abimelech has been installed on the throne by the Lords of Shechem, he soon falls out with them and a civil war ensues. The text (Judges 9) offers a theological meaning for this, and it is to punish him for his earlier crime of fratricide:

> [22]Abimelech ruled over Israel for three years. [23]But God sent *an evil spirit* between Abimelech and the Lords of Shechem; and the lords of Shechem dealt treacherously with Abimelech. [24]This happened so that the violence shown to the seventy sons of Jerubbaal might be avenged and their blood laid on their brother Abimelech, who killed them, and on the lords of Shechem, who strengthened his hand to kill his brothers.

Boling writes '*Evil spirits* from the deity are extremely rare in biblical narratives and they stand for the utterly inexplicable, as for example the near insanity of Saul'. In the Abimelech story it is the 'evil spirit of the Lord' which causes the civil war between Abimelech and the citizens of Shechem, who had only just installed him on the throne. His complete lack of gratitude and cruelty towards them is described in the succeeding verses:

> [44]Abimelech and the company that was with him rushed forward and stood at the entrance of the gate of the city [Shechem], while the two companies rushed on all who were in the fields and killed them. [45]Abimelech fought

against the city all that day; he took the city and killed the people that were in it; and he razed the city and sowed it with salt.

Butler, citing Olson, writes:

> Having destroyed most of the soldiers Abimelech turns to the rebel city itself. Abimelech's frenzied attacks of unwarranted and extreme revenge shows a portrait of a madman out of control.... One senses that Abimelech is randomly slaughtering people for no apparent reason.

The description here suggests Abimelech may have been a murderous psychopath.

In the ancient world to lay salt in the fields around a town was a way of imposing starvation on its surviving citizenry because once the soil is impregnated with salt, the land will be sterile and yield no crops for many years to come. The story of Abimelech's vindictive cruelty continues when he hears how the Lords of Shechem and its people have fled and sought refuge in the city stronghold of the Tower at the Temple of El-Berith. When they are trapped inside it, he sets fire to them:

> [49]So every one of the troops cut down a bundle and following Abimelech put it against the stronghold, and they set the stronghold on fire over them, so that all the people of the Tower of Shechem also died, about a thousand men and women.

Butler points out that Abimelech's mother and her relatives would have lived in Shechem and so probably also have perished in this great fire. There is also some archaeological evidence of a major fire on the site of the Shechem shrine dating to around the 12th century, possibly corroborating the story of Abimelech's fire. Much hated by this time, Abimelech's end comes in the final battle during his attack on the city of Thebez.

> [50]Then Abimelech went to Thebez and encamped against Thebez and took it. [51]But there was a strong tower within the city, and all the men and women and all the lords of the city fled into it and shut themselves in; and they went to the roof of the tower. [52]Abimelech came to the tower and fought against it and came near to the entrance of the tower to burn it with fire. [53]But a certain woman threw an upper millstone on Abimelech's head and crushed his skull. [54]Immediately he called the young man who carried his armour and said to him, 'Draw your sword and kill me, so people will not say about me, "A woman killed him".' So the young man thrust his sword through and he died. [55]When the Israelites saw that Abimelech was dead they all went home....

In the ancient world there was considerable ignominy at being killed by a woman and commentators sometimes link the story of Abimelech's death to that of Sisera to support of this. Sisera was a cruel Canaanite general who ruled over and tormented the early Israelites. The people then rose up against him and Sisera took refuge in the tent of a Kenite woman called Jael. Weary from the battlefield, Sisera fell into a deep sleep in her tent and Jael promptly drove a tent peg through his temple, nailing his head into the ground and killing him.

The final two verses of the story of Abimelech give a moral and religious meaning to his death.

> [56]Thus God repaid Abimelech for the crime he committed against his father in killing his seventy brothers. [57]And God made all the wickedness of the people of Shechem fall back on their heads and on them came the curse of Jotham son of Jerubbaal.

The final verses of the story are thought to have been added at a later date, possibly by the Deuteronomist(s). Boling explains:

> Deuteronomic theology also helps to clarify hostility towards Abimelech. Unlike King Josiah (a much venerated reforming 7th-century king and a contemporary to the Deuteronomist) Abimelech had become king through his own initiative, and to the later Jerusalem historian this meant that Abimelech had assumed the prerogatives of God and brought about a ruination of the venerable Temple covenant together with a mass of victimised citizens.... With all that is now known about the struggle of early Israel to actualise a new society, based on religion when God alone was King, it is not difficult to see through the bias of the Abimelech narrator, as he portrays a hot bed of conspiratorial action and reactions....

Abimelech seems to have been a 'bad character'; he charms the Lords of Shechem into giving him money to hire assassins to kill his brothers; he associates with criminals and psychopaths who assist him in the murder of his brothers; he massacres the citizenry of his own town, probably setting fire to his own mother. And all this is accomplished in just three years. More recent studies have shown that many of the cruel tyrants of history have had psychopathic personality disorders and the life of Abimelech as a vengeful and murderous ruler is compatible with him being a psychopath. Such individuals may have elevated death rates through both murder and suicide, often through violent means.

The actual mode of Abimelech's death – at his own request – is nonetheless a suicidal act, although, like that of Saul, is at the hands of his armour bearer. This is only briefly mentioned by the narrator; it receives no condemnation or any further comment in the text, or in any of the later commentaries on the Book of Judges, and seems to be little more than a passing incidental to the story.

## The death of Samson: suicide and vengeance

The life and death of Samson as portrayed in the Book of Judges is a rich and complicated tale of love, power, riddles, deceit and finally vengeance. Israel at the time (circa 1100 BCE) was under the rule of the Philistines, who were regarded as the oppressors. However, there was a considerable intermingling between the two peoples. Thus Samson chose a Philistine wife and when he deserted her, he was offered her younger sister to be his next bride. He also had dalliances with a prostitute from Gaza and finally fell for the seductive Delilah, who were all Philistine women, yet his principal driving force, at least as portrayed by the Book of Judges, seems to have been the destruction of the Philistines. Thus he sets fire to the tails of 300 foxes and then lets them loose on the Philistine stores of grain. With the single jaw of an ass he kills 1,000 Philistines. No wonder the Philistines were out to destroy him but this proves to be an almost impossible task. According to the biblical story this is because he has super-human strength, as he is a Nazirite. This means he cannot shave his head (see also page 546). Samson's secret is safe until he falls in love with Delilah. Three times she tries to coax out of him the secret source of his strength, but each time he gives a false reason. The Lords of the Philistines pay Delilah and on the fourth occasion she is successful in discovering the secret source of Samson's strength, which lies in his hair.

When Samson was asleep they shaved him and so when he woke up he was too weak to fight them off. Taken captive by the Philistines, he was thrown into prison and his eyes were gouged out but his hair began to grow again, thus renewing his strength. Some time later the Philistines were making sacrifices to their god Dagon and celebrating the capture of Samson. They wanted Samson to entertain them and the account of his dramatic end and the death of the Philistines is given in Judges 16:

> [25]And when their hearts were merry, they said, 'Call Samson, and let him entertain us.' So they called Samson out of the prison, and he performed for them. They made him stand between the pillars; [26]and Samson said to the attendant who held him by the hand, 'Let me feel the pillars on which the house rests, so that I may lean against them.' [27]Now the house was full of men and women; all the lords of the Philistines were there, and on the roof there were about three thousand men and women, who looked on while Samson performed.
> [28]Then Samson called to the Lord and said, 'Lord GOD, remember me and strengthen me only this once, O God, so that with this one act of revenge I may pay back the Philistines for my two eyes.' [29]And Samson grasped the two middle pillars on which the house rested, and he leaned his weight against them, his right hand on the one and his left hand on the other. [30]Then Samson said, 'Let me die with the Philistines.' He strained with all his might; and the house fell on the lords and all the people who were in it. So those he killed at his death were more than those he had killed during his life. [31]Then his brothers and all his family came down and took him and brought him up and buried him between Zorah and Eshtaol in the tomb of his father Manoah. He had judged Israel for 20 years.

God does not figure prominently in the Samson saga, but just before the end Samson prays for additional strength to help him bring down the house of the Philistines, but there is no particular moral or religious message to the story. The theological meaning of the Samson story is obscure, with different scholars offering a variety of interpretations and this is extensively reviewed by Butler (pp. 306–360). Themes concerning the significance of a Nazirite birth, the dangers of consorting with foreign women and the risks of losing cultural identity through intermarriage are thought to be relevant to the story. One author, Wurtzel (1998), even saw the story of Samson and Delilah as the archetypal tale of cross-cultural love between members of warring nations – the story of Romeo and Juliet – and one of fatal love, when someone is bound to die.

Commenting on Samson's death, Butler (p. 353) writes, Samson's motif is not religious; he does not ask God to help him to fulfil a forgotten mission. He wants payback for the loss of his two eyes and his blinding. His motif is revenge. Van Hooff (p. 106) discusses revenge suicide in the ancient world and calls them 'Samsonic'. In his series of 960 Graeco-Roman suicides he identified 19 (2%) of a similar type. Thus in his monologue on the beach, Ajax invokes the furies to take revenge on his enemies. Cicero took revenge when he had been betrayed by Octavian by killing himself next to the house of Octavian, hoping to send a revenging demon into his house.

Today, people who have attempted suicide often give a story of revenge against a rejecting partner, or an overly harsh employer, or some other oppressor, as the cause of their self-destructive act. The motivation behind the modern suicide bomber who carries out his deadly deed in a large theatre or in the market has the clear intention of causing the maximum number deaths, sometimes in the name of religion, his nation, or some political cause, and in many ways this resembles the suicide of Samson.

## King Zimri: suicide by arson in the royal palace

Little is known about Zimri, who reigned for only seven days. He was deposed by Omri, who became a rather more substantive monarch and whose existence is also recorded in an extra-biblical source, the Mesha stele. 1 Kings chs 14–18 describes a series of political assassinations in the northern kingdom of Israel, where each new king perpetrates a palace coup, then kills the preceding monarch, reigns for a short period before he too is assassinated in yet another palace coup. The narrator always points out that the particular king who is assassinated 'did evil in the eyes of the Lord' and that is why he lost the throne. Zimri is the fourth of these Kings of Israel, following Jeroboam I, Nadab, Baasha and Elah. Zimri seizes power by murdering his predecessor, King Elah, while Elah is drunk.

> In the twenty-sixth year of King Asa of Judah, Elah son of Baasha began to reign over Israel in Tirzah. He reigned for two years; [9]But his servant Zimri commander of half his chariots, conspired against him. When he (Elah) was at Tirzah drinking himself drunk in the House of Arza, who was in charge of the palace at Tirzah. [10]Zimri came in and struck him down and killed him in the twenty-seventh year of King Asa of Judah and succeeded him. (I Kings: 16[8])

As soon as Zimri took power he set about murdering all the relatives of his predecessors, King Baasha and King Elah. His coup d'état was unpopular with the army, who installed Omri as their commander, with the aim of wresting power back from Zimri. The ensuing battle and Zimri's suicide by arson then follow:

> [15]In the twenty-seventh year of King Asa of Judah, Zimri reigned for seven days in Tirzah. Now the troops were encamped against Gibbethon which belonged to the Philistines, [16]and the troops who were encamped heard it said 'Zimri has conspired and killed the King'; therefore all Israel made Omri the commander of the army, King over Israel that day in the camp. [17]So Omri went up from Gibbethon and all Israel with him and they besieged Tirzah. [18]When

Zimri saw that the city was taken, he went into the citadel of the King's house; he burned down the King's house over himself with fire and died, [19]because of the sins he had committed, doing evil in the sight of the Lord, walking in the way of Jeroboam and for the sin he had committed, causing Israel to sin.

The cause of Zimri's demise is suicide by arson and the text offers two contrasting explanations. The first is military and historical: facing defeat at the hands of Omri and his army, death is inevitable and the grand finale is played out with Zimri setting fire to the royal palace with himself inside it. Added on to this explanation the theology is superimposed: 'He committed sins and did evil in the sight of the Lord', or as Gray (p. 325) puts it, 'the Deuteronomic epilogue closes the account of the reign and fall of Zimri'.

While the death of Zimri may be down to his sins, the narrator makes no comment about the arson or the suicide itself. Coggan (2000, p. 413) notes that other Near Eastern Kings perished in a similar fashion. Thus Shamash-shum-ukin was the Assyrian King of Babylon from 668 to 648 BCE. He was the second son of the Assyrian King Esarhaddon. His elder brother, crown prince Sin-iddina-apla, had died in 672, and in his place Esarhaddon's third son, Ashurbanipal, was invested as crown prince and later King of Assyria, while Shamash-shum-ukin (the oldest brother) remained crown prince of Babylonia.

When Esarhaddon unexpectedly died on a campaign against a rebellion in Egypt in 669, Ashurbanipal assumed the throne, even though he was the youngest son, and he did this in the face of opposition by court officials and some of the priesthood. Shamash-shum-ukin, his older brother, became Viceroy of Babylonia. However, in May 652 Shamash-shum-ukin rose up in rebellion. The reasons for this are unknown, as no Babylonian sources have been preserved. After a two-year siege, during which cases of cannibalism were reported, Babylon yielded in June 648 BCE. Shamash-shum-ukin threw himself into his burning palace as Babylon fell to the conquering Assyrian army.

Similar parallels can be found in the Graeco-Roman literature. Thus Croesus attempted suicide by burning but was saved just in time by Apollo and Cyrus, who saved the city. Cesius burned himself alive in 43 BCE to escape being liquidated by the second Triumvirate (Van Hooff, 1992). Andreasen and Noyes (1975) found suicidal ideation was present in 2% of those admitted to a burns unit, and occasionally inpatient suicides occur today when patients, particularly those with schizophrenia, set fire to themselves.

## Suicide and violence

The suicides of Saul, Abimelech, Zimri and Samson were all by violent means and these were all also undoubtedly men of great violence. Saul massacres 85 priests at Nob, Abimelech murders 70 of his brothers, Zimri thrusts a sword through King Elah, and Samson takes pride in killing many thousands of Philistines. In addition the Sicarii, also known as 'the dagger men', were assassins of the Romans and they later perpetrated a mass suicide at Masada. There are strong known associations between violence and suicide; the topic is reviewed in detail by Plutchik *et al.* (2011). Hildebrand (1992) found that out of 50 habitually aggressive men in a forensic facility 15 (30%) had made suicide attempts. A survey of a school population in North Carolina showed that those with severe suicidal behaviours also had high rates of assaultive behaviours towards fellow pupils and teachers (Garrison *et al.*, 1983). Among hospitalised adolescent psychotic patients, 67% were violent, 43% were suicidal and 27% were both violent and suicidal. A study of a large number of patients in Missouri mental hospitals found that suicidal thoughts were the highest single predictor of homicidal ideas and the reverse was true as well (Altman *et al.*, 1971).

This association between suicidal and homicidal thoughts is important today as a small number of murders are committed by depressed men who then go on to commit suicide. Such double tragedies, which sometimes involve the death of whole families, are often reported in the newspapers. In the routine assessments of suicidal patients it is always necessary to enquire whether they are harbouring any thoughts of 'wanting to take someone with them'.

King and Barraclough (1997) showed that of those who died by a violent suicide, over half had a lifetime history of psychiatric treatment and over a third were psychiatric patients at the time of their death. The relative risk of a violent death for those who died within a year of their last psychiatric contact was 27 times greater than that of residents with no recent psychiatric contact. Suicide and homicide rates show an overall correlation. Rutz and Zihmer (2009) in a study of suicide in Russia in the 1990s, which was a period of massive societal upheaval in the early post-Communist era, found a nine-fold increase in both suicide and homicide rates, in parallel with an increase in alcohol-related deaths. Several mechanisms have been proposed for the association between suicide and violence. Rutz suggests the common link is related to untreated male depression, as men more often commit suicide and tend not to report their emotional states as often as women. He views untreated male depression as a major problem today and suggests that identifying and treating it might help reduce male suicide rates. Saul probably had bipolar disorder, which may have contributed to both his violence and his suicide.

## The suicides of shame and betrayal

The suicide of Judas Iscariot is well known and is found in the New Testament, while the much less well known suicide of Ahithopel is in the Old Testament, and the almost completely unknown case of Macron, a Greek governor, is in the Apocrypha.

### Ahithopel: the death of the king's counsellor

The death of Ahithopel (Heb. = my brother is folly) takes place in the immediate aftermath of David's defeat of Absalom's rebellion. It occurs in the context of the vicious internecine fighting between David and his sons and the dynastic power struggles among a group of jealous siblings.

The biblical writers, especially the Deuteronomist(s), have transformed this story of fratricide and rebellion in Israel's first family into an anti-monarchic polemic and a moral drama which highlights the powers of Yahweh in family matters and affairs of state, and so give this sordid tale a religious meaning.

David's great sin had been in stealing Bathsheba from her husband, Uriah, and then worst of all arranging for Uriah to be sent to the battle front to await a certain death in the war against the Ammonites. His sin was not the lust, but the cruelty with which he despatched Uriah – Bathsheba's lawful husband. Many years later three of David's sons were all to meet unnatural deaths, being murdered by each other, and the narrator attributes these deaths to the sins of their father, David.

Ammon is David's oldest son and he rapes his half-sister Tamar, a crime which David fails to deal with adequately, so Absalom, who is Tamar's half-brother and another of David's sons, arranges for the murder of Ammon by getting him drunk at a sheep-shearing festival. Another son, Adonijah, seizes the throne while David is still dying, but as soon as Bathsheba hears of this she tells her own son, Solomon, David's designated heir, and Solomon quickly arranges for Adonijah's murder. Absalom then leads a rebellion against David, in which he gets killed by David's lieutenant, Joab. It is during this rebellion that Ahithopel, one of David's long-serving counsellors, makes a disastrous decision to switch his allegiance from David to Absalom. Soon after, when Absalom is defeated, Ahithopel knows that torture and death will be his punishment for his treachery in such a blood-thirsty household, and so he hangs himself.

The story of Absalom's rebellion reads like a spy thriller, replete with tales of espionage, counter-espionage and treachery, and is told in 2 Sam. 13–18, and the final events are briefly outlined below.

> 15[30]But David went up the ascent of the Mount of Olives, weeping as he went with his head covered, and walking bare feet; and all the people who were with him covered their heads and went up weeping as they went. [31]David was told that Ahithopel was among the conspirators with Absalom. And David said 'O Lord, I pray you turn the Counsel of Ahithopel into foolishness....

As well as praying for divine assistance to crush Absalom's rebellion he takes practical steps and asks Hushai, another trusted advisor, to infiltrate Absalom's camp with the aim of getting Absolam to reject Ahithopel's strategies – a mission which Hushai succeeds in doing.

> 17[14]Absalom and all the men of Israel said the counsel of Hushai the Archite is better than the counsel of Ahithopel. For the Lord has ordained to defeat the good counsel of Ahithopel, so that the Lord might bring ruin on Absalom....

Hushai is the spy appointed by David but the narrator is at pains to show that in reality Hushai is the agent of the Lord and ultimately it is the Lord who is the true master of events and will determine the fate of kings and nations. Once Ahithopel hears that Absalom has rejected his advice, and there has been an unexplained change of strategy in Absalom's camp, Ahithopel realises the game is up and the end comes quickly.

17[23]When Ahithopel saw that his counsel was not followed, he saddled his donkey and went off home to his own city. He set his house in order and hanged himself: he died and was buried in the tomb of his father....

Ahithopel was a senior advisor to the court. He had committed treason and knew that to do so in a household as murderous as that of King David meant a certain death.

Josephus gives a more positive slant to the biblical story and writes:

> Therefore he [Ahithopel] said it would be better for him to remove himself from the world in a free and noble spirit than surrender himself to David to be punished for having helped Absalom against him. (Josephus, Ant. 7.229; 1st century CE, translated and republished 1957)

There are many Greek and Roman parallels. Thus Dimnos was discovered planning an assault on Alexander's life and so could not expect to live once the conspiracy had been uncovered. Calpernes Piso was betrayed as the instigator of an attempt on Nero's life. Self-chosen death was the only way out for the conspirators (Van Hooff, 1900).

When viewed from a psychiatric perspective, the most authentic feature of the whole Ahithopel saga lies in the very minor detail that 'he set his house in order'. Sometimes, those who plan their suicide will have a short delay between their decision and the execution of the act, and this is usually used to arrange their affairs, for example by writing a suicide note to explain their actions, or to arrange their financial matters. During this period they become calm, and while still in a settled state they take their own lives. Perhaps Athithopel's official position was akin to that of a senior civil servant today and so he may have been a thoughtful man accustomed to giving advice and planning, but here it his own death that he plans.

## Suicides in the Apocrypha

Three suicides are described in the Apocrypha: first, the case of Macron, the Greek governor considered in this section; second, the martyrdom of Razis, one of the Jewish elders; and third, the deaths of the mother (Hannah) and her seventh son.

The Apocrypha is the term used to describe the 15 books which come after end of the Hebrew scriptures but before the New Testament, also known as 'the deutero-canonical books', the latter term meaning these works were of secondary canonical value. Catholics, Orthodox and Eastern Christians accept these books as part of their canon but Protestants and Jews do not.

Even though they are not part of the Jewish scriptures, they were written by Jews with a Jewish readership in mind. They have come to us through their Greek versions and their earliest texts formed the Codices of the Septuagint. More recent archaeological studies, particularly the discovery of the Dead Sea Scrolls and the fragments found in the Cairo *Genizah* have established that some of these works were probably originally composed Aramaic. They provide an opening into the world of Hellenic Jewish life and Judaism during the inter-testamentary period, and so this may be one reason why they are held in high regard by the Church.

Maccabees 2 relates mainly to events of the 2nd century BCE and includes the revolt of the Jewish hero Judas Maccabeus. It is thought to have originally been a very large book, comprising five volumes known as the *biblion*, and written by Jason of Cyrene, but the book was shortened by an unknown editor and the version we now have is said to have been written by 'The Abridger'. Other texts from non-Jewish sources, particularly the 'Seleucid Chronicles', were also incorporated into this work, and a detailed account of its history and authorship can be found in Goldstein (1983).

The book was written during the Hellenistic period of Jewish history, which starts with the conquest of Judea by Alexander the Great in 332 BCE and extends to 141 BCE, when the land once more came under Jewish control, under the Hasmonaens, although under the overall aegis of the Romans. During this period the Greek empire was divided in two. The eastern empire, mainly Syria and Phoenecia, came under the Seleucid Kings, while the western empire of Egypt was ruled by the Ptolomeys. Tensions between these two empires resulted in the Syrian wars, of which there were at least five.

During the first part of the Greek occupation, from 300 to 200 BCE, Judea came under Egyptian Ptolomaic rule and Hellenic–Jewish relations were generally good. The Ptolomaic administrators accepted the Jewish ethos and culture, and this was an era of religious tolerance. However, later on, under the rule of the Seleucids, all this was to change, particularly under Antiochus IV, also known as Antiochus Epiphanes (175–164 BCE), who instituted a regime of cruel religious persecution of the Jews.

The books of Maccabees contain stories of persecution by the wicked Seleucid generals, while the Jewish rebels such as Judas Maccabeus were heroes, who became a part of Jewish folklore, and it is in the midst of this cultural turmoil the book records its two cases of suicide: that of Ptolomey Macron, a Greek governor, said to have been too friendly to the Jews, and secondly the suicide of Razis, a Jewish elder and a martyr to his religion.

## The death of Macron: a friend of the Jews

Macron was a senior administrator for the Seleucids in Syria and Phoenicia, a region which included Judea. He had been a governor of Cyprus when it was under the rule of Egyptian King Ptolemy Philometer. During one of the Syrian wars in Cyprus, Macron had switched sides from supporting King Ptolomy Philometer and had joined the side of the Seleucid King, Antiochus IV Epiphanes, and it was this switching of sides and his betrayal of Philometer that led to the charge of Macron being a traitor.

Once appointed to the administration in Judea, Macron became apologetic about the persecutions of the Jews instituted by Antiochus IV and tried to repair relationships between the Seleucids and the Jews, but such a move proved to be unpopular with the local gentile population. Indeed, Goldstein (pp. 388–390) suggests that it was the local Syrian Seleucid officials who tried to undermine Macron, because of his pro-Jewish stance. Feeling humiliated as a public servant and perhaps ashamed, he committed suicide by drinking poison, and this is described in 2 Maccabees 10[10-13]:

10¹⁰   Now we will tell what took place under Antiochus Eupator, who was the son of that ungodly man, and will give a brief summary of the principal calamities of the war.

   Eupator (Gk. = son of a noble sire) ascended to the throne aged 9. The ungodly man was Antiochus IV

¹¹   This man, when he succeeded to the kingdom, appointed one Lysias to have charge of the government and to be chief governor of Coelesyria and Phoenecia.

   Lysias was appointed guardian to the young King; Macron was the Seleucid administrator but he was friendly to the Jews

¹²   Ptolemy, who was called Macron, took the lead in showing justice to the Jews because of the wrong that had been done to them, and attempted to maintain peaceful relations with them....

The text suggests that shortly after the period of religious persecution the then Seleucid administrator Ptolomy Macron tried to reach out to the Jews to repair the damage caused by the Antiochan persecution – but this was not a wise policy because the Jews were unpopular at the time.

¹³   As a result he was accused before Eupator by the King's friends. He heard himself called a traitor at every turn because he had abandoned Cyprus, which Philometer had given to him, and had gone over to Antiochus Epiphanes. Unable to command the respect due to his office he took poison and ended his life.

   A reference to his switching sides when he was an administrator in Cyprus

We can never know the true reason for Macron's suicide, but the narrator provides some insights into how the suicide of a high official was understood at the time. The explanation seems to lie exclusively within his professional role, in the politics of the day, and the ebb and flow of pro- or anti-Jewish sentiment, and whether a man could be trusted or not, or considered to be a traitor. In contrast to some the earlier Bible suicides, the death of Macron has no religious dimension, possibly because he was a not a Jew. It is not Yahweh who has dictated his death. Like the death of Ahithopel, a senior administrator of an earlier generation, the suicide is neither impulsive nor violent but deliberate and achieved in a state of calm. There is no mention of any sort of sadness or personal distress, and all that seems to matter is the ongoing political saga of the day. The story of the death of Macron is placed in the middle of the Hanukkah Chanucah story, an important Jewish festival which is still celebrated today, yet, despite Macron's pro-Jewish stance, neither his life nor his death gains any mention in the Chanucah liturgy or in any later Jewish and Christian theology. Instead, his suicide seems to be in the classical Greek style of drinking poison, and Van Hooff found that around 8% of all suicides in his Graeco-Roman series died by taking poison.

## *The suicide of Judas Iscariot: the remorse of a traitor*

The betrayal of Jesus by Judas for 30 pieces of silver is one of the best-known stories of the New Testament. It is of course not a part of the Old Testament, which is the main focus of this book. However, I have chosen to include it as it is perhaps the best-known of the Bible suicides.

Judas has remorse and realisation that his actions led to the death of his friend and hero Jesus. The account of his death by hanging only appears in the gospel of Matthew. A second and different account is given in Acts, thought to be written by Luke.

Judas was one of the 12 disciples and was also a close friend of Jesus and had even lived with him for three years. His act of betraying Jesus to Caiaphas and the Temple authorities makes him one of the archetypal informers, a much-hated role that has always existed in society. The account of Judas's betrayal is given slightly different meanings in each of the four gospels. The version in John is the most vituperative and ascribes a pecuniary motive and accuses Judas of being a thief and as a result of this Judas became increasingly demonised in later Christian history. He became the archetypal Jew and his role in the crucifixion of Jesus formed a major part of the later damaging Christian charge of Jews killing Christ (the religious basis for much anti-Semitism).

The name Judas is derived from the Hebrew *Yehudah* (Judah) and Iscariot is thought to be derived from a town in southern Judea called Kerioth, which is mentioned in Josiah 15[25]. Judas was the son of a man named Simon. Otherwise nothing is known about his origins.

There are three different versions of his death. In Matthew it is a death by hanging and is clearly a suicide. In Acts his body swells up and he falls forward on his stomach, which bursts open, and thirdly in the early Christian writings of Papias it is also a death through his flesh becoming bloated and this is thought to be the death of sinners. The account of Judas' death is preceded by his famous betrayal of Jesus, which is a central part of Christian religious tradition. Jesus was a charismatic leader and had become increasingly powerful. Many listened to his teachings and this greatly upset the religious authorities at the Jerusalem Temple. His condemnation of the Pharisees, the Sadducees and the priests of the Temple as being hypocritical, greedy and corrupt was the final straw and this is described in Matthew 23. The Temple priests then conspired to get rid of him by handing him over to Pontius Pilate, the Roman governor.

> 26[3] Then the chief priests and the elders of the people gathered in the palace of the high priest who was called Caiaphas and they conspired to arrest Jesus by stealth and kill him but they said not during the festival or there may be a riot among the people....

A little further on a passage describes the treachery of Judas:

> [14] Then one of the twelve who was called Judas Iscariot went to the chief priests and said what will you give me if I betray him to you? They paid him 30 pieces of silver. [15] And from that moment he began to look for an opportunity to betray him.

The actual act of betrayal was to be through a specially prearranged signal to identify Jesus by a kiss, the so-called 'kiss of Judas', and this is described in Matthew 26[47-51]:

[47] While he was still speaking, Judas, one of the twelve, arrived: with him was a large crowd with swords and clubs, from the chief priests and the elders of the people. [48] Now the betrayer had given them a sign, saying 'the one I shall kiss is the man; arrest him'. [49] At once he came up to Jesus and said 'Greetings Rabbi!' and kissed him. [50] Jesus said to him 'Friend, do what you are here to do'. Then they came and laid hands on Jesus and arrested him.

After his arrest Jesus was taken to Caiaphas, then handed over to Pontius Pilate and soon after was crucified. Judas then became remorseful at the betrayal and realising he had done wrong, returned the money, as described in Matthew 27:

[3] Then when Judas, who had betrayed Him, saw that He had been condemned, he felt remorse and returned the thirty pieces of silver to the chief priests and elders, [4] saying, 'I have sinned by betraying innocent blood'. But they said, 'What is that to us? See to that yourself!' [5] And he threw the pieces of silver into the temple sanctuary and departed; and he went away and hanged himself. [6] The chief priests took the pieces of silver and said, 'It is not lawful to put them into the temple treasury, since it is the price of blood.'

A different account of his death is given in Acts 1[15-20]. Peter is speaking to the crowd (Acts 1[15]).

In those days Peter stood among the believers, together the crowd numbered about 120 people [16] and said 'Friends, the Scripture had to be fulfilled, which the holy spirit through David foretold concerning Judas who became a guide for those who arrested Jesus, [17] for he was numbered among us and was allotted his share in the ministry. [18] Now this man acquired a field with the reward of his wickedness and falling headlong, he burst open in the middle and all his bowels gushed out.

A third account the death of Judas is given by Papias, a Christian writer of the 2nd century:

his flesh became bloated to such an extent that he could not walk through the space through which a wagon could easily pass, the huge bulk of his head could not go through. (Papias fragment 6, *Patres Apostolici*, quoted in Flanagan, 1967)

A death through swelling was the death of sinners. Flanagan explains the different accounts as representing two different theological traditions. The death by hanging for being a traitor rests on the Ahithopel tradition, as he had been a traitor to King David. The later versions in Acts and that of Papias rest on symbolism based on the Book of Wisdom, which condemns the bodies of sinners, who would be struck down speechless and they should die prostrated (swollen). Thus the versions in Matthew and in Acts do not portray the actual historical circumstances of the death of Judas but rather point to its differing theological meanings (Flanagan, 1967).

### Shame and betrayal – a modern perspective

Ahithopel betrays his master, King David, by switching sides to join the revolt of Absalom, Macron betrays his King, Ptolomey Philometer, in the

Cyprus wars by switching sides and joining with Antiochus IV, and Judas Iscariot betrays his master, Jesus. In the written accounts of all three suicides the narrators appear to highlight the role of shame associated with the treachery. Shame was also important in the suicide of Abimelech, who says he would feel shame if people thought 'he had been killed by a woman'.

Although these four suicides all occur in very different historical eras and cultural settings, it is of interest that the more recent psychoanalytical literature also highlights the importance of shame over and above that of depression in the act of suicide. Thus Lansky (1991) writes 'shame is the most significant affect in suicidal patients, while depression, guilt and anger are secondary to the shame in driving the suicide'. Shame is the feeling associated with the failure to live up to ideals and to achieve important aspirations and goals. Shame is a response to feedback from others indicating incompetence or inefficiency and may be indistinguishable from hopelessness. Sometimes it is also associated with exhibitionism and falling short in the context of an ambitious driving quality, as in the case of some brilliant students who feel they have not lived up to expectations. Excessive primitive shame triggered by the experience of incompetence or inadequacy or lack of control can provoke cognitive impairment and bodily reactions and even a sense of self-disintegration. Shame may be related to the loss of, or impossibility of, meaningful bonding (Ronningstam *et al.*, 2009).

Although the biblical writers had no knowledge of mental illness or its connection to suicide there seems to have been some understanding that the emotion of shame played a role in suicide and so perhaps they fashioned their texts to incorporate this into their final versions.

## The suicides of martyrdom

Jewish martyrdom first appears in the late post-exilic period when Judea was occupied by the Greeks and then later again under the Romans. At first cases were occasional and death was usually at the hands of the occupiers but there were a few instances where the final act was a self-killing and there were also several episodes of mass suicide. The Romans made many martyrs of the early Christians; the topic of early martyrdom is covered in detail in the book *A Noble Death: Suicide and Martyrdom Amongst Christians and Jews in Antiquity* (Droges and Talbot, 1992). In this section only the death of Razis, the mother and the seventh son are considered.

### The death of Razis: suicide and martyrdom together

The dramatic death of Razis took place in 161 BCE and is described in 2 Mac. 14; it is one of the earliest stories of Jewish martyrdom and has as its backcloth the complexities of Jewish-Hellenic relationships, the religious persecution of the Jews by the Seleucids, and the Jewish counter-rebellion led by their champion Judas Maccabeus. Additional commentary below is taken from the works of Goldstein (1983) and Schwartz (2008).

King Seleucid IV (187–175 BCE) reigned over the Eastern Seleucid Empire and he had sent his son Demetrius to Rome as a hostage. Soon after

Demetrius returned from Rome, he was dispatched to quell the disorder and rebellion in Palestine. His fleet landed in Tripolis (modern Tarablus in Lebanon) and with a large army he headed straight to Jerusalem. An embittered former high priest of the Jerusalem Temple, Alcimus, approached Demetrius, who by now had become King, and warned him that the local Jewish leader, Judas Maccabeus, was stirring up rebellion:

14⁶Those of the Jews who are called Hasideans whose leader is Judas Maccabeus are keeping up war and stirring sedition and will not let the Kingdom attain tranquillity.... ⁸For the folly of those whom I have mentioned our whole nation is now in no small misfortune ... for as long as Judas lives it is impossible for the Government to find peace.

This speech of Alcimus so inflames King Demetrius that he orders his General, Nicanor, to kill Judas and scatter his forces. Demetrius then rewards the manipulative Alcimus by appointing him as high priest to the Temple.

14¹⁴And the gentiles throughout Judea who had fled before Judas flocked to join Nicanor thinking that the misfortunes and calamities of the Jews would mean prosperity for themselves.

Such persecutions of the Jews were popular at the time. Nicanor was, however, greatly troubled by the order to destroy Judas. He had only recently been defeated by the armies of Judas and in the ensuing peace treaty the two had made up and become friends.

14²⁴ And he [Nicanor] kept Judas always in his presence, he was warmly attached to the man.

The scheming Alcimus, observing their friendship, reported this back to King Demetrius, complaining about Nicanor's disloyalty to his Seleucid master, even hinting that Nicanor wanted Judas to become his successor:

14²⁷ But he [Alcimus] found an opportunity that furthered his mad purpose when he was invited by Demetrius to a meeting of the council. ²⁸The King became excited and provoked by the false accusations of that depraved man [Alcimus] and he wrote to Nicanor stating he was displeased with the covenant and commanded him to send Maccabeus to Antioch as a prisoner without delay.

Nicanor was even more troubled by the reiteration of the order to arrest Judas and this time he knew he could not disobey the royal edict. As a result Nicanor became cold and distant in his dealings with Judas, and Judas picked this up and, so sensing danger, he fled. Outwitted by his escape Nicanor was unable to find Judas. He went to the Temple and in his anger demanded that the local Jews should turn Judas over to him.

14³³ If you do not hand Judas over to me as a prisoner, I will level this shrine to God to the ground and tear down the altar and build here a splendid temple to Dionysus [a Greek god].

Judas Maccabeus could not be found, but instead an elderly Jewish man called Razis was found and denounced to Nicanor as 'the father of the Jews' and was made to face the full wrath of Nicanor in the place of Judas. The death of Razis is a dramatic tale, with the Jewish martyr Razis as the hero and the Seleucid General Nicanor as the villain.

The story also shows how friendships and alliances between the Jews and the Greeks alternated with periods of persecution during the Hellenic period. Thus Alcimus, the assimilated Jewish high priest, is an advisor to Demetrius; Nicanor and Judas are both military men and they fight each other but for a brief period become friends. Added to this melee are conflicts and tension within the Jewish community itself around the issue of assimilation, and this, together with the ongoing religious persecution, results in instability, to the point where rebellion and violence ensue. It is in this dangerous climate that Razis, a Jewish elder, sacrifices himself in the name of his religion. The botched suicide attempt of Razis, and his prayer for resurrection immediately prior to his gory end, is described in 2 Maccabees:

| | | |
|---|---|---|
| 14³⁷ | A certain Razis, one of the elders of Jerusalem, was denounced to Nicanor as a man who loved his compatriots and was very well thought of and for his goodwill was called Father of the Jews. | Gk *Gerousia* = city elders *Razis* possibly an Iranian name |
| 38 | In former times, when there was no mingling with the gentiles, he had been accused of Judaism and he had most zealously risked body and life for Judaism. | assimilation is now the problem Razis 'tried' for his Judaism |
| 39 | Nicanor, wishing to exhibit the enmity he had for the Jews, sent more than five hundred soldiers to arrest him; | Nicanor, the Seleucid general Expecting resistance, hence the |
| 40 | for he thought by arresting him he would do them an injury. | 500 soldiers |
| 41 | When the troops were about to capture the tower and were forcing the door of the courtyard, they ordered that fire be brought and the doors burned. Being surrounded, Razis fell upon his sword, | Honourable self-killing to avoid |
| 42 | preferring to die nobly rather than fall into the hands of sinners and suffer outrages unworthy of his noble birth. | torture |
| 43 | But in the heat of the struggle he did not hit exactly and the crowd was now rushing in through the doors. He courageously ran up the wall, and bravely threw himself down into the crowd. | Botched suicide attempt The narrator emphasises the super-human strength of Razis |
| 44 | But they drew back quickly, a space opened and he fell in the middle of the empty space. Still alive and aflame with anger, he rose, and though his blood gushed forth, and his wounds were severe He ran through the crowd and standing on a steep rock, with his blood now completely drained from him, he tore out | Second attempt by jumping |

| his entrails took them in both hands | Third suicide attempt, |
| and hurled them into the crowds, | by self-disembowelment, |
| calling on the lord of life and spirit | prayer for resurrection |
| to give them back to him again. | |
| This was the manner of his death. | |

Goldstein (1983) writes that this account probably includes legendary additions which serve to heighten the drama. Scholars sometimes compare the initial botched suicide attempt of Razis to a similar episode in one of the plays by Euripides where Meneocceus dies for the salvation of his city but his first attempt to kill himself with a sword thrust failed and so he tried again by hurling himself down into enemy lines. The suicide of Razis had an exhibitionistic quality and Van Hooff (1990) termed such suicides *iactatio*, or showing off. Exhibitionistic suicide was an acknowledged category within Roman jurisprudence and the verdict was 'suicide with ostentation as some philosophers do' – the latter referring to the death of the philosopher Empedocles, who threw himself into the crater of the volcano Mt Etna. During the great persecution of the early Christians in Nicomedia in northern Turkey, as many as 20,000 Christian martyrs hurled themselves into the flames of the fire at the imperial palace started by the soldiers of the Emperor Maximian (285–304 CE), who forbade Christianity.

## Self-disembowelling

Self-disembowelling is a very rare form of suicide. Most famously it occurs in the Japanese ritual of *Hara-Kiri* as well as in the second account of the death of Judas Iscariot. Ash (1996) provides a psychoanalytic explanation. Shame is the main affect involved in the suicidal act and disembowelling seems to have the aim of exorcising the shameful part of the body in order to regain face and to be purified. The relationship between the external object and the shameful interject is even more apparent when the *Hara-Kiri* victim throws his viscera at his object (Tarachow, 1960), establishing the union by contaminating him with his shameful parts.

The martyrdom of Razis and his prayer for resurrection set a precedent for many later acts of religious martyrdom. The manner of his death was much lauded by the Donatists, an extreme Christian sect of the 4th and 5th centuries CE who were renowned for the high frequencies of their suicides. This was one of the groups that eventually led Augustine and the Church to proscribe suicide.

## The death of the seventh son and his mother: suicide and martyrdom

The first account of the story and how the seven sons and their mother Hannah are tortured and then burned alive in defence of their religious faith is in 2 Maccabees (circa 135 BCE) and is thought to relate to the Antiochan persecutions of 166/167 BCE. However, this account includes no mention of suicide. Some 200 years later, a second version of the story appeared in 4 Maccabees (circa 50–100 CE) but in this account the seventh son and his mother hurl themselves into the flames and so their deaths are seen as voluntary and hence as suicides.

The author of 4 Maccabees was a religious Jew with a strong belief in the Torah and Jewish national identity but he was also well versed in Greek philosophy, as the book is written in the style of Greek rhetoric. The book is concerned with religious persecution, and rabbinic sources suggest it refers to martyrdom during the Hadrianic persecutions of the 1st century CE, possibly in Antioch. Linguistic and historical analysis also place its composition towards the end of the 1st century CE. The martyrs, Hannah and her seven sons, are venerated in the Roman Catholic Calendar of Saints on 1 August; according to Antiochene Christian tradition, their relics were interred in a synagogue (now a church) in the Kerateion quarter of Antioch.

The original story in 2 Maccabees was mainly concerned with issues of assimilation and Hellenisation which had culminated in the Antiochian persecutions. In this story each brother is asked by the tyrant Antiochus to break the strict Jewish dietary laws by eating swine flesh. This the brothers steadfastly refuse to do, and then one by one they are all tortured in front of the King before being burnt alive. The death of the seventh son and his mother is described in 2 Mac. 7[39-40]:

> [39]The king fell into a rage, and handled him worse, being exasperated by his scorn. [40]So he died in his integrity, putting his whole trust in the Lord. Last of all, the mother died, after her sons.

In this first version of the story there is no mention of suicide. Schwartz (2008) expresses his doubt as to the historical truth of this original story and writes:

> As with historicity while there definitely were martyrs in the Antiochian persecutions, no one would claim that this story is anything more than a stylised, didactic narrative perhaps deriving from a historicisation of Jeremiah 15[9] which refers to the death of the unfortunate mother in the same way as they died.

The original story in 2 Maccabees takes up only one chapter of 42 verses. The *same* story in 4 Maccabees but written some 200 years later takes up 10 chapters with 255 verses and so it is a huge elaboration of the original story. If Schwartz is correct that 2 Maccabees is a mainly legendary work then the story's elaboration in 4 Maccabees and the change of the mode of death to suicide is most likely a later fictional embellishment. Any sort of clinical analysis would therefore be pointless, but the story and in particular the speech of the mother before her death give some insight into the theology and logic that lay behind the suicides of martyrdom for faith among both the Jews and Christians of the 1st century CE.

Thus King Antioch tells the seventh son that his brothers were all very stupid to die because they disobeyed him. He feels compassion for the youngest son and offers him friendship and even a place in his government if he obeys the King but, if not, he too will be burned to death. His mother intervenes and the narrator highlights that her exhortation to refuse the King and not to give up his faith is made in Hebrew. The seventh son follows his mother's wishes and in defiance says to the King:

| | |
|---|---|
| 12[16] 'I do not desert the excellent example of my brothers | |
| [17] and I call upon the God of our ancestors to be merciful to our nation | Adherence to religious tradition is paramount |
| [18] but on you he will take vengeance both in the present life and when you are dead'. | Vengeance and hatred are also motives for the |
| [19] After he had uttered these imprecations he flung himself into the braziers and so ended his life. | suicide He kills himself. |

The death of the mother is preceded by her lengthy speech ($16^{12-13}$, $16^{18-23}$ and $17^1$), which gives a justification for martyrdom, and the role of suffering in religion and the need to steadfastly hold one's belief that it is better to die than to be coerced into changing one's faith, provides a helpful exposition for the thinking underlying a religious martyrdom:

| | |
|---|---|
| 16[12] Yet that holy and God-fearing mother did not wail with such a lament for any of them from dying, nor did she grieve as they were dying. | Dissociation from all normal feelings, including grieving for one's dying sons |
| [13] On the contrary, as though having a mind like adamant and giving rebirth for immortality to the whole number of her sons, she implored them and urged them on to their death for the sake of religion | Strong belief that resurrection will occur and this is used to overcome fears of death Religious faith all important |
| [18] Remember it is through God that you have had a share in the world and have enjoyed life | Martyrdom is for God |
| [20] For the sake also our father Abraham was zealous to sacrifice Isaac, the ancestor of our nation; and when Isaac saw his father's hand wielding the knife and descending on him he did not cower.... | Identification with Hebrew patriarchs and so the martyrdom is specifically Jewish Isaac possibly is the original Jewish martyr |
| [23] It is unreasonable for people who have religious knowledge not to withstand pain... | ? Masochism. Religious faith will let the martyr withstand pain |
| 17[1] Some of the Guards said that when she was about to be seized and put to death she threw herself into the flames so that no one might touch her body | ? a rumour of being put to death but she commits suicide to maintain her sexual purity |

Whether or not the mother herself truly spoke these words we will never know, but the narrator by putting these words into the mouths of the seventh son and the mother explains the complex motivations that lie behind martyrdoms by suicide: there is a fanatical degree of religious faith; the religion is specifically identified through naming its patriarchs; dissociation through faith will dispel ordinary emotions such as grief; there is a suggestion of masochism as pain and suffering are integral to religious faith and are to be expected; there are powerful feelings of vengeance directed at the foreign oppressor; resurrection to an afterlife will be the reward for such martyrdom. To a limited degree such thinking applies to many of the later Christian and Jewish martyrdoms as well as to the more recent suicide martyrdoms such as the Buddhists monks of Tibet, who immolate themselves in protest at the Chinese occupation. Their great fear is of losing their Tibetan cultural identity – and this was the fear of many religious Jews under the Greek occupation.

There is very little comment about the mother's suicide in the Old Testament literature. I have found only one comment in the Midrash, in Lamentations Rabbah 1.50. This Midrashic writer is unwilling to condone voluntary suicide but he explains the mother's death as follows.

> The mother had become insane after watching the execution of her sons and that is why she killed herself.

This was written sometime between the 4th and 8th century CE, probably during the post-Augustinian period, by which time both the Jewish and Christian faiths were strongly opposed to suicide. Nevertheless, the above comment shows that even during this very early period, which was long before the advent of psychiatry, there was some understanding that insanity might lie behind a suicide and there was also a degree of compassion for the mentally ill, who should be spared from the full moral condemnation of a suicide which by that stage was widespread (Goldstein, 1983, p. 493).

## Suicide today – a brief overview

Suicide is a major public health problem. In the UK today around 5,000 people a year commit suicide, in the USA around 30,000 and worldwide around 1 million. It ranks as the world's 10th leading cause of death. In the UK, where deaths due to a medical illness are uncommon among the young, suicide is now the leading cause of death in those under 50 years of age. Suicide is a multi-determined act with many different risk factors, including biological causes, a specific genetic predisposition to suicide, the major mental disorders, adverse personal circumstances and a wide variety of socio-cultural factors as well.

There is a huge and poorly understood variation in rates for suicide between different nations. The overall average world rate is 14.5 per 100,000 for both sexes, but in some countries and certain sub-groups these rates may be grossly elevated. Rates per 100,000 for men are given in parentheses after the nation in question, and the data are derived from the World Health Organization, quoted in Bertolote and Fleischmann (2009). These rates are highest in Eastern Europe: Lithuania (70), followed by Belarus (63), Russia (61) and Hungary (45). Sri Lanka also has a high rate (45), as do the Scandinavian countries: Finland (31), Estonia (35). The rates are lower for the UK (11) and the USA (18), Germany (20), Australia (17) and France (20). Israel has a fairly low rate (7.5). Rates are low for South and Central America and also for Muslim countries. The strictures against suicide in the Quran are so strong that a suicide verdict is rarely given and so figures from these countries are probably unreliable.

The reasons for such variation in rates are poorly understood. France and Italy, both Catholic countries, are neighbours but France has double the rate of Italy. Studies based in countries which have high immigrant numbers such as the USA and Australia have revealed that the suicide rates appear to follow a person's country of origin rather than their current domicile. Within countries there are considerable regional variations. Census data suggest that areas of high social fragmentation as evidenced by the number of persons in single households and high levels of population mobility appear to have high rates of suicide, consistent with the Durkheim's notion that levels of social integration are a critical factor. Thus in Vienna and Berlin, elderly women living on their own who are physically frail have very high rates.

The overall sex ratio for suicide is about 3:1, with males predominating, but the sex ratio also varies widely. All the Old Testament suicides are in men, but female suicides were well documented in the Graeco-Roman literature and in Rome the male–female ratio was 5:1 while in ancient Greece it was 3:1 (Van Hooff, 1992). In China today the sex ratio is almost equal at 0.8:1. Suicide rates tend to rise with age and some of the highest rates overall are found among elderly men. Thus for males over 75 the following figures per 100,000 are given: China (140), South Korea (130), Austria (93), Lithuania (82), but for the UK the rate for elderly males is only 10.4. Rates are higher in rural than urban communities, particularly in China and India. Thus one recent study of suicide in the south of Vellore in rural India found that 11% of *all deaths* were due to suicide (Bose *et al.*, 2006). It should be noted that ancient Israel was essentially a rural society.

Rates are higher for those in social classes 4 and 5 and certain occupations such as physicians and dentists. Recent studies have shown there are complex interactions between social class, occupation and cultural expectations (for a review, see Platt, 2011).

A psychiatric autopsy of a case of suicide entails interviewing family members about the mental health of the recently deceased relative. In the series of Barraclough *et al.* (1974) 93% of cases had a psychiatric disorder and only 7% were well in the weeks prior to the suicide. Of those with a psychiatric disorder, 70% had depression, 27% had a personality disorder and 19% had substance abuse – mainly alcoholism – and their finding that about 90% were mentally ill around the time of their deaths has been replicated in six other psychiatric autopsy studies. Partly because of this strong association with mental illness, the management of suicidal patients has now become a part of medicine and psychiatry in particular, but this has not always been the case.

Mental illness is clearly a major cause and Harris and Barraclough (1997) pooled the results on 227 studies of suicide which had also recorded a psychiatric diagnosis prior to the death and estimated the standardised mortality rate for suicide for each psychiatric disorder. Anorexia nervosa emerged as the most lethal psychiatric disorder and carries a 23-fold increased rate. The risks for other disorders were major depression (× 20), bipolar disorder (15), opiate use (14), anxiety neurosis (10), schizophrenia (9), personality disorders (7) and alcoholism (6), but for learning difficulties the risk was 0.88, which indicated no increased risk. Factors which raised the risk were: a previous suicide attempt, by a factor of 40; previous compulsory detention (38); and previously having been a psychiatric inpatient (7).

The 15-fold increased risk for bipolar disorder may be relevant to the case of Saul, who may have had bipolar disorder, while the 7-fold risk for personality disorder may be relevant in the case of Abimelech, who may have been an aggressive psychopath.

Around 10% of those with schizophrenia ultimately kill themselves, usually as a result of associated depression but sometimes as a result of command hallucinations, where loud voices direct them to do so. The lifetime risk for alcoholics is also high at around 2.4–3.4%. This usually occurs after many years of heavy drinking, commonly after a relationship break-up or some other loss, and alcoholic subjects are usually depressed at the time.

Social factors are also important and the scientific study of suicide starts with the work of the great French sociologist Durkheim, who published his book *Le Suicide* in 1897. Durkheim thought the most important personal factor in suicide was the extent to which an individual was either integrated or alienated from society. He identified four types of suicide: egoistic, altruistic, anomic and fatalistic. Egoistic suicide results from poor integration to society, for example due to mental illness. By contrast, altruistic suicide is due to over-integration into society, as in the Japanese *Hara Kiri*. Perhaps the suicides of Ahithophel and Macron, two dutiful civil servants, were of this type. Anomic suicide occurs when the bonds between an individual and society have become loosened and there is no regulation; possibly the criminal excesses and suicide of Abimelech relate to this. In a fatalistic suicide there is excessive regulation by society and the individual has no personal freedom; the suicide of a slave is perhaps an example.

Sociological theory has moved on from Durkheim but his statistical methodology of comparing suicide rates in different social groups remains the cornerstone of modern suicidology. Thus the rates for the unemployed are higher than for those in work and in the USA rates peaked during the great economic depression of the 1930s with its high unemployment, only to fall during World War II, when unemployment fell and the nation joined together in a common purpose.

Marriage may protect – rates are lower for married people than for single persons, while for those who are separated, widowed or divorced rates may be increased fourfold. However, among some cultural sub-groups marriage is not protective. For example, young married Indian women in the UK have much higher rates than the indigenous population, possibly as a result of family pressure to succeed in an arranged marriage with a partner not necessarily of their own choosing.

A strong affiliation to religion is generally also held to have a protective effect against suicide and the initial observation by Morselli (1881) showed that the Catholic states in Germany had consistently lower rates (6 per 100,000) than Protestant states (19 per 100,000). This was further explored by Durkheim (1897). The explanation offered at that time was that the Catholic religion had many more beliefs, rituals and practices than Protestantism and hence demanded a much greater degree of religious participation and it was the strength of affiliation that gave protection from suicide.

A review of the 162 studies completed between 1882 and 2008 found that 82% reported a protective effect but 18% did not. Religion also offers some protection from depression, which is a common precursor to suicide. However, the protective effect against suicide is very complex. It seems to operate both at the national and the individual levels. Thus nations dominated by religions which strongly condemn suicide, such as Catholicism and Islam, appeared to have lower rates of both completed and attempted suicide. At an individual level the picture is also complicated, and the protective effect does not appear to derive from the religion itself but from the individual's degree of religiosity (i.e. the strength of commitment, strength of belief, and frequency of church attendance). It is also thought that regular meetings with co-religionists provide helpful social interactions and 'a moral community' where there is very little in the way of deviant behaviour of any sort, combined with a much lower level of suicide acceptability than in the wider community. For those who have religious beliefs discussions with priests or a spiritual approach to problems is sometimes helpful (Cook *et al.*, 2009). The scientific literature on the topic of the protective effect of religion and suicide is both vast and complex and the interested reader is referred to a review by Stack and Kposowa (2011).

Stress in the form of recent adverse or negative life events may be important as a proximal cause. However, Maris *et al.* (2000) point out that stress and adversity tend to repeat over a person's lifetime and the vast majority of people do not respond to social adversity by committing suicide. The predisposition to mental illness is present in only a minority of the population, which may explain why only a few people succumb to suicide in the face of adversity. Life events entailing a loss are sometimes called 'exit events' and these are more frequent in the months preceding a suicide; their risk is increased by a factor of 10 among those who have made a suicide attempt (Paykel *et al.*, 1975).

Suicide can sometimes be 'contagious' and occur in clusters. This is sometimes known as 'the Werther effect', the name given to the media influence on social suicidal behaviour, after an apparent epidemic of suicides by shooting which occurred following the publication of Goethe's book *The Sorrows of Young Werther*, in which the hero dies by shooting himself when his love for a woman is not reciprocated (Philips, 1974). These epidemic effects may be relevant to the mass suicides of biblical times as well as those in the modern era and episodes of group self-mutilation, for example in the case of Elijah and the Prophets of Baal.

Hereditary factors are also important. One of the best-known suicides of the 20th century was that of the Nobel Prize-winning author Ernest Hemingway. At the age of 61, he shot himself in Ketchum, Ohio. Hemingway had had four wives, numerous affairs, drank to excess and was a lifelong depressive. He greatly enjoyed his writing, which helped to relieve his depression, but despaired towards the end of his life because he could no longer write. At the time of his death he was being treated with ECT in the Mayo Clinic. What is less well known is that his father, one of his sons, as well as himself all suffered from bipolar disorder, and that his father, his brother, sister and granddaughter all also committed suicide. At a later date his granddaughter told a journalist that she thought the whole Hemingway family was 'very, very dysfunctional', just before she also committed suicide (after Jamison, 1993). A family history of completed suicide is usually taken as a serious risk factor among those who have survived a suicide attempt.

More formal analysis of whether a familial trait is truly genetic or a learned experience depends on twin and adoption studies and these confirm a significant and specific hereditary component to suicide. Psychoanalytic theories of suicide abound, but no single personality type or dynamic can be found to explain the large variety of different suicides; the topic is reviewed by Maltsberger and Goldbatt (1996).

For those who are unsuccessful in their attempts or those with mental illness expressing suicidal thoughts, a great deal can be done, usually by trying to treat the underlying mental illness. Antidepressants and a wide variety of different psychotherapies are employed and at least in the short term are generally helpful. Most countries have suicide prevention programmes, mainly educational in direction, and these may also help in the short term, but have yet to show any impact on national rates, and, overall, the global suicide rate appears to be rising. The huge efforts that now go into treatment and prevention of suicide are well covered in Wasserman and Wasserman (2009) and Platt (2011) and other textbooks of psychiatry.

## Suicidal thoughts

There are several characters in the Old Testament who express a weariness with life. Thus Rebecca exclaims 'I am weary of my life because of the Hittite women. If Jacob marries one of the Hittite women such as these, one of the women of the land, what good should my life do to me?' (Gen. 27[46]). She says this when she hears that Esau plans to kill his brother Jacob for stealing the birthright and she despairs that she will lose both her sons and so advises Jacob to flee to her brother Laban, who lives in Haran, a Hittite city – but if they do this, there will be a risk of him marrying a Hittite woman.

Elijah also expresses a wish to die after hearing that Jezebel has planned to kill him because Elijah has killed all the prophets of Baal, a group whom she favoured (see page 278).

> [3]Then he [Elijah] was afraid: he got up and fled for his life, and came to Beersheba, which belongs to Judah; he left his servant here. [4]But he himself went a day's journey into the wilderness and came and sat under a solitary broom tree. He asked that he might die: 'It is enough: now, O Lord take my life away for I am no better than my ancestors.' (I Kings 19)

Perhaps he felt some remorse as well as fear after he had killed all 250 prophets of Baal.

In the next section, only the depression and suicidal thoughts of Sarah and Tobit, as described in the Book of Tobit, are considered in detail.

### *Tobit: suicidal thoughts and suicide planning in depression*

Depression is the most common affect linked to suicide, but depression is not mentioned in any of the earlier suicides in the OT, appearing for the first time only in the much later Book of Tobit, which provides an excellent account of suicidal ideation associated with depression. Tobit comes to us through its early Greek translations, and was thought to have first been written in Greek. However, with the discovery of the Dead Sea Scrolls in 1952, five fragments from the Book of Tobit were found in Cave 4; four of these fragments were in Aramaic and one was in Hebrew, and so it is now thought the original composition was probably in Aramaic.

The book is a romantic Jewish novella and expresses the moral values of the time: prayer, faithfulness to only one God, observance of the dietary laws, devotion to one's family, high personal ethical standards, and being charitable to the less well advantaged and so forth. Though entertaining, its primary purpose was to provide religious and moral teaching in the form of an adventure story. Moore (2009) suggests it was composed between 250 and 175 BCE, although Fitzmyer (2003), on the basis of the Qumran Aramaic texts, places it at around 300 BCE, but it is generally agreed that it was composed during the Hellenic period. Because much of the story is located in Media (Persia), it is thought to have been written somewhere in the Jewish diaspora, but exactly where and by whom is unknown.

The Book of Tobit does not have canonical status in the Jewish religious scriptures or for Protestants but is canonical for the Roman Catholic and Eastern Orthodox Churches. This was for *halachic* reasons. Thus the great lay Pharisee of the first century BCE, Simon Ben Shetah, insisted that the Ketubah (the marriage document) must be written by the bridegroom, whereas in the Book of Tobit the Ketubah was written by Raguel, who is the bride's father. From a modern perspective, this seems to be a relatively trivial reason for excluding such a literary gem from the Jewish canon.

## The story of Tobit

Tobit is a Jewish exile who lives in Nineveh with his wife Hannah and their son Tobias. He is a pious man who does many good deeds, such as feeding the poor and burying the corpses of those without families. One day during the Pentecost feast, his son tells him there is a corpse of a dead Jew in the street. He immediately leaves his meal and rushes out into the street to give the dead Jew an honourable burial, and afterwards takes a well earned rest in the courtyard. Unfortunately, while he is resting, sparrows who are flying above the courtyard let their droppings fall into his eyes and this blinds him. His wife must now support the family and she berates him for this. Fed up with her nagging and his blindness he prays to God to end his life.

At the same time, in Ectabana, a town in Media, a parallel story is taking place. Sarah, the daughter of Raguel and Edna, who is a distant relative of Tobit, has become depressed because all her seven marriages have failed. It is the same every time: the bridegroom dies on the wedding night and this is all due to the wicked demon Asmodeus. The final straw comes when her maidservant chides her and says she will remain unmarried and childless and so Sarah becomes depressed and prays to God to take her life.

Fortunately, God hears the prayers of both Tobit and Sarah and sends his angel Raphael to heal both of them. In the guise of a mortal named Azariah, Raphael accompanies Tobit's son, Tobiah, to Ectabana, where he is to wed Sarah. As they are crossing the river Tigris, a big fish jumps out and grabs Tobiah's foot. Raphael says that Tobiah must kill the fish and prepare a medicine from the fish's gall, liver and heart. When Tobiah and

Raphael arrive in Ectabana, they meet Sarah and put drops of the extracted fish medicine onto burning embers – and the odour is so powerful that it exorcises the wicked Asmodeus out of Sarah's body so she is free to marry Tobiah. To everyone's surprise Tobiah survives the wedding night.

The newly married couple then journey back to Nineveh to Tobit's household, but they are late and Tobiah's mother, Hannah, has an anxiety attack, thinking they have died on the journey. When they finally arrive in Nineveh, on Raphael's instruction the fish medicine is placed on Tobit's eyelids and this cures his blindness. Tobit and Sarah then pray to God to thank Him for being healed and go on to live lengthy and fruitful lives.

The description of depression and its close association with suicidal thoughts here is unique in the biblical literature and is given in ch. 3, which mentions numerous depressive symptoms and is quoted below. It is also a part of the Catholic liturgy. Thus in the two-year cycle, in the Proper of Seasons on the Wednesday of the ninth week of year one, Tobit 3[1-11,16] is read in Catholic churches.

| | | |
|---|---|---|
| 3[1] | Then with much grief and anguish of heart | Depression, anxiety, |
| | I wept, and with groaning began to pray: | crying, agitation |
| [2] | You are righteous, O Lord, and all your | Prayer to God for relief |
| | deeds are just; all your ways are mercy | |
| | and truth; you judge the world. | |
| [3] | And now, O Lord, remember me | Personal prayer for a favour |
| | and look favourably upon me. | |
| | Do not punish me for my sins | Guilt |
| | and for my unwitting offences | Guilt for sins I am unaware of |
| | and those that my ancestors | Guilt for my ancestor's sins |
| | committed before you. | |
| | They sinned against you, | |
| [4] | and disobeyed your commandments. | |
| | So you gave us over to plunder, exile, | Their sins caused the exile |
| | and death, to become the talk, the | |
| | byword, and an object of reproach, | Low self-image |
| | among all the nations among | |
| | whom you have dispersed us. | |
| [5] | And now your many judgements are true | |
| | in exacting penalty from me for my sins | My problems are due to my sins |
| | For we have not kept your commandments | |
| | and have not walked in accordance with | |
| | truth before you. | |
| [6] | So now deal with me as you will; | |
| | command my spirit to be taken from me, | My soul should leave me |
| | so that I may be released from the | Release me from life |
| | face of the earth and become dust | suicidal wish |
| | For it is better for me to die than to live | Death better than life |
| | because I have had to listen to undeserved | too much criticism |
| | insults, and great is the sorrow within me. | I am very depressed |
| | Command, O Lord, that I be released | Prayer to let me die |
| | from this distress; release me to go to the. | |
| | eternal home and do not, O Lord, turn | |
| | your face away from me. | |

For it is better for me to die than to see
so much distress in my life and to listen
to insults.

Death better than the
suffering I must endure

7      On the same day, at Ecbatana in Media,
it also happened that Sarah, the daughter
of Raguel, was reproached by one of her
father's maids.

The story switches to Sarah
berated by her maidservant

8      For she had been married to seven
husbands, and the wicked demon
Asmodeus had killed each of them before
they bad been with her as is customary
for wives. So the maid said to her, 'You
are the one who kills your husbands!'
See you have already been married to
seven husbands and have not borne the
name of a single one of them.

Repeated relationship failure
All her husband's die before
consummation of marriage
The maid blames Sarah

9      Why do you beat us? Because your
husbands are dead? Go with them! May we
never see a son or daughter of yours!

You beat us (maidservants)
You should also die
You will be childless

10     On that day she was grieved in spirit and
wept. When she had gone up to her
father's upper room she intended to hang
herself but she thought it over and said
'Never shall I reproach my father, saying
to him 'You had only one beloved
daughter but she hanged herself because
of her distress.' And I shall bring my father
in his old age down in sorrow to Hades.
It is better for me not to hang myself.
but to pray to the Lord that I may die
and not listen to these reproaches anymore.

Low spirits, depressed, crying
Active suicide planning
reconsiders the intended suicide

Guilt at the thought of the hurt
she might cause her father
My father will probably die
of depression if I kill myself
Better not for me to do the act
but I still have suicidal thoughts
God should help me die

11     At the same time with hands outstretched
towards the window, she prayed and said,
Blessed are you merciful God!
Blessed is your name forever;
Let all your works praise you forever

Prayer; however, the prayer
is for God to help her to die
and so she is still suicidal

12     And now Lord, I turn my face to you
and raise my eyes towards you.

13     Command that I be released from the earth     Further expression of wish to die
and not listen to such reproaches anymore.

14     You know O Master that I am innocent
of any defilement with a man

15     And that I have not disgraced my name
or the name of my father in the land of
my exile. I am my father's only child:
He has no other child to be his heir
he has no close relative or other kindred
for whom I should keep myself as wife
already seven husbands of mine have died.
Why should I still live? But if it is not
pleasing to you, O Lord, to take my life.
Hear me in disgrace

The story is in the diaspora
compassion to her father
Worries about her father,
hold her back from the brink

My life is pointless, futile

I wish to be dead

<sup>16</sup> At that very moment the prayers of both
of them were heard in the glorious presence
of God.

<sup>17</sup> So Raphael was sent to heal both of them:    Raphael is a healing angel
Tobit by removing the white films from        who cures Tobit's blindness
his eyes, so that he might see God's light
with his eyes; and Sarah daughter of Raguel,
by giving her in marriage to Tobias, son of
Tobit and by setting her free from the
wicked demon Asmodeus.                         Healing relationship problems
For Tobias was entitled to have her before
all others who had desired to marry her
At the same time that Tobit returned
from the courtyard into his house
Sarah daughter of Raguel                       Intention to hang herself
came down from her upper room                  now gone

In contrast to much of the OT, the story is about two ordinary people
with no connection to the monarchy, the priesthood or religion. They are
the victims of apparently senseless suffering: for Tobit it is his blindness;
and for Sarah it is repeated marital failure. Both are plunged into depression
and in moments of suicidal despair both pray to God for death as a release
from their suffering. Their stories run in parallel; de Salers has produced a
small table (given in Moore, 1996) which demonstrates these parallels and
to this table I have added their self-reports of depression. Table 7.1 shows

**Table 7.1** Depression and suicidal thoughts for Tobit and Sarah

| *Tobit* | *Sarah* |
| --- | --- |
| His piety ($2^{1-7}$) | Sarah's innocence ($3^{14)}$) |
| His blindness ($2^{9-10}$) | The demon Asmodeus destroys her marriages($3^8$) |
| Reproached by his wife ($2^{14}$) | Reproached by her maidservant ($3^8$) |
| *Expressions of depression* | |
| Much grief and anguish ($3^1$) | Grieved in spirit ($3^{10}$) |
| Great is the sorrow within me ($3^6$) | because of her distress ($3^{10}$) |
| See so much distress in my life ($3^6$) | |
| *Suicidal ideation* | |
| May be released from the face of the earth ($3^6$) | Command I be released from the earth ($3^{13)}$) |
| Better for me to die than to live ($3^6$) | Why should I still live ($3^{14}$) |
| Release me to go to the eternal home ($3^6$) | Oh Lord take my life ($3^{14}$) |
| *Suicidal planning* | She intended to hang herself, she hanged herself because of her distress ($3^{10}$) |

that phrases suggestive of depression occur six times (four for Tobit, two for Sarah); suicidal ideation in the form of a wish to die also appears six times (three for Tobit, three for Sarah). Suicide planning, which is a marker of a more severe level of suicidal intent, appears only for Sarah, who intends to hang herself after going into the upstairs bedroom. The association of depression with suicidal thoughts is quite explicit here. These thoughts are repeated many times but there is conflict and guilt in Sarah's mind as to how her death might affect her father, which pulls back from the brink. Such a repetitious quality of the suicidal thoughts and counter-arguments involving loved ones in the family, particularly children, are characteristic of the way suicidal thoughts are reported in clinical populations today.

The narrator in the Book of Tobit has some sense that depression can recur and that depressives like Sarah need looking after to prevent this. Thus just before Tobias and Sarah set off for Nineveh to return to Tobit's house, Sarah's father, Raguel, expresses his concerns to his new son-in-law, Tobias:

> 8[20] Then he called for Tobias and swore on oath to him these words: 'You shall not leave here for 14 days but shall stay here eating and drinking here with me; and *you shall cheer up my daughter who has been depressed*'.

This is the only place in the Bible where the notion that a depressed person can be cheered up by someone else talking to them appears, and by implication suggesting that sometimes a talking treatment works.

Some of the more minor characters in the Book of Tobit also seem to suffer from anxiety or depression. Thus because Tobias and Sarah are delayed by two weeks in the start of their return journey back to Nineveh, they are late arriving back and this worries Tobit's wife, Hannah, to the extent that she has a fit of anxiety:

| | |
|---|---|
| 10[1] Now, day by day, Tobit kept counting how many days Tobias would need for going and for returning, and when the days had passed and his son did not appear | Tobit gets anxious about the delay in his son's return |
| 2 He said, Is it possible that he has been detained? or that Gabael has died, and there is no one to give him the money? | |
| 3 And he began to worry. | |
| 4 his wife Hannah said 'My child has perished and is no longer among the living.' and she began to weep and to mourn for her son saying | Fears of death in her anxiety |
| 5 'Woe is me, my child, the light of my eyes'. But Tobit kept saying to her, 'Be quiet and stop worrying, my dear he is all right. Probably something unexpected has happened there. The man who went with him is trustworthy and is one of our own kin. Do not grieve for him, my dear; he will soon be here'. | Weeping and depression Self-blame/misery Tobit tries to reassure her His wife is depressed. |
| 7 She answered him, 'Be quiet yourself, do not deceive me! My child has perished.' | Does not believe him |

| | |
|---|---|
| She would rush out every day and watch the road her son had taken, and would heed no one. When the sun had set she would go in and mourn and weep all night long, getting no sleep at all. | Convinced son is dead<br><br>Reassurance fails<br>At night, a low mood,<br>Weeping and insomnia |

Hannah gets into quite a state about the delay in her son's return. She has become tearful, agitated, irritable and depressed and cannot sleep as a consequence. Although this is quite understandable she shows most of the features of what in modern terminology would be called a 'mixed anxiety and depressive state' from which she can neither be comforted or reassured. The condition of mixed anxiety and depression is described in one of the appendices of DSM-5 (APP, 2013). The essential feature is a dysphoric mood lasting for at least a month together with four out of 10 symptoms. Here, after each symptom the verse in which it appears is given in parentheses. These are irritability (7), easily moved to tears (7) hypervigilance (7), sleep disturbances (7), pessimism about the future (4) and feelings of worthlessness (4). There is no suggestion of the other symptoms of fatigue, difficulties in concentrating or memory difficulties. Hannah has six of these symptoms as well as the dysphoria.

Sarah's mother, Edna, also seems to be quite an emotional person as well. Thus, when the family in Media hear about Tobit's blindness, she weeps:

> 7[8] ... His wife Edna also wept for him, and their daughter Sarah likewise wept....

A little further on, Edna has to get the marriage bed ready for Sarah. She is full of trepidation because the seven previous husbands all perished on their wedding night.

> 7[16] So she went and made the bed in the room as he had told her and brought Sarah there. She wept for her daughter. Then wiping away the tears she said to her 'Take courage my daughter, the Lord of Heaven grant you joy in place of your sorrow: take courage my daughter'. Then she went out.

### Making sense of the account of depression in the Book of Tobit

The earlier emotionless suicides of the defeated kings of the Old Testament are difficult to identify with or see in today's clinical populations. However, in this tale Tobit and Sarah are just ordinary people of no cultic importance. Tobit is a kindly elderly family man with an incurable medical condition, blindness, giving him depression with suicidal despair, and as such might have been a frequent visitor to the general medical outpatient clinic of today. The problems of Sarah and her failed relationships and suicidality are also frequently encountered in today's psychiatric clinics, as well as populating the couches of numerous psychotherapists.

There are only six characters in the story and five of them show some evidence of depression and so presumably the writer himself was familiar with depression. Tobit is depressed because of his blindness, Sarah because of her repeated marital failure. Hannah gets into a state about her son's delayed return journey, believing him to be dead. Edna weeps when she hears about Tobit's blindness and worries about the forthcoming wedding, while Raguel, Sarah's father, will die of 'sorrow' if Sarah carries out her plan to hang herself. The story is generally held to be a piece of fiction and so probably assigning an individual diagnostic label to each character will add little to our understanding. What stands out is how the writer has probably superimposed his own depression and suicidal thoughts onto the main players of this drama. Perhaps he did this to relieve his own depression, in the same way as the author of the Book of Job obtained relief through his writing. The description of suicidal thoughts here seems clinically accurate. For the reader or a worshipper hearing these passages, and who might also currently be afflicted with depression or suicidality, the mention of such suicidal despair will bring immediate personal engagement with the story. However, the story has a good ending: prayer brings healing.

## Suicidal thoughts – the modern perspective

Suicidal thoughts are very common and an epidemiological study by Paykel *et al.* (1974) gave an annual prevalence of suicidal thoughts as follows: 'Felt life not worth living', 7.8%; 'wished you were dead', 5.0%; 'thoughts of taking one's life', 2.3% (this is the most commonly quoted figure); 'seriously considered taking one's life', 1.5% ; 'made a suicide attempt', 0.4%. Other thoughts such as 'no one loves me', 'I have no future', 'my life has no meaning', 'I would be better off dead', 'no one understands my depression', 'there will never be an end to my misery' and similar thoughts are also commonly reported.

Fewer than 1 in 200 (or 500 per 100,000) of those suffering from suicidal thoughts go on to complete a suicide, but this is still 45 times more than the 14/100,000 base rate for suicide in the general population. Among patients with depression, around 40% may also have suicidal thoughts but for those in the depressed phase of a bipolar disorder this figure rises to 72%, indicating that bipolar depressed subjects are at a much greater risk. International surveys of suicidal thoughts separate straightforward thoughts from those where there are thoughts associated with suicidal planning, which is taken as a more dangerous sign. A routine psychiatric assessment of a suicidal patient will always entail enquiring whether they are actively planning such an outcome and how far they have progressed in this endeavour – and Sarah does admit to suicide planning.

What is rather less well known is the extent and degree of intrusiveness of such thoughts. Kerkoff and Spijker (2011) found that many of their suicidal patients experienced repetition of their suicidal thoughts several hundred times a day and the total amount of time these suicidal thoughts intruded into their mind sometimes amounted to 10–15 hours a day. In times of crisis such suicidal thoughts would keep them awake and account for their distressing insomnia. Some reported the impossibility of stopping their suicidal thoughts and this proved to be the tipping point for their suicide attempt. The Samaritans, who operate a suicide help line, receive over 20,000 desperate calls each year from those experiencing such intense suicidal ideation. Certain features in suicidal thoughts point to a higher risk and these include: hopelessness, high levels of anxiety, insomnia, and depression, very intense emotions and, rarely, psychotic features, such as hearing voices or having depressive delusions. Thoughts associated with suicide planning are especially dangerous.

Suicidal thoughts are repeated several times in the stories of both Tobit and Sarah. They are also repeated many times in the lengthy Egyptian poem 'The man who was weary of life', which is briefly described in the Appendix to this chapter. In neither case is there any actual attempt at or a suggestion of a completed suicide but they are both good examples of the ruminative and repetitive quality of suicidal thoughts and their association with depression.

## Self-mutilation

Self-mutilation is a common problem today, and those who cut themselves are commonly seen in both psychiatric clinics and prisons. Cutting the skin is mentioned several times in the OT and the priests chose to ban it, so it must also have been quite a frequent problem in ancient times as well. In this section, two episodes of individual self-cutting are briefly reviewed (an episode of severe self-cutting with mourning in the Ugaritic literature is described in the Appendix). Self-mutilation is known to be highly 'infectious' and today spreads like contagion rapidly through psychiatric hospital wards and prisons. There is a lengthy history of group self-mutilation in a religious context and two early examples of this are given in the OT, the first among a group of pilgrims and the second during Elijah's challenge to the prophets of Baal.

### *Self-mutilation and its ban by the priesthood*

Self-mutilation is forbidden in the Books of both Leviticus and Deuteronomy. Leviticus is thought to be one of the priestly compositions and is about the work and duties of the priests, or *Cohanim,* said to be the sons of Aaron. The book is thought to have been written among priestly circles of the exiles sometime in the 5th or 6th century BCE but its priestly editor (P) was unknown. The first part (chs 1–16) concerns the 'priestly material', but chs 17–27 contain a series of personal and ethical standards, which all should aspire to, as well as rules of social justice, sexual conduct, the dietary regulations and laws on a wide variety of other topics. This section is also known as the 'Holiness code' and pronouncements in this section are often preceded or followed by the phrase 'I am the Lord', as if to give the command extra authority. In Jewish religious liturgy and practice the Holiness code remains one of the most important tracts in the Old Testament as it provides a detailed guide as to how Jews should conduct their day-to-day lives. Chapter 19 contains the ban on self-mutilation:

> [27]You shall not round off the hairs of your temples or mar the edges of your beard. [28]You shall not make any gashes in your flesh for the dead or tattoo marks. I am the Lord.

In the ancient world, hair was sometimes taken as a sign of a person's vitality. It reaches a magical and almost super-human quality in the Samson saga. Shaving the hair, tearing clothes and gashing the flesh were all parts of the funeral rites. In a Jewish funeral today, the mourner must still tear an item of clothing as he buries the dead. The command not to round off the hairs of your temples is retained by Orthodox Jews, who let their hair grow down in ringlets by the sides of their face.

A similar rule banning self-mutilation is given in Deuteronomy. Again, it is couched in religious terminology and the ban is imposed because the Israelites must not indulge in such pagan practices as they are 'a holy people consecrated to God':

> 14[1] You are the children of the Lord your God. You must not lacerate yourselves or shave your forelocks for the dead. [2]For you are a people holy to the Lord your God, it is you the Lord has chosen out of all the people on earth to be a holy people, his treasured possession.

Tigay (1996, p. 136) writes 'Gashing the flesh until the blood runs out and removing hair feature as a part of the mourning rites the world over and such practices have differing meanings in different cultures'. In some cultures the belief is that there can be an effect on the ghost of the dead person and as offerings to the ghost of the dead person blood or hair will strengthen the ghost in the nether world and assuage the ghost's jealousy of the living by showing how grief-stricken they are. Similar laws against the expression of grief by cutting occurred in Athens when Solon (6th century BCE) forbade 'mourners tearing themselves to raise pity' and in Roman laws (5th century BCE) which forbade mourning women to lacerate their cheeks.

The ban is given added weight by making it an offence against the notion of holiness; it is something 'the chosen people should not do'. It is only for pagans. Possible psychiatric reasons for this ban are discussed on pages 281–282.

## Hosea: an episode of self-mutilation

Hosea is one of the 8th-century prophets who was active in the Northern Kingdom shortly before its destruction by the Assyrians in 722 BCE. His writing is difficult to understand and indeed Anderson and Freedman (1985) write 'The text of Hosea competes with Job for the distinction of having more unintelligible passages than any other book of the Hebrew Bible'. The book is largely about politics, and how Israel's sins and idol worship will lead to its destruction, but Hosea applies the metaphor of his own problematic marriage to convey his message. Thus his own wife, Gomer, was unfaithful, and he had an unhappy marriage. He makes a parallel with his own poor marriage and Israel's marriage to God, now also in a deteriorated state as Israel has sunk into a state of moral corruption. This complicated mixing of metaphors and personification of Israel's troubles helps us understand the episode of self-mutilation described in 7[11-14].

Hosea ch. 7 starts by describing a palace coup when there has been a drunken assassination in the royal court. The text then goes on to describe how Ephraim (Israel) is caught like a bird between its two great neighbours, Assyria and Egypt, and its leaders conduct a disastrous foreign policy while the people rebel against God and eventually they gash themselves.

| | | |
|---|---|---|
| 7[11] | Ephraim has become like a Dove | |
| | silly and without sense they call upon | In its foreign policy Ephraim |
| | Egypt, they go to Assyria. | flits between the two superpowers |
| 12 | As they go, I will cast my net over them | A 'bird catching' image |
| | I will discipline them according | Discipline is needed because the |
| | to the report made to their assembly | treaties made with others has led |
| 13 | Woe to them for they have strayed | to the worship of foreign Gods |
| | from me! Destruction to them, for they | |
| | have rebelled against me. I would redeem | |
| | them but they speak lies against me. | The people are dishonest, |
| 14 | They do not cry to me from their heart, | their crying is insincere |
| | but they wail from their beds | ? histrionic wailing |
| | *they gash themselves* for grain and wine | Manipulative cutting for sustenance |
| | they rebel against me. | Anger against God (authority) |

Anderson and Freedman interpret this passage as a critique of Ephraim's foreign policy. Ephraim has no sense – the Hebrew *en leb* means literally 'no heart' but because the heart was thought to be mind, Anderson translates this as 'brainless'. The dove is a fluttery bird, brainless and simple-minded, and perhaps naïve, and Ephraim is behaving foolishly – like the dove. The politics is realistic and there is a danger to Ephraim (the Northern Kingdom) because it is a small state sandwiched between the two great titans of Egypt and Assyria. Ambassadors have been sent to both countries and Anderson translates *edutam* not as assemblies as in the NRSV above, but as 'treaties'. 'The Treaty made with Assyria will inevitably mean paying tribute to Assyria and hence the worshipping of Assyrian gods. This is the meaning of "they have strayed from me" and that is why Yahweh must discipline his people' (Anderson and Freedman, 1985).

With regard to the episode of 'gashing', both a cultic and psychiatric explanation are appropriate and are not mutually exclusive. The cutting results in the flow of human blood and this imitates the release of fertilising forces such as rain by God. This is the meaning of 'calling upon god' in the pagan Canaanite fertility rights, for example in their response to Elijah's challenge to the prophets of Baal.

The psychiatric explanation hinges on how the national failings have become personified. Quite abruptly in the middle of verse 13, Ephraim, previously a nation, becomes a person. This character is one who lies (*they speak lies against me*) and who is insincere or superficial in his professed state of misery (*they do not cry from their heart*) and he seems to be prone to rather gross exhibitionistic behaviours (*they wail from their beds*) and then he cuts himself for gain – a manipulative gesture which in this case is to obtain grain and wine (*gash themselves for food and grain*) and they are also angry at the same time (*they rebel against me*).

Such a character will be unfamiliar to most people and we have no reason to expect a priest, a rabbi or a biblical scholar to have any acquaintance with such a type. By contrast every psychiatrist, psychiatric nurse and most of the nursing staff in the A&E department will be all too familiar with the manipulative cutter who is a frequent visitor to the hospital. He turns up in the late evening to the A&E department with cuts on his arm and wrists and gives a tale of a terrible depression and destitution, seeking a meal and a bed for the night – but once achieved, his depression miraculously disappears, with the psychiatric background usually being one of a personality disorder. We have no idea how Hosea stumbled onto this metaphor. Perhaps in his role as a priest at one of the sanctuaries such a person came to him repeatedly seeking help. The description of this type of cutter in $7^{13-14}$ is too close to the modern reality of the manipulative self-mutilator to be a mere chance affair. Such cutters are generally undesirable characters and Hosea weaves this unpleasantness of character into his metaphor about Ephraim's stupidity and faithlessness.

## *Ezekiel: an episode of possible genital self-mutilation*

Chapters 16 and 23 of the Book of Ezekiel describe the two sisters Ohalah and Ohilabah, who are both whores, and Ezekiel uses this sexual metaphor to describe the political and moral failings of the cities of Jerusalem (Ohilabah) and Samaria (Ohalah). The language is lurid and pornographic and these cities will be punished by the Babylonians because of their whoredom (discussed in the chapter on Ezekiel on pages 336–339). Towards the end of the passage their punishment will be drunkenness, depression and the tearing out of their breasts.

$23^{32}$    Thus says the Lord God:
     You shall drink your sister's cup deep and wide
     You shall be scorned and derided it holds so much
[33]    You shall be filled with drunkenness and sorrow
     A cup of horror and desolation is the cup of your sister Samaria;
[34]    You shall drink it and drain it out and gnaw its sherds
     *and tear out your breasts*,
     For I have spoken says the Lord God

This doom-laden oracle is explained by Greenberg (1997, pp. 488–493):

> Israel's relation to God has been allegorised as one of morbid marital infidelity with the two sisters Ohalah representing Samaria and Ohilabah representing Jerusalem – and their excesses and bad end are set out in ch. 23. The oracle starts in the first part of the chapter with the sexual awakening of the sisters at the hands of the Egyptians.

> $23^3$ they played the whore in Egypt; they played the whore in their youth; their breasts were caressed there and their virgin bosoms fondled.

> The reference to Israel's youth is understood as the beginnings of the Israelite peoples because of their exodus from Egypt. The explicit sexual and voyeuristic nature of this metaphor needs no elaboration. Israel continues to have alliances with Egypt and an Egyptian influence remained strong. Ezekiel is highly critical of this, because of the realpolitik of the day, as he believed this

closeness to Egypt would incense the other powerful paramours of Assyria and Babylon – and ultimately this will result in its catastrophic destruction. The passage continues to explain that God will put an end to this political closeness with Egypt, and Ezekiel once more applies a sexual metaphor to this change of allegiance.

23²⁷ So I will put an end to your lewdness and your whoring brought from the land of Egypt; you shall not long for them or remember Egypt anymore....

It will all end with terrible vengeance and this culminates in a horrifying finale where Ohilabah tears out her breast, the very same organs originally caressed by Egypt and the reason for this is Israel's unfaithfulness:

23²⁴ You shall drink it, and drain it out and gnaw its sherds and *tear out your breasts*
23³⁵ because you have forgotten me and cast me behind your back, therefore bear the consequences of your lewdness and your whorings.

The psychiatric interest in this verse lies in the image of the woman tearing her breasts out. The image is so horrific that it is apparently omitted from the Septuagint translation of the Book of Ezekiel. Breast self-mutilation probably occurred in the ancient world and an earlier example is given in the Ugaritic literature which describes the Goddess Anat harrowing her chest (see the Appendix on page XX at the end of this chapter).

Self-mutilation of the breast also occurs in clinical populations today. Thus in Favazza's series of female self-mutilators around 18% of the sample cut their chests and Simiopolous (1974) also reports the case of a woman who at 14 became preoccupied with religious ideas and then began to cut herself on her chest and abdomen to relieve states of tension. I have looked after patient with a severe drug-resistant schizophrenia who over a 10-year period repeatedly slashed her breasts as well as her arms and legs. Possibly, this verse was just the product of Ezekiel's vengeful and misogynistic imagination, but also it is possible that in his role as a priest while attending funerals he may have witnessed bereaved women in states of grief cutting their breasts in much the same way as he describes in this verse.

## The pilgrims who mourn for Jerusalem: group self-mutilation

Jeremiah 41⁴⁻⁷ describes a strange episode occurring shortly after the fall of Jerusalem in 586 BCE. The Babylonians had installed a new governor, Gedaliah, to Jerusalem but after three months he was murdered by Ishmael, the son of Nathaniah. A group of 80 pilgrims who are mourning the fall of Jerusalem arrive in the city – but they too are murdered by Ishmael.

Jer.41⁴ On the day of the murder of Gedaliah, before anyone knew of it, ⁵eighty men arrived from Shechem and Shiloh and Samaria with their beards shaved and their clothes torn, *and their bodies gashed* bringing grain offerings and incense to present at the Temple of the Lord. ⁶And Ishmael son of Nathanial came out from Mizpah to meet them, weeping as he came. As he met them, he said to them 'Come to Gedaliah, son of Ahikam'. ⁷When they reached the middle of the city Ishmael and the men with him slaughtered them and threw them into the cistern.

Carroll (1986, pp. 708–711) explains:

> On the second day after the assassination of Gedaliah, eighty pilgrims arrive from a variety of famous sanctuaries and cities on their way to the Jerusalem temple. Their long pilgrimage is endured in a state of mourning – beards removed, clothes torn, bodies gashed – and it must be presumed they are responding to the fall of the city and the destruction of the temple. The pilgrimage is in the seventh month and so perhaps it is for the Day of Atonement. Ishmael tricks the pilgrims by persuading them to meet Gedaliah, but then he assassinates 70 of them.

The description of the self-mutilation is of interest. It goes with the usual accompaniments of mourning – shaving the beard and the tearing of the clothes – but it seems to have occurred in a group setting and this group gashing resembles the group cutting of the prophets of Baal (described below). Again, there is misery and depression because of the fall of Jerusalem but no funeral or actual bereavement of a named person.

## *Elijah and the prophets of Baal: an episode of group self-mutilation*

A particular genre in the prophetic literature is the 'prophet versus prophet contest'. The purpose of these stories is to enhance the power of their God and in this instance it is to enhance the status of the monotheistic deity Yahweh, as opposed to the Canaanite deity Baal, who was one of many gods. It is said to have the force of a didactic legend and demonstrates the power of Elijah, who is God's prophet, and by inference the power of his God over other gods. The actual passage forms part of the Jewish liturgy and the Haftarah, which is read usually in mid-February, in the 21st week of the annual cycle.

The story is set during the third year of the drought during the rule of King Ahab (873–852 BCE). The drought has led to a severe famine in Samaria. God has summoned Elijah and instructed him to go to Ahab so that rain can be sent to relieve the drought. However, there has been a problem with apostasy in the land. Ahab's wife, Jezebel, who was originally Assyrian, has brought in the prophets of the Assyrian gods Baal and Aserah and she has been killing the prophets of the Lord. The persecution of the prophets of the Lord has been so bad that Obadiah, who is the head of the royal palace, has had to hide the prophets of the Lord in local caves. King Ahab has become confused by all this and says he no longer knows who the true prophets are. In response to this Elijah claims to be the one and only remaining prophet of the Lord and he issues a challenge to the prophets of Baal to settle the matter. Two bulls are to be sacrificed, one by Elijah and the other by the prophets of Baal, but it will be up to their respective gods to send the fire to start the sacrifice off.

> 1 Kings 18[19] Now therefore have all Israel assemble for me at Mt Carmel with four hundred and fifty prophets of Baal and the four hundred prophets of Asherah who eat at Jezebel's table....

[25] Then Elijah said to the Prophets of Baal 'Choose for yourself one bull and prepare it first, for you are many, then call on the name of your God, but put no fire in it'. [26] So they took the bull that was given them, prepared it and called on the name of Baal from morning until noon crying 'O Baal, answer us!' But there was no answer; they limped about the altar that they had made.

[27] At noon Elijah mocked them saying 'Cry aloud! Surely he is God, either he is meditating or he has wandered away or he is on a journey or perhaps he is asleep and must be awakened'. [28] They cried aloud and, as was their custom, *they cut themselves with swords and lances until the blood rushed over them.* As midday passed they raved on until the time of the offering of the oblation but there was no answer and no response....

The story continues with Elijah asking the people to drench the sacrifice with water and when he calls upon his God to set it alight, the fire consumes everything – including the bull, the stones, the wood and even the water. Then the much needed rain arrives and the story ends with Elijah asking the people to seize the prophets of Baal and he kills them all. We do not know whether or not he has remorse for this act but in the following chapter he becomes suicidal and expresses a wish to die: 'O Lord take away my life, I am no better than my ancestors'.

Gray (1964) makes two interesting comments on *they slashed* (Hebrew *gadar*) themselves. Thus although the shedding of blood was usually associated with mourning rites, in this instance the self-laceration of the prophets of Baal and their shedding of blood may have been a rite of imitative magic. The hope was that it would prompt a liberal release of the vital rain that all life depended on. In verse 27 the Hebrew word for rave, *hittnabi'i,* denotes the extent of the prophetic experience; thus a *nabi* was a prophet – and their ecstatic behaviour was often indistinguishable from the conduct of the madman, which is sometimes denoted by the same verb (Gray, p. 355).

However, the most interesting parallel is cited by Roberts (1970). Although the Ugaritic tablets from the Ras Shamra excavations date from 1500–1200 BCE, a much older tablet, written in Old Babylonian, from this site and thought to originate in the early Kassite Babylonian period (circa 1700 BCE) recounts the failure of cultic experts to diagnose the problems of a sick man. It has the line 'My brothers bathed in their own blood like an ecstatic'. Since an ecstatics in the ancient world were sometimes psychotics this may be a very early reference to psychotic self-mutilation, a dangerous but rare category of self-mutilation.

## Self-mutilation today

A comprehensive account of self-mutilation today is given in *Bodies Under Siege* by Favazza (1996) and only a brief description will be given here. He classified self-mutilation as either being culturally and religiously sanctioned, or being morbid and pathological. In both types of cutting, the skin is broken until there is a flow of blood and this is its defining feature. Some of the episodes in the OT are religiously sanctioned and most often occur in mourning rituals but in other instances its purpose is directed at placating the gods, pleading for rain, seeking healing or achieving spirituality. The ban on cutting in the OT suggests that the practice was widespread and that most of these episodes would not have been religiously sanctioned.

Mortification of the flesh was important in Christianity in the Middle Ages, resulting in epidemics of self-mutilation, most notably the Flagellants of the 14th century, who wandered across Europe whipping themselves. Two examples of religiously sanctioned self-mortification of the flesh from modern Islam will be briefly mentioned. Crapanzano (1973) describes the Hamadsha, an extreme Sufist brotherhood in Morocco who engage in head slashing. They do this as part of their role as Muslim healers and ill persons are said to dip bits of bread or sugar lumps into their blood and then eat them. Therapeutic powers are thought to rest in the healer's blood. At other times they indulge in extreme behaviours 'of wild ecstatic dances, drinking boiling water, eating spiny cactus, charming poisonous snakes and all this is combined with numerous acts of self-mutilation' (Favazza, 1996).

In Shia Islam today much attention is paid to the martyrdoms of Ali, Hasan and Husain. During annual passion plays the deaths of these martyrs are fervently re-enacted with both the actors and the spectators inflicting wounds on themselves. During the festival of Husain many thousands of Shiites flagellate themselves while reciting the words 'Trial afflictions and pains, the thicker they fall on man, the better they prepare him for the journey to Heaven'. In the OT two groups probably showed religious group self-mutilation and these were the prophets of Baal during their contest with Elijah, and the pilgrims who gash themselves in mourning before their visit to Jerusalem after its fall.

Culturally sanctioned cutting of the type described in the OT are rare in Western countries today, but cutting itself remains common. Instead of the religious self-mutilation of the past, the psychiatric clinics of today are confronted by a near epidemic of pathological self-mutilation, mainly among young people. This is of two types: first, there are the very severe and dangerous psychotic episodes which include slashing the throat, self-castration, enucleation of the eye and the severing of major nerves or arteries. These episodes often occur as part of a genuine suicide attempt in the context of a psychotic illness (either severe depression or schizophrenia) and often end in a compulsory admission to a psychiatric hospital. They tend to be one-off episodes and are relatively rare.

The second group of cutters are far more common and the cutting is usually more superficial. These episodes are less dangerous and usually do not have a suicidal intent. Around 11% of those who attempt suicide and who are admitted to poison units in hospitals are admitted because of their cutting or self-mutilation. The condition is not rare and population estimates give a figure of around 1 in 600 people per year deliberately wounding themselves to the extent that they require hospital treatment. In the study of Favazza and Conterio (1989) the most common method of self-injury was cutting (72%), burning (35%), hitting or punching parts of body (22%), interfering with wound healing (22%), scratching (22%), hair pulling (10%) and breaking bones (8%). The most common site for the cutting was the wrist and arms (74%), the legs (44%), the abdomen (25%), head (23%) and chest

(18%) and the genitalia (8%), including the vagina. The onset is usually in the late teens and the habit persists for 5–10 years. More than half of their sample had wounded themselves on more than 50 occasions, suggesting it may be an addictive process. Studies of the associated psychiatric diagnoses usually reveal the presence of a psychiatric disorder in 90% of subjects, especially borderline personality disorder and in some cases antisocial personality disorder, but sometimes there is also depression, schizophrenia, substance abuse and eating disorders as well. Sometimes there is a history of childhood physical and sexual abuse but in many instances the family background is unremarkable.

Theories of causation abound: thus the early psychoanalysts such as Menninger termed self-mutilation 'a partial suicide' and suggested that it was an act of healing and served as a substitute for real suicide. Stengel also made the distinction between a suicide attempt and other forms of self-harm where there was no intention to cause death. Novotny (1972) noted that for many women, self-mutilation offered some erotic gratification and on this basis postulated it was primarily a masochistic phenomenon. As an explanation for the more positive aspects of self-mutilation, Kafka (1969) described a young female cutter who reported 'the exquisite border experience of becoming alive at the moment of cutting'. She also described how 'the flow of blood has been like a voluptuous bath with pleasant warmth spreading all over her body'. She was at a loss to understand why everyone did not indulge in blood baths routinely, especially since they were readily available 'by simply unzipping one's skin'.

Many patients today report similar positive feelings, namely tension relief, relief from dead feelings, particularly depersonalisation and depression, and they also welcome the comforting sensation of the warm blood flowing over their skin. Pain is not experienced during the cutting.

In a hospital setting, self-mutilation and cutting are often learned behaviours. Episodes occur in clusters, particularly among adolescents, and cutting can spread rapidly through an inpatient ward from one patient to another in an almost infectious fashion. Cutting can also form part of a threat or manipulation or an angry gesture to hurt a partner following the ending of a relationship.

Rates of cutting are very high in prisons, particularly among women. Toch (1975) reported rates of 7.7% among youth offenders, in adult male prisoners of 6%, and among women prisoners of 10.8%. Self-mutilation in prison may be a symptom of depression or personality disorder, or a manipulation to gain medical attention or a protest against incarceration. In Russian prisons self-mutilation was found only among the criminal prisoners but not among the political prisoners. Numerically, the problem is substantial.

Most cases of repeated cutting do not respond to treatment but many will remit spontaneously after 5–10 years. Even so, these subjects have an increased lifetime risk of completed suicide.

There is a mystery as to why the Torah should impose a law which bans the act of self-mutilation, which usually has only relatively temporary and minor consequences for the person, but says nothing at all about a completed suicide, which results in the death of an individual. Favazza (pp.

288–289) explains the difference through the different feelings that these acts elicit in those around:

> Put simply no one loves self-mutilators. Their very presence seems to threaten the sense of mental and physical integrity of those around them.... Even experienced psychotherapists are hard pressed to maintain equanimity with chronic self-mutilators.

Frances (1987) writes:

> Of all the disturbing patient behaviours, self-mutilation is the most difficult to understand and treat. The typical clinician, treating a patient who self-mutilates, is often left feeling a combination of helpless, horrified, guilty, furious, betrayed, disgusted and sad....

Although suicide is shocking, the grief of mourning may be assuaged by a host of convenient rationalisations such as 'It is all part of God's plan' or 'At the least the victim is dead'. But self-mutilation is horrific in its seeming senselessness, and the victim is very much alive and able to haunt us in the flesh. The priests of ancient Israel were regularly confronted by self-mutilation at funerals and, like the bereavement counsellors of today, they might have been tasked with comforting those in mourning. Self-mutilation seems to evokes very powerful feelings of revulsion, much more so than a completed suicide, and so it is no wonder that the priests tried to ban it.

## Summary and conclusions

Suicide is a major problem for all societies today, but curiously in the ancient world it does not seem to have been a problem, or at least so much of a problem. When it occurred in an important person such as a king, it would always be recorded by the scribes of the day. There was no criticism or condemnation of those who took their own lives in the OT, nor are there any laws prohibiting suicide in the Torah or anywhere else in the Bible. Three of those who killed themselves in the OT, Saul, Samson and Ahithopel, were given proper burials with full funerary rites, an indication that suicide was not held to be a sin. Had their deaths occurred 1500 years later, they might have been buried at the crossroads, excommunicated and had a stake driven through their hearts, with their families being disinherited. Civilisation does not always advance in a straight line. By contrast the laws against the far lesser but related problem of self-harm are repeated twice in the Torah.

Although both the ancient Greeks and the Romans had some early laws proscribing suicide, van Hooff (1990) has shown how suicide was quite common among the elite in the classical world and held to be an honourable way to die. The somewhat strange phenomenon of martyrdom for one's faith first appeared among the Jews during the period of the Greek occupation around 200 BCE and then became a part of the story of early Christianity and continued intermittently right through to the late Middle Ages among both Christians and Jews. Sometimes in the face of intense religious persecution suicides appeared to be logical and the only honourable way out, but many of the earlier martyrdom suicides occurred in a spirit of joy, as a way of demonstrating absolute faith and obedience to the deity. Martyrs chose to demonstrate the strength of their faith through their own deaths, usually at the hands of their persecutors, but occasionally as individual suicide or episodes of mass suicide. Such unnecessary deaths alarmed the Catholic Church and so not surprisingly there was a powerful reaction against suicide, culminating in Pope Augustine decreeing suicide to be a crime against God.

The same debate continues today – whether a person is free to take his own life, or whether to do so is a crime against God. Some European countries have legislated that it is no longer a crime to commit euthanasia and those who assist in a suicide are not committing any crime. In the UK today the debate continues and cases regularly appear before the courts where the issues revolve around an assisted suicide, when a person is so ill that they are unable to perform the act themselves, and whether those who assist in a such a suicide are committing a murder or not.

The Catholic Church maintains an absolute position in such cases, but even the most secular of those working in psychiatry would be anxious if the attitude to suicide in society became more permissive, as almost certainly numbers would rise. In addition, those with severe and difficult-to-treat depression would perhaps also seek a way out through euthanasia, and their numbers are very large indeed – yet quite a high proportion of them will eventually get better.

All the three main categories of self-destructive behaviours – completed suicide, suicidal thoughts, and self-harm – are all well represented in the Bible. A fourth category, attempted (unsuccessful) suicide, is not mentioned in the OT but it certainly occurred in the ancient world; thus Josephus reports on the four attempts that King Herod made on his own life and there are numerous Greek examples as well. Although the accounts of martyrdom may possibly have additional fictional embellishments, the other biblical suicides appear to be realistic and include clinical details that tally well with modern clinical experience. Examples are Ahithopel's delay between the decision and the act, Zimri's arson, Saul's depression, Judas Iscariot's remorse, and Samson's pleasure in the mass killing which accompanies his death. The repetition of suicidal thoughts in the Book of Tobit is a clinically accurate account of their intrusiveness.

Because suicide was never a crime in the Old Testament, most of the suicides described do not carry great religious importance, nor are they particularly controversial. The only two suicides that have some religious significance are those of King Saul in the Old Testament and Judas Iscariot in the New Testament. Nevertheless, a suicide is always a very disturbing event, evoking powerful feelings of fear and fascination in those around and always demands an explanation. A thread common to both ancient and modern suicides is that these explanations almost always seem to lie in a failure of human relationships, some sort of defeat or humiliation, but will be expressed in the language and culture of the day. For the kings of the Old Testament, it may have been a defeat in battle, the end of their kingship and the loss of their palaces that culminated in their suicides. Today the immediate causes may be rather more modest, such as the loss of a job, desertion of a spouse, or an eviction from a house for non-payment of rent.

Abemelich and Zimri had both been assassins and the Deuteronomist applies a morale dimension to their deaths, as he says 'they did evil in the sight of the Lord'. By contrast, Samson, who takes several thousand people with him when he commits suicide, receives no criticism, gaining praise and honour instead. His modern counterpart might be the suicide bomber.

The suicides of betrayal of Ahithopel and Macron also have little religious significance and are mentioned in the text only in passing. The explanation of their deaths seems to lie entirely in the politics of the day and how these characters were out-manoeuvred and ended up on the losing side. Judas Iscariot, however, knows he has done wrong and is full of remorse for his act of betrayal and hangs himself. Many later Christian writers suggest that 'Justice was done and that he deserved to die', but God is not invoked as either causing or sanctioning his suicide.

The position of God in the suicide debate has moved many times over the last 3,000 years and has come almost full circle and reverted back to its original position of neutrality. Thus in the early part of the Old Testament and in ancient Egypt, God is *neutral* and has no part in causing, praising or criticising a self-killing. Later on, particularly at the height of the Deuteronomistic period, it was *God who determined the death as a punishment*, for example in the case of Saul's unfaithfulness in Chronicles (4th century BCE). A couple of centuries later, in the 2nd century BCE, as martyrdom took hold, martyrs committed suicide *for God to demonstrate their faithfulness and devotion to God*. Everything then switches again after Augustine (5th century CE onwards) when *suicide becomes a crime against God* in all three Abrahamic faiths and this position lasts until the end of the Middle Ages. Gradually, with increasing secularisation, suicide became a crime against the state (and in the 20th century no crime at all). As the role of mental illness in suicide became increasingly understood, suicide came under the aegis of medicine, and *God has left the scene altogether* – perhaps similar to the initial neutral stance assumed by God in the earlier part of OT and the ancient Egyptian literature some 3,000 years ago.

Not all are in agreement that suicide should be placed in the domain of medicine and psychiatry, however. Szaz (1979), an anti-psychiatrist, argues that this medical ownership of the suicide domain, especially when accompanied by claims that psychiatry can successfully treat mental illness, has resulted in grossly over-optimistic expectations in the public that psychiatrists can prevent suicide. Thus, in the USA a failure to prevent a suicide may lead to a legal action against the psychiatrist and such cases are now beginning to appear in the UK as well. Things were easier for the profession when all of this was the responsibility of God.

This review has shown that suicide was a common problem in biblical times just as it is today, adding to the notion that suicide itself is a part of the human condition. In the ancient world its description was clothed in the language of religion, history and philosophy. In the modern world it is covered with a mantle of medical science, statistics and psychiatry – but the tragedy of the unnecessary loss of life, and the devastation left among its survivors, remain the same today as in times gone by.

# Appendix

Two pieces of para-biblical literature are presented here. The first is the Egyptian poem 'The man who was weary of life'. It is included because it is probably the oldest account of depression and suicidal thoughts. The second is an account of self-mutilation from the Ugaritic literature, as it parallels Ezekiel's unusual mention of breast self-mutilation.

'The man who was weary of life' is a lengthy ancient Egyptian poem. It is about a debate between a man who is weary of life and his own soul (his *ba*). Since he finds life unbearable, the man contemplates suicide. His *ba* or spirit vacillates: he first agrees that his suicide will not be followed by a mortuary service for his survivors, then proposes an abandonment to a life of careless pleasures and finally agrees to stay with the man in any case. The whole poem is far too long to quote in full here but a few couplets showing depression and taken from the translation by Simpson (2003) are given below. The interested reader is referred to the works of Simspon (2003) and Lichtheim (1973) for further details. The original papyrus known as Berlin Papyrus 3024 is in the Berlin State Museum.

> [18]My *ba* is senseless in disparaging the agony of life
> And impels me to death before my time
> And yet the west will be pleasant for me as there is no sorrow there

> [28]For my longing is too intense to bring me joy
> and only the Gods will purge my innermost pain

> [56]My *ba* opened his mouth to me in answer to what I had said:
> If you are obsessed with burial, it will only cause sadness of heart
> for it brings tears to grieve a man

> [127]Whom can I trust today
> I am laden with sorrow
> and there is none to comfort me

The text dates from the Middle Kingdom and probably from the turbulent times between the Old and Middle Kingdoms (end of the third millennium BCE) when the established order had broken down and men were struggling to find new values. Lichtheim (1973) suggests the 12th dynasty, circa 1900 BCE. The poem has no connection to the Old Testament depressive literature and was probably unknown to the Old Testament writers, but it is relevant to the history of psychiatry because it is more than 1,000 years older than the OT itself, and perhaps represents the very first written account of depression.

The Ugaritic texts describe El's grief at the death of Baal, a case of severe cutting in mourning. The Baal cycle is a very complicated Ugaritic tale on seven tablets found in the Ras Shamra excavations of the 1920s. Ugaritic is the first alphabetic language and the precursor of both the Canaanite and Hebrew languages. The origins of the Hebrew religion also owes much to this earlier culture, which dates from 1500–1200 BCE, and these particular tablets are thought to date from at least 1200 BCE, long before the OT was written. The bodily cutting described here is by far the oldest written description of self-mutilation. The two Ugaritic gods mentioned in this lament, Baal and El, also feature in the OT. Thus El is probably the precursor of the Hebrew God Elohim, later called Yahweh, while Baal is the son of El, and Baal worship is repeatedly criticised in the OT.

In this passage El is in deep sorrow, mourning the death of his son Baal, and there is a description of mourning rituals with what seems to be repeated and extensive cutting:

KTU 1.5 VI 11–25: El's Grief (Translation by A. Gianto)

Thereupon the kind-hearted El, the Benign
went down from the throne sat down on the footstool,
and from the footstool he sat down on the earth.
Pouring the dirt of lament on his head,
the dust of mourning on his crown,
with a clothing he covered the loins.
*He scraped his skin with a flint,*
*rows of slitting with a blade,*
*cutting his cheeks and chin,*
*repeating three times to his arm,*
*slitting all over his chest,*
*doing the same three times, deeply, to his back.*
Raising his voice he exclaimed:
Baal is dead! If only, Oh people
The Son of Dagan! If only, Oh crowd,
I could go down to the underworld in place of Baal!

Gianto (2010) explains that El's grief becomes visible through the actions he performs during the mourning: descending from the throne, he sat on the footstool, only to end up sitting on the ground. Similar imagery of a god's descent from a throne to a footstool is also described in Isaiah 66[1]: 'Heaven is my throne and the earth is my footstool.' While in this position, he poured 'the dirt of mourning' on his head, the 'dirt of rolling' on the crown of his head, and he was covered only with a loincloth. El scrapes his skin with a flint and more dramatic moments are described when he cuts his cheeks and his chin, lacerates his own arms three times and slits his chest and also lacerates his back. Scraping the skin with a stone is also described in the Book of Job (2[8]): 'Job took a potsherd with which to scrape himself and sat among the ashes'. When Anat, a female goddess, learns of Baal's death she reacts in the same way, except she cries profusely as well, suggesting she is unhappy and possibly depressed at the time of the cutting. Gianto does not offer a translation of Anat's grief and so the translation is that of Pardee.

Anat's Grief: KTU 1.6 I:2–8 (translation by Pardee, 2012)

*She harrows her upper arms*
*Ploughs (her) chest like a garden*
*Harrows her back like (a garden in) a valley*
Balu is dead what (is to become of) the people
The son of Dagan is dead

What is (to become of) the hordes (of the earth)
After *Balu*, we shall descend into the earth,
With him *Sapu*, luminary of the Gods shall descend.
*She drinks (her weeping) until she is sated,*
*(She drinks her) tears like wine.*

In both these laments there is extensive self-mutilation of most parts of the exposed body. Anat cries in her grief so she is possibly depressed while she is cutting. As might be expected when one god mourns the death of another, their show of grief must be both profuse and dramatic but the author must have drawn his observations of the cutting which took place at funerals and the burial rites associated with the mourning of ordinary citizens of this ancient state.

# References

Altmann H., Sletten I.W., Eaton M.E., and Ulett G.A. (1971) Demographic and mental status profiles Patients with homicidal, assaultive, suicidal, persecutory, and homosexual ideation. The Missouri Automated Standard System of Psychiatry *Psychiatric Quarterly* 45, 57–64.

Anderson, F.I. and Freedman, D.N. (1985) The Anchor Bible: *Hosea, A New Translation and Commentary*. Garden City, New York: Doubleday and Company.

Andreasen, N.C. and Noyes, R. (1975) Suicide attempted by self-immolation. *American Journal of Psychiatry* 132, 554–556.

Asch S.S., (1996) Suicide and the Hidden Executioner. Ch. 24, pp. 379–396 in *Essential Papers on Suicide*. Edited by John Maltsberger and Mark Goldblatt, New York: New York University Press Books.

Barraclough B.M. (1992) The Bible Suicides *Acta Psychiatric Scandinavica* 86, 64–69.

Barraclough, B.M., Bunch, J., Nelson, B. and Sainsbury, P. (1974) A hundred cases of suicide: clinical aspects. *British Journal of Psychiatry*, 125: 355–373.

Bels, J.(1975) La Mort voluntaire dans l'oevre de saint Augustine *Revue de l'histoire des religions* 187: 147–80.

Bertolote, J.M. and Fleischmann, A. (2009) A global Perspective on the Magnitude of suicide Mortality. Chapter 13 pp87–90 in *Oxford Textbook of Suicidology and Suicide prevention* Eds Wasserman D. and Wasserman C. Oxford: Oxford University Press.

Boling, R.G. (1975) *Anchor Bible: Judges Introduction, Translation, and Commentary*. Garden City New York. Doubleday and Company.

Bose A., Konradson F., John J., *et al* (2006) Mortality rate and years of lost life lost from unintentional injury and suicide in South India. *Tropical medicine and International Health;* 11: 1533–1556.

Butler, T. C. (2009) *Judges: Word Biblical Commentary* Volume 8. Nashville: Thomas Nelson.

Carroll, R.P. (1986) *Jeremiah A Commentary* London: SCM Press.

Cogan, M. (2000) The Anchor Bible. *I Kings, A new translation with Introduction and Commentary*. New York: Doubleday.

Cohn, H.H. (2007) Saul entry in *Encyclopaedia Judaica. vol 19 p296* Jerusalem: Keter Publishing Company.

Colt, G.H. (1987) *The History of the Suicide Survivor. The Mark of Cain*. In E. J. Dunne and J. L. Mackintosh and K. Dunne-Maxim, *Suicide and Its Aftermath: Understanding and Counselling the Survivors*. New York: Norton.

Cook, C.H. Powell, A. and Sims, A. (2009) *Spirituality and Psychiatry*. London: Royal college of Psychiatrists.

Crapanzano (1973) *The Hamadsha* Berkeley: University of California Press.

Droge (1992) Suicide. *The Anchor Bible Dictionary Volume 6:* Ed. D.N Freedman. New York: Doubleday: 225–231.

Droge, A. J. and Tabor, J.D. (1992) *A Noble Death: Suicide and Martyrdom amongst Christians and Jews in Antiquity*. San Francisco: Harper.

Durkheim, E. (1951) *Suicide: A study in sociology*. New York: Free Press (original work published in 1897).

Favazza, A. (1996) *Bodies Under Siege: Self-Mutilation and Body Modification in Culture and Psychiatry*. Second edition. Baltimore: Johns Hopkins University Press.

Favazza, A. and Conterio, K. (1989) Female habitual self-mutilators. *Acta Psychiatric Scandanavica* 79: 283–289.

Fishbain, D.A., Achille, L., Barsky, S. and Aldrich, T. (1984) A controlled study of suicide pacts *Journal of Clinical Psychiatry* 45, 154–157.

Fitzmyer, J. A. (2003) '*Tobit*' *Commentaries on Early Jewish Literature*. New York: Walter de Gruyter.

Flanagan, N. M. (1967) Judas Iscariot. *New Catholic Encyclopaedia Volume 8*, pp. 15–16. New York: McGraw Hill Book Company.

Francis, A. (1987) Introduction to the section on self-mutilation in *Journal of the Personality Disorders* I, 316.

Garrison, C.Z., Mckeown, R.E., Valois, R.F. and Vincent, M.L. (1993) Aggression, substance abuse and suicidal behaviours in High school students *American Journal of Public Health*, 83, 179–184.

Gianto, A. (2010) Grief, joy and anger in Ugaritic literary texts. In W. H. van Solat (ed.), *Society and Administration in Ancient Ugarit*. Leiden: Nino, pp. 45–57 = Pihans, 14, 45–57.

Goldstein, J. A. (1983) *The Anchor Bible 2 Maccabees. A New Translation and Commentary*. Garden City New York: Doubleday and Company.

Gray, J. (1964) *I and II Kings: A commentary*. London: SCM Press.

Greenberg, M. (1997). *The Anchor Bible Ezekiel 21–37 A New translation and Commentary*. pp. 482–484. New York: Doubleday.

Harris, E.C. and B. Barraclough (1997) Suicide as an outcome for mental disorders. A meta-analysis. *British Journal of Psychiatry* 170, 205–228.

Hillbrand, M. (1992) Self-directed and other directed aggressive behaviour in a forensic service. *Suicide and Life Threatening Behaviour*, 23, 333–340.

Huisman, M. (2007) Work related Stress and depression *Journal of Epidemiology and Community Health* 61(10), 890.

Jamison, K.R. (1993) *Touched with Fire: Manic Depressive illness and the artistic Temperament*, New York: Free Press.

Jobes, D.A. Luoma, J.B., Hustead, L.A., Mann, R.E. (2000) In the wake of suicide: postvention. Ch.22 in *Comprehensive Textbook of Suicidology* by Ronald W. Maris, Alan Berman and Morton M., Silverman New York: Guildford Press.

Josephus, F. (1987) *The Works of Josephus. Complete and Unabridged*. Translated by William Whiston. Peabody Massachusets: Hendrickson Publishers.

Kafka, J.S. (1969) The Body as a transitional object; A Psycho-analytic study of a self mutilating patient. *British Journal of Medical Psychology* 41: 207–212.

Kerkoff A., and Spijker B. (2011) Worrying and Rumination as Proximal risk factors for Suicidal behaviour. Chapter12 p199–210 in *International handbook on Suicide Prevention research Policy and practice*. Eds Rory C. O'Connor, Stephen Platt and Jacki Gordon. Chichester: Wiley Blackwell.

King, E. and Barraclough, B. (1990) Violent death and mental illness. A study of a single catchment area over eight years. *British Journal of Psychiatry*, 156: 714–720.

Klein, R. W. (2006) *I Chronicles: A Commentary*. Minneapolis: Fortress Press.

Koch, H.J. (2005) Suicides and suicidal ideation in the bible: An empirical survey. *Acta Psychiatrica Scandanavica* 112, 167–172.

Lansky, M. (1991) Shame and the problem of Suicide. *British Journal of Psychotherapy* 7, 230–242.

Lichtheim, M. (1973) *Ancient Egyptian Literature*, vol.I, University of California Press.

Littman, S.K. (1981) King Saul: persecutor or persecuted. *Canadian Journal of Psychiatry* 26(7): 464–467.

Maltsberger, J.T. and Goldblatt, M.J. (1996) *Essential Papers on Suicide*. New York, New York University Press.

Maris, R.W., Berman, A.L. and Silverman, M.M. (2000) The Social Relations of Suicides. Chapter 10:pp 240–265 in *Comprehensive Textbook of Suicidology*. Eds. R. W. Maris, A. L. Berman and M.M. Silverman. New York: Guildford Press.

McCarter, P. J. (1980) *The Anchor Bible I Samuel: A New Translation and Commentary.* Garden City New York: Double Day and Company.

Menninger K. (1938) *Man Against Himself.* New York: Harcourt Brace World.

Moore, C. A. (1996) *The Anchor Bible. Tobit. A New Translation and Commentary.* Garden City: New York: Doubleday and Company.

Morselli, H. (1881) *An Essay on Comparative Mortality Statistics.* London; Kegan Paul.

Novotny, P. (1972) Self-cutting. *Bulletin of the Menninger Clinic* 36: 505–512.

Pardee, D. (2012) The Ugaritic Texts and the Origins of West-Semitic Literary Composition (Schweich Lectures on Biblical Archaeology): British Academy.

Paykel E.S., Myers J.K., *et al* (1974) Suicidal feelings in the general population. *British Journal of Psychiatry* 124, 460–69.

Paykel, E.S., Prusoff, B.A., and Myers, J.A. (1975) Suicide attempts and recent life events. A controlled comparison. *Archives of General Psychiatry* 32(3) 327–333.

Phillips, D.P. (1974) The influence of suggestion on Suicide: Substantive and theoretical implications of the Werther effect *American Sociological Review* 39, 340–354.

Platt, S. (2011) Inequalities in suicidal behaviour Ch.13: 211–234 in *International Handbook of Suicide Prevention* Eds. O'Connor R.C. Platt S. and Gordon J. Chichester: Wiley-Blackwell.

Plutchik, R. (2011) Aggression, violence and suicide. Chapter 17. pp. 407–419 in *Comprehensive Textbook of Suicidology* by Ronald Maris, Alan Berman and Morton M. Silverman. New York: Guildford Press.

Regier, C.A., Boyd, J.H., Burke, J.D., *et al.* One month Prevalence of mental disorders in the United States. *Archives of General psychiatry* 45, 977–986.

Ronningstam, E., Weinberg, I. and Maltsberger, J. T. (2009) Psycho-analytic theories of suicide: historical overview and empirical evidence. Chapter 24 pp 149–158 in *Oxford Textbook of Suicidology and Suicide prevention* Eds. D. Wasserman and C. Wasserman. Oxford: Oxford University Press.

Rutz, W. and Rihmer, Z. (2009) Suicide in Men Chapter 35 pp249–255 in *Oxford Textbook of Suicidology and Suicide prevention* Eds D. Wasserman and C. Wasserman. Oxford: Oxford University Press.

Schwartz, D. R. (2008) *Commentaries on Early Jewish literature. 2 Maccabees.* New York: Walter de Gruyter.

Seigel, S. (1979) Religion: A Jewish View, pp. 83–90 in *Suicide: Theory and Clinical practice* Eds. LD Hankoff and B. Einsidler: PSG Publishing.

Simpson, W.K. (2003) The Literature of Ancient Egypt. Newhaven: Yale University Press.

Siomopoulos, V. (1974) Repeated self-cutting: an impulse neurosis. *American Journal of psychotherapy* 28:85–94.

Stack and Kposowa A.J. (2011) *Religion and Suicide: Integrating four theories Cross-Nationally* Chapter 14 in *International handbook on Suicide Prevention research Policy and practice.* Eds Rory C. O'Connor, Stephen Platt and Jacki Gordon. Chichester: Wiley Blackwell.

Szasz, T.(2011) *Suicide Prohibition. The Shame of Medicine.* Syracuse New York: Syracuse University Press

Tarachow, S. (1960) Judas. The Beloved Executioner. *Psycho-analytical Quarterly* 29,528–554.

Tigay, J.H. (1996) *The JPS Torah Commentary Deuteronomy. The Traditional Hebrew Text with the New JPS Translation.* Philadelphia. The Jewish Publication Society.

Toch, H. (1975) *Men in Crisis* Chicago. Aldine Press.

Van Hooff, A. J. L. (1990) *From Autothanasia to Suicide. Self-killing in Classical Antiquity.* London: Routledge.

Wasserman, D. and Wasserman, C. (2009) *The Oxford Textbook of Suicide Prevention. A Global perspective* Oxford: Oxford University Press.

Wurtzel, E. (1998) *Bitch: In Praise of Difficult Women.* New York: Doubleday, p. 329.

# Chapter 8

# Ezekiel: schizophrenia or schizo-affective disorder?

The Book of Ezekiel is the third large collection of Israel's ancient prophecies, taking its place alongside the other major prophetic works of Isaiah and Jeremiah. In Hebrew, the word 'Ezekiel', *Jehezkel,* means 'May God make strong'. Not much is known about Ezekiel the man, save that he was a priest and was the son of Buzi, also a priest. He is thought to have been deported to Babylon in 597 BCE and the conditions of this first deportation were probably more benign than those following the later siege and destruction of Jerusalem in 586 BCE. Ezekiel's prophecy commenced in Babylonia in the fifth year of King Jehoiachin's exile, a date generally accepted as 593 BCE, and Ezekiel's prophecy is thought to extend between 593 and 571 BCE. He lived in exile in Babylonia in a small village called Tel-abib, near Nippur on the Chebar Canal, corresponding to an area in present-day southern Iraq. There is even a mosque dating back to the 12th century CE where his grave is, in the village of Kefil near Birs Nimrud, on the Euphrates to the south of Baghdad.

As a Zadokite priest by training he would have been literate and knowledgeable about the Israelite texts, such as the Torah, but Greenberg (1983) points out that with his residence in Mesopotamia, which at the time had become a fairly literate society, he might have been familiar with ancient Sumerian texts as well, although some of these were written in Akkadian.

Most of Ezekiel's prophecies address an audience in Jerusalem, which was many hundreds of miles away, and in his visions he is transported to Jerusalem and so is able to visualise what the people of Jerusalem are doing. This ability to prophesise at a distance has puzzled many generations of biblical scholars. The first half of the book concerns the city of Jerusalem and the Temple, which Ezekiel condemns as corrupted beyond hope, and his prophecies of doom were, unfortunately, realised when both city and Temple were completely destroyed by the Babylonians. The latter part of the book prophesises an era of restoration, giving a message of hope, while the final section of the book is concerned with a utopian image of the new Temple, its architecture, the role of its priests and its place in the restored community. Within the book itself, chs 1–24 are said to contain all the oracles of doom, chs 25–32 are the prophecies against the nations, while the book ends with passages of consolation and hope in chs 32–48.

The psychiatric interest in the book lies in its plentiful and detailed description of psychotic phenomenology buried within the religious text; it seems likely that Ezekiel suffered from a psychotic illness, most probably schizophrenia or schizo-affective disorder. Ezekiel stands out from the other prophets because of the many bizarre things he says and does, and most of which were thought to be 'strange' even by his contemporaries, as well as by many later commentators, even though he has always been held in high esteem by the religious hierarchies of both Judaism and Christianity.

## The Book of Ezekiel

The Book of Ezekiel has always been considered to be among the stranger and more obscure works of the Old Testament and, indeed, there was much controversy as to whether it should have been included in the canon at all. This was because there are numerous discrepancies between edicts in the Book of Ezekiel and the cultic regulations of the Torah itself. A detailed discussion of exactly what these differences are is given in the Talmud and is covered by Sweeney (2011). From a modern perspective, most of these discrepancies appear to be quite trivial; however, Jewish tradition in the Talmud holds that the inclusion of Ezekiel in the canon is thanks to the heroic efforts Rabbi Hanina ben Hezekiah.

Rabbi Yehuda said to the Rav:

> That a man is to be remembered for good by the name of Hanina ben Hezekiah, for but for him the Book of Ezekiel would have been hidden, because the words contradict the Torah. What did he do? He brought three hundred measures of oil to his room and he toiled day and night and explained it, ... and in this way the Book of Ezekiel was included in the canon. (b. Menahot 45, Babylonian Talmud)

The book itself is mainly written in the style of typical Old Testament rhetoric, an almost unique genre in the literature of the world. It comprises of an odd mixture of different topics: some oral prophecies, tirades against foreign nations, invectives with strong sexual innuendos, ecstatic visions, much legal material, architectural designs for the second Temple, regulations for the priests, as well as lists of items that were regularly traded in the ancient world, and it also has several different literary formats.

Although mostly written in prose, there is also some poetry. Duhm (1901) argued that poetry was the natural expression of the ecstatic state in which the prophets proclaimed their messages. Composition in verse, with frequent rhyming, is sometimes also a feature of the writing found in excited psychotic states and so may also be relevant to his psychopathology.

## Who wrote the Book of Ezekiel?

Exactly how, when, or by whom the Book of Ezekiel was written is a question shrouded in mystery and only a brief summary of this debate will be presented here.

Older Jewish tradition in the Talmud (*Baba Bathra* 15a) attributed the writings of Ezekiel to the men of the Great Assembly which flourished soon after the return from the exile. A Jewish scholar of the 11th century, Judah Halevy (1075–1141, Spain) is quoted in Shalsheleth Hakabbalah (a part of the Kabbalah) as saying:

During Nebuchadnezzar's reign, Ezekiel the prophet was exiled to Babylon, where he was imprisoned for five years and when he was 30 years old he wrote his book. Others say that he did not write his book, but that other sages wrote it. He was very handsome and was slain by Jews at the age of 58. (After Rosenberg, 1991)

We have no idea whether he was truly slain by his fellow Jews, or indeed whether he was a very handsome man, but the literature on Ezekiel is replete with many such speculations.

Two important biblical exegetes of the 19th and 20th centuries, Smend and S. R. Driver (1954), held that the whole book was written by Ezekiel himself. Smend (1880) states:

> The whole work is the logical development of a series of logical ideas according to a well considered schemata or plan; no part could be taken away without destroying the whole ensemble. Thus it is highly probable the whole book was written down all in one piece.

A diametrically opposed view was taken by the German scholar, G. Holscher (1924), who thought that Ezekiel himself was responsible for only a tiny portion of the book, namely all the sections written in verse, with redactors writing the greater part. He suggested that only 16 oracles and five poems – a total of only 170 out of 1,270 verses – were actually written by Ezekiel.

One of the greatest puzzles within the book is the issue of where the prophet lived. His prophecies all relate to the people of Jerusalem but the text repeatedly refers to him living among the exiles in Babylon and this has greatly mystified biblical scholars, resulting in some bizarre solutions to the authorship problem. Herntrich (1933) offered a wonderful two-person solution: Ezekiel, the great religious prophet, resided in Palestine and preached his oracles to the people in Jerusalem; there was then a second person, the 'Babylonian editor', who lived in Babylonia, and he was the one who experienced all the fantastic visions and delivered the oracles of salvation because these are set in Babylon and his writings give repeated references to the exiles. This second editor's purpose was to give the deportees of 597 BCE in Babylon some spiritual leadership and also to demonstrate that Yahweh was an effective God even in Babylonia. Needless to say, this rather bizarre solution has been rejected by most scholars. Greenberg (1983, 1997) and Zimmerli (1979, 1983) both provide an extensive review of the issue of authorship but refrain from making any specific assertion apart from suggesting that Ezekiel was the editor of the book that bears his name.

Regardless of who actually wrote the Book of Ezekiel, there are two early texts, the Septuagint version (LXX) and the Masoretic text (MT) from which our present version is taken. Unfortunately, the MT of Ezekiel is thought to have been poorly preserved and has numerous additions, errors and deletions. Thus there are many small differences between the MT and the LXX. Of these texts, the Septuagint is thought to be the oldest and closest to the Hebrew Vorlage (the original Hebrew version) of Ezekiel, which was translated into Greek around 200 BCE and is held to be the more authentic version. The earliest surviving Greek text is the Chester Beatty-Scheide

Papyrus 967 (also known as P967), which is thought to have originated in the in the first half the 3rd century CE (see Wurthwein, 1995). The German scholar G. Jahn (1905) compared the MT and LXX versions and came down firmly in favour of the LXX as being the better text, complaining that the MT had diluted much of Ezekiel's venom:

> There is scarcely a book in the whole world of literature which has been so mishandled as Ezekiel by the *Soferim*.... The *Soferim* have removed the fangs of this most passionate prophet and have made him into a senile pulpiteer!

Small fragments of Ezekiel were also found in the Qumran collection (Dead Sea Scrolls) and there are also passages from Ezekiel quoted in the Damascus document found in the Cairo Genizah. Fragments from Ezekiel were also discovered at Masada by the Israeli soldier archaeologist Yigdal Yadin.

From a psychiatric point of view, controversies as to when Ezekiel lived and whether his residence was Jerusalem or Babylon are of little consequence. Since the book is in part autobiographical, the only issue of importance is whether those sections which describe Ezekiel's life and some of his abnormal behaviours were written at the time Ezekiel himself lived and reported his visions, because these then most likely would have been written by him.

The arguments used to place a date on the book are quite strange and relate to Ezekiel's prophecies of doom. Greenberg (1983, p. 14) points out that many of Ezekiel's prophecies relating to Israel's neighbours failed to materialise. For example, Ezekiel predicted that Nebuchadnezzar would destroy Tyre but this never happened. He also foretold that the end of Babylon would be bloody; however, the eventual collapse of Babylon in 539 BCE was quite bloodless, with King Cyrus of the Medes just walking into Babylon without encountering any sort of resistance. This 'failure to predict the future correctly' goes very much against the Old Testament tradition of post-event prophecy, where a prophecy was always correct because the outcome was already known. Such literary religious devices were widely used in the OT to enhance the status of a prophet. A prediction of the future *which was wrong* must have been written before the said events had occurred, and therefore would have genuinely been written at the stated time. This means that the actual writing of the book took place during the reign of King Nebuchadnezzar II (605–562 BCE), decades before the collapse of the Babylonian empire in 539 BCE. Other biblical and extra-biblical sources have tended to confirm the dates of the events in the Book of Ezekiel and its contents fall between 593 and 571 BCE.

Because the period of Ezekiel's prophecy comes immediately after that of Jeremiah, the earlier part of the history of this period is also described on pages 75–79 (Chapter 3, on Jeremiah). After the capitulation of Jerusalem, the King, the Queen Mother and the chief officials (who included Ezekiel) were all taken to Babylon in the first deportation of 597 BCE. Conditions during the first Babylonian exile were reasonable: freedom of association was permitted and the elders are depicted meeting in the house of Ezekiel while Jeremiah encouraged the exiles to build houses and to take wives and have families. Many of the Israelite émigrés became artisans and prospered, although religious worship and cultic sacrifice could not take place in Babylon as it was considered an unclean land – such religious rites were permitted only in the Jerusalem Temple.

## Ezekiel's contribution to law religion and ethics

Although the main focus of this chapter is Ezekiel's mental illness, it is important to note that he made important contributions to ethics and theology, as one of the first religious leaders of the exile. His most lasting contribution is thought to have been his teaching of the doctrine of individual responsibility in law. He starts his exposition with a proverb – which he says is to be rejected.

> 18[1] The word of the Lord came to me. [2] What do you mean by repeating this proverb concerning the land of Israel, 'The parents have eaten sour grapes, and the children's teeth are set on edge'? [3] As I live, says the Lord God, this proverb is no more to be used by you in Israel. [4] Know that all lives are mine; the life of the parent as well as the life of the child; it is only the person who sins shall die.

Grapes were a common harvest for the rural community of ancient Israel, and Eichrodt (1970, p. 274) explains that the eating of unripe or sour grapes will leave a peculiar and unpleasant sensation in the mouth, setting the teeth on edge – but in this proverb it is the children's teeth which are set on edge, and so this proverb is an allegory of blood guilt – the children will be punished for their parents' crimes. The doctrine of blood guilt is set out specifically in the second of the ten commandments, where the punishment for idolatrous worship is given: 'For I the Lord your God am a jealous God, punishing children for the iniquity of parents to the third and fourth generations'. Ezekiel is emphatic that such ideas are to be rejected.

The notion of individual responsibility which Ezekiel promotes here is nowadays taken for granted but would have represented revolutionary thinking in ancient Israelite society, where tribe and family assumed much greater importance than the individual, and a whole family might be punished for the crime of one of its members.

Ezekiel was not the first to write about redemption, forgiveness and the ability to change but he writes very eloquently on these themes; thus the great Protestant theologian Martin Luther particularly liked verse 33[11]: 'As I live says the Lord God, I have no pleasure in the death of the wicked, but that the wicked should turn from their ways and live'. This powerfully expresses his compassion for the wicked, his wish for change and redemption as well as his distaste for capital punishment, which at the time was probably the only way of keeping some sort of order in society. Similarly, in 36[26]: 'A new heart I will give you, and a new spirit I will put within you and I will remove from your body the heart of stone and give you a heart of flesh.' Sometimes Ezekiel's writings seem almost incomprehensible, but in other instances they are inspirational and they provide for eight of the Haftarot used in the liturgy of the Sabbath services to this day (see Talmon).

The principal source for the present chapter is the Book of Ezekiel itself, particularly the first 12 chapters. In addition, to try to understand the historical and religious significance of these passages I have been much en-lightened by Greenberg's (1983, 1997) masterful treatises on Ezekiel, and the monumental work of W. Zimmerli (1969). In a few instances I have quoted from the more specific Jewish interpretations offered in the Midrash, the Talmud and the views of the great rabbis of the Middle Ages, as given in Rosenberg (1991), and also from other more recent commentators.

## The clinical psychiatry of Ezekiel

The central theme of this chapter is that Ezekiel suffered from an episodic mental disorder – probably schizophrenia or possibly a closely related condition known as schizo-affective disorder. The text is rich in its descrip-tion (in autobiographical form) of the main symptoms of mental illness. However, because the psychiatry is interspersed with moral, religious and other historical material, the original clinical record is somewhat obscured. Fortunately, most of the passages depicting his mental illness do not have great religious significance. Schizophrenia is by far the most serious of the major mental illnesses but, in contrast to depression, its symptoms do not occur in the wider community and so most people will be quite unfamiliar with them and so they will seem to be bizarre and incomprehensible to the layman.

In the sections which follow each of the main schizophrenic symptom groups that Ezekiel displays is followed by a brief summary as to how Talmudic and later biblical exegetes have viewed this material. This is followed by an exposition of the relevant psychiatry. There is a huge cultural gap between the religious prophecy of the 6th century BCE and 21st-century secular psychiatry, so the attempt to marry two such unlikely bedfellows is problematical. On the other hand, the clinical description of schizophrenia given in the Book of Ezekiel is very accurate and closely resembles the histories communicated in psychiatric clinics by patients today. Thus it may be of interest to consider how a patient would be diagnosed today if he said or did some of things Ezekiel is said to have done. The order of symptoms discussed in this chapter is as follows:

- mutism and catatonia
- auditory phenomena
- visual phenomena (visions)
- morbid jealousy
- other Schneiderian 'first-rank symptoms' (explained below).

After this explanation of the symptoms, further sections give a summary of the psychopathology and describe the lifetime course of Ezekiel's illness. Before some concluding remarks are made, a diagnostic formulation is presented in terms of the diagnostic glossary of DSM-5 (schizophrenia and schizo-affective disorder are also described in the appendix to this chapter).

Perhaps a preliminary warning should be given to the reader, that this chapter is the longest and most difficult in this book. It needs to be long because the issue of whether Ezekiel has schizophrenia or not has been controversial since 1877 and still remains unresolved, and only a detailed examination of key individual verses will be able to provide any sort of answer. Also, this is a technical chapter, as schizophrenia is a difficult condition for the layman to understand. Moreover, the Book of Ezekiel is almost completely incomprehensible to those lacking biblical knowledge, and even those familiar with the Bible consider it an obscure text. There is therefore the risk of drowning in a swamp of incomprehensible schizo-phrenic phenomenology to the accompaniment of Old Testament rhetoric laden with doom and gloom.

## The episodes of mutism and catatonia

Klostermann (1877) was the first to suggest that Ezekiel was suffering from *katalepsia odersucht* (catalepsy and addiction) and this explained Ezekiel's dumbness, which seemed to come and go without clear reason. He was the first scholar to suggest Ezekiel's feeling of being bound for 390 days on one side and then 40 days on the other side was catatonia. Klostermann had no intention to disparage Ezekiel or to cast doubt on his divine inspiration but felt sorry him: his article is entitled *Der arme Ezekiel* ('the poor Ezekiel').

The biblical text describes four separate episodes of muteness, but during the second episode, which is also the longest, there a clear description of his associated immobility and this suggests catatonia. Literally, catatonia refers to a state of increased tone in muscles at rest which can be abolished by voluntary activity. Characteristically, patients remain immobile for long periods and are mute but they are just about able to eat and carry out vital bodily functions. Catatonia used to be a fairly common presentation of schizophrenia. Thus, at the turn of the last century, Kraepelin (1908) found that around 20% of his cases of *dementia praecox* (an early term for schizo-phrenia) presented with catatonia. Assuming a general population prevalence rate for schizophrenia of 1%, and that 20% of these cases had catatonia, then around 2/1000 of the population would have had catatonic schizophrenia, making the condition unusual but not unheard of.

### The first episode of muteness

The first episode describes only muteness rather than a full-blown catatonic syndrome. Ezekiel experiences a period of dumbness lasting for seven days. The episode is buried within a text rich in religious content and can readily be overlooked.

> 3[14] The spirit lifted me up and bore me away; I went in bitterness in the heat of my spirit, the hand of the Lord being strong upon me. [15] I came to the exiles at Tel-abib, who lived by the River Chebar. *And I sat there among them, stunned, for seven days.* [16] At the end of seven days, the word of the Lord came to me: [17] Mortal, I have made you a sentinel for the house of Israel; whenever you hear a word from my mouth, you shall give them a warning from me.

The traditional rabbinical and Talmudic explanation for these verses is given by Rosenberg (1991).

- *I went in bitterness.* This means it was distasteful to me to chide the children of my people. Rashi wrote that it meant 'like a person who brings foreboding tidings and goes with a dejected spirit, wishing to conceal the matter'. Mezudath David explains that the prophet was grieved and troubled because he saw the departure of the Shechinah (seeing God in his glory) from the holy Temple.
- *The hand of the Lord being strong upon me.* Rashi wrote that this was coercion – Ezekiel being led against his will. He also says that *the hand of the Lord* sometimes signifies an episode of insanity (see page 333).
- *I sat there among them, stunned, for seven days.* Rashi translates *māsmayim* as 'bewildered', 'a man silenced and unable to speak'. The Hebrew word is *māsmayim*, meaning 'stunned', and Greenberg translates this as 'numbing, wretchedness, unnerving shock, aloneness and desolateness', which is quite a good description of depressive mutism. Zimmerli (p. 139) has 'The experience weighed so heavily upon him, inhibiting all free activity, that he remained for 7 days completely overwhelmed'. Zimmerli also a suggests an abnormal mood and ecstasy, and writes 'the receiving of a message in which visionary and trance like features occur, is sometimes introduced by the reference to the hand of the Lord' (vol. 1, p. 118). Carley (1974, p. 25) suggests 'the spirit which transports the prophet in his visionary experience leaves him overwhelmed and speechless for a week'. Catatonia may also present with excitement, and in modern terminology this particular episode of ecstasy might be termed catatonic excitement – but he does not speak.

## The second and third episodes of mutism may be catatonia

The description of the second episode is much more explicit and more readily recognisable as catatonia since there is a clear description of mutism – failure to speak – as well as akinesis – lack of movement. The duration of these episodes is again specified, as is Ezekiel's extremely poor diet and poor level of personal functioning during these phases. The accuracy of the clinical description makes it quite likely that such an episode genuinely occurred because it would be almost impossible to conjure up such a description purely from imagination. The emphasis is more on his immobility and low level of subsistence during this phase, but the account is in keeping with the description of catatonia as found in older psychiatric textbooks, from a period when catatonic presentations were more frequent than today (there are now effective treatments for catatonia so full-blown cases are rarely seen).

> 3[24] The spirit entered me and set me on my feet; and he spoke with me and said to me: Go, shut yourself inside your house. [25] As for you, mortal, *cords shall be placed on you and you shall be bound with them so that you cannot go out among the people.* [26] And I will make your tongue cling to the roof of your mouth, *so that you shall be speechless* and unable to reprove them; for they are a rebellious house. [27] But when I speak with you, I will open your mouth and you shall say to them, 'Thus says the Lord God'; let those who will hear, hear; and let those who refuse to hear, refuse; for they are a rebellious house.

*Traditional rabbinical explanation of 3²⁴⁻²⁶*

Redak says that '*shut yourself inside your house*' means that this will show them that they are not even worthy of reproof. From verse 3²⁵, *cords shall be placed on you* means you will be imprisoned in your house as if you were bound with ropes. Verse 3²⁶ means 'It is as though your tongue clings to your palate, and you will be dumb i.e. you will not talk to them or reprove them'. Verse 3²⁷, *I will open your mouth*, Redak says means 'I shall permit you to talk to them'. Mezudath David writes: 'When I shall speak to you to proclaim to them the prophecy, then I shall open your mouth to enable you quickly to speak with eloquence although you are not accustomed to telling people to improve their ways' (from Rosenberg, 1991, pp. 24–25).

It is noteworthy that none of the earlier rabbinical commentaries questions the fact that Ezekiel was both silent and immobile, but explain this as house arrest rather than as clinical disorder. Thus the traditional religious explanation for this passage is that Ezekiel is to cease his prophesying to the people because he is so critical of them. Even when this period ends, the prophet once more starts to berate the people for being rebellious and not listening to God.

*Psychiatric aspects*

The phrase *cords shall be placed on you* describes a state of immobility. The phrase in 3²⁶ *and I will make your tongue cling to the roof of your mouth so that you shall be speechless* indicates he could not talk. A state of silence or the absence of speech would have been noticed by those around him. Perhaps they remarked on it and recorded how this once loquacious and hypercritical prophet had suddenly been reduced to silence. Possibly this is Ezekiel's own explanation for the subjective sensations he was experiencing during the catatonia. Certainly it is a unique metaphor and does not appear anywhere else in the Bible.

The picture is therefore of the prophet being both speechless and motionless for a prolonged period. Both the onset and offset of the episode is attributed to God, as is the placing of the cords, indicating no obvious triggering or external causation; hence this is a spontaneous and unexplained onset and a spontaneous remission. This is how an episode of catatonia develops: it comes for no particular reason, and then after a time it goes. Catatonia responds well to electroconvulsive therapy (ECT) and anti-psychotic drugs and so has become much less frequent, but a stroll through the wards of any mental asylum before the 1950s, prior to the advent of the antipsychotic drugs, would have found many 'Ezekiels' sitting in their chairs or lying on their sides on their beds in mute and catatonic states.

*The duration of the dumbness and immobility*

The period of immobility and muteness is prolonged. He has two separate episodes: the first is for 390 days (190 days in the LXX) and the second, described in 4³⁻⁸, for 40 days (this is the third episode of muteness).

> 4³ Then take an iron plate and place it as an iron wall between you and the city; set your face towards it and let it be in a state of siege and press the siege

against it. This is a sign for the house of Israel. [4] Then lie on your left side and place the punishment of the house of Israel upon it; you shall bear their punishment for the number of the days that you lie there. [5]*For I assign to you a number of days, 390 days, equal to the number of the years of their punishment and so you shall bear the punishment of the house of Israel.* [6] When you have completed these, you shall lie down a second time, but on your right side, *and bear the punishment of the house of Judah; forty days I assign you, one day for each year.* [7] You shall set your face towards the siege of Jerusalem, and with your arm bared you shall prophesy against it. [8] See, I am putting cords on you so that you cannot turn from one side to the other until you have completed the days of your siege.

## Rabbinical comments on the duration of the silence of 4[4-8]

The rabbis provide an elaborate explanation for the prolonged duration of Ezekiel's confinement and silence. But where do the 390 days come from?

Rashi took his explanation from the Talmud, as originally proposed in *Seder Olam*, ch. 26. Here, Rabbi Joseph made a computation that 'Israel sinned for three hundred and ninety years from the time they entered the land until the time the ten tribes were exiled from there'. There then follows a listing of all the kings and judges of Israel, giving their names and the duration of their respective reigns. When this is summed it comes to only 350 years, but there is then some dispute over the duration of the reigns of King Jehoahaz and King Jeroboam and with 'appropriate Talmudic mathematical adjustments' to the duration of the reigns of these monarchs, the computation eventually ends up with a total of 390 years, which corresponds to the 390 days of Ezekiel's immobility (see Rosenberg, 1991, pp. 26–27).

Rashi adopts a similar rationale for the 40 days of verse 4[6] ('you shall ... bear the punishment of the house of Judah; forty days I assign you, one day for each year): 'This teaches us that the house of Judah sinned from the time that the ten tribes were exiled until Jerusalem was destroyed which was forty years'. There then follows a piece of complicated piece of mathematics summing the duration of the reigns of all the Kings of Judah (Ahab, Manasseh, Ammon and Jehoiakim) and again with 'appropriate Talmudic mathematical adjustment' this totals 40 years.

Neither the fact of Ezekiel's silence nor its duration was questioned by the rabbis of the Talmud or by Rashi, who took the duration to be authentic, but instead they offered a somewhat fanciful explanation based on the duration of the reigns of the Kings of Judah and of Israel.

The phrase *I am putting cords on you* is used once more to describe the immobility, which was presumably Ezekiel's own explanation for his abrupt and unpleasant discovery that he could no longer move.

## Catatonia in the medical literature

The description of being unable to speak (your tongue cleaving to your mouth) and being immobile (cords put on you) describes a state of akinetic mutism or stupor which is consistent with catatonia. Schizophrenic catatonia can last for several years and then remit, leaving the individual undamaged. There are several series of cases of stupor in the psychiatric literature (see Cutting, 1997). Catatonia itself has a long list of causes, with the majority of cases being due to schizophrenia and some to schizo-affective disorder; however, organic brain diseases such as tumours, encephalitis, metabolic disorders such as high blood calcium levels, and liver failure encephalopathy, can all result in catatonia. A person can emerge from such severe catatonic illnesses with their intellect completely intact, with an ability to recall everything said to them during their catatonic phase, and this seems to have happened to Ezekiel.

Such a prolonged episode of stupor or stupor-like behaviour which Ezekiel experienced and that lasted for over a year and yet from which he emerged completely intact can only be explained by catatonia as occurs in schizophrenia or schizo-affective disorder. This is because all the other causes of catatonia listed above are usually rapidly fatal.

## Surviving on lowly rations and the coprophagia

Patients who are mentally ill, particularly those with a chronic psychoses, often suffer from self-neglect and a very poor diet. They cook simply and sparingly, although in some cases they may fail to accomplish even this. Immediately following the description of how Ezekiel is to lie on his side in a silent immobile state there is a clear description in $4^{9-15}$ of his very impoverished diet during this episode:

> $4^9$ And you, take wheat and barley, beans and lentils, millet and spelt; put them into one vessel, and make bread for yourself. During the number of days that you lie on your side, three hundred and ninety days, you shall eat it. $^{10}$ The food that you eat shall be twenty shekels a day by weight; at fixed times you shall eat it. $^{11}$ And you shall drink water by measure, one-sixth of a hin; at fixed times you shall drink. $^{12}$ You shall eat it as a barley cake, *baking it in their sight on human dung.* $^{13}$ The Lord said, 'Thus shall the people of Israel eat their bread, unclean, among the nations to which I will drive them'. $^{14}$ Then I said, 'Ah Lord God! I have never defiled myself; from my youth up until now I have never eaten what died of itself or was torn by animals, nor has carrion flesh come into my mouth'. $^{15}$ Then he said to me, 'See, I will let you have cow's dung instead of human dung, on which you may prepare your bread'.

This passage describes the extremely poor diet that Ezekiel must have eaten during his catatonic phase. The account is very detailed, suggesting that either Ezekiel himself or those around him must have observed and recorded his strange diet. It is noteworthy that subjects with catatonia have an excellent recollection of everything that they did or heard during their catatonia once their episode has resolved. Thus once he was better he recorded the terrible food he had eaten while he was catatonic. It is clear that for at least a part of the time he must have been cooking his food by burning human faeces (his own?) and only later used cow dung ($^{15}$ I will let you have cow's dung). Its symbolic and religious meaning is given in the next two verses, which liken Ezekiel's starvation diet to the starvation of the people of Jerusalem:

> $4^{16}$ Then he said to me, Mortal, I am going to break the staff of bread in Jerusalem; they shall eat bread by weight and with fearfulness; and they shall

drink water by measure and in dismay. [17] Lacking bread and water, they will look at one another in dismay, and waste away under their punishment.

## Traditional rabbinical explanations for the starvation diet

Redak commented, 'God intimated to Ezekiel that he was to eat this bread when lying on his right side because the people of Judah were also afflicted by famine'. Commenting on the limited quantity of fluid, Redak added 'his thirst was never quenched and this was symbolic of the dire thirst that would prevail in Jerusalem during the siege, which lasted from the ninth year of Zedekiah until his eleventh year' (after Rosenberg, p. 29). The narrator in the Bible says the prophetic meaning of Ezekiel's starvation diet will be a sign for the house of Israel – a portend of the future siege of Jerusalem and the starvation of its citizens – the catastrophe that is yet to come.

On verse 12, *baking it in their sight on human dung*, Rashi writes 'They shall bake it with their coals that dry it out and burn it'. Redak also explains the Hebrew word *teoneneh* as the feminine plural, meaning that the women will bake the cake with coals made of dried human excrement. He quotes others who render 'you shall bake' as the prophet himself should bake the cakes. The word *Gaylelae* denotes dry excrement, which can roll (*galil*). God commanded the prophet to bake in this repulsive manner as a sign to the Jews that they would have to eat unclean bread when they were among the other nations.

The Babylonian Talmud (Erubin 81a) tells of an experiment made in the third century CE which showed that Ezekiel's bread was not only uneatable, but would not even be touched by a dog.

The English poet William Blake, probably a manic depressive himself, who was fascinated by Ezekiel, was puzzled by his eating human dung. In his book *The Marriage of Heaven and Hell* he wrote:

> After dinner I then asked Ezekiel why he ate dung, and lay so long on his right and then his left side? He answered, it is the desire of raising other men into the infinite; it is this the North American tribes practise. Is he honest who resists his genius or conscience for the sake of present ease or gratification? (Quoted in Rowland, 2009, p. 233)

## Psychiatric aspects

The diet described in $4^{9-15}$ is extremely poor. The amount of bread Ezekiel eats, 20 shekels in weight, corresponds to around 8 ounces a day (one shekel is 4/10 of an ounce) and the amount of water he must drink is also limited. One hin is a gallon and so one-sixth of a hin would be equal to about 1⅓ pints, which would be barely enough to survive on in a hot Middle Eastern country such as Babylonia (southern Iraq).

The use of human dung in the preparation of his bread ($4^{12}$) suggests that Ezekiel must have been both desperate and disturbed at the time. He broke the religious dietary laws as well as moral taboos and this could only have occurred if all of Ezekiel's normal inhibitions had broken down, as might happen in severe mental illness. The use of human excrement in cooking is against religious laws and Greenberg comments (p. 107) that human dung was considered to be ritually unclean and was always buried to prevent defilement (see Deut 23$^{12-14}$). The text describes Ezekiel eating food as if he were living under siege conditions, but in Babylonia *there was no siege at that time.* The link with a siege is therefore only symbolic and is used as a *sign action* to prophesy the later conditions of starvation that the people of Jerusalem would have to endure. This is confirmed in the verses immediately preceding this account of his strange starvation/coprophagic diet, which describes him being catatonic state for more than a year.

Eating human faeces is known as coprophagia and taboos in all cultures against this are strong. However, it can occur in certain illnesses, including schizophrenia, seizure disorders, cerebral atrophy and tumours, mental retardation, alcoholism, autism, dementia and a variety of other less common disorders. In Ezekiel's case schizophrenia seems to be the most likely cause.

### The fourth episode of muteness

The fourth episode of muteness follows soon after the death of his wife, and it appears to occur in the context of an atypical grief reaction. He is commanded not to mourn. The passage begins by describing the death of his wife and ends with a period of mutism. A date for this episode is given as the 10th day of the 10th month of the 9th year (of the exile) which corresponds to January 588 BCE. Although there can be no certainty, it seems likely that Ezekiel himself recorded this precise date for his wife's death (a very important occasion for himself personally, but not really for anyone else). He obtains relief from this mutism only when a messenger from Jerusalem arrives:

> 24$^{15}$ The word of the Lord came to me: $^{16}$ Mortal, with one blow I am about to take away from you the delight of your eyes; *yet you shall not mourn or weep, nor shall your tears run down.* $^{17}$ Sigh, but not aloud; make no mourning for the dead. Bind on your turban, and put your sandals on your feet; do not cover your lip or eat the bread of mourners. $^{18}$ So I spoke to the people in the morning and at evening my wife died. And on the next morning I did as I was commanded.

Ezekiel's failure to mourn is then given prophetic significance – that the people are not to mourn after the killings of their sons and daughters who remain in Jerusalem, which will soon fall to the Babylonians:

> 24$^{19}$ Then the people said to me, 'Will you not tell us what these things mean for us, that you are acting in this way?' $^{20}$ Then I said to them: The word of the Lord came to me: $^{21}$ Say to the house of Israel, Thus says the Lord God: I will profane my sanctuary, the pride of your power, the delight of your eyes, and your heart's desire; and your sons and your daughters whom you left behind shall fall by the sword. $^{22}$ And you shall do as I have done; you shall not cover your upper lip or eat the bread of mourners. $^{23}$ Your turbans shall be on your heads and your sandals on your feet; you shall not mourn or weep, but you shall pine away in your iniquities and groan to one another. $^{24}$ Thus Ezekiel shall be a sign to you; you shall do just as he has done. When this comes then you shall know that I am the Lord God.

Thus Ezekiel's private grief and his unusual failure to mourn the death of his wife seems to have been used by the biblical narrator as an instruction to the people not to mourn Israel's forthcoming disaster. This is another of Ezekiel's sign actions. The third section of this mourning passage goes on to describe Ezekiel's muteness:

> 24²⁵ And you, mortal, on the day when I take from them their stronghold, their joy and glory, the delight of their eyes and their heart's affection, and also their sons and their daughters, ²⁶ on that day, one who has escaped will come to report to you the news. ²⁷ *On that day your mouth shall be opened to the one who has escaped, and you shall speak and no longer be silent.* So you shall be a sign to them; and they shall know that I am the Lord.

One can infer from 24²⁷ that Ezekiel had been silent for some unspecified period of time after the death of his wife, but he was now able to speak – hence he had been through another episode of mutism.

*The rabbinical comments on Ezekiel's failure to mourn (from Rosenberg, 1991)*
The rabbis try to link the death of Ezekiel's wife (588 BCE) to the destruction of the Temple in 586 BCE. R. Johanan (Palestine 3rd century CE) wrote:

> When a man's wife dies on him, it is as though he experienced the destruction of the Temple. The text says, 'Man I am going to take away your eye's desire by a stroke'; It goes on to say 'My wife died in the evening' and then 'I am going to desecrate my Temple ... your eye's desire'. (b. sanhedrin 22a; Greenberg, vol. 2, p. 515)

Redak writes that Ezekiel's wife's death was sudden and not preceded by illness; the 'desire of their eyes' actually refers not to Ezekiel's wife but to the Temple, which will soon also be quite suddenly destroyed. Just as Ezekiel is not to weep over the loss of his wife, so Israel is not to weep over the forthcoming destruction of its Temple.

Carley (1974, p. 166) writes that this moving passage concerning Ezekiel's wife's death has been taken to indicate the prophet's heartlessness in turning his own personal grief into an act of prophecy. Although Ezekiel was prepared to subject his own feelings to the prophetic task, the narrative of his wife's death is presented as the climax of his first period of prophetic activity, culminating in his last words before news of Jerusalem's fall reached the exile. Jeremiah was also instructed not to share in mourning rites, as this was to be a sign of the overwhelming national disaster which lay ahead. At that time all feelings would be numb. The dead would not be honoured by the living and the living would find no one to comfort them in their sorrow (Jer 16⁵⁻⁹). Rashi expressed similar sentiments and said the people should not mourn because they will have no comforters. 'For no one among you is not a mourner, and there can be no mourning except where there are consolers.' When everyone is dead or dying there is no point in carrying out mourning rituals. No mourning rituals were observed at Auschwitz.

*Psychiatric aspects*

Atypical grief, or failure to mourn in the face of personal tragedy, may occur in schizophrenia and the grief may itself result in an exacerbation of the schizophrenia. In this instance it appears that Ezekiel's failure to mourn in the traditional way was substituted by an episode of mental illness, either catatonia or depressive mutism.

The text records that Ezekiel was very fond of his wife, as she is referred to as 'the delight of your eyes', although Zimmerli suggests such sentimental language may have been in common use at the time and be relatively meaningless. Instead of mourning, he became mute. It is unclear whether this is simple depressive muteness or a further episode of catatonia. What is of importance is that Ezekiel notices when the messenger comes that he can now speak again, and his condition has improved; this is the only acknowledgement that he has been unwell and silent following the death of his wife.

Some years ago I looked after a female patient with chronic schizophrenia who lived with her mother and both were devoted to each other. Her mother always ensured her daughter took her medication and so she remained well for many years. When her mother died, she had no one to remind her to take her medication and she soon became floridly ill. While in this state, instead of grieving for her mother, she denied her mother's death completely, and began laughing whenever someone spoke about it; she refused to let her mother be buried and became quite paranoid. She was then placed on section, admitted to hospital and treated with antipsychotic medication; as her condition improved she became sad and wept and started to grieve over her mother's death, eventually consenting to her mother's burial. Such atypical grief reactions are common in schizophrenia and this may account for Ezekiel's strange reaction as well.

## The fifth episode of mutism

The fifth episode of mutism is dated to the 12th year of the exile.

> 33[21] In the twelfth year of our exile, in the tenth month, on the fifth day of the month, someone who had escaped from Jerusalem came to me and said 'The city has fallen'. [22] Now the hand of the Lord had been upon me the evening before the fugitive came to me in the morning; *so my mouth was opened and I was no longer unable to speak.*

The passage continues with Ezekiel launching into one of his prophecies of doom concerning the woes of the land of Israel, the sins of the people and how God will make the land one of desolation if the iniquitous practices of the people continue. R. Malbim provides a theo-political explanation for this episode:

> Since Ezekiel lived in Babylon, he was not chosen to foretell the destruction of the Jerusalem Temple. That mission was delegated to Jeremiah, who lived in Judah and it was Jeremiah's task to admonish the people so that they would repent and so avert the disaster. He also advised Zedekiah to surrender to Nebuchadnezzar. When Jeremiah's admonitions went unheeded and the

destruction came about, Jeremiah's mission ended, and it was only then that Ezekiel could commence his prophecies for the Jews in Babylon. This explains why up until the destruction of Jerusalem, Ezekiel's mouth was sealed. Those prophets who did speak were the many false prophets who said that the Temple would not be destroyed. After the destruction of Jerusalem the people were more likely to heed Ezekiel's prophecies. (Malbim, quoted in Rosenberg, 1991, vol. 2, p. 288)

## Summary

Thus there are five episodes when Ezekiel became mute. In the second and longest of these episodes he is more than mute – he becomes immobile and speechless for more than a year and eats a starvation diet. As early as 1877, Klostermann suggested that this episode represented catatonia, which at that time had only recently been described in the German psychiatric literature. Broome (1946) and Jaspers (1968) also agreed that this episode represented catatonia. If the five episodes are taken as discrete, then the possibility that Ezekiel suffered from recurrent catatonic episodes is raised.

Some authors, such as Ellen Davis (1989), somewhat implausibly propose the dumbness was merely a literary device created by Ezekiel. Both Greenberg and Davis link Ezekiel's episodes of dumbness to a later episode when he eats the scroll, providing a quasi-religious explanation for this: 'Ezekiel must fall "silent" and let the scroll which he has swallowed speak through him'. However, a more likely link between his recurrent episodes of muteness and his eating the scroll is that both are manifestations of an underlying schizophrenic illness.

## The auditory phenomena

Like any other prophet, Ezekiel hears the voice of God and delivers his message to the people. In ancient Israel the prophet's task was to serve as an intermediary between the deity and his people, as well as to educate the people. There are numerous examples of the prophets hearing the voice of God in the Old Testament and passing on his message to the people. This forms an important part of religion and has no pathological significance. However, in Ezekiel's case the phraseology and the content of what he hears are unique and have a much more schizophrenic flavour than that found for any of the other prophets, none of whom appears to have had a psychosis. In addition, Ezekiel also hears voices and other noises that are *not* attributed to the deity, and are phenomena not shared by any other prophet. In order to understand how the voices and other sounds that Ezekiel experiences are unusual – even for a prophet, I describe below how other 'normal' prophets experienced the voice of God.

### Hearing the voice of the deity – normal prophetic voices

Apart from Ezekiel, it seems that Jeremiah hears the voice of God most often, and Jeremiah did not suffer from any sort of psychosis or schizophrenia (see Chapter 3).

Some examples of how the voice of God is heard by prophets are given in Table 8.1.

**Table 8.1** How the prophets hear the voice of God

| Prophet | Scripture |
| --- | --- |
| Jeremiah | 1[14]Then the Lord said to me 'Out of the north disaster shall break out on all the inhabitants of the land....' |
| | 3[6] The Lord said to me in the days of King Josiah; have you seen what she did – the faithless one Israel.... |
| Hosea | 3[1] The Lord said to me again 'Go love a woman who has a lover and is an adulteress just as the Lord loves the people of Israel....' |
| Joel | 1[1] The word of the Lord that came to Joel son of Pethuel 'hear this oh elders.... |
| Jonah | 1[1] Now the word of the Lord came to Jonah son of Amittai saying [2]Go at once to Nineveh that great city and cry out against it.... |

Ezekiel is also a prophet but as well as hearing the voice of God, he has a much wider range of auditory experiences, and these differ substantially from the stereotyped format evident in Table 8.1. Thus Ezekiel has six different types of auditory experience, five of which are consistent with psychotic illness:

- normal prophetic voices – similar to those described for other prophets (Table 8.1) and *not* of a schizophrenic type
- voices associated with spirits that enter him and perform strange actions
- voices occurring in the context of command hallucinations, giving bizarre instructions, which he obeys
- voices experienced at other times, which have some features of schizophrenic auditory hallucinations
- voices that occur during visions (discussed together with the visions in the next section)
- peculiar sounds (non-verbal auditory hallucinations) which seem to occur in association with Ezekiel's visual hallucinations.

All these auditory experiences may all have religious meaning but they may all, except the first, also be symptoms of schizophrenia.

### Ezekiel's version of prophetic voices

Like any other prophet, Ezekiel hears the voice of God, and it is his task to relay the prophetic message to the people. Ezekiel is frequently addressed (over 80 times throughout the book) by God as 'man' or 'mortal', the Hebrew being *ben adam* ('son of man'). For instance:

> 7[1] The word of the Lord came to me: [2] You, O mortal, thus says the Lord God to the Land of Israel: An end! The end has come upon the four corners of the land.

15:1 The word of the Lord came to me: 2 O mortal, how does the wood of the vine surpass all other wood....

Greenberg (1993, pp. 61–62) states that this type of address is unique to Ezekiel in the prophetic literature, as other prophets such as Jeremiah, Amos and Hosea are addressed by their own names. Most of the references to Ezekiel hearing the voice of God are of this type, and are probably non-psychotic.

## Voices associated with spirits

Voices associated with spirits are more likely to be psychotic in origin because they occur in the presence of other psychotic phenomena.

> 1:28 Like the bow in a cloud on a rainy day, such was the appearance of the splendour all around. This was the appearance of the likeness of the glory of the Lord. When I saw it, I fell on my face, and *I heard the voice of someone speaking.*
> 2:1 He said to me: O mortal, stand up on your feet, and I will speak with you 2And when he spoke to me, *a spirit entered into me and set me on my feet; and I heard him speaking to me.* 3 He said to me, Mortal, I am sending you to the people of Israel, to a nation of rebels who have rebelled against me*; they and their ancestors have transgressed against me to this very day.

Block summarises the traditional and more recent interpretations for this passage:

> Ezekiel is in a prostrate state and he hears a voice commanding him to rise because the speaker desires to converse with him. But whose voice is it? The text is unclear since *wayyo'mer* could be translated 'It said' or 'he [Yahweh] said'. The question may be academic. In the meantime Ezekiel is infused with an energizing *ruah* (spirit) that picks him up and sets him on his feet. And what kind of *ruah* is this? Is it a sudden gust of wind? Or is it the spirit of Yahweh, the holy spirit? The text notes the raising of the prophet occurs at the same time as the sound of the voice, which suggests that this *ruah* must be the same *ruah* that had animated the wheels as in (1:12,20, and 21) and that will control Ezekiel's movements throughout his ministry. (Block, 1997, p. 115)

### Psychiatric aspects

This passage occurs at the end of the chariot vision (ch. 1), where the text states he hears 'the voice of someone'. Block indicates that it is 'unclear' whose voice it is. The LXX has a slightly different version, 'the voice of one speaking', which also implies an uncertain origin for the voice – either man or God (Greenberg, 1993, p. 61). Although most commentators assume that it is the voice of the God, nowhere is this explicitly stated. This is important because an ancient prophet could hear the voice of God: this would be his professional privilege and would not imply any sort of mental disorder or psychic abnormality.

The voice then instructs him to stand up, but it is a *ruah* or spirit which enters him and actually makes him stand up. In terms of schizophrenic phenomenology this might qualify as an example of a passivity experience or of a 'made influence' (an alien, usually delusional influence, which takes over some bodily function) and counts as a Schneiderian first-rank symptom of schizophrenia, which has important diagnostic implications (see pages 340–341).

The phrase 'I heard him speaking to me' may represent another psychiatric symptom – audible thoughts. Greenberg (1983, p. 62) states the Hebrew here is unusual, *et middabber*, and means 'one speaking to himself'. Such a translation shows some resemblance another Schneiderian schizophrenic symptom, namely thought echo (hearing one's own thoughts aloud).

Thus, in this very short passage (only two verses), placed at the end of the chariot of vision, there is a wealth of psychopathology. It contains evidence of Ezekiel of seeing things (*like a bow in a cloud on a rainy day* – visual hallucinations?) and hearing things (*he said stand up on your feet* – auditory hallucinations?), and having the experience that *a spirit entered me and set me on my feet* (?passivity phenomena), in the form of a made influence.

Only a person in the middle of a schizophrenic episode could have put all these symptoms together in a single short stanza and the likelihood is that Ezekiel himself recorded all his thoughts and feelings while he was in a state of excitement – or prophetic ecstasy. The symptoms of psychosis were completely unknown at the time and so it would be almost impossible for any author or later editor to just randomly create such an unusual constellation of symptoms – unless he was actually experiencing them. It is the accumulation of several psychotic symptoms together which make it most probable that this was a genuine psychotic episode.

### Voices occurring during the visions

It is quite common for patients with psychotic illness who are experiencing visual hallucinations to also hear voices emanating from figures within their visual experience. There are a few examples of Ezekiel reporting voices of this type during his visions. In ch. 1, immediately after Ezekiel hears the noise of wings of the cherubim he reports hearing a voice:

> 1²⁵And there came a voice from above the dome over their heads; when they stopped they let their wings down.

It is important to note that the voice Ezekiel hears in this section is not described as the voice of God, and hence is not a 'normal' prophetic voice. Also, when Ezekiel is exiled in Babylon, he hears the voice of God while at the same time experiencing a vision that he is inside the Jerusalem Temple. However, both these examples are also replete with prophetic messages, with much religious significance.

> 8¹⁴ Then he brought me to the entrance of the north gate of the house of the Lord; women were sitting there weeping for Tammuz. ¹⁵ Then he said to me 'Have you seen this O mortal. You will see still greater abominations than these'.

The psychiatry is straightforward. Ezekiel hears a voice of God while he is visiting the temple and he sees the abominations that were going on there, suggesting that he was hearing a voice during his vision.

A further example of Ezekiel hearing the voice of God during a vision is given in 11$^{1-4}$. This describes how Ezekiel sees a group of 25 men who are prostrating themselves to the east and by implication worshipping idols. Again, the text is rich in prophetic and religious meaning but is included here because he hears the voices within a vision:

> 11$^1$ The spirit lifted me up and brought me to the east gate of the house of the Lord, which faces east. There, at the entrance to the gateway, were 25 men; among them *I saw* Jazaaniah son of Azur, and Pelatiah, son of Benaniah, officials of the people. $^2$ *He said to me*, 'Mortal these are men who devise iniquity and who give wicked counsel in this city. $^3$ They say 'The time is not near to build houses; this city is the pot and we are the meat'.

Carley (1974, p. 66) thought this was a waking vision and wrote 'although a waking vision should be distinguished from dreams perhaps the experience of an exceptionally vivid dream from which we awake feeling "I was really there" is the closest most people come to appreciating this type of sensation'. In psychiatric parlance this state of mind might correspond to an *oneroid* (dream-like) state and usually occurs in subjects with severe psychiatric disorders such as organic brain disorders or schizophrenia.

The image of the city being the pot and 'we are the meat' is a powerful metaphor of dread, and not psychotic material. It refers to the fate of the city of Jerusalem and its forthcoming destruction, with the pot being filled with the choicest morsels. In ch. 24 the image of the pot and the meat is repeated but given a more ominous turn by including the fire beneath the pot.

In these verses Ezekiel experiences rather more than simply hearing the voice of God as it is occurring *during his visionary experiences,* a combination also known to occur in psychosis. Thus Deahl (1987) in a study of psychotic patients who had visual hallucinations showed that around a third often also had a variety of auditory hallucinations as well.

With the exception of Zechariah, this combination is not shown by any of the other prophets. There is nothing unusual in the message Ezekiel delivers, with the content of the message being typical of other Old Testament oracles of woe, but the combination of hearing voices within these visions points to a possible psychotic origin.

## Command hallucinations

Ezekiel hears voices throughout his life – more often than any other prophet. There are three instances where Ezekiel receives instructions which take the form of a command which he hears, and that he should carry out some bizarre act, an act which even during his own lifetime people would have thought to be quite strange. The first of these is a command to eat a scroll, the second is that he must shave his head and the third is that he must dig a hole through a wall in the Temple. There are well known and widely accepted religious-historical interpretations for all these acts, and the events are sometimes termed 'sign actions' – a dramatic and visual demonstration that the prophet makes to communicate the word of the God to his people. However, strange actions of this type, carried out under the command of voices, are also a well known feature of schizophrenia. It is noteworthy that the more bizarre actions are unique to Ezekiel: none of the other Old Testament prophets engage in behaviours anywhere near as strange, even though they all hear the voice of God and may also communicate through sign actions – but these are of a far more understandable type.

### Eating the scroll ($2^8$–$3^2$)

Ezekiel eats the sacred scroll and this is perhaps the strangest action performed by any person in the whole of the Old Testament.

> $2^8$ But you, mortal, hear what I say to you; do not be rebellious like that rebellious house; open your mouth and eat what I give to you. $^9$I looked and a hand was stretched out to me and a written scroll was in it. $^{10}$He spread it before me; it had writing on the front and on the back, and written on it were words of lamentation and mourning and woe. $3^1$*He said to me O mortal eat what is offered to you; eat this scroll and go, speak to the house of Israel.* $^2$So I opened my mouth and he gave me the scroll to eat. $^3$*He said to me: Mortal, eat this scroll that I give you and fill your stomach with it. Then I ate it*; and in my mouth it was as sweet as honey.

### Traditional rabbinical and more recent commentary

Although the rabbis of the Talmud and the Middle Ages usually gave a literal meaning to almost every phrase in the OT, in this particular instance they do their utmost to avoid a literal interpretation, preferring a figurative explanation instead. It seems as if the great rabbis just could not bring themselves to believe that Ezekiel could do such a crazy thing as to eat a scroll.

Arbabanel (13th-century Spain, republished 1957) explains that 'God exhorted the prophet to absorb the contents of the scroll so that he could not later shirk his mission by claiming to have forgotten the prophecy'. R. Malbim explained that God wanted the words of the scroll to become as much a part of Ezekiel as the food he eats. According to Mezudath David, the instruction to eat means 'learn and accept the statements in the scroll', and this is followed by the word 'go', which, he says, means after you have digested all the words of the scroll 'go and tell them to the people', while 'feed your stomach' means 'pay attention to the words and do not let them escape your mind lest you forget them'. When the prophet does actually eat the scroll, Rashi interprets this as acquiescence: 'I accepted it and its words were in my mouth, as sweet as honey'.

More recent students of Ezekiel, such as Zimmerli (1969, p. 136), have taken both a literal and a figurative meaning for this passage. Zimmerli compares these verses to a similar passage in Jeremiah $15^{16}$: 'Thy words were found so I ate them and they became to me a joy'. He suggested that eating the divine word was only a simile. By contrast, Greenberg (1983), perhaps the best of the modern commentators, believed the event actually happened, Ezekiel did truly eat the scroll and this was a monstrous act:

> the reality of the scroll event makes it signify the absolute subjugation of the prophet to the will of God ... what follows is something of an ordeal intended to try the prophet's obedience as is suggested by a gradual series of commands over-riding the prophet's hesitation about his capacity to perform

the monstrous feat he has been commanded to carry out.... How monstrous may be gauged by comparison with the imbibing of the curse-filled potion by the suspected adulteress (Num 5) or the ingestion of magical formulas known from Greek-Egyptian magical papyri. In these examples the main purpose was to ingest the words alone, which would be washed or licked off or drunk down, but the papyrus or writing material itself was never eaten. Here an intractable and indigestible mass had to be swallowed, as emphasised by the threefold iteration of the word scroll, suggesting the episode was probably authentic. (R. Olsson cited in Greenberg, p. 78)

## Psychiatric aspects

The clinical psychiatry is relatively straightforward. Ezekiel has an auditory experience in the form of a command hallucination telling him to eat the scroll. The command is repeated several times over and eventually he succumbs to the voices and does eat the scroll. This is the precise pattern of a schizophrenic command hallucination. Patients with schizophrenia who are suffering from command hallucinations requiring them to perform a bizarre act tend to hear the command repeatedly before they eventually 'cave in' and carry out the instructions. Thus those with suicidal auditory hallucinations repeatedly hear the command to commit kill themselves; they usually try to resist the instruction but some will eventually succumb to the command – more often than not, as a way of escaping from the voices.

Although Ezekiel did not have an eating disorder, Lyketsos *et al.* (1964) in a study of eating disturbances among patients with schizophrenia found that around 17% experienced hallucinations instructing them to eat something strange. Eating the scroll was indeed a very strange action and it is almost impossible to conceive that those close to Ezekiel would have made up such a story because it does little to enhance his reputation. Almost certainly they would have just faithfully recorded the event. What makes this most likely to be an action of a person with schizophrenia is that it occurs in the context of voices and command hallucinations which are repeated several times over and these are well recognised schizophrenic symptoms.

## The act of shaving his hair and burning it ($5^{1-2}$)

Ezekiel shaves off the hair from his head and burns a third of it. This follows from an instruction from God. Such an act is rich in symbolic and historical meaning but would be out of character, indeed forbidden, for a priest in ancient Israel.

> $5^1$ And you, O mortal, take a sharp sword; use it as a barber's razor and run it over your head and your beard; then take balances for weighing, and divide the hair. $^2$ One-third of the hair you shall burn in the fire inside the city, when the days of the siege are completed; one-third you will take and strike with the sword all around the city; and one-third you will scatter to the wind, and I will unsheathe the sword after them.

## Rabbinical comments (from Rosenberg, 1991, p. 22)

In contrast to the scroll-eating episode, the rabbis do not question the event itself; they accept that Ezekiel did shave his beard and the hair on his head and burnt his hair, but they provide a historical-religious explanation for the event.

Rashi explains that the sword used for the shaving symbolised the sword of Nebuchadnezzar; the burning of one-third of the hair was a sign that a third of the people would perish in the city dying by fire, famine or plague; the third of the hair that was to be cut by the sword represented the third of the population of the city who would be killed by the sword; while the third of the hair that remained was to be scattered in the wind and this represented the Jews who would flee to other lands.

According to Abarbanel (1957, originally 13th century) the unsheathed sword would pursue this last third, symbolising the massacres and persecutions that were to later follow the Jews in their new and foreign lands – and the subsequent history of the Jewish diaspora more than confirms such a tragic history of repeated massacres.

Maimonides, a physician of the 11th century CE and an important biblical commentator, was perhaps the first to point to the contradiction between the command to shave the head hair with priestly prohibitions on doing so in Lev. 21[5] and Ezek. 44[20], and adds that to do this would have been out of character for a priest like Ezekiel. Greenberg (p. 127) makes a link with the breaking of this religious taboo here, with the prophet defiling himself by eating unclean food (human faeces) and the eating of the scroll, as these behaviours would be out of character for a member of the priesthood.

The notion of a threefold division and sifting of the nation first appears with Elijah (1 Kings 19[17]) but is repeated in the Book of Zechariah (13[8]). The emphasis throughout this passage is on the fate of the survivors, and how the calamity will pursue even them.

Shaving the beard is a normal activity but shaving the scalp is unusual and burning one's hair in public even more strange. Burning one's hair can occur in any psychiatric disorder, including schizophrenia. The presence of an auditory command is less obvious here than in the scroll-eating episode but the passage starts 'And you, O mortal, take a sharp sword'. No other psychotic symptoms are reported at the same time, and so this bizarre and out-of-character behaviour here may or may not be psychotic, but in Jewish religious tradition a specific historical meaning appertaining to later anti-Semitic persecutions have been given to these verses.

### Hearing voices to kill

In his Temple vision (8[18] – 9[9]), Ezekiel describes voices similar in content to the way patients today might describe their voices, including distressing voices about killing. Diagnostically this is important, as voices giving instructions to kill only really occur in psychotic depression and schizophrenia. Patients who are acutely hallucinated often feel physically quite ill as well and in this vision Ezekiel sees a scene of terrible killing but feels so distressed by it that he collapses to the ground.

| | | |
|---|---|---|
| 8[18] | Therefore I will act in wrath; my eye will not spare, nor will I have pity; and though *they cry within my hearing* with *a loud voice*, I will not listen to them. | Hearing others speak ?conversations<br>Loudness; attempt to resist voices |

| 9¹ | Then he cried within my hearing with a loud voice, saying 'Draw near, you executioners of the city, each with his destroying weapon in his hand'. | Hearing others speak; quality of loudness repeated. The content of the voice is killing |
|---|---|---|
| 2 | And six men came from the direction of the upper gate, which faces north, each with his weapon of slaughter in his hand; among them was a man clothed in linen with a writing case at his side. | Visual experience<br><br>Content is killing |
| ... | | |
| 4 | 'Go through the city, through Jerusalem, and put a mark on the foreheads of those who sigh and groan over all the abominations that are committed in it.' | |
| 5 | *To others he said in my hearing* ... your eyes shall not spare, and you shall know no pity. | The voice is not that of God. Command hallucination to kill |
| 6 | Cut down old men, young women, little children but touch no one who has the mark. And begin at my sanctuary.' So they began with the elders who were in front of the house. | |
| 7 | Then he said to them 'Defile the house and fill the courts with the slain. Go!' So they went out and killed in the city. | |
| 8 | While they were killing and *I was left alone, I fell prostrate on my face* and cried out 'Ah Lord God! | Feeling acutely lonely; distressed collapses? feeling very ill? |

There are three instances in this passage where Ezekiel hears the voice of God and both the phrasing and content, which is about killing, are reminiscent of how patients with schizophrenia might describe their voices. No other prophet reports anything like this and this may represent psychotic material.

> 9⁵*To the others he said in my hearing* 'Pass through the city after him and kill; your eyes shall not spare...'.

The description in 9⁵ suggests that Ezekiel can hear the voice talking to other people. Greenberg (1983, p. 175) says the Hebrew for the phrase 'in my hearing', *qara be'zne*, literally means 'call' or 'cry' 'in the ears of', and has several meanings. In this case he writes 'Here the ears merely overhear what is addressed to others, hence the rendering "in my hearing"'. This is remarkably close to the phenomena that some patients with schizophrenia report – that they can hear the voices talking to each other or they can overhear conversations, when no other person is present, and this counts as one of Schneider's first-rank symptoms (see pages 340–341).

The content of the voice, 'to kill', is also quite common among patients with schizophrenia and a clinician confronted by such a patient today would have to act quickly to admit and treat the patient, sometimes even on a compulsory order, because voices with this type of content are dangerous and result in occasional tragedies.

$9^1$ *Then he cried in my hearing with a loud voice, saying* 'Draw near, you executioners of the city....'.

The phrase 'with a loud voice' means the voice Ezekiel heard must have been loud. Patients with acute schizophrenia often complain that their voices are screaming at them. Medication is sometimes successful in abolishing these voices but even if the drugs fail it is usually possible to obtain a reduction in the volume of the voices. No other OT prophet complains of the loudness or volume of the voices they hear, but this is a very frequent complaint of those with schizophrenia. The phrase 'cried within my hearing' implies the voice is emanating from external space somewhere nearby – also typical of schizophrenic voices.

$8^{18}$ Therefore I will act in wrath; my eye will not spare, nor will I have pity; *and though they cry in my hearing with a loud voice, I will not listen to them.*

The verse is difficult to interpret because the *I* of *I will act in wrath* probably refers to God, who is angry with the idolators in the Temple, whereas in the second part of the verse, the *my* of *cried in my hearing* refers to Ezekiel and what he heard. In the latter part of the verse, which is in italics, three features typical of schizophrenic voices are very accurately described: third parties talking, loudness and a tendency to try not to listen to the unpleasant voices. Today, patients often use earphones, iPods or stuff their ears with cotton wool to try to get rid of these unpleasant voices.

### Ezekiel digs through a wall ($12^{4-7}$)

$12^4$ You shall bring out your baggage by day in their sight, as baggage for exile; and you shall go out yourself at evening in their sight, as those do who go into exile. $^5$ *Dig through the wall in their sight and carry the baggage through it.* $^6$ In their sight you shall lift the baggage on your shoulder, and carry it out in the dark; you shall cover your face so that you may not see the land; for I have made you a sign for the house of Israel. $^7$ *I did just as I was commanded. I brought out my baggage by day, as baggage for exile, and in the evening I dug through the wall with my own hands;* I brought it out in the dark carrying it on my shoulder in their sight.

### Rabbinical religious explanations

Redak says that this passage refers to how Zedekiah (the last king of Jerusalem) and the young princes escaped from the palace when the officers of the King of Babylon entered Jerusalem. Although no mention is made of Zedekiah digging a hole, from verse 12 implies that he was about to do so. Moreover, it appears that Zedekiah and his men went out through a hole in the wall because they escaped by way of the King's garden (Jer $39^4$), signifying that they came into the garden through its entrance and fled through the facing wall. They dug through the wall by hand because they had no iron tools with them (Rosenberg, 1991).

More recently Greenberg (1983) has rejected this traditional medieval rabbinical explanation which links Ezekiel's digging the hole in the wall with King Zedekiah's attempt to escape from the siege of Jerusalem. Instead, he suggests that burrowing through the wall of a house was a sign of urban destruction; or desperate efforts to escape; or to escape furtively and so circumvent the besiegers. Burrowing could only occur if the wall was made of mud or clay which was the most common building material used in Babylonia (southern Iraq today) where Ezekiel lived.

In the account, the text mentions 'in their sight' four times, indicating that Ezekiel's contemporaries presumably in Babylonia would have seen him actually digging the hole in the wall, so this strange act was witnessed and so probably did really happen.

## Psychiatric explanations

An explanation is possible in terms of his schizophrenia. The hole in the wall is dug in the context of a voice the prophet hears – the voice of God. The instruction to dig the hole is given repeatedly and such repetition is characteristic of schizophrenic command hallucinations, where patients report hearing the same command many times over before they actually carry out the instruction. Digging holes in walls is odd behaviour but such behaviour is known to occur in schizophrenia. It usually occurs in paranoid schizophrenia, where the subject is tormented by voices which they believe emanate from the walls of their house. In this context, it is of interest to read later in the book that Ezekiel did seem to hear voices coming from the walls of houses. In this later verse ($33^{30}$) God tells him that people are gossiping about him by the walls: 'As for you, mortal, your people *who talk together about you by the walls,* and at the doors of the houses, say to one another, each to a neighbour, "Come and hear what the word is that comes from the Lord".' Such a statement is not particularly bizarre or psychotic and is consistent with its situation within a religious text. This verse seems to suggest he is hearing something either coming from or around the walls.

By making holes and digging into their walls, patients with schizophrenia seek to locate the source of their tormenting voices and sometimes they attack or destroy the wall itself, or electrical fittings in the wall. In a 30-year career I have encountered two such patients who burrowed into the walls of their houses and tried to destroy the electrical and gas fittings, leaving their houses in a dangerous state, because they believed these devices were the sources of the voices they heard.

This simple act of a man digging a hole in the wall with his bare hands has attracted a plethora of explanations. Does it symbolise Zedekiah's escape from the palace? Or is it Ezekiel's desperate attempt at escape during the siege of Jerusalem? Or is it simply all part of a psychotic illness and a way of attacking the source of his voices due to schizophrenia? We shall never know.

## Non-verbal auditory hallucinations

Many patients with schizophrenia also hear noises which are non-verbal sounds, such as the sound of rustling. The symptom is non-specific for schizophrenia but is fairly common. The SCAN (Wing *et al.*, 1990), an established glossary of psychiatric symptoms, defines this symptom as follows:

*Non-verbal auditory hallucination* (item 17.3). The symptom includes noises other than words which have no real origin in the world outside, and no explicable origin in bodily processes which respondents regard as separate from their own mental processes.... Noises such as music, tapping, bird cries, hissing, etc.

During his first vision, Ezekiel sees two cherubim who make a loud noise:

> 1[23] Under the dome of their wings were stretched out straight, one towards another; and each of the creatures had two wings covering its body. [24] When they moved, I heard the sound of their wings like the sound of mighty waters, like the thunder of the Almighty, *a sound of tumult like the sound of an army.*

A similar example of non-verbal auditory hallucinations is given in 10[4-5]; this may be no more than a repeat of the above verse or it may represent a separate episode.

> 10[4] Then the glory of the Lord rose up from the cherub to the threshold of the house; the house was filled with the cloud, and the court was filled with the brightness of the Lord. [5] *The sound of the wings of the cherubim was heard as far as the outer court, like the voice of God Almighty when he speaks.*

A strange rumbling noise is also reported:

> 3[12] Then the spirit lifted me up, and as the glory of the Lord rose from its place, I heard behind the sound of loud rumbling. [13] It was the sound of the wings of the living creatures brushing against one another, *the sound of the wheels beside them, that sounded like loud rumbling.*

These three examples of sounds that Ezekiel hears all appear to emanate from the cherubim, themselves fictional figures, possibly the precursors of angels, but seems to imply an imaginary source for the sounds, rather than them emanating from real objects in his environment. This excludes a basis in reality. Nor are they described as the voice of God or indeed as emanating from God, and so they seem not to have any significant religious meaning; they are just sounds he reports hearing. A psychiatric explanation would be that these are 'non-verbal auditory hallucinations' as defined above and this gives a reasonable fit to Ezekiel's descriptions of these noises.

## Summary of the auditory phenomena

Ezekiel experiences a wide variety of auditory experiences, some of which are also described in association with schizophrenia. He has voices which instruct him to carry out bizarre actions, which seem to be *command hallucinations*, as, for example, they instruct him to eat the scroll. On several occasions he hears *non-verbal auditory hallucinations*, especially during his visions. Later in this chapter we find he also has *voices which comment on his thoughts* and *voices which have conversations* with third parties. Perhaps most important of all is the contrast with the voices heard by other prophets, who are not psychotic. In all these instances the prophet hears only the voice of God, the content is of a typical religious message and not bizarre in its content; the prophet passes the message on to the people and it seems to make sense in the context of the time. The fact that Ezekiel experiences both schizophrenic auditory hallucinations as well as the more normal type of prophetic voices must have been a source of much confusion for Ezekiel himself, his people at the time, the later rabbis, as well as for more recent biblical scholars. Confusion arises here because Ezekiel is a great prophet who repeatedly hears the voice of God, but he also describes frequent auditory psychotic experiences, making it likely that he was *both* a prophet and a psychotic.

## The visual phenomena

Ezekiel experienced several dramatic visions during his lifetime. Some of the symbolism within these visions can readily be explained in terms of cultic practices of the ancient Israelites, ancient Near Eastern iconography, and the historical events of Ezekiel's lifetime. His original visions may have been elaborated on by his followers, with the later biblical redactors amplifying the description and enhancing the written style, rendering them as exquisite and memorable poems, which later came to hold great religious significance, especially for deeply religious Jews, but it has generally been held that Ezekiel was their original author.

Not much is written about exactly how the distinction is made between a schizophrenic visual hallucination, or an anomalous visual experience, or just the product of a vivid imagination. In general, a visual hallucination is more likely to be schizophrenic if it occurs in the presence of other psychotic symptoms, or is bizarre, or its content has unreal or fantastic objects. A psychiatrist in daily contact with his schizophrenic clientele will know after a few minutes that he is listening to an account of a schizophrenic visual hallucination, but if asked how he came to this conclusion he will have difficulty explaining this, beyond saying he had heard it all before. A further difficulty relates to the fact that there are a wide variety of anomalous visual experiences, ranging from simple visual imagination to visual illusions, visual pseudo-hallucinations, true visual hallucinations and oneroid states. Working out which of these different phenomena is being reported is difficult enough in practice today, but would be a very uncertain exercise when applied to an ancient religious text. Caution therefore must be exercised before making any diagnostic inferences solely on the basis of Ezekiel's visions and it is best to leave the question open.

The first of Ezekiel's visions, the vision of the divine chariot, was experienced while he was walking among the exiles along the banks of the River Chebar (probably the Euphrates or one of its tributaries). This vision is repeated almost in its entirety in ch. 10 and there are several further references to 'the vision he saw at the River Chebar', indicating it may have been a recurrent vision. The vision has a deeply sacred meaning for Orthodox Jews, to the extent that the Talmud even prohibits its study.

The vision provides a vibrant picture of shining lights, bright jewels, angels, cherubim and wheels, and ends with Ezekiel seeing God in the clouds in his glory. A first reading gives an impression of watching an exciting film at the cinema. Carley (1974) writes 'we should take seriously the visionary nature of Ezekiel's experience and appreciate these verses as a kind of moving dream, fantastic in some features and observing as much as it reveals of the divine glory'. It was probably experienced while Ezekiel was in a state of prophetic ecstasy.

From the 3rd and 4th centuries CE onwards, there has grown an extensive literature describing the conditions for the mystical descent, which includes the palaces literature (Hekalot) and the Jewish mysticism literature of the Kabbalah, as described in an important book *Major Trends in Jewish Mysticism* (Scholem, 1946). The chariot vision and certain other passages in Ezekiel are also thought to have been the inspiration for much of the Book of Revelation in the New Testament.

In the section below, the whole of the NRSV account of the chariot vision is quoted verbatim. Different types of interpretations are given, including the traditional rabbinical explanations, Greenberg's (1983) explanation of the symbols in the vision in terms of the contemporary Near Eastern iconography, as well as a modern explanation in terms of the possible psychiatry.

| | | |
|---|---|---|
| 1[1] | In the thirtieth year, in the fourth month, on the fifth day of the month, as I was among the exiles by the River Chebar, the heavens were opened, and I saw visions of God. | Accurate dating? abrupt onset Thirtieth year refers to either 30 years after the Josianic reforms, or the age of Ezekiel |
| 2 | On the fifth day of the month (it was the fifth year of the exile of King Jehoiachin) | This date corresponds to Nisan (April) 593 BCE |
| 3 | the word of the Lord came to the priest Ezekiel son of Buzi, in the land of the Chaldeans by the River Chebar and the hand of the Lord was on him there. | Chaldeans were the Babylonians 'Hand of the Lord' see page 333 Rashi says in the Book of Ezekiel this phrase is usually an expression of the prophecy seizing him, 'like a person going mad' |
| 4 | As I looked, a stormy wind came out of the north: a great cloud with brightness around it and fire flashing forth continually, and in the middle of the fire something gleaming like amber | For 'wind from the north', see note 1 ? heightened perception *Hashmal* for amber see note 2 on *Hashmal* |
| 5 | In the middle of it was something like four living creatures. This was their appearance, they were of human form. | 'something like' – see note 3 Mixed animal and human forms |
| 6 | Each had four faces and each had four wings | Similar anthropomorphic deities have also been found in temples |
| 7 | Their legs were straight and the soles of their feet were like the sole of a calf's foot and they sparkled like burnished bronze. | and on tablets in the ancient Near East but may also occur in schizophrenic hallucinations burnished bronze ?*hashmal* |
| 8 | Under their wings on their four sides they had human hands. And the four had their faces and their wings thus: | The number four is of special significance – see note 4 |
| 9 | Their wings touched one another; each of them moved straight ahead without turning as they moved. | Motion within the vision; cinematographic sensation |

10 As for the appearance of their faces: the four had the face of a human being, the face of a lion on the right side, the face of an ox on the left side, and the face of an eagle.

Detailed descriptions of strange mixed animal forms? A scenic visual hallucination (see page 324)

11 Such were their faces. Their wings were spread out above; each creature had two wings, each of which touched the wing of another while two covered their bodies.

12 Each moved straight ahead; wherever the spirit would go they went without turning as they went.

13 In the middle of the living creatures there was something that looked like burning coals of fire, like torches moving to and fro among the living creatures; the fire was bright and lightning issued from the fire.

heightened perception, *hashmal* (see note 2)

14 The living creatures darted to and fro like a flash of lightning.

movement within the vision

15 As I looked at the living creatures I saw a wheel on the earth beside the living creatures, one for each of the four of them.

16 As for the appearance of the wheels and their construction: their appearance was like gleaming of beryl and the four had the same form, their construction being something like a wheel within a wheel

Hebrew, for beryl is *Tarsis*, from Tartessus in Spain
Gleaming= ?heightened perception (see note 2)
?psychotic imagery (see page 324)

17 When they moved they moved in any of the four directions without veering as they moved

18 Their rims were tall and awesome for the rims were full of eyes all around.

possibly psychotic imagery (see page 324)

19 When the living creatures moved, the wheels moved beside them and when the living creatures rose from the earth the wheels rose.

motion within the vision, suggesting excitement or ecstasy

20 Wherever the spirit would go they went, and the wheels rose along with them; for the spirit of the living creatures was in the wheels.

21 When they moved the others moved; when they stopped the others stopped; and when they rose from the earth, the wheels rose along with them for the spirit of the living creatures was in the wheels.

Suggestion of passivity phenomena

22 Over the heads of the living creatures there was something like a dome, shining like crystal spread out above their heads.

23 Under the dome their wings were stretched out straight one towards another and each of creatures had two wings covering its body.

Imaginary creatures with wings

24 When they moved I heard the sound of

sounds within the vision

| | | |
|---|---|---|
| | their wings, like the sound of mighty waters, like the thunder of the almighty, a sound of tumult like the sound of an army, when they let down their wings. | Suggests non-verbal auditory hallucinations (see note 6) |
| 25 | And there came a voice from above the dome over their heads. When they stopped, they let down their wings. | voice = ?auditory hallucination but *not* the voice of God |
| 26 | And above the dome over their heads there was something like a throne in appearance like a sapphire; and seated above the likeness of a throne was something that seemed like a human form. | 'Something like' = Hebrew *Kemare* (see note 3) |
| 27 | Upwards from what appeared like the loins I saw something like gleaming amber; something that looked like fire enclosed all around; and downwards from what looked like the loins I saw something that looked like fire and there was a splendour all around. | *Hashmal* ?heightened perception<br><br>*Hashmal* (see note 2) |
| 28 | Like the bow in a cloud on a rainy day such was the appearance of the splendour all around. This was the appearance of the likeness of the glory of the Lord. When I saw it, I fell on my face and I heard the voice of someone speaking. | See note 6 on seeing the glory of God<br>?auditory hallucination. NB not God, but 'someone' speaking |

*Note 1. The north.* Mythical belief of the Babylonians that the Gods lived in the north. Also the wind from the north may relate to the climate of ancient Babylonia (modern-day Iraq). A regular north-westerly wind called the shamāh blows over the whole of Iraq, with strong winds producing sandstorms. This is at its worst in July – the month when Ezekiel experienced his vision.

*Note 2. The Hashmal.* The phrase 'something that looked like gleaming amber' is used in $1^4$ and $1^{28}$ and elsewhere in the Book of Ezekiel. The Hebrew word for amber is *Hashmal*. The Septuagint has *electron*, from which the word for the sub-atomic particle electron is derived and the Vulgate has *electrum*. This word is said to be at the heart of this vision of the deity. Although the etymology is uncertain, a similar word, *elmešu*, also occurs in Ugaritic, for example 'his lower cheeks constantly flash like lightning' (Landsberger, 1967).

Rashi saw some danger in the study of the word itself. 'When they asked what is *Hashmal*? Rav Judah replied "Living beings of fire that speak. In a breath we learn sometimes silence, sometimes speaking – when the speech emanates from the mouth of the holy one".' There is a large Talmudic literature on the topic and this is reviewed by Sweeney (2011). In modern Hebrew the word *Hashmal* means electricity.

### Psychiatric explanations

The psychiatric significance of brightness or flashing colours, or of very bright amber lights, may relate to the symptom of 'heightened perception' and this appears frequently in Ezekiel's visions. The SCAN psychiatric glossary (Wing *et al.*, 1990), defines this:

> *Heightened perception*: Sounds seem unnaturally clear or loud or intense, colours appear more brilliant or beautiful, details of the environment seem to stand out in a particularly interesting way and any sensation may be experienced more vividly.

The symptom can occur in mania, schizophrenia, excited states and especially in schizo-affective disorder. It has not previously been linked to Ezekiel's visions but it seems to be the most likely explanation of the vivid quality of his experiences.

*Note 3. 'Something like'.* Greenberg (1983, p. 52) makes an important observation that the word *kemaré*, which means 'like the appearance of', is used throughout the chariot vision. Thus 1⁴ has 'something like the appearance of amber', verse 1³ has 'something that looked like burning coals of fire', verse 1¹⁶ 'like the gleaming of beryl', and verse 1²⁶ 'something like a throne' and 'something that looked like a human form'. Greenberg states that this phrase 'reflects a desire to be faithful and exact while indicating consciousness of the visionary nature of the event'.

However, this is also very similar to the phraseology used by patients with schizophrenia when they try to describe their visual hallucinations, although, at the same time, are aware of the fantastic or bizarre nature of what they see, even though they believe it to be real. Thus they often qualify the scene they visualise with words such as 'it looked like', 'it resembled' or 'it had the appearance of' and so forth. Greenberg's observation suggests that much of the chariot vision must have been both experienced and written by Ezekiel himself, because this style of reporting, with 'a something like' quality, also seems to occur in the self-reports of schizophrenic hallucinations.

*Note 4.* The number four is said to have special significance in Ezekiel, suggesting the idea of completeness, as in the phrase 'the four corners of the earth' – a popular idiom also given in Isa 11⁴². Even earlier references to the four directions are given in Genesis 13¹⁴ and are thought to symbolise the divine capacity to control the whole world. The Babylonian literature is also replete with references to the four regions of the world. Thus the *sar erbetti* (Greenberg, p. 58) or the four winds is a notion that appears frequently in the Bible, from the Babylonian period onward. This particular verse is also thought to be the origin of the Tetramorph, later to become important in Christian art and iconography. Thus the four apostles are portrayed as archers defending truth and the order of Christ with Matthew being the winged man, Mark the lion, Luke the ox and John the eagle.

*Note 5, verse 24.* Within his vision Ezekiel hears loud noises. He likens them to the sound of running water, thunder and the tumult of an army. This description is consistent with the psychotic symptom *non-verbal auditory hallucinations* (see pages 315–316).

The passage continues in verse 25 to describe how Ezekiel also hears a voice, which suggests he is experiencing verbal auditory hallucinations. It is important to note that the voice he hears is not reported as the voice of God, but only as 'a voice', and hence is not a normal prophetic experience.

In Cutting's (1997) series, non-verbal auditory hallucinations were accompanied by verbal auditory hallucinations in 97% of his cases, and this association also seems to be true for Ezekiel.

*Note 6*, verse 1[28], 'The glory of God', *Kabod-adonai*. Normally, a person is not allowed to see God and this phrase is translated as 'the glory of God' (or 'majesty of God'). The only other time God makes his appearance is also in a fire, when the Israelites received the Ten Commandments on Mount Sinai. The link made between Moses seeing God on Mount Sinai and Ezekiel seeing God in the chariot vision occurs in the annual cycle of reading the Jewish liturgy, as this is the passage that is read as the Haftarah to accompany the Torah portion on Shavout, the festival which celebrates Moses accepting the law from God on Mount Sinai. So what, then, is this link? There are many Talmudic commentaries on this question but perhaps the most intriguing explanation is to be found in the much later Kabbalah literature:

> According to a tradition preserved in the Kabbalah, we learn how Moses rose through the throne world of God like any mystical voyager depicted in the Merkavah tracts.... At the apex of his ascent all the cosmic vaults are opened to Moses and he sees the majesty of the heavens! – but not only to Moses. With the opening of the heavens all Israel sees the glory face to face. As the words 'I am the Lord' (Ex 20[1]) blast forth, the entire people, all 600,000, die in ecstasy. Revived by divine mercy, God sends forth 1,200,000 angels to enable the entire nation to receive the divine revelation and live. Each person is therewith supported by two angels, one to hold the head, so that he may withstand the vision; the other to hold the heart, so that he would not escape in awe.... (Fishbane, 2002, p. 444)

*An explanation in terms of the contemporary iconography of the symbols in the chariot vision (after Greenberg, 1983)*

Apart from the psychiatric explanation given below Greenberg's (1983) explanation for the content of the chariot vision is based on the contemporary iconography of the region and is perhaps the most realistic. He suggests that almost every item reported in the vision has a specific cultic meaning which would have been known to the ancient Israelite people and their priests. Thus the image of God as a rider on a chariot in the sky with the blazing clouds is common to both the Bible and Ugaritic texts. Baal's stock epithet was of a rider in the clouds (Pritchard, 1969, p. 1306). A similar image for one of the Babylonian gods, Ashur, was found on a coloured piece of ceramic pottery and shows Ashur floating amidst rain clouds accompanying his army and shooting with a bow: 'The flying God is unusually beautiful, the head and uppermost part of his body seems to be white, and the wing feathers yellow and blue, and there is a double yellow ring in his flaming nimbus while great flaming streamers fly back from him' (Andrae, 1925). The appearance of the deity in cloud and fire also occurs in the wilderness narratives in Exodus, and the image of God riding a chariot in the sky is also common to many other cultures.

The winged cherubs which occur in this vision have also been found in other Middle Eastern excavations, and these have been compared to the winged sphinxes and other composite quadrupeds that support the thrones of other ancient Near Eastern kings, such as King Ahiram (Pritchard ANEP, 332 and 458). Ezekiel's composite creatures, which have faces of both man and beast, were quite common in the ancient world. Thus J. Cerný (1957) in his book *Ancient Egyptian Religion* explained that the Egyptians frequently combined zoomorphic and anthropomorphic ideas in a composite whole. These anthropomorphised gods were sometimes given a human body, but only rarely a human head, because the head was usually replaced by that of the animal in whose form the god used to appear:

> For the purposes of the art ... some personification of the deities was indispensable. The human bodies of the Gods retained the heads of various animals because this was a convenient way of distinguishing their various personalities and the head of the animal was used to recall the qualities attributed to that particular God. (Cerný, 1957)

Winged quadrupeds with human faces as described in Ezekiel's visions have also been found on tablets in Mesopotamia. Thus two tiny bronzes from Babylonia show a god and goddess with four identical faces.

The eyes, which figure prominently in Ezekiel's vision, also figure in ancient Phoenecian iconography. Sanchuniathon described the Phoenecian god El, or Kronos:

> the God *Tauthos* devised for *Kronos* as an insignia of Royalty, four eyes before and behind (of which two were waking and two quietly closed). This meant that *Kronos* could see when asleep and sleep while waking.

Similarly, the tiaras of the statues of the Assyrian gods were frequently adorned with numerous eye-stones. Thus the rim of the wheel that Ezekiel saw was surrounded by eyes; likewise there were 26 eye-stones for the tiara of the god Nabu. The four animals that comprise the faces in Ezekiel's vision also have their own iconography. The lion is traditionally the fiercest of beasts, the eagle the most dominant bird, the bull the most valued of domestic animals and all of these animals figure prominently in ancient Near Eastern iconography.

The four wheels that appear in Ezekiel's vision are the wheels of a chariot, which is the chariot of God, and this has been called a throne chariot. An Assyrian palace relief dated to around the 8th century BCE, some 200 years before Ezekiel, depicts servants carrying an empty wheeled throne. A relief of the high-backed wheeled sedan chair of Aššurnasirpal II was found in an excavation on some bronze gates in the town of Balawat in Iraq (Solberger, 1974).

While all these pictures and statues can explain the many images that Ezekiel saw, the iconography alone cannot account for *their simultaneous appearance all together in a single visual episode.*

### The psychiatry of the chariot vision

As noted previously, prominent theologians and biblical exegetes who studied Ezekiel, such as Wevers, Zimmerli and Greenberg, have drawn attention to the striking differences between the visions of most of the other prophets, such as Amos or Jeremiah, and those of Ezekiel. Thus, Amos sees a basket of over-ripe summer fruit, while Jeremiah sees the branch of an almond tree, both of which are well recognised plants and objects in the real world but here symbolising the forthcoming destruction of Israel. Zimmerli (1969) also comments on the greater participation Ezekiel has in his vision and how he participates in the event itself. He eats the scroll; he is transported by the spirit, or by Yahweh's hand ($3^{12-15}$, $8^3$, $37^1$, $40^{1-3}$) to see events at a great distance (while in Babylon, he walks through the Jerusalem Temple). While it is not possible to make a diagnosis of schizophrenia solely on the content of the visual hallucinations, their fantastic nature bears a striking resemblance to the content of those found among patients today and reported in the psychiatric literature. The whole of the chariot vision is repeated again with only minor differences in ch. 10. A psychiatric explanation for the repetition might be that Ezekiel has a further episode of illness, and re-experiences the vision in this subsequent episode since visual hallucinations tend to recur in an identical form with each subsequent relapse. A literary explanation might be that the beautiful poem-vision of ch. 1 was reworked by later biblical redactors, who felt it merited a second inclusion, albeit in a slightly different form.

Although there is no official recognised classification of visual hallucinations, the terms 'elementary', 'formed' and 'panoramic' are sometimes used. Panoramic hallucinations are complex scenarios of events, processions, historical scenes, or other events. Ezekiel recognised he was seeing a vision and the text also conveys the impression that the vision was totally real to him and his visions seem to be of the panoramic type.

Cutting (1997) studied the visual hallucinations of some 250 patients with schizophrenia; the catalogue of their contents can be usefully compared to the material found in the visions of Ezekiel. Some of the items given in Cutting (1997, pp. 94, 113) show many similarities to the items found in Ezekiel's chariot vision. In Table 8.2 more specific parallels are made with the items in Ezekiel's chariot vision and the content of visual hallucinations as described by Bleuler (1951) and Cutting (1997). The 'fantastic' nature of the content of Ezekiel's vision shows many similarities with the visual hallucinations of patients with schizophrenia today. The state of obvious excitement and the presence of auditory hallucinations within these visual hallucinations suggest he was in a state of psychotic excitement at the time. Their poetry, literary quality and its religious meaning may have been an original contribution of Ezekiel but also quite possibly the work of later biblical redactors.

## The vision of the defiled Temple

The next major vision in the Book of Ezekiel – of the defiled Temple – is rather more complex, has less obvious psychotic elements and rather more in the way of moral rhetoric; it also seems to be more contrived than the chariot vision. Greenberg (1983, p. 199) states that most recent commentators regard it as a patchwork of additions laid on an earlier original kernel. Only one section, $8^{1-13}$, may find its origin in a psychotic experience, but even within this short section there are insertions which take the form of

**Table 8.2** Comparison between the content of the chariot vision and of visual hallucinations among patients with schizophrenia

| *Chariot vision (Ezekiel 1$^{1-28}$)* | *Visual hallucinations, data from Bleuler and Cutting* |
|---|---|
| 1$^4$ Storms, clouds, fire flashing forth | Flashes of light |
| 1$^{5-6}$ Animals with human appearances | Mixed animal and human faces. Everyone looks like a wolf: man with a frog where his head should be |
| 1$^{11}$ Winged creatures | Pterydactyls, green and slimy |
| 1$^{13}$ Living creatures like burning coals of fire | Orange yellow faces; flashes in the sky |
| 1$^{16}$ Gleaming beryl sapphire and amber | Numerous examples of bright colours |
| 1$^{16}$ Wheels | Geometric shapes |
| 1$^{16}$ Wheels within wheels | Face within a face; real world within the world |
| 1$^{18}$ Eyes all around the wheels | Second pair of eyes above a normal pair; eyes have special meaning; people's eyes look white and popping |
| 1$^{24}$ Creatures with wings making noises | Flies and insects bearing supernatural messages; 'angels no bigger than wasps fly around him' |
| 1$^{25}$ Dome with a shining voice | |
| 1$^{26}$ Like a human form | Words coming out of the top of a head |

moral exhortations, condemnation of sin and so on which may have been later additions made by priests with a more specific religious purpose.

The vision describes how Ezekiel is lifted from Babylon by a lock of his hair and taken to Jerusalem to the inner court of the Temple and then asked to dig a hole in the wall and go inside. Once inside the Temple he sees many different creatures, which include some human forms, as well as some of the elders of Israel. People in the Temple are committing all sorts of abominations – worst of all, worshipping idols. There is an admixture of bizarre material, suggestive of psychosis, combined with oracles of woe, suggestive of a later a priestly influence.

| 8$^1$ | In the sixth year, in the sixth month, on the fifth day of the month, as I sat in my house, with the elders of Judah sitting before me, the hand of the Lord God fell on me there. | Accurate dating? Ezekiel records his own experiences at the time<br><br>Hand of the Lord (see page 333)<br>He recognises a strange feeling |
|---|---|---|
| 2 | I looked and there was a figure that looked Like a human being; below what appeared to be its loins was fire, and above the loins | *Hashmal* brightness |

| | | |
|---|---|---|
| | was like the appearance of brightness like gleaming amber. | ?heightened perception |
| 3 | It stretched out the form of a hand and took me by a lock of my head and the spirit lifted me up between earth and heaven and brought me in visions of God to Jerusalem, to the entrance of the gateway of the inner court that faces north, to the seat of the image of jealousy, which provokes to jealousy. | Note transportation is within the vision, suggesting delusional levitation. See note 7. Ezekiel in Jerusalem or Babylon? Ezekiel may have had morbid jealousy (see pages 336–339) |
| 4 | And the glory of the God of Israel was there like the vision that I had seen in the valley. | Reference to the chariot vision where Ezekiel saw God |
| 5 | Then God said to me 'O mortal, lift up your eyes now in the direction of the north'. So I lifted up my eyes towards the north, and there north of the altar gate was this image of jealousy. | |
| 6 | He said to me, 'Mortal, do you see what they are doing the great abominations that the house of Israel are committing here, to drive me far from the sanctuary? You will see still greater abominations. | Kara states that this is a reference to idol worship under King Manassah (Greenberg, p. 168) |
| 7 | And he brought me to the entrance of the court; I looked and there was a hole in the wall. | |
| 8 | Then he said to me, 'Mortal, dig through the wall and when I dug through the wall there was an entrance. | Command hallucination? |
| 9 | He said to me, 'Go in and see the vile abominations that they are committing there. | |
| 10 | So I went in and looked there portrayed on the wall all around were all kinds of creeping things and loathsome animals and all the idols of the house of Israel. | Bizarre and unreal animals suggestive of psychotic content. See note 7 for parallels in ancient Near Eastern iconography |
| 11 | Before them stood seventy of the elders of Israel with Jazaniah son of Shephan standing among them. Each had his censer in his hand and the fragrance of incense was ascending. | Ezekiel experiences smells within this vision. Suggests an olfactory hallucination. See note 8 |

*Note 7.* Greenberg (1983, p. 169) attempts to explain 'loathsome creatures' in this vision in terms of the contemporary Near Eastern iconography. The Hebrew *kol sĕqĕs*, meaning 'every detestation', is combined with *gillul*, to read, *sĕqĕs*, meaning loathsome thing or idol. In Leviticus 11[10-42] the word *sĕqĕs* is a term reserved for vermin which is forbidden as food. Greenberg suggests the 'idols' in this passage were actually engravings of animal figures on the walls. He cites the Ishtar gate in Babylon, which has lions and serpent dragons inlaid on it, and also the rock carving at Maltaya, which has Babylonian gods riding in a procession on the backs of all sorts of real or imaginary creatures. These pictures are given in Pritchard ANEP (1975, pp.

537, 760). Egyptian theriomorphic deities and possibly even totem animals may also have served as the source for this scene.

*Note 8.* Greenberg writes that the incense (Heb. *qetoret* = incense) may refer to the cloud of incense at awesome ceremonies of the Day of Atonement (Lev. 16$^{2,13}$). More significantly, the phrase is preceded by the hapax *tv*, related to the Syriac *etra*, meaning 'vapour' or 'fume', implying anything offered in sacrifice, and the word also may have pagan overtones. Incense also played an important role in idolatrous private cults, which by that time would have been strictly forbidden.

The psychiatric explanation is that they may be olfactory hallucinations; Ezekiel is writing about the smells he experiences but, not understanding them, he tries to explain them away. Ezekiel is in Babylon at the time but he experiences these smells in the Jerusalem Temple. Olfactory hallucinations are the third most common type of hallucination found in schizophrenia but they are very much less frequent than either visual or auditory hallucinations. Cutting (1997, p. 86) gives a prevalence of 6% among people with schizophrenia. These smells are either unpleasant, such as a sick, burning or fishy odour, or pleasant, such as the smell of roses or pine. Ezekiel smells incense, which sounds rather pleasant.

The passage continues to describe the 'abomination' that Ezekiel has seen in his vision. Most of the references are to idol worship or other forbidden practices, and the tone is one of a religious condemnation of idolatry.

### Psychiatric aspect of the vision of the defiled Temple

This vision is not as florid as his other visions, nor does Ezekiel experience it in the same state of excitement, but more with a feeling of dread, which makes him feel quite ill. However, what strikes the psychiatric reader is the accumulation of numerous other psychotic symptoms within this vision. Thus the whole section from 8$^1$ through to 11$^{24}$ is interspersed with occasional psychotic material, albeit it is buried within typical OT moral rhetoric and other oracles of woe. At various points Ezekiel indicates he may be unwell and possibly psychotic at the time, and a large number of well known schizophrenic symptoms are recorded in this section:

- 8$^3$, 11$^1$ and 11$^{24}$, delusional transportation
- 8$^8$, command hallucination to dig a whole in the wall
- 8$^{10}$, visual hallucinations (bizarre animals, etc.)
- 8$^{11}$, olfactory hallucinations (see page 326)
- 8$^{18}$, auditory Hallucinations (see page 314)
- 9$^1$, auditory Hallucinations with instructions to kill (see page 313)
- 9$^5$, auditory Hallucinations which are loud (see pages 314, 316)
- 10$^9$, heightened perception, or *hashmal*
- 10$^{13}$, auditory and visual hallucinations together
- 11$^5$, thought broadcasting.

The accumulation of a great deal of psychotic phenomenology all of which seems to occur within visual hallucinations is characteristic of an acute psychotic episode in schizophrenia. This is far beyond the type of visual imagery resulting solely from simple imagination. Complex visions of this type with other associated psychotic symptoms are unique to Ezekiel in the OT. By contrast, the visions of the other OT prophets are usually confined to only one or two real objects, such as fruits or plants, which serve as a metaphor or a sense of hope for the future; they never contain the bizarre material, voices, smells or actions characteristic of Ezekiel's visions.

## *The vision of the dry bones – the resurrection of the dead Israel*

Ezekiel's vision of the valley of the dry bones is perhaps the most famous and dramatic of his visions. It is a brief, vivid and extremely powerful allegory about man's concern with the end of life and his resurrection, and has been the subject of countless paintings and songs. Its symbolism extends far beyond its original setting as a prophecy of the destruction of Israel with its subsequent restoration. The traditional religious meaning, as Redak explains, is that God shows the dry bones to Ezekiel and these symbolise the death and destruction of Israel because of the exile, but while he is looking at the bones they are restored to life: the bones join together and then a spirit from God breathes life into them. Most of the passage is thought to be the authentic writing of Ezekiel, with the possible exception of verses 11–13, which may have been inserted by a later redactor. Thus, Zimmerli (1969) wrote 'that of all the passages of the book, analysis of its form suggests extreme proximity to the genuine work of Ezekiel'.

| 37[1] | The hand of the Lord came up upon me and he brought me out by the spirit of the Lord and set me down in the middle of the valley: it was full of bones | Rashi, writes 'Every time the hand of the Lord' appears in a prophecy it means he is like a madman and must go to the place the spirit desires (see page 333) Transportation by the spirit |
|---|---|---|
| 2 | He led me all around them, there were very many in the valley, and they were very dry. | Ezekiel is an active participant in his visions. The dry bones symbolise the great despair of the Israelites |
| 3 | He said to me, 'Mortal, can these bones live?' I answered 'Oh Lord God, you know'. Then he said to me 'Prophesy to these bones and say to them: O dry bones hear the word of the Lord'. | Auditory experience; conversation with God |
| 5 | Thus says the Lord God to these bones: I will cause breath to enter you, and you shall live. | breath = *Ruah* or breath of life or spirit. The sense here is the same as when God breathes life into Adam (Gen 2[7]), the *ruah* being the animating principle |
| 6 | I will lay sinews on you and will cause flesh to come upon you and cover you with skin, and put breath in you and you shall live, and you shall know I am the Lord. | |
| 7 | So I prophesied as I had been commanded and as I prophesied suddenly there was a noise, a rattling and the bones came together bone to its bone. | Non-verbal auditory experience |

8   I looked and there were sinews on them and flesh had come upon them, and skin had covered them but there was no breath in them

*Ezekiel in his priestly role was involved in ritual sacrifice, so had a good knowledge of basic anatomy as shown in this verse (Zimmerli, p. 261)*

9   Then he said to me 'Prophesy to the breath, prophesy, mortal, and say to the breath: Thus says the Lord God, Come from the four winds, O breath, and breathe upon these slain that they may live.

*The 'four winds' concept originated in Mesopotamia where he lived (see page 321) Possible reference to the* Erbetti *wind; see note 4 above*

10   I prophesied as he had commanded me and the breath came into them, and they lived, and stood on their feet, a vast multitude.

11   Then he said to me, 'Mortal these bones are the whole house of Israel. They say, 'Our bones are dried up and our hope is lost; we are cut off completely'

*Verses 11–13 provide historical and religious meaning to the vision but many biblical commentators now consider these verses to be later insertions*

12   Therefore prophesy and say to them, Thus says the Lord God: I am going to open your graves and bring you up from your graves, O my people and I will bring you back to the land of Israel

*Message of hope and restoration ?late insertion; non-psychotic material*

13   And you shall know I am the Lord when I open your graves and bring you up from your graves, Oh my people.

14   I will put my spirit within you, and you shall live, and I will place you on your own soil; then you shall know that I, the Lord, have spoken. and will act, says the Lord.

*This key phrase is absent from the LXX and hence may be a later addition (i.e. after 200 BCE)*

## Historical and religious aspects

The rabbis of the Talmud and the Middle Ages regard the vision of the dry bones as an allegory, and not to be taken literally. The restoration of life in this vision is in two phases: the bones are first joined together and flesh is given to them; and then a breath from God brings the bones to life. Zimmerli (1969, p. 265) writes that the vision was directed at the community in exile around 589 BCE, who were in a state of deep despair having lost their land, and the vision was meant to give them hope by drawing a parallel between the resurrection of the desiccated bones and the restoration of the exiles back to their homeland.

Greenberg (1997) suggests that the apparently bizarre image of a plain or desert filled with bones may have a basis in reality, having its origin in Mesopotamian and Sumerian accounts of battle. He argues that because Ezekiel was a literate person, he would have known of Akkadian texts, such as *The Annals of Sennacherib* (Luckenbill, 1924), where Sennacherib boasts 'with the bodies of the enemies, warriors filled the plain, like grass'. In another passage of the same text, the oath of loyalty to one of the vassal kings of Esarhaddon reads: 'If you are disloyal, may Ninurta, leader of the Gods … fill the plain with your corpses, give your flesh to eagles and vultures to feed on' (Pritchard, 1969, p. 583). The desert plains of southern Iraq where Ezekiel lived were battlegrounds and were frequently strewn with the skeletons of warriors slain in battle.

Even schizophrenic visual hallucinations can have some basis in reality and so a historical explanation that there were dead bodies in the desert may be quite realistic. The suggestion that this vision may have had its origin in a schizophrenic hallucination should not detract from the beauty of this passage. Later redactors may have given it symbolic meaning with its message of restoration, which resonates powerfully with the suffering and hopes of exiles and subjugated peoples the world over, giving this vision its timeless and universal quality. It has an important place in the liturgies of the Jewish synagogue worship, where it is traditionally read as the prophetic lesson (the Haftarah) on the Sabbath of the Passover week – a festival cele-brating the liberation from slavery in Egypt. Like the Passover, it is a story of rebirth. 'Our bones are dried up and our hope is gone', but on receiving God's command Ezekiel addresses the bones themselves and breathes life into them. In church services it is used to celebrate redemption and the giving of new life, and in Catholic Mass it is read at Pentecost The story has also acquired much popularity in the world of music and art. Perhaps the best-known song inspired by this vision is the spiritual 'Ezekiel saw dem bones'.

*Psychiatric aspects*
The vision starts with an experience of the 'hand of God', which, as noted below, denotes at the very least a state of religious excitement or ecstasy. Rashi, almost 1,000 years ago, wrote that, at least for Ezekiel, this means 'behaviour like a madman', indicating that the psychiatric explanation given in the present chapter is not original. The spirit enters Ezekiel and transports him within the vision – perhaps suggestive of passivity phenomena, where the subject experiences an alien force taking control over him (a Schneiderian first-rank symptom; see pages 340—341). Ezekiel is an active participant in his vision and this quality brings added authenticity to the scene but may also be a feature of schizophrenic hallucinations. The other OT prophets never enter into their visions or move around or share this dramatic quality. The mood changes from one of profound despair associated with the dry lifeless bones in the desert to one of huge excitement as the bones jump to life. The content of the vision also shows a limited resemblance to some of the examples of visual experiences of patients with psychotic depression and schizophrenia as documented by Cutting (1997, pp. 113, 117) in the following listing:

- people all looked elderly, like octogenarians
- everything quiet like a desert
- people plodding along unreal, things like in a dream
- people looked strange – nurses one day, patients next
- puzzled about how people act, as if in a dream
- everyone on the planet the same – all clones, all identical
- people look dead, pale, cold; doctors are elves

- people turn to skeletons
- people's faces look like skeletons but with a real head at the back.

While none of these images is identical to the vision of the dry bones in the desert, images of people looking strange or miserable are relatively common in depression, and Cutting (1997) even documents one example of a schizophrenic patient who saw people turning into skeletons in their visual experiences. Although we can never know exactly what Ezekiel experienced, a patient today who reported such experiences would most likely be diagnosed with a psychotic episode, either schizophrenia or psychotic depression.

## The vision of the new Temple

The final section of the book (chs 40–48) is presented as an account of single vision in which the prophet is led about by an angel and shown the ideal Temple of the future. The content of this vision is very different from the other visions of the book, and the material is almost all non-psychotic, as it describes the design, dimensions and structure of the new Temple. If parallels were to be sought in present-day literature, they would be found in manuals of architecture rather than textbooks of psychiatry. Wevers (1969, p. 295) writes that this portion is, stylistically, completely different from the rest of the book, and many scholars have questioned whether this section was actually written by Ezekiel. Zimmerli (1969, p. 327) comments on the contrast:

> While the earlier visions, especially in their original form, are filled with continuous movement and are in a narrative style, the effect of chapters 40–48 is that of a description of a static situation in which only what is at hand is revealed. There appears on a large scale to be legal regulations which recall the legal style of the Pentateuch and this may be why chapters 40–48 have been called for short 'the draft constitution'.

Thus although this section commences with a vision ($40^{1-7}$), most of this is a repeat of verses found in previous visions, giving the feel of an artificially recreated vision. It is dated in October 573 BCE, which is near the end of Ezekiel's period of prophecy. A second and similar vision appears in ch. 43. Although there is an occasional mention of mental symptoms in these passages, these verses have quite clearly been lifted from previous sections in the book and do not represent anything new. It takes the form of an ordinary religious vision and there is no question of this being a visual hallucination as in a psychotic illness.

## Summary of the visual material

Ezekiel's visions contain many themes, but there is usually a primary visual experience accompanied by other psychotic symptoms and superimposed on these are moral and historical insertions, possibly made by later redactors, giving a religious meaning to these passages. In some visions, particularly the chariot vision (ch. 1) and the vision of the dry bones (ch. 37), bizarre visual material is much more prominent and is typical of panoramic schizophrenic hallucinations. In the vision of the defiled Temple (chs 8–11) there is more in the way of moral reprobation, with bizarre visual material only just discernible. In the final Temple visions (chs 40 and 43) this is much less in evidence, leading to the suggestion of a non-Ezekiel authorship for these visions, and there is no question of them being schizophrenic visual hallucinations.

Where possible, I have tried to draw parallels between the contents of Ezekiel's visions and modern accounts of visual hallucinations as reported by patients with schizophrenia, and described by Cutting (1997) – but it is for readers to make their own decisions on the similarity between the writings of this ancient prophet and modern accounts of psychopathology. Some caution is required before making a diagnosis of a visual hallucination. Thus in a study of over 134 accounts of visions in the medieval religious literature, Kroll and Bachrach (1982) were able to assign only four of these visions a certain diagnosis of true schizophrenic visual hallucinations, indicating that such hallucinations were comparatively rare even among religious visions and so it may be best to leave the question of any underlying psychopathology to Ezekiel's visions open.

The visions of a prophet of any religion are usually held to occur during periods of prophetic ecstasy – in more modern psychiatric parlance, this might be a trance or a transient dissociative state but such visions or visual hallucinations can also occur in serious psychotic illnesses as well. The common assumption made by a majority of biblical scholars is that Ezekiel experienced his visions in *trance* states or states of religious ecstasy. How, then, can one make the distinction between such well known culturally recognised trance states and psychotic illness?

This dilemma commonly occurs today in cross-cultural psychiatry, as trance states are quite common in developing nations. DSM-IV (American Psychiatric Association, 1994) states: 'in the presence of other schizophrenic symptoms, trance states should not be diagnosed but rather the condition is schizophrenia'. Ezekiel has very many other schizophrenic symptoms, including catatonia, voices, hallucinations of smell and vision, and if a person today were to present with the same features as Ezekiel these ecstatic/trance-like states would be accorded a diagnosis of schizophrenia rather than of a simple trance state, which hitherto has been the traditional explanation for Ezekiel's ecstatic episodes.

Despite their possible status as schizophrenic hallucinations, Ezekiel's visions have served as an inspiration for great art over the centuries. The great English artist and poet William Blake, himself possibly a manic depressive, was fascinated by the chariot vision and painted his version 'The Whirlwind: Ezekiel's Vision of the Cherubim and Eyed Wheels' (*circa* 1803). The Church of St Maria and St Clement, in the village of Schwarzrheindorf, near Bonn, Germany, dedicated in 1151, has all its walls adorned with frescoes appertaining to Ezekiel's visions (see Odell, 2009) while the vision of the dry bones is depicted in the frescoes of the Dura-Europa Synagogue in eastern Syria, dated to 244 CE.

## A note concerning the phrase 'the hand of God'

The *hand of God* is a phrase that appears frequently in the Book of Ezekiel, perhaps more so than in any other book of the Bible. Zimmerli (1969) lists all its occurrences ($1^3$, $3^{12-15}$, $8^3$, $37^1$, $40^{1-3}$). For example:

> $1^3$ The word of the Lord was revealed to Ezekiel the son of Buzi the priest, in the land of Chaldeans, by the River Chebar and *the hand of the Lord* came upon him there.

Rashi was the first to intimate that whenever the phrase 'the hand of the Lord' appeared it might have medical significance, indicating either a seizure or an episode of insanity. He also wrote that the phrase suggested a compulsion, implying that prophecy seizes him against his will, like a person going mad; he likened the phrase to the old French *destreze*, which means compulsion. The Bible uses a similar phrase in association with Elijah.

J. J. Roberts (1971) has conducted an extensive survey of the use of the expression 'the hand of God' in both the Israelite literature and other ancient Near Eastern cultures. Most scholars take the expression to denote a specific reference to an ecstatic or trance-like state. Duhm (1901) said the expression designated a 'half-way cataleptic condition which the human spirit, because of a psychological reaction, resists as if a violence was inflicted upon it'.

In the Akkadian diagnostic texts, Labat found that the expression the 'hand of God' was used in association with 40 different deities as well as several demons and in all instances the phrase 'the hand of God' was specifically tied to the notion of sickness, either mental or physical. It usually denoted 'a disastrous manifestation of the supernatural power'. Thus in the Babylonian wisdom literature, the sufferer in the Babylonian Job, Ludlul bēl nēmeqi, says of God 'his hand was heavy [upon me]; I could not bear it'. In another Mari text, a woman, Šattukyazi, complains 'I came here, I have been sick and it is the hand of Ištara-danna [a Mari god] and my Lord knows it'. In the Atra-hasis epic, when Atra-hasis and his followers are praying to the god Namtara, asking him to lift the plague, the phrase 'let him lift/remove his hand' appears. Similar phraseology also has been found in the literature of the western Asiatic states. Thus a reference to Rasap, a Phoenician god, quoted in one of the Amarna letters, reads:

> Behold in my law, the hand of Rasap my lord has killed all the men of my land ... because the hand of Rasap was in my land and in my house, my wife had a son who is now dead, my brother.

In the Egyptian literature the phrase 'in the hand of God' had a more specific and psychiatric connotation to denote an insane person. Grapow (1956) sees 'a clear connection between the use of this phrase and the description of the journey of Wen-Amon, since the raving of the ecstatic and the madness of the insane person were both brought about by the seizure of the deity'.

Roberts points out that in Hebrew a similar verb is used to describe both the ecstasy of a prophet and the word 'insane' (Hebrew *Hatnab'ii*; Akkadian *Nambū*). This suggests that the ancient Semitic peoples probably found it difficult to distinguish between the behaviour of the religious man subjected to brief periods of ecstasy and the more genuinely insane individual: a diagnostic distinction which even today is sometimes difficult to make.

Roberts argues that the use of the term 'hand of God' is based on anthropomorphic considerations. Just as the hand of a man is used to carry out his actions, so an act of God, especially in the realm of unexplained sickness, would have to have been mediated by the 'hand of God'. Thus the manner of its use in the OT may be a reflection of ancient theories of illness causation as generally understood throughout the ancient Near East; that is, it is a sickness idiom (for references see Roberts, 1971).

## *The location of Ezekiel's prophecy and his transportation in visions between Babylon and Jerusalem*

According to tradition, Ezekiel was a priest who was taken captive and together with other important leaders of the Jewish community he was deported to Babylon, in exile, in 597 BCE . His entire prophetic ministry was spent in the village of Tel-abib on the River Chebar in southern Iraq. 'Tel-abib' is thought to be derived from the ancient Akkadian *Tel abubi*, which means 'mound of the flood' or 'mound of the fruit spring' and has given its name to Tel-Aviv, now Israel's largest city. For the first four years of his exile, from 597 to 593, little of note appears to happen to Ezekiel. The Book of Ezekiel itself starts with 'The chariot vision', which he dates as 593 BCE. Ezekiel never returned to Jerusalem in the flesh, although he frequently visited the holy city in his visions and would then castigate the people for their sins or issue warnings of forthcoming disasters. Because most of the material and oracles of the first part of the book pertain to the political and religious situation in Jerusalem, which would seemingly have been irrelevant to the exiles in Babylon, some scholars have suggested that he must have actually lived in Jerusalem or a neighbouring city. Arguments in the text which favour a Jerusalem location are: his appointment as a watchman for the people of Jerusalem; a first-hand knowledge of the conditions of the siege; and some awareness of the political intrigues between pro-Egyptian and pro-Babylonian factions in the capital ($17^{13-18}$ and $18^{23-29}$), because possession of such information would have been unlikely had he been domiciled some 700 miles away in Babylon.

Against this argument, Greenberg (1983) suggests the Babylonian domicile is implicit in the text, because of phrases like 'I was alone among the exiles' and 'come to the exiles', together with numerous references to Chaldea (Babylonia) and the River Chebar (possibly the Euphrates). People in Jerusalem are referred to as 'they' or 'them' ($12^{11}$) and the visits to Jerusalem occur only in his visions. The site of his domicile has puzzled scholars for more than a century (see Howie, 1950, for a review) but in his visions he seems to be often flitting between Jerusalem and Babylon and his mode of travel is of some psychiatric interest.

His initial journey to Babylon is described in mystical terms: he is borne away by a spirit and is stunned when he arrives. His next trip to Jerusalem is described in a vision where he is lifted up by a lock of his hair. The verses describing Ezekiel's transportation are given below:

2[14] The spirit lifted me and bore me away; I went in bitterness in the heat of my spirit, the hand of the Lord being strong upon me. [15]I came to the exiles at Tel-abib, who lived by the river Chebar. And I sat among them stunned for seven days.

8[3] It stretched out the form of a hand, and took me by a lock of my head and the spirit lifted me up between earth and heaven and brought me in visions of God to Jerusalem, to the entrance of the gateway of the inner court that faces north to the seat of the image of jealousy which provokes jealousy.

11[1]The spirit lifted me up and brought me to the east gate of the house of the Lord which faces east.

11[24] The spirit lifted me up and brought me in a vision by the spirit of God to the children, to the exiles. Then the vision I had seen left me. [25]And I told the exiles all the things that the Lord had shown me.

## Possible explanations for these journeys

Zimmerli (p. 236) assumes these verses describe ecstatic transportation. He says there is a heavenly mediator who seizes Ezekiel's hair, and Ezekiel may experience pain in the process. There is a merging of the man, the spirit and Yahweh himself and in this process Ezekiel is brought to the north gate of Jerusalem. Greenberg (1983) draws parallels with the Akkadian literature, citing the vision of the Netherworld: 'Valiant Nergal was seated on the Royal throne ... from his arms lightening was flashing ... he took me by the locks of my forehead and drew me before him' (Greenberg quoting Pritchard, 1969, p. 110a).

There are several possible psychiatric explanations for these mystical journeys. Thus, patients with schizophrenia, in their hallucinations, commonly experience themselves in places other than their usual domicile. It seems as if Ezekiel's true place of residence was Babylonia – but he writes very little about the daily life of his exile in Babylon (perhaps it was too humdrum to write about). However, in his fertile imagination he lives out his prophetic existence in Jerusalem. Much of Ezekiel chs 1–11 relates to Jerusalem and some of this material is delusional. Those with schizophrenia today who reside on an impoverished long-stay ward of a mental asylum sometimes hear voices which tell them they are a king and live in a royal palace, and they may be totally oblivious of the reality and poverty of their current surroundings. Could it be that Ezekiel, in the misery of the Babylonian exile, consoled himself in his visions with the thought that he was prophesying in the holy city of Jerusalem, and at the Temple, and in the city of the Davidic kings?

The sensation of being lifted up by the lock of his hair and transported is probably a passivity phenomenon, similar to the experience of levitation described by Lukianowicz (1967) in his paper 'Body image disturbances in psychiatric disorders'. Under the category of hypnogogic experiences of levitation he describes several cases such as the one below.

*Case no. 42*, a schizophrenic student nurse aged 22, claimed 'Every night just when I am falling asleep a man comes into my bedroom. He takes me into his arms and we begin to float, high over the mountains and over the seas. I become frightened and begin to twist and to wriggle, until I either become wide awake again or slip out of his arms and begin to fall into a black bottomless precipice. Then I lose consciousness and fall asleep.'

The sexual content of the above hallucination is obvious but otherwise the nurse here describes delusional levitation and transportation. Its occurrence during the hypnogogic phase (as one falls asleep) is non-pathological. The magical transportation of Ezekiel between Babylonia and Jerusalem seems to fit this pattern and so may also be an example of delusional transportation.

However, by far the best explanation for Ezekiel's journeys is surely that offered by W. H. Brownlee (1986), Professor of the Old Testament at Claremont. He wrote:

> Ezekiel must have actually made the journey from Babylon to Jerusalem ... Ezekiel either literally flew through the air from Babylonia to Jerusalem or he ran there from Gilgal in a state of ecstasy, in which it seemed he was flying.... If Ezekiel flew from Babylonia, he travelled much more slowly than a modern aeroplane but faster than an ordinary bird. On February 28th, 1948 Millar Burrows, also a biblical scholar, drove by automobile all the way from Baghdad to Jerusalem starting early and travelling late. If we allow that Ezekiel arrived at the scene in the Temple no later than 4.00 a.m. and the elders visited him no later than 4.00 p.m. it is feasible with extraordinary exertion (despite the difficulties of finding his way at night) he could have reached Jerusalem within that length of time. We do not know what was the wind that bore him, whether it was wholly subjective or whether there was an east wind at his back.

Who says psychiatrists are the only ones with fanciful ideas!

## Misogyny, jealousy and morbid jealousy: Ezekiel chs 16 and 23

In ch. 16, the prophet uses the old story of a female foundling who is cared for by a prince. When the foundling grows up, the prince marries her and decks her with riches but she becomes a wilful harlot. The story is meant to be an allegorical description of Israel's history – how Yahweh has nurtured and cherished her yet she repays this kindness by being unfaithful (Joyce, 2009). A similar parallel to Israel's infidelity to Yahweh is described in ch. 23, where Oholah and Oholibah, two sisters who represent the cities of Jerusalem and Samaria, respectively, become promiscuous and unfaithful. These chapters appear to be both somewhat pornographic and misogynistic and some feminist biblical commentators have expressed their concern at their inclusion in the Bible (for review see Mein, 2009). A complete analysis of the historical and symbolic meanings of these chapters is beyond the scope of this chapter and the interested reader is referred to the standard works on Ezekiel for explanations of its historical symbolism. The psychiatric interest lies in the explicit sexual and almost pornographic content and Ezekiel's clear obsession with infidelity and its punishment.

The biblical tradition of Yahweh taking Israel as his wife who then becomes unfaithful wife or a harlot starts long before Ezekiel, perhaps with Hosea, a prophet from the 8th century BCE. Hosea complains bitterly about his unhappiness because of the adultery of his own wife, Gomer, and he draws parallels between his own marriage and the faithlessness of Israel to her 'husband' Yahweh. However, the parallel ends there. By contrast, Ezekiel's jealousy and his obsession with female adultery concerns women who are also imaginary but who symbolise Israel, suggesting that the whole drama of these two chapters may have been played out only in Ezekiel's mind. Also, from the little we know about Ezekiel's wife, he was fond of her (he calls her 'the delight of my eyes'), never accuses her of being unfaithful, and when she dies he becomes quite ill and refuses to go into a state of mourning for her.

A few of the verses which show his obsession with sexual infidelity are given below:

> $16^{15}$ But you trusted in your beauty and played the whore because of your fame and lavished your whorings on any passerby.

> $16^{25}$ At the head of every street you built your lofty places and prostituted your beauty offering yourself to every passerby.

> $23^5$ Oholah played the whore while she was mine; she lusted after her lovers the Assyrian warriors....

> $23^7$ She bestowed favours among the choicest men of Assyria.

Several verses follow describing Israel as being promiscuous with the Egyptians, Chaldeans, the Philistines, etc., with the symbolic meaning that Israel has been worshipping foreign Gods. Her adultery will be punished by stoning her to death:

> $23^{38}$ I will judge you as women who commit adultery and shed blood are judged, and bring blood upon you as in wrath and jealousy.... $^{40}$ They shall bring up a mob against you and they shall stone you and cut you to pieces with their swords.

Note that it is the adultery which is the crime, and this has brought on powerful feelings of wrath and jealousy, and it is these emotions that will lead on to the stoning. In morbid jealousy, it is anger at the infidelity that leads to the violence.

There is also obviously sexually titillating material:

> $23^8$ For in her youth, men (Egyptians) had laid with her and fondled her virgin bosom and poured out their lust upon her.

An obsession with the semen of other men is also a feature of morbid jealousy, as subjects search through the clothing and underwear of their wives. Ezekiel also mentions semen in this passage:

> $23^{19-20}$ She played the whore in the land of Egypt and lusted after her paramours there whose members were like those of donkeys, and whose emissions were like those of stallions.

Ezekiel appears to be obsessed with sexual unfaithfulness to a partner but he distinguishes this from simple sexual gratification as occurs in prostitution:

> 16[34] So you were different from other women in your whorings: no one solicited you to play the whore; and you gave payment, while no payment was given to you: you were different.

In morbid jealousy the focus of the antipathy to the woman also relates to lovers and extramarital affairs, *but not to paid sexual encounters as occurs in prostitution*. If verses of this sexual type were to appear only once in these chapters, no one would consider this to be pathological; there is nothing psychotic in these chapters and similar content appears elsewhere in the Bible. What makes these passages indicative of an abnormality of mind or a psychiatric disorder (probably morbid jealousy) is their constant repetition and obsessive quality. It is written to imply that it is God who experiences these jealous thoughts but clearly they are Ezekiel's own thoughts – it is how he imagines God feels about these faithless sisters.

Morbid jealousy has three core themes: adultery/unfaithfulness; overt sexual/pornographic material; and vengeful punishment. In Table 8.3 the number of times these three types of thought appear in chs 16 and 23 is given. The table shows that Ezekiel clearly displays a repetitive obsession with pornographic sexual activity and female infidelity, which must be severely punished (he is quite vindictive in this). Such a picture is characteristic of the 'morbid jealousy' syndrome. We have no idea how severe it was in Ezekiel's case; there is no record of him actually doing anything about it, and it is possible that the whole thing just played out in his mind, or at worst he gave a few misogynistic sermons decrying female sexuality. Ezekiel uses the analogy of a faithless wife to describe Israel's complicated foreign policy, of which he is highly critical, as well as Israel's more usual sins of apostasy and corruption. The condition is also mentioned in association with the *sotah* on pages 372–377.

Morbid jealousy was first described by Ey (1954) and is a very strong form of sexual jealousy. Enoch and Trethowan (1979) thought it particularly important to distinguish jealousy which had a delusion of infidelity from understandable jealousy. Morbid jealousy is classified as one of the delusional disorders. The condition may occur in either sex and is regarded as a descriptive term for a syndrome rather than a disorder in its own right.

**Table 8.3** Frequency of verses alluding to adultery, sexual titillation and punishment in Ezekiel 16 and 23

| *Type of statement* | *Ch. 16* | *Ch. 23* | *Both chs 16 and 23* |
|---|---|---|---|
| Adulterous, unfaithful, whoring, paramours (as in 23[5]) | 9 | 13 | 22 |
| Sexually titillating or pornographic (e.g. breasts, nakedness, seductive) (as in 23[8]) | 7 | 5 | 12 |
| Punishment, stoning, murderous wrath, jealousy (as in 23[38]) | 6 | 8 | 14 |

Typically, a man might believe his spouse is being unfaithful to him on a daily basis, having affairs with anybody and everybody. The sufferer becomes so suspicious and obsessed that he inspects and smells his wife's clothing, searching for the semen of other men or any other evidence of sexual activity, and routinely confronts their spouse about supposed infidelities. In this context it is of interest that Ezekiel also has a verse that reads: 'whose members were like those of donkeys and whose emissions were like those of stallions'. Typically, when the wife goes out of the house the husband may follow her, or repeatedly phone her at work to check that she is really there. If the wife is late home from work, the husband will immediately assume she is being unfaithful and harass her about supposed infidelity.

Denials from the partner that no affair has ever happened falls on deaf ears and may even exacerbate the jealousy or be taken as evidence that the partner is lying as well. Shakespeare recognised this in his play *Othello* and the condition is sometimes also known as the Othello syndrome. Shakespeare also recognised its most serious complication, spousal murder, as Othello murders his wife Desdemona, who had done nothing wrong. Mowat (1966) studied all the murder cases in Broadmoor (a hospital prison for insane serious offenders) over a 20-year period and found 110 cases of morbid jealousy at the time of the offence; they comprised of 12% of male and 3% of female murderers. Of these, 13 had schizophrenia, indicating that the risk was very real. A much more common presentation than a full-blown homicide is repeated domestic violence, where the husband repeatedly attacks his wife because of his belief in her infidelity (see also pages 372–377 for a discussion of the *sotah*).

Its prevalence is unknown but morbid jealousy may occur in a wide variety of psychiatric conditions. Sometimes when it is due to an underlying delusional disorder it may respond well to antipsychotic drugs but more often than not these subjects refuse to take any medication, and in intractable cases only a geographical separation will help.

What, then, is the relationship between the morbid jealousy described in chs 16 and 23 and Ezekiel's schizophrenia? A recent study on the prevalence of morbid jealousy among a group of psychiatric in patients may throw some light on this question. Of 8134 psychiatric inpatients, 93 (1.1%) were found to have morbid jealousy. Delusions of jealousy were most common among subjects with organic disorders (7%); paranoid disorders (6.7%); alcoholic psychoses (5.6%); and schizophrenia (2.5%). For affective disorder the rate was only 0.1%. Because schizophrenia was by far the most common diagnosis among these inpatients overall, it was also the commonest underlying cause of morbid jealousy in this large inpatient sample (Soyka *et al.*, 1991). The suggestion, therefore, is that Ezekiel's morbid jealousy is *an associated feature or complication* of his schizophrenic illness, because around 1 in 40 (2.5%) of those with schizophrenia will also have morbid jealousy.

Although many feminist biblical scholars have taken objection to these chapters because of their distasteful pornographic passages, they flow from the same pen as the magic of the chariot vision and the hope inspired by the vision of the dry bones, yet all three passages find their origins in Ezekiel's illness – his schizophrenia.

## Schneider's 'first rank' symptoms and Ezekiel's illness

Kurt Schneider (1959) described a number of symptoms of schizophrenia which he considered 'features of the first rank'. These are cardinal symptoms, helpful in making the diagnosis, but they do not have any causal or prognostic significance. They may occur in other conditions, particularly organic brain disease, but their presence is strongly suggestive of schizophrenia. Mellor (1970) offered some reasonably clear definitions of these symptoms.

The task of linking particular biblical verses with modern definitions of Schneider's first-rank symptoms is problematical. Thus, many of the abnormal thoughts, voices or actions in the Bible are attributed to God and so would be in keeping with the norms of an ancient culture. The justification for trying to link Ezekiel's writings to Schneider's first-rank symptoms is that some verses show a remarkable resemblance to these symptoms.

*Auditory hallucinations* (discussing the subject or arguing about him/her and referring to him/her in the third person):

> 33[30] As for you, mortal, *your people who talk together about you by the walls*, and at the doors of the houses say to one another each to a neighbour 'Come and hear what the word is that comes from the Lord'.

In this verse Ezekiel believes that people by the walls and doors are talking to each other about his prophecies. The actual content of what he says is non-psychotic and is quite appropriate for a religious text. Freedman (2007) has commented that Ezekiel never went out to meet the populace or converse with them, and indeed never recorded a conversation with anyone else, so Ezekiel may have just had a strong feeling that other people were talking about him at the walls, although he never interacted with them.

*Thought insertion.* This is the experience of intrusion of alien ideas or thoughts into the subject's mind as a result of some external agency. One possible example is given in 38[10]:

> 38[10] Thus says the Lord God: On that day thoughts will come into your mind and you will devise an evil scheme.

Here the experience Ezekiel describes is of thoughts coming into his mind and this fits with the definition of thought insertion. It is important to note that these are not God's thoughts, but the introductory part of the verse 'Thus says the Lord God' is offered as an explanation for the strange phenomenon.

*Thought broadcasting.* This is the experience that the subject's thinking is no longer confined within his/her mind but is shared or is accessible to other people.

> 11[5] Then the spirit of the Lord fell upon me and he said to me 'Thus says the Lord: This is what you think O house of Israel: I know the things that come into your mind.

The feeling Ezekiel experiences here is that some outside being (in this instance God) knows what he thinks, and this may have some parallel with thought broadcasting. However, for a member of the ancient Israelite priesthood or even for a religious person today, God is omnipresent and all-knowing, and so might be expected to know the prophet's innermost thoughts. Such a feeling therefore might also be consistent with religious beliefs and not necessarily be indicative of any psychopathology. Nevertheless, the phraseology found in this verse is unique to Ezekiel and is not used by any of the other prophets.

*Made impulses (passivity experiences)*. Here the experience is of actions, sensations, bodily movements, emotions or thought processes being generated by an outside agency which usurps the will of the subject. There are numerous examples of this phenomenon where a spirit (but not the deity) interferes with his will and seemingly takes control and causes some physical action to occur.

> $2^2$ And when he spoke to me a spirit entered into me and set me on my feet and I heard him speaking to me....

In the symptom of a 'made impulse' the patient experiences an event as being inserted into the self from outside by some alien force (Sims, 1988, p. 122) and this fits the description given here. Carley (1974, p. 22), an important Ezekiel scholar, is also puzzled by the '*ruah*' or spirit in this verse:

> The word spirit which means 'wind' or 'breath' and thought to originate from God but in this case lacks the close association with God. In this particular passage, it is *spirit-undefined* – which raises Ezekiel to his feet, supplements and revives his physical powers like a fresh breath of life.

Carley, as a biblical scholar, would have been unfamiliar with schizophrenic passivity phenomena and so unable to make the connection between this verse and schizophrenia, but nevertheless he made a distinction between a spirit and a force from God.

Passivity phenomena of a similar type also occur in $2^{14}$, $8^3$, $11^1$ and $11^{24}$; in these verses there seems to be a reasonably good fit with passivity phenomena. The description is also consistent with spirit possession as occurs in 'possession states' but this is more often a non-psychotic phenomenon.

In summary, therefore, Ezekiel offers reasonable evidence for passivity phenomena, evidence for third-person auditory hallucinations and weaker evidence for thought broadcasting and thought insertion, giving him three or four first-rank symptoms. Schneider (1959) suggested that only one was needed to make a diagnosis of schizophrenia. Mellor (1972) found that 72% of subjects with schizophrenia had at least one first-rank symptom. The accumulation of three or four first-rank symptoms for Ezekiel adds some weight to the diagnosis of schizophrenia.

## Summary of the psychotic phenomenology

### Catatonia and mutism

These episodes are all dated, and have observer descriptions, and therefore are probably authentic. It is possible that Ezekiel himself recorded the dates, as no other person is mentioned in the text as recording them. The catatonia was first diagnosed by Klostermann (1877) and later confirmed by Broome (1946) and Jaspers (1967). There are two episodes of catatonia and three episodes of depressive mutism:

- definite episode of catatonia, lasting 390 days, in verse $4^{4-6}$
- second episode of catatonia, lasting 40 days, in verse $4^6$
- episode of mutism, lasting 7 days, probably depressive, in verse $3^{15}$
- episode of mutism following wife's death in verse $24^{25}$
- episode of mutism on hearing about the fall of Jerusalem in verse $33^{21}$.

### *Acts that are bizarre or out of character for a priest*

All four of these acts occur in the presence of other psychotic symptoms and so probably occur during psychotic episodes. If the account is autobiographical, which I believe it to be, Ezekiel is recording his thoughts and feelings at the time these actions are taking place. The traditional explanation for these episodes is that they are the 'sign actions' of a prophet. The four episodes are:

- baking bread on human dung during an episode of catatonia in verse $4^{12}$
- eating the scroll in response to an auditory command hallucinations in verses $2^8-3^3$
- shaving his head and burning his hair in verse $5^{1-2}$
- digging through the wall in verse $8^7$.

### *Auditory phenomena (probably authentic but may have been changed by later editors)*

- non-verbal auditory hallucinosis, verses $1^{24}$, $10^5$
- voices occurring during visions, verses $1^{28}$, $37^3$
- atypical address as 'son of man'; unique for Ezekiel (throughout)
- high frequency of hearing the voice of God (80 times)
- command hallucinations which are carried out, verses $3^2$, $8^7$
- voices which are loud, verse $9^1$
- hearing voices that talk to other people, verse $9^5$
- hears a voice of a man (in a vision) who is not there, verse $1^{25}$.

### *Visual phenomena*

The visual phenomena are of less certain authenticity, are difficult to distinguish from non-psychotic anomalous visual experiences and may have been changed by later editors. They are:

- fantastic visual scenes, not reported by other prophets
- visions suggestive of panoramic schizophrenic visual hallucinations (ch. 1, the chariot vision)
- the dry bones vision (ch. 37).

Ezekiel is a participant in the visions, a characteristic not seen with other prophets. They are of an ecstatic or manic quality, with the hand of God, with heightened perceptions, giving them a a moving, vibrant quality. Also, there is non-verbal and verbal auditory material in the visions.

## Schneiderian first-rank symptoms (uncertain)

Interpretation of the first-rank symptom is more uncertain because of cultic beliefs in an all-powerful, all-knowing deity. Nevertheless, they may include:

- auditory hallucinations commenting on thoughts or behaviour (?$12^{18}$)
- thought insertion, with thoughts inserted by an alien agency (?$38^{10}$)
- thought broadcasting (?$11^5$)
- passivitiy experiences ($2^2$, $8^3$, $11^{24}$, $11^1$)
- delusional transportation ($11^1$, $11^{24}$).

## The lifetime course of Ezekiel's illness

The Book of Ezekiel opens with the phrase 'In the thirtieth year'. Some authorities take this as the 30th year after the discovery of the Torah in the reign of King Josiah and the start of Josianic reforms. Others suggest it is the 30th year of the prophet's life, when the prophet received his call, in which case it would also give the age of onset of his disorder.

Ezekiel's episodes of illness fall into two broad categories. First, there are the excited manic phases, when he presents as the ecstatic prophet with florid visions, experiences the hand of God, or hears the voice of God or of some spirit who makes him perform strange things; he also delivers his moral tirades to the people. These excited phases may represent catatonic excitement, hypomania or schizo-mania (which are probably similar disorders anyway). Second, there are the catatonic/depressive episodes, when he is either frankly catatonic or in a mute depressed state. In addition, chs 16 and 23 describe a loathing of unfaithful women which probably represents a phase of morbid jealousy. Thus in ch. 16 the harlot Jerusalem is vilified and in ch. 23 it is the two sisters Ohalah and Oholibah who are decried. These chapters provide a good description of the rich fantasy life and thoughts of a person with morbid jealousy and would have been composed while Ezekiel was depressed, since such states usually occur during paranoid depressive phases.

When a precise date is given for the onset of a vision or an excited state, it suggests an acute onset for the episode, with abrupt changes in mental states, which are usually memorable to the subject and to observers around. Exactly who recorded these dates is not known, but the most likely source is Ezekiel himself (perhaps recording his thoughts and the events of his life in some kind of diary). Freedy and Redford (1970) constructed a table, which is reproduced in Greenberg (1983), that matches the events in Ezekiel's life to dates given in the biblical text, and this also incorporates information derived from Egyptian and Babylonian sources. To this table I have added his psychiatric episodes to produce Table 8.4. The table shows that Ezekiel had an episodic illness, with high/ecstatic/manic episodes alternating with mute/catatonic/depressive phases. Such a bipolar episodic pattern

**Table 8.4** Chronology of Ezekiel's illness (after Freedy and Redford 1970)

| Biblical event | Chapter and verse | Suggested date | Ezekiel's age | Possible type of psychiatric episode |
|---|---|---|---|---|
| Chariot vision | $1^1$–$2^8$ | 593 BCE | 30 | Excitement |
| Eating the scroll | $3^3$ | 593 | 30 | Excitement/mixed |
| Dumb for 7 days | $3^{14}$ | 593 | 30 | Depressive |
| Appointed as a watchman; repeat of chariot vision | $3^{22}$ | 593 | 30 | Excitement |
| Catatonia for over 1 year | $4^{48}$ | 593–592 | 31–32 | Depressive |
| Shaving and burning his hair | $5^5$ | 593–592 | 31 | Depressive/mixed |
| Vision of the defiled Temple | $8^1$ | September 592 | 32 | Excitement |
| Chariot vision | $10^{1-28}$ | ?? | 32 | Excitement |
| Morbid jealousy | Chs 16, 23?? | | ?? | Depressive |
| Start of siege of Jerusalem. Mute following wife's death | $24^{27}$ | January 588 | ?34 | Depressive |
| Arrival of fugitive after Jerusalem fell | $33^{21}$ | 585 | 38 | Depressive/mute |
| Vision of the dry bones | $37^{1-14}$ | ?? | ?? | Excitement |
| Vision of the new Temple | $40^1$ | October 573 | ?50 | Excitement |

is especially common among those with schizo-affective disorders and will be readily recognised by most hospital psychiatrists as having a so-called 'revolving door' pattern. Even if some of the dates are wrong or some of these episodes never occurred (such as the vision of the new Temple in 573, when he was 50) the explanation that he suffered from a recurrent and episodic psychosis would remain intact. The table shows a phase of frequent illnesses clustering early on in his prophetic career, when he was aged 30–35, starting around 593 BCE, four years after went into exile in 597 BCE. The pattern is shown in Figure 8.1. He seems to get better on his own, with what appears to be good inter-episode recovery, and in later life there are few, if any, episodes. Deterioration, which is a key feature of severe schizophrenia, is lacking. Had Ezekiel suffered from a deteriorating disorder or a chronic defect state with negative symptoms, thought disorder and personality deterioration, as can occur in schizophrenia, he could never have resumed his priestly work or completed his book. His disciples and those around would certainly have recognised such a change of character and rejected him. Thus those with a chronic schizophrenic defect state are commonly rejected by their families colleagues and employers. The conclusion must be that he did not have such a chronic deteriorating type of schizophrenia but suffered

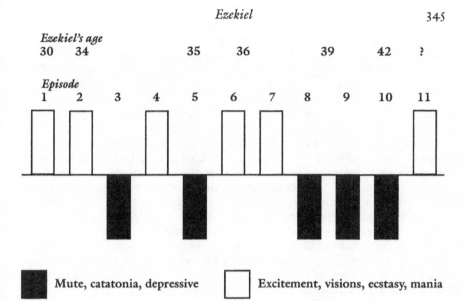

**Figure 8.1** Life chart of Ezekiel's episodes of mental disturbance. Chronology taken from Freedy and Redford (1970), in the order given in the book of Ezekiel. 1, vision of the heavenly bodies – ecstasy ($1^1$); 2, eating the scroll – ecstasy ($3^3$); 3, dumb for seven days – mute ($3^{15}$); 4, repeat of the chariot vision – ecstasy ($3^{22}$); 5, catatonia for one year – depressive ($4^{48}$); 6, vision in the Temple – ecstasy ($8^1$); 7, vision in the Temple – excitement ($10^1$); 8, morbid jealousy – depressive (16, 23); 9, mute following wife's death – depressive ($24^{27}$); 10, arrival of the fugitive from Jerusalem – mute ($33^{21}$); 11, vision of the dry bones – ecstasy ($37^{1-14}$)

from only acute florid episodes, with visions and voices – a far more benign type of schizophrenia than is usually encountered.

For the bulk of his life Ezekiel was probably quite well and free of psychosis. Thus, prior to the age of 30 he functioned as a priest in Jerusalem, until 597 BCE, when he was deported. Once he was in Babylonia, for the first four years until 593 BCE there is no evidence of any mental problems. He must have been quite traumatised when he found himself deported to a small rural village in southern Iraq and so it is not surprising that with the resulting 'culture shock' he became ill – but this was not immediately.

Such a pattern of a delayed onset of schizophrenia following migration has been shown for Swedish immigrants to Minnesota in America in the early 20th century (Ødegård, 1932) or from the West Indies to the UK in the 1950s (Sharpley *et al.*, 2001). These studies have shown that rates for schizophrenia are often much higher among immigrants than either in their new host communities or in their countries of origin; moreover, these illnesses do not come on straight after the migration but most commonly appear with a delay of some 5–10 years. Ezekiel was deported in 597 BCE but became ill only in 593 BCE, some four years after his deportation; this delayed onset seems to fit the pattern of onset for an immigrant psychosis.

Then there follows a period of five years, from 593 to 588 BCE, when he seems to have had many episodes of illness, but thereafter, apart from occasional relapses, he seems to have been quite well. His prophecy is thought to have ended around 570 BCE; in this later period no further breakdowns are recorded, and so for the bulk of his life he seems to have been reasonably well.

Long-term studies of the outcome of schizophrenia (e.g. Huber *et al.*, 1975; Ciompi and Muller, 1976) suggest that around 20–30% of patients with schizophrenia have an episodic course with good inter-episode recovery and do not show deterioration. Perhaps this is the type of schizophrenia that Ezekiel had. Alternatively, the primary disorder may have been schizo-affective disorder, which is rather more closely related to manic depression, where there is a pattern of recurrent episodes that may eventually burn out, also without evidence of deterioration. Catatonic excitement and catatonic stupor tend to favour a diagnosis of catatonic schizophrenia, but this type of schizophrenia often has an affective overlay, with mood disorders being prominent during episodes, and normality rather than deterioration characterising the inter-episode period. The conclusion must be that Ezekiel's schizophrenia was of a benign and recovering type, or that this was schizo-affective disorder.

## The application of DSM-5 criteria to Ezekiel's illness

DSM-5 (APA, 2013) is the 'bible' of modern psychiatry, particularly in America. It provides easily understood operational criteria for each disorder and it is possible to match verses in the Book of Ezekiel to in the individual DSM-5 criteria. In Ezekiel's case there are many features of schizophrenia and so although Ezekiel's possession and ecstatic states were deemed at the time and later to be a part of his religious experience and as religiously based trance states they should nowadays be viewed as part of his mental disorder, A matching of his symptoms with the DSM-5 definition of schizophrenia is given in Table 8.5.

DSM-5 also specifies that if catatonia is present, then the diagnosis should be catatonic schizophrenia, and as Ezekiel seems to have had at least two episodes of catatonia (the first lasting 390 days and the second for 40 days) a person presenting today with his symptoms would be diagnosed with catatonic schizophrenia according to the American scheme. It would also be possible to conduct a similar exercise applying ICD-10 criteria for schizophrenia.

Schizo-affective disorder is also a possible diagnosis because during his visions Ezekiel is in an ecstatic state, with evidence of overactivity and heightened perception, and such features are usually associated with a diagnosis of mania/hypomania, making these episodes schizo-mania. A study of patients with catatonia showed that around 25% of them had

**Table 8.5** DSM criteria for schizophrenia and verses from the Book of Ezekiel

| *DSM schizophrenia* | *Verses from Ezekiel* |
| --- | --- |
| Two or more of the following for at least one month | |
| (1) Delusions | Delusional transportation |
| (2) Hallucinations | Both non-verbal and verbal auditory hallucinations |
| | Panoramic visual hallucinations |
| (3) Disorganised speech | |
| (4) Grossly disorganised or catatonia | Catatonia in chs 3 and 4 |
| (5) Negative symptoms, affective flattening, alogia, or avolition | Not present |
| Note that only one of these symptoms is required if the delusions are bizarre, or if the hallucinations consist of a voice keeping up a running commentary on the person's behaviour and thoughts, or two or more persons conversing with each other | |
| (a) voices commenting on a person's behaviour or thoughts | – |
| (b) two or more voices conversing with one another | ? 'he cried within my hearing' |
| Social/occupational dysfunction in work, relationships or self-care | Severe self-neglect during catatonic phase. Baking with human dung |
| Continuous for at least six months | Catatonic for 390 days |
| Schizo-affective and mood disorder excluded | Ezekiel may have had schizo-affective disorder |
| Not due to a medical or developmental disorder | No evidence of any other ill health |

schizo-affective disorder rather than schizophrenia (Taylor *et al.*, 1977). On most of the occasions when Ezekiel's psychotic symptoms are florid, there is also a suggestion of mood disorder and this also favours a diagnosis of schizo-affective disorder, as does the relative absence of 'negative symptoms' (on which, see the Appendix to this chapter) and the episodic nature of the disorder. However, to speculate whether Ezekiel's illness was schizo-affective disorder or schizophrenia or some other related disorder within the schizophrenia spectrum is probably fruitless and goes far beyond the data available in this ancient text. Such distinctions are quite difficult to make even when the patient can be examined in depth.

## The views of the rabbis, theologians and others concerning Ezekiel's behaviour

Ezekiel's strange behaviour must have puzzled observers and commentators from the earliest times. No man, however great, who eats a scroll, burns his hair in public, lies down speechless and motionless for a year and then experiences voices and visions would have escaped from other people questioning his sanity. The issue of Ezekiel's sanity first appears in the Talmud, but because Ezekiel was a holy man, and his book is part of the sacred canon, no Talmudic rabbi could possibly dare to suggest he was mad, but instead must place such thoughts in the mouths of others. Thus, with regard to the first episode of catatonia, in $4^{4-8}$: 'A heretic said to Rabbi Abbahy, "Your God is a Joker – for he says to Ezekiel lie on your left side and then lie on your right side".' The rabbi then goes on to interpret this suffering as atonement for Israel's sin and suggests that the heretic who made such a suggestion was most probably a Christian (BT, Sanheddrin 39a). The fact that this story is quoted at all in the Talmud suggests that some of the rabbis must have raised the issue of Ezekiel's sanity – if only to dispel such a notion.

There are also mysterious Talmudic restrictions on the study of Ezekiel. Although the rabbis of the Talmud (3rd to 8th centuries CE) had no detailed knowledge of schizophrenia as a mental illness they retained a deep scepticism regarding visions of Ezekiel and placed restrictions on their study (Greenberg, 1983, p. 205). Thus, the first chapter of the book, which describes the vision of the journey of the ecstatic on the divine chariot through the celestial arena, was considered by the rabbis to be a mortally dangerous journey. The Mishnah specifically prohibits its study: 'One may not teach the Merkabah (chariot vision) to even a single student unless he is wise enough to fill in the clues by himself' (Mishnah Hagigah 2.1). The reason given was that a child 'who looked into the hashmal (the glowing amber) ... was consumed when fire leapt forth from the hashmal' (Talmud Hag 13a). However, the book was saved from withdrawal from the canon, once more by Rabbi Hananiah Ben Hezekiah, who pointed out that 'fortunately such children were very rare'. There is also an anonymous opinion in the Mishnah (Meg 4:10) forbidding the use of this passage for a *haftarah* (a part of the Sabbath service in the synagogue). There is a similar stricture in the Mishnah for using ch. 16, where Jerusalem is described as a harlot in a passage replete with sexual innuendoes, because this was an insult to the city of Jerusalem.

During the Middle Ages, the great Jewish physician and philosopher of Arabic Spain, Maimonides, issued a firm denial that Ezekiel might have been mad but by his very statement also acknowledged the question had been raised: 'God is too exalted that he should turn his prophets into a laughing stock and a mockery for fools by ordering them to carry out crazy actions'. He went on to explain such actions were merely visionary (Guide of the Perplexed II, 46). Certainly Rashi, the great French commentator of the 11th century, acknowledges there was an issue concerning Ezekiel's sanity and says that whenever the 'hand of God' appears Ezekiel is seized and behaves like a madman; he remarks on the frequency of his dramatic episodes, his so-called sign actions. Greenberg (p. 122) also comments on how Ezekiel has far more symbolic acts (or *mopet*) which portend an impending event than any other prophet: 'For the most part and always with Ezekiel, they are intended to impress a public – and are often accompanied by verbal explication to the witnesses'.

W. Zimmerli (1969, pp. 19–21), perhaps the foremost modern biblical scholar of Ezekiel, lists all the behaviours he identifies as abnormal, which are similar to those identified here, but he seems reluctant to make any diagnosis. The phenomena Zimmerli highlights as abnormal are: the catatonia, eating the scroll, groaning and hand clapping, loss of speech on his wife's death, the nightmare in which the eyes on the wheels pursue and stare at him, symbolic actions and visionary experiences, transportation by the spirit, walking through the Temple in his visions, walking through a field of dead bones, his participation in his visions and the dramatic element. Despite grouping all these features together and considering them to be strange, Zimmerli writes 'All these traits of physical weakness ... are scarcely sufficient for arriving at a specific diagnosis of an illness for the prophet'. Zimmerli's analysis of Ezekiel is very detailed and his reluctance to make a diagnosis might relate to a deeply held religious belief that a holy prophet could not suffer from a debilitating mental disorder, but more likely point to an obvious lack of familiarity with any of the features of schizophrenia. His biblical studies spanned the period from the 1930s to the 1960s and coincided with the peak of institutionalisation in psychiatry, so almost all patients suffering from schizophrenia were sequestered away in mental hospitals and thus were rarely seen in the community. A professor of religion working in an isolated academic environment, spending his days poring over manuscripts in the library and passing his hours of leisure socialising with like-minded souls would rarely if ever encounter a patient suffering from schizophrenia. If Professor Zimmerli had only taken a stroll down to his local mental asylum he would certainly have remarked on the striking similarity between the symptoms of the clientele residing there and Ezekiel's abnormalities which he so scrupulously documented and which even he found to be strange.

Brownlee (1986), another important Ezekiel scholar, wrote that he was a mystic but a normal, healthy man. Brownlee accepted an aphasic episode following his wife's death, with repeated aphasia due to strokes accounting for later episodes of dumbness. The episodes of immobility or catatonia were explained away as true binding by the people, as Ezekiel was perceived to be a public nuisance by the local population because of his preaching. Greenberg (p. 121), another important modern Ezekiel scholar, lists all the abnormal behaviour described in $3^{24}-4^8$ but he does not make any diagnosis.

D. J. Halperin (1993), in an otherwise erudite exposition of the book, offers a conventional Freudian explanation, based on notions of repressed sexuality, possibly because he was advised by his wife – a psychoanalyst. He believed Ezekiel to be a man suffering from deep inner torment, and he focuses on the issue of female sexuality. He linked chs 16 and 23, which are essentially pornographic tirades against promiscuous women (see above on morbid jealousy), with ch. 8, which describes Ezekiel digging a hole through the wall which he thought represented repressed sexual intercourse. His failure to mourn the death of his wife served as further evidence of repressed sexuality and on this basis Halperin postulated the central motif to Ezekiel's psychic life was a dread and loathing of female sexuality. Such an antiquated Freudian view is neither tenable nor shared by any other commentator today.

## Psychiatric opinions

Even before schizophrenia had been described in the medical literature, Klostermann (1877) was the first to suggest that Ezekiel might have had catatonia, as described on page 296. Broome (1946), an American psychiatrist heavily influenced by psychoanalytic thinking, was the first modern psychiatrist to formally suggest that Ezekiel had schizophrenia, which he characterised as paranoid schizophrenia. He also postulated schizophrenic withdrawal. In support of this, Freedman points out there is no evidence in the book that Ezekiel ever had a conversation with any other human being (*Encyclopaedia Judaica*, 2nd edition, Ezekiel Entry, p. 1083). When Broome wrote his paper, psychoanalysis ruled supreme, everyone had their own definition of schizophrenia and there were no agreed diagnostic criteria for schizophrenia. He also felt that Ezekiel's religious significance was not impaired by making a psychiatric diagnosis, a view also previously expressed by William James (1909) about other important spiritual leaders.

Karl Jaspers also considered Ezekiel had schizophrenia in a short paper entitled 'Der Prophet Ezechiel, Eine pathographische Studie', which initially appeared in Germany in 1947 and was later republished in 1968. In addition to the obvious episodes of catatonia, Jaspers thought that the visions which herald the onset of his episodes were typical schizophrenic episodes.

In a recent complete rebuttal of the thesis expressed here that Ezekiel had schizophrenia, Cook (2012) argued that the actual phenomenology described by Ezekiel was not compatible with current concepts of schizophrenia (all the voices Ezekiel experienced were those of God, and are quite in line with a wholly religious explanation for the auditory phenomena) and that Ezekiel himself is best considered a mystic. Quite possibly Ezekiel was a mystic, but mystics may also have schizophrenia.

Obviously there can never be any certainty about a diagnosis based solely on an ancient religious text but the present writer is in agreement with Klostermann (1877), Broome (1946) and Jaspers in 1946 (republished in 1967), who all also diagnosed schizophrenia. However, our understanding of schizophrenia and its protean manifestations has greatly improved over the last 50 years. There are now published checklists of symptoms which are themselves strictly defined so it is possible for any psychiatrist, doctor or even lay person to replicate the analysis given here and match the verses from the Book of Ezekiel with psychotic symptoms as defined in the current psychiatric diagnostic glossaries, principally DSM-5 and ICD-10. Although the use of the ICD-10 and DSM-5 can be criticised as being culturally inappropriate, it is important to note that nothing better is presently available. In this sense, the diagnosis of schizophrenia made here does not represent the personal view of the author, but it might also be reached by any present-day clinical psychiatrist applying standard and internationally accepted criteria.

# Concluding remarks

Ezekiel lived more than 2500 years ago, in the lands of Israel and Babylonia, during one of the great junctures in the history of religion. The land of Israel, its kings and its temple were destroyed and the educated remnant of the population of Jerusalem had been deported to Babylonia. Once there, the writings of the Israelite peoples were sifted and edited, the oral teachings of the great prophets recorded for posterity, leading to a gradual transition from an ancient cult bound to its land of origin and an oral tradition through to a much more universal religion independent of territorial restriction but now based on the written word alone. The Israelite peoples, who were later to become the Jews, survived in their exile as a people because of their laws, religious traditions and the writings of their scribes and prophets. Ezekiel lay at the centre of this transformation and was one of the great contributors to the literature of the time, which was so dramatically to influence history and religions of the world (Kaufman, 1960).

Ezekiel appears to have been the main religious philosopher of the earliest period of the exile, and helped to keep the Jewish religion alive. Joyce (2009, p. 20) writes:

> The catastrophe [of the exile] might well have proved to be the end of Israel as a religious community. That it did not owed everything to a small group of theologians who boldly attempted to account for the disaster within the framework of faith in Yahweh. In Judah, the prophet Jeremiah and also it seems the authors of the deuteronomistic history struggled to give a Yahwistic account of events. Among the exiled community, this task fell initially to just one person, namely Ezekiel.

Ezekiel's personal contribution to religion and literature is not to be underestimated. He is thought to be one of the fathers of the apocalyptic literature, and some of the later apocalyptic literature in both the Old and New Testament draws on his visions, his rhetoric and writing. He also made a lasting contribution to ethics in his doctrine of individual responsibility, and laid to rest the notion of blood guilt, proclaiming that only the person who commits a crime should be punished, and not his family – a relatively advanced notion for any ancient cult.

As an educated and highly intelligent literate priest of the Jerusalem Temple, he must have been quite traumatised when he found himself deported to a small rural village in southern Iraq, and so it is not surprising that, with the resulting 'culture shock', he became ill, although only after an interval of a few years, which seems to be the pattern for an immigrant psychosis. His illness seems to have been most severe during the early years, with the longest episode of catatonia lasting for just over a year. Otherwise, he appears to have suffered from short-lived episodes of excitement or depression characterised by muteness, paranoia and morbid jealousy. A diagnosis of schizophrenia or schizo-affective disorder is supported by extensive and detailed descriptions of the relevant phenomenology. However, the illness appears to have been at the more benign end of the spectrum for psychotic illness – he recovers spontaneously from each episode quite intact, with little in the way of inter-episode disturbance, and in his later years the illness appears to burn itself out, with little evidence of any psychiatric symptoms after the age of 40. However, the illness was rather more than a simple possession state or the excited frenzy of an ecstatic prophet and fulfils modern diagnostic criteria for schizophrenia.

Does his illness matter? The answer is that it probably does not matter very much. For the most part, the passages which describe his schizophrenia have little religious importance, and the only places where the psychiatry and religion intersect is in his visions, particularly the chariot vision and the vision of the dry bones. Perhaps these were written while he was in an acute psychotic state but great literature can sometimes flow from the pen of a writer in the midst of a psychosis; for example, Virginia Woolf's stream-of-consciousness work is thought to have been written while she was in a manic state.

His schizophrenia does not seem to have had much impact on his ability to perform his priestly duties or to function as a prophet, or to write great religious literature – although there is a suggestion that some of his psychotic thought processes have suffused his writings, particularly in the descriptions of the visions. He was never rejected by his contemporaries but they did record his strange behaviours. His religious poetry is often terse yet profound, conveying important religious ideas.

Ezekiel has little insight into his illness and fails to recognise when he is entering into an illness episode. This should not surprise us, as patients today rarely have much insight into their change from normality to a schizophrenic episode. In Ezekiel's day mental illnesses were generally un-recognised. However, he does seem to notice when he emerges from his illness phases. Thus, as he emerges from his year-long episode of catatonia, when he cooked with human dung, he notices a change for the better when God says to him '*See, I will let you have cow's dung instead of human dung* on which you can prepare your bread' ($4^{15}$). Similarly, when he emerges from an episode of mutism much later in his life he notices that he can now talk again and this seems to occur just before the messenger from Jerusalem arrives: 'but he [God] had opened my mouth by the time the fugitive came to me in the morning; so my mouth was opened, and *I was no longer unable to speak*' ($33^{22}$).

Much of the Book of Ezekiel is autobiographical and the account of his visions and voices is often accurately dated, suggesting he must have kept some sort of a diary – which perhaps he later collated and edited into a book. A modern example of this type of literary genre is *I Never Promised You a Rose Garden* by Hannah Green (1964), but there are many more.

His schizophrenia explains many of the great mysteries which have been the subject of Ezekiel scholarship for the last 2,000 years. The brightness of his visions or the *Hashmal* may be an example of heightened perception. The controversy of where he lived (Jerusalem or Babylon) is readily explained by him living his life in Babylon but in his imagination (?delusions) he lives in Jerusalem. His sign actions such as eating the scroll (command hallucina-tions); lying on one side for a year (catatonia) and burning his hair and cooking with human faeces are all accounted for by a single explanation:

that he had schizophrenia. Passages such as the pornography and misogyny of chs 16 and 23, which have puzzled students of religion for many generations, are *not* solely a reflection of a patriarchal society replete with physical abuse and the denigration of women as some feminist biblical commentators contend, but most likely are related to his morbid jealousy and are a part of his schizophrenia.

From a psychiatric perspective, the interest in this case lies not so much in the diagnostic issue but with the accuracy and clinical detail of his autobiographical description of the symptoms of his schizophrenia. Early descriptions of mental disorder first appeared in the European medical literature of the 17th century, with a more formal identification of schizophrenia occurring around 120 years ago, but it is only in the last four decades that accurate glossaries of the individual symptoms of schizophrenia have been published and these can be applied to the biblical or any other texts. Ezekiel's illness as described in the book which bears his name is one of the earliest descriptions, if not the first, of schizophrenia or schizo-affective disorder, and certainly it is by far the most detailed example of psychiatric phenomenology to be found anywhere in the literature of the ancient world.

There is an understandable and natural tendency to resist the notion that a holy man such as Ezekiel might have suffered from a serious mental disorder such as schizophrenia. This probably relates more to the lowly position, economic impoverishment and stigma and sometimes contempt with which the mentally ill are held in modern society. This was not always the case and attempts are now being made to reverse these unfortunate historical trends which have impacted so badly on the mentally ill in recent times. In ancient Israel, the less seriously mentally ill would probably not even have been noticed and except in cases of danger or violence certainly would not have been stigmatised in the same way as patients are today. A man's status would depend more on his wealth, his military prowess, his scholarly or literary ability, or his position in society. Thus, while all of Ezekiel's psychic abnormalities are faithfully recorded in the text, his contemporaries do not appear to have rejected him or downgraded his teachings because of his bizarre experiences and strange behaviour. It is only the later rabbis of the Talmud and the Middle Ages who began to question his sanity – albeit in a muted form, and then placed certain restrictions on the study of his works.

Fortunately, there is very little interplay between those passages in the book held to be sacred and Ezekiel's illnesses. Ezekiel's most famous vision – of the dry bones in the desert, which join up together and begin to dance when God breathes life into them – has served as a constant source of hope for those suffering persecution and despair. Not surprisingly, the slaves of the deep South in America used these images to create some of their most beautiful music in their spirituals. The Jewish people have also looked to these verses in their darkest hours of persecution and in them seen messages of hope. Outside the Knesset, the parliament of Israel in Jerusalem, there is a frieze with a picture of Ezekiel's vision of the valley of dry bones, with the bones joining together and dancing to life – so symbolising the restoration of Israel and the renewal of the Jewish state following the long nightmare of Jewish persecution throughout the ages.

# Appendix

## Schizophrenia

Schizophrenia is the most serious and common mental disorder treated by psychiatrists today and is one of the two major functional psychoses, the other being manic depression. For the layman, the illness is much more difficult to understand than manic depression, not least because until quite recently most patients with schizophrenia were sequestered away in distant mental hospitals with very little general knowledge of its features in the wider community.

The illness has a low incidence (number of new cases a year) – around 11 per 100,000 – but because it is a lifelong disorder, cases accumulate in the community and so it has a high prevalence (total number of cases in the community at any one time) – of between 0.5% and 1%. At least half the psychiatric beds in the UK are occupied by patients with schizophrenia and this condition presents the most important therapeutic challenge to the psychiatric services today.

The illness usually starts in the late teens or early 20s in men but a few years later among women, although it can start at any age. Typically, the illness follows a chronic course in which an acute episode of delusions and hallucinations (these are known as positive symptoms) is superimposed on more persistent and subtle disorders in the organisation of thought and behaviour. The latter are known as negative symptoms, and include disorganisation, lack of will, low energy levels, flattening of emotional response, or incongruous emotional responses and thought disorder. Negative symptoms can result in severe destruction of the personality, with an accompanying failure in social and occupational roles – and it is the negative symptoms more than the positive symptoms which cause a lifetime of social disability. The more florid positive symptoms of delusions and hallucinations usually resolve quickly with modern drug therapy. It should be noted that not all cases have negative symptoms, and cases with a later onset tend to have less personality deterioration. In Ezekiel's case, he had a later onset, when aged about 30, with mainly positive symptoms, in the form of delusions and hallucinations, with no suggestion of any negative symptoms. He probably had complete recovery between episodes and did not have a chronic persistent disorder, placing his illness among those with a more benign outlook.

Hebephrenia, the most florid subtype of the illness, usually presents with florid delusions and hallucinations and profound deterioration of thought and organising abilities and is found in younger patients. Dementia paranoides was initially regarded as a separate condition, but from the late 1880s onwards Kraepelin joined together catatonia, hebephrenia and dementia paranoides as one illness, which he called *dementia praecox*. The *dementia* referred to the deteriorating course and the *praecox* to its onset in youth. More importantly, he distinguished the illness from manic depression, which he claimed was associated with complete inter-episode recovery rather than a deteriorating course.

The illness was renamed 'schizophrenia' by Eugene Bleuler in 1911 (translated by Zinkin in 1951) and this term has remained. Bleuler discarded the term 'dementia' because many cases did not have a deteriorating course and he also dropped the 'praecox' since the illness could start at any time, including old age. Bleuler described certain fundamental symptoms – including affective flattening, loosening of associations, ambivalence and autism – which he thought represented the core of the illness. In recent years these have been classified as the 'negative symptoms', while delusions and hallucinations, though critical in making the diagnosis, he regarded as secondary or accessory symptoms, and these are now termed 'positive symptoms'.

Hallucinations in any sensory modality can occur in schizophrenia, although auditory hallucinations are by far the most common. These take the form of voices commenting, voices discussing or arguing or hearing one's own thoughts aloud. Often the voices are harsh or critical and they may be frightening. Patients sometimes carry out the instructions given by these voices, and these are known as command hallucinations. In schizophrenia the voices are said to be 'mood incongruent', in that their content cannot be readily understood as a consequence of the patient's mood, whereas in an affective psychoses (depression, mania, or schizo-affective disorder) the content of the voices appears to be related to the patient's current mood. In Ezekiel's case, when he hears voices, they are usually mood congruent: when he is excited or in a state of ecstasy, they have a glorious content, as in the chariot vision, but when he is miserable there is gloom, as in the vision of the dead bones.

Delusions are strongly held but false beliefs and are also common in schizophrenia. Most commonly, they have a paranoid content or are delusions concerning the self but they may encompass a very wide variety of different topics. Among the more severe and chronic cases, thought disorder and negative symptoms may prevail, but Ezekiel shows little evidence of these features. Ezekiel also shows many of Schneider's first-rank symptoms, which are generally held to have some diagnostic significance, as discussed on pages 340–341.

A detailed discussion of the cause of schizophrenia is beyond the scope of this brief overview and useful accounts are given in standard textbooks of psychiatry. Essentially, twin and family studies have demonstrated an important genetic contribution, so that around 80% of the cause is thought to be genetic. A small number of cases are thought to be related to intra-uterine infections or birth injuries. Brain scanning studies have shown abnormalities in the frontal and temporal lobes of the brain, although their significance is unclear. Earlier notions that families or mothers could somehow cause schizophrenia in their offspring have rightfully been discarded but the emotional environment and stress can influence the course of the disease. Prior to the asylum era, patients were looked after in their communities, but if their behaviour was outrageous or dangerous they might be chained up, imprisoned or even killed. Until the 20th century there was no treatment and the majority of sufferers with the severe forms of the illness languished for the greater part of their lives in mental hospitals.

In 1952 two French psychiatrists (Delay and Deniker, 1955) introduced a new potent anti-histamine drug – chlorpromazine – which had dramatic effects on the positive symptoms of schizophrenia and news of its effectiveness spread rapidly through the asylums of Europe and America. Its use gradually led the emptying of these institutions and heralded a change in attitude to the illness. The outlook greatly improved in the early 1990s when a new group of potent antipsychotic drugs appeared, the so-called 'atypicals', which are just as effective as the older drugs but have far fewer side-effects. The old asylums have now largely closed. Most patients live in the community and are largely symptom free but are still considerably handicapped, with only a minority being able to assume normal roles in family life or in the workplace, and the disorder remains both common and debilitating.

*Schizo-affective disorder*

Schizo-affective disorder is a closely related condition that is distinguished from schizophrenia by the presence of prominent symptoms of mood disorder, which occur at the same time as the psychotic or schizophrenic symptoms. Thus, when active positive symptoms such as delusions or hallucinations are present, the patient should also exhibit evidence of either mania or depression to qualify for a diagnosis of schizo-affective disorder. Similarly, episodes of paranoia or catatonia should be accompanied by depressive symptoms. The destructive negative symptoms and thought disorders of schizophrenia itself are uncommon in schizo-affective disorder and there is good inter-episode recovery. This seems to be consistent with the pattern Ezekiel displays.

## References

Abarbanel, D. I. (1957) *Peruš 'al nevi'im 'aharonim.* Jerusalem: Torah va-Da'at.

American Psychiatric Association (1994) *Diagnostic and Statistical Manual of Psychiatric Disorders,* 4th edition (DSM-IV). Washington, DC: American Psychiatric Association.

American Psychiatric Association (2013) *Diagnostic and Statistical Manual of Psychiatric Disorders,* 5th edition (DSM-5). Washington, DC: American Psychiatric Publishing.

Andrae, W. (1925) *Coloured Ceramics from Ashur,* 1925, London: K. Paul, Trench Trubner & Co.

Bleuler, E. (1911) *Dementia Praecox* Translated 1950 by J. Zinkin. New York: International Universities Press.

Block, D. I. (1997) *The Book of Ezekiel* Chapters 1–24. Grand Rapids Michigan. William B Eerdmans Publishing Company.

Broome, Edwin, C. (1946) Ezekiel's abnormal personality. *Journal of Biblical Literature,* 65, 277–292.

Brownlee, William H. (1986) Vol. 28 *Ezekiel The Word Biblical Commentary.* Pages xix–xxix, and 134–135 Dallas, Texas: Word Books.

Carley, K.W. (1974) *The Book of the Prophet Ezekiel.* The Cambridge Bible Commentary. Cambridge: Cambridge University Press.

Cerny, J. (1957) *Ancient Egyptian Religion* pp. 29–40. London: Hutchinsons University Library.

Ciompi, I. and Muller, C. (1976) *Lebenswegund alter der Schizophrenen: Eine Karamenertische langzeit bis ins Senium.* Berlin: Springer-Verlag.

Cook, C.H. (2012) Psychiatry in Scripture: Sacred Texts and Psychopathology: *The Psychiatrist* 36, 225–229.

Cutting, J. (1997) *Principles of Psychopathology.* Oxford: Oxford University Press.

Davis, Ellen F. (1989) *Swallowing the Scroll: Textuality and the dynamics of discourse in Ezekiel's prophecy.* Sheffield: Almond Press.

Deahl, M.P. (1987) Do patients see visions that talk? *Lancet*, ii, 812.

Delay, J., Deniker, and Harl, J. M. (1952) Utilisative en therapeutic psychiatric d'une phenothiazine centrale elective (4560 RP). *Annales Medicales et Psychologique (Paris)* 110: 112–117.

Driver, G.R. (1954) 'Ezekiel: Linguistic and Textual Problems'. *Biblica,* 35: 145–159, 299–312.

Duhm, B. (1901) Das Buch Jeremia *Kurzer Hand-Commentar zum alten testament,* Tubingen: Mohr

Enoch, M.D. and Trethowan, W.H. (1979) *Uncommon Psychiatric syndromes* (2nd edition) Bristol:John Wright.

Ey, H. (1954) *Etudes Psychiatriques: Structure des Psychoses aigues et Destructuration de la conscience.* Paris: Desclee de Brouwer.

Fishbane, M. (2002) Connection between the Haftarah and the Festival of *Shavout,* p. 444 In *The JPS Bible Commentary: Haftarot:* Philadelphia : Jewish Publication Society.

Fohrer, G. (1955) Ezechiel, mit einem Beitrag von K. Galling. *Handbuch Zur Alten Testamentum* 13. Túbingen: J.C.B. Mohr.

Freedman, D.N. (2007) Ezekiel Entry. *Encyclopaedia Judaica* 2nd edition. Eds Skolnik Vol p. 1083.

Freedy, K.S. and Redford, D.B. (1970) The dates in Ezekiel in relation to Biblical, Babylonian and Egyptian sources. *Journal of the American Oriental Society,* 90, 462–485.

Green, H. (1986) *I Never Promised you a Rose Garden.* Pavanne Books MacMillan Education Australia.

Grapow, H. (1956) *Kranker, Krankheiten und Arzt : Vom gesunden und kranken Ägypter, von den Krankheiten, vom Arzt und von der ärztlichen Tätigkeit,* Akademie Verlag, Berlin.

Greenberg, Moshe (1983) *Ezekiel 1–20: A New translation with introduction and commentary, Vol. 22 of the Anchor Bible.* Garden City, N.Y.: Doubleday.

Greenberg Moshe (1997) *Ezekiel 21–37: A New Translation with Introduction and Commentary* Vol 22A. Anchor Bible. New York: Doubleday.

Halperin, D.J. (1993) *Seeking Ezekiel.* University Park, Pennsylvania: Pennsylvania State University Press.

Herntriche, V. (1933) Ezechiel probleme. *Beihefte Zur zeitshrifte fur die alttestamentliche Wissenschaft* 61. Giessen: A. Topelmann.

Holscher, G. (1924) Hesekiel, der Dichter und das Buch, *Beihefte Zur zeitshrifte fur die alttestamentliche Wissenschaft* 39. Giessen:A. Töpelmann.

Howie, C.G. (1950) The Date and Composition of Ezekiel. *Journal of Biblical Literature Monograph Series, IV.* Philadelphia: Society of Biblical Literature.

Huber, G., Gross, G. and Schuttler, R. A long term follow up of schizophrenia: psychiatric course of illness and prognosis *Acta Psychiatrica Scandanavica,* 52: 49–57.

Jahn, G. (1905) *Das Buch Ezechiel.* Leipzig: E. Pfeiffer.

James, W. (1902) *The Varieties of Religious Experience. A Study in human nature.* London Longmans Green and Co.

Jaspers, Karl (1968) Der Prophet Ezechiel: Eine pathographische Studie. In Jaspers, *Aneignung und Polemik: Gesammelte Reden und Aufsätze zur Gescgucgte der Philosophie,* 13–21, Munich: Piper. Originally published 1947.

Joyce, P.M. (2009) *Ezekiel: A Commentary* New York: T&T Clarke.

Kaufman, Yehezkel (1960) *The Religion of Israel: from its beginnings to the Babylonian exile.* Translated from the Hebrew and abridged by Moshe Greenberg. Chicago: University of Chicago Press.

Klosterman, August (1877) Ezechiel: Ein Beitrag zu besserer Würdigung seiner Person und seiner Schrift. *Theologische Studien und Kritiken* 50, 391–439.

Kraepelin, E. (1909–1913) *Psychiatrie* (8th edition), vol. 3, part 2. Trans. 1919 by R.M. Barclay as *Dementia Praecox and Paraphrenia.* Livingstone, Edinburgh. Extracts from vols. 3 and 4 trans. 1921 by R.M. Barclay as *Manic-depressive insanity and paranoia.* Livingstone, Edinburgh.

Kroll, J and Bacharach, B (1982) Visions and Psychopathology in the Middle Ages. *Journal of Nervous and Mental Disease,* 170: 41–49.

Landsberger B. (1967) Akkadisch-Hebraische Wortgleichen. *Supplement Vetus Testamentum* 16

Luckenbill, D.D. (1924) *The Annals of Sennacherib.* Chicago: University of Chicago Press.

Lukianowicz, N. (1967) Body image disturbances in psychiatric disorders. *British Journal of Psychiatry*, 113, 31–47.

Lyketsos, G.C., Paterakis, P., Beis, A. and Lyketsos, C.G. (1985) Eating disorders in schizophrenia. *British Journal of Psychiatry*, 146, 255–261.

Mein A (2009) Ezekiel's women in Christian Interpretation: The case of Ezekiel 16 in *After Ezekiel: Essays on the Reception of a Difficult Prophet*. Edited by Paul Joyce and Andrew Mien. New York: T&T Clark International.

Mellor, C.S. (1970) First rank symptoms of schizophrenia. *British Journal of Psychiatry*, 117, 15–23.

Mowat, R.R. (1966) *Morbid Jealousy and Murder*. London: Tavistock.

Odell M.S. Reading Ezekiel, Seeing Christ: The Ezekiel Cycle in the Church of St. Maria and St.Clemens Schwarzrheindorf, Chapter 8 pp 115-136 in *After Ezekiel: Essays on the Reception of a Difficult Prophet*. Edited by Paul Joyce and Andrew Mien. New York: T&T Clark International.

Ødegård, O. (1932) Emigration and insanity: A study of mental disease in the Norwegian born population of Minnesota. *Acta Psychiatrica et Neurologica Scandanavica* Suppl. 4 1-206

Pritchard, J.B. (1969) *Ancient Near Eastern Texts Relating to the Old Testament (ANET)*. Princeton: Princeton University Press, 3rd edition.

Pritchard, J.B. (1975) Ancient Near Eastern Texts Volume 2 *A New Anthology of Texts and Pictures (ANEP)*. Princeton: Princeton University Press.

Roberts, J.J. (1971) The Hand of Yahweh. *Vetus Testamentum* , 21: 244-251

Rosenberg, A.J. (1991) *The Book of Ezekiel A New Translation of the Text, Rashi and a Commentary Digest*. Volumes 1 and 2. New York: Judaica Press.

Rowland, C. (2009) William Blake and Ezekiel's Merakabah. Chapter 9, pp. 230-245 in *After Ezekiel: Essays on the Reception of a Difficult Prophet*. Edited by Paul Joyce and Andrew Mien. New York: T&T Clark International.

Schneider, K., (1959) *Clinical Psychopathology* Trans. M.W. Hamilton. New York. Grune Stratton.

Sharpley, M., Hutchinson G., Mackenzie K., *et al*. (2001) Understanding the excess of Psychosis among the Afro-Carribean Population in England. A review of current Hypotheses. *British Journal of Psychiatry* 178, Suppl. 40, 560-568.

Silverman, J. (1967) Shamans and acute schizophrenia. *American Anthropologist* 69, 21–31.

Sims, A. (1988) *Symptoms in the Mind: An introduction to Descriptive Psychopathology*. London: Balliere Tyndall.

Smend, R. (1880) Der Prophet Ezechiel. *Kurzgefasstes exegetisches Handbuch zum alten Testament, VIII*. 2te Auflage. Leipzig: S. Hirzel.

Solberger, E. (1974) The White Obelisk of Assurnasirpal II *Iraq* 36, 232.

Soyka, M., Naber, G. and Völcker, A. (1991) Prevalence of delusional jealousy in different psychiatric disorders. An analysis of 93 cases. *British Journal of Psychiatry* 158:549-53.

Sweeney, M.A. (2011) The Problem of Ezekiel in Talmudic Literature. Chapter2 pp11-24. In *After Ezekiel:Essays on the reception of a difficult Prophet* Eds. Paul Joyce and Andrew Mein Library of Hebrew Bible/Old Testament studies. London: T&T Clark.

Talmon, S. (1960) 'Double Readings in the Masoretic Text'. *Textus* 1, 144–184.

Taylor M.A, and Abrams R. (1977) Catatonia: Prevalence and importance of the manic phase of manic depressive illness. *Archives of General Psychiatry*. (1977) 34, 1223-5.

Wevers, J. (1969) *Ezekiel*. The Century Bible, London: Nelson.

Wilson, R.R. (1972) 'An Interpretation of Ezekiel's Dumbness' *Vetus Testamentum* 22, 91–104.

Wing, J. K., *et al*. (1990) 'SCAN. Schedules for Clinical Assessment in Neuropsychiatry.' *Archives of General Psychiatry* 47.6 : 589-93.

Wurthwein (1995) *The text of The Old Testament: An Introduction to the Biblia Hebraica* 2nd Edition Grand Rapids: Eerdmans. Based on the 5th German Edition. *Der Text das Alten Testaments*. Stuttgart, 1988.

Zimmerli, W. (1979) *Ezekiel I: A commentary on the Book of the Prophet Ezekiel* (Vol. I; chapters. 1–24). trans. R Clements, Hermeneia. Philadelphia: Fortress Press.

Zimmerli, W. (1983) *Ezekiel 2: A commentary on the Book of the Prophet Ezekiel* (Vol. 2; chapters. 25–48), trans. R Clements, Hermeneia. Philadelphia: Fortress Press.

# Chapter 9

# Did chronic mental illness exist in the ancient world?

This chapter concerns evidence for severe and chronic mental illness in the Bible and some other literature of the ancient Near East. This means the chapter has little or no potential religious significance but it is of great psychiatric interest. Although severe and chronic mental illness is common today, with most countries reporting that around 1% of the population suffers from schizophrenia, in ancient times these conditions were unrecognised and so, unsurprisingly, rarely commented on; for instance, in Greek and Roman times there are almost no descriptions of schizophrenia (Evans *et al.*, 2003). This puzzle has led some epidemiologists to postulate that schizophrenia may have been a 'new disease', becoming much very much worse in the 18th and 19th centuries, and this is discussed at the end of this chapter. Although the Bible lacks any sort of comprehensive description of chronic mental illness, there are occasional asides in single verses or part verses as well as references to unnamed prophets that do suggest severe and chronic mental illness, providing some evidence that such conditions did exist in biblical times.

In the first section of this chapter citations that imply that some of the unnamed prophets may have been mentally ill are considered. None of the well known great literary prophets, such as Isaiah, Jeremiah, Hosea and the prophets of the Book of 12, suffered from psychotic disorder and the case of Ezekiel, who probably was mentally ill, is described in the previous chapter. It is among the numerous other mostly unnamed prophets that we find suggestions of both acute and chronic mental illness.

In addition, the book *Psyche: The Cult of Souls and Beliefs in Immortality among the Greeks* by Erwin Rhode (1925) has a whole chapter on Dionysiac and Ecstatic religion that gives a detailed account of the prophetic and oracular tradition of ancient Greece, as well as a few references to the insanity of prophets in the (mainly) Greek religious literature of the 8th to 6th centuries BCE, that is, at the same time as the main prophetic era of ancient Israel.

Two delusional disorders, lycanthropy (in the Book of Daniel) and morbid jealousy (in Numbers), that suggest psychotic conditions are also included here. A section on the para-biblical literature follows that gives two cases of possible psychosis in the ancient Egyptian literature as well as a case of possible schizophrenia in the Ugaritic literature dating *circa* 1300 BCE.

## Prophecy and chronic insanity in Israel

The interest here lies with many lesser and unnamed prophets, who had no literary or religious importance. Some but not all of these prophets were ecstatics, and some may also have been mentally ill, as states of psychotic excitement can closely resemble states of religious ecstasy. The distinction between the ordinary ecstatic and the psychotic ecstatic is nowadays based on the presence of other features of schizophrenia which separate those who are mentally ill from those who are ordinary 'uncomplicated religious ecstatics'. Not surprisingly, with the exception of Ezekiel, the Bible does not tell us whether a particular prophet has other schizophrenic features and so this test cannot readily be applied. All we can do is presume that some of these prophets were simple ecstatics who just went home to their families after having danced all day in a state of religious ecstasy, while there were others who were separated from their families and lived in prophetic communes. In these cases the ecstasy may have been rather more than simple religious ecstasy and circumstantial evidence is presented here to suggest that at least some of these prophets may have been mentally ill. Four topics are of relevance to this issue:

(i)   the explicit labelling of madness given to some of the prophets
(ii)  the killing of prophets, which may have resembled the killing of the insane
(iii) the existence of religious regulations to detain the insane
(iv)  encampments near the main religious sanctuaries where groups of prophets lived in communes.

## Evidence that some of the prophets may have been regarded as mad at the time

In 2 Kings 9, the story is told of Elijah instructing one of the prophets in his circle to seek out Jehu, an army commander, and anoint him king. Neither Elijah nor the unnamed prophet is initially described as mad, but when Jehu returns to the camp his fellow officers think that the unnamed prophet must be mad:

> 2 Kings 9[11] When Jehu came back to his master's officers they said to him, 'Is everything alright? *Why did that madman come to you?*' He answered them, 'You know how they babble.'

The Hebrew for 'madman' here is *mesuggah* and is used disparagingly to refer to ecstatic dervish-like behaviour (Cogan and Tadmore, 1985). The fact that the soldiers presumed that the prophet was mad suggests that during this period it was common knowledge that people who called themselves prophets were sometimes mad.

A second, more explicit statement that some of the prophets were mad comes from Hosea.

> 9[7]   The prophet is a fool,
>        the man of the spirit is mad!

The Hebrew for the last line is *hanebi'ii meshugah*, literally 'the prophet is mad', and the NIV translates this as 'the inspired person a maniac'.

A further reference to madmen being quite common at the time also occurs in the David and Saul stories. Thus, when Saul is pursuing David in Judah he escapes to the land of the Philistines and he pretends to be mad in order to obtain asylum with King Achish:

> 1 Sam 21[14] King Achish said to his servants, 'Look, you see the man is mad; why have then you bought him to me? [15]*Do I lack madmen, that you have brought this fellow to play the madman in my presence?* Shall this fellow come into my house?'

His rhetorical question 'Do I lack madmen?' suggests he has quite a lot of madmen in his kingdom, while his follow-up comment, 'Shall this fellow come into my house?', suggests the king may have had some responsibility for the insane within his kingdom.

In his book *The Religion of Israel*, Kaufman (1960) explains:

> by the 9th century prophets are numbered in their hundreds and are found everywhere. After the time of David, ecstatic bands are no longer heard of; in their stead a new phenomenon appears, that of the *Bene' Nebi'im*, the sons of the prophets, and they appear in groups of prophetic orders. They are not ecstatics, nor do they act as mantics or messengers.... In all likelihood the prophets and the *bene nebi'im* were for the *most part psychically abnormal men of wild imagination, visionaries, neurotics, epileptics.* Like men of God everywhere they differed from the rest of the people; sometimes they appeared bruised and bleeding and at other times they ran as if possessed; they were popularly regarded as fools and madmen. (Kaufman, 1960, pp. 275–276)

It may be that within this group of prophets and the sons of the prophets some of the mentally ill of the ancient world are to be found.

Kaufman is suggesting that many of the so-called 'prophets' and the 'sons of the prophets' who roamed ancient Israel were actually either social misfits or frankly mentally ill. This leads on to the question, 'What exactly was the "prophetic frenzy" of the Bible?' Modern survey data of people with diverse psychotic disorders (schizophrenia, schizo-affective disorders, delusional disorder, bipolar disorder, psychotic depression) show that 22–39% of those with a severe psychosis have delusions with religious content (Lukoff *et al.*, 2010). This figure is hardly likely to have been any less in ancient Israel, where the influence of religion on society was very much greater than it is today in the West. It suggests that a large (though unspecified) proportion of those who went around in overactive excited religious states were probably psychotic, with religious mania being a common presentation for a psychosis. This would have been very confusing for the local population at the time because there was no concept of psychosis and a man who went around preaching religion would seemingly be a man of God. However, here and there some observers who thought that some of these religious people were mad, hence the comment of Hosea quoted above.

This is very different from the religious ecstasy that is found in some developing nations today, where the picture is more one of devout religious belief, combined with joy, singing and dancing and so on, and not usually one of psychosis.

## Ancient Greek parallels

The description of groups of prophets roaming the land subject to periodic bouts of ecstasy is much clearer in the ancient Greek literature. Rhodes (1925) writes:

> The worship of Dionysus descended from the North from Boeotia and spread through Thrace and the Peloponnese. It seems as if the women were the first to give in to the invading worship. We are told of the irresistible progress and success of Bacchic dance worship and its exaltation reminds us of similar religious epidemics of more recent times.... A few strange accounts come to us of how such brief attacks of transitory insanity ran through whole cities like infectious epidemics.... The Korybantic form of the malady, which was religious in character, arose from the Phrygian mountains. Those affected by such fevers saw strange figures that correspond to no objects of reality [? visual hallucinations) and heard the sounds of invisible flutes [? auditory hallucinations]. The Dionysian cult was based at the shrine at Delphi, where the priests gave their oracles in a state of 'enthusiasm' or 'possession' by the God.

Such states were deemed to be conditions requiring treatment:

> The ecstatic element was expelled or suppressed by music.... This skill taken up as a special disciplinary process by the physician priesthood.... Cure was effected through an intensification of the Dionysian frenzy.

Saul also uses music as his therapy, but for him this is only for his depressions and not during his manic ecstatic phases.

Men and women began to appear who on their own initiative began to act as intermediaries between the gods and individuals. Apollo assumed the mantle of Dionysis, the enthusiastic, the Bacchic god, and Aeschulus strikingly calls him 'Ivy-crowned Apollo, who more than any other God calls forth in men's souls *the madness that makes the clairvoyant...*'. Is Aeschulus suggesting that, sometimes the prophet is mad? This seemingly took place in the darkness and ferments of the period between the 8th and 6th centuries BCE, before the philosophical period of ancient Greece. This seems to be very similar to the biblical accounts of the numerous self-appointed prophets and false prophets found in ancient Israel during roughly the same historical epoch.

The Sybils and Bakids were not attached to any particular temple and wandered through the land like the previous generation of Homeric omen interpreters (Rhodes, 1925, pp. 282–232). The Sybils, who were important female oracles, were often overcome with *furor divinus* and perhaps this was the same as the Israelite prophetic frenzy. Were these states of simple prophetic ecstasy or was this psychotic excitement? Further descriptions of prophetic *Ekstasis* in the Greek literature are given in Rhodes (1925) and his account has the advantage of providing references to the original sources. Prophecy in both ancient Israel and ancient Greece seems to share many commonalities, such as groups of prophets and group ecstasy, and both literatures include references to the insanity of prophets. There is, however, one important difference: only the Israelites have a tradition of literary prophecy culminating in the great prophets of the Bible, who write extensively on religion, ethics and morality and other social issues. The period of Greek prophecy ended around the 6th century BCE and was replaced by the era of the Greek philosophers, with their writings being almost entirely secular, although their literature seems to have covered similar ground to the Israelite literary prophets while being far more extensive in scope.

## The killing of prophets

Before the advent of asylums, people had no way of managing a dangerous insane person and so it is no surprise that sometimes they were killed. Indeed, such killings have occurred right up until modern times. Deuteronomy has laws against prophets who divine through dreams, and states that these prophets should be killed:

> Dt 13[5] But those prophets or those who divine by dreams shall be put to death for having spoken treason against the Lord your God – who brought you out from the land of Egypt....

Many years later, the book of Chronicles (5th century BCE) records the killing of several prophets. Some (possibly ecstatic or mentally ill) were possessed but others were not.

> 2 Chr 24[20] Then *the spirit of God took possession of Zechariah* son of the priest Jehoiada; he stood above the people and said to them, 'Thus says God: Why do you transgress the commandments of the Lord, so you cannot prosper? Because you have forsaken the Lord, he has also forsaken you.' [21] But they conspired against him, and by the command of the king they stoned him to death in the court of the house of the Lord.

The phrase being 'the spirit of God took possession' suggests a possession state – perhaps no more than simple religious ecstasy, but quite possibly one of psychotic excitement and of religious mania. 2 Chronicles lists other prophets with similar experiences:

> 15[1] The spirit of God came upon Azariah son of Oded.
> 20[14] Then the spirit of the Lord came upon Jahaziel.

Both these prophets were 'possessed' but were not killed.

Jeremiah gives a lengthy diatribe against the false prophets, who he says should be put to death. They are false because they give the people an overly optimistic view of what is to come, and fail to warn the nation of the imminent dangers. Two other prophets, Ahab and Zedekiah, are accused of prophesying a lie and are killed by being given over to the cruel tyrant Nebuchadnezzar, who promptly roasts them in public (Jer 29[21-22]). By contrast, another prophet, Uriah, the son of Shemiah, offers the same grim prophecies as Jeremiah, and King Jehoiakim orders him to be killed. Uriah flees to Egypt, only to be tracked down by Jehoiakim, who 'struck him down with the sword and threw his dead body into the burial place of the common people' (Jer 26[21-24]). Jeremiah himself was nearly killed, but was saved by the intervention of Ahikam, son of Shampam (Jer 26[24]).

Rhodes (p. 300) describes the case in ancient Greece of Hermotimus of Klazomenai, who was among those with the magic gift of prolonged *ekstasis*. His soul could desert his body 'for many years' and on its return from its ecstatic voyages brought with it much mantic lore and knowledge of the future. Eventually, enemies set fire to the tenantless body of Hermotimus when his soul was away, and thereafter his soul never returned again. Might this repeated departure of the soul of Hermotimus serve as a Greek parallel to the delusional wanderings of Ezekiel? And was he murdered because of his insanity?

Prophets in ancient Israel seem to have had a high mortality rate. A prophet might be an ecstatic and possessed, and he might or might not get killed. He might be overly optimistic and a false prophet, or too pessimistic; either way, he might get killed. Internecine fighting between prophetic schools believing themselves to be the true prophets with opposing groups being the false prophets sometimes broke out. A prophet might be detained and placed in the stocks because he was mad. There are frequent references to the 'false prophets' and some of their deaths may have been politically inspired, as the prophets were critics of the establishments of the day. But perhaps also their mental disorder made them more vulnerable. They also had a lowly position in society. Thus, as quoted above, the dead body of the prophet Uriah 'was thrown into the burial place of the common people'. Florid psychotic states are not cited as the reason for the killing, although the word 'possessed' is sometimes used. The manner of their deaths seems to be without any crime being committed or any judicial process being instituted – and they are killed by the mob, sometimes with the complicity of the king.

## Laws to detain the mentally ill

All societies have laws to arrest and detain the mentally ill. Jeremiah tells us of his experiences and provides perhaps the first example of a government directive to detain the insane:

> Jer 29[24] To Shemaiah of Nehelam you shall say: [25] Thus says the Lord of hosts, the God of Israel: In your own name, you sent a letter to all the people who are in Jerusalem, and to the priest Zephaniah son of Maaseiah, and to all the priests, saying, [26] The Lord himself has made you a priest instead of Jehoiada, so that *there may be officers in the house of the Lord to control any madman who plays the prophet, to put him in the stocks and collar.* [27] So why have you not rebuked Jeremiah of Anathoth who plays the prophet for you?

These verses tell us that one of the duties of the officers assigned to the first Temple was the controlling of madmen, a role that the state continues to play to this day in its management of the insane. As a working psychiatrist I derive much comfort from this particular verse. Thus, in my post as a community psychiatrist in a London suburb for nearly 30 years it was part of my job to detain the insane in my particular district, a task I undertook perhaps two or three times a month. I was not an employee of the Jerusalem Temple of the 7th century BCE, but of the NHS in London in the 20th century, and yet these verses tell us something about the sacred origins of such duties. Many will criticise psychiatrists for their actions in depriving the insane of their liberty and for detaining them in hospital. However, this is almost always a highly successful and lifesaving manoeuvre. Unfortunately, it was greatly abused by the Soviet regime in the middle of the 20th century, who used it to control their political opponents and dissidents by locking them up on the grounds that they were insane– but this seems to be exactly the same behaviour and thinking that the priesthood of the Jerusalem Temple showed towards Jeremiah in the 6th century BCE.

## Regulations for Qumran community meetings

The religious life of the Qumran community, who were probably all Essenes, is laid out in the Dead Sea scrolls. One section of these ancient scrolls covers the 'Charter of a Jewish Sectarian Society' and one part of this charter sets out the rules for the behaviour expected of those attending 'public meetings and communal meetings of the chapters' and the sanctions to be applied for flouting these rules (Wise *et al.*, 2005, p. 127):

- whoever speaks foolishness: three months (of exclusion)
- anyone interrupting his companion while in session: 10 days
- anyone who lies down and sleeps in a session of the general membership: 30 days
- anyone who walks about naked in the presence of a comrade, unless he is sick, to be punished by reduced rations for six months
- a man who spits in the midst of a session of the general membership is to be punished by reduced rations for 30 days
- anyone who brings out his penis from beneath his clothing – that is, his clothing is so full of holes his nakedness is exposed – is to be punished by 30 days of reduced rations.
- anyone *who bursts into foolish horse laughter* is to be punished by reduced rations for 30 days.

Extreme and inappropriate laughter can occur in both mania and acute schizophrenia, although uncontrollable laughter does not necessarily signify mental illness. These regulations seem to be about the correct decorum for public meetings, and they set out to punish those who are sexually disinhibited or who seem to be behaving in an insane fashion.

## Ecstatics at the Temple of Serapis in ancient Egypt

Greek papyri concerning the regulations at the religious sanctuary at the Temple of Serapis mention a group of ecstatics labelled the κάτοέχοΐ, who lived in the Temple and might have been detained in the Temple against their will. This is described in the book *Possession, Demoniacal and Other, Among Primitive Races in Antiquity, the Middle Ages and Modern Times* by T. K. Oesterreich (1930, republished 2002). He cites the views of several early-20th-century German Egyptologists, although not all concur with the notion that detention was against their will. Thus K. Sethe advances the hypothesis that the κάτοέχοῖ should not be taken to mean 'possessed' but merely denoted men who did not have the right to leave the sanctuary at Serapis. Basing his views on the records within these Temple papyri, Sethe wrote that certain constellations give rise to disturbances in hearing and speech among men born under their sign, and these men become possessed in the Temple so that they prophesy and fall sick in mind (references here and below in Oesterreich, 2002). Kroll wrote that this was not merely a question of dreams, but seemingly of possession in the true sense of the word, and that it was misfortune in their lives that brought these men to the sanctuary. A differing view was expressed by Wilcken, who rejected the idea of imprisonment to explain the prolonged stay of the κάτοέχοῖ at the Temple and argued for

> an entirely inner relationship of a mystic kind between Serapis and his worshipper. The God holds him, takes possession of him (κάτοέχοῖ) so that he is a possessed of God. We cannot conceive of a lasting ecstasy, for this state often continued for several years. Only the God could liberate him, after which he generally returned to his own country, whereas formerly in his state of sub-jugation he had no rights to leave the precincts of the Temple.

Sudhoff interprets the documents in question thus:

> To be possessed by the God that is what the κάτοέχοῖ are. When he experiences this feeling of possession, the κάτοέχοῖ goes to the Temple to be delivered from the malady or from some other affliction. He sleeps in the Temple and either is directly delivered from the demon of sickness or he receives in sleep the indication of what he must do in order to be cured.

It seems as if these κάτοέχοῖ often stayed for several years at the Temple and only when their state of possession (or mental illness?) left them were they permitted to leave. Their lives seem to have been regulated by the Temple priests. These Greek Egyptian papyri relate to the 2nd century BCE but the suggestion is that the κάτοέχοῖ may have had some kind of chronic mental illness and were held in the Temple at Serapis, sometimes for years. This ancient Greek Temple literature seemingly describes a regime of resi-dential care and detention for the κάτοέχοῖ in ancient Egypt, making these temples the very first true mental health asylums.

It is important to note that all the articles cited above are more than 100 years old and in German, while the papyri they quote from are all in Greek, and so being certain of their meaning may be problematical for a non-classical linguist.

## Where did the prophets live? The significance of the word 'Naioth'

We do not know where members of these prophetic orders lived but King Saul has two encounters with groups of prophets, who infect him with their ecstasy. The first group reside in Gibeath-elohim (the hill of the Lord) and the second encounter was at the Naioth at Ramah. Gibeath corresponds today with the site of Tell-el-ful, north of Jerusalem, first excavated by

Albright in 1924 (and repeatedly since then). It seems to have been a sizeable settlement and may have been Saul's original capital. Saul meets a group of prophets from Gibeath-elohim:

> I Sam 10[5] After that you shall come to Gibeath-elohim, at the place where the Philistine garrison is; there, as you come to the town, you will meet a band of prophets coming down from the shrine with harp, tambourine, flute and lyre playing in front of them; they will be in a prophetic frenzy.

This verse suggests that this particular set of prophets lived as a group at or near the shrine of Gibeath-elohim. This passage ends with Saul going into a prophetic frenzy:

> 10[11] When all who knew him before saw how he prophesied with the prophets, the people said to one another, 'What has come over the son of Kish? Is Saul also among the prophets?' [12]A man of the place answered, 'And who is their father?' Therefore it became a proverb, 'Is Saul also among the prophets?' [13]When his prophetic frenzy had ended, he went home.

Saul behaves like an ecstatic prophet but when the episode is over he goes home. The prophets here do not seem to have a father, nor do they go home. 'Father' may in fact refer to the leader of this group of prophets. Perhaps they were born out of wedlock, but more likely it seems they are separated or alienated from their families of origin, and this is why they do not have a father, and so, unlike Saul, they do not go home. Throughout history, families have commonly rejected relatives who became mad, especially those who developed schizophrenia, and so possibly family alienation also lies behind the phrase of 'who is their father?'

The other site associated with Saul's ecstasy is the Naioth at Ramah.

> I Sam 19 [19] Saul was told, 'David was at Naioth in Ramah'. [20] Then Saul sent David messengers to take David. When they saw the company of prophets in a frenzy, with Samuel standing in charge of them, the spirit of God came upon the messengers of Saul, and they also fell into a prophetic frenzy....

The word *Naoith* does not appear outside this passage (Gordon, 1986, p. 164). Some scholars suspect it may be a plural form of *naweh*, meaning 'a shepherd's dwelling camp'. Here the frenzied prophets seem to live at the '*naoith*' attached to the city of Ramah. Malamat (1962), in his study of Mari society (Mesopotamia 18th century BCE), compares the Hebrew word *naweh* with the Akkadian word *nawum:*

> The concept of *nawum* is central to the tribal organisations mentioned in the Mari documents. A good example of the *nawum* type of settlements may be found in the traditions of the Hebrew Patriarchs who did not dwell in the Canaanite settlements as such, but they pitched their camps on the outskirts and then moved on.... *Very likely the prophetic fraternities of Israel dwelt in such settlements.*

Thus the obscure word *Naoith* referred to in I Sam 19[19] as the dwelling place of a band of prophets is not the proper name of a particular spot at or near

Ramah but is a common name *nawoe(h)* denoting an encampment – in this case situated at Ramah. Gordon(1986, p. 117) writes 'Ecstatic prophets of this sort were inclined to operate in groups *which attached themselves to cult centres.* The cult centres of the time were the great religious shrines'.

The Talmud (Zeb 54b) has '*Naioth*: literally dwellings, a place of seclusion in or near Ramah where Samuel taught his disciples the Torah'. Also, those aspiring to prophecy were trained to purify their thoughts and deeds, to enable the prophetic spirit to rest upon them. J. renders 'in the house of study' (Rosenberg, 1976, p. 163).

Further references to such prophetic encampments are given in tales about Elisha in the book of Kings:

> 2 Kings 6[1] Now the company of prophets said to Elisha, 'As we see, the place where we live under your charge is too small for us'.

The suggestion here is that this particular company of prophets was too large for their current housing and so they asked their leader to find them a bigger place.

Taken together, these very early biblical references all point to communal living by these groups of prophets who were prone to prophetic frenzy, and that these were in encampments often adjacent to the major religious shrines.

The earliest true mental hospitals probably appeared in several sites across the Middle East during the 8th to 9th centuries CE. Okasha (2010) suggests the first Islamic mental hospital was established in Baghdad around 705 CE, but he states that this was modelled on eastern Christian monastic infirmaries, although he gives no further details on these monasteries. In Egypt, Sultan Kalaoon al-Mansour established a general hospital in Cairo in 683 CE; the Kalaoon hospital was by 1284 noted to have separate departments, including one for mental patients. In Syria, to the north of Israel, a mental hospital appeared in Aleppo in the 8th century CE (Wallace and Gach, 2008). Through the influence Arabic medicine and culture in Spain, mental hospitals appeared in Valencia and Seville, from which they gradually spread to northern Europe as well. These mental asylums dating from the 8th to 9th century CE did not appear until at least 1500 years after the biblical texts describing how the encampments (*naioth*) at important religious shrines where fraternities of prophets (?the mentally ill/psychotics) congregated together. This suggests there may be a lengthy pre-asylum history on diverse models of care for the mentally ill (prior to their recognition as suffering from mental illness), and the Bible indicates that the encampments at Ramah and also possibly at Gibeah may have served such a role.

## The lycanthropy of King Nebuchadnezzar II

The Book of Daniel was probably completed in the Maccabean period, around 164 BCE. Chapters 1–6 consist of six court legends, sometimes written in the third-person narrative, which describe the adventures of Jewish heroes in the courts of the Persians. The episode of Nebuchadnezzar's lycanthropy occurs in this first section in the fourth chapter. 'Lycanthropy' in the psychiatric literature refers to a delusion that one has turned into a wolf, but it also covers all delusions that one has turned into any animal, and in the case of Nebuchadnezzar this seems to have been an ox or a cow.

The second half of the book, comprising chapters 7–12, describes a series of apocalypses within the period of the Maccabean revolt. The book is written in two languages, Hebrew and Aramaic, the latter being probably the *lingua franca* of the ancient Near East. Common religious themes join the two sections of the book: God's sovereignty over history and foreign monarchs; the special insight and wisdom given to one devoted to God; and the idea of heroic obedience to God, even to the point of death. The book links two periods Jewish of persecution, the first under Nebuchadnezzar, in the 6th century and probably written in the 5th century, and the second under the Seleucids, by Anthony IV Epiphanes, in the 2nd century BCE, and probably written at that time.

King Nebuchadnezzar II (605–562 BCE) experiences a frightening dream but he cannot understand it. His Babylonian dream interpreters are also at a loss to explain it, and so the Jewish exile Daniel is called in. Selected verses describing the king's dream and his ensuing madness are given below.

> Dn 4⁴ I, Nebuchadnezzar, was living at ease in my home, and prospering in my palace. ⁵ I saw a dream that frightened me; my fantasies in bed and the visions of my head terrified me....
> ¹³ I continued looking, in the visions of my head and as I lay in bed, and there was a holy watcher, coming down from heaven. ¹⁴ He cried out aloud and said 'Cut down the tree and chop off its branches...'.

The text continues to describe the tree and its branches, which are all to be cut down. Daniel explains to the king that this has the symbolic meaning that the king will soon lose his empire and will eventually go mad:

> 4¹⁶ Let his mind be changed from that of a human, and let the mind of an animal be given to him.

The description of Nebuchadnezzar's change into an animal then occurs during a vision. The story continues to describe his fall from grace and transformation into an ox or a cow. This is to be a punishment for his arrogance, a traditional religious motif in the Bible used to humble the powerful and previously also meted out to Saul, David and many others.

> Dn 4²⁸ All this came upon King Nebuchadnezzar. ²⁹At the at the end of 12 months he was walking on the roof of the royal palace of Babylon ³⁰ and the king said, 'Is this not the magnificent Babylon, which I have built as the royal capital by my mighty power and for my glorious majesty?' ³¹ While the words were still on the king's mouth, a voice came from heaven: 'O King Nebuchadnezzar, to you it is declared: The kingdom has departed from you! ³² You shall be driven away from human society, and your dwelling shall be with the animals of the field. You shall be made to eat grass like oxen, and seven times shall pass over you until you have learned that the Most High has sovereignty over the kingdom of mortals and gives it to whom he will'. ³³ Immediately the sentence was fulfilled against Nebuchadnezzar. He was driven away from

human society, *ate grass like oxen* and his body was bathed with the dew of heaven, until *his hair grew as long as eagles' feathers and his nails became like birds' claws.* [34] When that period was over, I, Nebuchadnezzar, lifted my eyes to heaven and my reason returned to me.

The description is both the first and third person and is of a man who leaves polite society and goes into the forest and begins to eat grass like a cow, and grows hairs and claws, and this carries on for a period of 'seven times', which is assumed to be seven years. Afterwards he recovers his sanity. The madness is to be a punishment for his sin of pride in his royal palaces in Babylon.

This biblical account of King Nebuchadnezzar's descent into madness is not now thought to have much in the way of historical veracity. Thus a great deal was recorded in the Babylonian literature about Nebuchadnezzar II's 43-year reign. He was an extremely busy monarch and no seven-year gap exists; nor is there any mention of him being deprived of the throne or going mad or going off to live in a forest. Rather, it seems as if another, much later king, Nabuniad or Nabonides (556–539 BCE), was ill and went off to live in the desert. The Nabonidus Chronicle (see Pinches, 1882) describes how Nabonides left the city of Babylon for several months at a time when he was ill and sojourned in Teima, a remote oasis in the Arabian desert. Documents found among the Dead Sea scrolls in cave 4 confirmed the existence of Nabonides, his illness and his seven-year departure from Babylon, some fragments of which are quoted below:

## The healing of King Nabonides (4Q242)

Fragments 1–3 are the words of the prayer of Nabonides, the King of Babylon, 'the great king, when he was smitten with a severe inflammation in the command of God in Teima'.

> I, Nabonides, was smitten with a severe inflammation lasting for 7 seven years. Because I was thus changed, I prayed to the most high and he forgave my sins. An exorcist – a Jew, in fact a member of the community of exiles – came to me and said, 'Declare and write down this story and so ascribe greatness and glory to the name of God most high'. Accordingly I have written it down. I was smitten with severe inflammation while at Teima by the command of God most high. I continued praying to the gods made of silver and gold and bronze and iron, wood, stone, and clay for I used to think they were really gods. (Cited from Wise *et al.*, 2005, p. 340)

The passage has obvious similarities to Daniel ch. 4: the illness/exile lasts for seven years; the names of both kings begin with similar sounds; and there is a Jewish exorcist/dream interpreter. Scholars have postulated that both Daniel 4 and the Nabonides story drew on some earlier and unknown common source, perhaps written some 200 years previously (Wise *et al.*, 2005). The main difference in the two texts is that Nabonides suffered from an inflammation but Nebuchadnezzar is described as being insane and suffering from lycanthropy.

Nabonides was the fourth successor to Nebuchadnezzar and the last king of Babylon. He relocated himself to Teima, an oasis in the Arabian desert, and he appointed his son Belsharusur as his regent (this is King Belshazzar of the Book of Daniel). After 10 years Nabonides returned to Babylon, only to be overthrown by King Cyrus of the Medes in 539 BCE. The overthrow of Babylonian power must have been a source of joy for the Jews. However, as Nabonides had not been particularly unkind to the Jews during his reign, the ire of the Jewish writers of the day was directed instead at the much-hated Nebuchadnezzar II (Wise *et al.*, 2005; Hartmann and di Lella, 1978).

## Lycanthropy

The condition is rare and refers to a delusional belief that one has become an animal. It may have had its origins in folk tales describing mythological figures such as the gods. For instance, Odin, a Norse god, turns into an eagle, the Roman God Hecuba into a bitch, and Jupiter into a bull, while Actaeon becomes a stag.

In clinical settings, metamorphosis is always delusional. A variety of different animal transformations in delusional states are described, changes into a dog or wolf being the most common and this is lycanthropy. Changes into a cow are known as bo-anthropy. Changes into snakes, bees, frogs and various other animals have been reported in single cases. Zo-anthropy refers to mixtures of animals, such as a cow and a wolf, and this appears to be the case with Nebuchadnezzar, who eats grass like a cow but also grows claws and hairs like an eagle. The text is fairly clear that Nebuchadnezzar experiences a disorder of the mind, as Daniel 4[16] states 'Let his mind be changed from that of a human, and let the mind of an animal be given to him'. Thus the transformation is delusional rather than a true metamorphosis.

Today, lycanthropy is an overall term used to describe *all* the different animal-based delusions and is sensitive to the social conditions of the day.

Most of the cases in the classical era or Middle Ages were religiously or culturally sanctioned. Some people may even have deliberately sought to transform themselves into a wolf by drinking potions, or drinking water from the footpath of a wolf. Others claimed to have fallen victim to magical or diabolical forces. During the Middle Ages there were epidemics of lycanthropy, most notably during the period of the French Inquisition (1560–1630), when more than 30,000 cases were reported. Blom (2013) who reviews the condition (56 cases in the world literature from 1850 to the present day) and provides a modern perspective. In his series there were 34 females and 22 males and almost all of the cases had a psychiatric diagnosis. Thus schizophrenia was present in 25%; psychotic depression in 23%; bipolar disorder in 19%; and psychotic disorder NOS (not otherwise specified) in 13%. Full remission was achieved in 36%, and partial remission in 46%, after standard electroconvulsive therapy (ECT) and psychotropic medication. Mortality rates were high, at 13%, and the causes of death were starvation, TB, suicide or execution.

Sims (2010, p. 259) considers the differential diagnosis of the lycanthropy mentioned in Daniel 4 to be most likely bipolar affective disorder with a current episode of mania with psychotic symptoms, and as a second alternative he proposes schizo-affective disorder, but rejects an organic brain psychosis. In fact, though, there is no evidence in Daniel 4 for depression or mania, making both bipolar and schizo-affective disorder unlikely, whereas the text presents the lycanthropy as an isolated delusion, making delusional disorder a more probable explanation.

In a fascinating paper entitled 'Lycanthropy alive in Babylon: the existence of an archetype', Younis and Mohselhy (2009) report their visit to the southern Iraqi province of Babylonia where Nebuchadnezzar II had developed his lycanthropy, and they searched the psychiatric records of two hospitals in the region for similar cases. Over a 20-year period they found 8 cases of lycanthropy, indicating that the condition described in Daniel 4 still continues to appear in modern Babylonia. Seven of these cases came from a rural rather than an urban environment, which the authors suggest may be due to the closer contact with farm animals. Two of their cases had schizophrenia and 6 cases had psychotic depression with lycanthropic delusions. All the patients in their series had severely threatening life events and major losses prior to the onset of their psychosis. These authors also cite a much earlier case of bo-anthropy in Babylonia, reported by the famous Arab physician Avicenna (980–1037). His patient claimed to be a cow and bellowed like one. In an attempt to cure him Avicenna describes an early attempt at prokaleptic (confontational) therapy. Thus Avicenna bound his patient's hands and feet and then told the patient that a butcher was about to come and slaughter him. Avicenna then left the room and later returned dressed in a butcher's outfit and proclaimed to the cow (the patient) that he was too lean to slaughter and had to be fattened up. He then untied the patient, who promptly fled. He began to eat enthusiastically and gained strength, and was completely cured of his lycanthropy.

With regard to the biblical case, Nabonides is said to suffer from ' inflammation' and not lycanthropy; Nebuchadnezzar was too busy to have had any sort of mental illness during his lengthy reign, nor is any recorded, so neither did he have lycanthropy. Rather, it must have been some other person who suffered from this delusion but who was familiar to the writers of Daniel 4. The Jewish writers of the day, perhaps overjoyed at the fall of Babylon, would have known that the king at the time, Nabonides, had been ill. Then, in an act of literary vengeance, perhaps they placed this illness onto Nebuchadnezzar II, who had been a cruel and hated torturer of the Jews. To add insult to injury, they changed his illness from one of a simple inflammation to one of insanity, and moreover gave him one of the most degrading insane delusions they knew of, namely lycanthropy. While this is perhaps only speculation, we can nevertheless conclude that the rare and strange delusion of lycanthropy seems to have been known in the ancient world.

## The *sotah* and morbid jealousy

Brichto (1975) writes that there are few texts in the OT that give more discomfort to exegetes and translators than that describing the *sotah*, a harrowing religious ritual, presided over by a priest, that was performed on a woman suspected of adultery, as described in the Book of Numbers. The passage begins with the report of the husband:

Num 5$^{12}$ ... If any man's wife goes astray and is unfaithful to him, [13] if a man has had intercourse with her but it is hidden from her husband, so that she is undetected though she has defiled herself, and there is no witness against her since she was not caught in the act; [14] if a spirit of jealousy comes on him and he is jealous of his wife who has herself defiled herself; *or if a spirit of jealousy comes on him and he is jealous of his wife, though she has not defiled herself,* [15] then the man shall bring his wife to the priest.

It is noteworthy that some more recent translations of the Bible use the word 'suspicion' instead of 'spirit of jealousy' in verse 15:

if he has a fit of suspicion, suspecting his wife even though she may not have defiled herself, he must take his wife before the priest. (Moffat Bible, 1972)

or if he is jealous or suspects her even though she is not impure – then he is to take his wife to the priest. (New International Version; Kohlenberger, 1987)

or if this spirit of suspicion comes over him and makes him suspicious of his wife even when she is innocent – the man will bring his wife before the priest. (Jerusalem Bible, 1966)

Brichto (pp. 67–68) writes:

our argument seems to culminate in something of a conundrum. A jealous husband, possessing not a scintilla of evidence against his wife, is asked to subject her to a test in which all the cards are stacked in her favour.... The author seems to have known what he was doing; he gave weight to a stylistic charade of pomp and ceremony in which the tragic figure of the accused wife seems to hold centre stage whilst the cognoscenti in the audience have their attention fixed on the *clownish figure of the insanely jealous husband* hovering in the wings.

Brichto is a biblical scholar and not a psychiatrist but he infers that at least in part this bizarre ritual is about the insanely jealous husband and this is akin to the modern concept of morbid jealousy. DSM-5 describes 'delusional disorder, jealousy sub-type' as follows:

The central theme of the person's delusion is that his or her spouse or lover is unfaithful. This belief is arrived at without due cause and is based on incorrect inferences supported by small bits of evidence (e.g. disarrayed clothing or spots on the sheets) which are collected and used to justify the delusion. The individual with the delusion usually confronts the spouse or lover and attempts to intervene in the imagined infidelity e.g. by restricting the spouse's autonomy, secretly following the spouse, investigating the imagined lover, or attacking the spouse. (DSM-5, 2013, p. 325)

The ancient Israelites also seemed to have recognised that the suspicion of infidelity was a serious matter and that even *if such suspicions were false,* suspicious men needed urgent mollification. In the UK today about two women are murdered every week and jealousy and suspected infidelity, whether factually based or not, is the most common precipitant.

Laws about infidelity also appear in the Code of Hammurabi (LH, *circa* 1750 BCE) which precedes the Book of Numbers by more than a 1000 years.

LH 131 is about suspicion on the part of the husband. LH 132 concerns public suspicion of the infidelity, and this was taken more seriously. Israelite law corresponds to LH 131.

The circumstance of the *sotah* is repeated in Numbers 5$^{29-31}$:

> $^{29}$ This is the law in cases of jealousy, when a wife, while under her husband's authority, goes astray and defiles herself, $^{30}$ *or when a spirit of jealousy comes on a man* and he is jealous of his wife; then he shall set the women before the Lord, and the priest will apply this entire law to her. $^{31}$ The man shall be free from iniquity, but the woman shall bear her iniquity.

Thus even if the women is innocent the husband is not punished for making such false accusations. The woman is humiliated by having to undergo the ritual, whether innocent or guilty, but is subjected to punishment only if is she is guilty. The text does not state exactly what will happen to her but only states 'shall bear her iniquity'. Capital punishment was typically the punishment for adulterous wives in the ancient Middle East – just as it is in some places like Iran today. However, no cases of women being killed for adultery are given in the OT and certainly none is reported after the *sotah* ritual. An abbreviated version of the actual ritual is given below:

> Num 5$^{17}$ The priest shall take holy water in an earthen vessel and take some dust that is on the floor of the tabernacle and put it into the water. $^{18}$ The priest shall set the woman before the Lord, dishevel the woman's hair, and place in her hands the grain offering of remembrance, which is the grain offering of jealousy.... $^{21}$ let the priest make the woman take the oath of the curse and say to the woman – 'the Lord make you an execration and an oath among your people, when the Lord makes your uterus drop, your womb discharge; $^{22}$ now may this water that brings the curse enter your bowels and make your womb discharge, your uterus drop!' And the woman shall say 'Amen. Amen'.
> $^{27}$ When he [the priest] has made her drink the water [the water of bitterness], then, if she has defiled herself and has been unfaithful to her husband, the water that brings the curse shall enter into her and cause bitter pain, and her womb shall discharge, her uterus drop, and the women shall become an execration among her people. $^{28}$ But if the woman has not defiled herself and is clean she will be immune and be able to conceive children.

In the ancient world the blame for the husband's suspicions was placed entirely on the woman (even when she was innocent), who, as a consequence, had to bear a most awful punishment. This was to undergo the *sotah*, the ritual described above and, if she had defiled, in this ordeal her womb would fall out of her vagina. Most biblical scholars believe this corresponds to a prolapse of the womb, where in severe cases the uterus can fall out through the vagina. A quick look at the symptoms and severe social consequences of uterine prolapse provides some clues as to how this very strange ordeal may have come about.

## Uterine prolapse

The main symptom of uterine prolapse is urinary incontinence. This can occur at any time but particularly on standing or on coughing. A meta-analysis of uterine prolapse by Walker and Gunesekra (2015) of 30 studies in the developing world (i.e. where there is little in the way of treatment) found an overall prevalence of 19.7%, with a peak in women aged around 45. Urinary incontinence was the main and most distressing symptom, being present in 28.7% of cases, and 6.9% also had faecal incontinence. Additional symptoms included uncomfortable feelings in the vagina, back pain, poor sleep, low energy and impairment of sexual function. In a Nepalese study (Shrestha *et al.*, 2011) key risk factors included extensive physical work during pregnancy as well as after delivery, multiparity and the use of unskilled birth attendants – all conditions that would have been present in ancient Israel. These workers also found that for the milder levels of uterine prolapse (where the uterus had descended into the vagina), even if symptoms were present most women tended not to seek help. However, once the uterus became visible outside the vagina, then the women became desperate and sought emergency medical help. Measures of its effects on quality of life, marriage, social and family relationships, and economic activity showed increasing impairment with increasing severity of symptoms, with shame being understandably associated with the symptoms of urinary and faecal incontinence, to the extent that the affected women were very reluctant to talk about their problems. The condition is not usually fatal but very distressing. Medical treatments in ancient Israel were lacking and so the picture that appertained in ancient times was probably similar to that described in modern Nepal where medical facilities are very poor. It now becomes possible to explain how the *sotah* arose.

The *sotah* describes the linking of two common but unrelated devastating medical disorders, namely female uterine prolapse and male morbid jealousy. How could such a bizarre linkage come about? Brichto (1975) argues that there was only one priest who wrote about the *sotah*, mainly on the grounds that it is so bizarre and there is nothing like it elsewhere in the Judaeo-Christian literature, nor indeed in any other religion of the world. This particular priest must have been a medically observant person. So how did he think?

A *sitz im leben* (place in life) explanation concerning the many roles of the priesthood may be helpful here. In the absence of any doctors, the priests of the ancient world often assumed many other functions and among these was sometimes a quasi-medical role. Thus in Leviticus there are extensive tracts written by priests on various skin lesions, Hannah consults the priest Eli about her infertility, and here in the *sotah* the priest reports on the causes of prolapsed wombs.

A prolapse of the womb would have been as common then as it today. The condition is described in the Egyptian medical literature and is mentioned three times in the Kahun Medical Papyrus (*circa* 1800 BCE), discovered by Flinders Petrie in 1889. It is also the first gynaecological condition found on the Ebers Papyrus, a large Egyptian medical text dated around 1550 BCE. This is all long before biblical times and the Book of Numbers.

In biblical times, women with severe prolapse (the womb hanging out of the vagina) would have rushed to see the nearest available healer/authority figure and this would have been the priest. The priest who saw these women would have empathised with their distress, and be shocked when he saw a womb hanging out, but also puzzled as to its cause. It was so awful that to him it must have represented some terrible punishment from God. So what had these women done wrong? The only available explanation for medical conditions at the time was that sin caused sickness, so these women must have committed some terrible sin!

Because prolapse occurs as a result of perineal muscle damage as a result of childbirth, all the women who presented with prolapse would have previously borne children *and therefore been married*. Of all the sins that married women commit, surely, this priest must have thought, infidelity is the most heinous. At the same time, as part of his pastoral duties this priest was seeing many enraged jealous men who were accusing their wives of being unfaithful. Local gossip would also confirm that marital infidelity was rife in his parish, just as it is today. In a flash of genius this one priest put together his medical observations on prolapsed wombs together with the irate jealous husbands he encountered and concluded that some of these men may have been right about their unfaithful wives. This explained to him the many prolapsed wombs that he encountered in his pastoral work. Probably at this point other writers joined in because not all these women were guilty of infidelity and so a test was needed to distinguish the guilty from the innocent and this was to be the *sotah* ritual. It is noteworthy that all the elements of the ritual can be found in the literature of other ancient Near Eastern cultures (see Levine, 1993, pp. 205–212) and so the ritual itself is probably not original, but the linking of the prolapsed womb to the morbidly jealous husband is unique. The above may only be speculation but it provides a possible explanation for the strange linkage between uterine prolapse and morbid jealousy within a religious ritual. The direction of the *sotah* ritual in the Book of Numbers is:

- Suspicion of infidelity → report wife to the priest → drink the bitter water → womb drops out

However, the ritual can be much more readily understood if the order is reversed:

- Prolapsed womb → terrible punishment from God → must be due to sin → worst possible sin is infidelity → suspicious men are often correct → need to devise a test of guilt → *sotah* ritual.

Although the *sotah* seems at first glance to be misogynistic and degrading to women, it may have acted in their favour by offering some protection from their insane deluded husbands. Thus the jealous husband complains to the priest, who takes his suspicions seriously. He humiliates the woman in front of her husband, by dishevelling her hair and making her drink some bitter water, and this serves to reassure the jealous spouse that someone was taking his suspicions/delusions seriously. This would diminish the severity and associated anger of these delusions and hence decrease the risks of marital violence and spousal murder. When it came to the woman drinking the bitter water, this never caused a uterine prolapse because no cases are recorded of this actually happening, either in the Bible or anywhere else.

We should not be surprised at this because uterine prolapse is the result of difficult childbirth and multiparity – not drinking funny water! The *sotah* ritual may have worked as a way of mollifying angry jealous husbands in early biblical times. By the time of the second Temple, the practice had fallen into disuse and Rabbi Johannan ben Zakkai (30 BCE to 90 CE), a famous sage and contributor to the Mishnah, abolished the ordeal altogether (Milgrom, 1990, p. 43).

## References to psychotic disorders in other ancient Near Eastern literature

There are very few references to serious mental illness in the literature of the ancient world. In this section, two citations from the ancient Egyptian literature are included, as well as a description of an acute psychotic episode in the Kingdom of Ugarit, in what is now northern Syria. The last dates from around 1300 BCE and may be the first reported case of schizophrenia.

### *The Journey of Wenamon (after Simpson, 2003)*

This is presented on a papyrus of the 21st dynasty (*circa* 11th century BCE). Wenamon was a representative of King Amon Re and he voyaged in the Syrian seas. The papyrus gives an account of all his adventures and is a secular document. It tells us he was robbed at the port of Dor, a Philistine city on the northern coast of Palestine, and then took refuge in the port of Byblos for 29 days, until the Prince of Byblos ordered him to leave his harbour. The account includes an episode on the boat when a young member of the crew suddenly went mad.

> Now when he offered to his Gods, the God took possession of a lad from the circle of his boys and put him in an ecstatic state, he (the ecstatic) told him 'Bring the God up and bring the envoy who is carrying him'. *For when the youth became ecstatic that night,* I located on to a freighter heading for Egypt and had already loaded all my possessions onto it so as to prevent another evil eye from seeing the God. I was waiting till darkness for that I might see the God. (Simpson, 2003, p. 118)

The tale continues to describe all the maritime adventures of Wenamon. The reference to ecstasy here is very brief, and appears only as an incidental in the tale of Wenamon, who, because he became frightened of the evil eye, seems to have jumped ship and switched to another boat bound for Egypt immediately after this crew member developed his ecstasy. There is little further comment in the Egyptology literature as to what this ecstasy of the crew member might have been. A footnote in Pritchard (1969) suggests this might be epilepsy but an acute manic or psychotic episode is more likely.

### *The Bentresh stela (after Simpson, 2003, p. 361)*

This stela is in the Louvre in Paris. It dates from the 4th century BCE but draws on legendary material from the period of Ramses II (*circa* 13th century BCE) and concerns a hostile spirit or ghost who inhabits a princess in the land of Bakhtan, a land which is otherwise unknown.

> [O]ne came to say to his Majesty that a messenger of the Prince of Bakhtan has come with many gifts for the Queen; then he spoke kissing the ground before his Majesty and said 'I have come to you concerning Bentresh the younger sister of Queen Neferure, a malady has pervaded her body, may your Majesty send a wise man to examine her'.
>
> The king said 'Bring me one who is skilled in his mind who can write with his fingers'.
>
> So the royal scribe Tothemheb came before his Majesty and his Majesty commanded that he should go to Bakhtan with the messenger. So the wise man (Tothemheb) arrived in Bakhtan and he found Bentresh in the condition of one who has a ghost. He found in her an enemy with whom he could contend. The Prince of Bakhtan sent word again before his Majesty's command and he commanded that a God be brought to contend with the ghost. Then Khonsu-in-Thebes-Neferhotep was conducted to Khonsu-the-Authority, the great God who expels wandering spirits. He reached Bakhtan after the completion of a journey of one year and five months and he went to the place where Bentresh was. Then he made magical protection for the daughter of the Prince of Bakthan and she was well at once.

This seems to be a tale of a mysterious possession by a ghost. The relatives are very distressed and seek help from the supreme King of Egypt. A clever scribe, Tothemheb, who can write with his fingers, is summoned and asked to visit the afflicted princess. He makes a diagnosis of 'ghost possession' and then calls on another god, Khonsu-the-Authority, to effect a cure. It is all first-rate teamwork!

## A case of possible schizophrenia in Ugarit

In 1928, a farmer in north-west Syria (near the coast, around 12 km from Latakia), while ploughing his field dislodged the top of a stone tomb. This turned out to be the roof of a burial mound of the Mycenaean type, now known as the Tel at Ras Shamra. Within this burial site there was a vast treasure trove of ancient tablets in cuneiform, hieroglyphic and alphabetic scripts and these were written in seven ancient languages: Akkadian, Cypro-Minoan, Egyptian, Hittite, Hurrian, Sumerian and Ugaritic – the last language hitherto being unknown. Ugaritic was one of the very earliest alphabetic languages; indeed, it may have been the original proto-Canaanite language and hence the first alphabetic language from which both the Hebrew and Greek alphabets and hence ultimately the English alphabet are derived. This whole body of literature is now known as the Ras Shamra collection and the Ugaritic texts in this collection have been reliably dated to the Bronze Age, somewhere between 1200 and 1500 BCE. Excavations in northern Syria have continued more or less continuously since then and in 1978, at a nearby village, Ras Ibn Hani, a satellite of the Bronze Age city of Ugarit (modern Ras Shamra), another important find was made, of a text entitled 'An incantation for the exorcism of a possessed adolescent' (text KTU 1.169; also known as find number RIH 78/20). It was first translated into French by Cacquot (1979) and has attracted considerable interest among Ugaritic scholars but hitherto has been unknown to psychiatry. Although the tablet has only 16 lines, the patient it reports on is considered to be insane and his main psychotic symptoms are described in this incantation. In the passage below, the English translation by N. Wyatt (2002) is given on the left and the possible psychiatry on the right. Numbers on the left are the line numbers on the original tablet. The brackets [ ] indicate missing letters and words which have been guessed.

| | | |
|---|---|---|
| 1 | Exorcising the demons of an adolescent. | Title: A case of Demon Possession |

TO THE DEMON

| | | |
|---|---|---|
| 2 | May the w[ord] of Baal expel you, | Prayer to Baal for the Demon to go |
| | may it expel you so that you come out | |
| | at the voice of the exorcist. | At the command of the exorcist |
| 3 | Like smoke through a chimney, | the demon should disappear quickly |
| | like a snake into a green tree, | like smoke out of a chimney |
| 4 | like goats to a summit, | |
| | like lions to a lair, | |

TO THE STAFF

| | | |
|---|---|---|
| | Wand, rouse yourself! | The magic staff of the exorcist |
| | And draw near, wand! | ? to the demon |
| | May you be amiss as to your back, | ? Possible self-mutilation |
| 6 | and may you be ill with regard | |
| | to your face! | ? Also possible self-mutilation |
| 7 | May you eat the bread of fasting; may | Not eating ? loss of appetite |
| | you drink mere drops without a cup, | Not drinking ? thirst |
| 8 | in the heights, in the water-meadows, | |
| | in darkness, in the sanctuary. Thus, | |
| 9 | O sorcerers, O demons, | Appeal to the demons |
| 10 | May Horon expel (your) familiars, | Horon will expel your |
| | and the Divine Assistant (your) | |
| | acquaintances. | Acquaintances – the other demons |

TO THE PATIENT

| | | |
|---|---|---|
| | Depart! | Command to the demons to go |
| 11 | Let no words of scorn bring (you) down; | Derogatory voices causing the low |
| 12 | let not your tongue stammer; | mood; Stammering and |
| | let no dribbling affect you! | dribbling ?causing raving. |
| 13 | May the God clothe you, | ?stripping naked; God will |
| | May the God put a garment on you, | heal you by clothing you |
| 14 | (turning) into a man | The man will be cured |
| | and one who has breath on earth, | |
| 15 | the madman into a son of man. | The patient was a madman |
| | from delirium restored, | he had delirium |
| 16 | lo, by the breath of Athirat | Athirat: Goddess and wife, |
| | | the Great Lady of El; |
| 17 | in the h[eart] may you be moulded. | |
| | I shall recognise you [ ] | I can recognise the demon |

TO THE DEMON

18  [To the] house (to which) I come,
    you shall not come,                    The demon is forbidden
19  [in the dwelling in which I dwell]     to return to this house
    you shall not dwell!

Fleming (1981) writes that KTU.1.169 is neither a mythic story nor a prayer, but is a spell directed to the attacking sorcerer, commanding his departure. The spell appears to be spoken by the *ṯʿy*, an Ugaritic official not usually associated with incantations and healing. The young man is described as 'mad' or 'strange'. The text explicitly states that this is a case of madness and provides considerable detail about what precisely the purported demons are doing to the young man and hence the poem gives a brief catalogue of his symptoms.

Gross observable disorders of behaviour are reported. He is delirious and said to be raving and dribbling and is described as being insane. He gets undressed and seems to be naked and those around pray to the gods to clothe him again and once clothed this will signify he is cured. He seems to be hurting his own body, suggesting self-harming. There is evidence that he is hearing scoffing (?derogatory) voices and this seems to send him down in mood, possibly into depression. Disturbances in sleep, appetite and thirst are also observed. The picture is of an acute psychotic episode and so assigning a label of 'acute psychosis' seems reasonable.

Those around seem him seem to be very worried by his condition, to the extent that an official of the cult (the officiant/exorcist) is called in to perform an exorcism. Demon possession is held to be the cause of this man's affliction and the incantation prayer of the exorcist is directed at getting rid of the demon, as this will lead to his cure. The exorcist invokes the assistance and the powers of four important and powerful gods, El, Baal, Athirat and Horon, to try to get rid of the demons. El was the chief god in the Canaanite pantheon and in some texts Baal was his son. El and Baal are often associated with the bull in Ugaritic texts, as a symbol both of strength and fertility, and both gods also appear in the Old Testament. Athirat is the earth mother goddess and is both the sister and wife of El and is known for her kindness towards her many children. Horon has healing powers and is able to cure snakebite by removing the power of its poison, and so may be able to help in this case of possession. To call on the assistance of so many powerful deities implies that the plight of this young man must have been fairly desperate, or in modern terminology he seems to have elicited considerable 'therapeutic concern' among those around him.

A young man presenting with such an acute psychotic episode today is generally assigned a differential diagnosis of acute schizophrenia, schizoaffective disorder, mania, a transient psychotic disorder or occasionally an organic psychosis. Probably it would be a futile exercise to assign such 20th-century diagnostic refinements to this ancient text, as the clinical data required to clarify the differential diagnosis is lacking.

This account precedes the biblical account of Ezekiel and his illness, and of any Greek record of insanity, by at least 600 years, and is the only possible description of a case of schizophrenia in the second millennium BCE. It may therefore be the earliest description of schizophrenia in the world literature.

## Concluding remarks

The main purpose of this chapter is to document any evidence of severe chronic psychotic illness in the ancient world and refute the argument that schizophrenia did not exist in ancient times. This evidence is summarised in Table 9.1.

Why should this be important? Edward Hare (1988), writing about the statistically confirmed dramatic rise in the admission rates for insanity in the 19th century, claimed his data supported the 'recency hypothesis' for schizophrenia, originally suggested by Torrey (1980), which proposed that this rise was explained in part by a real increase in the incidence of cases of young-onset schizophrenias during the 19th century. Although accepting that much of this rise was also due to social changes as a result of industrialisation, as previously proposed by Cooper and Sartorius (1977), Hare argued that because this increase in hospital admissions was very large it could not be *solely* accounted by the adverse social consequence of urbanisation and industrialisation. Torrey had argued that such fluctuations in prevalence,

**Table 9.1** Indirect evidence for chronic psychotic illness in the first and second millennium BCE

| Item | Citation | Century BCE |
|---|---|---|
| Prophets are sometimes mad | 2 Kings 9[11]; Hos 9[7]; 2 Sam 21[13] | 8th |
| Prophetic ecstasy and *furor divinus* | 1 and 2 Samuel; Rhodes (1925 Greek literature) | 6th |
| Killing of the prophets | 2 Chr 24[20]; Jer 26[23]; Jer 29[21-22] and others | 5th |
| Killing of Greek prophets | Rhodes (1925) | ?6th |
| Spirit possession by the prophets | 2 Sam 21[13]; 2 Chr 24[20] and more | 10th and 5th |
| Temple officials to detain the insane | Jer 29 [24] | 7th |
| Qumran regulations on decorum in public meetings | | 2nd |
| Possible detention of ecstatics at Serapis | Oesterreich, pp. 151–157 | 2nd |
| Prophetic encampments | 1 Sam 10[5]; 1 Sam 19[19]; 2 Kings 6[1] | 11th |
| Egyptian literature | Bentresh stela (Simpson, 2003) | 4th |
| Egyptian literature | Journey of Wenamon (Simpson, 2003) | 11th |
| Ugaritic literature | The demons of an adolescent (Wyatt, 2002) | 14th |

which are known to occur for infectious diseases, offered some support for a possible viral aetiology or at least viral contribution to schizophrenia. Hare (p. 127) admits that the 'recency hypothesis' itself rests on what he called 'flimsy evidence'. In this chapter, although no single item when taken on its own, is sufficiently convincing to prove that severe chronic mental illness existed in ancient Israel, when all the evidence from this chapter is taken together it seems as if psychosis and severe chronic mental illness must have existed in biblical times and indeed was probably quite common. Schizophrenia does not seem to be a new disease and the historical data presented here do not offer support for the 'recency hypothesis' and hence the viral theory of causation.

# References

Blom, J. D. (2013) Why doctors cry wolf: a systematic review on the literature of clinical lycanthropy. *History of Psychiatry*, 25(1) 97–102.

Brichto, H. C.(1975) The case of the Sotah and a reconsideration of Biblical Law. *Hebrew Union College Annual* 46: 55–70.

Caqout, A. (1979) Ras Ibn Hani 78/20. *Annuaire du Collège de France 79* . Resume de cours et travaux, Annee Scolarire.

Cogan, M. and Tadmor, H. (1985) *The Anchor Bible II Kings. A New Translation with Introduction and Commentary*. New York: Doubleday and Company.

Cooper, J. E. and Sartorius, N. (1977) Cultural and temporal variations in schizophrenia: A speculation on the importance of industrialisation. *British Journal of Psychiatry*, 130: 50–55.

Evans, K., McGrath J. and Milns, R. (2003) Searching for schizophrenia in ancient Greek and Roman literature: a systematic review. *Acta Psychiatrica Scandanavica* 107 (5), 323–332.

Fleming, D. E. (1981) The voice of the incantation priest (RIH 78/20) *Ugarit-Forschungen*, 23, 141–54.

Gordon, R. P. (1986) *I and II Samuel: A Commentary*. Carlyle: Paternoster Press.

Hare, E. H. (1988) *On the History of Lunacy: The 19th Century and After*. London: Gabbay.

Hartmann, L. F. and Di Lella, A. A. (1978) *The Anchor Bible: The Book of Daniel. A New Translation with Notes and Commentary*. Garden City: Doubleday.

Kaufman, Y. (1960)*The Religion of Israel* . Chicago: Chicago University Press.

Kohlenberger, III, J. R. (1987) *The Interlinear NIV Hebrew–English Old Testament*. Grand Rapids, Michigan: Zondervan.

Jerusalem Bible (1966) London: Darton Longman and Todd.

Levine, B. A. (1993) *The Anchor Bible Numbers 1–20. A New Translation with Commentary*. New York: Doubleday.

Lukhoff, D., Cloninger, R., Galanter, M., *et al.* (2010) Religious and spiritual considerations in Psychiatric Diagnosis: Considerations for DSM-5 Chapter 4.6 ,pp 423–444 in *Religion and Psychiatry: Beyond Boundaries*, editors Peter Verhagen, Herman Von Praag, Juan Lopez-Ibor, John Cox and Driss Moussaoui. Chichester: John Wiley.

Malamat, A. (1962) Mari and the Bible: Some patterns of tribal organisation and institutions. *Journal of the American Oriental Society* 82: 143–150.

Milgrom, J. (1990) *The JPS Torah commentary Numbers*. Philadelphia: Jewish Publication Society.

Moffat Translation of the Bible (1972) London: Hodder and Stoughton.

Pinches, T. G. (1882) The Nabonidus Chronicle. *Transactions of the Society of Biblical Archaeology* 7, pp. 153–169.

Oesterreich, T. K. (1930) *Possession demoniacal and other, among primitive races in antiquity, the middle ages and modern times*. 1st edition 1930; 8th edition republished 2002. London: Kegan Paul Trench and Trubner.

Okasha, A. (2010) Religion and Mental Health in Islam. Chapter 2.3 pp. 119–242. In *Religion and Psychiatry: Beyond Boundaries* Editors Peter Verhagen, HermanVon Praag, Juan Lopez-Ibor, John Cox and Driss Moussaoui. Chichester: John Wiley.

Pritchard, J. B. (1969) *Ancient Near Eastern texts relating to the Old Testament. (ANET)* Princeton: Princeton University Press, 3rd edition.

Rhode, E. (1925) *Psyche: The Cult of Souls and beliefs in Immortality among the Greeks.* Translated from the German 8th edition by W. B. Hillis. Originally Published 1925 by Kegan Paul, Trench and Trubner Co Ltd. Republished (2006) Eugene, Oregon: Wipf & Stock.

Rosenberg, A. J. (1976) *The Book of 1 Samuel. A New English translation of the Text, Rashi and a Commentary Digest.* Brooklyn. New York: Judaica Press.

Shrestha, B., Onta, S., Choulagai, B., *et al.* (2015). Uterine prolapse and its impact on quality of life in the Jhaukhel-Duwakot Health Demographic Surveillance Site, Bhaktapur, Nepal. *Global Health Action.* 2015 Aug 10;8:28771. doi: 10.3402/gha.v8.28771.

Simpson, W. K. (2003) *The Literature of Ancient Egypt.* Newhaven: Yale University Press.

Sims, A. (2010) Religion and Psychopathology: Psychosis and Depression. Chapter 3.3, pp. 253–270, in *Religion and Psychiatry: Beyond Boundaries* Editors Peter Verhagen, Herman Von Praag, J., Lopez-Ibor, J., Cox, J. and Driss Moussaoui. Chichester: John Wiley.

Torrey, E. F. ( 1980) *Schizophrenia and Civilization* New York: Jason Aronson.

Walker, G. J. and Gunasekera, P. (2011) Pelvic organ prolapse and incontinence in developing countries: review of prevalence and risk factors. *International Urogynecology Journal.* 22: 127–35.

Wallace, E. and Gach, J. (2008) *History of Psychiatry and Medical Psychology* New York: Springer.

Wise, M., Abegg, M. and Cook, E. (2005) *The Dead Sea Scrolls.* New York: Harper One.

Wyatt, N. (2002) *Religious texts from Ugarit,* 2nd edition revised. London: Sheffield Academic Press.

Younis, A. A., and Mosehly (2009) Lycanthropy alive in Babylon: The existence of an archetype. *Acta Psychiatrica Scandinavica* 119(2) 161–164.

# Chapter 10

# Proverbs and personality disorders: male types of antisocial personality disorder

The Book of Proverbs forms part of the Wisdom literature of the Old Testament. The title, Proverbs, derives from the Septuagint's *Paroimiai Solōmōntas*, which corresponds to the Hebrew *mišlê s'lomoh*, which means the 'Proverbs of Solomon', abbreviated to *Mišlê* in modern Hebrew versions. The early Christian writers referred to the book as 'Wisdom' or 'All Virtuous Wisdom' and in the Hebrew canon Proverbs is found in the third division, known as the *K'tubîm* (writings), which also include Psalms, Job and Ecclesiastes (Whybray, 1990, p. 3).

The prologue and opening verses set out the purpose of the book, which is addressed to the 'young' and the 'simple' in the hope that they will be able to acquire wisdom, or *Hochma*. This is not primarily a religious construct, but describes how, through the power of intellect, reason and the acquisition of experience, a person can be helped to better navigate through the vicissitudes of life. Good and worthy qualities are extolled, while bad and antisocial behaviours are condemned as 'folly', and this is accompanied by dire warnings that such bad ways are not to be emulated. The psychiatric interest lies more in the description of wickedness and folly than in the delineation of wisdom, because the descriptions of the 'fools' of the OT show a remarkable resemblance to the features of antisocial personality disorder as found in the contemporary psychiatric literature, as well as in the real life of our psychiatric wards and prisons.

Crenshaw summarises the concept of wisdom as it was understood in the ancient world:

> The search for specific ways to ensure personal well-being in everyday life, to make sense of extreme adversities and to transmit this knowledge to successive generations ... within the Hebrew bible this takes several different forms: advice usually from parents to children, brief sayings, sometimes longer instructions, observations aimed at labelling things and expressing judgments on different types of character. Some of this is achieved through literary devices such as the personification of wisdom as for example in Lady Wisdom but there is much debate, diatribe, catalogues of items, poems and occasional prayers. (Crenshaw, 1998, pp. 1–16)

The realms covered by the Wisdom literature of Israel, Egypt and other ancient Near Eastern nations were family life, personal morality, contented marriage, having children who are a source of joy to their parents, and avoiding the excesses of alcohol and sexual depravity because of their harmful and destructive effects. Much of the book is devoted to describing 'wise' behaviour in society and the book ends with a description of the 'ideal wife', the *esset hayyil*, who is a paragon of female virtue.

The sages who wrote the Book of Proverbs were concerned with individual happiness and personal morality. Order was very important to them, and disorder an anathema. In contrast to the prophets, the sages did not protest or involve themselves in social reform, or campaign on behalf of the poor, widows or orphans; nor did they involve themselves in fighting the political order of the day. They believed in political obsequiousness, as did the writers of the ancient Egyptian wisdom literature, who described how to behave humbly in the presence of a king. The sages were generally 'yes-men' with regard to the authority structure. Bribery is only partially condemned and there is even one verse advocating its use. The book is also very different to the histories of the OT, such as Kings and Chronicles, because there are no famous people and no great political events or wars; nor does the earlier history of Israel and its great patriarchs gain any mention, a feature shared with the other Wisdom books – Job and Ecclesiastes.

The religious value of the Book of Proverbs stems from its description of what is moral as well as sensible behaviour – the exposition of wisdom. Preachers from both the Jewish and the Christian faiths have used the text to teach their congregations about wisdom and morality from the earliest times. The fascination for the psychiatrist is at the opposite pole, what the scribes regarded as wicked behaviour or 'folly'. Psychiatrists are not Sunday school teachers, and their interest lies with the deviant, the psychopath and the destructive side of human nature. Proverbs contains a detailed account of antisocial personality disorder under the label 'scoundrels and fools' and their bad character traits are all described in rich clinical detail.

Schneider (1923) was the first to offer a readily understood definition of personality disorder, as the condition 'of a person who suffers or makes others suffer because of his abnormal personality'. This should be compared with Fox's definition of the fools of Proverbs, and on whose commentary much of this chapter is based. He writes: 'Proverbs here and elsewhere, is well aware that society includes fools and troublemakers ... *They are aberrant individuals, just stupid folk who cause harm above all to themselves and whose punishment is inevitable*' (Fox, 2000, p. 342, emphasis added).

The degree to which these ancient descriptions correspond to the modern concepts of personality disorder is quite remarkable and forms the main theme of this chapter and the next one. Two personality types are particularly well described: the 'scoundrel' (the *belial*) corresponds well to an aggressive psychopath; and the 'strange woman' (the *issah zarah*) corresponds to the modern concept of borderline personality disorder. There is condemnation of such bad characters in strongly moralistic terms, consistent with the religious ethos of the day, and this is accompanied by repeated advice to avoid such people at all costs.

The psychiatric study of personality disorder has moved the debate away from the moralistic good–evil dichotomy of the Bible and has encouraged a more clinical, neutral and scientific approach to this timeless problem, although within the wider community the 'good–bad' dichotomy for such character types still remains widely held.

## Authorship and setting

None of the authors of the biblical Wisdom literature is known. The traditional Jewish rabbinic view on authorship is given by Rosenberg (1993):

> Although the Scripture explicitly states that the book consists of the Proverbs of Solomon, the Talmud (*Baba bathra* 15a) attributes authorship of the Book to Hezekiah and his followers. *Rabbi Joseph Ibn Nachmaish* maintains that Solomon's Proverbs were committed to memory by the sages of the generations from Solomon to Hezekiah. However, Hezekiah who excelled in poetry and realised the power of the Proverb or allegory, decided that these *mashalim* authored by King Solomon through divine revelation should be committed to writing.

The book opens with a superscription attributing the Proverbs to King Solomon (961–922 BCE): 'The Proverbs of Solomon, Son of David, King of Israel ... to know wisdom'. The Book of Kings claims that Solomon himself wrote some 3000 proverbs. However, no modern biblical scholar accepts a Solomonic authorship for any of the Proverbs. Hezekiah (727–698 BCE) is also mentioned but, equally, he is not thought to have been an author.

Anonymous scribes attached to the royal court were the most likely authors as few people could read and write, let alone compose sophisticated verse. These scribes were intellectuals and were also known as 'sages' and insofar as the ancient cult had a class system they would have been drawn from the middle and upper classes. Their writings reflect their mainly middle-class values, which show a strong resemblance to the middle-class values of today: high standards of honesty and personal morality; the merits of self-sufficiency and hard work; marital and family harmony. Great importance was placed on the education and training of the young. This was all accompanied by a hatred of crime, antisocial behaviour and any form of social disorder. These are the themes that pervade the whole book.

The role of the sages in ancient society can only be inferred from their writings. Gammie and Perdue (1990) write: 'a sage is one who has composed a book belonging to the Wisdom literature of the ancient Near East'. However, Carol Fontaine (p. 125), a biblical scholar writing from a feminist perspective, believes they had a much more extensive social function:

> Sages are persons who perform one or more of the following tasks associated with the Wisdom tradition: authorship, scribal duties (i.e. collecting, copying and editing), but also counselling, conflict resolution, economic management, teaching and healing. There can be little doubt that the sages who wrote Proverbs must have been teachers of some sort. Almost all the addresses are from 'father to son' but it is likely that they also served a general educational role. In other biblical works, e.g. the Histories, the word scribe is used instead of sage, giving more weight to their role as writers, recorders and notaries.

However, the case will be argued that some scribes/sages must have been quite heavily involved in the work of the court and the legal system and they may have also had some kind of quasi social worker role as well. The scribes who wrote during the monarchic periods must also have assumed a role as royal or state officials – as is clearly recorded in ancient Egyptian society. The

Wisdom literature of Israel drew heavily from the much older Sumerian and Egyptian Wisdom literature (as described in the appendix to this chapter).

Like the older Wisdom literature of Egypt and Mesopotamia, the Book of Proverbs is not a religious text but mainly a secular work. Fox points out that Proverbs makes no pretence to having an origin in divine revelation or inspiration. God is never quoted or addressed, only 'fear of God' is mentioned and this refers more to a respectful attitude to family and religious authority rather than to the deity as such. As a consequence, the book had little role in the spiritual or ritual life of Israel during the era of the Temple or after its destruction, in later synagogue life or worship, although it is often quoted in the Mishnah.

## Dating

The Book of Proverbs as a whole cannot be dated. It was written by many different and unknown authors. There is no reference to any major historical event such as a war or invasion which could provide a point of fixity; nor are any known important Israelite characters mentioned, with the exception of Solomon and Hezekiah. It is thought that first proverbs began to appear in an oral form around 800 BCE. They were gradually written down so that a large collection, particularly chs 10–31, comprising the latter part of the book, already existed prior to the exile in 586 BCE. Evidence in support of a pre-exilic dating for at least some of the book derives from numerous proverbs which describe how to behave before a king or how the king should treat his subjects (ch. 23). Since the royal household ceased with the Babylonian conquest, these sections must have been written during the period of the First Commonwealth, when kings reigned over Israel, and this ended with the exile.

However, the first part of the book, Proverbs 1–9, which comprises a rather lengthy introduction (and summary) to the rest of the book, is rather more organised and is thought to have been written after the exile, during the 'Persian period'. It includes a series of lectures and poems, some of which describe personality disorder. Three arguments are used to support a post-exilic authorship for this section. First, Fox (2000, p. 48) argues that there are certain wisdom concepts expressed in this first part of Proverbs (chs 1–9) which show an awareness of Greek thinking, and this would place the dating to after the Macedonian conquests of Alexander the Great in 323 BCE. Secondly, the book's diatribe against the 'strange woman' and the dangers of sexual relations with foreign women is thought to relate to social and political conditions during the Persian period. There was a great mixing of peoples in Babylon following the exile and this continued as the returnees resettled Judah. The dominant community fear of the time, particularly as expressed in the Books of Ezra and Nehemiah, was of intermarriage, and consequent loss of land entitlement and Hebrew identity (discussed on page 438 in the next chapter). Third, many of the mores about family life seem to tally with the teachings of the Book of Malachi, placing the composition of Proverbs around the same time as Malachi, which was during the 5th century BCE. However, even Fox admits that these arguments are speculative.

## Literary aspects

The whole of the Book of Proverbs is written in verse. It must be one of the few places in literature where the psychopath is accorded the privilege of being described in poetry. Some of the sayings in the book are 'one liners' but most are two liners, in the form of parallel couplets; there are also occasional tristiches (three liners) and quatrains. Whybray (1990, p. 13) speculates on why the authors of Proverbs chose to write in a poetic form, even though a prose style would have conveyed the meanings just as well. Poetry has greater force and power than prose. The bulk of the book is a rather random assortment of two-line couplets or proverbs, termed *māsāls*. The Hebrew word *māsāl* carries two meanings: to be similar to, and to rule over. Both elements are reflected in most of the proverbs in the book. First, there is some kind of analogy, which stresses its paradigmatic or exemplary character. The second part has an element of teaching – but with some force, a didactic impulse. It may be a warning or an exhortation (a particular path is good or bad, or some benefit or harm might arise). A proverb also has a quality of immediate cogency, and brevity is essential for proverbs in all cultures.

Poetry has a mnemonic value as well. It seems as if proverbs were one way a pre-literate society had to disseminate moral education, as short proverbs could easily be remembered (which holds true today). Thus Naré (1986) found a total of 1900 proverbs used by a West African tribe, many of them similar to the ancient Hebrew proverbs.

Whybray (1990, p. 5) suggests there are two main categories of writing in Proverbs: popular sayings or aphorisms that circulated among ordinary folk during times going back to monarchic or even pre-monarchic periods; and sayings that were composed by an upper class of educated officials, as purely literary works. The ancient Hebrew Proverbs display another literary quality – parallelism, although this poetic technique is also shown in Egyptian and other Wisdom literature (see pages 150–151).

In addition to the parallel couplets, there are several short poems or 'epigrams' in the Book of Proverbs which describe a single character type. In particular, the account of the *belial* (scoundrel) in Proverbs 6 corresponds well to modern descriptions of antisocial personality disorder and the poem about the *issa zarah* (strange woman) in Proverbs 7 describes a woman with a personality disorder approximating to the modern concept of borderline personality disorder. The suggestion that one of the main themes of the Book of Proverbs is personality disorder and the problems people with personality disorder pose to society is both novel and far from obvious. At a superficial level, the book seems to be arranged in an almost random order. Thus Waltke (2005), who wrote a massive treatise on Proverbs, writes:

> There are a total of 930 ancient sayings in the Book of Proverbs. For the logical mind, the book seems to be a hodge-podge collection having no rhyme or reason in its groupings of sayings. They jump from one topic to another like scatterbrains in a living room conversation. How does one make sense of such a mish-mash?

The answer to Waltke's question is that book can be readily decoded once all the verses describing a particular topic are placed together. When this is done for the topic of 'adverse personality traits', almost all the mal-adaptive traits we now associate with antisocial personality disorder emerge, accurately described in sublime biblical verse. In addition to those who are clearly aggressive criminal psychopaths, the *belial*, other character types to emerge are those with lowish intelligence, the *pethi*, and an intelligent but highly malicious type known as the *lēs*.

The ancient Hebrews had a dichotomous view of the world. Men were either righteous and wise or sinners replete with folly. A strongly moral dimension was placed on their assessment of personality. Such a moral position is reminiscent of the influence of the Deuteronomist, an editor of large tracts of the Old Testament who placed a religious-ethical dimension onto Israel's history. A moral approach was lacking in much of the earlier Wisdom literature of ancient Egypt and Sumeria, and is also formally excluded from the modern concept of personality disorder (as in DSM-5 and ICD-10), although the notion that many psychopaths are bad or intrinsically evil people persists and remains widely held in most societies today.

Proverbs sets out two opposing realms, wisdom and folly, each with many facets, subtypes and subdivisions. The various types of 'fool' in the text correspond to some degree to what today we call personality disorder, particularly 'antisocial personality disorder'. The description is largely in rhyming couplets and a particular category of fool or his action is placed in a parallelism opposite an attribute of wisdom. This pairing of opposites helps to sharpen the meaning of the traits of the fools. To a limited extent therefore *wisdom constitutes the antithesis of personality disorder* – with wisdom representing positive personality strengths and useful traits. The ostensible purpose of the Book of Proverbs was to educate the young. The reality which disturbed society at the time, and still does today, was the harm caused by its 'fools'. This was the main driving force leading the sages to write about the chaos and crimes caused by these malevolent characters. The hope was that with knowledge acquired through education, the young would choose wisdom over folly.

The order of topics discussed in this chapter is as follows:

- character typology and a description of the biblical terms used for wisdom and folly
- the biblical description of the *belial* (the scoundrel)
- application of the DSM-5 criteria for antisocial personality disorder (ASPD) to the *belial*
- other personality disorders in men in Proverbs (the *pethi* and the *hasar leb* and learning difficulties)
- a trait-based approach to the diagnosis of psychopathy (the application of Hare's Psychopathic Checklist to Proverbs)
- aspects of antisocial personality disorder (forensic issues and prognosis)
- the concepts of wisdom and folly in the Proverbs and their relation to personality disorder
- a modern perspective on antisocial personality disorder.

After a summary and conclusion, there is an appendix on the Egyptian Wisdom literature and other descriptions of antisocial personality disorder in the ancient Near East.

## Character typology in the Book of Proverbs: wisdom and folly

The book opens with a prologue which contains most of the words associated with the concepts of wisdom. The intention of the author was to 'dazzle the audience with all the wonderful range of qualities that could be acquired from studying this book' (Whybray, 1990, p. 31). The introduction to the book serves as a sort of glossary on the various types of wisdom and folly (denoting bad character types) and reflects a fairly sophisticated level of thinking on these topics. This introductory section (Proverbs 1[1-7]) is annotated below:

| | | |
|---|---|---|
| 1[1] | The Proverbs of Solomon son of David, King of Israel | Authorship is attributed to Solomon |
| 2 | For learning about wisdom and instruction, | wisdom = *hochma* |
| | | instruction = *musar* |
| | for understanding words of insight. | understanding = *binah* |
| 3 | For gaining instruction in wise dealing, | wise dealing = *sēkēl* |
| | righteousness, justice and equity. | |
| 4 | To teach shrewdness to the simple, | shrewdness = *ormah*; simple = *pethi* |
| | knowledge and prudence to the young | knowledge = *da-at*; |
| | | prudence = *m'zima* |
| 5 | Let the wise also hear and gain learning | the wise = *Hakam*; learning = *da-at* |
| | and the discerning acquire skill | discerning (person) = *nabon*; |
| | | skill = *Tahbulot* |
| 6 | To understand a proverb and a figure, | proverb = *māsāl*; |
| | the words of the wise and their riddles. | the wise = *Hākām* |
| 7 | The fear of the Lord is the beginning of | |
| | knowledge; | knowledge = *da-at*; |
| | fools despise wisdom and instruction. | fools = *'ĕwil* or bad character |
| | | wisdom = *hochma*; |
| | | instruction = *musar* |

The Hebrew word *hochma* means wisdom, but the sense is not quite the same as in the English. It also denotes craftsmanship, skill, knowledge, qualities of astuteness and good judgement, particularly in the realm of inter-personal relationships. *Binah* designates intellectual discernment, ability to reason, and is similar to the modern concept of intelligence. A *nabon* is one who possesses *binah* and 'knowledge comes easily to him'. In the Book of Daniel, *binah* also refers to the ability to interpret esoteric messages. *Da-at* is a very broad word covering almost any sort of cognition, knowledge or good sense. *Musar* is an important concept in the context of personality disorder and its management, and means teaching, correction or disciplining. In the Book of Proverbs, *musar* is frequently applied; it helps the wise but fools are resistant to it (13[18]). *Sekel* refers to discretion, diplomatic skills and insight and the ability to grasp a situation. A person's *sekel* gives him the sense and patience which helps him avoid interpersonal

**Table 10.1** Hebrew words for wisdom, associated character types, and their meanings

| Words for wisdom | Associated character type and meaning |
| --- | --- |
| *Hochma* – wisdom | *Hakam* – possessor of wisdom |
| *Binah* – intelligence | *Nabon* – astute man |
| *Da'at* – knowledgeable | *Yodea* – knowledgeable man |
| *Esah* – planning, design | *Yo'es* – adviser, planner |
| *Sēkel* – discretion | *Maskil* – discreet man, man of good sense |
| *Tahbulot* – guidance through life | – |
| *T'bunah* – good sense | *Mebin* – intelligent sensible man |
| *Tusiyyah* – resourcefulness | – |
| *Musar* – discipline, education | – |
| *M'zzimah* – discretion | – |
| *Ormah* – cunning | *Arum* – cunning person |

conflict. *Ormah* refers to cunning and political skill or adroitness. It is a useful skill which Lady Wisdom offers to teach (8⁵). *Tahbulot* is a political word meaning strategy or guidance; it can be used for both good planning and evil scheming. *Tebunah* is competence and the ability to deal with all the exigencies of life, particularly in the realm of interpersonal affairs. *Tusiyyah* denotes clear thinking and resourcefulness in the realm of power and confers personal and political power on the individual.

Table 10.1 presents the Hebrew words in the general rubric of wisdom (Fox, 2000). They represent good character attributes and useful personality assets; they are the antithesis of folly and by implication of personality disorder.

## Folly

The Book of Proverbs describes several different types of fool, each of whom has a slightly different character, yet all malevolent. English translations do not differentiate between the various categories of 'folly' and so there is considerable loss of meaning in translation. In particular, three different categories of Hebrew 'personality' types – the *'ĕwil*, the *kesil* and the *pethi* – are all translated by the one English word 'fool', which fails to convey quite large differences between them. For instance, the *'ĕwil* and the *kesil* are much more malignant characters than a simple fool. Readers may think the fools of Proverbs are merely stupid people and the wise are the clever ones, but this is far from the original Hebrew. The Book of Proverbs has eight different categories of bad character types, most of whom are called 'fools', indicating the scribes made quite serious attempts to sub-classify bad character, as shown in Table 10.2, much in the same way as modern psychiatry tries to sub-type its personality disorders.

**Table 10.2** Hebrew words for folly and personality disorder

| Hebrew word | English translation | Character type | IQ |
|---|---|---|---|
| petayyat | Gullible; fool | Pethi (plural p'ta'im) | Low IQ; some learning difficulties |
| hasar leb | Lacking a mind; fool | Thoughtless person | Lowish IQ; some learning difficulties |
| 'ĕwil | Immoral character; fool | 'Ĕwil, plural 'ĕwillim; psychopathic traits | Normal IQ |
| kesil | Immoral character; fool | Kesil, kesilut; more extrovert than the 'ĕwil; psychopathic traits | Lacks intellectual keenness; brighter than the pethi, but not as bright as the 'ĕwil |
| lās | Scornful man | Lēs, plural Lason; arrogant contemptuous man; narcissistic and psychopathic traits | Normal IQ |
| ba-ar | Animal brutishness | Occasionally mentioned | Simple brute |
| belial | Scoundrel; worthlessness | Criminal psychopath | Normal or high IQ |
| nabal | Oaf | Oaf-boor, churlish man; nabal also means wine skin, so linked with alcoholism | |

## The *belial* (scoundrel)

The *belial* (scoundrel) is not considered under the general rubric of folly. He is regarded as a wicked man and a villain whose life will come to an abrupt end, possibly through capital punishment. He has a perverted mind and devises evil schemes. He is arrogant, lies and is violent. He abuses his wife and children. In today's terminology he corresponds to the severe psychopath (aggressive psychopath or criminal psychopath). The descriptions in Proverbs 6[12-19] and 16[27-30] are analysed below. Commentary on both passages is based on Fox (2000). Jeremiah 5[26-28] also has a short section on this particular villain. First, Proverbs 6[12-19]:

| | | |
|---|---|---|
| 6[12] | A scoundrel and a villain goes around with crooked speech | for origin of the word *belial* see note 1 below |
| [13] | Winking the eyes, shuffling the feet pointing the fingers | for significance of allusions to different body parts, see note 2 |
| [14] | with perverted mind devising evil continually sowing discord. | stirring trouble, malevolent and manipulative |
| [15] | On such a one calamity will descend suddenly In a moment damage beyond repair. | ? death through being murdered or executed |

| | | |
|---|---|---|
| 16 | There are six things the Lord hates<br>seven that are an abomination to him | numbers and lists are a common literary device; similar to operational criteria; see note 3 |
| 17 | Haughty eyes, and a lying tongue<br>and hands that shed innocent blood | psychopathic traits: arrogance, dishonesty and violence |
| 18 | A heart that devises wicked plans<br>feet that hurry to run to evil | scheming/manipulation<br>? impulsivity |
| 19 | A lying witness who testifies falsely<br>and one who sows discord in the family | lies, ? perjury<br>? wife or child maltreatment |

Second account, in ch. 16:

| | | |
|---|---|---|
| 16²⁷ | Scoundrels concoct evil<br>and their speech is like a scorching fire | fire often used in the OT as a symbol of total destruction (Whybray, 1990) |
| 28 | A perverse person spreads strife<br>and a whisperer separates close friends | for 'perverse' see note 4<br>a manipulative trouble maker |
| 29 | The violent entice their neighbours<br>and lead them in a way that is not good | euphemism for disaster, or crime |
| 30 | One who winks the eyes plans perverse things;<br>One who compresses the lips brings evil to pass | shifty looks are linked to crimes or malevolent plans<br>? silence or lying linked to bad deeds |

*Note 1.* The etymology is the word *belial* is uncertain. It is translated as 'scoundrel' and is thought to derive from two separate words, *beli*, meaning without, and *ya'al*, meaning usefulness. It can therefore be rendered 'without use' or 'good-for-nothing' or 'worthless person'. In later Hebrew literature the *belial* became demonised as the Prince of Wickedness. In the Book of Jeremiah (2⁸) the concept of a false god (Baal) and lack of profit are linked together.

The traditional rabbinical explanation for the word *belial* is also relevant. According to Mezudoth (Rosenberg, 1993, p. 33) *belial* derives from *beli* = without; and *ya-al* = yoke, and he explains this as 'without a yoke', meaning this is a person who has cast off the yoke of the Torah. Since the Torah meant the law and codes of personal morality, and all the conventions of society, the meaning would be of a man who had no respect for the law, or a lawless person. This interpretation is very similar to the lead clauses of the definition of antisocial personality disorder as in DSM-5 and ICD-10, the two main modern psychiatric glossaries. For DSM-5 the lead clause is: 'A pervasive pattern of disregard for and the violation of the rights of others...'. For ICD-10, dissocial personality disorder is defined as 'A condition coming to attention because of a gross disparity between behaviour and the prevailing social norms...'. Thus the rabbinic interpretation of the word *belial* is close to the core of the modern definitions of antisocial or dissocial personality disorder.

*Note 2.* Reference to body parts (eyes, fingers, feet, etc.) is linked to specific character traits in the Bible. In the literature of the ancient world personality was explained as part of the mind–body interaction (Fox, 2000, p. 220).

The three body zones were: the heart and eyes; the mouth and ears; and the hands and feet. These three zones represented the totality of personality, but each had a separate function. Thus the eye was the point of entry to the heart. The word *leb* (heart) was often used to represent the functions which we now ascribe to the mind and therefore a person's will. A winking eye might have indicated hostility. For example, Job says his enemy sharpens his eyes against him (Job 16[19]). The hands and the feet put a person's will into action, while the mouth – which in the case of the *belial* is crooked – gives expression to his thought and will. Thus this very brief description of the features of the *belial* (scoundrel) has been organised around the three body zones associated with personality, highlighting the strong mind–body link with regard to personality disorder in the ancient world.

*Note* 3. The lists in 6[16] – 'There are six things the Lord hates / and seven are an abomination to him' – follow the pattern *n* and then *n* + I to describe things which God either approves or disapproves of. This was a common literary device in the ancient world. Haran (1972) lists 12 places in the OT where lists of this type occur and the device also appears in the Proverbs of Ahiqar and other Egyptian Wisdom literature. According to Fox (2000, p. 223) the list of seven items in this epigram that 'the lord hates' consists of five psychopathic traits, each of which is linked to body parts: (1) arrogant eyes, (2) a lying tongue, (3) hands that spill innocent blood, (4) a heart that crafts wicked plans, (5) feet that run quickly to evil, (6) a lying witness, and (7) a fomenter of strife – the last two items being actual characters rather than body parts. Malbim (cited in Rosenberg, 1993) wrote that the seventh, 'fomenter of strife', was the worst of them all because by inciting quarrels one destroys society.

I have highlighted this list of malevolent traits because it parallels present-day diagnostic methods. Thus, the definitions of *almost all* psychiatric disorders comprise an initial statement of the core features, accompanied by lists of diagnostic criteria which are said to characterise a particular disorder. Thus for antisocial personality disorder, DSM-5 has a core statement about 'violating the rights of others' and then it stipulates 'and is accompanied by three or more of the following items'. It proceeds to list seven items; the actual definition is given in Table 10.3 (page 397). The list in the Old Testament is very similar and at least three of the traits of the *belial* 'which the Lord hates' are the same as the DSM-5 criteria: repeated lying (DSM-5), corresponding to 'a lying tongue' (6[17]); impulsivity to 'feet that run to do evil'(6[18]); irritability and aggressiveness to 'hands that spill innocent blood' (repeated physical assaults) (6[19]).

The use of such lists is of immense historical importance, as it indicates that the sages of ancient Israel seem to have applied a similar type of diagnostic thinking by using lists of adverse personality traits in their diagnostic formulary, in a similar manner to modern operational criteria. All the sage had to do to confirm whether he was dealing with a *belial* was to tick off which of the seven items 'the Lord hates' that the man before him seemed to possess, and if he had some of these he could confidently be called a scoundrel.

*Note 4.* The Hebrew word for 'perverse' is *tahpūkot,* which mainly occurs in Proverbs (and once in Deuteronomy). For instance, Proverbs $2^{14}$ has 'who rejoices in doing evil and delight in the perverseness of evil'. Thus the man of perverted speech uses his speech to achieve evil ends (Whybray, p. 53). Mezudath David writes about the perverse man as 'One who misrepresents the facts. The sages interpret this as a reference to the serpent, who distorted God's word and brought about a quarrel between man and God.'

Some modern theologians have also recognised the antisocial qualities of the *belial.* Thus W. McKane (1970, p. 493) calls him 'The Mischief Maker' and entitles his comments on $6^{12-19}$ 'Antisocial behaviour'. McKane writes:

> The types of behaviour under consideration have this in common, that they are all disruptive in their tendency, that they are characterised by self-assertiveness or malice or violence and they break the bond of confidence and loyalty between man and man. Whether it be an abuse of inventiveness for evil purposes, or in the contempt for law and the rights of others or in lying, particularly as perjury, these are men who employ their talents in order to destroy the basis of common life. What is described is a deep seated corruption of motives which gives rise to a constant and dedicated malevolence tantamount to total incapacity for neighbourliness. When such chronic bad will is allied to resourcefulness, thoroughness and deceit, it assumes its most dangerous shape and wreaks havoc in the community.

In respect of Proverbs $16^{26-28}$ McKane writes:

> the *ish belial* (scoundrel) is a deranged or destructive man rather than a worthless man. This confusion is a deep seated malevolence – a contamination of the springs of sociability and it sets a man at enmity with all other men. He has no urge to use language creatively in order to make friends and enlarge brotherhood; he is obsessed with the thought of hurting his fellows. He 'digs mischief' and his words have the destructive fury of a blazing fire.

Mckane's interpretation of the *belial* in both epigrams ($6^{12-19}$ and $16^{27-30}$) give a good description of psychopathic or antisocial personality disorder. Thus the present author cannot claim to be the first to make the link between the *belial* and the psychopath. However, it is important to note that McKane's explanation was *not* written by a psychiatrist or a lawyer but is the work of a Professor of Theology in Aberdeen, probably with little or no professional contact with such types, and he bases his formulation of this character entirely on the biblical description of the *belial.* This particular character type seems to have been well known and could be accurately described in ancient Israel.

## The *belial* and the DSM-5 concept of antisocial personality disorder

How close is the concept of the *belial* of the Book of Proverbs to the modern concept of antisocial personality as defined in DSM-5? The short poem in Proverbs $6^{12-19}$ consists of seven verses and ninety-three words. Such poems are called epigrams, tightly written poetry used to make a single point, in this case the description of the scoundrel. DSM-5 represents the best of modern thinking about psychiatric diagnoses and like 'the seven things the Lord hates' it also has diagnostic criteria. In Table 10.3 (on the following page) the two descriptions are compared. The following notes relate to the table.

*Note 5.* Conning others (DSM-5 criterion 2). This is not described in the epigram of Proverbs 6, but is well described in Jeremiah's account of the *belial:*

5²⁶     For scoundrels are found among my people;        *belial*
        they take over the goods of others
        like fowlers they set a trap;
        they catch human beings
²⁷      Like a cage full of birds,
        their houses are full of treachery;
        therefore they have become great and rich.
²⁸      They have grown fat and sleek
        They know no limits in deeds and wickedness:

The account of the scoundrel in Jeremiah is of historical interest because Jeremiah wrote just before the exile and it indicates that both the word and concept of the *belial* was presumably well established in pre-exilic times even though the introduction section of Proverbs is thought to be post-exilic.

DSM-5 criterion 6, 'failure to sustain work', is alluded to in Proverbs 10²⁶:

> Like vinegar to the teeth and smoke to the eyes
> So are the lazy to their employers.

Financial irresponsibility of a psychopathic type (again, DSM-5 criterion 6) is suggested in Proverbs 21¹⁷:

> Whoever loves pleasure will suffer want;
> whoever loves wine and oil will not be rich.

Table 10.3 shows that the compact epigram of Proverbs 6¹²⁻¹⁹ describing the *belial* has at least five of the seven DSM-5 criteria for antisocial personality disorder: failure to confirm to social norms; deceitfulness; impulsivity; irritability; and recklessness. The verses thus give a reasonably good description of antisocial personality disorder. The remaining two criteria *not* found in this epigram (inability to sustain work and honour financial obligations; and lack of remorse) are all described elsewhere in the Book of Proverbs. This is quite remarkable considering this poem was probably composed by a single scribe more than 2500 years ago.

What possible explanation is there for this astounding degree of clinical acumen? It is possible that the scribe who wrote this epigram was a man of very great insight, as certain great authors are. Thus for example Thomas Hardy in his description of Sergeant Troy in *Far From the Madding Crowd* (1874) provides an excellent account of a psychopath and doubtless there are other accounts in the world of literature.

**Table 10.3** DSM criteria for antisocial personality disorder compared with the epigram of 'the scoundrel' (belial) in Proverbs 6$^{12-19}$

| DSM antisocial personality disorder | Features of the 'scoundrel' in Proverbs 6$^{12-19}$ |
| --- | --- |
| Pervasive violation of the rights of others, from the age of 15, as shown by three or more of the following seven items | 6$^{14a}$ 'with a perverted mind', devising evil; see also meaning of *belial*, in note 1 above; a person who throws off the yoke of the Torah<br>6$^{18a}$ with a heart that devises wicked plans<br>For onset before 15 see 17$^{21}$ and 17$^{25}$ |
| (1) Being unable to conform to social norms; unlawful behaviours | 6$^{19}$continually sowing discord<br>6$^{17b}$ 'hands that shed innocent blood'<br>Also the rabbinic interpretation of *belial* as disregarding the Torah, violating the law and social norms |
| (2) Deceitfulness (e.g. lying, use of aliases, conning people) | 6$^{19}$ 'a lying witness who testifies falsely; conning others for profit; see note 5 below. |
| (3) Impulsivity/failure to plan | 6$^{18b}$ 'feet that hurry to run to do evil' |
| (4) Irritability, aggressiveness (e.g. repeatedly involved in fights) | 6$^{17b}$ 'hands that shed innocent blood; also irritability as described on page 411 |
| (5) Recklessness/disregard for safety of self or others | 6$^{15}$ 'On such a one calamity will descend suddenly, in a moment' |
| (6) Irresponsibility (e.g. in employment, finance) | Not described here; see note 5 below, but described in 10$^2$, 10$^{26}$ and 11$^1$ |
| (7) Lack of remorse | 6$^{19}$ Hurt and mistreated others = ? 'sows discord in the family'; lack of remorse, 14$^9$ see page 409 |
| The person has to be over 18 years of age | |
| There should be evidence of conduct disorder from before the age of 15 years | Numerous references to 'fool' in childhood, see page 413 |
| The behaviour does not occur in the context of mania or schizophrenia | The distinction is made in 26$^{17}$, see page 420 |

Fox (2000, p. 225) offers another possible explanation. He points out that the Book of Proverbs is in two sections. Proverbs 1–9 is the more recent and post-exilic section and is said to be an introductory review, while Proverbs 10–31 represents the older, pre-exilic section, which has a rather more random and haphazard collection of sayings. He shows that most of the verses in 6$^{12-19}$ are repeats taken from the older part of the book, particularly 16$^{27-30}$. Fox goes on to suggest that the scribe who rewrote the scoundrel epigram in ch. 6 selected only those verses from the older part of the book (ch. 16) appertaining to psychopathy and which seemed to him to represent a unified character type and then added in other characteristics he deemed to be relevant and wove them together into his short poem. His genius was that his selection from the menu of malevolence was almost identical to that made by the modern psychiatrists who wrote DSM-5.

DSM-5 (APA, 2013) represents the zenith of modern psychiatric thinking in the description of psychiatric disorders. This last edition is the sixth major revision of the *Diagnostic and Statistical Manual* (DSM) of the American Psychiatric Association and its definitions form the basis on which all American psychiatrists are supposed to make their diagnoses. A huge effort has gone into each revision: committees of experts spent many years convening and reviewing the relevant literature and deriving an agreed and optimal definition for each psychiatric disorder. Yet one passage comprising only seven verses in the Book of Proverbs ($6^{12-19}$) has a description of the *belial* that incorporates most of the main features of DSM-5 antisocial personality disorder. The biblical version is also slightly more succinct than the DSM-5 summary table, comprising only 93 words in the English translation but only 46 words in the original Hebrew, compared with 127 words for DSM-5 and, amazingly, precedes DSM-5 by more than 2500 years.

## Other personality disorders affecting males in Proverbs

While the description of the *belial* is clear and easy to recognise as a man with antisocial personality disorder, the Book of Proverbs describes several other character types. Two types, the *'ĕwil* and the *kesil*, are both translated into English as 'fool', although they describe slightly different psychopathic types. A third character, the *lēs*, is a contemptuous man full of arrogance and he is translated as a 'scorner' in the RSV and 'scoffer' in the King James and older versions. The *lēs* is a psychopathic person with narcissistic traits rather than someone with a primary narcissistic personality disorder. Another group of characters are highlighted because they seem to be of low intelligence, but in the OT this is perceived as more of a moral failing – almost a crime. These include the *pethi*, the *hasar leb* and the *ba-ar*, and some of these characters might nowadays be classed as having low or borderline IQs, or even learning difficulties.

Unlike the *belial*, there is no single epigram describing these types and their characteristics have to be inferred from the verses they feature in and how they are placed opposite different types of wisdom. Donald (1963), in his important paper 'The semantic field of folly in Proverbs, Psalms, Job and Ecclesiastes', studied all the verse couplets where a particular type of fool was mentioned and used the second line of the couplet, placed in antithetic parallelism, to infer the characteristics of the fool specified in the first line of the couplet. The descriptions of the different characters given below are based on Fox (2000), Donald (1976) and Waltke (2005 ) and their interpretations of these verses.

## The kesil (oaf)

The *kesil* is the most common type of fool described in Proverbs (mentioned 49 times). The word *kesil* means both stupid and confident (Gesenius dictionary, translated from the German by Brown *et al.*, 1906). Fox infers from this that the *kesil* is an over-confident person and this will destroy him:

> The *kesil* is not as intelligent as the *'ĕwil*. He is an over-confident oaf who talks too much. He stumbles into other people's quarrels. He is self-satisfied and stirs up trouble and brings trouble onto himself through his disinhibited talk.

The kesil appears in Proverbs 18:

| 18[6] | A fool's lips bring strife | *kesil* |
|---|---|---|
| | and a fool's mouth invites a flogging | *kesil* |
| 18[7] | A fool's mouth is his undoing | *kesil* |
| | and his lips are a snare to themselves | |

His stupidity permits him to slide into wickedness and he tends to stay there (Proverbs 1[32]):

> For waywardness kills the simple
> and the complacency of fools destroys them     *kesil*

In terms of morality he seems to derive pleasure from his wrongdoing, which suggests a callous streak (Proverbs 10[23]):

> Doing wrong is like a sport to a fool     *kesil*
> But wise conduct is pleasure to a person of understanding

Donald (1976) considered him to be a more malignant character than the *'ĕwil*. The only distinction that seems clear is that the *kesil* is less intelligent than the *'ĕwil*. Like all the other categories of fool, he fails to respond to punishment (Proverbs 17[10]):

> A rebuke strikes deeper into a discerning
> person than a hundred blows a fool.     *kesil*

He is also an impulsive person capable of very great anger, a quality also shared with the *'ĕwil* (Proverbs 17[12]):

> Better to meet a she-bear robbed of its cubs
> than to confront a fool immersed in folly     fool = *Kesil*; folly = *'ĕwillet*

The potential for violent anger of a dangerous type is clear in this metaphor. The pattern of folly seems to be lifelong (Proverbs 26[11]):

> Like a dog that returns to his vomit
> is a fool who reverts to his folly.     *kesil*

This failure to respond to punishment, or therapy, or anything at all, and the lifelong nature of the disorder is today recognised as the major stumbling block to improving the outlook for a person with antisocial personality disorder.

He cannot save but squanders whatever comes his way (Proverbs 21[20]):

> Precious treasure remains in the house of the wise
> But the fool devours it                                                   *kesil*

The *kesil* dies a poor man and, like the *ba-ar* in the end, neither has any wealth to pass on (Psalm 49[10]):

> When we look at the wise, they die
> Fool and dolt perish together,                        *kesil* and *ba-ar*
> leaving their wealth to others

In Donald's (1976) analysis the *kesil* is placed opposite *hochma* (wisdom) 13 times, *nabon* (wiseman) twice, *mebin* (understanding perceptive person), *sekel* (discretion), *tebunah* (good sense, competence) and also *kavod* (honour) and *da-at* (knowledge). He is aligned together with the *ba-ar* and *nabal* (brutish oafs) against *hochma* (wisdom), and also paired together with *lēs*, the scorner, on four occasions.

There is no exact equivalent for the *kesil* in the modern personality disorder lexicon, yet the type is clearly recognisable. He harms others and he harms himself, so according to Schneider he has a personality disorder. There are some antisocial features such as great anger and a pleasure in doing wrong but probably there is insufficient detail to qualify for a formal diagnosis of antisocial personality disorder, whereas the *belial* qualifies for a full diagnosis. There are elements of a learning difficulty – he is not very bright; but again he seems to be above the learning difficulties threshold, and so perhaps it is best to let him remain in the 6th century BCE rather than try and unsuccessfully force him into some modern diagnostic box.

## The *'ĕwil*

The *'ĕwil* appears in English translation as a 'fool' but more in the sense of a knave than in the sense of a stupid person, such as the *pethi*. The *'ĕwil* is mentioned 19 times, and his quality, *'ĕwillett*, is mentioned 22 times; he is the second commonest type of fool mentioned in the Book of Proverbs. He is a morally bad individual, who is quarrelsome, licentious, lacks guilt. He is wayward and recalcitrant and difficult to change. However, he is not of low intelligence and is described as 'skilled in doing evil' (Jer. 4[22]). The *'ĕwil* dislikes knowledge (Proverbs 1[7]):

> The fear of the Lord is the beginning of knowledge;
> but fools despise wisdom and instruction.                      *'ĕwillet*

The *'ĕwil* is similar to the *kesil*. Both are hot tempered men, self-opinionated and cannot take advice (Proverbs 12[15-16]):

> Fools think their own way is right,                            *'ĕwillim*
> but the wise take advice.
> Fools show their anger at once,                                *'ĕwillim*
> but the prudent ignore an insult.

They are badly behaved from quite young and their parents cannot discipline them (Proverbs 15[5]):

> A fool despises a parent's instruction.    *'ĕwil*

This verse is important as it recognises the early onset of this personality disorder, and early onset is a key feature of antisocial personality disorder.

In Jeremiah (4[22]) the *'ĕwil* is likened to a stupid child:

> For my people are foolish,             *'ĕwil*
> they do not know me;
> they are stupid children,             *kesillim*
> they have no understanding.
> They do not know how to do good.

Applying Donald's (1976) analysis of what he lacks, the *'ĕwil* is placed opposite *hochma* (wisdom) on nine occasions and opposite *da-at* (knowledge) on five occasions. In addition, he lacks *musar* (discipline); *sekel* (discretion); *esah* (careful thinking, and planning); and *kavod* (honour). Fox considered the *'ĕwil* to be some kind of immoral knave. He is more intelligent than the *kesil* but not as malevolent as either the *lēs* or the *belial*. Like the *kesil*, he shows some features of antisocial personality disorder, but perhaps not the complete picture.

As an interesting aside on the rabbinical literature on the *'ĕwil*, Rabbi Moshe ben Hayyim Alsheikh (1508–1601, Safed), a Talmudic scholar, identified the primary defect: 'that *'ĕwillim* are not idiots or madman for these would not even bother to esteem or despise discipline. Rather one is called an *'ĕwil* who vacates (*yᵉhassar*) his mind from choosing good and rejecting evil' (from Fox, p. 40). The insight here that the *'ĕwil* is neither insane nor an idiot but only has a defect in his moral sense. Some 200 years later Prichard (1835) defined moral insanity, which was central to the concept of the psychopath and the earlier definitions of antisocial personality disorder:

> a morbid perversion of the natural feelings, affections, inclinations, temper, habits, moral dispositions *without* any remarkable disorder or defect of the intellect or knowing or reasoning facilities and particularly *without* any insane illusion or hallucination.

Prichard's definition of moral insanity is fundamental to the modern concept of the gross immorality of the psychopath – but it can be seen that the key element of moral deficiency, namely the exclusion of insanity and idiocy, is common to both Prichard and the writings of Alsheikh, a rabbi, hitherto unknown to psychiatry, who passed his life living in the religious mountain town of Safed in Palestine of the 16th century.

## The pethi

The *pethi* is the most benign type of fool (where the English word is used in the sense of 'stupid' rather than 'knave'). He is a common character, appearing 15 times in Proverbs and three times in Psalms. His quality, *p'tayyut*, means inexperience or gullibility. The *pethi* probably corresponds to the simpleton, the man of low or borderline intelligence, and this may represent one of the OT's references to the category that modern psychiatry now labels as 'learning difficulties'. However, the IQ level is in range of mild rather than severe learning difficulties because the *pethi* can learn some things and he appears to be teachable. The prologue to Proverbs (1⁴) says the instruction is directed at the *pětha'im* (plural of *pethi*):

> To teach shrewdness to the simple,                    *pětha'im*
> knowledge and prudence to the young.

The second line is a parallelism and indicates the *pethi* lacks *da-at* (knowledge) and *ormah* (prudence). The *pethi* is gullible and does not think about the future (Proverbs 14¹⁵, King James):

> The simple believeth every word                    *pethi*
> but the prudent looketh well to his going          *arum*          (King James)

The antithetic parallel here is *arum* (prudent), a person who thinks and plans ahead. The *pethi* suffers on account of his stupidity – but the prudent man can spot trouble ahead (Proverbs 22³, King James):

> A prudent man seeth the evil and hideth himself
> But the simple pass on and suffer for it          *pětha'im*          (King James)

In the Book of Psalms, references to the *pethi* are solely to their learning difficulties, and a more compassionate approach is taken; they are given protection in the same way as people with depression or passing through a life crisis. For example, Psalm 116⁶:

> The Lord protects the simple                    *pethi*
> When I was brought low, he saved me

In Hosea the word is also used to describe foolishness in the sense of stupidity and Ephraim's foreign policy is described as being without sense as she changes her alliances between Assyria and Egypt (Hosea 7¹¹):

> Ephraim has become like a dove,
> silly and without sense;                    *poteh*, derived from *pethi*
> they call upon Egypt, they go to Assyria.

The authors of Proverbs, according to Fox (2000, p. 43), tended to assume the moral high ground far too easily and interpreted any intellectual flaw as tantamount to a moral one. One explanation for this assessment of the *pethi* might be that the authors were focusing more on those individuals with a low IQ *combined* with personality disorder in their description of the *pethi*, because this particular combination (a low IQ together with a personality disorder) is both common and troublesome in the general population and today individuals with both disorders commonly end up in prison (discussed further on page 429).

## The hasar leb (literally empty heart; the senseless)

The *hasar leb* is similar to the *pethi*, but he may be even more stupid and so it is possible that he is within the modern learning difficulties range. The word *leb* means heart, but in the ancient world all cognitive functions were thought to take place in the heart and so the word really should translate as mind or head. A translation 'empty headed' may be more appropriate than empty heart. In tracing the origin of this word, Fox (2000) suggests that the concept of 'lacking a heart' (*hasar leb*) meaning lacking a mind has an exact Egyptian equivalent. He quotes Shuppak (1993, p. 187) and the Egyptian equivalent is *iwty-ibf*, which also means 'lacks a heart'. This also refers to a senseless impudent fool rather than an arrogant or wicked person. Fox argued that because this phrase is found only in the Hebrew Wisdom literature it is likely to be an 'Egyptianism', suggesting that the problems posed to society by people of low intelligence was probably also recognised in Egypt and presumably in other cultures of the ancient world as well.

The *hasar-leb* is dumb and slothful and neglects to look after himself and his property (Proverbs 12[11] and 24[30]):

12[11]    Those who till the land will have plenty of food
          those who follow worthless pursuits have no sense.    *hasar leb*

24[30]    I passed by the field of one who is lazy by
          the vineyard of the stupid person and see,    *hasar leb*
          it was all overgrown with thorns and the
          ground was covered with nettles.    (NRSV)

The *hasar leb* is incapable of looking after even his small-holding from which he is meant to gain his living and in effect this means he cannot feed himself. In the description of the strange woman (see page 458), the term *hasar leb* is used interchangeably and with the same meaning as the *pethi*, where the character is seen as weak willed and easily seduced by the strange woman (Proverbs 7[8]):

And I beheld among the simple ones    *péthayim*
I discerned among the youths
A young man void of understanding    *hasar leb*
Passing through the street near her corner
And he went the way to her house.    (King James)

The gullibility of the simple minded and their risks for sexual exploitation as described here also gains mention in DSM-5. Included under the heading of associated features of those with intellectual disability the text states 'Gullibility and lack of awareness of risk may result in exploitation by others and possible victimization, fraud, unintentional criminal activity, false confessions and sexual abuse.

## The ba-ar (stupid or animal like)

The *ba-ar* has only two appearances in Proverbs and three in Psalms, which means working out the typology of this character is difficult. In Psalms the connotation is with animal-like brutishness. For example (Psalms 73[22]):

> But I am stupid and ignorant, lacking knowledge     stupid = *ba-ar*
> I am a beast with you.

The word *ba-ar* does not necessarily denote a pernicious defect, but only non-human-like qualities. In Proverbs 30[2]:

> Surely I am too stupid to be human;     stupid = *ba-ar*
> I do not have human understanding

And in Proverbs 12[1]:

> Whoever loves discipline loves knowledge
> but those who hate to be rebuked are stupid.     stupid = *ba-ar*

Indeed, the King James version has 'brutish' instead of 'stupid'.

There is no equivalent to the *nabal* or the *ba-ar* in the modern psychiatric lexicons of personality disorder, but the meaning is of a rather primitive and stupid person. It is possible that the *ba-ar*, who is very stupid, might today also fall under the rubric of learning difficulties.

The *nabal* appears only three times in Proverbs, although more often in the Psalms. He is perceived as an enemy, one who reproaches and doubts God. A related word means 'wineskin', suggesting the association between alcoholism and personality disorder, which appears in I Samuel 25 (see Chapter 14, page 520).

The complaint that the scribes of Proverbs have against the *pethi*, the *hasar leb*, the *ba-ar* is that they are all stupid. This is not only a moral failing but their mention indicates that they must also have been a burden on this ancient society. Today, such people might find themselves unable to sustain a job because of their poor intelligence and capabilities, and so they live on state benefits, while those with more severe defects are under the learning difficulties services. Intellectual disability is further discussed in Chapter 15 (page 572).

## A trait-based approach to the psychopath in Proverbs

A second way of assessing the question as to whether the Book of Proverbs is describing a severe and malignant personality disorder such as antisocial personality disorder is by considering the adverse personality traits it condemns. 'Traits' are defined in DSM-5 as:

> enduring patterns of perceiving, relating and thinking about the environment and oneself over a wide range of social and personal contexts. They describe the underpinnings of the behavior patterns but not the specific behaviors themselves. Maladaptive traits can be combined to form a limited number of personality disorder categories.

What, then, are the traits which define antisocial personality disorder? An early modern author on psychopathy, Cleckley (1941), in his famous book *The Mask of Sanity*, gave a detailed description of the condition. A later author, Hare, based his analysis largely on Cleckley's work isolated a number of key traits which he believed were the core features of psycho-pathic personality disorder. His original scale, the Psychopathic Checklist (PCL), had only 20 items listed below but the latest revised version has 22 items (PCL-R; Hare, 1991). Subjects in high-security prisons score very highly on this scale, indicating that it is a valid descriptive tool for a severe antisocial type; the scale also provides some kind of quantitative measure of the severity of the disorder. The scale is extensively used in research into psychopathy and in Canada it is used by the parole boards to assess risks of relapse among prisoners seeking parole All the items described in this scale are traits which are universally recognised as being of bad character and these are listed below:

a. Glibness/superficial charm
b. Grandiose sense of self-worth
c. Need for stimulation/proneness to boredom
d. Pathological lying
e. Conning/manipulative
f. Lack of remorse or guilt
g. Shallow affect
h. Callous, lack of empathy
i. Parasitic lifestyle
j. Poor behavioural control
k. Promiscuous sexual behaviour
l. Early behavioural problems
m. Lack of realistic long-term goals
n. Impulsivity
o. Irresponsibility
p. Failure to accept responsibility for one's actions
q. Many short-term marital relationships
r. Juvenile delinquency
s. Revocation of conditional release
t. Criminal versatility

Do these same traits appear in the Book of Proverbs? Below, I have attempted to match specific biblical verses from Proverbs with the items on Hare's Psychopathic Checklist listed above. The definition of the trait according to Hare is given in the first part of the item, and this is then matched to verses as given mostly in the King James version of Proverbs, as this sometimes seems to give a better translation of the malevolent character traits. Where the word 'fool' is used the Hebrew type of fool in Proverbs is given in parentheses. Some of these traits are also mentioned in the Wisdom literature of other ancient Near Eastern cultures and these have also been included.

## Item a. Glibness/superficial charm

The individual is glib, voluble and verbally facile; he exudes an insincere and superficial sort of charm. He is able to tell unlikely but convincing stories that place him in a good light. He may succeed in presenting himself well and may even be quite likeable but he generally seems too slick and smooth to be entirely believable, but when tested his knowledge is only superficial.

There are several verses alluding to this trait and the association between superficial charm and bad character was obviously well understood in biblical times:

26²⁸    And a flattering tongue worketh ruin

5³      For the lips of a strange woman drop as an honeycomb,
        And her mouth is smoother than oil

16²⁹    A man of violence enticeth his neighbour.                    (King James)

Note that here enticing behaviour is linked to violence

## Item b. Grandiose sense of self-worth

The individual has a grossly inflated view of his abilities and self-worth. He may impress as a braggart. He often appears self-assured, opinionated and cocky during an interview. His inflated ego and exaggerated regard for his own abilities are remarkable given the facts of his life. He is convinced his present circumstances are the result of bad luck, unfaithful friends or an unfair and incompetent criminal justice system. He feels that the trades taught in prison are worthless or beneath him.

14¹⁶    The wise man is cautious and avoids misfortune
        But the fool is arrogant and confident            *(kesil)*

21²⁴    The proud and haughty man, scorner is his name  *(lēs)*
        He worketh in the arrogance of pride.                        (NRSV)

The RSV has scorner; the King James version has scoffer. The Hebrew is *lēs*.

12¹⁵    Fools think their own way is right           *('ĕwil)*
        but the wise listen to advice

Fools are self-opinionated, and their failure to take advice from others is implied in the second line as a synthetic parallelism. The foolish (*'ĕwil*) is placed opposite the wise (*hacham*).

15²⁵    The Lord tears down the house of the proud.                  (NRSV)

## Item c. Need for stimulation/proneness to boredom

The individual demonstrates a chronic and excessive need for novel and exciting stimulation and an unusual proneness to boredom. He expresses a strong interest in taking chances, 'living in the fast lane' or 'being where the action is'. School, work and long term relationships are all boring and he may take drugs. He comments that he has itchy feet and needs to be on the go, and cannot imagine working at the same job for any length of time.

Some psychopaths have a need for stimulation and are constantly novelty seeking. Cloninger *et al.* (2000) attributed this trait to a dysfunctional brain dopaminergic system.

Proneness to boredom is not described in Proverbs, but the need for stimulation is clearly alluded to in the description of 'the contentious man', who in the realm of interpersonal relationships is likened to an arsonist:

26²⁰ When there is no wood, then the fire goeth out;
    so when there is no tale bearer, the strife ceaseth.
²¹     As coals are to burning coals, and wood to fire;
    so is a contentious man to kindle strife.                  (King James)

The verse describes the harm caused by the contentious man who goes around stoking up fires and trouble, and his need for stimulation or excitement is clear. A kind of dysphoric restlessness akin to boredom is also described with the 'strange woman' who has a need to go out into the street and seduce young men:

7¹¹ She is loud and wayward;
    her feet do not stay at home.
¹²  Now in the street, now in the square.                      (NRSV)

Note that Hare's definition of 'proneness for boredom' includes the phrase 'has itchy feet, needs to be on the go'.

## Item d. Pathological lying

Lying and deceit are a part of the individual's interactions with others. He is capable of fabricating elaborate accounts of his past. His readiness to lie and the apparent ease with which he can carry it off may be quite remarkable. He has an explanation or excuse for everything and often makes new promises 'on his word of honour'. He often lies for obvious reasons but deceiving others also seems to have some intrinsic value for him.

There are numerous references in Proverbs to the harm caused by lying. The first two examples may be a description of perjury:

14⁵ A faithful witness does not lie
    but a false witness breathes out life.                     (NRSV)

14²⁵ A true witness delivereth souls;
    but a deceitful witness speaketh lies.                     (King James)

Whybray comments that the references to lying in the OT usually signify lying in court or perjury and the OT takes a particularly harsh line against this. McKane (1970, p. 469) writes. 'The two verses 14⁵ and 14²⁵ are forensic in character'. A truthful witness does not lie, but a perjurer utters falsehoods. Thus the truthful witness 'saves lives' insofar as his honest testimony enables the judicial process to function effectively (Whybray, 1990, p. 221). The witness who perjures the judge may bring about a false conviction and as capital punishment occurred this could lead to the death of an innocent person. The observation that most of the references to lying seem to occur in the context of perjury or lying in court has implications concerning the role of the sages in the legal system. Possibly some of them were tasked with the questioning of witnesses in court, as a barrister might do today.

Lying is also specifically linked with the scoundrel (*belial*).

6¹⁹   A lying witness who testifies falsely,
     and one who sows discord in the family.                     (NRSV)

12¹⁹  Truthful lips endure forever,
     but a lying tongue lasts only a moment.

The Talmud (Shabbath 104a) offers a very quaint explanation for the second verse. The word for a 'lying tongue' or falsehood has three Hebrew letters, ש (*shin*), ק (*kof*) and ר (*resh*), as in שׁ ק ר *sheker*. These three letters all stand on one foot, but to stand on one foot is very unstable. However, the Hebrew word for truth, המא (*emet*) has three letters, א (*aleph*), מ (*mem*) and ה (*hay*), which either stand on two legs or stand firmly on the line, hence the saying 'truth stands, but falsehood lasts only a moment'.

Lying with slander is also condemned and associated with the *kesil*.

10¹⁸  He that hateth is of lying lips,
     And he that uttereth slander is a fool.    *(kesil)*     (King James)

There are other parallels in the ancient Wisdom literature of Assyria in the the Proverbs of Ahiqar. This manuscript was originally in Aramaic and an early version was found among the Elephantine papyri (Cowley, 1923):

> My son if thy will is to be wise, refrain thy tongue from lying and thy hand from theft, and thou shall become wise. (Proverbs of Ahiqar)

### Item e. Conning/manipulative

Although this item is similar to the previous item of lying, the deceit and deception are used to cheat, defraud or manipulate others. There may be schemes or scams motivated by a desire for personal gain with no concern for the effects on victims. Some of his schemes are well thought out and may be carried out in a cool self-assured and brazen manner. He may be involved in two or three intimate relationships at a time which are unknown to his partners. He may use dishonest and unethical practices that are of dubious legality or make use of loopholes in the law.

Behaviour of this type and its link with a bad character were well understood in ancient times, and Jeremiah's account of the *belial* places the trait of conning and cheating in at its core (quoted on page 396).

For conning:

11¹   A false balance is an abomination to the Lord
    But an accurate weight is his delight.                (NRSV)

And for manipulation:

6¹⁸   A heart that devises wicked plans.

16²⁸    A perverse man spreads strife
and a whisperer separates close friends.

18⁸    The words of a whisperer are as dainty morsels
and they go down into the innermost parts of the belly.                (NRSV)

The implication of the last verse is that the whisperer's words go down into
the belly to stir up some trouble or action, and so the verse is similar in
meaning to the English expression of a 'shit-stirrer'. The classical medieval
Jewish interpretation of this verse is quite different and has a more medical
connotation. Thus Mezudath David has 'The words of the whisperer are like
stunning blows that penetrate. They do not cause superficial wounds, but
internal injuries. Just as it is difficult to cure internal injuries, so it is difficult
to cure the blows delivered by the grumbler' (Rosenberg, 1993, p. 165).

22²⁶    though hatred is covered with guile
the enemy's wickedness will be exposed in the assembly.                (NRSV)

Here, the hatred is concealed by guile, suggesting manipulativeness, and this
is linked to wickedness. This trait is also described with the 'strange woman'.

7¹⁰    ... a woman with the attire of a harlot, and wily of heart.

## Item f. Lack of remorse or guilt

The individual shows a lack of concern for the negative consequences
for others of both his criminal and his non-criminal actions. He is more
concerned with the effects his actions have upon himself than about any
suffering caused to his victims or damage to society. Lack of remorse may
also be indicated by failure to appreciate the seriousness of his actions or
by arguing that the victim, society or extenuating circumstances were all to
blame.

14⁹    Fools mock at the guilt offering            (*'ēwillim*)
but the upright enjoy the Lord's favour.                (NRSV)

## Item g. Shallow affect

The individual is unable to experience a normal range and depth of
emotion and may appear cold and unemotional. Displays of emotion are
generally dramatic, shallow and short-lived; they leave the observer with
the impression that he is play acting. He may admit that he is unemotional
or that he shams emotions. Sometimes the individual claims to experience
strong emotions yet seems to describe the subtleties of various emotional
states. He may equate love with sexual arousal, sadness with frustration,
anger with irritability.

This trait is familiar to most psychiatrists but is not well described
anywhere in Proverbs.

## Item h. Callous/lack of empathy

The individual has attitudes and behaviours that indicate a profound lack of empathy and a callous disregard for the feelings, rights and welfare of others. He is cynical and selfish. Any appreciation of the pain, anguish or discomfort of others is merely abstract and intellectual. He has no hesitation in mocking other people, including those who have experienced misfortune or those who suffer from mental or physical handicap. There may be reports of callous or sadistic treatment of others, or the use of excessive violence for no apparent reason.

10²³    It is a sport to a fool to do mischief,                    *(kesil)*
        but a man of understanding hath wisdom.

26¹⁹    So is the man that deceiveth his neighbour
        And saith, am I not in sport?                         (King James)

A sport implies a game, and so the fool (*kesil*) does not care about his victim. The second line indicates that this trait is an opposite of wisdom, and is an integral part of the fool's character. The metaphor of a sport is used again in 19²⁶ in the context of being deceitful, also suggesting an uncaring attitude to the victim.

## Item i. Parasitic lifestyle

Financial dependence on others is an intentional part of the individual's lifestyle. Although able-bodied, he avoids steady, gainful employment, but instead continually relies on family, friends and social security. He obtains what he wants either by presenting himself as helpless or by using coercion or threats, or by exploiting his victims' weaknesses. His use of others to support himself is not simply the result of temporary circumstances that prevent him from working but is seen over the longer term as well.

This trait is not described as such in Proverbs, but lazy people are condemned.

21²⁶    The craving of the lazy person is fatal,    Heb.: *asel* = sluggard, lazy person
        for lazy hands refuse to labour.

6⁹     How long will you lie there,
        O lazybones                             *asel* = sluggard            (NRSV)

The concept of the lazy person or sluggard (Heb. = *asel*) is described in Waltke (2005, pp. 115–116) but it does not include a notion of living off others, although it may be implied. It is possible that the concept of parasitic existence did not exist in the ancient world because there was no welfare state. Nowadays it is possible to live off the state but this is a comparatively recent social development, perhaps first occurring only during in the twentieth century. Parasitic existence within the family for the young, the old or the sick might occur but this is very different. In the ancient world a man could live through his honest labour and failing that he might survive through a life of crime, but it was probably just not possible to survive as a parasite for a prolonged period in any ancient society and so this may explain why there is no description of this item but only of the trait of extreme laziness.

## Item j. Poor behavioural control

The individual has poor behavioural control. He may be described as short-tempered or hot-headed. His response to criticism, attempts to discipline him and frustration is with threats, verbal abuse or even violence. He takes offence easily and becomes angry and aggressive over trivialities. His outbursts are often short-lived and he acts as if nothing out of the ordinary has happened. His behavioural controls, not ordinarily very strong, may be further weakened by alcohol.

There are numerous descriptions of this trait in Proverbs, with the lack of control usually appertaining to outbursts of temper.

17¹² Better to meet a she bear robbed of its cubs
than to confront a fool immersed in his folly.    fool, *kesil;* folly *'ĕwillet*

It is difficult to imagine a more dangerous situation than an enraged bear robbed of its cubs, but the inflamed *kesil* seems to be similarly inflamed.

20³ It is an honour for a man to keep from strife
but every fool will be quarrelling.    *'ĕwil*    (NRSV)

20¹¹ A fool gives full vent to anger    *kesil*
but the wise quietly hold it back.    (NRSV)

14²⁹ Whoever is slow to anger has great understanding
but one who has a hasty temper exalts folly.    *'ĕwillet*    (NRSV)

In these verses the antithetic parallelism is used to contrast hasty temper against restraint.

16³² He that is slow to anger is better than the mighty
he that ruleth his spirit is better than he that taketh a city.    (King James)

14¹⁷ A quick tempered man acts foolishly
and a man of sinful plots is hated.    *'ĕwil*

Note the association above between irritability and malice (sinful plots) in the last verse.

29²² One given to anger stirs up strife
And the hot head causes much transgression.

19¹¹ It is a discretion in a man to restrain his anger
And it his glory to forgive transgression.

23²⁴ Associate not with a passionate man
Nor go with a wrathful man.

There are nine separate verses expressing the undesirability of the trait of uncontrolled anger, some of which are accompanied by praise for the ability to exercise restraint or control one's anger. Are these the work of nine separate authors? This particular trait gave the greatest concern then, just as it does now, because of its potential to lead to violence. Not surprisingly, the trait of unrestrained anger is also well described in the Wisdom literature of ancient Egypt and Assyria. An ancient Egyptian Wisdom parallel is:

> Be not angry; to be friendly is good. Let the memory of thee abide because of thy loving kindness. (Teaching of Meri-ka-re)

Meri-ka-re is extremely old Egyptian wisdom literature, circa 2100 BCE.

> Associate not with a passionate man
> Nor approach him for conversation.
> (*Teaching of Amenemope* $9^{11}$)

A similar saying describing poor behavioural control in association with homicide is found in the Assyrian Wisdom literature:

> My son, stand not in the house of those that are in strife; because from a word there cometh a quarrel, and from a quarrel is stirred up vexation, and from vexedness springeth murder. (Proverbs of Ahiqar; see Lindenberger, 1983)

The trait of inordinate or uncontrolled anger has been recognised since ancient times as being very harmful. Modern studies such as Stone's (1990) follow-up of borderline personality disorder have demonstrated that those borderlines who also had the trait of inordinate anger did particularly badly.

## Item k. Promiscuous sexual behaviour

This item describes an individual whose sexual relations with others are impersonal, casual or trivial. There may be frequent casual relations (e.g. one-night stands), indiscriminate selection of sexual partners, frequent infidelities, prostitution or a willingness to participate in a wide range of sexual activities. The individual may coerce others into sexual activity and there may be convictions for sexual offences.

Proverbs has criticisms of men who consort with prostitutes, which suggests promiscuity on the part of the man.

$29^3$   A child who loves wisdom makes a parent glad,
        but to keep company with prostitutes is to squander one's substance.

$6^{26}$   For on account of a whorish woman
        a man is brought to a piece of bread.

The Talmud (Sotah 4a) comments on the last verse: 'Whoever consorts with or patronises with a harlot will be reduced to poverty and seek a loaf of bread and not find it'.

Promiscuous behaviour is also described in association with the 'strange woman' and the fate of her many lovers who come to an unfortunate end (see page 444 in the next chapter).

## Item 1. Early behaviour problems

The individual has had serious behavioural problems as a child (i.e. age 12 and below). These may include persistent lying, cheating, theft, fire-setting, truancy, bullying, early violence and running away from home. There are reports of disruptive behaviour both at home and at school. The subject may be described as the black sheep of the family or as hyperactive or unmanageable.

These items from Hare's psychopathic checklist indicate that psychopathy may manifest itself in childhood or adolescence and cause despair to the parents.

| 22¹⁵ | Foolishness is bound up in the heart of a child | ? *'ĕwillet* |
| | but the rod of correction shall drive it far from him. | (King James) |

The description here is of a manifestation in childhood. Punishment is still applicable and just might work because the 'fool' is young and the parents are still responsible. Although the advice is stern, there is hope the child will change. The next three quotes describe parental distress at having a 'fool' (*kesil*) for an offspring. The words *'ĕwil* and *kesil*, both translated as 'fool', denote rebelliousness, bad temper and badness in the case of the *kesil*, while for the *'ĕwil* a degree of stupidity is implied as well.

| 10¹ | A wise child makes a glad father | |
| | But a foolish child is a mother's grief. | *kesil* (NRSV) |

| 17²⁵ | Foolish children are a grief to their father | *kesil* |
| | and bitterness to her who bore them. | (NRSV) |

| 17²¹ | He that begetteth a fool doeth it to his sorrow | *kesil* |
| | and the father of a fool hath no joy. | (King James) |

The classical medieval Jewish interpretation for 'the foolish son' of 10¹ and 17²⁵ is given by Rashi, who says the foolish son refers to Jeroboam, the son of Nebat, while 'he who bore him' refers to Esau, who caused distress to his parents Isaac and Rebecca (Rosenberg, pp. 54, 106). These three verses describe how parents feel about having a 'deviant/disturbed' child and how miserable they seem to be (discussed further in Chapter 13, on page 500).

Difficulties with one's children, or the bringing up of disturbed children, were a universal source of despair, not solely confined to the Israelite people. Not surprisingly, there are references to this problem in the much older Mesopotamian and Egyptian Wisdom literature. One of these documents in the Sumerian Wisdom literature written about 2500 BCE entitled 'A scribe and his delinquent son' consists almost entirely of a father's bitter denunciation of his ungrateful son, whom he claims hates school and learning, hates the scribal art and is generally perverse, constantly seeking materialistic and other depraved pleasures. However, instead of ending his diatribe with a curse, the scribe proceeds to bless him as fatherly love overcomes his parental disappointment. This ancient document was translated from the Cuneiform into German as 'Der Vater und sein Misratener Sohn' (A. W. Sjoberg, 1973).

## *Item m. Lack of realistic long-term goals*

The individual is unable or unwilling to formulate long term plans or goals. He tends to live day to day and to change his plans frequently. He does not give a serious thought to the future nor does he worry about it very much. This probably refers to an inability to plan for the future, as well as a desire for instant gratification and both these elements are described in Proverbs.

12[11]   He who works his land will have abundant food
         But he who chases fantasies lacks judgement                          *hasar leb*

Long-term planning is clearly needed to be a successful farmer, to work the land. One who lacks judgement (the *hasar lab*) is one of the categories of fool, possibly with learning difficulties. The notion of long-term planning or goals – such as bringing in the harvest – is therefore placed in a parallelism but antithetically to the concept of a fool (in this case the *hasar leb*), meaning that the fool does not have long-term goals.

10[5]   A child who gathers in summer is prudent
        But a child who sleeps in summer brings in shame.

The agricultural metaphors are fitting for a peasant agrarian society. The reference here, however, is to a child and not to a fool. A wish for short-term gratification or pleasure-seeking behaviour is also described.

21[17]   He that loveth pleasure shall be a poor man.
         He that loveth wine and oil shall not be rich.

Pleasure-seeking behaviour is central to the modern concept of antisocial behaviours and poverty is the consequence of such impulses. An association between pleasure-seeking and drinking is also implied in this verse.

## *Item n. Impulsivity*

The individual is generally impulsive and lacking in reflection or forethought. He acts on the spur of the moment or because he feels like it. He is unlikely to weigh the pros and cons of a course of action. He will often break off relationships, quit jobs or move from place to place on little more than a whim and without bothering to inform others.

There are numerous references to this trait in Proverbs, which was obviously regarded as very troublesome then just as it is today.

14[17]   One who is quick tempered acts foolishly   *'ĕwillim*
         and a crafty man is hated.

In this verse actions based on quick temper (impulsivity?) are linked to the crafty man – both different attributes of the psychopath.

14[29]   He that is hasty of spirit exalteth folly    *'ĕwillim*
                                                      hasty of spirit = ?decides or acts
                                                      quickly, and the trait is linked to
                                                      folly

19²   Desire without knowledge is not good
and one who moves hurriedly misses
the way                                   (NRSV)

The above verse is not obviously about impulsivity, but this meaning may have been lost in translation. Toy (1899) offers a different translation of the same verse which is nearer the concept of impulsivity:

19²   To act without reflection is not good
he who is hasty in action fails in his aim.

6¹⁸   A heart that devises wicked plans     *belial*
feet that hurry to run to do evil.                   (NRSV)

Note again the association of 'run to do evil' (impulsivity?) and bad character.

Taken together with the numerous references to bad temper and poor control, it is clear that the traits of behavioural disinhibition and impulsivity were of major concern to the sages of old – just as they are for the courts of justice today.

## Item o. Irresponsibility

The subject habitually fails to fulfil or honour obligations and commitments to others. He has no sense of duty or loyalty to family, friends, employers or causes. Irresponsibility is shown in financial areas (e.g. defaulting on loans), work behaviour (e.g. sloppy performance), business relationships and failure to support a spouse or children, causing them unnecessary hardship.

This is not well described in Proverbs.

## Item p. Failure to take responsibility for one's actions

This refers to the way a psychopath will often rationalise or deny any wrongdoing or by offering all sorts of excuses or place the blame on others.

10¹⁸   When words are many, transgression is not lacking.     (NRSV)

20²³   Like the glaze covering an earthen vessel
are smooth lips with an evil heart.                (NRSV)

26²⁴   He that hateth dissembleth with his lips
and layeth up deceit within him           (King James)

The NRSV has 'enemy' and the NIV has 'malicious man' for 'he that hateth', which is consistent with linking this behaviour to that of the psychopath. However, all translations have 'dissembleth'.

The *Oxford English Dictionary* defines 'to dissemble' as 'To alter the semblance of (one's character, a feeling, design, *or action*) so as to conceal or deceive as to its real nature; to give a false or feigned semblance to; to cloak or disguise by a feigned appearance'. This description is similar though not quite identical to 'failure to take responsibility for one's actions'. Rationalising is familiar behaviour among psychopaths, particularly in court when they try to explain away their wrongdoing.

### Item q. Many short-term marital relationships

Although divorce existed in the ancient world it was greatly frowned upon. For example, Malachi 2[16] states 'For I hate divorce says the Lord, the God of Israel'. If a man married for a second or third time the expectation was for a prolonged marriage and not for a series of short-term relationships. There is no direct description of this phenomenon, but the lecture in Proverbs 5[15-20] gives a strong exhortation for a man to remain in a monogamous relationship and by advocating a single long-term monogamous pattern as the preferred path, the authors imply that a pattern of shorter-term relationships probably existed for some individuals in the community.

### Item r. Juvenile delinquency

See item l, early behaviour problems, above.

### Item s. Revocation from conditional release

This implies that conditional release from prison has occurred, but the subject has reoffended and has had to be recalled back to prison.

Prison probably did not exist for common criminals in ancient Israel and so this item should be considered under the general rubric of recidivism. A person who reoffended after being admonished would have posed a threat to society. There are two references to serious recidivism, both suggesting that such behaviour might be punishable by death:

| 29[1] | One who is often reproved yet remains stubborn | ?recidivism |
| | will suddenly be broken beyond healing. | ?capital punishment |

| 19[16] | Those who keep the commandment will live | |
| | Those who are heedless in their ways will die. | ?capital punishment |

The translation of the latter by Toy (1899) is even more clear.

| 19[16] | He who obeys the law preserves his life. | |
| | He who despises the word will die. | |

Toy also comments that the Masoretic text has 'put to death' for 'will die', which is even more explicit. An ancient society with no prisons might have no alternative to capital punishment as a way of dealing with the problem of severe recidivism, which is implied in this particular item.

The item can also be interpreted as 'failure to learn through punishment' and there are numerous references to the difficulties in changing the character of a fool – through punishment or any other means. This is an important insight in the light of modern difficulties in changing the behaviours of the severe psychopath. These individuals just don't change, either with the harshness of punishment or with the kindness of therapy.

$27^{22}$  Crush a fool in a mortar with a pestle   *'ĕwil*
along with crushed grain
but the folly will not be driven out.   *'ĕwillet*

$17^{10}$  A rebuke strikes deeper into a discerning person
than a hundred blows into a fool.   *kesil*   (NRSV)

$13^{1}$  A wise son heareth his father's instruction;
but a scorner heareth not rebuke.   *lēs*
$^{2}$  A man shall eat good by the fruit of his mouth;
but the soul of the transgressor shall eat violence.   (King James)

Note that the scorner (*lēs*) is also associated with not being able to learn and in the next verse he is linked to treachery and violence, all of which are prominent psychopathic traits.

## Item t. Criminal versatility

The main description of antisocial personality disorder is contained in the description of the *belial* or scoundrel ($6^{12-19}$). Fox (2000) describes how this word is used in association with many other crimes in different books of the OT. It is used to describe rapists (Judges $19^{22}$) and perjurors (I Kings $21^{10}$) and in Jeremiah ($5^{26}$) it is linked to conning and taking the goods of others. Although Hare's definition refers to a single individual committing diverse crimes, the *belial* was capable of many different crimes and so may have displayed 'criminal versatility'.

## Summary

The sages of Proverbs seem to have been very familiar with the character of the psychopath and ancient Israel seems to have found them to be just as great a burden to the harmony of their society as we find them today. Almost all of the items of Hare's Psychopathy Check List are lucidly described in Proverbs, but appearing in a rather haphazard order, seemingly randomly distributed throughout the Book of Proverbs. They are attached to different types of character, the *'ĕwil*, the *kesil*, the *lēs* and the *belial*. Traits that are poorly described are: many short-term marital relationships and shallow affect, and irresponsibility is not described at all. Parasitic existence is not described, but this may relate to the lack of recognition of such a concept in the ancient world, where there was an exclusively dichotomous (righteous or sinful) view of man and his actions.

All eighteen other items are well described with remarkable accuracy in biblical verse and so virtually the whole of Hare's PCL-R is reproduced in the Book of Proverbs – a religious text written probably more than 2500 years before either Cleckley or Hare published their work.

## Aspects of antisocial personality disorder

A brief clinical description from a modern textbook by Casey (1998) provides a useful overview and gives a good match to the character typology described in Proverbs. She writes:

> These individuals may be charming, brusque or occasionally belligerent in their manner. There is generally an inner coldness coupled with insensitivity to the feelings of others and a lack of empathy. The more severe cases are obviously callous, and some will have committed serious crimes. In social or family situations there is a tendency to try to dominate, or at the very least demean other people. Confrontation on some personal issue may provoke revenge, and among those with poor impulse control this may rapidly escalate into violence.
>
> People with antisocial personality disorder usually have a clear grasp of the moral values of society and may even superficially acknowledge that they should change their behaviour. They repeatedly fail to learn from experience or fail to respond to more conventional punishment regimes. A few, especially the more simple types, may be so grossly insensitive as to be genuinely unaware of the feelings of others. However, most are all too aware of the foibles and weaknesses of other people and take advantage to prey on them. The defect in affectional responsiveness is serious and it is probably this aspect which permits the callous behaviour. There is little capacity to share tender feelings or experience any genuine affection or love. A sham apology, or expression of contrition, may sometimes appear after hurting someone, or following a serious crime, but there is little or no genuine experience of guilt or remorse.

Boredom and a low tolerance of frustration are common. Many of these individuals are unable to sustain the tedium of a job or the day-to-day responsibilities of a marriage. They may resort to thrill-seeking behaviours, such as gambling, promiscuity or substance abuse. In spite of their almost total lack of respect for the rights of others, many have a superficial charm and a mask of civility. However, before long the charmer will display his true colours as a con man or fraudster and sooner or later hostile feelings and vindictiveness usually appear. Antisocial personalities usually explain their aggressive or hostile behaviour with explanations and rationalisations (e.g. 'the world is tough place where dog eats dog'). Often they blame other people, such as their spouse or their employers, for their relationship difficulties and ascribe their malevolent impulses to others, as an explanation or rationalisation for their behaviour. Attacks (physical or verbal) then become justified as the subjects view themselves as the persecuted victim.

Antisocial personality disorder is a common condition. Werner *et al.* (2015) review estimates of the lifetime prevalence of the disorder in the general population and these range from approximately 1% to 4%, with 12-month prevalence rates between 2% and 3.3%. These estimates are broad. Gender also seems to play a role, as males are three to five times more likely to be diagnosed with antisocial personality disorder than females; 6% of men and 2% of women meet DSM-IV criteria for antisocial personality disorder in the general population, which holds as well for clinical samples based on primary care clinics (8% of men versus 3% of women). Most studies give figures in the 2–3% range and it is noteworthy that all the biblical 'fools' are male. Prevalence rates are higher among young people, as the condition attenuates as people get older and more mature. For those who turn to crime, 'criminal burn-out' may occur as subjects get older. Rates are higher among those of lower socio-economic status, the unemployed, widowed, separated and divorced, with lowest rates among the married. Poor education is associated with higher rates of the disorder, but this may be a consequence of the disorder rather than a cause, because these individuals are much more difficult to educate, a problem frequently mentioned in the biblical text. High concentrations of psychopaths are found in prisons because of the association with crime, particularly with recidivism, and up to 80% of those in prison showing recidivism may have an antisocial personality disorder.

## Forensic aspects: a note concerning culpability in the Old Testament

It is important at the outset to make a distinction between the criminal and the psychopath. Most crime is committed by 'normal' people who do not have a personality disorder, and only a minority of individuals who carry the label 'psychopath' go on to commit crimes. Although psychopathic people can commit almost any sort of crime, they are particularly associated with the more severe and callous crimes, and crimes of impulsive violence, including murder. An important difference between a 'normal criminal' and one with a severe personality disorder is that the usual punitive and corrective measures, such as prison and rehabilitation programmes, may improve the outcome for a more normal individual and can often result in a change for the better, but they have little effect on those with personality disorder, especially on those with antisocial personality disorder. Dolan and Coid (1993) provide a comprehensive review of all the available treatment studies for antisocial personality disorder over the last 50 years, almost all of which were ineffective, and they concluded:

> most treatment methods currently being provided for people suffering from psychopathic disorder could not prove their efficacy in order to pass a treatability test.... It seems strange that so little advance has been made over the last fifty years.

Had these authors also included the account of treatment resistance given in the Book of Proverbs they might have concluded their review by writing 'It seems strange that so little advance has been made over the last 2500 years'!

Because of their inability to change, people with antisocial personality disorder have high rates of recidivism and so account for a large and disproportionate number of the crimes committed. They also tend to accumulate in prison populations, and in some prisons account for the majority of inmates.

Is the psychopath responsible for his actions? This debate has raged at least since the 19th century. What is interesting is that a similar type of discussion appears to have taken place with regard to different character disorders of the Old Testament. Thus Donald (1963), in his analysis of the meaning of the different types of fool, was able to provide a hierarchy as to who were the less culpable and which types were more culpable when they committed a crime. The least culpable were the *pethi* (the simpleton), the *hasar leb* (those without heart) and the *ba-ar* (the animal brute). These types are fools in the sense of being stupid with low intelligence. The *kesil* (oaf) is a more blameworthy fool and the *'ĕwil* (knave) is more definitely responsible for his actions (Fox, 2000, p. 39; Donald, 1976, p. 292). The *belial* (scoundrel) was punished for his criminal activities, and the text refers to capital punishment solely for this category. Such a gradation in the degree of culpability, and therefore severity of punishment, displays some compassion as well as a degree of legal sophistication in the management of severe personality disorder, perhaps not dissimilar to present-day court practice.

In the DSM-5 definition of antisocial personality disorder, criterion D states that the condition can be diagnosed only if 'The occurrence of the antisocial behaviour does not occur exclusively in the course of schizophrenia or a manic episode'. This clause was included because the behaviour of an inflamed psychopathic person and an insane (psychotic) person are often similar so readily confused but have very different origins. The sages in Proverbs were also able to note this similarity, yet different origin:

29¹⁷  Is one who meddles in the quarrel
        of another.
¹⁸     Like a maniac who shoots deadly          Heb. *mitlameah* = maniac
        firebrands and arrows,
¹⁹     so is one who deceives and says
        'I am only joking'.

The Hebrew word for maniac, *mitlameah*, literally means 'madman' or like-man-being-mad (Kohlenberger, p. 558). This verse compares two characters who 'meddle in the quarrels of others': one is a maniac, and the other is one who deceives people and regards this as a joke and so presumably this one has a psychopathic personality disorder. The verse conveys the similarity between mad and bad behaviour but differentiates between the two possible causes: the mad from the bad or, in modern terminology, between psychosis and psychopathy. Psychiatrists, particularly those with forensic expertise, are commonly called to write reports to assist the courts in making this distinction, which lies at the heart of much medical jurisprudence for the mentally ill today.

## Prognosis

Proverbs places a poor prognosis on its fools. Modern studies, reviewed below, show that people with low intelligence or those with severe personality disorder (of either sex) often have a poor outcome. Not only are their lives far more chaotic and disorganised but there is statistical evidence of raised mortality rates, with much of this excess mortality being explained by sudden and violent deaths. There is also the problem of high rates of associated alcoholism with personality disorder, and alcoholic violence (discussed in Chapter 14 on page 534). Sometimes the sages explained this raised mortality in moralistic terms (e.g. God might favour the good or the wise and punish the wicked) but in other places only the observed fact of a greater risk of an early death is recorded. Because there are eight separate verses describing the premature mortality of those with folly, it is possible that each represents the observations of several different scribes. They are randomly scattered throughout the Book of Proverbs. The simpletons (*pethi*) die because of their lack of intelligence, as they cannot feed or look after themselves properly:

10¹⁸ The lips of the righteous feed many
    but fools die for lack of sense.                    *pethi*

Also:

1³² For waywardness kills the simple          *pethi*
    and the complacency of fools destroys them.   *kesillim*

Today, those with learning difficulties need to be looked after and fed, and if left to their own devices would probably starve or become ill and die. However, in the ancient world, a simpleton, without the support of his family, might have perished early, and perhaps this was the reality of the time that the sages wrote about.

In the description of the *belial* (scoundrel) there is a suggestion of an execution:

6¹⁵ ... on such a one calamity
    will descend suddenly
    in a moment damage beyond repair.

A further reference to premature death is given for the 'wicked man' (*eesh rashah*):

5²² The iniquities of the wicked ensnare them,    *eesh rashah*
    and they are caught in the toils of their sin.
²³ For they die for lack of discipline
    and because of their great folly they are lost.          (NRSV)

Similarly:

13⁹ The light of the righteous rejoices
    but the lamp of the wicked goes out.      *rashah*

Verse 10²⁶ provides a similar comment on premature death, again with the implication that it is the wickedness that leads to punishment and a shorter life. The proverb is to be understood literally (Whybray, p. 172):

10²⁶ The fear of the Lord will prolong life
    but the years of the wicked will be short    *rashayyim*

Premature death for the young who have difficult hostile relationships with their parents is also commented on:

30[17]   The eye that mocketh at his father
        and despiseth to obey his mother,
        the ravens of the valley shall pick it out
        and the young eagles shall eat it.                          (King James)

The ravens of the valley refers to vultures and the scene described here is the death of a young person who was abusive to his parents (mocks his father); the death is away from home, probably sudden and violent, and no burial has taken place because a proper burial would have given protection from the carrion birds (Murphy, 1998, p. 295).

A similar scenario is described in 20[20]:

20[20]   If you curse father or mother
        Your lamp will go out in utter darkness.

Ibn Ezra sees the lamp as representing the soul, while the flickering lamp alludes to the death penalty, which is imposed on one who curses his father or mother. Darkness is a metaphor for troubles (Rosenberg, 1993, p. 123). Whybray (1994) suggests the phrase 'Your lamp goes out in darkness' refers to an execution, and a person who is abusive to his parents is of a similar type to one who later in life commits a capital offence.

The scribes of Proverbs have picked up on the high mortality among young delinquents, and this is also confirmed by modern studies. Thus Fok *et al.* (2012) studied a large cohort of people with personality disorders ($n = 1836$) who had been admitted to a psychiatric units in south-east London and compared their mortality to the expected general population rates. Men with personality disorders had a life expectancy of 59.1 years compared with the general population figure of 76.8 years – a shortfall of 17.7 years. Women with personality disorder had a life expectancy from birth of 63.3 years compared with the expected 82 years –a shortfall of 18.7 years. Zilber *et al.* (1989) studied the five-year mortality, using the standardised mortality ratio (SMRs), of all the patients admitted to psychiatric hospitals in Israel in the year 1978 ($n = 16,147$). These workers found the SMR for those with personality disorder was 6.9, which was similar to the rates for schizophrenia (SMR = 6.3) but lower than the rates for depression (SMR = 8.5). In their study around half the deaths for personality disorder were due to natural causes, and half were due either to violence or suicide.

A Swedish follow-up study of male antisocial adolescents found that 13% had died in the follow-up period, compared with an expected rate of 1–3% among healthy Swedish adolescents. They also found that 88% of the dead boys had met 'sudden and violent deaths', which they listed as accidents, suicides, murder/manslaughter, alcohol/drug abuse and death from uncertain causes. Robertson (1987) studied prisoners with very severe personality disorders, a group who would have caused great concern to any ancient society lacking prisons, and found that around 29% met a violent death in the 10-year follow-up period.

The sages who wrote the Book of Proverbs must have been all too aware of these premature deaths, as they refer to them on eight occasions, and may have been shocked by them, possibly in the same way as modern psychiatry is also concerned about the high early mortality of this group. The solution of the sages was, through education, to try to persuade young men to pursue a path of wisdom instead, as well as urging their parents to beat the 'folly' out of them (and when that didn't work to beat them even harder). While it may be all too easy to criticise the thinking of these ancient sages, young antisocial people still continue to die prematurely in their droves, and psychiatry has yet to find an answer for this all too common tragedy.

## Personality disorder and the concept of wisdom in Proverbs

Wisdom and its characteristics form the central theme of the Book of Proverbs, but wisdom is placed opposite folly in many places of the book. As demonstrated in this chapter, much of what is described as 'folly' in Proverbs appertains to personality disorder, especially antisocial personality disorder, and therefore wisdom, which is the opposite of folly will, to some degree, represent the antithesis of personality disorder. This antithesis was also recognised by Westerman (1995), the German theologian who devotes a whole chapter to this theme in his book *The Roots of Wisdom*. Donald (1963) sought to clarify the meaning of the different words used for folly by examining words placed in parallel with, or in opposition to, the words for 'wisdom' in the large number of parallel couplets which comprise the Book of Proverbs. This has made it easier to clarify the main features of the different categories of 'fool', as well some more subtle aspects of their personalities, such as their intelligence levels and their degree of malevolence.

The Old Testament concept of wisdom is somewhat nebulous but one way of enhancing its definition may be to examine how it is placed opposite to folly. In order to do this, every reference to 'wise' or 'wisdom' or related concepts must be scrutinised to see if it falls in a parallelism with some aspect of folly. Fortunately, to make this task easier there are huge lexicons which list the exact location(s) of every single word in the Bible. The most important of these is the Gesenius dictionary, *Lexicon Manuale Hebraicum et Chaldaicum in VT Libros*, published in 1833 by William Gesenius, which was revised many times and translated into English by Brown *et al.* (1906). The Gesenius dictionary has three words for 'wisdom':

- *hacham*, to be wise (verb; 49 entries; placed opposite a folly word 19 times)
- *hacham*, wise (adjective; 34 times; placed opposite a folly word 18 times)
- *hochma*, wisdom (15 times; placed opposite a folly word 4 times).

In total, wisdom is placed opposite a word for folly (or its modern equivalent, personality disorder) on 36 of 98 occasions (37%). This simple statistic implies that personality disorder, particularly antisocial personality disorder, would have had a significant impact on the formation of the biblical concept of wisdom as given in Proverbs.

It would take up too much space to repeat every single one of the 36 verses where a wisdom/folly pairing occurs; instead, a few of the most relevant ones are selected which yield a particular quality of wisdom described by the pairing.

Some verses just state that wisdom and folly are opposites:

14²⁴   The crown of the wise is their wisdom
       but folly is the garland of fools

However, other verses ascribe opposite character traits to folly and wisdom, and the wise are cautious and the fools are reckless:

14¹⁶   The wise are cautious and turn away          caution
       from evil
       but the fool throws off restraint            fool = *kesil*
       and is careless.                             reckless

Recklessness is a key characteristic of antisocial personality disorder (and forms part of the diagnostic criteria both for DSM-IV and ICD-10) and is clearly a very troublesome trait. Its opposite is the trait of caution and therefore caution becomes incorporated as one of the qualities of wisdom. Caution on its own, without being placed opposite recklessness, though a helpful trait, would not merit reaching such a lofty status as wisdom. However, by pairing it opposite the qualities of the *kesil* it becomes much more significant because 'not being a *kesil*' (a personality disorder) is the key to wisdom.

There are several other instances where a negative personality disorder trait is condemned and its opposite is hailed as an attribute of wisdom. In these instances *it is the maladaptive personality disorder trait which is the harmful social reality providing the driving force for selecting its opposite*, which then becomes an attribute of wisdom. These are shown in Table 10.4.

**Table 10.4** Attributes of wisdom derived from being the opposite to traits of folly (personality disorder?) in antithetic parallelisms in Proverbs

| Verse | Folly trait | Derived wisdom trait |
|---|---|---|
| 9⁸ | Difficulty in rebuking | Accepts advice/listens |
| 10²³ | Callous | Doing good |
| 10⁸ | Babbling/disinhibited talk | Obedient |
| 10¹⁴ | Babbling/disinhibited talk | Acquires knowledge |
| 11² | Pride | Humility |
| 12¹⁵ | Headstrong | Takes advice |
| 14¹⁰ | Insolence | Takes advice |
| 14¹ | Destructiveness | Constructiveness |
| 14³ | Gossip | Tact |
| 14¹⁶ | Careless | Cautious |
| 21²⁰ | Profligate | Saves money |
| 20¹ | Heavy drinking | Not destroyed by drink |

The central topic of the Book of Proverbs is 'wisdom' and how to lead a prosperous, successful and moral life. Folly (personality disorder) is one of several topics covered in the book yet this mini-analysis has shown that personality disorder through its antithesis has had an important effect on defining some of the qualities that lie behind biblical wisdom.

The ancient Israelites must have been much troubled by people with serious personality disorders for it to have had such an impact on their religious literature. The Old Testament concept of wisdom came to dominate Judaeo-Christian thinking in Europe over the next two millennia. This may go some way to explaining why Western cultures have so often taken a moralistic approach to the problem of personality disorder, having a dichotomous view of the good being equated with the wise, and the wicked to those with a personality disorder – even in the absence of any crime.

## Personality disorders: the modern perspective

Personality disorders are both common and damaging and have become a major medical, psychiatric and above all social problem. These individuals have chronic – often lifelong – impairments in their ability to work, sustain loving relationships, sustain education and function over a wide variety of areas. As a consequence they are more commonly single, or involved in crime, drug or alcohol abuse and are generally less well educated. Among the severe antisocial types there may be high rates of criminal recidivism, suicide rates are raised and there may also be a generally raised mortality.

In day-to-day clinical psychiatric practice around half the patients encountered will have some sort of personality disorder. This is partly because personality disorder may predispose to many common psychiatric conditions such as anxiety, substance abuse disorder, impulse control disorder and eating disorders. People with personality disorder – particularly those with 'the dramatic disorders' that is, the borderline and antisocial types – are often manipulative and demanding and will test the limits of any physician's skill and tolerance.

The concept of personality disorder is not easily grasped; these are conditions which are poorly defined, have little in the way of effective treatments, are lifelong and at their less severe end blur into normality but at the more severe extremes are both damaging and dangerous. Schneider defined psychopathic personalities 'as those abnormal personalities that suffer from their abnormality or whose abnormality causes society to suffer'. An eccentric university professor might have an abnormal personality in the statistical sense, but Schneider would not have included him as a personality disorder as no harm results from his eccentricity. An aggressive psychopath might also have an unusual personality, but because he beats people up and causes harm he is said to have a personality disorder.

Both the DSM-5 and the ICD-10 schemes provide broadly similar descriptions and definitions of the various types of personality disorder. Both texts also state the personality disorder should start early in life, either in childhood or in adolescence, be manifest across a broad range of personal and social situations, be of long duration, be relatively inflexible to change, and result in a significant degree of distress for the individual concerned and in some cases to others as well. Shorter-term deterioration in behaviours and personality function due to depression or some other psychiatric (or medical disorder) should be excluded. DSM-5 has the advantage that its definitions consist of simple lists of easily recognisable traits and so it is relatively easy to check if a person fulfils the diagnostic criteria. It has 10 types of personality disorder, which it groups into three major clusters, A, B and C:

## Cluster A: the eccentric group

- *Schizoid personality disorder* describes a pattern of isolation, detachment from social relationships, and severely restricted emotions
- *Schizotypal personality disorder* (not the same as schizophrenia) is a pattern of detachment, acute discomfort in social relationships combined with eccentric ideas, unusual perceptual experiences, suspiciousness, few close friends and odd thinking – all of a lesser degree than found in schizophrenia
- *Paranoid personality disorder* is a lifelong pattern of distrust, suspicious-ness such that others' motives are interpreted (falsely) as malevolent, a tendency to bear grudges, a combative sense of personal rights which can sometimes lead to an excessive amount of litigation, and an excessive sense of self-importance and a self-referential attitude.

None of these types are described anywhere in the Bible or in the literature of the ancient world. However, paranoid personality disorder is described in medieval rabbinic literature, and is included in the prayer book for the Yom Kippur services (Day of Atonement) in one of the study passages entitled 'Sin and Envy':

> The sixth type is the complainer. The complainer is the man who is always grumbling and whining and finding fault with his friend's conduct and speech even though the friend is quite innocent of any desire to harm him. Such a person always finds reason for accusing, never for excusing. He treats every un-intentional slight as if it were intentional. He imagines himself to be victimised and is full of his neighbour's sins against him, whereas in reality he is the offender.... Keep yourself far from the way of the complainers for they harm only themselves and know not of peace.... (R. Jonah ben Abraham Gerondi, 1200–1263, a prominent Kabbalistic scholar and cousin of Nachmanides, quoted in *The Prayer Book*, 1985, p. 714)

This early description of paranoid personality disorder is of importance to the history of psychiatry and precedes by more than eight centuries the later accounts of paranoid personality disorder as found in the writings of Kraepelin and Schneider in the early 20th century.

## Cluster B: the dramatic group

This group plays an important role in the Book of Proverbs. Four main types are described: antisocial, borderline, histrionic and narcissistic.

The *antisocial personality disorder* (psychopaths in the older terminology), discussed extensively above, is associated with a gross disregard for the rights of others. Among women *borderline personality disorder* is the most frequent type and is described in connection with the *issa zarah* (the strange woman) in the next chapter. *Histrionic personality disorder* is also more common among women and has a pattern of excessive emotionality, attention seeking, suggestibility and shallowness and is also described in association with the *issa zarah* in the next chapter. The fourth type, *'narcissistic personality disorder*, encompasses a pattern of grandiosity, need for admiration, lack of empathy for others, a sense of entitlement, and haughty or arrogant behaviour. The *lēs* in the Book of Proverbs has some narcissistic features, but also psychopathic features as well.

## Cluster C: anxious group

Like the cluster A group this group probably does not appear in the Old Testament. The three types are *avoidant* ('anxious' in the ICD-10 scheme) where the pattern is only of social inhibition, feelings social inadequacy and hypersensitivity. People with *dependent* personality disorder have a lifelong pattern of submission and clinging behaviours, an excessive need for reassurance, nurturance and support. *Obsessional* personalities have a lifelong preoccupation with orderliness, perfectionism and control.

## Summary and conclusions

The Book of Proverbs is ostensibly about wisdom, and its prescription of wisdom was meant to be imbibed by the young in ancient Israel. In later centuries Proverbs came to be used by the clergy of both the Jewish and the Christian faiths to preach the merits of a life of wisdom. But the reality in the ancient Near East was not that there was a problem with people who were wise, but rather there was a vast excess of those afflicted by 'folly' or, as this chapter has shown, there was a large number of people with severe personality disorder, particularly antisocial personality disorder. No one knew where the 'folly' came from but education of the young was seen as the best way of preventing the problem. Wisdom was the opposite of folly and so if wisdom could be drummed into the young, then the hope was that in later life they might not become fools or scoundrels. Many of the wisdom passages in both the Israelite and Egyptian traditions start with 'A lecture from a father to his son', suggesting a primary educational role for these texts.

Antisocial personality disorders present a major challenge to all societies, both ancient and modern. In the ancient world there were no police, prisons or hospitals or any other organisation to assume these functions which might protect the community by confining its more antisocial and dangerous members. A society without prisons would find it difficult to cope with severe recidivism and so it is not surprising that the sages of the Old Testament were well acquainted with these characters, who would have repeatedly been seen in the courts.

This chapter has shown a reasonable correspondence between ancient Israelite types of folly and present-day categories of personality disorder, particularly antisocial personality disorder. The *belial* (scoundrel) even fulfils DSM-5 diagnostic criteria for antisocial personality disorder. The comparison between Hare's Psychopathy Check-List and verses in Proverbs shows that the profile of malevolence of humankind in the ancient world was little different to that of today and that both the Bible and the DSM-5 texts are describing the same group of people. The *belial* (scoundrel) is particularly well described. The English word 'fool' is reserved for the four Hebrew types the *pethi, 'ĕwil, kesil* and *hasar leb*. These immoral personality types show some limited parallels with modern typology. As a character typology it is both older and more sophisticated than the Greek scheme of Theophrastus, which is usually recorded as the earliest character typology. What is of some historical interest is that there are no other personality typologies between the time of the ancient Israelite scheme (6th century BCE) and appearance in the late 19th century of more modern definitions of personality disorder.

Ancient Egyptian and Sumerian descriptions of abnormal personality exist, and are described in the appendix to this chapter, but the descriptions are thin and do not cover the whole field. The detail with which antisocial types are described in the ancient world contrasts with the almost complete lack of any record of schizophrenia or insanity. Why should this be? A psychotic person is only occasionally dangerous, but the psychopath is frequently extremely dangerous. Schizophrenics can commit murder but psychopaths are much more likely to do so, probably with a ratio of 10:1 (UK data only). Today, the majority of those with severe psychopathy are locked up in prisons and studies have shown that somewhere between 39% and 76% of the prison population comprises people with severe antisocial personality disorders. If a prisoner should escape, the matter immediately becomes an item on national TV news, with people being advised not to approach the escapee. In ancient Israel there were no prisons for ordinary criminals; the man in the farm next door might be a *belial* or an aggressive psychopath who beats his wife and children; the local market trader might be a con-man. The village tavern might find itself full with *pethis 'ĕwils* and *kesils,* bringing with them the ensuing problems of drunken violence (see Chapter 14, page 525). Most people would have been all too familiar with the stupid, the wicked and the dangerous characters in their community. This may be why the sages gave these categories specific names and chose to write about people with personality disorders with both precision and passion.

Certain dimensions of modern psychopathology were well recognised by the ancients:

- low intelligence
- arrogance
- aggression and violence
- resistance to changing their behaviours.

First, they recognised the importance of poor intellect and the influence this could have on personality, competence and moral behaviour and devoted at least one whole character type – the *pethi* – to this defect. Two other types – the *hasar leb* (lacking in heart/mind) and the *kesil* (stupid oaf) – also appear to have some intellectual defect. The *'ĕwil*, *lēs* and *bēlial* all have normal intelligence and in the main are just malevolent individuals.

Why should those with lowish intellect be singled out? One can turn again to modern prison statistics for a possible explanation. A review by Winters (1997) of studies on the prevalence of learning difficulties in juvenile correctional institutions in the USA found that 28–43% of individuals had special educational needs, while 15% of adult inmates had at least mild learning difficulties. A UK study of arrests and people detained in police custody in Cambridge found that 25% could neither read nor write and 10% had attended a special school, with 4% attending a school for learning-disabled children (Lyall *et al.*, 1995). The modern data also point to a high degree of contact between those with learning difficulties and the criminal justice system, and if the same trend operated in the ancient world this might explain why the scribes, who sometimes worked in the courts, chose to separate off people with learning difficulties, even giving them names such as *pethi* and *hasar leb*, as being especially troublesome types.

The second dimension identified is one of arrogance, scornfulness and contempt. One whole character type – the *lēs* – is given over to this trait, but the trait also sometimes appears in the *'ĕwil, kesil* and *belial*. Contempt is a very common trait among narcissists and more severe psychopaths, but not all psychopaths show this trait and so separating off this group may have some validity. Stone (1990) has suggested that contempt is of fundamental importance in the assessment of treatability. Some characters are just too contemptuous of their fellow man to engage in any sort of correction or therapy and therefore never change.

A third dimension is the degree of malevolence and evil. The *belial* – translated as a scoundrel or villain – is violent, abusive to his family, continuously plotting, arrogant, and epithets such as wickedness are used to describe him even today. He is highly malignant and corresponds well to the aggressive or criminal psychopath (sheds innocent blood). As a trait, 'malevolence' shows a wide range in modern psychopathic populations, with some just being 'creative' in devising fraudulent schemes while others are highly malicious, aggressive and therefore very dangerous, as for example with a vengeful Mafiosi boss.

A fourth dimension is their failure to respond to punishment or failure to learn, and this is frequently mentioned in Proverbs.

These four themes which the Book of Proverbs mentions repeatedly bear a striking parallel to the day-to-day management problems posed today by people with antisocial personality disorder in the psychiatric and prison services. Only those who have had a considerable degree of first-hand contact with these difficult types would be capable of focusing on just these themes with such a high degree of insight. Because the courts of justice are the only institution that also existed in ancient Israel where these individuals regularly appear it seems likely that in their 'day job' the sages worked in the courts.

The sages were able to capture the problematic aspect of antisocial personality disorders in their writings. Wisdom was the by-product of this endeavour and was also meant to be the cure. If only the young would acquire wisdom, then there might be no crime and all could live in harmony. The fool who is stupid is the *pethi* and has as his counterpart the wise man, or the *hacham*, who has wisdom, or *hochma*. But if there were no *pethis*, or simpletons, would the qualities of *hochma* (wisdom) or *binah* (intelligence) have been so highly venerated? Equally, if there had been no *belials* or those with antisocial personality disorder, would wisdom have included qualities such as *sekel* (discretion) and *musar* (self-discipline, education). Wisdom was the opposite of folly but without folly, or the reality of the pain that people with severe personality disorder inflict on society, would there have been any point in having wisdom, and a huge wisdom literature? The suggestion of this chapter is that, at least in part, the Book of Proverbs tells the story of an ancient society and its struggles with the problems of severe personality disorder, but all written in exquisite biblical verse.

## Appendix: the Wisdom literature of other ancient societies

Wisdom literature was ubiquitous in the ancient Near East, probably going back at least 4000 years in both Egypt and Sumeria. A comprehensive review of the foreign Wisdom literature is beyond the scope of this chapter, but there is general acceptance that the Book of Proverbs was influenced by foreign wisdom, particularly the Egyptian Amenemope.

### Instruction of Amenemope

The Instruction of Amenemope is thought to have been composed in the Ramesside era circa 1240–1070 BCE. The author was the scribe Amenemope, the son of Kanakht; his home town was Tieny near Abydos some 60 miles south of Luxor. Amenemope himself worked in the civil service and probably held a very senior position, being responsible for the regulation of arable land and the collection of grain tariffs either for the whole of Egypt or at the very least for one region. At the end of the scroll, the scribe Senu declares that he is the person who has written it, or at least copied it out, and it is this version that rests in the British Museum, known as 'Papyrus B.M. 10474'.

In 1923 the whole text was photographed, and the hieroglyphics were translated and published by Sir Ernest Budge as the second series of *Facsimilies of Egyptian Papyrii at the British Museum*. It soon became apparent that a section of the Book of Proverbs ($22^{17}$–$24^{22}$) had drawn heavily from the Instruction of Amenemope. The latter is quite long, at around 30 chapters, although each chapter is only 10–15 lines, and it goes over roughly the same sort of ground as the Book of Proverbs. It covers many topics, including: the merits of honesty; the search for wealth; respect for other people's property; the tricks of the 'corn measurer'; human dignity and sincerity; how to talk in law court; and respect for the elderly. The section entitled 'The teaching of Amenophis the son of Kanakht' describes a man with severe personality disorder. It was translated by F. L. Griffith(1926) and is too long to be quoted in full but ch. 6 of that text is devoted to a comparison of 'The passionate man and the tranquil man' and ch. 9 is entitled 'Avoid the passionate man and his ways'. In the latter chapter a cluster of character traits are associated with the 'passionate man': hot temper, trickery through speech, impulsive speech, lies, quarrelsomeness , committing crimes, provoking trouble and anger. Both chapters describe the character traits associated with psychopathic behaviour. The passionate man appears to be an irritable type of psychopath, and the text is replete with animal and plant metaphors which are not always easy to understand. The full description has most of the features of antisocial personality disorder according to DSM-5.

The Instruction of Amenemope precedes the Hebrew description of personality disorder by at least 300 years and must therefore count as one of the oldest descriptions of personality disorder.

## Ptah-hotep

The instruction of Ptah-hotep, is also very long, comprising 37 sections, and most of it has nothing to do with mental illness or personality disorder. The complete translation is given in Lichtheim (1973, pp. 62–76). Ptah-hotep belongs to the period of the Old Kingdom and set in the reign of Isesi in the Fifth Dynasty (2388–2356 BCE) and is therefore also very old , although the earliest existent books containing his Wisdom are from the 12th dynasty. The present-day version is known as the 'Prisse Papyrus', after the French Egyptologist who first acquired it at Thebes. This scroll is in the Biblothèque Nationale in France; two later papyrii are in the British Museum and a wooden tablet, the Carnavon tablet, is in the Cairo Museum.

Oesterley (1929) has linked all the parallels with Proverbs, but only a very few verses, less than 5% of the whole instruction, appertain to personality disorder. In the section below I have selected a few verses which give a suggestion that the author had some knowledge of 'bad character types', but it is probably not sufficiently detailed to qualify as a psychiatric description.

> Instruction of the Mayor of the City, the Vizier Ptah-hotep, under the Majesty of King Isesi, who lives for all eternity. The Mayor of the City Ptah-hotep said:

| | | |
|---|---|---|
| | Oh King my lord | |
| | Age is here, old age arrived | |
| | Feebleness came, weakness grows ... | |
| | He spoke to his son ... | |
| 6[1] | Do not scheme | |
| | God punishes accordingly | |
| 8[5] | Guard against reviling speech | |
| | Which embroils one great with another | |
| | Keep to the truth. Do not exceed it | |
| | But an outburst should not be repeated | |
| 25[4] | He who provokes gets into trouble | Stirring; manipulation |
| | Don't be haughty lest you be humbled | contempt |
| | Don't be mute lest you be chided | |
| | When you answer one who is fuming | Temper |
| | Avert your face, control yourself | Don't be provoked |
| | The flame of the hot heart sweeps across | Anger |
| | He who steps gently, his path is paved | |

| | | |
|---|---|---|
| | He who frets all day has no happy moment | ? Anxiety |
| | He who is gay all day can't keep house | irresponsibility |
| 31[11] | A quarreller is a mindless person | A character who quarrels |
| | If he is known as an aggressor | aggressive, hostile person |
| | The hostile man will have trouble in the | |
| | neighbourhood | |

These abstracts describe a hostile aggressive person with some suggestion of an antisocial character type – but, as this text is over 4000 years old, perhaps we should not expect an exact parallel with modern antisocial personality disorder.

## The cuneiform literature of ancient Mesopotamia

Mesopotamia is the Greek name of the land that lies between two great rivers, the Tigris and Euphrates, which constitutes present-day Iraq. An excellent description of antisocial character traits is given in the Surpu. This is a famous Mesopotamian prayer, first translated into English from ancient Akkadian, by Erica Reiner in 1958. The largest collection of the Surpu texts consists of nine tablets from the royal library of King Assurbanipal (668–627 BCE) at Sultantepe. This library was first excavated by the English archaeologist A. H. Layard in 1849, at a place called Kouyunjik, which corresponds to the site of ancient Nineveh the capital of Assyria. The bulk of this collection now resides in the British Museum.

The Surpu text contain a series of incantations, prayers and instructions for use by the Asipo, the priests of Mesopotamia. The name 'Surpu' is Akkadian for 'burning' and refers to the Asipo ceremony that was carried out while the incantations and prayers were recited. One of the copies from the Sultantepe library bears the date 670 BCE. However, the original works came from a much earlier times and some of the Sumerian incantations that make up tablet IX can be dated back to the Old Babylonian period, probably to the Kassite period (circa 1700–1600 BCE). Reiner suggests that the purpose of the Surpu was for 'the healing of a sick person'. She made this remark in spite of the lack of any physical symptoms, which implies that condition described (psychopathy) may have been regarded as some sort of a mental disorder in ancient Mesopotamia (Reiner, 1958, p. 4).

This tablet starts with the following statement:

> Be the mystery resolved in that 'so and so' does not know it is wrong.... When he gives a small measure ... uses a false balance ... takes money not lawfully his.... Set up a false boundary stone.... Enters a friend house, has intercourse with his friend's wife, shed his blood and steal his clothes.... When his mouth says yes; his heart says no and whatever he says is completely untrue, when ... shakes/and trembles (with rage), destroys (things), throw them out (of house) or makes them disappear; when he accuses, incriminates, spreads gossip, wrongs, robs or incites others to rob.

The tablet then gives a long list of antisocial traits and behaviours which the English archaeologist Kinnier Wilson (1965, p. 924) considered fitted the picture of the psychopath. He wrote: 'Here is the Babylonian psychopath – the pathological liar, the swindler, the kleptomaniac, the gossip monger, the social misfit, the sexual criminal, the murderer – an unmistakable picture'.

It lists a large number of adverse personality traits (for details, see Abdul-Hamid and Stein 2012) and the text fulfils both DSM-5 and ICD-10 criteria for antisocial personality disorder. After each adverse trait or crime is described the spirit of a named God is invoked to bring about healing. In this incantation prayer antisocial personality disorder is viewed as a sickness which the gods can heal. There is no moral condemnation of the character as in the Book of Proverbs.

## *Theophrastus*

Most accounts of the history of personality disorder start with the ancient Greek writer Theophrastus, although the analysis in this chapter has shown that there are many much earlier and better descriptions of personality disorder. Theophrastus was born in 371 BCE at Eresus on the island of Lesbos, which was around 15 years after the foundation of Plato's Academy in Assos. He formed an early friendship with Aristotle, and after Plato's death, Aristotle and Theophrastus worked together at Plato's Academy, After Aristotle died, Theophrastus took over the school and was its head for the next 36 years until he died in 287 BCE (Fortenbaugh *et al.*, 1993).

Like Plato and Aristotle, Theophrastus was a great intellectual polymath, who wrote extensively on botany, law, logic, physics, politics and poetry. He was a prolific author with some 225 works being attributed to him, the lengthiest being a 24-volume textbook of law, but at least in psychiatric circles he is best known for his 'Book of Characters', which was published in 319 BCE – probably well after the completion of the Book of Proverbs.

The style of character description given in Theophrastus is very different from the Book of Proverbs. Theophrastus writes in prose, like a gossip columnist, and it is much lighter reading than the Book of Proverbs. There is a blunt description of how one of his characters might behave in the marketplace, and the text has no moralising or religious quality; it also lacks any clinical depth. Each character is defined by his epithet, for example 'The boastful man', 'the man of petty ambition', 'the unseasonable man', or 'the unpleasant man', and most of his 30 character types do not show any resemblance to modern personality disorders. Only two of his character types resemble modern antisocial personality disorder: 'the reckless man' and 'the evil man'. Below is a description of the 'reckless man', taken from Jebb's (1909) translation of Theophrastus:

> Recklessness is tolerance of shame in word and deed. The reckless man is one who will lightly take an oath being proof against abuse and capable of giving it. In character a coarse fellow, defiant of decency, ready to do anything; just a person to dance a *cordax* (a Greek dance) in a comic chorus. At the conjuror's performance too, he will collect the pence going along from man to man and wrangling with those who have a free pass and claim to see the show for nothing. He is apt also to become an innkeeper or a tax farmer; he will decline no sort of disreputable trade, a crier's or a cook's. He will gamble, and neglect

to maintain his mother; he will be arrested for theft, and spend more time in prison than in his own house.

And he would seem to be one of those persons who collect and call crowds to them, ranting in a loud cracked voice and haranguing them. Great is he too in lawsuits, now as a defendant, now as a prosecutor. He will not disdain either to be a captain of marketplace hucksters, but will readily lend them money exacting as interest upon ten pence, two and a half pence a day; and will make the round of the cook shops, the fishmongers and the fish picklers thrusting into his cheek the interest which he levies on their gains. These are troublesome persons, for their tongues are easily set wagging abusively; and they talk in so loud a voice that the marketplace and the workshops resound with them.

The description is in a very different genre to that of Proverbs. The account is readily understood; religion does not enter into it, nor are there several layers of meaning or the thought-provoking quality of Proverbs. Even so, the reckless man of Theophrastus appears to have some of the characteristics of antisocial personality disorder, but it is probably too threadbare to be worth comparing it to modern diagnostic criteria such as DSM-5.

The Egyptians, Mesopotamians and the ancient Israelites all gave much better and more detailed accounts and which were also all much earlier as well, but it seems as if as soon as writing became a medium for communication, the topic of the psychopath and his damaging ways began to feature in the literature of almost all ancient societies.

## References

Abdul-Hamid, W.K. and Stein, G.S. (2012) The Surpu: Exorcism of anti-social Personality Disorder in Ancient Mesopotamia. *Mental Health Religion and Culture* 2012: 1-15.

Babylonian Talmud (1935) Translated into English by Rabbi I. Epstein, *Baba Bathra* 15a, p. 71, London Soncino Press.

Babylonian Talmud (1938) Translated into English by Rabbi I. Epstein and Rabbi H. Freedman. *Shabbath* 104a, p. 501. London Soncino Press.

Babylonian Talmud (1948) Translated into English by Rabbi I. Epstein and E. Cashan. *Seda Kodashim, Hullin* 57b, p. 316. London Soncino Press.

Brown, F., Driver, S.R. and Briggs, C.A. (1952) *A Hebrew and English Lexicon of the Old Testament, based on the Lexicon of William Gesenius as translated by Edward Robinson,* Oxford: Clarendon Press.

Casey, P. (1998) Personality Disorders. Chapter 18, pp. 753-815. *College Seminars in Adult General Psychiatry* Eds. George Stein and Greg Wilkinson. London: Gaskell Press.

Cleckley, H. (1941) *The Mask of Sanity.* St. Louis MO: C.V. Mosby.

Cloninger, C.R. and Svrakic, D.M. (2000) Personality disorders. In *Kaplan and Sadock's Comprehensive Textbook of Psychiatry,* eds. B. Sadoch and V. Sadoch, page 1755; Philadelphia: Lippincott Williams and Wilkins.

Cowley, A.E. (1923) *Aramaic Papyri of the Fifth Century BCE* (repr. 1923). Osnabruck: O. Zeller.

Crenshaw, J.L. (1998) *Old Testament Wisdom. An Introduction.* Westminster: John Knox Press, Louisville, Kentucky.

Donald, T. (1963) The Semantic Field of 'Folly' in Proverbs, Job, Psalms and Ecclesiastes. *Vetus Testamentum,* Leiden, 13: 28–92.

Driver, G.R. (1956) *Canaanite Myths and Legends.* Edinburgh: T&T Clark.

Fok, M.L., Hayes, R.D., Chang, C.K., *et al.* (2012) Life expectancy at birth and all-cause mortality among people with personality disorder. *Journal of Psychosomatic Research* 73(2): 104–107.

Fortenbaugh, W.F., Huby, P.H., Sharples, R.W. and Gutas, D. (1993) *Theophrastus of Eresus. Sources for his life, writings, thoughts and influence,* pp. 1–3. Leiden: E.J. Brill.

Forms of Prayer for Jewish Worship(1985) *III Prayers for the High Holy Days: Sins of Slander* pp. 713–714. Edited by the Assemblies of Rabbis of the Reform Synagogues of Great Britain: London: Reform Synagogues of Great Britain.

Fox, M.V. (2000) *Proverbs 1–9. The Anchor Bible.* New York: Doubleday.

Gammie, J.G. and Perdue, L.G. (1990) *The Sage in Israel and the Ancient Near East.* Winona Lake: Eisenbraun.

Griffiths, F.L. (1926) The teaching of Amenophis, the son of Kanakht. Papyrus B.M. 10474. *Journal of Egyptian Antiquities* xii: 191–231.

Haran, M. (1972) The Graded Numerical Sequence and the Phenomenon of 'Automatism' in Biblical Poetry. *Vetus Testamentum supplement,* Leiden 22: 238–267.

Hardy, T. (1874) *Far from the Madding Crowd.* London: Smith Elder and Co.

Hare, R.D. (1991) *Manual for the Psychopathic Check list Revised.* Toronto: Multi-Health Systems.

Jebb, R.C. (1909) *The Characters of Theophrastus: An English Translation from a revised text with introduction and revised notes by R.C. Jebb.* A new edition edited by J.E. Sandys. London: Macmillan.

Kinnier Wilson, J. V. (1965) An introduction to Babylonian Psychiatry. In *Studies in honour of Benno Landsberger,* pp. 280–298. Chicago: Oriental Institute of the University of Chicago.

Kohlenberger, III, J.R. (1987) *The Interlinear NIV Hebrew-English Old Testament,* p. 558. Grand Rapids, Michigan: Zondervan.

Lambert, W.G. (1960) *Babylonian Wisdom Literature.* Oxford: Clarendon.

Lichtheim, Miriam (1973–80) *Ancient Egyptian Literature.* Vols 1–3 Berkeley: University of California Press.

Lindenberger, J.M. (1983) *The Aramaic Proverbs of Ahiqar.* Baltimore: John Hopkins University Press.

McKane, W. (1970) *Proverbs a new approach.* London: SCM Press.

Masoretic Text (1944) *The Holy Scriptures according to the Masoretic Text.* Eighteenth Impression, Philadelphia: The Jewish Publication Society of America.

Moffat Translation of the Bible (1972). Hodder and Stoughton, London.

Naré, L. (1986) *Proverbs Solomiens et Proverbes Mossi. Etude comparative a partir d'une nouvelle analyse de Proverbes,* 25–29. Frankfurt.

New Revised Standard Version of the Bible (1989). Oxford; Oxford University Press.

Oesterley, W.O.E. (1929) *The Book of Proverbs.* London: Methuen.

Prichard, J.C. (1835) *Treatise on Insanity.* London: Gilbert and Piper.

Reiner, E. (1958) *Surpu: A collection of Sumerian and Accadian incantations.* Graz: Selbstverlage des Herausgeber.

Robertson, G. (1987) Mentally abnormal offenders: manner of death. *British Medical Journal,* 295: 632–634.

Rosenberg, A.J. (1993) *Proverbs. A New English Translation of the Text, Rashi and a Commentary Digest.* New York: Judaica Press.

Schiffman, L.H. (1991) *From Text to Tradition: A History of Second Temple and Rabbinic Judaism.* Hoboken, NJ: Ktav Publishing House.

Schneider, K. (1923) *Die Psichopathishen Personlicheiten* Vienna: Deuticke

Schupak, Nili (1993) Where can Wisdom Be Found? *Orbis Biblicus et Orientalis,* Freiburg, Switzerland 130. Göttingen: Vandenhoeck and Ruprecht.

Sjoberg A.W. (1973) Der Vater und sein Misratener Sohn. *Journal of Cuneiform Studies* 25: 105–169.

Toy, Crawford H (1899) *The Book of Proverbs.* International Critical Commentary. Edinburgh: T. & T. Clark (reprinted 1959).

Waltke B., (2005) *The Book of Proverbs. Chapters 1–15* Grand Rapids. Michigan: William B Eerdmans Publishing Company.

Werner K.B, Few L.R, and Bucholz K.K. (2015) Epidemiology, Comorbidity, and Behavioral Genetics of Antisocial Personality Disorder and Psychopathy. *Psychiatry Annual* 45(4): 195–199.

Westerman, C. (1995) Proverbs dealing exclusively with the wise and the Foolish. Chapter 3.2 pp 52–58 , in *The Roots of Wisdom.* Edinburgh: T&T Clarke.

Whybray, R.N. (1990) *Proverbs: New Century Bible Commentary.* William B. Eerdmans Publishing Company, Grand Rapids, Michigan, pp. 4, 5, 13.

Whybray, R.N. (1994) *Proverbs. New Century Bible Commentary.* William B. Eerdmans Publishing Company, Grand Rapids, Michigan.

Winters C.A. (1997) Learning Difficulties, Crime, Delinquency, and Special Educational Placement. *Adolescence* 32 (126): 451–462.

Zilber, N., Schufman, N. and Lerner, Y. (1989) Mortality among psychiatric inpatients, the groups at risk. *Acta Psychiatrica Scandinavica* 79: 248–256.

# Chapter 11

# The 'strange woman' of Proverbs

The Book of Proverbs has a description of women, their virtues and their vices, their role in marriage, child rearing and in wider society. However, throughout the Old Testament women are thought of and spoken of almost wholly from the point of view of men. Marriage is for the man's benefit, not the woman; she is useful to him, attends to his needs, looks after the household and above all bears his children. The woman's own personal needs are rarely mentioned. A worthy woman is her husband's pride and joy, but an unworthy woman is said to be his disgrace. In practice, however, women probably held a rather more dominant role, particularly in the realm of family life (Crenshaw, 1998); indeed, even Abraham, the first of the great patriarchs, is told by God 'Whatever Sarah says to you, do as she says' (Gen 21$^{12}$). There are also exhortations for the young to listen to the voices of *both* their father and mother.

The Book of Proverbs describes five different female character types:

1 *Lady Wisdom* – the attributes of wisdom are personified in a fictional character
2 *the virtuous wife* – a perfect wife, but still a real human being
3 *the contentious wife* – a wife who nags too much, a very real character
4 *Lady Folly* – a personification of the bad attributes of the strange woman
5 *the strange woman* – a promiscuous drama queen, possibly a real character.

The 'strange woman' is of psychiatric interest as she shows character pathology suggestive of a borderline/histrionic type, and to a lesser extent the fictionalised Lady Folly may be relevant as she too has a character problem.

There are three passages describing the strange woman (2$^{16-19}$, 5$^{1-9}$ and 7$^{1-27}$) and she appears only in Proverbs. She has mystified scholars throughout the ages. She is described as a sexually predatory female who lures young men into her trap and then leads them on to personal disaster and death, an archetypal tale often appearing in the mythology of the ancient world. She is painted as the classical 'whore' type but a few verses also contain references to non-sexual character traits and these are of great psychiatric significance. Biblical feminist writers, whose views are considered later, point out the androcentricity of the description – which refers mainly to the harm which will befall any young man who consorts with her. This has resulted in a lack of compassion for the strange woman's personal distress and means that her subjective psychology is poorly described.

After briefly describing the social context of the time, the chapter proceeds with a note concerning translation and terminology, before looking in some detail at the three descriptions of the strange woman. This is followed by a discussion of the modern conceptions of borderline and histrionic personality disorders, and their possible application to the strange woman. The other female characters in the Book of Proverbs are also considered towards the end of the chapter.

## Social context

It may be useful first to consider the social concerns of early post-exilic Israel, to explain why the literature on the 'strange woman' arose. Thus, some 50 years after the deportation of the Jews from Jerusalem to Babylon (586 BCE), Babylon itself was conquered, by King Cyrus II of Persia. He adopted a benevolent policy towards the Hebrew deportees and later encouraged the repatriation of the exiles and the rebuilding of national shrines. In 538 BCE King Cyrus decreed that the Temple in Jerusalem was to be rebuilt and all the exiles who wished could return to Judea, by then a part of the Persian Empire and known as the province of Yehud. This repatriation ushered in the era of the Second Temple, also known as the Second Commonwealth. At first, the population of Judah was small, perhaps less than 20,000 souls living around Jerusalem, but under Persian rule the province prospered and in the 5th century BCE the population is thought to have doubled (Schiffman, 1991). The whole of the Persian period (also known as the Achaemenid period) extended from circa 550 to 333 BCE and it is now thought that it was during this period that the introduction to Proverbs (chs 1–9) was written and it is within this section that the strange woman appears. A major anxiety for the community elders at the time was inter-marriage, because this hastened assimilation, and could lead to loss of land, as land tenure in the ancient world was determined by blood lineage and marriage. Thus sexual relationships with foreign women were seen as a danger to property inheritance and this may explain some of the fears associated with sexual promiscuity, adulterous relationships and an exogamous marriage because these would have represented a major economic threat to the stability and homogeneity of society.

## A note concerning the meaning of English word 'borderline' and the Hebrew word *zar*

An important source of confusion has been the translation of the word *zar*. Older translations such as the King James (1611) version and the Rall Bible (1884) preserve the Hebrew 'strange', but more recent translations such as the Moffat Bible (1926) and the Revised Standard Version (RSV) and the New Revised Standard Version (NRSV) have 'the loose woman'. The insipid word 'loose' at a single stroke removes all the bizarreness and the psychiatric connotation of a woman with a peculiar personality and changes her into a woman who only has loose morals and a penchant for extramarital affairs, rather than one considered strange. The NRSV, however, in its footnotes indicates that the word 'strange' could be used as an alternative, and so in the sections that follow below the NRSV translation is used but the word 'strange' is used instead of 'loose'.

There is no Hebrew dictionary which gives the exact meaning of any particular biblical word, but the *Gesenius Dictionary* list all the places and contexts where a particular word occurs. By examining these verses it is possible to infer more precisely what a particular word might mean. Fox (2000) provides a detailed analysis of the meaning of the word *zar* as it is used in different places and contexts in the OT. He writes:

> A lay Israelite is a *zar*, or outsider or alien in situations permitted to priests alone (Exodus 29[33]) or to enter into the sanctuary (Num 1[51]). In Levirate law the 'strange man' is a man belonging to another family (Deut 25[5]). In Lev 22[12] the 'strange man' is an outsider only in the sense that he belongs to a different caste. While Tobit (4[12]) warns his son against taking a 'strange' (*zar*) wife who is not from the tribe of your father. These meanings also all carry the notion of some sort of a boundary with a person who is just outside a particular social group, such as the family, or tribe.

The English word 'borderline' is defined in the *Oxford English Dictionary* as the 'strip of land' along the borders between two countries or districts. Figuratively it may be the boundary between areas, classes, etc. The phrase 'borderline case' has two meanings: verging on the indecent or obscene; or verging on insanity. The *Oxford English Dictionary* quotes an early use: 'Therapeutic suggestive conversation with these early borderline cases is never wasted'. The word 'borderline' was probably first used in the context of personality disorder by Hughes (1884), when he wrote 'The borderline of insanity is occupied by many persons who pass their whole life near that line, sometimes on one side sometimes on the other.' Its use in the context of personality disorder dates to Stern (1938), who applied it to a group of patients who failed to show any response to psychoanalysis, the main treatment at the time, yet who were not obviously psychotic. Thus in psychiatry the border of 'borderline' initially appeared as the area between neurosis and insanity rather than with the boundaries of a particular social grouping. Otherwise, the Hebrew word *zar* and the psychiatric term 'borderline' share certain common meanings appertaining to boundaries, even if they are not used in exactly the same sense.

## The strange woman in ch. 2[16-19]

The first appearance of the strange woman is in ch. 2 and follows on immediately after a passage giving advice to a young man (addressed as 'my son') to avoid 'the evil man', who is described in the preceding verses and is clearly quite a psychopathic individual (*eesh rashah*). This sequence implies that the 'strange woman' is equally noxious and perhaps a female counterpart to the 'evil man'.

| | | |
|---|---|---|
| 2[16] | You will be saved from the strange woman, from the adulteress, with her smooth words, | On 'strange', see above |
| [17] | who forsakes the partner of her youth and forgets her sacred covenant; | ?ignores parental instruction<br>?breaking the covenant<br>?breaking marriage vows, adultery |

| | | |
|---|---|---|
| 18 | For her way leads down to death, | see note 1 |
| | and her paths to the shades | shades = *rephaim*, who inhabit Sheol – see note 2 |
| 19 | those who go to her never come back | go to her = sexual intercourse |
| | nor do they regain the paths of life. | relationships with her are difficult and usually end badly or even fatally |

*Note 1.* In verse 18, the Hebrew for 'leads down' is *allup*, which also means 'leader'. McKane (1970) proposes 'paternal educator of youth' or father, suggesting a break with the father or father's code. The second part of the verse 17, 'forgets her sacred covenant', may refer to the sacred religious vows or may also imply adultery (Fox, 2000, p. 121). Either way, verse 17 implies some sort of deviancy and the breaking of moral codes.

*Note 2.* In 2$^{18}$, the *rephaim* (the shades) are the inhabitants of Sheol. The etymology is probably from the Ugaritic *rpūm*, who are chthonic deities: the Hebrew *rp* (bound up) and Arabic *rf* are joined together. Driver (1956) suggests in his book *Canaanite Myths and Legends* that the dead are envisaged as a massed community leading a common life in the underworld. McKane (1970, p. 287) writes the imagery in the first part of the verse (her ways lead down) alludes to the Canaanite god *Mot*, whose gaping throat is the gateway to Sheol, and the second part (the *Rephaim*) refers to the massed community of the world of the dead. The 'strange woman' who is an outsider inhabits the borders of the land between the living and the dead and so her paths lead to Sheol, the land of the dead.

## The strange woman in ch. 5$^{1-9}$

The account given in ch. 5 also takes the form of parental guidance to avoid the strange woman, and repeats most of ch. 2, but in one critical section (verse 6) describes how the strange woman has lost her way in life and does not know where she is going, but she has little insight into this. Although this notion is expressed in only one verse, from a psychiatric perspective this may be the key to our understanding of the strange woman because it alludes to the concept of 'identity disturbance' – one of the core features of borderline personality disorder (see page 447 for fuller description).

| | | |
|---|---|---|
| 5$^1$ | My child, be attentive to my wisdom, incline your ear to my understanding | Guidance from father to son |
| 2 | So that you may hold on to prudence and your lips may gain knowledge. | |
| 3 | For the lips of the strange woman drip honey for her speech is smoother than oil | Seductive charm, through speech Relationships start nicely but end in disaster |
| 4 | But in the end she is bitter as wormwood | ?tumultuous relationships of borderline personality disorder? bitter side to her character – |
| | sharp as a two-edged sword | see note 3 |
| 5 | Her feet go down to death her steps follows the path to Sheol | risk of harm or death, in associating with her |

| | | |
|---|---|---|
| 6 | She does not keep straight to the path of life; | She does not follow the usual life path for a young woman ?identity problem |
| | her ways wander, and she does not know it | ?she is unstable ?no insight ?promiscuous see note 4 |
| 7 | And now, my child, listen to me, and do not depart from the words of my mouth | advice is repeated from father to son; 'do what I say' |
| 8 | Keep your way far from her and do not go near the door of her house; | avoid this woman |
| 9 | or you will give your honour to others and your years to the merciless. | |

*Note 3.* In Arabic and Hebrew the word for 'wormwood' also means 'curse' and in the Bible the word generally denotes bitterness. Today, extracts from the wormwood plant, *Artemisia absinthium*, are used to make absinthe, vermouth and mead.

*Note 4.* The traditional explanation of the rabbis for verse 6 points to deviancy but expressed in religious terminology: thus Mezudath David renders 'Lest you compare the way of life – the wisdom of the Torah – to her, you should know that her paths have wandered very far from it, so far that you will not know any comparison or likeness to the wisdom of the Torah' (Rosenberg, 1993, p. 30). Because the Torah means 'the law', wandering away from the Torah implies social deviancy perhaps similar to deviancy of the scoundrel (*belial*). Correct translation is crucial in making any parallel with modern personality disorder, and there are several different translations, particularly for the Hebrew word *navu* (crooked, moveable, unstable):

- King James (1611), 'Lest thou shouldest ponder the path of life, / her ways are moveable, that thou canst not know them' (*navu* = moveable)
- Rall translation (1885), 'So that she findeth not the level path of life / Her ways are unstable and she knoweth it not' (*navu* = unstable)
- Moffat (1972), 'The high road of life is not for her / Shifty and slippery are her tracks'
- NRSV, 'She does not keep straight to the path of life / Her ways wander and she does not know it'.

Oesterly (1929) also translates *navu* as unstable. The NIV (Kohlenberger, 1987) has *navu* = crooked. No sexual pathology is mentioned here. By taking all the translations together it is possible to make an analogy with two aspects of borderline personality disorder. The first is identity problems (findeth not the level path of life; does not keep to the straight path of life; the high road of life is not for her) and the meaning of identity problems in personality disorder is discussed on page 448. The second aspect is some sort of instability. It is unclear whether this is instability of mood, or instability of relationships or occupation, but the four separate translations 'her ways are moveable', 'her ways are unstable', 'shifty and slippery are her tracks' and 'her ways wander' all seem to describe instability – one of the hallmarks of borderline personality disorder. Indeed, before borderline personality disorder (BPD) became the more fashionable term, the older Schneiderian term for this category was of *labile personality disorder* and verse 6 conveys the notion of lability quite well.

The passage is short, and is a repeat of the warning not to be seduced by the sweet-talking strange woman, because an adulterous relationship with her can end only in disaster. As in the description of the strange woman in ch. 2, only one verse is dedicated to describing non-sexual aspects of her character, namely her emotional instability her lacking any idea of where she is going in life – suggestive of identity disturbance.

## The strange woman in ch. 7$^{1-27}$: a tale of seduction

The seduction tale in ch. 7 opens with an admonition to the young to keep away from the 'strange woman'. She is described as an adulteress who gazes out from her window searching for simple and foolish youths with whom she can enjoy a love tryst while her husband is away on business. She seizes a young man and kisses him, then takes him back to her house, which is one of relative luxury, and then seduces him – but the outcome is disaster for the young man, who ends up in Sheol. He is but one of many she has previously seduced. The focus of the text and moral message are the dangers of adultery, but in this case it is for the man who sleeps with her, while the risks for the married woman herself are not described, yet they must have been considerable because at the time female adultery was punishable by death.

A few verses describe non-sexual aspects of her character and it is these passages that are of psychiatric significance. Rather than being a description of a real character or person, the text portrays a character type, but it does not have quite the same degree of clinical accuracy as the various male characters ('fools') who correspond more or less exactly to our present-day concept of antisocial personality disorder.

| | | |
|---|---|---|
| 7$^1$ | My child, keep my words and store up my commandments with you; | Parent–child address, typical of Proverbs |
| 2 | Keep my commandments and live, keep my teachings as the apple of your eye | |
| 3 | Bind them on your fingers, write them on the tablet of your heart. | Possible reference to *Phylacteries* See note 5 |
| 4 | Say to wisdom, 'You are my sister' and call insight your intimate friend, | Personification of wisdom as a close relative, a term of endearment (Fox, p. 240) |
| 5 | That they may keep you from the strange woman, from the adulteress with her smooth words | Heb. *Hehliqah* = smooth, also insincere |
| 6 | For at the window of my house I looked out through my lattice | The wives of David, Sisera and Ahab, also wait and look out of the window |
| 7 | And I saw among the simple men I observed among the youths<br><br>a young man without sense, | Simple men = *pethi* without sense = *haser leb*, both simpletons described in the previous chapter |

8     Passing along the street near her corner taking the road to her house

'Twilight is the time when people think they can remain unrecognised.' A similar passage in Job 24[15]

9     in the twilight, in the evening at the time of night and darkness

10    Then a woman comes towards him decked out like a prostitute, wily of heart

The woman is predatory and although dressed up, she is not a prostitute; wily of heart – see note 6

11    She is loud and wayward;

Loud – see note 7; wayward – see note 8

      her feet do not stay at home

Describes motor restlessness, ? agitation Subjective distress as well

12    Now in the street, now in the square and at every corner she lies in wait.

itchy feet

13    She seizes him and kisses him

Hebrew seizes = *te-erob*, also means ambush

      and with an impudent face says to him:

Predatory behaviour. Impudent face – see note 9 Kissing in public would have been frowned on

14    'I had to offer sacrifices and today I have paid my vows.

15    So now I have come out to meet you, to seek you eagerly and I have found you!

16    I have decked my couch with coverings, coloured spreads of Egyptian linen;

Ancient Israel was within Egypt's trading sphere, and Egyptian culture was still a dominant influence

17    I have performed my bed with myrrh, aloes and cinnamon

aloes – see note 9; myrrh – see note 10; cinnamon – see note 11

18    Come, let us take our fill of love till morning; let us delight ourselves with love.

Obvious description of lovemaking

19    For my husband is not at home; he has gone on a long journey

'Not at home' – see note 12 identifies the strange woman as a married woman having an affair

20    He took a bag of money with him; he will not come home till the full moon

? husband is a prosperous merchant She reassures the youth that they will not be caught

21    With much seductive speech she persuades him; With her smooth talk she compels him.

22    Right away he follows her and goes like an ox to the slaughter, or bounds like a stag to the trap

Heb. for 'right away' = *pit'om*, meaning 'impulsively' or suddenly The youth is quite unaware of what is happening to him

23    until an arrow pierces its entrails. He is like a bird rushing into a snare

The woman is a *femme fatale* A bird is a biblical epitome of

| | | |
|---|---|---|
| | not knowing it will cost him his life. | mindless gullibility and he is caught in a trap |
| 24 | And now, my children, listen to me and be attentive to the words of my mouth. | |
| 25 | Do not let your hearts turn aside to her ways, do not stray into her paths. | Relationships with this type of woman are a disaster for the man |
| 26 | For many are those she has laid low and numerous are her victories | She has destroyed many men through her affairs with them |
| 27 | Her house is the way to Sheol | Sheol = underworld, indicating these men come to a bad end |

*Note 5.* Phylacteries (*Tefillin*) are prayer bands bound around the head and the hands and the middle fingers and are still used in prayer today by Orthodox Jews. However, it is uncertain as to when this religious practice started and whether it was before or after the composition of Proverbs (Waltke, 2005, p. 369).

*Note 6.* The Hebrew for 'wily of heart' is *n'suat leb*, which literally means 'guarded of heart' or 'hidden'. Of itself, being guarded is more of a virtue, but in the context of a sinister character such as the strange woman this may be a danger. Fox (p.. 244) quotes Delitzch, a German biblical scholar who wrote a large treatise on the strange woman, and he attached a narcissistic significance to this phrase:

> The strange woman is of a hidden mind, of a concealed nature; for she feigns fidelity to her husband and flatters her paramours as her only beloved, while in truth she loves no one, and each of them to her is only a means to an end, namely the indulgence of her worldly sensual desire.

Ego-centricity, narcissism and stealth are described here, and this suggests that the sages of Proverbs and their later commentators were writing about character traits, perhaps in a similar way as psychiatry does today, and so making a comparison with modern typologies is a valid exercise.

*Note 7.* The Hebrew word for 'loud' here is *homiyyah*. The King James and the Rall Bibles have 'clamorous'; the Hebrew also means 'noisy, boisterous and unsettled'. Toy (1899) gives the meanings 'loud, clamorous, excited, vehement, passionate, boisterous' and quotes the Vulgate, which also has 'garrulous'. These words are very close to the modern personality disorder lexicon as applied to the cluster B personality disorders, which include borderline personality disorder as one of the 'dramatic' types.

The word and especially its root, *hāmāh*, has a related meaning, 'to groan'. This may also be critically relevant to understanding the nature of the mood disturbance of the strange woman and its relationship to borderline personality disorder. Thus Fox (p. 244) writes that *hāmāh* may be applied in a transferred sense to the inward groaning of a disturbed soul as occurs in certain psalms, and is translated as 'disquieted'. Psalm 42[5] has the lines

> Why are you cast down, O, my Soul
> and why are you disquieted within me?'    '*hāmāh*'

If the meaning of *hāmāh* is taken as 'disquieted', it suggests a feeling of anxious dysphoria – the mood which is said to typify borderline personality disorder. The single word *homiyyah* which is applied to the strange woman, as well as to Lady Folly, conveys this dysphoria and some of the more subtle features of the affective disturbance found in borderline personality disorder.

*Note 8.* The Hebrew word for 'wayward' here is *soreret*. Fox (p. 244) quotes G.R. Driver who suggests *sororet* means 'restless, fickle as well as rebellious'. Driver (1932) suggests the etymology is derived from the ancient Akaddian word *sarāra*, which means to be unstable or inconstant. Toy (1899) has rebellious, self-willed and wilful, which are obvious personality disorder epithets. *Sorer* is always used to describe a person who is incorrigible and defiant of authority, as in Isaiah 30[1]:

30[1]    Oh, rebellious children, says the Lord,        rebellious – *sorer*
         who carry out a plan, but not mine.

The words *homiyyah* (loud/dramatic) and *sororet* (wayward) are adjectives which describe people's character and not their sexual behaviours and lend weight to notion that the sages were writing about character typologies, *and that women of this type were troublesome to their societies.* There is also some degree of fit with the modern concepts of borderline and histrionic personality disorders as described in DSM-5.

*Note 8.* Rather than 'impudent face', both the Masoretic Text and the Revised English Bible have 'brazen', which is better. Fox (p. 245) says a hard forehead connotes obduracy and callousness in other biblical passages, and also means bold, or not inhibited. Excessive anger is one of the criteria for borderline personality disorder.

*Note 9.* A woman was not allowed to make sacrifices when she was menstruating. Fox (p. 246) interprets this verse as meaning that 'because she has made her sacrifices, she is not menstruating, and is therefore sexually available'.

*Note 10.* Myrrh is a gum resin which exudes from the plant *Balsamendron myrrha*, a shrub which grows in Saudi Arabia and the Sudan. It is reddish brown in colour and has a pleasant odour and an aromatic bitter taste. It was pulverised into a fine powder and placed in a sachet worn between a woman's breasts (Song of Songs 1[13]).

*Note 11.* Aloe (Hebrew=*ᵃhalim*) is a precious spice from the south-east Asian and north Indian eaglewood tree (*Aquillaria agallochum*).

*Note 12.* Cinnamon is the aromatic bark of a Ceylonese tree and was an ingredient of the sacred oil of the ancient Israelites. Its inclusion here indicates wealth and luxury (Toy, 1899), as well as trade between Judea and Ceylon, probably via Arabia.

*Note 13.* She cannot tolerate being alone for one moment. Borderline subjects collapse quickly when their main support is no longer around. DSM-5 states 'their abandonment fears are related to an intolerance of being alone and a need to have other people with them'. Although verse $7^{19}$ describes her sense of loneliness when her husband is away, fears of abandonment are not mentioned directly, but biblical commentators from the Middle Ages onwards (Rashi and Ramaq) as well as modern scholars have picked up a sense of abandonment. For example, Fox (p. 248) writes:

> The phrasing 'his house' is suggestive of alienation and emotional distance, because a woman's house is normally called 'her house'. Rashi basing himself the Talmud on b. *Sanheddrin* 96b identifies the man as God who has removed his *Shechinah* from Israel (*Shechinah* = the presence of God). This gives an interesting picture of sin set in atmosphere of national desperation as in Ezekiel $8^{12}$. While the national scope is irrelevant here *the insight that the woman feels deserted and neglected seems pertinent.* (Emphasis added)

The statement that 'the woman feels deserted and neglected' with her persistent running out into the street is virtually synonymous with the first criterion of today's DSM-5: 'Individuals with Borderline Personality Disorder make frantic efforts to avoid real or imagined abandonment'.

## Summary of the description of the strange woman

The description of the strange woman in the three passages $2^{16-19}$, $5^{1-9}$ and $7^{1-27}$ is of a particular character type. She is not reported as a clinical case history but appears only as a hypothetical type, in a tale of seduction and as a warning to young men to avoid becoming involved or committing adultery with such a character because this may have a bad or even lethal outcome. She is described as 'strange' throughout – a word which suggests an abnormality of personality. Thus she is defiant and wilful ($7^{11}$) and breaks her agreements or covenants ($2^{13}$) whether these are with God or her husband. She can be quite charming, her lips drip honey ($5^3$), but relationships with her usually become 'as bitter as wormwood' ($5^4$). Although she is a married woman she is still compelled to have a string of extramarital affairs, most of which end in a disaster for the man as 'numerous are her victims' ($7^{26}$).

She is unable to follow the normal life trajectory for a young woman as 'she does not keep straight to the path of life' ($5^6$), and this may be a biblical rendering of the modern concept of identity disturbance. The expected or ideal path for a young woman is described for the *essat hayil*, the ideal wife as described below, and the strange woman falls far short of this. There is good evidence of some kind of affective disturbance but this is not described as simple depression. She is described as 'unstable' ($5^6$); there is motor restlessness and agitation – 'her feet do not stay at home, now in the street, now in the square' ($7^{11-12}$). She is also 'loud' ($7^{11}$) and dramatic, or the same Hebrew word meaning 'loud' (*hamah*) can also signify an inner dysphoria. Some translations have 'clamorous'. McKane (1970, p. 367) suggests 'wanton and feverish' and his description is worth quoting:

The *issa zara* (strange woman) leads a feverish tempestuous existence; she gads about unpredictably; she lives in the way a drunken driver steers his car. She is not tranquil.

It would be difficult to improve on McKane's interpretation of the strange woman as this is exactly what borderline personality disorder is like, yet Mckane was a theologian and his understanding of this character type is derived entirely from the biblical texts.

She is cunning or 'wily of heart' ($7^{10}$), suggestive of a manipulative quality, and is capable of acting impulsively in sexual matters – she seizes the young man and kisses him ($7^{13}$). Her long-term relationships (e.g. with her husband) are obviously poor, while relationships with her paramours never last and have a bad or even fatal outcome. The story is a simple tale of seduction but within it is an attempt to describe a female character who causes much trouble for others – in this case young men. This is consistent with the basic Schneiderian concept of personality disorder of 'one who causes suffering to themselves or others by virtue of their personality'. There is no question of all of the above being due to a mental illness, as she seems to be quite sane and so she seems to have some sort of personality disorder.

It is a secondary consideration to see precisely which of the modern categories of personality disorder in the DSM-5 glossary give the best fit to the strange woman of Proverbs. The suggestion here is that she shows many of the features of borderline personality disorder and/or possibly also histrionic personality disorder, as described below.

## Borderline personality disorder

Psychiatrists are all too familiar with problems raised by borderline personality disorder (BPD) in their clinical practice. The account below is derived from the accounts by Casey (1998) and DSM-5 (2013).

This personality type has a frequency of around 1% in the general population, around 15% among psychiatric outpatients and around 25% among inpatients. Some 75% of the subjects are female. Schneider (1923), in his monograph, described 'the labile personality', a forerunner of the modern concept of borderline personality disorder, as follows:

> The labile has no chronic moodiness but is specifically characterised by the abrupt and rapid changes of mood which he undergoes. Sometimes the smallest stimulus is sufficient to arouse a violent reaction. Labile persons present a picture of shiftless social instability ... as a group the more irritable ones are apt to get into trouble through impulsive violence, and the more inconstant ones have all sorts of chance lapses.

Further developments came from an American psychoanalyst, Stern (1938), who identified a group of patients whom he called 'borderline', who did very poorly with conventional psychoanalytic treatment and who defied the existing classification schemes – which at that time focused on the distinction between psychoses and neurosis. Stern's term 'borderline personality disorder' remains in use.

*Clinical description*

The hallmark of this disorder is instability: instability of mood and of relationships. There is a pattern of intense unstable relationships which may be tumultuous. When things are going well the partner is idealised and seen as wonderful, but when the partner fails to fulfil some need they are devalued and the relationship is viewed in angry or hostile terms and may sometimes break, with consequent traumatic depressions for all concerned. The pattern is recurrent, although many borderline women eventually mature out of this pattern and settle with one partner, although the same associated emotional intensity may persist even within a monogamous relationship.

There is also a marked instability of mood. Depression is common but the dominant pattern is not of a continuous depressed mood, but rather of rapid and reactive shifts into and out of depression. The mood is characterised by complaints of boredom and intolerance of being alone (see below) and is said to be associated with an unpleasant sense of frustration and emotional emptiness. Some analysts such as Kohut (1971) describe this as 'affective hunger', which they believe is so unpleasant as to drive subjects into impulsive or addictive behaviours such as binge eating, gambling and alcoholism, as a relief from their strange dysphoric emotional state.

Identity disturbance, a concept derived from developmental psychology, is found in around three-quarters of subjects in clinical samples. Erikson (1956), a child psychiatrist, proposed that during adolescence the individual should be able to negotiate the maturational steps involved in the development of a commitment to physical intimacy, occupational choice and normal competition, and achieve their own personal and social definition as well as a sense of identity. DSM-5 explains this criterion presents as sudden and dramatic shifts of self-image, shifting goals and shifting vocational aspirations. These individuals may suddenly change from the role of being a needy supplicant to becoming a righteous avenger of past mistreatment. Their self-image is often based on being bad or evil but some subjects may have no self-image at all. There is a suggestion of this feature in the strange woman because she is said to be someone who has 'lost the level path of life' (5[6]).

Impulsivity is a maladaptive trait shared with antisocial personality disorder and presents with recurrent suicidal threats, overdoses or self-mutilating behaviours. Sometimes by accident, sometimes by intention, there is a completed suicide, and the overall death rate from suicide may be around 5–10%. Impulsive behaviours are usually of a self-damaging type, such as binge eating, substance abuse disorders, engaging in unsafe sex or other reckless behaviours.

Excessive anger is also common, sometimes presenting as irritability, usually reported by relatives, but sometimes becoming apparent only during treatment. One unusual but well recognised fear of borderline subjects is the fear of abandonment, which may be intense. These are the patients who cannot tolerate their therapist taking a vacation, or who become acutely distressed if a friend is late for an appointment or a partner cancels a date. Their underlying fear is that they are 'bad' in the other person's eyes and because of this they have been rejected or abandoned, in what may have been no more than a routine or even expected change. Gunderson (2001) refers to this as an 'intolerance of aloneness'. Masterson (1981) first suggested that abandonment fears were related to childhood separation fears, but it is now clear that childhood sexual abuse is the more relevant trauma, rather than simple separation in childhood.

## Cause

The cause of borderline personality disorder is unclear and a comprehensive review of the huge literature on the topic is beyond the scope of this chapter. Gunderson (2001) points out that around 75% of subjects are female. In the stress–diathesis model of psychiatric disorder, both nature (diathesis) and nurture (stress) contribute, and the innate contribution is presumed to be genetic. Gunderson suggests that the heightened aggression, impulsivity and poor emotional control found in both antisocial and borderline personality disorders probably have their origin in innate and genetically determined characteristics, while the noxious early environment which many borderline subjects grow up in (broken homes, severe marital disharmony, physical and sexual abuse) leads to the formation of negative self-images, later mood disorder, excessive vengeance, etc., which are all characteristic of borderline subjects. A twin study of borderline personality disorder estimated the size of the genetic component to be responsible for about 69% of the cause (Torgerson *et al.*, 2000).

The outlook for borderline personality disorder is somewhat better than for antisocial types and there are now drugs, such as the antidepressants (e.g. Prozac), which appear to have beneficial effects on impulsivity, and the abnormal moods of the borderline, and there are also extensive psychotherapy programmes, which, if not curative, can certainly ameliorate the severity of the disorder (Bateman and Fonagy, 2004). Many psychiatric units will enrol patients with borderline personality disorder, but not those with antisocial personality disorder, into comprehensive treatment programmes applying both pharmacological and psychotherapeutic approaches.

## Can a diagnosis of the strange woman be a valid exercise?

An attempt is made below to compare the biblical account of the strange woman (*issa zarah*) with the modern definition of borderline personality disorder as defined by DSM-5. A much greater degree of caution needs to be taken when applying modern diagnostic criteria to the descriptions of female character types than their male equivalents in the Old Testament. Thus the descriptions of the *belial* (scoundrel) and of the various types of fools in Proverbs are of common criminals and obvious psychopathic types, and are readily recognisable. However, the 'strange woman' is deviant only in the realm of sexual morality, and her main appearance is in a fairy tale of seduction, making her character difficult to evaluate, as it occurs in a strongly patriarchal society. Thus, issues concerning marriage, the social position of women in society and the inheritance of land may be paramount when deviancy labelling is considered. In addition, the biblical description of the

**Table 11.1** Comparison between the DSM criteria for borderline personality disorder and the case of the strange woman

| DSM borderline personality disorder | The strange woman of Proverbs |
|---|---|
| There has to be pervasive instability in relationships, self-image and affects, as well as impulsivity from early adulthood, in a variety of settings, with at least five of the following | 5⁶ She does not keep to the straight to the path of life: her ways wander, and she does not know it<br>See also McKane's description (page 447)<br>7¹³ She seizes him and kisses him (impulsive behaviour) |
| (1) Efforts to avoid abandonment | 7¹¹⁻¹² When her husband is away she cannot stay still – 'Her feet abide not in the house, Now she is in the street, now in the squares'. Itchy feet |
| (2) Unstable but intense personal relationships, alternating between extremes of idealisation and devaluation | Initially there is great charm – 'From the lips of the strange woman drops honey' (5³), 'But in the end she is bitter as wormwood' (5⁴) |
| (3) Unstable self-image or self-worth | She does not keep straight to the path of life (NRSV 5⁶). The Rall translation is 'She findeth out not the level path of life' |
| (4) Potentially self-damaging impulsivity (e.g. in spending, sex, substance abuse, binge eating) | Many affairs: 'Numerous are her victims' (7²⁶). Adultery, punishable by death was a high risk reckless behaviour for a married woman |
| (5) Suicidal gestures or threats or self-mutilation | 'Her feet go down to death' (5⁵). No references to suicide or self-mutilation but several to death (2¹⁸, 7²⁵ and 7²⁷ ) |
| (6) Mood instability (e.g. intense but brief dysphoria, irritability or anxiety) | Probably conveyed by words *homiyyah* and *sororet* in 7¹¹: 'She is loud and wayward' (see notes 7 and 8 on pages 444–445) |
| (7) Chronic feelings of emptiness | 7¹¹ ?The word *hamah* (for loud) also means 'inner disquietude' |
| (8) Inappropriate anger, temper, physical fighting | ? 7¹³ 'Talks with an impudent face'; (impudent = anger); also 7¹¹, 'wayward', *sororet*, which Toy (1899) translates as 'rebellious, wilful' |
| (9) Stress-related paranoid ideation or severe symptoms of dissociation | Not present. Note that this criterion was not present in earlier definitions |

strange woman contains far more in the way of archetypal material, which means that anthropological, cultic and religious factors need to be taken into account to interpret its metaphors and this is discussed further on pages 454–456. However, an attempt is made here to apply the modern diagnostic criteria of DSM-5 (APP, 2013) of borderline personality disorder to the verses describing the strange woman of the Book of Proverbs.

From Table 11.1 it is apparent that five of the DSM-5 criteria (unstable relationships, identity disturbance, reckless behaviour, affective instability and inappropriate anger) are reasonably well identified in the biblical text. Criterion 4 specifies that two self-damaging behaviours should be present, but only one type of self-damaging behaviour (sexual) is described. Two items which describe subjective affective status – fears of abandonment (criterion 1) and chronic feelings of emptiness (criterion 7) – are hinted at through the restlessness of the woman, constantly rushing out into the street to seek a new paramour. Some sort of inner distress is implied in this behaviour; however, the women's subjective state is not described. The sages who were men had little interest in the inner emotions or psychological state of the 'strange woman', but were more concerned with the upset she caused to the men who strayed across her path. Recurrent suicidal behaviour is not described, but the violence is implied in the repeated deaths of her paramours, which may be an equivalent. The final item, 'transient paranoid ideation', is not mentioned but this has only recently been included in the definition of borderline personality disorder and its status is still uncertain.

The biblical text is quite clearly intending to depict an odd or 'strange' female personality type: she meets at least five out of the nine criteria for borderline personality disorder. An alternative, however, might be histrionic personality disorder, as described below.

## The strange woman and histrionic personality disorder

The description of histrionic personality disorder given below is taken from the text of DSM-5 (APP, 2013, p. 711).

The essential feature of histrionic personality disorder is pervasive and excessive emotionality and attention-seeking behaviour. They like to be the centre of attention (criterion 1) and so they are often lively and dramatic. They have charm, initial enthusiasm, apparent openness and flirtatiousness. They like to be the life and soul of the party and do dramatic things. They may flatter the physician or have dramatic descriptions of physical and psychological symptoms. These individuals often dress in an inappropriate sexually provocative or seductive way. Emotional expression may be shallow and rapidly shifting. Individuals with this disorder use their physical appearance to draw attention to themselves. They are overly concerned with impressing others with their appearance and spend excessive amounts of time, energy and money on clothes or grooming. They may have a style of speech that is excessively impressionistic yet lacking in detail. Individuals with this disorder show self-dramatisation, theatricality and an exaggerated expression of emotion. They may embarrass friends and acquaintances with an excessive display of emotions in public, e.g. embracing casual acquaintances, sobbing uncontrollably or having temper tantrums. Emotions may be quickly turned on or off, leading others to suspect they are faking these feelings. Histrionic individuals are highly suggestible, easily influenced by others and by current fads. They may be overly trusting of authority figures who they believe magically may solve their problems. They may consider relationships more intimate than they actually are and longer-term relationships may be neglected to make way for new relationships which have greater excitement. Borderline, narcissistic, antisocial and dependent personality disorders may often coexist. The type is more common among females and prevalence studies suggest a rate of around 2% in the general population, but rates of 10–15% have been reported in mental health settings when structured interviews have been used.

Table 11.2 compares the DSM-5 diagnostic criteria for histrionic personality disorder to the features of the strange woman. The biblical description of the strange woman in chs 5 and 7 gives a reasonable fit. There is good evidence for being inappropriately sexually seductive (item 2); shallow

**Table 11.2** Comparison between DSM histrionic personality and the strange woman

| *DSM histrionic personality* | *The strange woman of Proverbs* |
| --- | --- |
| Pervasive and excessive emotionality and attention seeking from early adulthood, in a variety of contexts, with at least five of the following | |
| (1) Uncomfortable where they are not the centre of attention | 7$^{11}$ She is loud and wayward (this is attention-seeking behaviour) |
| (2) Interaction with others is often inappropriately sexually seductive or provocative | 7$^{13}$ She seizes him and kisses him 7$^{17}$ 'I have perfumed my bed with myrrh, aloes and cinnamon' |
| (3) Rapidly shifting and shallow expression of emotions | 5$^{3-4}$ Her speech is smoother than oil but in the end she is as bitter as wormwood |
| (4) Uses physical appearance to draw attention | 7$^{10}$ Then a woman comes to him decked out like a prostitute |
| (5) A style of speech that is excessively impressionistic and lacking in detail | 5$^{3}$ 'For the lips of the strange woman drip honey, and her speech is smoother than oil' |
| (6) Self-dramatisation, theatricality and exaggerated expression of emotion | 7$^{11}$ She is loud and wayward (see above for translation of *homiyyah* and *sororet* |
| (7) Suggestible/easily influenced | Not present |
| (8) Considers relationships to be more intimate than they actually are | ? 7$^{21}$ 'With her smooth talk she compels him'. A seduction but no relationship |

emotions (item 3); seductive dress (item 4); impressionistic speech (item 5); and theatricality (item 6). Evidence for 'being the centre of attention' (item 1) and 'presumes relationships to be more intimate than they really are' (item 8) is rather less certain, while there is no description of suggestibility (item 6). This trait was recognised as dangerous to the individual in Proverbs and is described elsewhere as gullibility and in association with simpletons (*pethi* – see page 453) but not specifically with regard to the strange woman.

Thus the description of the strange woman appears to fulfil criteria for both borderline and histrionic personality disorder, but it is important to realise that fulfilling the criteria for two different personality disorders does not mean the person has two personalities, but rather that the personality disorder is more serious and complex, and therefore has an increased number of maladaptive traits. Diagnoses of this type are artificial, reflecting no more than the inadequacies of present-day personality disorder taxonomy. The combination of both borderline and histrionic features is quite commonly encountered in clinical practice and precise labelling does not really matter. What is important is that the strange woman does seem to have some sort of a character problem or, in modern jargon, a personality disorder.

## Who was the strange woman of Proverbs?

Just as the strange woman attracted lovers, so she has also drawn the attentions of numerous scholars throughout the ages who have offered multiple explanations as to who she might be. The explanation offered here, that she represents a particular personality type, perhaps corresponding to the modern concept of borderline or histrionic personality disorder, is only one of several equally valid and competing explanations. The review given below is a summary of a very large literature extending back to the Talmud (5th century CE) and is based on the detailed analysis by Fox (2000) in his book *Proverbs 1–9* and the work of Athalaya Brenner (1995) in *A Feminist Companion to Wisdom Literature*, which considers the origins of the strange woman from both an anthropological and a feminist perspective.

### The strange woman is a real character

Fox (2000, p. 252) maintains that she represents a real character and this is the view taken by the present author as well. Fox points out that this feeling of reality is only in evidence in the description of the seduction of the young man in ch. 7, where there is a portrayal of a young woman who has feelings, motivations and some degree of pathology. Like the present author, he also focuses on the words used to describe her non-sexual pathology; for example, in verse 7[11] she is *homiyyah*, or clamourous, and *soreret*, or defiant or rebellious, adjectives which relate to a character disorder. McKane (1970), another biblical scholar, also writes that she is a real person but one who is extremely unstable. Readers are told to avoid such a person, but beneath her sensuous veneer Fox (p. 254) feels she is a sad and shabby character and even mentions that he has met such women.

Academic theologians, such as Fox and McKane would not have known that the average psychiatrist meets with a 'strange woman' almost every week in their clinics while psychotherapists encounter these types on an almost daily basis, when they lie on the couch and unravel their complicated love lives during therapy. A particular hazard of working with these clients is that every now and again a therapist succumbs to the sexual charms of the a 'strange woman' and so violates their professional boundaries. Once the affair ends, as it usually does, the vengeful client reports the misconduct to the professional authorities. This leads to the debarring of the therapist from any further work, a termination of their career, and sometimes even financial ruin, or, as the scribe of Proverbs wrote some 2000 years ago, 'Do not stray into her path, for many are those she has laid low and numerous are her victories. Her house is the way to Sheol' ($7^{25-27}$).

## *A foreign secular woman – and the risk of exogamous marriages*

H. Washington (1995) provides a powerful historical argument based on an economic analysis of the conditions which appertained in Judah following the return of the exiles. He proposes that the 'diatribe' against the strange woman should be seen as part of an ongoing campaign against exogamous marriages, as these were threatening the identity and fabric of Jewish society during the Persian period (circa 500 BCE). Christl Maier (1998) concurs with Washington's formulation and suggests that land tenure was the critical issue for a people returning from exile and reclaiming the land of their ancestors. She suggests that strangeness may mean 'foreign women'.

Land tenure in the ancient world was determined by blood lineage and marriage, and under these circumstances an exogamous marriage would have represented a major economic threat to the stability and homogeneity of society. This was because the land that King Cyrus had now restored to the Jewish community could once more be lost to foreigners, not through war and expropriation, but through legal mechanisms such as inter-marriage.

Also in support of his hypothesis that economic factors were paramount, Washington argues that the earlier pre-exilic part of the Book of Proverbs (chs 10–31) takes a much more benign line on adultery and prostitution than Proverbs 1–9, which is the post-exilic section of the book. He argues that in this post-exilic section the 'strange woman' or 'foreign woman' has been demonised and there is a vicious diatribe against her. A sexual liaison with her is seen as threatening the life of any young man who consorts with her. Evidence from other books in the OT, particularly Ezra and Nehemiah, probably written at around the same time, tell the same story and describe vigorous campaigns against marriages to foreign women. There is even one report of an episode in which more than 100 foreign wives were deported.

## *Mythological and anthropological parallels*

Myths surrounding the seductive powers of women, especially foreign goddesses, abound in the literature of the ancient world. Eve and the serpent entice Adam to take a bite from the apple and as a result they are barred from the Garden of Eden. Clifford (1993) proposes that the story of the strange woman is not a warning against sex or promiscuity but more a warning against a false marriage or a false relationship.

Claudia Camp (1995) makes a powerful analogy between the ubiquitous folk tales that revolve around 'the trickster' motifs and the story of the strange woman. She draws heavily on an anthropological analysis by Pelton (1980), entitled 'The Trickster in West Africa'. The trickster is portrayed as a combination of a liar and a buffoon yet at the same time is a folk hero and is described in culture-specific terms. The trickster is able to break all social boundaries and the conventions of proper sexual behaviour and in so doing is able to demonstrate in a subtle and sometimes humorous way the mores and traditions of a particular society.

The female imagery of Proverbs also plays largely on opposites which are personified. Lady Wisdom represents creation, love, social order and wisdom, whereas the strange woman represents death, falsehood, social disorder and folly, and she strays over the accepted sexual boundaries. The strange woman and personified wisdom represent a certain literary unity which conveys a much more complex situation than an over-simplistic division of the world into good and evil to be found in most of the Old Testament.

The reason such tales are both universal and popular is that they bring the forces of disorder, chaos and death into a more human realm or, as Pelton suggests, 'they are not on or outside the margins of society, but deep in its midst'. Trickster tales grapple with the mysteries of death, deceit, boundaries and chaos and many other unresolved psychological and social issues. Moreover, these themes, together with their associated fears, frequently come up during psychotherapy.

There are also a multitude of feminist interpretations, but for reasons of space only one is included here. Fontaine (1993) suggests the story is one of childlessness and male infertility. She writes:

> We take the position that our strange woman is no mother, but seeks to become one. Thus in verse $7^{10}$ she is only dressed as a prostitute but does not practice such a trade. In the same verse she is *n'surat leb* (guarded of heart) and so her thoughts and motivation are hidden. In verse $7^{20}$ 'the time is the dark side of the moon', the mid-point of her menstrual cycle meaning she is fertile, and her mention of completing her sacrifices in $7^{14}$ means that she is sexually available. Her husband is away and will be absent at a time when she might possibly conceive – even if she had any lingering hope that she might be able to gain a child by him. She chooses a young fertile partner of little experience because he can easily be manipulated. His implied lustiness can be channelled for her own satisfaction. Denied the one thing – a child, that will make her a women of value in her culture, she takes the matter into her own hands. Neither prayers for fertility, or an accessible husband can meet her need so she manages the situation herself. Thus she functions as a temptation to other women who might imitate her actions and given that this arises in the male dominated literature of the sages, such a woman is strange indeed!

## Allegorical interpretations

There are numerous allegorical interpretations of these passages which suggest she is not a real person at all but describes some important social or religious theme. Rashi identifies the *issā zārāh* (strange woman) with the heretical church and Christianity. He wrote 'What would the excellence of the *Torah* (Wisdom) be if Solomon, the author of Proverbs, said here that it would save you from the adulteress above and not from other transgressions?' By this he meant that adultery was a very tiny misdemeanour in comparison with defection from Judaism, which encompasses all transgressions, and therefore being unfaithful with the strange woman represented a defection to Christianity (cited in Rosenberg, 1993). Malbim identifies the strange woman with foreign philosophy, specifically with Greek philosophy (Friedlander, 1904, pp. 68–76).

Maimonides interpreted the attack on 'the strange woman' as an attack on the physical, worldly and sensual pleasures, especially the sex drive. Hame'iri believed it was a warning against the prostitute while Alsheikh thought the strange woman was a cipher for evil inclinations, which also basically meant the sex drive (see Fox for references). In contrast to the male character disorders in Proverbs, such as the *belial* (the scoundrel), about whom there can be no doubt that they describe real people with little or no fictional or allegorical content, the *issā zārāh* (strange woman) is far less definitely a real character and this has left the field wide open to a multitude of differing explanations, among which personality disorder is but one.

## Other female characters in the Book of Proverbs

There are four other female characters in the Book of Proverbs, but three of them seem to depend on the strange woman, suggesting that the wider societal issues raised by her character were a central preoccupation for the writers of Proverbs. The (*essat hayyil*) is the capable or virtuous wife and the antithesis of the strange woman. The contentious wife (*essāt midyanot*) is the wife who nags too much; she is a real person, a universal and familiar character. She depicts bad and unhappy marriages but she bears no relationship to any of the other women in the Book of Proverbs. The other two characters are personifications of wisdom and folly.

### The virtuous wife (*essat hayyil*)

This worthy wife is described in Proverbs 31[10-31] and *essat hayyil* is sometimes translated as the 'capable wife' or 'valiant wife'. She works hard at her domestic tasks of spinning, weaving and sowing. She rises very early in the morning (while it is still dark), prepares food for everyone in her house and delegates tasks for the servants. She manages her household with great competence and provides stores of food to insure against a short-fall and for the snow in the winter. She knits her own clothes and is so skilled at making clothes that she is able to sell some of them. Her business acumen enables her to assess the value of property and she manages her own vineyard. She laughs and her children call her happy, her husband praises her, and he has become an important elder of the city, trusted implicitly.

This description is of a stereotype who fulfils the male concept of the woman's role in marriage. She is the opposite of the strange woman. The description has some socio-historic significance as it describes the values of an idealised marriage of this period, but it has no psychiatric relevance.

## The contentious wife (*ēssāt midyanot*)

This character appears surprisingly frequently in the Book of Proverbs and is also of little psychiatric significance. The sages were concerned about unhappy marriages, which they appear to blame on wives who quarrel too much. The problem is mentioned on four occasions. The verse in ch. 21[9] is repeated in 25[24]:

> It is better to dwell in the corner of a housetop
> than with a contentious woman in a wide house.

The same thought is repeated again, though this time not word for word:

17 It is better to dwell in a desert land
    than with a contentious and fretful woman

Hebrew 'fretful' also means vexation and quarrelsome.

20[13] A foolish son is a calamity for his father
    and the contentions of a wife are a continued dropping.

Toy (1899, p. 373) in his comment on this verse quotes an old Arab proverb: 'There are three things that make a house intolerable: *tak* (rain leaking through), *nak* (a wife's nagging) and *bak* (bugs)'.

15 A continual dropping in a very rainy day
    and a contentious woman are alike
16 to restrain her is to restrain the wind
    or to grasp oil in the right hand....

This verse tells how the contentious (fretful) wife wears the marriage down, but the following verse describes the sheer impossibility of trying to change the situation – it is like trying to grasp oil.

Biblical feminist writers point out that this is a patriarchal way of describing marital unhappiness – it is all the woman's fault (she nags too much). There is only one mention of abusive husbands or men who destroy their marriages in Proverbs (the *belial*) as a result of their violence (wife beating). The figures of the nagging wife and her long-suffering husband are not usually held to be mentally ill, but are a universally familiar couple.

## Lady Wisdom and Lady Folly

Lady Wisdom (*esset hochmot*) and Lady Folly (*esset kesilut*) are personifications of their respective qualities. Lady Folly is derived from the strange woman and the verses describing her are drawn from the seduction passages of the strange woman story given above. Lady Wisdom is her antithesis and so she also depends in part on the strange woman. Proverbs ch. 9 gives an account of how each provides a meal for 'the simple and mindless' in the town. It is written as a brief playlet of two scenes with the cast drawn from the lexicon of the other personality disorders of Proverbs. These include the *pethi ,the hasar leb* (both simpletons) and the *les* (a narcissistic psychopath).

The banquet of Lady Wisdom is analysed first below. She slaughters her cattle, prepares her wine and sets her table. Servant girls are sent from the top of the town to seek out the simple minded (*pethi*) who eat her bread and wine; she then urges them to become more mature and insightful. Lady Wisdom is part literary, part human and part mythological. The human element is represented by a personification of a wise and sensible woman. The second scene is the meal with Lady Folly, who gives her fools a diet of illicit adulterous sex, which leads to their death.

| | | |
|---|---|---|
| 9[1] | Wisdom has built her house, she has hewn seven pillars. | Origin of T. E. Lawrence's book *The Seven Pillars of Wisdom* |
| 2 | She has slaughtered her animals she has mixed her wine, she has set her table. | Feasts with wine and wisdom – see note 14 |
| 3 | She has sent out her servant girls she calls from the highest place in the town | Servant girls ? teachers of wisdom LXX has 'man servants', to |
| 4 | You that are simple, turn in here! | preserve female propriety. simple = *pethi*; |
| | To those without sense she says | without sense= *hasar leb* |
| 5 | 'Come eat my bread and drink of the wine I have mixed. | |
| 6 | Lay aside immaturity and live and walk the way of insight'. | It is still possible to give moral education to the simple |
| 7 | Whoever corrects a scoffer wins abuse; whoever rebukes the wicked gets hurt. | Scoffer = *les* (narcissistic, antisocial type, who attacks back if criticised) |
| 8 | A scoffer who is rebuked will only hate you; the wise when rebuked will love you. | impossible to impart moral education to the *les*. See note 15 |
| 9 | Give instruction to the wise, and they will become wiser still; teach the righteous and they will gain in learning | Verses 7–10 thought to be later insertions |
| 10 | The fear of the Lord is the beginning of wisdom, and the knowledge of the Holy One is insight. | religious element added in later Insight=*binah* |

Note 14. The sequence

building a house – slaughtering animals – feasting – debating wisdom

is also described in the Ugaritic literature when El gives a banquet inviting the gods to 'Eat, gods, and drink wine unto Satiety, unto drunkenness'. Waltke (2005) also likens the occasion to a Greek symposium, where a feast with wine would be followed by a learned discussion.

*Note 15.* The scribe observes that the *pethi* and the *hasar leb* who are two simple-minded characters are actually able to learn and take guidance from Lady

Wisdom – but the *les*, who is narcissistic, contemptuous and psychopathic, cannot even receive instruction, let alone change. The sheer impossibility of changing the ways of the psychopath are sharply observed here and will be all too familiar to anyone working in psychiatry or the prison service.

Secondly, the meal hosted by Lady Folly is described:

| | | |
|---|---|---|
| 9¹³ | The foolish woman is loud, she is ignorant and knows nothing | Heb. loud = *homiyyah*. The MT has 'turbulent', foolish (*kesillit* from *kesil*) |
| ¹⁴ | She sits at the door of her house on a seat at the high places of the town | Possibly where a prostitute would have plied her trade |
| ¹⁵ | Calling to those who pass by who are going straight on their way | People with no intention of any wrong-doing, she leads astray |
| ¹⁶ | You who are simple, turn in here and to those without sense | simple = *pethi* without sense = *hasar leb* (see page 403) |
| ¹⁷ | Stolen water is sweet and bread eaten in secret is pleasant | Stolen water and the quenching of thirst allude to adultery Similarly bread eaten in secret also suggests adultery |
| ¹⁸ | But they do not know that the dead are there, that her guests are in the depths of Sheol. | Wisdom imparts life; folly leads to death; the dead = *rephaim* or shades As in the strange women passages 7²⁶⁻²⁷ |

The characters of this little play all denote a particular category of personality disorder. The 'strange woman', perhaps a case of borderline personality disorder, hovers behind Lady Folly and her antithesis, Lady Wisdom, the fools with learning difficulties, the *pethi* and *hasar leb*, can just about be trained but this is a hopeless task for the *les* (the psychopath).

Lady Folly has a similar character to the strange woman but is much more of an abstraction of her bad qualities, existing only as a foil to highlight the good characteristics of Lady Wisdom. G. Bostrom (1935) offers a historic-cultic explanation similar to that of Washington (1995), suggesting that all the 'bad' female figures in Proverbs 1–9 represent a prostitute of another cult. This was linked to fears of social disintegration and loss of cultic identity, which was paramount among the elders during the Persian period, as discussed above. Equally plausible is Perdue's (1981 ) argument that Lady Folly is a personified foreign fertility goddess such as Ishtar, Asherah or Anat and her invitation to 'drink stolen water and eat bread in secret' represents participation in foreign fertility rights and by implication a defection from the Israelite cult.

## Concluding remarks

One of the great charms in trying to interpret the Old Testament Wisdom literature is that although the text is rich in meaning, it is often written with such generalities to convey a multitude of different explanations. None perhaps more so than the 'strange woman' of Proverbs, who has already acquired religious, moral, socio-economic, anthropological and mythical explanations, and to this pot pourri, here is added the notion that she may have a personality disorder as well. The sages who wrote about her had no intention of describing a personality disorder – that is a purely modern perspective. Their concerns lay in the preservation of order, physical and emotional survival, ensuring the stability of society and the avoidance of chaos. Then, as now, marriage lay at the root of social organisation, and a bad marriage was a disaster for all concerned, while an exogamous marriage had serious economic implications for the family and the whole community.

The intention of the sages seems to have been to provide a guide to young men about different prospective brides. Some were truly wonderful, like the *ēssāt hayyil* (the virtuous wife), while others could be most unpleasant to live with, such as the *ēssāt midyanot* (the contentious wife), but there was one type that was positively dangerous – the *issa zarah* or the strange woman. This woman brings great harm to the young men she leads astray, who will end in Sheol; even if they do not die, they will end up in a bad place.

The strange woman by virtue of her personality causes harm to others and this is one of the central features of Schneider's definition of a personality disorder. It is a matter of secondary importance as to which particular personality disorder she has in accordance with the modern diagnostic glossaries. Here it is suggested she fulfils criteria for both borderline and histrionic personality disorders, neither of which was formally delineated until the 20th century.

The description of borderline personality disorder in the context of the strange woman is reasonable, but not nearly as accurate or coherent as that for the male antisocial types such as the *belial* (scoundrel) or the fools described in the previous chapter, with nothing in their typologies pointing to mythical characters. The strange woman presents with a veritable feast of possible interpretations and readers are invited to choose for themselves as to who she actually might be.

## Appendix: female personality disorder in other ancient Near Eastern texts

### The Wisdom of Anii

This work dates from the period of the New Kingdom (1580–1085 BCE) in Egypt, and the preserved papyri are dated between the 8th and the 11th century BCE. It also takes the form of parental instruction but in this case both father and son are scribes. Oesterly (1929, pp. xxxiii–lv) draws a parallel with the passage below taken from the Wisdom of Anii and the strange woman of Proverbs:

> Beware of the strange woman, who is not known in her city. Ogle her not and have no intercourse with her. She is a deep expanse of water and her turning is not known. A woman is away from her husband says daily unto thee 'I am beautiful', when no witness is present. That is a great crime worthy of death.

## The Proverbs of Ahiqar

By far the most important Assyrian influence on the Book of Proverbs, is a book of antiquity known as the Proverbs of Ahiqar. This document, which dates from the 8th century BCE, was known to many peoples of the Middle and Near East and versions exist in Syriac, Armenian, Arabic, old Turkish, Slavonic, Russian, Ethiopian and a variety of other ancient languages. For many generations the Proverbs of Ahiqar were included as an appendix to the Arab classic *A Thousand and One Nights*, and so these sayings were widely known in the Arab world, but little known in Western circles. Their history will therefore briefly be recounted here, with the account being derived from Lindenberger (1983).

Ahiqar was an advisor and cabinet minister to Sennacherib, King of Assyria (704–681 BCE). While still a youth, Ahiqar had been warned by astrologers that he would have no children. When he reached adulthood, the prophecy came true, despite prodigous efforts on his part to disprove it, including marriages to no fewer than 60 wives.

Some sections in Proverbs resemble the sayings of Ahiqar and all the parallels are given in Oesterley (1929).

### A parallel with the strange women

> My son lift not up thine eyes and look upon a woman that is bedizened and painted; and do not lust after her in thine heart; for if thou shouldst give her all that is in thine hands, thou findest no advantage in her; and thou will be guilty against God.

Ptah-hotep also makes a comment on 'the approaching woman', a seductive female type to be avoided, which Oesterly (1929) likened to the strange woman of Proverbs as follows:

> In whatsoever place thou enterest beware of approaching women. The place where they are is not good. On their account a thousand go to ruin; A man is mocked by their glistening limbs, which soon become as Herset stones. A little moment and what was like a dream became death in the end.

Herset stones are a sign of grief.

### Babylonian Wisdom literature

The following description of a harlot is taken from Lambert's (1960) *Babylonian Wisdom literature*. He assigns this text to the Cassite Period of 1500 – 1200 BCE, which is considerably older than Proverbs (800 – 300 BCE), and may even be older than Amenemope (circa 1040-1200 BCE). The account is not sufficiently detailed to provide a firm identification with borderline personality disorder, but Oesterley (1929) has linked it to the description of the 'Strange Woman' .

> Do not marry a prostitute whose husbands are legion
> A temple harlot who is dedicated to a god

A courtesan who favours many
In your trouble she will not support you
In your dispute she will be a mocker;
There is no reverence or submissiveness with her
Even if she dominates your house get her out
For she has directed her attention elsewhere.

(Lambert, 1960, lines 72–79, p. 102)

## The Qumran texts

These are dated around 200 BCE and come after the Book of Proverbs. One scroll found in cave 4 was translated by John Allegro; he entitled it 'The Wiles of the Wicked Woman' (4Q184). It contains a lengthy poem which repeats much of the tale of the strange woman of Proverbs. As such it is not independent of Proverbs but indicates that the problem of the *femme fatale*, which seems to have been relevant to the mores of society during this later period. It is too long to be included here but complete versions can be found in Wise *et al.* (2005).

## References

Bateman, A. and Fonagy, P. (2004) *Psychotherapy for Borderline Personality Disorder: Mentalization Based Treatment*. Oxford: Oxford University Press.

Boström, G. (1935) *Proverbiastudien: Die Weisheit und das fremde Weib in Spruche 1–9*. Lund: C.W.K. Gleerup.

Brenner, A. (1993) Proverbs 1–9: An F Voice? Pp. 113–130 in *On Gendering Texts*. Ed. By A. Brenner and F. van Dijk-Hemmes. Leiden: Brill.

Brenner, A. (1995) Some observations on the figurations of women in Wisdom Literature. In *A Feminist Companion to Wisdom Literature*. Ed. A. Brenner, pp. 50 – 66. Sheffield: Sheffield Academic Press.

Camp, C.V. (1995) Wise and Strange: An interpretation of the female imagery in Proverbs in light of Trickster Mythology in *A feminist companion to Wisdom literature*. Ed. A. Brenner, pp.131 – 156. Sheffield Academic Press, Sheffield.

Clifford, R.J. (1993) Woman Wisdom in the Books of Proverbs. Pp. 61–72 in *Biblische Theologie und geselleschaftlicher Wandel* (FS N. Lohfink). Ed. By G. Baraulik, W. Gross and S. McEvenue, Freiburg; Heider.

Crenshaw, J. L. (1998) *Old Testament Wisdom. An Introduction*. Westminster John Knox Press, Louisville, Kentucky.

Driver, G. R. (1932) Problems in Proverbs. *Zeitschrift fur die Alttestamentliche Wissenschaft*, Berlin 50: 141–148.

Driver, G. R. (1956) *Canaanite Myths and Legends*. Edinburgh: Clark.

Erikson, E. H. (1956) The problem of ego identity *Journal of the American Psychoanalytical association* 4, 56-121.

Fontaine, C. R. (1993) The social roles of women in the Words of Wisdom. In *A Feminist Companion to Wisdom Literature*. Ed. A. Brenner, pp. 24–29. Sheffield. Academic Press, Sheffield.

Fox, M.V. (2000) *Proverbs 1–9. The Anchor Bible*. New York: Doubleday.

Friedlander, M. (1904) *Griechische Philosophie im Alten Testament*. Berlin: Reimer.

Gammie, J.G. and Perdue, L.G. (1990) *The Sage in Israel and the Ancient Near East*. Eisenbraun. Winona Lake.

Gunderson, J.G. (2001) *Borderline Personality Disorder: A Clinical Guide*. Washington DC: American Psychiatric Press.

Hughes, C.H. (1884) Moral (affective insanity): Psychosensory Insanity *Alienist and Neurologist*, 5, 296-315.

Kohlenberger, III, J.R. (1987) *The Interlinear NIV Hebrew-English Old Testament*, pp. 5–58. Grand Rapids, MI: Zondervan.

Kohut, H. (1971) *The Analysis of the Self.* New York International University Press.

Lambert, W.L. (1960) *Babylonian Wisdom Literature*. Oxford: Clarendon.

McKane, W. (1970) *Proverbs a new approach.* London: SCM Press.

Maier, C. (1998) Conflicting Attractions: Parental wisdom and the strange women in Proverbs 1–9 in *The Feminist Companion to the Bible* (second series). Eds. A. Brenner and C.R. Fontaine. Sheffield: Sheffield Academic Press.

Masoretic Text (1944) *The Holy Scriptures according to the Masoretic Text*. Eighteenth Impression, Philadelphia. The Jewish Publication Society of America.

Masterson J.F (1981) *The Narcissistic and Borderline Disorders*. New York: Brunner Mazel.

Moffat Translation of the Bible (1972). London: Hodder and Stoughton.

New Revised Standard Version of the Bible (1989) Oxford: Oxford University Press.

Oesterley, W.O.E. (1929) *The Book of Proverbs*. London: Methuen.

Pelton, R.D. (1980) The trickster in West Africa: a study of mythic irony and sacred delight. *Hermeneutics. Studies in the History of Religions*. Berkeley, CA: University of California Press.

Perdue, L.G. (1981) Liminality as a social Setting for wisdom instruction *Zeitschrift fur die Alttestamentliche Wissenschaft* 93: 324.

Rall Bible (1885) *The Parallel Bible*. Cambridge: Cambridge University Press.

Rosenberg, A.J. (1993) *Proverbs. A New English Translation of the Text, Rashi and a Commentary Digest*. New York: Judaica Press.

Schiffman, L.H. (1991) *From Text to Tradition: A History of Second Temple and Rabbinic Judaism*. Hoboken, NJ: Ktav Publishing House.

Stern A.,(1938) Psychoanalytic investigations of and therapy in the Borderline group of neuroses. *Psychoanalytic Quarterly*, 350–354.

Torgerson, S, Lygren, S., Andersen, P., *et al.* (2000) A twin study of personality disorders. *Comprehensive Psychiatry* 41: 416–425.

Toy, Crawford H. (1899) *The Book of Proverbs*. International Critical Commentary, Edinburgh: T. & T. Clark (repr. 1959).

Washington, H.C. (1995) The Strange women of Proverbs 1–9 and Post-Exilic Judaen Society in *A Feminist Companion to Wisdom Literature*. Ed. A. Brenner, pp. 157–187.

Waltke B. (2005) *The Book of Proverbs. Chapters 1–15*. Grand Rapids, MI: William B. Eerdmans.

Wise, M.O., Abegg, M.G. and Cook, E.M. (2005) *The Dead Sea Scrolls: A New Translation*. New York: Harper.

# Psychosomatic disorders and other miscellaneous episodes

This chapter contains a collection of miscellaneous cases which do not fit neatly into any particular psychiatric or religious category. The first part consists of psychiatric cases that, had they occurred today, might be found in a general hospital setting and such cases fall into the category of 'consultant liaison psychiatry', a relatively new sub-specialty. As a part of modern holistic medicine it has become increasingly apparent that many medical disorders are often accompanied by a psychiatric problem which also needs attention. All the larger general hospitals now have their own psychiatric teams led by a consultant who specialises in general hospital or 'liaison' psychiatry. Examples of this in the Bible include the depressions associated with Hezekiah's boil, Hannah's infertility and the pre-senile dementia of King Ptolomey IV Philopater, as described in Maccabees 3. These cases are all described in the first part of the chapter. Following on from this are those episodes of depression and anxiety not present in prophetic literature but found in other books of the Old Testament and the Apocrypha.

Apart from the story of Hannah and her infertility, these stories have little religious significance and therefore are largely unknown to the general reader. There is no unitary theme to link these conditions apart from the general empathy of the biblical writers towards mental disorder, a category these writers knew nothing about, yet instinctively felt were important enough to record in their religious literature.

## Hezekiah's boil

> In those days Hezekiah became sick and was at the point of death.... (2 Kings 20[1])

Hezekiah has a boil which the prophet Isaiah heals by the application of a poultice of figs. There are two accounts of this episode. First, a factual version is given in 2 Kings 20, where the only mention of any emotion is that Hezekiah wept bitterly. However, in the second account, in Isaiah 38, there is a much more complicated story, which includes a lament similar to the sickness psalms, and this includes a possible episode of depression. Although the text attributes authorship to Hezekiah and it is placed within the Book of Isaiah, neither is thought to be the true writer, but rather the composition is attributed to some unknown priest – a scribe attached to the Temple. The text is rich in religious meaning and was probably written for the comfort of the post-exilic community.

Blenkinsop writes:

The story of Hezekiah's sickness, and near-death experience, recovery, and subsequent liturgical celebration may well have been read in the post-exilic period as foreshadowing the experience of the people ... also implicit but nearer the surface is the contrast between the death of the Assyrian King Sennacherib, brutally murdered by his power-hungry sons, as compared to the happy recovery from the near death of the Judean King Hezekiah, who prays to Yahweh and thanks him for his healing.

Comments on this passage (Isaiah 38$^{12-22}$) are taken mainly from Blenkinsop (2000, p. 483).

| | | |
|---|---|---|
| 38$^{12}$ | My dwelling is plucked up and removed from me like a shepherd's tent; | Pastoral metaphor for sudden loss of home/or life |
| | like a weaver I have rolled up my life; he cuts me off from the loom; | Weaving metaphor as in Job 7$^7$ transitory nature of life |
| | from day to night you bring me to an end; | 24-hour distress with |
| 13 | I cry for help until morning; | depression, weeping at night |
| | like a lion he breaks all my bones; from day to night you bring me to an end | Accuses Yahweh of causing the pain, which is both day and night |
| 14 | like a swallow or a crane, I clamour I moan like a dove. | The sounds of birds are similar to the sounds of the ghosts of Sheol |
| | My eyes are weary with looking upwards. | Weariness; exhaustion |
| | O Lord I am oppressed; | Heb. *Oskachs* = social exploitation |
| | be my security! | *arar* = security, a money lender's term |
| 15 | But what can I say? For he has spoken to me, and he himself has done it. | |
| | All my sleep has fled because of the bitterness my of my soul. | Severe insomnia, because of ? depression |
| 16 | O Lord by these things people live, and in these is the life of my spirit | |
| | O restore me to health and make me live! | Prayer for life and health |
| 17 | Surely it was for my welfare that I had great bitterness; that you held back my life from the pit of destruction | It was for my own good that 'you gave me' this depression and then saved my life |
| | for you have cast all my sins behind your back. | My sins are forgiven; a precondition before any healing |
| 18 | For Sheol cannot thank you. Death cannot praise you; | Once dead you can no longer praise God |
| | those who go down to the pit cannot hope for your faithfulness. | loss of hope |
| 19 | The living, the living, they thank you, as I do this day; fathers make known to children your faithfulness. | Prayer of thanks for salvation |
| 20 | The Lord will save me and we will sing to stringed instruments all the days of our lives at the house of the Lord. | Music played as in the Temple |
| 21 | Now Isaiah said let them take a lump of figs and apply it to the boil so that he may recover. | |
| 22 | Hezekiah also had said 'What is the sign that I shall go up to the house of the Lord?' | |

This psalm of lament has much beauty and an uplifting quality; perhaps this is why it came to be included in the liturgy. As an explanation for its meaning the Book of Isaiah starts with an accusation that 'The children God has brought up have rebelled against me' and they are 'a sinful nation of people laden with iniquity' (Isa. 1[2,4]). It is thought this psalm may refer to their healing after they have been forgiven by God for their transgressions. Thus, this passage starts as a psalm of lament, but after verse 17 it turns into a prayer of thanksgiving, as God has forgiven the sick man his sins, and only then can healing and redemption take place (after Blenkinsop, 2000).

The psychiatry is similar to that in the other psalms of lament. The writer mentions weeping (13), weariness (14), low mood (13, 14), thoughts of death (12, 13), hopelessness (18) and insomnia (13), and this is attributed to 'his bitterness of soul' (15), which is presumably some sort of negative thinking or depression. These are all depressive symptoms, perhaps sufficient to imply that the writer was personally familiar with depressive symptomatology, but there are not quite enough depressive symptoms to diagnose a full-blown episode of major depression according to modern diagnostic criteria.

While the depression is obvious, its association with a physical illness, namely Hezekiah's boil, is unusual for a biblical psalm. However, psychiatric reactions, particularly to physical illness, are well recognised today. Thus, an epidemiological study by Feldman *et al.* (1987), using a structured psychiatric interview, found that around 15% of patients admitted to a general hospital with a medical condition had a diagnosable affective disorder, most commonly anxiety or depression. This contrasts with the general population one-week prevalence of 1.8–2.7% for psychiatric disorder in the British National Psychiatric Morbidity survey (Jenkins *et al.*, 1997), suggesting a 6- to 8-fold increased risk of depression during a physical illness.

We shall never know why the later redactors of the Book of Isaiah placed this lament adjacent to the story of Hezekiah's boil, but perhaps they had some inkling that a person suffering from a physical illness might also become depressed. More likely the thinking was that a prayer of lament for an illness should be dedicated to an important personage such as the King, and as such prayers frequently contained elements of depression, an appearance is given of a depression associated with his boil.

### Hannah: a case of infertility and depression

Childlessness was a tragedy for a woman in the ancient Near East and the barren wife was likely to be despised by her husband, her family and society at large. The topic gains frequent mention in the OT. In some cases the infertility is never relieved, as in the case of David's first wife, Michal, but in other cases a late child appears. Thus three childless women are described in the Old Testament whose infertility was relieved by divine intervention, resulting in the birth of later important patriarchal leaders.

Sarah, the mother of Isaac, was 90 years old when she heard she was to have a baby. Genesis 18[13] reads:

> And the Lord said to Abraham, 'Why did Sarah laugh and say "Shall I indeed bear a child now that I am old?"'

The only other recorded emotional reaction Sarah has to her infertility is her cruel treatment of Haggai, Abraham's other wife and the mother of Ishmael: 'Then Sarah dealt harshly with her [Haggai] and she ran away from her' (Gen. 16⁶).

We know even less about the infertility of the mother of Samson, whose story is described in the Book of Judges (13¹³):

> And the angel of the Lord appeared to the woman and said to her 'Although you are barren, having no children you shall conceive and bear a son'.

In due course she gave birth to Samson. Her story in the Bible relates solely to her maternal function, and the text says nothing about her personal feelings, her relationships, or even her own name, and she is identified only through her husband – as 'the wife of Manoah'.

Hannah eventually gives birth to another important biblical prophet, Samuel, but her story is very different and the Book of Samuel gives a sympathetic account of her feelings, which is in marked contrast to the earlier, more impersonal accounts of the infertility of Sarah and the wife of Manoah. Her sadness at her infertility, her relationship with her husband, Elkanah, and the problematic rivalry of living with Elkanah's other wife, Peninnah, who did have children, as well as her depression are all described in considerable detail in the first book of Samuel (I Sam. 1²⁻¹⁹):

| | | |
|---|---|---|
| 1² | He [Elkanah] had two wives: the name of one Hannah, and the name of the other Peninnah. Peninnah had children, but Hannah had none. | Polygamy for important people 'Hannah' means charming 'Peninnah' means fat or fecund |
| 3 | Now this man used to go up year by year from his town to worship and to sacrifice to the Lord of Hosts at Shiloh, where the two sons of Eli, Hophni and Phineas, were priests to the Lord. | He was a religious man Modern Khirbet Seilun, a shrine, north of Jerusalem |
| 4 | On the day when Elkanah sacrificed he would give portions to his wife Peninnah and to all her sons and daughters. But to Hannah he gave a double portion because he loved her, though the Lord had closed her womb. | Her fertility is emphasised he still loves her despite the infertility |
| 6 | Her rival used to provoke her severely, to irritate her because the Lord had closed her womb | irritability third mention of her infertility |
| 7 | Therefore Hannah wept and would not eat. | weeping and anorexia |
| 8 | Her husband said to her 'Hannah why do you weep? Why do you not eat? Why is your heart so sad? Am I not more to you than ten sons? | Elkanah observes her depression and is puzzled by it Heb. *yeh'ra levavechah* = sad heart |
| 9 | After they had eaten and drunk at Shiloh, Hannah rose and presented herself before the Lord. Now Eli the priest was sitting on the seat beside the doorpost of the Temple of the Lord. | Heb. *mezuzat* = doorpost |

The story of Hezekiah's sickness, and near-death experience, recovery, and subsequent liturgical celebration may well have been read in the post-exilic period as foreshadowing the experience of the people ... also implicit but nearer the surface is the contrast between the death of the Assyrian King Sennacherib, brutally murdered by his power-hungry sons, as compared to the happy recovery from the near death of the Judean King Hezekiah, who prays to Yahweh and thanks him for his healing.

Comments on this passage (Isaiah $38^{12-22}$) are taken mainly from Blenkinsop (2000, p. 483).

| | | |
|---|---|---|
| $38^{12}$ | My dwelling is plucked up and removed from me like a shepherd's tent; | Pastoral metaphor for sudden loss of home/or life |
| | like a weaver I have rolled up my life; | Weaving metaphor as in Job $7^7$ |
| | he cuts me off from the loom; | transitory nature of life |
| | from day to night you bring me to an end; | 24-hour distress with |
| 13 | I cry for help until morning; | depression, weeping at night |
| | like a lion he breaks all my bones; | Accuses Yahweh of causing the |
| | from day to night you bring me to an end | pain, which is both day and night |
| 14 | like a swallow or a crane, I clamour | The sounds of birds are similar to |
| | I moan like a dove. | the sounds of the ghosts of Sheol |
| | My eyes are weary with looking upwards. | Weariness; exhaustion |
| | O Lord I am oppressed; | Heb. *Oskachs* = social exploitation |
| | be my security! | *arar* = security, a money lender's term |
| 15 | But what can I say? For he has spoken to me, and he himself has done it. | |
| | All my sleep has fled because of the bitterness my of my soul. | Severe insomnia, because of ? depression |
| 16 | O Lord by these things people live, and in these is the life of my spirit | |
| | O restore me to health and make me live! | Prayer for life and health |
| 17 | Surely it was for my welfare that I had great bitterness; that you held back | It was for my own good that 'you gave me' this depression |
| | my life from the pit of destruction | and then saved my life |
| | for you have cast all my sins behind your back. | My sins are forgiven; a precondition before any healing |
| 18 | For Sheol cannot thank you. | Once dead you can no longer |
| | Death cannot praise you; | praise God |
| | those who go down to the pit cannot hope for your faithfulness. | loss of hope |
| 19 | The living, the living, they thank you, as I do this day; fathers make known to children your faithfulness. | Prayer of thanks for salvation |
| 20 | The Lord will save me and we will sing to stringed instruments all the days of our lives at the house of the Lord. | Music played as in the Temple |
| 21 | Now Isaiah said let them take a lump of figs and apply it to the boil so that he may recover. | |
| 22 | Hezekiah also had said 'What is the sign that I shall go up to the house of the Lord?' | |

diagnostic criteria and so the diagnosis cannot be refined any further. Most of the depressions in the Bible are autobiographical accounts but here is a very early observer account of depression. Two well respected men, Elkanah, Hannah's husband, and Eli, the priest, are puzzled by her symptoms. Elkanah cannot understand why she is so miserable and protests that she has no good reason to be miserable because he loves her deeply and he gives her more gifts than her rival Peninnah. Eli cannot make any sense of her curious loss of voice while she prays. The loss of voice is partial, occurring only during her prayer. Perhaps this is no more than silent prayer, as she is mouthing the words. Eli, unable to find any other explanation, accuses her of drunkenness, but Hannah protests she has not had any drink (this might a description of aphonia, as discussed below).

The biblical feminist literature holds Hannah's tale in high regard. Thus Nunally-Cox (1981, p. 63) writes:

> Hannah is something of an undefined figure. We know her as a woman of prayer, and something of a gentle soul. She is rarely outwardly angry, either with her rival and provoker, Peninnah, or with Eli, who makes quite erroneous assumptions. Rather she seems to be more melancholy. She also seems to fit more into the stereotype of a submissive, obedient woman; she is careful not to offend the priest, but in reality it is he who offends her. But Hannah receives what she asks for, a son, and that is most important for her. Hannah comes at the end of a long line of women, once barren and who bear unusual sons late in their life, Sarah, Rebekah, Rachel and the mother of Samson. Hannah is more often remembered for the little coat she makes for Samuel than for the beautiful song attributed to her. Hannah's song is a model for the *Magnificat*, Mary's song of Thanksgiving in the New Testament....

Hannah's tale is also of great importance to psychiatry, particularly to the history of psychiatry, as there are very few accounts of depression in the literature of the ancient world, and the few that exist appertain only to men, even though depression is more common in women. Hence it is likely that Hannah's depression may be the very first described in a woman. This is more than two millennia before the more definitive accounts of depression written by Burton in the 17th century CE.

A recent study of women attending an infertility clinic in America (Holley *et al.*, 2015) found that 39% met criteria for major depressive disorder. However, a population survey in Norway found that a history of infertility (having tried to conceive for more than 12 months) was not associated with raised levels of depression (Biringer *et al.*, 2015). The authors suggest it is the *act of trying to conceive and its associated failure* that is the cause of the depression, rather than the long-term childless status.

It is the aphonia in this story that is of most psychiatric interest. This is now considered a conversion symptom. (Conversion denotes the expression of psychological distress as a physical symptom and replaces the previous term 'hysterical'.) In Hannah's case it seems to be partial, appearing in one setting, her praying, but not otherwise (she can converse with Eli).

Hysterical aphonia is uncommon nowadays, particularly in Western societies. An Indian study reported on 25 cases (Bhatia and Vaid, 2000).

These authors collected all the cases of conversion disorder presenting to an Indian teaching hospital over a three-year period ($n$ = 796). Of these, 25 (3.2%) had aphonia. All were examined by an otolaryngologist to exclude an organic cause. In most cases the presentation was as a psychiatric emergency, with the symptoms being present for less than 2 weeks, and it was more common among young women (mean age 21 years). In the majority of cases the underlying cause was exam stress, or failure in an examination, or family quarrels. Urban residence predicted a presentation to the hospital, whereas rural residence usually led to seeking help from a traditional healer. Psychiatric comorbidity was present in 80% of the cases, most commonly mixed anxiety and depression.

These observations may help us to understand Hannah's story. She was also under stress, as she was a continued failure in the 'produce a baby test', while serious family tensions were present because of the complex polygamous marital situation she found herself in. The text records many features of an anxiety depressive syndrome. Because today most cases of aphonia present as an emergency to an A&E department, the above Indian study suggests that it may have been the aphonia itself which triggered the psychiatric consultation. Possibly this was why Elkanah took Hannah to a traditional healer (Eli the priest) at the shrine of Shiloh, rather than the associated infertility and depression. However, Eli (or whoever the writer was) soon picked up on the infertility, the depression and her impossible marital situation.

One must admire the sensitivity of this particular Old Testament writer for the way he unravels the psychiatric history: he accurately reports on the aphonia, a strange symptom which he neither recognised nor understood; he then elicits the underlying social and medical causes – the infertility and the complicated polygamous marital situation lying behind it. He would have obtained a distinction in history taking had he been a psychiatric trainee today.

Liaison psychiatry concerns the co-occurrence of psychiatric disorder with a general medical disorder. Infertility is an accepted gynaecological disorder and so Hannah's depression is likely to be the first recognisable case in the history of liaison psychiatry.

The expression of emotional distress can appear as a psychological complaint, such as anxiety or depression, or as a somatic symptom, such as headache or stomach ache or physical weakness. Among the cultures of developing nations, somatic expressions of distress are more common than their psychological equivalents. Mumford (1992) took this observation to examine to what extent somatic distress appeared in the Hebrew Bible. He counted the number of times particular bodily organs were mentioned and whether the emotional states of distress were associated with each reference. The Hebrew word *leb* (heart) was most frequent, occurring over 700 times, and was associated with a wide variety of different emotions, and in ancient times the heart was thought to be the seat of the soul. There were 29 references to *meim* (bowels) and this was usually linked to emotional distress. Similarly *beten* (belly) occurred 30 times and on a further 38 occasions it signified 'womb' and this was also linked to somatic distress. The word *etsem* (bones) appeared 105 times and on 13 occasions this was linked to emotional distress but sometimes *etsem* signified distress of the whole body. Some of the bodily sensations relate to the autonomic symptoms of panic attacks, particularly those reported by Jeremiah and Job, who both suffered from panic disorder.

## A neuropsychiatric case: the failing memory of King Ptolomey IV Philopater

An account is given in Maccabees 3 of the life of King Ptolomey IV Philopater, an Egyptian Pharaoh, and persecutor of the Jews, who seems to have developed a failing memory, perseverative behaviours, fits and a premature death, all suggestive of a neuropsychiatric disorder, possibly a pre-senile dementia. Philopater was the son of Ptolomey III and his wife, Queen Berenice II of Egypt. He had a love of wine, banqueting and lascivious behaviour, and was considered to be a corrupt and degenerate king. He lived 244–204 BCE, and ascended the throne aged 23 in 221 BCE; the high point of his reign was in 217 BCE, when he defeated the Macedonian Emperor Antiochus III at the battle of Raphia. This preserved the independence of the Egyptian Ptolomaic empire for a further 150 years, until it was finally conquered by the Romans. His existence is confirmed on the Rosetta Stone, which also records his wife's name, Arsinoe, and the date of birth of his son.

Early in his reign he came under the malign influence of an Alexandrian called Sosobius, who was one of his ministers, who feared competition for power from other members of the royal family. Thus, under the influence of Sosobius, Philopater killed his brother Magas by having boiling water poured over him, then murdered his uncle, poisoned his mother, Queen Berenice II, and then married his own sister, Arsinoe. Sometimes members of the royal families of the ancient world were not very nice to each other.

Maccabees 3 is thought to have been written in the first century BCE. Biblical scholars consider it to be primarily a religious work concerned with the power of the Jewish God over the Jews' gentile persecutors and with the need to preserve the Jewish identity in the face of foreign occupation. It was written in the style of a religious romance.

After his victory at Raphia, Philopater sought to visit the religious shrines of Israel and this included the Temple in Jerusalem. The high priest of the Temple at the time, Simon, perhaps aware of Philopater's appalling history, objected to this visit and prayed to God to intervene and prevent it (3 Maccabees 2):

> [14]In our downfall this audacious and profane man undertakes to violate the holy place on earth dedicated to your glorious name.... 2[17] Do not punish us for the defilement committed by these men or call us into account for this profanation.

God seems to have listened to this prayer and achieves his goal by inflicting some sort of neuropsychiatric disorder on Philopater, which starts with what appears to be an epileptic fit:

2²¹ Thereupon God who oversees all things, the first father of all, holy among the holy ones, having heard the lawful supplication scourged him who had exalted himself in insolence and audacity. *He shook him [Philopater] on this side and that, as a reed is shaken in the wind, so that he lay helpless on the ground and besides being paralysed in his limbs was unable even to speak* since he was smitten by a righteous judgment.... ²⁴ After a while he recovered, and though he had been punished, he by no means repented but went away uttering bitter threats.

In this passage there is a description of the king's body shaking like a reed in the wind, a fall to the ground, a brief period of unconsciousness, temporary paralysis accompanied by an inability to speak, and then a full recovery, with the whole episode being suggestive of an epileptic fit.

After this, the king turned against the Jews, and sought to have them destroyed, but first he ordered a census to know how many Jews there were. The scribe who takes this instruction goes on to observe the king's mental state as quite bizarre:

4¹⁶ The king was greatly and continually filled with joy, organising feasts in honour of all his idols, with a mind alienated from the truth and with a profane mouth praising speechless things that are not even able to communicate or come to one's help, and uttering improper words against the supreme God.

The presence of elation (filled with joy), delusions (a mind alienated from the truth) and profanities (swearing/blaspheming) is suggestive of a state of mania or some sort of psychotic excitement. The king's madness continues and he sought to destroy the Jews:

5¹ Then the king, completely inflexible was filled with overpowering anger and wrath; so he summoned Hermon, keeper of the elephants, ² and ordered him on the following day to prepare all the elephants, five hundred in number, with large handfuls of frankincense and plenty of unmixed wine, and to drive them in maddened by the lavish abundance of drink so that the Jews might meet their doom.

Once more the Jews prayed to their God to be rescued, and God saved them again, but on this occasion by giving Philopater episodes of hypersomnia accompanied by severe forgetfulness.

5¹⁰ Hermon, however, when he had drugged the pitiless elephants until they had been filled with a great abundance of wine, and satiated with frankincense, presented himself at the courtyard in the morning to report to the king about these preparations. ¹¹ But the Lord sent upon the king a portion of sleep, that beneficence that from the beginning of night and day is bestowed by him who grants it to whomsoever he wishes. ¹² And by the action of the Lord, he [Philopater] was overcome by *so pleasant and deep sleep* that he quite failed in his lawless purpose and was completely frustrated in his inflexible plan. ¹³ Then the Jews, since they had escaped the appointed hour, praised their holy God and again implored him to show the might of his all-powerful hand to the arrogant Gentiles.

In the above passage an episode of hypersomnia is described in verse 12 (a pleasant and deep sleep), and a further episode afflicted the king soon afterwards, when he held a banquet:

[14]... the person in charge of the invitations, seeing that all the guests were assembled, approached the king and nudged him. [15] And when *he had with difficulty roused him*, he pointed out that the hour of the banquet was already slipping by and he gave him an account of the situation. The king, after considering this, returned to his drinking.... [18]After the party had been going for some time, the king summoned Hermon and with sharp threats demanded to know why the Jews had been allowed to remain alive through the present day.... [20] The king, possessed with a savagery worse than that of Phalaris, said that the Jews had benefited by today's sleep, 'but', he added, 'tomorrow without delay, prepare the elephants in the same way for the destruction of the lawless Jews'.... [26]... Hermon arrived and invited him [the king] to come out indicating that what the king desired was ready for action. [27] But he, on receiving the report, and being struck by the unusual invitation to come out – since he had been *completely overcome by incomprehension* – inquired what the matter was for which this had been so zealously completed for him. [28] This was the act of God who rules over all things, for God *had implanted in the King's mind a forgetfulness of the things* previously devised....

These verses describe a confusional state (incomprehension) and loss of short-term memory, both of which suggest a dementing process. When the king realises his order to kill the Jews has not been carried out he becomes angry and blames his commander, Hermon, but this time his officials question his mental state. He summons Hermon and in a threatening tone says:

[37] How many times, you poor wretch, must I give you orders about these things? [38] Equip the elephants now once more for destruction of the Jews tomorrow.' [39] But the officials who were at the table with him wondering at *his instability of mind* remonstrated as follows: [40] 'O King how long will you put us to the test, as though we were idiots, ordering now for a third time that they be destroyed and again revoking your decree in the matter?'

The king's mental instability and his perseverative behaviours have become obvious to the courtiers. A further attack of possible epilepsy in the king seems to follow:

6[20] Even the King began to shudder bodily and he forgot his sullen insolence.

The phrase 'shudder bodily' suggests possible epilepsy. The story ends on a happy note, with the king rescinding his order to persecute the Jews, giving them food and wines for a banquet of deliverance to last seven days, instead of death at the feet of his elephants.

There is a reasonable description of epileptic fits, possible delusions, a manic state, verbal disinhibition, uncontrollable rages, episodic hypersomnia, severe short-term memory loss and perseverative behaviours, which were all observed by his courtiers, and then presumably recorded by the royal scribes. Diagnosis is far from obvious but an organic brain disorder is most likely. Severe alcoholic brain damage with a Korsakoff's psychosis is possible, with the fits being a part of an alcoholic withdrawal syndrome of delirium tremens. The king is only 40 years old when he dies, having become a recluse in his later years, but there is a record of him earlier leading a degenerate alcoholic life. Other possibilities include a pre-senile dementia or even a brain tumour. The story clearly has many fictional elements. Thus the story of the elephants is thought to relate to a popular legend circulating in the last two centuries BCE but are linked to another king of Alexandria, namely King Ptolomy IX Physcon (146–117 BCE). The psychiatric importance of this story lies in the way that it records observer accounts of key neuropsychiatric symptoms such as fits, hypersomnia and short-term memory loss, as well as perseverative behaviours, even though the actual diagnosis is unclear and in this respect it appears to be unique as a very early neuropsychiatric case history.

## Mentions of depression in Proverbs

There are three verses in Proverbs which refer to how difficult it is to bear 'the broken spirit'. Although the English translation in the NRSV for the phrase 'broken spirit' are slightly different in the three verses, the original Hebrew uses the same words for all three.

15<sup>13</sup>  A glad heart makes a cheerful countenance
But by sorrow of heart, the spirit is broken     Heb. *ruah* = spirit;
*nechay'a* = broken

The writer suggests that the low and sad mood can break the person. Is the writer describing what now we call a 'nervous breakdown' or is this a reference to depression?

17<sup>22</sup>  A cheerful heart is good medicine          Happiness helps your health
But a downcast spirit dries up the bones.   Heb. *nechay'a* = downcast

Happiness is good for you, but low mood causes poor health – it dries the bones up. Perhaps this phrase refers to the drawn depressed facies, or possibly to the emaciated appearance of a depressed subject.

18<sup>14</sup>  The human spirit will endure a sickness:
But a broken spirit, who can bear.          Heb. *nechay'a* = broken

The writer says that most people can usually tolerate a sickness (? a physical illness) but a broken spirit (? depression) is so painful it is almost impossible to bear. Many people today who suffer from a depression say how much worse it is to endure a depression than a physical illness.

Although the NRSV translates the word *nechay'a* in three different ways, other translations use only one word. Thus the Interlinear Bible has 'stricken spirit' and Murphy has 'crushed spirit' for *ruah nechay'a*. When all three verses are put together – a spirit that is broken, a spirit that is very difficult to bear and one which dries up the bones, and all this is caused by sorrow – then it would be reasonable to infer this scribe is writing about depression. But one can go no further than an intelligent guess that the condition here is depression. By contrast, for most of the autobiographical biblical accounts of depression the writer usually provides an extensive catalogue of his symptoms, permitting far greater diagnostic clarity, sometimes even to the extent of being able to compare the OT's subjective accounts to the 21st-century psychiatric glossaries.

## *The corrosive effect of depression*

The psychiatrist today is all too aware of the damaging effects of a depression. Careers are lost, relationships are ruined, once pleasurable hobbies are relinquished, the whole personality may change for the worse, and the longer the depression goes on, the more corrosive the effects of the depression seem to become, and this essence is captured in the verse below.

| 25²⁰ | Like vinegar to a wound is one who sings songs to a heavy heart. Like a moth in clothing, or a worm in wood, sorrow gnaws at the human heart. | Vinegar worsens an open wound complaints about low mood both creatures do damage, like depression gnaws at the person |
|---|---|---|

The poetry here is exquisite and its metaphors powerfully convey the destructive effects of depression just as eloquently as the countless modern scientific papers on the adverse consequences of depression. Unlike a physical disorder, an external observer will see only the gradual social and personal decline in a depressive. Perhaps this is what the scribe of Proverbs observes here and alludes to in this verse.

## *Stress is the cause of depression*

12²⁵   Anxiety weighs down the human heart
      but a good word cheers it up.

Depression is not mentioned as such, but a human heart that is weighed down is at the very least suggestive of a low mood, if not an actual depression. This neat little verse gives both the cause and the cure. Anxiety is the cause, and a good word (possibly provided through support or psychotherapy in a modern context) alleviates the low mood.

## *Mood lability/switching*

People with depression can suddenly switch into a happier mood. Conversely, those who are ostensibly quite happy can abruptly switch into a depression. A good subjective account of the experience of mood switches is given in Psalm 30 (see pages 174–176) but the phenomenon is also briefly mentioned in Proverbs:

14¹³   Even in laughter the heart is sad
      and the end of joy is grief.

## Other accounts of depression in the OT

There are many accounts of depression in the Bible, even though the condition was not formally recognised at the time. Some accounts are very lengthy and detailed while others are quite terse and are barely recognisable. One useful way of classifying these depressions is whether the text is reporting an autobiographical account of the writer's own depression, or whether it is an observer-based account (a third-person account). Differences between these two types of report are shown in Table 12.1.

**Table 12.1** Comparison between first-person (autobiographical) and third-person (observer-based) descriptions of depression in the OT

|  | *First person* | *Third person* |
|---|---|---|
| Quality of description | Good; detailed | Brief; barely recognisable |
| Literary genre | Verse (poets often depressives) | Usually prose |
| Symptoms mentioned | Many symptoms, often florid | Very few; |
| Severity | Sometimes severe (Job) | Usually mild, reactive |
| DSM-5 can be applied | Sometimes with success | Never |
| Authorship | Prophets, Psalms, Job | Proverbs, Sirach |
| Cause | Punishment from God for sin | It just occurs – unrelated to sin |
| Cure | Pray to God | Shake yourself out of it or drink wine (Qoheleth) |
| Insight they are ill | Unusual | Generally present |

From a modern perspective it is easy to see that both the first-person and the third-person descriptions are reporting the same condition – but from different perspectives. However, in biblical times depression was unrecognised, and so no link between these two different ways of recording psychic distress were made. Melancholia had been described by Hippocrates had from the 5th century BCE onwards, but it was probably not until Roman times and the early Christian era that a single condition called *acedia* came to be recognised.

## Objective descriptions of panic in Proverbs

In one of the opening passages in the Book of Proverbs (Proverbs 1[22-26]), Lady Wisdom cries out about all the 'foolish' ways in which people behave. No one seems to listen to her, especially the simpletons and the scoffers (those with learning difficulties and personality disorders in today's language) and she says how she will mock these people because they will inevitably suffer from panic attacks:

| 1[22] | How long O simple ones will you love being simple | People of low IQ should stop being simple, implying they have a choice |
|---|---|---|
| [23] | How long will scoffers delight in their scoffing and fools hate knowledge .... | Psychopaths should stop being so contemptuous and learn to change their ways |
| [24] | Give heed to my reproof... | |
| ... | | |

| 26 | I will laugh at your calamity; | I will laugh at your panic |
| | I will mock *when panic strikes* you | Heb. *pahad* = panic |
| 27 | when panic strikes you like a storm | Panic is a punishment |
| | and your calamity comes like a whirlwind | Heb. *shoah* = calamity |
| | when distress and anguish come upon you. | |

The passage is brief but of great interest from a psychiatric perspective. Three types of fool are mentioned: the *petayim* (simpletons), the *lesim* (the contemptuous psychopaths) and the *kesilim* (those with antisocial personality disorder). These types are explained in Chapter 10 (pages 398–404).

Lady Wisdom asks them all to listen to her and to change their ways. There is an underlying assumption that change is possible because all men have free will. If they fail to change then, just like the *lesim* who laughs and mocks everyone, so Lady Wisdom will also laugh and mock them, as they will inevitably get into a state of panic (after Fox, p. 100). By merely writing about these types the scribe implies that such characters were a recognised problem in ancient Israel. There is an expectation that these characters could change for the better if only they would listen to wisdom. We now know that those with learning difficulties and the more severe personality disorders never really change, nor is it within their power to do so, and treatment rarely works, but in biblical times there seems to be the forlorn hope that if only they would listen to Lady Wisdom, then they might change.

What if they don't change and don't listen to wisdom? The writer then punishes them. But he does this with yet another psychiatric disorder, *pahad*, or panics. The theme of panic being a type of punishment is repeated once more in Proverbs 3:

| 3²⁵ | Do not be afraid of sudden panic | |
| | Or the storm which will strike the wicked | storm = *shoah*, calamity, holocaust |
| 26 | for the Lord will be your confidence | |
| | and will keep you from being caught. | |

The observation here is that panic comes on suddenly and is a punishment for the wicked. This is contrasted with how the Lord will protect you, so that you do not get caught in a sudden panic. Panic as punishment is also described by Jeremiah, who seeks to inflict his panics onto his jailer, Pashur.

## World weariness in Ecclesiastes

Ecclesiastes is one of the most obscure yet beautiful books of the Bible. The Hebrew title is Qoheleth (Teacher), the name used by the author of the book.

Crenshaw explains its message:

> Life is profitless, totally absurd. This oppressive message lies at the heart of the Bible's strangest book. The writer advises people to enjoy life because soon old age will overtake you. And as you enjoy things, know that the world is meaningless. Virtue does *not* bring reward. The deity stands at a distance, abandoning humanity to chance, fate, and death.

The book adopts a very different tone to all the other books of the Bible, and it is almost free of any religion. Qoheleth repeatedly exhorts people to enjoy their transitory stay on earth and says that much that consumes their energy is vanity – by which he means it is totally futile. His theology has a refreshing freedom from that of the prophets, according to whom good deeds lead to wealth and happiness, and sin to the most terrible punishments, including sickness and national disasters. In contrast, Qoheleth says it makes little difference what you do in life, and that wisdom will get you no further than folly (Longman, 1998, p. 30). He assumes a hedonistic position that many in the 21st century might also share. Such anti-moral themes in the book led to scepticism among the rabbis and there were even some sages who argued against its inclusion in the canon (Shabbat 30b; Yadayim 3.5) but it seems to have been included as a religious text from quite early on.

Jewish religious tradition attributes its authorship to King Solomon, who is said to have written the 'Song of Songs' in his youth, Proverbs in his middle age and Qoheleth as an old man. Nowadays the book is thought to be a relatively late composition but it pre-dates Sirach (about 180 BCE), which draws on it, and most scholars suggest composition somewhere between 250 and 200 BCE. There is a suggestion that it may have originally been written in Aramaic (Ginsberg, 1950) because of the presence of numerous Aramaisms in the text, but this hypothesis was discounted by linguistic analysis (Gordis, 1952) and the discovery of numerous Hebrew fragments in the Qumran scrolls, dating from around 200 BCE. True authorship is unknown but as it is a part of the Wisdom literature a scribe working in the second Temple seems a possible author.

The poetry of the book has great beauty and a timeless quality and so not surprisingly many sections have become a part of the religious liturgy. Thus it is read on Succoth (festival of booths). One very well known poem is read on the Day of Atonement in Jewish services and is also widely used in funeral liturgies:

> 3$^1$ For everything there is a season, and a time for every matter under the sun:
> $^2$ A time to be born, a time to die...

Qoheleth was not a depressive and thought people should cheer themselves up by drinking wine. Certain verses distributed across the book point to a low-grade pessimism and anxiety but there is no picture of a full-blown depression, rather only allusions to states of chronic anxiety. However, there is a single reference to a specific phobia – the fear of heights.

### Gloom and anxiety in Qoheleth

In some verses the text is in the first person, suggesting the writer is the subject of the misery, but in most other instances Qoheleth writes in the third person about the woes of others, and he writes as an observer of the human condition.

| | |
|---|---|
| 1$^8$  All things are wearisome<br>more than one can express. | Heb. *yege'im* = wearisome, weary, tired |

The Latin *tedium vitae* or the German *weldtshcmerz* convey the sense of world weariness suggested here. Murphy writes 'there is nothing new because everything is only a futile repetition what has happened in past generations'. However, Longman emphasises the negative mood in this phrase.

| | | |
|---|---|---|
| 1[18] | In much wisdom is vexation | Heb. *ka'as* = vexation, frustration |
| | and those who increase knowledge | Heb. *ma'acouv* = sorrow, grief |
| | increase sorrow. | |

Murphy (p. 14) suggests the setting for this verse may have been a school: the teacher would have encouraged the student but the acquisition of wisdom is never without work or pain (even corporal punishment). Longman (p. 85) gives the verse a psychiatric significance: 'It is most likely that the suffering Qoheleth envisages as a result of the increase in knowledge is mental anguish and not corporal punishment'.

| | | |
|---|---|---|
| 2[20] | So I turned and gave my heart up to despair concerning all the toil of my labours under the sun. | Heb. *ya'es* = despair; *amal* = toil, burden |
| 2[21] | Because sometimes one who has toiled with wisdom and knowledge and skill must leave all to be enjoyed by another who did not toil for it. | miserable person (in Job) |
| | This is also vanity and a great evil. | |

Murphy writes (p. 25): 'Qoheleth is despairing not only about his experience but what he sees as the lot of many people; how their wealth obtained by hard work is often acquired by others who have done nothing for it'. The despair here is more about the nature of inheritance, and the exploitation of other people, rather than being the despair of clinical depression.

| | | |
|---|---|---|
| 2[22] | What do mortals get from all the toil and strain with which they toil under the sun. | Heb. *uvrayun libbi* = striving of the heart |
| 23 | For all their days are full of pain, and their work is vexation; even at night their minds do not rest; this also is vanity. | Life is painful *ka'as* = frustration; insomnia due to worry; Heb. *hebel* = vanity |
| 24 | There is nothing better for mortals than to eat and drink and find enjoyment in their toil This also I saw is from the hand of God. | |

In verse 22 the Hebrew *uvrayun libbi* literally means 'striving of the heart'. Other translations such as the NIV have 'anxious striving'; Longman has 'anxious'. The suggestion here is of some sort of anxiety. Qoheleth writes in the third person as an observer of people who seem to be in pain and anxiety and who cannot sleep. The way out is to eat, drink and enjoy their work or *amal*, a message he reinforces by giving it an endorsement from God.

In chapter 5 he addresses the problems of the wealthy and what happens when they lose their fortunes. This, he says, makes them all end up in a dark place, and seemingly quite sick as well:

| | | |
|---|---|---|
| 5[13] | There is a grievous ill that I have seen under the sun: riches were kept by their owners to their own hurt, | *Qoheleth* is the observer |
| 14 | and those riches were lost in a bad venture... | Loss of fortune |
| ... | | |
| 16 | This is also a grievous ill; just as they came so they shall go; and what gain do they have from toiling in the wind? | |
| 17 | Besides, all their days they eat in darkness, in much vexation and sickness and resentment. | darkness, anxiety sickness and bitterness |
| 18 | This what I have seen to be good: It is fitting to eat and drink and find enjoyment in all the toil with which one toils under the sun the few days of the life God gives us; for this is our lot. | just enjoy your life as it will be all too brief |

The wealthy have striven hard all their lives to acquire possessions but then sometimes they lose it all. So what was the point of all that hard work? Even worse, they can end up 'eating in a dark place, in much vexation, and sickness and resentment'. The observation here is of some kind of unpleasant mental anguish which Qoheleth has observed among people who lose their fortunes.

I have included this passage because it is written by an observer who cites a cause (loss of wealth) for becoming mentally unwell and provides an explanation in terms of the person's lifestyle (constant striving for wealth) that underlies their breakdown, and he also offers a cure – eat, drink and find enjoyment. Losses of any type are known as 'exit events' and are strongly associated with depression (Paykel *et al.*, 1975) and these verses indicate that such a link, at least for financial losses, was well understood during Old Testament times.

## *Fear of heights*

Chapter 12 is the finale of the book and so not surprisingly is about old age and death. One early commentator in his book entitled *The Dirge in Ecclesiastes 12* argued that the whole chapter describes a funeral cortege (Taylor, 1874):

| | | |
|---|---|---|
| 12[5] | When one is afraid of heights, and terrors are on the roads: the almond tree blossoms.... | Fear of heights Terror = ? panic, as in Jeremiah |

Only one scholar, Fox (1989, p. 305), identifies this as a specific phobia. He writes:

> Most commentators suppose this to mean that old people are afraid of heights either because they develop acrophobia (is that true?) or because they do not like walking uphill then this would represent a fear of hills, rough ground and the like....

In fact, old age is more usually associated with a fear of falling because many older people suffer from falls, rather than from fear of heights, which is more common in young people. Terrors on the road may refer to the panic attacks which are often associated with the specific phobias such as fear of heights.

Qohelet is one of the great observers of the human condition, and excessive worry or anxiety is something he has noticed, and such thoughts are futile and should be banished. Perhaps Qoheleth himself was a sufferer, or he had seen the condition in a friend or relative. We have no idea why he mentions this unusual but common phobia, also known as acrophobia.

Acrophobia (from the Greek ἄκρον, *ákron*, meaning 'peak, summit, edge', and φόβος, *phóbos*, 'fear') is an extreme or irrational fear or phobia of heights, especially when one is not particularly high up. It belongs to a category of specific phobias, called space and motion discomfort, that share both a common aetiology and options for treatment. Most people experience a degree of natural fear when exposed to heights, known as the fear of falling. On the other hand, those who have little fear of such exposure are said to have a head for heights. Acrophobia sufferers can experience a panic attack in high places and become too agitated to get themselves down safely. Approximately 2% of the general population suffers from acrophobia, with twice as many women affected as men.

## The Wisdom of Solomon

There is a suggestion of panic, anxiety disorders and specific animal phobia in the Wisdom of Solomon, one of the later books of the Apocrypha. Almost certainly the book was originally written in Greek, because its language draws on the translated Hebrew of the Septuagint. This suggests it might have been composed after the 3rd century BCE, possibly in the Egyptian diaspora. Conventional thinking places the book between the 1st century BCE and the period after the Roman conquest of Egypt in 47 BCE. Although it is written in Greek, the author is thought to be Jewish, as the book covers mainly Jewish theological and wisdom themes, including basic morality, the righteous contrasted to the wicked, the ambiguity of death, knowledge and ignorance, and immortality of the soul; it is severely critical of idol worship and polytheism. Today, the book is a part of the Roman Catholic and Greek Orthodox canon but is not included in either the Jewish or Protestant canon (Grabbe, 1997).

Chapter 17 of the book is a diatribe against the Egyptians, who are perceived as the 'lawless ones' or the 'unrighteous ones'. A plague of darkness will descend upon them and they will become prisoners of the night. This plague includes spectres and phantoms, which cause great fear and are difficult to get rid of. The magical arts of the Egyptians can do nothing to alleviate this. The Egyptians seem to suffer from a bad conscience and their punishment will be terrifying fears.

The psychiatric interest of the book concerns the anxiety disorders, unrelated to the religious themes; these disorders appear only as occasional metaphors to describe punishments to be meted out to the 'unrighteous', which include 'terror' (possible panic) and perhaps also a specific animal phobia. The passage is quite long but almost every verse has a reference to a symptom of either fear or anxiety (these two emotions were not properly distinguished in the ancient world):

| 17[2] | For when lawless people supposed that they held the holy nation in their power, They themselves lay as captives of darkness and prisoners of the long night, shut in under their roofs exiles from eternal providence. | Lawless people = Egyptians Holy nation = Israel<br><br>The plague of darkness |
|---|---|---|
| 3 | For thinking in their secret sins they were unobserved behind a dark cloud of forgetfulness, they were scattered, terribly alarmed, and appalled by spectres. | Hide their sins in the darkness<br><br>High anxiety levels |
| 4 | For not even the inner chamber that held them protected them from fear but terrifying sounds rang out around them, and dismal phantoms with gloomy faces appeared. | No protection them from fears Terrifying sounds ?hyperacusis<br><br>Greek *indalma* = hallucination |
| 5 | And no power of fire was able to give light Nor did the brilliant flames of the stars avail to illumine that hateful night | Even the lights of the stars cannot alleviate the distressing nocturnal symptoms |
| 6 | Nothing was shining through to them except a dreadful self-kindled fire, and in terror they deemed the things that they saw to be worse than that unseen appearance. The delusions of their magic art lay humbled And their boasted wisdom was scornfully rebuked. | All they can feel is an unpleasant inner turmoil terror = panic or severe anxiety their imagination makes things worse than they really are. criminal skills become futile |
| 8 | For those who promised to drive off The fears and disorders of a sick soul were sick themselves with ridiculous fear | Gk. *ephybristos* = magical shams ? their fears are like a sickness people claiming to help had even more severe fears |
| 9 | For even if nothing disturbing frightened them yet, scared by the passing of wild animals and the hissing of snakes, | wild animals scare them, as does the hiss of a snake |
| 10 | They perished trembling in fear refusing to look even at the air, though it nowhere could be avoided | *through* fear of the snake avoid looking at wild animals |
| 11 | For wickedness is a cowardly thing, condemned by its own testimony; distressed by conscience, it has always exaggerated the difficulties | Gk. *Syneidesis* = conscience *synechei* = anguish |
| 12 | For fear is nothing but a giving up of the helps that comes from reason: | This type of fear is irrational See definition of anxiety below |
| ... | | |
| 15 | and now they were driven by monstrous spectres, and now paralysed by their souls' surrender: for sudden and unexpected fear overwhelmed them. | unpleasant visual scenes<br><br>paralysis due to abrupt fear suggests a panic attack |

...

<sup>19</sup>   ... Or an echo thrown back from a hollow
of the mountains,
it paralysed them with terror          Paralysis through terror ?panic

The moral message of the passage is that those who are lawless or unrighteous will be punished by anxious thoughts and disturbed nights, and terrors
(probably panic attacks) so they do not 'get away with it'. The psychiatric
interest lies in exactly what sort of disturbance this was. It is not depression,
as with Job, but episodes of severe fear or anxiety (3, 8, 9 and 12), actual
terror (3, 4, 5, 6 and 19) or being paralysed or perishing through terror,
which probably also signifies a panic attack (10, 15 and 19), and by disturbed
nights (5). There is also a disturbing inner turmoil, 'a dreadful self-kindled
fire' (6). This is all suggestive of a person who is overwhelmed by fears and
probably experiencing panic attacks and so the passage is consistent with an
anxiety disorder. The fear is severe and there is no protection from it, thus
'not even the inner chamber that held them could protect them from fear'
(4). There are people who claim to be able to cure such fears, but they are
magical shams and they suffer from even higher levels of anxiety/fear or
'ridiculous fear' (8).

The writer appears to be well acquainted with the experience of high
levels of fear from which there is neither protection nor cure and so he
may have been a sufferer of panic disorder and anxiety. He almost assumes
a medical model and writes about it as if it is some kind of a sickness: 'the
fears and disorders of a sick soul' (8). The word *syneidesis*, translated as
conscience (11), is a legal or philosophical term, connoting interrogation or
cross-examination. The idea of a conscience does not appear elsewhere in
the Hebrew Bible, and seems to be a mainly Greek concept, but one which
assumed much importance later on in almost all religions.

In the ancient world no distinction was made between an anxiety disorder
and fear itself and this explains why the author writes only about fear.
However, in verse 12 he shows a very high degree of insight and captures the
essence of the distinction between anxiety and fear:

<sup>12</sup> For fear is nothing but a giving up of the help that comes from reason;

That is, fear (or anxiety in this verse) is a type of fear without good reason.

Such a distinction between fear and anxiety probably did not appear
again in the psychiatric literature until the mid-19th century, when Georget
(1840) in France first formulated the modern concept of the neuroses as
non-fatal, non-psychotic disorders, which included hysteria, nervous palpitations, gastralgia and neuralgia. In the American Civil war Da Costa
(1871) described a condition of 'irritable heart', a type of cardiac anxiety experienced in the chest but occurring in fit young men.

Lewis(1970) characterised the main features of anxiety as follows:

- anxiety is an unpleasant emotional state with the *subjective experience of fear*
- the emotion may be accompanied by *a feeling of impending death*
- it is directed at the future, with feeling of *some kind of threat*

- there *may be no recognisable threat*, or it may be one that by reasonable standards is insufficient to provoke the degree of anxiety.

Fear, on the other hand, is an adaptive response to a *real threat* and enables the organism to take appropriate action to ensure its survival. It may provoke the emergency *fight and flight* reaction in animals. In man, the subjective experience of fear and anxiety is the same, but the anxiety that is common in psychiatric disorders is *not* usually associated with any external threat, and this essence is captured in verse $17^{12}$, where the fear exists without good reason.

Within this passage there is also a suggestion of an animal phobia. Thus it is the sight of wild animals or the noise of a hissing snake that provokes the terror. It is not the attacks of wild animals or the bite of the snakes which worry this writer but only his fears of seeing or hearing them. In $11^{18-19}$ he repeats this fear:

$11^{18}$    ... Or of newly created unknown beasts
        full of rage, or such as breathe out fiery
        breath or belch forth a thick pall of smoke   A fire-breathing dragon
        or flash terrible sparks from their eyes;
$19$       Not only could the harm they do destroy
        people, *but the mere sight could kill by*
        *fright.*                                damage done is through fright

However, there is more than only anxiety in this passage. The writer seems to be very frightened of snakes and wild animals and this is known as an animal phobia and is one of the specific phobias.

## Phobias

The term 'phobia' refers to a group of anxiety symptoms brought on by certain objects or situations. A 'specific phobia', formerly called a 'simple phobia', is a lasting and unreasonable fear caused by the presence or thought of a specific object or situation that usually poses little or no actual danger. Exposure to the object or situation brings about an immediate reaction, causing the person to endure intense anxiety (nervousness) or to avoid the object or situation entirely. The distress associated with the phobia and/or the need to avoid the object or situation can significantly interfere with the person's ability to function. Adults with a specific phobia recognise that the fear is excessive or unreasonable, yet are unable to overcome it. There are different types of specific phobias, based on the object or situation feared,. These include animal phobias, examples of which are fear of dogs, snakes, insects or mice. Animal phobias are the most common specific phobias, particularly in children. They may be associated with panic attacks and antici-patory anxiety, which involves becoming nervous ahead of time about being in certain situations or coming into contact with the object of the phobia; for example, a person with a fear of dogs may become anxious about going for a walk because he or she may see a dog along the way. Children with a specific phobia may express their anxiety by crying, clinging to a parent, or throwing a tantrum. DSM-5 criteria for specific phobia are shown in Table 12.2, in which they are matched with verses from ch. 17 of the Wisdom of Solomon.

**Table 12.2** DSM criteria for phobia and ch. 17 in the Wisdom of Solomon

| *DSM specific phobia* | *Wisdom of Solomon, ch. 17 (verse number in parenthesis)* |
|---|---|
| Marked and persistent unreasonable fear, cued by the presence of a specific object or situation (e.g. flying, heights, animals, injections) | Scared by the passing of wild animals and the hissing of snakes ($17^9$) |
| Exposure to the phobic stimulus almost invariably provokes anxiety or panic | They perished trembling in fear ($17^{10}$) their souls surrender for sudden and unexpected fear ($17^{15}$) |
| The person recognises the fear is un-reasonable | Fear is nothing but a giving up of the help from reason ($17^{12}$) |
| The phobic situation is avoided or else is endured with intense anxiety or distress | Nowhere could it be avoided ($17^{10}$); not even the inner chamber protected them from fear ($17^4$) |
| The avoidance, anxious anticipation or distress of the feared situation(s) interferes significantly in the person's life | These fears are so severe they will be punishment for the unrighteous ($17^{15}$) |

The description here is of a fear of wild or imaginary animals and/or of snakes. These will make people perish through the fear of just seeing them rather than any actual animal attacks or the bites of snakes. It is for the reader to decide on how well the account of the fears described in ch. 17 fit the picture of a specific animal phobia.

Finally, the writer describes in $7^{22-24}$ a personified female Wisdom character who has many wonderful and desirable characteristics. The list comprises of 21 epithets borrowed largely from Greek philosophy. Winston (1979) cites other examples of such lists of virtues in religious literature, such as the Mithras Liturgy; Cleanthes lists 26 divine attributes in the Apocalypse of Abraham; and in the Indian literature, the Perfect wisdom text Prajnaparamita is praised by a litany of her 32 great attributes.

What is of striking interest in the list given by the writer of the Wisdom of Solomon is the inclusion of the item *free from anxiety* – a trait not attested to directly anywhere else in the Wisdom literature.

$7^{22}$  There is in her a spirit that is intelligent,   a list of 21 good attributes
  holy, unique, manifold ...   follows on but not all quoted
$7^{23}$  beneficent, humane, steadfast sure, *free
  from anxiety*, all-powerful, overseeing all....

In his praise of Wisdom, this unknown writer of the Wisdom of Solomon can think of nothing more wonderful than to be *free from anxiety*, suggesting that he may have been a person who suffered from anxiety, an animal phobia (snake phobia) as well as possibly panic attacks. We shall never know.

## Psychiatric episodes associated with King David

David is one of the great Jewish heroes. He is very important in both Jewish and Christian religious traditions because he is said to have composed the Psalms, and Jesus Christ is his direct descendent. His life is described in 1 and 2 Samuel. Unlike his predecessor King Saul, David was quite sane. However, during his long and colourful life there are four episodes which show some psychiatric features:

- an episode of acute stress following the birth and death of Bathsheba's baby
- an episode of feigned insanity when he sought refuge among the Philistines
- a guilt-ridden, tortured relationship with his rebellious son, Absalom
- a strange (and fatal) disease which made him go impotent and cold.

### *King David: an episode of acute stress disorder*

The 2 Samuel 11 tells the story of how King David took a fancy to the beautiful Bathsheba, who was at the time the wife of another man. When their first child was born, David abruptly became mute, refused to eat or drink and even appeared to be considering self-harm for a brief period. However, as soon as the child had died, he recovered quickly, a picture suggestive of an ICD-10 acute stress disorder.

> 11² It happened, late one afternoon, when David rose from his couch, and was walking about on the roof of the King's house that he saw a woman bathing; the woman was very beautiful. ³ David sent someone to inquire about the woman. It was reported 'This is Bathsheba, daughter of Eliam, the wife of Uriah the Hittite'. ⁴ So David sent messages to fetch her and she came to him and he lay with her. (Now she was purifying herself after her period.) Then she returned to her house. ⁵ The woman conceived and she sent and told David 'I am pregnant.'

The story goes on describe how David gets rid of her husband, Uriah, by arranging for him to be sent to the front in the war against the Aramaeans where the fighting was most intense and where a certain death in battle awaited him:

> 11²⁶ When the wife of Uriah heard that her husband was dead, she made lamentation for him. ²⁷ When the mourning was over David sent and brought her to his house and she became his wife and bore him a son.
>
> 12 But the thing that David had done displeased the Lord, ¹ and the Lord sent Nathan to David.

The prophet Nathan admonished David for the crime of stealing Uriah's wife, and even worse for arranging that he should be killed. Nathan told him that he would be punished for this and said 'the child that is born to you, shall die'.

> 12[15] The Lord struck the child that Uriah's wife bore to David, and it became very ill. [16] David pleaded with God for the child; David fasted and went in and lay all night on the ground. The elders of his house stood besides him, urging him to rise from the ground: but he would not, nor did he eat food with them. On the seventh day the child died. And the servants of David were afraid to tell him that the child was dead; for they said, 'While the child was alive we spoke to him, and he did not listen to us; how then can we tell him the child is dead? He may do himself some harm.'

When David heard that the child was dead he recovered rapidly and once more talked to his servants, then anointed himself and started to eat again.

McCarter (1984) discusses the origins of this story. He believes that the original story of David, Bathsheba and Uriah, one of his senior commanders, was probably all true and represents the older original material. The narrator inserts his own theological narrative on to this story through the agency of the prophet Nathan: David is punished by the death of the baby for his unscrupulous behaviour. The story has mystified commentators because David seems to get better when the baby actually dies, which is odd for a bereavement reaction. In his thoughtful commentary McCarter (p. 301) writes:

> The story of David's vigil is very strange. David's behaviour during the child's illness is like that of a man mourning the dead; but when the child dies David does not mourn.... From the servants' point of view, David seems to be mourning at the wrong time. David is not mourning at all, he is imploring Yahweh to spare the child....

This confusion can be resolved by understanding the psychiatry here. Thus ICD–10 describes a type of anxiety disorder called acute stress reaction as follows:

> a transient disorder of significant severity which develops in an individual in response to exceptional physical and/or mental stress and which usually subsides within hours or days. The symptoms typically include an initial state of daze ... followed by further withdrawal from the surrounding situation (to the extent of a dissociative stupor) or by agitation or overactivity. Symptoms usually appear within minutes of the impact of the stressful stimulus and disappear within 2–3 days.

Following the birth and subsequent illness of his baby, David is acutely distressed, he becomes dazed and he is mute; he fails to respond to his servants, does not eat or drink, and the servants think he may harm himself. This corresponds to the picture of acute stress reaction. Moreover, the condition resolves rapidly once the baby dies (the whole episode lasts less than seven days). Thus, rather than it being a bereavement reaction, it is a stress reaction, and rather than grieving, in his anxiety he is praying for the life of the child. Once the baby dies there is no more illness, and no more stress, no point in praying, and so he gets better.

## An episode of feigned insanity

David is pursued by Saul across the deserts of southern Judah and eventually has to escape from Israel altogether. He seeks asylum with King Achish of the Philistines, as described in 1 Samuel 21:

> [10] David rose and fled from that day from Saul; He went to King Achish of Gath. [11] The servants of Achish said to him, 'Is this not David the King of the land? Did they not sing to one another of him in dances "Saul has killed his thousands and David his tens of thousands"?' [12] David took these words to heart and was much afraid of King Achish of Gath. [13] So he changed his behaviour before them; he pretended to be mad when in their presence. He scratched marks on the door of the gate, and let his spittle run down his beard. [14] Achish said to his servants 'Look you see the man is mad; why then have you brought him to me? [15] Do I lack madmen that you have brought this fellow to play the madman in my presence. Shall this fellow come into my house?' ...
> 22[1] David left there and escaped to the cave of Adullam....

The passage raises a number of psychiatric issues. First, it suggests that madness itself existed in Israel, and was well recognised at the time. Secondly, a mad person might be able to obtain asylum, or perhaps be treated with more leniency than a sane person in similar circumstances. Thirdly, the king asserts he has too many mad people in his kingdom. Madness was not only common but troublesome to the king, and this may indicate that the state took some kind of responsibility for the insane.

Sims (2014) suggests that the simulation saved David's life and was therefore successful. In fact, a close reading suggests that King Achish saw through the ruse and knew that David was pretending: 'You have brought this fellow to play the madman in my presence'. Achish was able to distinguish between genuine insanity and feigned madness.

The issue of feigned madness remains a current problem today, termed a 'factitious disorder' and the term 'malingering' is also sometimes applied.

### Feigned insanity, factitious disorder and malingering

Two separate conditions of simulated insanity are recognised today. In factitious disorders the symptoms are intentionally induced so that the patient can assume the sick role. These clients often have a nursing or paramedical background and use their knowledge to simulate both physical and mental disorders. They may tamper with their wounds to make them worse, interfere with drips or use medications to make themselves ill. Sometimes they even admit to this but generally once their actions are exposed they enter into denial, become angry or flee from one hospital to another.

In malingering there is an intentional production of false or grossly exaggerated physical or mental symptoms. The motivation is generally obvious, such as some threat or some financial gain. David's simulation fits this picture quite well.

It is in fact quite easy to simulate insanity and to fool qualified psychiatrists. Thus, in a famous experiment to highlight the poor quality of diagnosis at the time, Rosenhan (1973), a psychologist in California, devised an experiment in which 'pseudo-patients' presented with symptoms of auditory hallucinations (but nothing else) to psychiatric hospitals and gained admission. They remained on the ward for two to three weeks and all had to take the usual antipsychotic medication; they all behaved normally and despite a fairly lengthy period of observation their simulation was not spotted. After the experiment was over, examination of the medical records showed that seven received a diagnosis of schizophrenia, and one of manic depression.

King Achish did well to see through David's ruse, but simulated madness remains a problem for psychiatry today. Sometimes it occurs in prisons as an attempt to avoid court proceedings but it is found more commonly in civilian practice. Thus claims made after a traumatic event will sometimes include a gross exaggeration of the subject's mental symptoms, specifically with the purpose of increasing a financial claim. Rodgers *et al.* (1994) in a large survey of psychiatric reports found rates of malingering in 15% of forensic cases and 7% in civilian cases. The task of the assessing psychiatrist is to sort out the fact from fiction, but sometimes this is very tricky, as the fakers of today employ far more sophisticated ruses than David did.

## David and Absalom: a conflicted father–son relationship

David's sons are in conflict with each other, and one of them, Absalom, provokes a serious rebellion against David himself. The religious explanation for these disastrous family relationships is that this is a punishment from God for David's behaviour over Bathsheba and the killing of Uriah. It is, however, the biblical portrayal of David's agony and depression in dealing with Absalom which provides a vivid account of how a conflicted relationship can result in an understandable depression.

2 Samuel 13 tells how Ammon, who is one of David's sons, lusts after and then rapes Tamar. She is the sister of Absalom, who is so incensed by the crime that he seeks revenge by killing his half-brother Ammon. He does this while the latter is in a drunken state at a sheep-shearers' festival. David is deeply upset by this episode of fratricide among his children: 'David mourned for his son day after day' ($13^{37}$). The phrase 'day after day' suggests quite prolonged mourning following his loss of Ammon. Absalom then went on to start a rebellion against David, with intention of seizing the throne, and several verses describe David's weeping and distress over this rebellion by his son.

> $15^{30}$ But David went up the ascent of the Mount of Olives, weeping as he went, with his head covered and walking barefoot; and all the people who were with him covered their heads and went up, weeping as they went....
> $16^{12}$ [David said] 'It may be that the Lord will look upon my distress and the Lord will repay me with good for this cursing of me today'.

Absalom's rebellion is eventually defeated, but David expressly commands that his son should not be killed: 'Deal kindly with the young man Absalom' ($18^8$). Absalom flees the battleground but his horse runs under an oak tree and he is caught by a branch. News of this accident reaches Joab, who is David's henchman, and together with 10 of his soldiers he goes and stabs

Absalom to death. When David hears about the death of his son, he is distraught:

> 18³³ The King was deeply moved, and went up to the chamber over the gate and wept: and as he went he said 'O my son Absalom, my son, my son Absalom! Would that I had died instead of you. O Absalom, my son, my son.'

When David's soldiers hear that the King is grieving for his rebellious son, they are upset because they had acted to crush a rebellion and save David's life. Joab has to confront David and tell him there is a near mutiny on hand:

> 19⁵ Today you have covered with shame the faces of all your officers who have saved your life today.... ⁶ For love of those who hate you, and hatred of those who love you, You have made it clear today that commanders and officers are nothing to you; for I perceive that if Absalom were alive and all of us dead today then you would be pleased....

McCarter (pp. 410–411) writes that the narrator goes to great lengths to exonerate David from the charge of murdering his own son. Not only does he tell the troops to deal kindly with his son but he has no involvement with the actual killing. He weeps so profusely that his troops are nearly in revolt, because David places his piety and grief over his son's death above the very safety of the state.

David's depression is readily explained; using older psychiatric terminology, it seems to be a reactive depression: he mourns the loss of two sons, Ammon and Absalom. The conflicted father–son relationship caused by Absalom's rebellion practically gives him a nervous breakdown. Depression can commonly arise from conflicted family relationships. As a depiction of intra-familial conflict leading to depression in their father, the tale of David and his murderous sons is unsurpassed in its poignancy.

## The death of David

Right to the end of his life David remains the scheming politician and perhaps also a little paranoid as he seeks to settle old scores. As he hands over the reins to his son Solomon he instructs him to kill Joab, his loyal henchman, because he is a dangerous man, and also to kill Shimei, who many years previously sided with Absalom in his rebellion. David had a long, vengeful memory and both men are to die in the same way:

> 1 Kings 2⁹ 'You must bring his grey head down with blood to Sheol.' ¹⁰ Then David slept with his ancestors and was buried in the city of David....

David's final illness and his decline into senility is described in the opening of 1 Kings:

| 1¹ | King David was old and advanced in years, he could not get warm | Estimated to be about 70 years Hypothermia; most common |
| 2 | So his servants said to him, 'Let a young virgin be sought for my Lord the King | cause today is hypothyroidism |

and let her wait on the King and be his attendant; Let her lie in your bosom So that my Lord the King may be warm
3 So they searched for a beautiful girl throughout all the territory of Israel and found Abishag the Shunamite
4 The girl was very beautiful. She became the King's attendant and served him but the king did not know her sexually.

Heb. *sokenet* = nurse, not concubine, but to have sex with him or to just warm him up?

Shunem: ?Arab village of Sulem 7 miles from Nazereth

The King is impotent

The demonstration that the king was impotent is significant, as Gray (1977) suggests that a king's authority and indeed his life might depend on his ability to prove his virility. In support of this he cites the older Ugaritic Ras Shamra text about the life of King Keret, whose sickness disqualified him from ruling.

The most intriguing aspect of this tale is the suggested method of using a young virgin to warm his body up: 'Let her lie in thy bosom so that my Lord the King may be warm'. This seems to have been a recognised therapeutic intervention in the ancient world. Thus Montgomery and Gehan (1951) write:

> The proposed remedy of procuring a virgin is correctly attributed by Josephus as being on the advice of physicians (Antiquities vii, 14.3) and such practices are corroborated by one of Galen's prescriptions, *'iis vero quae extrinsicus applicanter puellus una sic accubans abdomen eius contiget'*, which translated from the Latin reads: 'in addition to remedies applied from the outside, a young girl lying with him touches his abdomen'. This interesting remedy had no effect on David and so now not surprisingly is no longer applied.

An Israeli physician (Ben-Noun, 2002) has commented that the description given of David being cold despite being given many warm clothes is consistent with hypothermia and she lists several causes of hypothermia. Her diagnosis is malignant disease, but my own diagnostic preference is that this is hypothyroidism (low thyroid hormone levels), as this is a much more common problem amongst the elderly, with a prevalence of around 5% (Bensenor *et al.*, 2012).

# References

Ben-noun, L. (2002) Was the Biblical King David Affected by Hypothermia? *Journal of Gerontology A: Biological Science; Medicine.*

Bensenor, I., Olmos, P.D. & Lotufo, P. (2012) Hypothyroidism in the elderly: diagnosis and management *Clinical Interventions in Aging* 7: 97–111.

Bhatia, M.S. and Vaid, L. (2000) Hysterical aphonia – an analysis of 25 cases. *Indian Journal of Medical Science*, 54: 335–338.

Biringer, E., Howard, L.M., Kessler, U., *et al.* (2015) Is infertility really associated with higher levels of mental distress in the female population? Results from the North-Trondelag Health Study and medical birth registry of Norway. *Journal of Psychosomatic Obstetrics and Gynaecology* 36(2): 38–45.

Blenkinsop, J. (2000) *Isaiah 1-39. A New Translation with Introduction and Commentary* Anchor Bible. New York: Doubleday.

Crenshaw, J.L. (1988) *Ecclesiastes: A Commentary.* London: SCM Press.

Da'Costa, J.M. (1871) On irritable heart: A clinical case study of a functional cardiac disorder and its consequences. *American Journal of Medical Science* 61, 17–52.

Feldmann, E., Mayou, R., Hawton, K., *et al.* (1987) Psychiatric disorder in Medical inpatients. *Quarterly Journal of Medicine* 63: 405–412.

Fox, M.V. (1989) *Qohelet and His Contradictions*. Sheffield: Almond Press.

Ginsberg, H.L. (1950) *Studies in Koheleth*. New York: Jewish Theological Seminary.

Gordis, R. (1952) Koheleth The original Language – Hebrew or Aramaic? *Journal of Biblical Literature* 71.

Grabbe, L.J. (1997) *Wisdom of Solomon*. Sheffield: Sheffield Academic Press.

Gray, J. (1964) *I and II Kings: A Commentary*. London: SCM Press.

Holley S.R. Pasch L.A. Bleil M.E. *et al* (2015) Prevalence and predictors of major Depressive Disorder for fertility treatment patients and their partners. *Fertility and Sterility (2015)* 103(5): 1332–1339.

Jenkins R., Lewis G., Bebbington, P., *et al.* (1997) The National Psychiatric Morbidity Surveys of Great Britain – initial findings from the household survey. *Psychological Medicine* 27: 775–779.

Josephus (1st century CE republished 1987); The Antiquities of the Jews Book 7 Ch.14.3. p. 207 in *The Works of Josephus: Complete and Unabridged*. Translated by William Whiston (1667–1752) Peabody, MA: Hendrikson Publishers.

Lewis, A. (1970) The ambiguous word 'anxiety'. *International Journal of Psychiatry* 9: 62–79.

Longman, T. (1998) *The Book of Ecclesiastes*. Grand Rapids Michigan: William B Eerdmans Publishing Company.

McCarter, P.K. (1980) *The Anchor Bible. I Samuel.: A New Translation with Introduction, Notes and Commentary*. Garden City, NY: Doubleday.

McCarter, P.K. (1984) *The Anchor Bible. II Samuel: A New Translation with Introduction ,Notes and Commentary*. Garden City, NY: Doubleday.

Montgomery, J.A. and Gehman, S.H. (1951) *The International Critical Commentary: A Critical and Exegetical Commentary on the Book Kings*. Edinburgh: T&T Clark.

Mumford, D.B. (1992) Emotional Distress in the Hebrew Bible: Somatic or Physical. *British Journal of Psychiatry* 160(1): 92–97.

Murphy, R.E. (1992) *Ecclesiastes Word Biblical Commentary* Vol 23A. Dallas, Texas: Word Books.

Nunnally-Cox, J. (1981) *Foremothers: Women of the Bible*. New York: Seabury Press.

Paykel, E.S., Prusoff B.A. and Myers, J.A. (1975) Suicide attempts and recent life events. A controlled Comparison. *Archives of General Psychiatry* 32(3): 327–333.

Rodgers, R., Sewell, K.W. & Goldstein (1994) Explanatory models of human behaviour. *Law and Human Behaviour* 22: 273–285.

Rosenhan, D. (1973) 'On being sane in insane places'. *Science* 179 (4070): 250–258.

Sims, A. (2014) Feigned insanity – Psychiatry in sacred texts. *British Journal of Psychiatry* 204(1): 35.

Taylor, C. (1874) *The Dirge in Ecclesiastes 12*. Edinburgh: Williams and Norgate.

Winston, D. (1979) *The Anchor Bible. Wisdom of Solomon: A New Translation with Introduction and Commentary*. Garden City, NY: Doubleday.

# Chapter 13

# Children

There are only a few references to children and parenting in the Old Testament and , as might be expected, they are all from the perspective of adults. Children had little or no independent status in the ancient world but poor parenting seems to have been a problem in ancient Israel just as it is today. In this short chapter only three stories will be covered: the Judgement of Solomon; neglectful parents; and the fate of the stubborn and rebellious son. The latter two stories do not have much in the way of religious significance and so are not widely known.

## The Judgement of Solomon

Each day in the UK judges sit in the family division of the High Court and must make heart-wrenching decisions on child care, such as whether or not a mother can keep her child or whether a child who has been removed from her can be returned. In disputes between parents the judge is required to adjudicate on who is best placed to bring the child up in the long term. In the face of neglectful or dangerous parenting the state assigns to social services the task of assessing just how damaging a defect in parenting is, and whether it is no longer safe, or in the child's best interest, for a child to remain with the parents, a position usually fiercely disputed by the parents or the mother alone. Ultimately, it will be the judge's task to make such a life-changing decision, which even today is sometimes known as the 'Judgement of Solomon'.

Inadequate parenting is not of itself a psychiatric condition, but mental illness in the mother is one of its more frequent causes. It may result in psychiatrically damaged children who grow up to have difficulties in later life, with a corresponding cost to society as a whole. Psychiatrists, especially child psychiatrists, are now increasingly being drawn into the world of child protection, and such cases form a significant part of the child psychiatrist's workload. Adult psychiatrists are also sometimes called to assist the court in making these very difficult decisions, especially in cases of maternal mental illness. Although the biblical story of the Judgement of Solomon is primarily a religious parable concerning the source of divine wisdom, the case example chosen to illustrate the divine quality of Solomon's wisdom was one of disputed child care, and perhaps selected because these are the most taxing of cases – both in ancient Israel and in the modern world.

The story is described in I Kings 3$^{15-27}$ and is no more than a brief legal case report of two women who quarrel over who is the natural mother of a newborn infant. The ultimate theological message of the story can only really be understood by taking into account Solomon's dream which immediately precedes the court case in I Kings 3$^{4-12}$. In this dream, God asks

Solomon what he would most want now he has become the King of Israel. Solomon replies with modesty what he would like is to have an 'understanding mind'. The word used here for 'mind', *leb*, actually means 'heart', but throughout the ancient world the heart was the seat of the soul, where all emotions were felt. In the Akkadian literature wisdom is ascribed to the ear (*uznu*) 'with great wisdom and wide understanding that the wisest of the Gods presented me'. In ancient Egypt, the expression the 'hearing heart' refers to the heart as the agent of understanding and throughout the ancient Near East the ability to listen was perceived as the source of wisdom (Cogan, 2000). Even today, it is the judge's special ability to listen and carefully weigh the evidence presented in court that is central to judicial capacity. Solomon also asks that he should be able 'to distinguish between good and evil' (i.e. between right and wrong), a requirement that goes to the core of the task of the judge. These qualities were held to emanate from the deity but the notion that such judicial ability might also reside within the person of the king had also been recorded for the much earlier kings of Canaan in the Krt and 'Aqht Ugaritic texts of the Ras Shamra literature, which predates the Solomonic period by around four centuries.

God then thanks Solomon that his requests were not for riches, long life or the death of his enemies, and so to reward his modesty God bestows on Solomon fabulous wealth, as well as a long life. The chapter then provides a legal case example to demonstrate just how wise Solomon has now become.

The legal case described in 1 Kings 3$^{15-28}$ and sometimes known as the Judgment of Solomon is one of the best-known stories of the Old Testament. There is some question as to whether the original story was of Israelite origin because the central theme has a universal origin: similar stories are found in the folklore of many nations (some of these are described below). The Book of Kings provides a poetic yet legally well balanced account of the dispute between the protagonists. As in the story of Solomon's dream, it is thought that the Deuteronomist redactor played a major role in crafting the tale, by making it both exciting, and logical, subtly emphasising the divine presence in Solomon's judicial prowess as well as in his compassion. The biblical tale has primarily a religious purpose and informs on the relationship between the monarchy, the judiciary and religion, but remains relevant today as it considers the role of the judiciary in disputes over the right to parent a child.

Nowadays these parental rights are most frequently questioned in cases of child abuse or neglect, where the protagonists are generally the state (as represented by social services) and the mother. The story is quoted below in full, before a brief commentary is given on each verse and then a few similar stories from other nations are discussed. To give the passage a modern psychiatric relevance a brief summary of the role that child and adult psychiatrists have in assisting the court in such cases today is also included below.

## The biblical account (1 Kings 3$^{16-28}$)

[16] Later two women who were prostitutes came to the king and stood before him. [17] One woman said, 'Please, my Lord, this woman and I live in the same house; and I gave birth while she was in the house. [18] Then on the third day

after I gave birth, this woman also gave birth. We were together; there was no one else with us in the house, only the two of us were in the house. [19] Then this woman's son died in the night, because she lay on him. [20] She got up in the middle of the night and took my son from beside me while your servant slept. She laid him at her breast, and laid her dead son at my breast. [21] When I rose in the morning to nurse my son, I saw that he was dead; but when I looked at him closely in the morning, clearly it was not the son I had born.' [22] But the other woman said, 'No, the living son is mine, and the dead son is yours'. The first said, 'No the dead son is yours, and the living son is mine.' So they argued before the king.

[23] Then the King said, 'The one says, "This is my son that is alive, and your son is dead"; while the other says "Not so! Your son is dead and my son is the living one".' So the king said, 'Bring me a sword', and they brought a sword before the king. [25] The king said, 'Divide the living boy in two; then give half to one and half to the other'. [26] But the woman whose son was alive said to the king – because compassion for her son burned within her – 'Please, my lord, give her the living boy; do not kill him!' The other said, 'It shall be neither mine nor yours; divide it.' [27] Then the king responded: 'Give the first woman the living boy; do not kill him. She is his mother'. [28] All Israel heard of the judgement that the king had rendered; and they stood in awe of the king, because they perceived that the wisdom of God was in him, to execute justice.

*Verse 16. Two women who were prostitutes came to the king*
The women are both harlots and Cogan (2000) writes that there is no moral condemnation of the women or their trade here. They are both treated fairly and given their day in court, the same as for any other Israelite, as if to reflect the spirit of equality before the law regardless of their social standing.

*Verse 17. This woman live and I live in the same house*
The Targum has 'feminine inn-keepers'. Harlots would unashamedly visit an inn, but most commentators (e.g. Cogan) suggest the house was a tavern where the women had taken up a semi-permanent residence to ply their trade.

*Verse 18. We were together; there was no one else with us in the house, only the two of us were in the house*
This verse has legal significance because there could be no witnesses to the events that later took place. Conventional court practice, both today and in the ancient world, relies on hearing evidence from witnesses and in the absence of any independent evidence conventional legal methods and judgements will be difficult to apply. Cogan (2000) suggests this verse may be a Deuteronomistic insertion to reflect that now an inspired and divine-like quality will be required to judge where the truth lies because there are no witnesses nor any factual evidence on which to base a decision. This will mean that sacral and religious methods will be needed to make the judgement, and this in turn has an echo with Solomon in his dream asking God for the ability to discern between good and evil. It was the Deuteronomist's intention for the whole story to be regarded as a verification of Yahweh's granting to Solomon the gift of judicial wisdom, a gift that ultimately derives from God.

*Verse 19. This woman's son died during the night, because she lay on him*
The suggestion here is that the woman herself, presumably by accident, killed her infant. Subtly, the writer prepares us for Solomon's final decision, because one of the women has been proven to be negligent, at the very least, and failed to preserve the life of her child. There is no condemnation or even accusation for her role in the death of the child because there is no proof, yet this phrase alludes to maternal incompetence. Mothers should not sleep on top of their infants and this is given as the cause of death.

*Verses 20–27*
An open quarrel develops between the two women in the courtroom. Solomon's reaction to this dispute, like that of any judge, is to summarise the positions of the two litigants. The king cannot work out which of the women is telling the truth so he devises a test which will obviously be stressful for the participants and shocking for the audience. He asks for a sword to be brought to him and threatens to cut the baby in half. This might have been a fair solution had the baby been no more than a lifeless possession. However, since the test will inevitably mean the death of her child, the true mother reacts with very strong emotion. The actual words are important here. The word *chāmār* means 'hot' and *rahamaim* (the plural of 'womb') signifies womb or bowels as the seat of the emotions. This might then be rendered as 'her bowels were in ferment', but other translations for *rachamaim* have 'maternal compassion'. It is in the heat of her emotional reaction to the thought that her child might die that she relinquishes her claim. She does this to save the life of the child and in so doing she demonstrates her maternal empathy and compassion. By contrast, the second woman, perhaps in trying to please the king, goes along with his apparently cruel suggestion to cut the baby in half.

Solomon, on witnessing the display of maternal compassion in the first woman, then bases his judgement on the selflessness of her emotions and gives her the child. De Vries (2006), a biblical scholar, writes, 'The choice is now between the claim of motherhood and the claim of life itself. Thus the true mother finds herself willing to suffer in order to save her child's life, and is even prepared to lose her child in order to let him live.'

*Verse 28. The wisdom of God was in him*
As might be expected, this is the moral of the whole story. The people stood in awe because Solomon's wisdom was more than could be expected from a mere mortal, and so it must have come from God. 'The wisdom of God was in him'. This particular type of wisdom was about *mishpat* – the ability to judge, or judicial wisdom.

Two elements in this story remain relevant today. First, Solomon found it impossible to make the judgement purely on the statements of the two disputing women. To solve this dilemma he sent for a sword and proposed to cut the infant in half; this was a shock but it elicited the quality of maternal compassion and empathy from the true mother. Today, a stress test is also sometimes applied in child-care cases that cannot be resolved on evidence or depositions alone. Mothers are sent away with their infants for a residential parenting assessment, where their parenting skills can be readily observed, and an important part of this assessment is looking at maternal empathy and competence.

Also, one of the cornerstones of a modern social worker's assessment of whether a mother is an adequate parent is the demonstration that she is able to place the child's needs over and above her own needs, as for example in the case of a drug-addicted mother where the need to satisfy addictive cravings may take precedence over attending to the infant. This principle of placing the infant's needs above all else seems to have been recognised in this ancient biblical parable.

## Similar anthropological stories

The actual story of disputed motherhood and it ending up in a legal case is very old and may be ubiquitous rather than an original Israelite tale. Hugo Gressemann in his study *Das Salomonische Urteil* (1907) identified no fewer than 22 stories of an abused mother and her endangered child in the folklores of various peoples, and suggested that the Solomonic story may have originated in India, since many of these tales were from there.

A Buddhist Jataka tale preserved in a Singalese version of the fifth or sixth century CE relates that a female cannibal demon (*yakinni*) once stole the child of a woman who was bathing in the river. The demon and the mother appealed to Buddha for a judgement. He drew a line on the ground and ordered the two of them to draw the child across the line in a tug of war. The true mother refused.

In another Indian (Pakrit) tale, two women set out for a feast, each with an infant child. While they were asleep in the forest, a wolf killed one of the children. The mother substituted the dead baby for that of her companion before the latter awoke. At the court of Gopicandra, a wise parrot advised that the child be cut in half. The true mother revealed herself by demurring at this suggestion.

In a Tibetan tale, a man has both a wife and a concubine. The wife is barren but the concubine bears a son. When the man dies, the wife claims the son as hers in order to inherit the estate. The sage Vicakha orders a tug of war. The true mother refuses.

Gaster (1969) describes many other similar tales from around the world, including an English version, but with the possible exception of the Indian stories most of these take place long after the reign of King Solomon. In most of these tales the underlying problem is one frequent perinatal death as the mortality of infants and young children in the ancient world was very high. Today, infant mortality is greatly reduced and the underlying problem the courts face in their 'Judgement of Solomon' cases is usually the adequacy or otherwise of parental care.

## Neglectful parents

Child psychiatry is a very recent sub-speciality of psychiatry, probably finding its beginnings after World War I, when August Hamberger set up the first child psychiatry clinic, in Heidelberg, and at around the same time Emanuel Miller set up a similar clinic in the East End of London. Later there were concerns about criminal and delinquent children as well as those with educational problems and soon they also came under the general rubric of these early clinics. Both the Old and New Testaments give occasional mention to difficult and problematic children, poor relationships between parents and their children and parents who seem to upset their children (in the New Testament only) – all topics that are nowadays an everyday part of child psychiatry.

## Neglect of infants

Although the vast majority of women take readily to the challenge of a new infant, it has always been a mystery as to why a tiny minority of are unable to rise to the task of motherhood. This conundrum is mentioned by Deutero-Isaiah but he uses it as a metaphor in the context of Yahweh's relationship to Zion (Isaiah 49):

14    But Zion said, 'The Lord has forsaken me,
      And the Lord has forgotten me.'
15    *Can a woman forget her nursing child,*
      or show no compassion for the child of her womb?
      Even these may forget,
      Yet I will not forget you.

The passage has many differing interpretations, mostly devolving around Yahweh's covenant with Israel. The verses express a lament of Zion (symbolising the people) that Yahweh has forgotten them. There is an allusion to a nursing mother (v. 15), as a metaphor, who is not compassionate to her own infant, suggesting some sort of defect in the mother–child relationship.

Most traditional explanations hinge on the ending of the tale. Thus, while the accusation is that Yahweh has abandoned his wife (Zion), in the end the text says he has not forgotten her and so this verse becomes a message of hope and salvation. Baltzer (1999, p. 321) suggests this represents a scene where a woman appeals to a judge because her husband has left her. The word 'forsaken' probably means she is not divorced but merely separated. Were she to be formally divorced she could at least demand her dowry back, return to her own family or remarry, but the situation will require clarification in court.

However, it is verse 15 which is of psychiatric interest as it describes the unusual situation of a mother who seems to be both uncaring and oblivious of her newborn infant. Such an image cannot be just made up, or created from the imagination, and most likely would have been based on the writer witnessing a new mother failing with her newborn infant, or at the very least the writer hearing a story about such a case.

Today, we have some understanding of the causes of such a lack of maternal capacity and poor bonding. Most often poor-quality early maternal attachment and care occurs as a result of personality disorder, chronic schizophrenia, low IQ and a whole catalogue of mental disorders, notably post-natal depression or a post-partum psychosis. But there is no hint of any maternal mental illness in this passage.

Our understanding even today is incomplete, and few remedies are at hand to reverse this situation, although the state, through the agency of social services, is obliged to intervene. Infants who are not being cared for adequately by their mothers are placed on the Child Protection Register, most commonly for neglect (35%), physical injury (23%), emotional abuse (17%) and sexual abuse (12%), or combinations of these categories. Almost certainly all these defects in maternal care would have existed in the ancient world but in the face of very high infant and child mortality such deficiencies in parenting might hardly have been noticed. It is of interest therefore that Deutero-Isaiah selected a case of poor maternal attachment and bonding failure for his metaphor to question Yahweh's attachment to Zion.

## Neglect of older children

Older children who suffer at the hands of a negligent or uncaring parent may show behavioural disorder or emotional distress at school or in other settings. In biblical times there was no knowledge of child psychiatry or that a disturbed child was anything other than the product of neglectful parenting. This seems to apply to the cases of child neglect observed by the author(s) of Proverbs:

29[15]    The rod and reproof give wisdom
         but a mother is disgraced by a neglected child....

29[17]    Discipline your children, and they will give you rest;
         they will give delight to your heart.

McKane (1970, p. 634) explains:

> Verses 15 and 17 are concerned with parental discipline, corporal punishment and education. Corrections by the rod produce wisdom, but the youth who is not under discipline is running to waste. Apparently free as the wind, he is in fact abandoned to the chaos of destructive impulses whose slave he is, and he will bring shame to his mother....

It seems as if the neglected child refers to one who is undisciplined and has run wild. Such children today are sometimes given a diagnosis of 'conduct disorder', and their mention in this verse suggests that such children probably existed and were recognised in ancient Israel. The solution was more discipline and more beatings with the rod. Today we know better, and administering more of the rod is not only unhelpful but can make matters worse and might even invite a charge of physical abuse.

Behaviour disorders – which are beyond the range of normal childhood naughtiness – are less common and have a wide variety of causes, including coercive parenting, attention deficit hyperactivity disorder (ADHD) or developmental disorders, such as learning difficulties.

Further mentions of unhappy child–parent relationships as a result of the child himself being very difficult are given in Proverbs:

10[1]   A wise child makes a glad father,
        but a foolish child is a mother's grief.

17[21]  The one who begets a fool gets trouble;
        the parent of a fool has no joy.

17[25]  Foolish children are a grief to their father
        and bitterness to her who bore them.

In these three instances it is the disturbed child who brings about the parental misery. Disturbed and disobedient children can sometimes cause much distress to their parents, sometimes even precipitating maternal depression. In the Book of Proverbs the word 'fool' denotes something akin to the modern concept of personality disorder (mainly antisocial) and it is the parental despair at having a fool as a child which is described here.

The recent child psychiatry literature has numerous studies replicating an association between maternal depression and having children with conduct disorder and so confirming the observations of the scribes of the Book of Proverbs. A study of the mothers of over 1,000 twins found a strong association between maternal depression and antisocial behaviours in their children but the causal direction was that it was the mother's depression which resulted in their child's antisocial behaviour problems (Kim-Cohen *et al.*, 2005) rather than the antisocial child being the cause of the parental depression as Proverbs suggests. Either way, it is of interest that the scribes of ancient Israel were seeing and writing about such dysfunctional families.

Parents who seem to cause their children's disturbance and may even abuse their children are common today. This scenario is not mentioned in the Old Testament but in the New Testament there are two possible warnings against overly harsh parenting:

> Ephisians 6[4]: Fathers do not provoke your children to anger, but bring them up in discipline and instruction of the Lord.

> Colossonians 3[21]: Fathers do not exasperate your children so they will not lose heart.

Both verses allude to what seems to be a novel concept for the ancient world, namely that it is the parents who destabilise the child. This goes against the more usual Old Testament rhetoric of 'Spare the rod and spoil the child' but overly angry parents are all too frequent visitors to the child psychiatry clinic today.

## The stubborn and rebellious son: a very severe case

Among the many laws in the Book of Deuteronomy, ch. 21 contains several 'Laws on respect for life'. These include what to do about 'the rebellious and stubborn son':

> 21[18] If someone has a stubborn and rebellious son who will not obey his father and mother, who does not heed them when they discipline him, [19] then his father and mother shall take hold of him and bring him out to the elders of his

town at the gate of that place. [20] They shall say to the elders of his town, 'This son of ours is stubborn and rebellious. He will not obey us. He is a glutton and a drunkard.' [21] Then all the men of the town shall stone him to death. So you shall purge the evil from your midst; and all Israel hear, and be afraid.

In the earlier patriarchal period of ancient Israel and also in ancient Rome, parents had the absolute right to execute their children. However, Tigay (1996) points out that under this Deuteronomic ruling such an execution could occur only after a trial and on the authority of the elders, and the killing was conducted by all the men of the town, not the parents. The ruling represented a means whereby the parents could share the guilt of killing their own unmanageable son with the rest of the community. Tigay also suggests that this option was rarely if ever applied, but the law was used to strike fear into defiant youngsters. Curiously, the punishment for the insubordinate son in ancient Mesopotamia as recorded in the much older Code of Hammurabi (*circa* BCE 1800) was rather less severe, comprising only the cutting off the delinquent's hands.

Stoning one's own child seems to be very cruel and grossly out of tune with the rest of the Torah's laws on family life. This was certainly the view of the rabbis of the Talmud (4th–8th century CE) and they produce a lengthy discussion (Sanhedrin 70a: 473–489) on who might qualify to be a 'stubborn and rebellious son'. In a fascinating discourse, applying the best of Talmudic logic, they find so many exclusions that such a person could never have existed and so this cruel punishment never have been applied. The argument runs as follows.

First is the age. The Mishnah states: 'A stubborn and rebellious son, when does he become liable to the penalty of a stubborn and rebellious son? From the time he produces two hairs until he grows a beard right round' (by which is meant the hairs of the genitals, not of the face, but the sages spoke in polite terms).

Second, 'the son' means not a full-grown man, but a minor is also exempt, since he does not fall within the scope of the commandment. This means not a minor but nor a full-grown adult.

Third, 'If he ate *tartema* [an unknown food] in a company celebrating a religious act' Rabbi Abbahu then commented he is not liable, unless he eats in a company consisting entirely of good-for-nothings. Thus, even if they were all wastrels, because they were celebrating a religious act he is not punished.

Fourth, the Talmud also provides exemption clauses based on the phrase 'he is a glutton and a drunkard'. R. Hanan b. Moledach and in R. Huna's name said: 'He is not liable unless he drinks and he buys meat and wine cheaply and consumes them for it is written "he is a *zolel* ( glutton)".'

Fifth, R. Hanan b. Moledach also said he is not liable unless he eats raw meat, and drinks undiluted wine, and by this is meant insufficiently diluted wine, and raw meat means only partially cooked meat, like the charred meat cooked by thieves.

Sixth, Rabbah and R. Joseph both said 'If he eats pickled meats or drinks wine from the vat [i.e. new wine before it has matured] he does not become a stubborn and rebellious son'.

Finally, the passage concludes 'With whom does the following *Baraitha* agree: There never has been a stubborn and rebellious son, and so why was the law written? That you may study it and receive an award.' Thus the Talmud, perhaps with the purpose of trying to preserve a more compassionate impression of Torah, argues away the very existence of the stubborn and rebellious son, so such cruel punishments were never administered.

However, there is plenty of evidence that 'the stubborn and rebellious son' continues to thrive today. Society still has no answer for the drunken, violent adolescent, but at least today we should be thankful that we have secure adolescent psychiatric provision for such dangerous youths. A study from one such unit reveals the scale and nature of the problem. Hill *et al.* (2012) report on 37 admissions to an adolescent secure forensic psychiatric unit in Southampton. These clients were responsible for 2,388 violent incidents over 6161 admission days; of these incidents, 761 were violent physical assaults, of which 8.4% were patient-on-patient and 91.6% were patient-on-staff. The underlying psychopathologies found in these clients included developmental disorders such as learning difficulties, previous histories of conduct disorder, previous histories of child abuse and domestic violence in their families of origin, but not psychotic disorders. A follow-up study of children discharged from a similar unit in Birmingham found that around one-third of subjects subsequently developed substance abuse (Harrington *et al.*, 2005).

Perhaps the word 'rebellious' in the biblical phrase 'stubborn and rebellious son' actually refers to verbal and physical attacks on their parents. How could an ancient Israelite family possibly cope with such children? Today, the vast majority of these violent attacks are directed at the nursing staff, but there were no such secure units staffed by nurses in ancient Israel and so the parents would have been at the receiving end of these repeated severe assaults, perhaps occurring at a frequency of one attack every couple of weeks. Many of these children in modern studies also had learning difficulties and so were incapable of changing their ways; perhaps this is the meaning of the word 'stubborn' in this phrase. Finally, around one-third of these adolescents later developed substance abuse, and perhaps this is the meaning of the phrase 'he is a glutton and a drunkard'. In ancient Israel the only substance involved would have been alcohol and hence the inclusion of the term ' drunkard' to describe this challenging clientele.

Children presenting with repetitive assaultive behaviours are uncommon but are nowadays removed from their parents and cared for on compulsory detention orders in institutions. It is little wonder that in the ancient world they were killed, but this passage in Deuteronomy legitimises such a killing by making it a judicial execution conducted by the whole community, enabling the guilt of the parents to be shared. The priests who wrote the Torah were perhaps more in touch with the painful reality of their flock than were the later rabbis of the Talmud, who tried to debate away the existence of such youths from the safety of their academies in Babylon. While there can never be any certainty that the 'stubborn and rebellious sons' of Deuteronomy correspond to present-day aggressive and delinquent adolescents, there do not appear to be any other candidates who fit this job description quite so well.

# References

Babylonian Talmud *Sanhedrin* 68a–70a pp. 465–479. Editor Rabbi I. Epstein. London: Soncino Press.

Baltzer, K. (1999) *Deutero-Isaiah: A Commentary on Isaiah 40–55*. Translated by Margaret Kohl. Minneapolis: Fortress Press.

Cogan, M. (2000) *I Kings. The Anchor Bible. A new translation with introduction and commentary*. New York: Doubleday.

De Vries, S. J. (2006) *I Kings*. Word Biblical Commentary. Vol. 12 B. Dallas: Word Books, Thomas Nelson.

Gaster, T. H. (1969) *Myth Legend and Custom in the Old Testament*. New York: Harper and Row.

Gressemann, H. (1907) Das Salomonische Urteil. *Deutsches Rundschau* 13: 212–224.

Harrington, R.C., Kroll, L., Rothwell, J., *et al.* (2005) Psychosocial needs of boys in secure care for serious or persistent offending. *Journal of Child Psychology and Psychiatry* 46(8): 859–866.

Hill, S. A., White, O., Lolley. J., *et al.* (2012) Incidents in an adolescent secure inpatient service. *Medicine Science and Law* 52(1): 27–31.

Kim-Cohen, J., Moffitt, T. E., Taylor, A., *et al.* (2006) Maternal depression and children's antisocial behavior: nature and nurture effects. *Archives of General Psychiatry* 62(2): 173–181.

McKane, W. (1970) *Proverbs: A New Approach*. London: SCM Press.

Tigay, J. H. (1996) The Punishment of the Insubordinate Son, pp. 196–197, in *The Jewish Publication Society Commentary on Deuteronomy*. Philadelphia: Jewish Publication Society.

# Alcoholism in ancient Israel

Most societies, both ancient and modern, have an ambivalent attitude to alcohol, on the one hand enjoying its relaxing and mood-elevating effects, while on the other hand being much concerned about the consequences of alcoholism. Few have expressed this ambivalence more eloquently than the writers of the Old Testament in their account of wine drinking in ancient Israelite society. Wine gave pleasure to many and the possession of a vineyard was a sign of personal wealth. Wine played an important part in family celebrations and religious festivals, including the Sabbath. The drinking of both wine and beer, as well as drunkenness, had been previously well documented in the ancient Egyptian and Sumerian literature long before Israel came into existence but the Old Testament account is unique in its detail and its coverage of the dire social consequences of alcoholism, as well as some of its neuropsychiatric complications.

The description of alcoholism in the Old Testament is not systematic; a few verses here and there may contain a polemic against drinking or perhaps a metaphor is applied to a political matter, or some issue of foreign policy alludes to alcoholic deterioration. There are mentions of alcohol in the castigations of the major prophets, especially Isaiah and Jeremiah, who railed against its use. A more objective and clinical approach is given in a lecture from a father to his son in the Book of Proverbs, while guidance on the merits of drinking in moderation is given in the Book of Sirach. The harm caused to society by alcohol was sufficient to provoke a reaction that resulted in two separate teetotal movements, the Nazirites and the Rechabites.

Some of the verses selected for a more detailed analysis in this chapter are well known, others less so. The criterion for inclusion is whether the verse mentions a symptom or problem related to alcohol that might be encountered in a psychiatric clinic today. More so than any other chapter in this book, this chapter is concerned with the history of psychiatry, specifically the early history of alcoholism and the way its complications were perceived in the ancient world. This is a more factually based topic and has relatively less in the way of spiritual and religious meaning, and so hopefully this will make the chapter relatively less controversial.

## The early history of wine and alcoholic drinks

There is archaeological evidence of wine production from grapes going back to around 5000–6000 BCE in Georgia and northern Iran. In his book *Viticulture and Brewing in the Ancient Orient*, Lutz (1992) argues, as do others, that Eurasian grape cultivation and wine making probably originated in the southern Caucasus, in the area of modern-day Georgia, and probably spread south from this region through to northern Iran and the Levant. Organic alcoholic residues have been found in ceramic vessels recovered from archaeological sites in the area covered by northern Iran. One of the best-known of these is the Godin Tepe archaeological site. This was an Elamite village located in the Zagros mountains. This site pre-dates Mesopotamian civilisation and is thought to have been a trading station for lapis lazuli (a gem) mined in Afghanistan. Storage jars found on this site (circa 3500–3100 BCE) have been found to contain tannin crystals, tartrates and tartaric acid, indicating they once held beer. References to grapes, wine and raisins become increasingly frequent in cuneiform sources of ancient Sumeria from around the second half of the third millennium BCE and thereafter. There is good evidence from the cuneiform literature for the consumption of wine at banquets in Sumeria.

A similar picture emerges from excavations in ancient Egypt, with scenes of wine making depicted on the walls of tombs from the middle of the 3rd millennium BCE onwards. By the end of the Old Kingdom (2600–2152 BCE) there is evidence of at least five separate types of wine being produced in the Nile delta region. A study of trace chemicals taken from five clay amphorae from the tomb of Tutenkhaman (1323 BCE) yield traces of white wine. Ancient Egypt was also an important early site for beer production in the pre-dynastic period (Geller, 1992). One of the most important and best-known ancient Egyptian archaeological sites is Hierakonpolis. This may have been the pre-dynastic capital of ancient Egypt, and is dated circa 3800–2980 BCE. It corresponds to the modern city of Nekhen. This site was large, around 1.5 km², and comprises of a complex of buildings, temples and cemeteries; within this complex there are two parallel rows of vats for brewing. Residues found in these vats contained several stable carboxylic acids, which are organic compounds and the fermentation by-products derived from uncarbonised wheat and barley, as found in beer and grapes. The scale of beer production at this site is thought to have been up to 1100 litres per day. Beer formed an important part of the ancient Egyptian diet, as well as having a place in funeral and burial ceremonies of the king.

Joffe *et al.* (1998), in their review 'Alcohol and social complexity in ancient western Asia', provide a detailed description of the manufacture and trade of wine and beer, and of their political importance throughout the ancient Near East. Mazzoni (1998) emphasised the high calorific value of alcoholic drinks, combined with their ease of storage for long periods, which made them valuable commodities. The manufacture and storage of beer were usually under the control of the monarch or the government. Even though alcoholic drinks were essentially food stuffs in the ancient world, their psycho-stimulant effects were well known, giving them a special place in religious festivals as well as in the world of commerce.

In the Levant, an area just to the north of Israel, jars containing traces of wine and olive oil have been found in the excavations in the area of Mt Hermon (southern Lebanon) dating to the early Bronze Age (circa 3500–2300 BCE) and much of this wine was exported to Egypt. Olive oil production depends on the steady growth and the nurturing of olive trees for at least 12 years. A vineyard can take three to five years to mature. The discovery of these agricultural commodities at several archaeological sites in southern Lebanon and Syria suggests there would have been a settled agrarian village life in this area, as opposed to a purely nomadic existence, which is often mentioned in the Old Testament. Thus, there were probably stable agricultural communities inhabiting the Levant, an area just to the north of Israel and Jordan, from at least the third millennium BCE onwards.

Thus long before the pre-exilic biblical era (1100–586 BCE) there is ample evidence from archaeological and other sources for both viticulture and beer production in the region now thought to have been ancient Israel. Wine production had probably been going on for at least one millennium (i.e. an era of about 40 generations) and possibly even for two millennia before Old Testament times. The ancient Israelites probably added little new to knowledge of the day – but they were the first to write about it in detail, describing the place of wine in an ancient society, and its role in religious festivals and social life, as well as recording the high frequency of drunkenness and detailing some of the more devastating consequences of alcoholism.

Wine continues to play an important role in Jewish religious festivals today. After the Sabbath service, a small glass of wine is drunk to celebrate the holy day of rest and this is known as the Kiddush. Wine is also drunk when the candles are lit in the Havdalah service on Friday night to welcome in the Sabbath bride. Four glasses of wine are drunk at the Passover Seder service, two cups are drunk at weddings and one at circumcisions. A cup of wine is offered to the bereaved after the funeral at the 'meal of comfort'. Originally this was ten glasses of wine to which four more had been added, but in modern times this practice has been discontinued. Before the drinking of wine, a blessing is recited, which does not actually mention wine but gives thanks for the fruit of the vine, and this dates to Old Testament times, when a person's vineyard was regarded as a symbol of his wealth. Wine drinking in moderation is seen as a positive and life enhancing and when drinking wine in company it is customary to wish one another *Le-hayyim*, which means 'to life' (*Encyclopaedia Judaica*, 2nd edition, 2007).

However, on the negative side alcoholism is a common and serious condition today and both DSM-5 and ICD-10 recognise two conditions: alcohol abuse and alcohol dependence. The order of topics given in this chapter is as follows:

- general descriptions in the Old Testament of the problems associated with alcohol
- acute alcoholic intoxication (drunkenness, drunken vomiting, alcoholic stupor, coma and death)
- alcohol dependency and withdrawal
- alcohol, anger, violence and homicide
- alcohol, mood changes and depression
- alcohol and antisocial personality disorder
- alcoholic sleep disorder
- alcoholism in women
- alcohol and incest
- the teetotal sects – the Rechabites and the Nazirites
- drinking in pregnancy.

After a summary and conclusions, an appendix sets out how alcoholism is understood today.

## General descriptions of the problems associated with alcohol

There are two general but brief descriptions in the Old Testament of the problems associated with alcohol. The first is in the Book of Proverbs (23$^{29-35}$) and the second is in the Book of Sirach, which is included in Chapter 15. Both are in the Wisdom literature and are written in the form of an address from a father to a son and provide recognisable descriptions of the more salient features of alcoholism.

### *A lecture from father to son on the bad effects of wine: Proverbs 23$^{29-35}$*

23$^{29}$ Who has woe? Who has sorrow? Who has strife? Who has complaining? Who has wounds without cause? Who has redness of eyes?

$^{30}$ Those who linger late over wine, those who keep trying mixed wines.

$^{31}$ Do not look at wine when it is red, when it sparkles in the cup and goes down smoothly.

$^{32}$ At the last it bites like a serpent, and stings like an adder.

$^{33}$ Your eyes will see strange things and your mind utter perverse things.

$^{34}$ You will be like one who lies in the midst of the sea, like one who lies on the top of a mast.

$^{35}$ 'They struck me', you will say, 'but I was not hurt; they beat me, but I did not feel it. When shall I awake? I will seek another drink.

This passage describes several features of alcoholism. Alcoholic-induced mood disorder is described in the opening phrases 'Who has woe? Who has sorrow?' Alcoholic irritability is evident in 'Who has strife? Who has complaining?' The red eyes of the chronic alcoholic is noted: 'Who has redness of eyes?' And there is a suggestion of alcoholic visual hallucinosis: 'Your eyes will see strange things'. Talking out of character is also mentioned: 'your mind [will] utter perverse things'. The final verse describes the addictive nature of the wine and the phenomenon of morning drinking: 'When shall I awake? I will seek another drink.' Toy (1899) concludes that this brief passage in Proverbs gives 'the fullest and liveliest description of drunkenness in the Old Testament', but it is of interest to see what the great rabbis of the Talmud made of this passage.

### *Talmudic and Midrashic comments on Proverbs 23$^{29-35}$*

This passage has attracted much commentary in the Talmud. The brief and select account below draws on a book entitled *Mishlei* (Ginsburg and Weinberger, 2007), which gives the rabbinic commentary on the Book of Proverbs.

$^{29}$ Who has woe? Who has sorrow?

R. Yonah says the woe is a more of a heartfelt groan. The drunkard bewails the sins he commits under the influence of alcohol.

$^{29}$ Who has strife?

Midrash Mishlei writes that a drunk person tends to be argumentative and is liable to reveal people's secrets, thereby angering them and instigating conflict.

The Talmud (Pesachim 49a) lists the ill effects of the Torah scholar who parties too much.

[30] To those who linger over wine.

'A person who abandons Torah will turn into a drunkard. These are the people who are the first to arrive at the tavern and the last to leave' (Midrash, Vayikra Rabbah 12[1]).

[32] At the last it bites like a serpent.

R. Yonah writes, 'Initially the victim of the snake bite is not aware of being poisoned. Gradually however the venom spreads through his body until it kills him. In the same way a drinker initially thinks all is well; eventually, however, the drinking will take its toll.'

Midrash Mishlei explains that wine can be literally deadly, just like a serpent.

[33] Your eyes will see strange things.

Ralbag (1288–1344) writes that this verse is speaking of the hallucinations to which a confirmed drinker is susceptible.

[33] ... and your mind utter perverse things.

Bamidbar Rabah (ch. 102) says that once drinking has drawn a person to some sins he will eventually find himself committing other sins that once were foreign to him. R. Saadah Gaon says that the poison of wine so changes a person's nature and outlook that what had previously been alien to him now finds favour in his eyes. Both these rabbinical comments express in religious terminology the deterioration in character sometimes seen in alcoholism, or in modern psychiatric terminology the change of character for the worse as well as the association of alcoholism with a personality disorder.

[34] You will be like one who lies down in the midst of the sea, like one who lies on the top of a mast.

Radak and R. Ben Schlomo wrote: 'This verse compares a drunkard's dizziness to sea sickness. As though he were on a ship rising and plunging with the waves or balancing on top of the mast that is swaying to and fro, so the drunkard is unable to stand.' Rashi mentions suicidal ideation in this context: 'the verse compares the drunkard's irrationality to that of a suicidal person ready to throw himself into the sea or to lie down on top of the mast'.

[35] ... they beat me, but I did not feel it.

Ralbag writes that alcohol numbs the drunkard's senses to such an extent that if he is beaten he does not feel the pain. He exposes himself in an unseemly fashion to that to which he is oblivious (Midrash Tanchuma).

These knowledgeable comments from the rabbis indicate that such complications of heavy drinking were both common and well recognised even before the Middle Ages.

## The dispute of the three courtiers of King Darius: 1 Esdras 3 and 4

Alcohol is ubiquitous in most societies and probably always has been. It may also have profound effects on society which today can be quantified but in the ancient world could not but such big effects were observed and recorded in the idiom of the day.

The Book of 1 Esdras is in the apocrypha and is non-canonical for Jews and Protestants but is canonical for the Eastern Orthodox churches. It contains a story of a dispute between the three pages of King Darius, who all agree to write 'one thing that shall be strongest' and to let King Darius bestow great honour on him whose answer is the wisest. The first writes 'Wine'; the second, 'The King'; the third, 'Women, but above all things truth'. Then they explain their answers. The third, who is the victor, asks as a reward the return of the Jews to their homeland, and his name is given as Zerubbabel in I Esdras 4[13]. The speech of the first guard, who argued that wine was the strongest, is given below:

> 3[17] Then the first who had spoken of the strength of wine began and said:
> [18] 'Gentlemen, how is wine the strongest? It leads astray the minds of those who drink it. [19]It makes equal the mind of the king and the orphan, and the slave and the free, and the poor and the rich. [20] It turns every thought to feasting and mirth, and forgets all sorrow and debt. [21] It makes all hearts feel rich, forgets kings and satraps, and makes everyone talk in millions. [22] When people drink they forget to be friendly with friends and kindred, and before long they draw their swords. [23] And when they recover from wine they do not remember what they have done. [24] Gentleman, is not wine the strongest, since it forces men to do these things?' When he had said this he stopped speaking.

This parable shows that wine was seen as a major force for both good and bad by this Jewish writer in Persian society around the time of the rule of King Darius. Today we express the global and destructive effects of alcohol on society in a less amusing style but more in statistical terms of overall cost to the community, hospital admission rates, death rates and so forth. The overall burden of disease due to alcohol is immense. Thus Vonghia *et al.* (2008) estimated that alcohol and alcohol-related problems accounted for 6–8% of the gross national product of Italy. A study of the burden of disease in the USA estimated that alcohol accounted for 7.1% of all deaths and 4% of 'years lost to disability'. In a South African study, where the prevalence of alcoholism is particularly high, the community burden was mainly accounted for by interpersonal violence (39%), neuropsychiatric conditions (18%) and road traffic accidents (14%), and because up to 26% of women had alcoholism the burden due to foetal alcohol syndrome was also extremely high (18%) (Schneider *et al.*, 2007). The overall destructiveness of alcohol to whole communities is what drives the clergy, politicians and legislators to try to restrict its consumption, much in the same way as the prophets and scribes of the Old Testament railed against its use.

## *The poor prognosis of alcoholism*

There are three separate references in the OT to the poor long-term outcome of alcoholism. Two occur in Proverbs:

21[17]  Whoever loves pleasure will suffer want;
       whoever loves wine and oil will not be rich.

23[20]  Do not be among winebibbers,
       or among the gluttonous eaters of meat;
21     for the drunkard and the glutton will come to poverty,
       and drowsiness will clothe them with rags.

McKane (1970, p. 553) writes 'that the use of the phrase "wine and oil" is suggestive of a *simḥā*, or having a good time, but is used pejoratively here. Feasting and drinking are recipes for poverty, and the man who has a fondness for the extravagances of high living will always be short of money and is on his way to becoming a pauper'.

A third comment in the poor prognosis is given by Ben Sira in the Book of Sirach:

31[25]  Do not try to prove your strength by wine drinking
       for wine has destroyed many.

Ben Sira writes about the 'macho' quality sometimes found among alcoholics – competitions about who can drink the most alcohol, which appear to have occurred in the ancient world just as they do among young students today. He warns against this and adds his observation that alcohol has destroyed many people – an allusion to the increased mortality and morbidity and the general destructiveness of alcohol.

These Old Testament speculations about the prognosis of alcoholism are confirmed by everyday observations as well as more formal and long-term studies today. Thus alcoholism is often a lifelong disorder. Edwards *et al.* (1997), summarising previous work, estimated that if 100 patients aged 45 with alcohol dependence were followed for 20 years, then about 40% would have died by the 20th anniversary, and of the remainder 30% would have attained abstinence but 30% would still be drinking.

## *An admonition against drunkenness in the Book of Tobit*

The Book of Tobit is part of the Apocrypha. The life of Tobit, a pious Israelite, is described is more fully Chapter 7. Here, it is sufficient to note a brief mention of drunkenness:

4[15]   And what you hate, do not do to anyone.
       Do not drink wine to excess or let drunkenness go with you on your way.

## Acute alcoholic intoxication – drunkenness

Acute alcoholic intoxication, or drunkenness as it is more commonly known, is a common condition, not usually deemed to be a medical disorder;

indeed, drunkards are regularly ejected from the accident and emergency departments of most hospitals. However, acute intoxication involves more than simply drunkenness and can be a clinically dangerous condition and so it is included as a separate DSM-5 disorder; the main criteria for acute intoxication are:

A  recent ingestion of alcohol
B  clinically significant maladaptive behavioural or psychological changes (e.g. inappropriate sexual or aggressive behaviour, mood lability, impaired judgement, impaired social or occupational function) that developed during or shortly after ingestion of alcohol
C  one (or more) of the following signs developing during or shortly after alcohol use:
   1. slurred speech
   2. incoordination
   3. unsteady gait
   4. nystagmus
   5. impairment in attention or memory
   6. stupor or coma.

The above symptoms are all fairly frequent after acute intoxication and the common term 'drunken' is used to describe such states both today and in the Old Testament. Several of the symptoms described above are also covered in the OT and will be briefly reviewed here.

The Hebrew word for being drunk is *shākār,* which also means strong drink or beer. Three well known biblical characters – King Ben-Haddad (discussed immediately below), Nabal (see pages 520–522) and Noah (see page 503) – are described as being drunk, but the term is widely used and is cited in a further 15 places in the Old Testament.

## King Ben-Haddad

King Ben-Haddad of Aram is reported to be drunk together with his soldiers in 1 Kings.

> 20[16] They went out at noon, while Ben-Hadad was drinking himself drunk in the booths, he and the 32 kings allied with him.

Gray (1963) explains that Ben-Haddad was the 'King of the Aramaeans' whose capital was Damascus, while Ben-Haddad refers to the title of the King of Damascus, so all the kings of Aramaea in the Old Testament are called Ben-Haddad. The 32 kings referred to are therefore thought to be the tribal leaders in the region of Damascus. Ben-Haddad must have started his drinking early in the morning to have been so drunk by noon. A stele found in Aleppo in northern Syria has the Aramaic form of the name Ben-Haddad on it, but its original date is uncertain.

In the phrase 'drunk in the booths' the Hebrew word *Sūkkot* refers to shelters in the fields which may have been military bivouacs. However, today *Sūkkot* refers to the harvest festival and corresponds to the small out-houses decked in fruits and plants where prayers are said during the Jewish harvest festival of Sukkoth in the autumn. Yadin (1955), an Israeli general and later an archaeologist, suggests that the use of the term *Sūkkoth* in this verse refers to the proper name of the town of Succoth in the Jordan Valley where Ben-Haddad had set up his military camp.

## Drunken ataxia (unsteadiness)

People who drink to excess are commonly observed to stagger and the medical term for this is ataxia. It is possible that some of those described in the Old Testament as staggering around the city are brain damaged. There are references to drunken ataxia in Psalms and in Jeremiah, and a further four references to staggering under the influence of alcohol in Isaiah ($19^{14}$; $28^7$; $29^9$; $51^{17}$) – Isaiah seems to have been personally distressed at the sight of his fellow citizens staggering around the town. Priests were banned from drinking (Lev. $10^9$) and in the verse below from Isaiah he is critical of the drunken staggering and corrupt priests who have broken their vows not to drink:

$28^7$    These also reel with wine
        and stagger with strong drink
        The priest and the prophet reel with strong drink,
        they are confused with wine,
        they stagger with strong drink;

In a later passage Isaiah likens the weak sleepy inhabitants of Jerusalem to drunkards:

$51^{17}$    Rouse yourself, rouse yourself!
        Stand up, O Jerusalem,
        you who have drunk at the hand of the Lord
        the cup of his wrath,
        who have drunk to the dregs
        the bowl of staggering.

The metaphor of 'cup of wrath' is further explained on pages 524–525 but here the bowl is associated with another side-effect of alcohol – staggering.

The reference to staggering in Psalms is in Psalm 60:

$60^3$    You who have made your people suffer hard things;
        you have given us wine to drink that made us reel.

It all seems to be God's fault, as he has given the people the wine which causes all the trouble!

Staggering is also described in Psalm 107. This is a prayer of thanksgiving and starts with thanking God for his love and his powers of redemption; it then lists several groups that he has helped. Among these are the brave seamen who sail the seas for trade, but in the storms at sea they reel around like drunkards:

21    Some went down to the sea in ships
        doing business on the mighty waters;
...

26　　They mounted up to heaven, they went down to the depths;
　　　their courage melted away in their calamity;
27　　*they reeled and staggered like drunkards,*
　　　and were at their wits' end.
28　　Then they cried to the Lord in their trouble,
　　　and he brought them out from their distress;
29　　he made the storm be still.

Kraus (1989) explains these verses:

> another group of people obligated to give thanks to the Lord are of those
> sailors who are spared from a shipwreck. They are the merchants who sailed
> the sea, most likely from Phoenician ports. The theological message is also
> implicit. The violent sea obeys the orders of God. The wind is sent out like a
> messenger and whips up the waves. In 26 and 27 there is a vivid description
> of how the ship is tossed to and fro and is like a plaything of the waves and all
> the courage of the sailors is gone. When in such distress the seamen who had
> already surrendered to death, now cry for help to Yahweh, lived on to see the
> intervention of God who stilled the storm and the waves. The psalm attests to
> the omnipotent power of God, who can both cause the storm but then still it
> and so save the lives of the seamen....

The psychiatry here is more straightforward: the wind and storms at sea
make the ship and its sailors toss around and the metaphor of the staggering
drunkard is used to convey the unsteadiness of the ship in a storm.

Staggering in alcoholics may be due to acute intoxication, but is more
commonly an effect of chronic alcoholism. It may be due to acute on chronic
cerebellar damage. The staggering drunkard is repeatedly mentioned in the
Old Testament, but all these complications are the result of prolonged heavy
drinking and this points to at the very least, a moderate frequency of chronic
alcoholism in ancient Israel.

Both Isaiah and Jeremiah also give repeated references to the drunkard
who staggers around the town, perhaps also vomiting (on which, see
below), being generally out of control and in a deteriorated state. The folly
of the nation's leadership, the corruption and sinfulness of the people are
all compared to this degenerate character, who is a figure of contempt.
Such a picture is consistent with people sometimes nowadays referred to as
'skid row alcoholics', who can be found in every major city. They are well
described by Edwards *et al.* (1997):

> These people usually have a socially downhill path, often ending up as
> homeless vagrants, lacking any sort of kinship or family support; they may
> become involved in petty criminality and have poor nutrition and subsist by
> begging, or may be found sleeping rough or under railway bridges. They
> almost certainly have a very high mortality.

Such a deteriorated group has probably always existed, especially in cities,
and so it is no surprise that their drunken behaviours, frailty and vulnerability were noted by the Old Testament writers.

*Poor judgement, cognitive impairment and confusion*

Poor judgement, cognitive impairment and confusion are symptoms both of acute intoxication and of chronic alcoholism, the latter through brain damage. In a small number of alcoholics, a dementing picture emerges over the long term. There are several references to this in the Old Testament, including Hosea 4:

11      Wine and new wine
        take away the understanding

A further example is Isaiah 28

7       These also reel with wine
        and stagger with strong drink;
        the priest and the prophet reel with strong drink,
        they are confused with wine,
        they stagger with strong drink;
        they err in vision,
        they stumble in giving judgement.

These two verses are self-explanatory in portraying the impairment of judgement due to alcohol. A further passage from Isaiah is a pungent critique of the foreign policies of Egypt, which at that time held hegemony over Israel. Isaiah likens the foolishness and confused policies of the Egyptian political leaders to the confusion of an alcoholic:

19[13] The princes of Zoan have become fools, and the princes of Memphis are deluded; those who are the cornerstones of its tribes have led Egypt astray. [14] The Lord has poured into them a spirit of confusion; and they have made Egypt stagger in all its doings as a drunkard staggers around in vomit.

The meaning of the passage is clear: the Egyptian princes do not seem to know what they are doing. Isaiah is scathing in his contempt for them. Zoan (Egyptian Za'ame), in the Nile Delta, has been excavated and was at the time a royal city. Memphis was the Greek name for the capital of ancient Egypt and lies about 25 km south of Cairo.

*Vomiting associated with acute intoxication*

Two references to alcoholic vomiting appear in Isaiah. One has been quoted above – Isa. 19[14], 'as a drunkard staggers around in vomit'. The other is in Isaiah 28:

7 ... they are confused with wine....
8 All tables are covered with filthy vomit;
no place is clean.

Alcoholic vomiting is also described in Jeremiah:

25[27] Then you shall say to them, Thus says the Lord of hosts, the God of Israel: Drink, get drunk and vomit, fall and rise no more, because of the sword that I am sending among you.

Vomiting is usually a sign of serious intoxication and may indicate high blood levels of alcohol (Vonghia *et al.*, 2008). Edwards *et al.* (1997) write that vomiting is a potentially fatal symptom of alcoholism:

> self-neglect and the associated way of life, particularly among skid row drinkers, are also important factors predisposing to infections. Because heavy drinkers may both vomit and go into stupor they are prone to inhale material into their lungs and hence develop lung abscesses and bronchial infections. The aspiration of vomit is sometimes fatal.

## *Alcoholic stupor*

In Isaiah 29[5-9], a complicated passage, the leaders who make the wrong political judgements behave as if they are in a stupor. However, Isaiah pointedly remarks that this particular stupor is *not due to wine* – with the implication that he and his readership were well aware of wine-induced stupor.

29[8]   Just as when a hungry person dreams of eating
        and wakes up all hungry,
        or a thirsty person dreams of drinking
        and wakes up faint, still thirsty, ...
9       *Stupefy yourselves and be in a stupor*
        *blind yourself and be blind!*
        *Be drunk, but not from strong drink!*
10      For the lord has poured out upon you
        a spirit of deep sleep;
        he has closed off your eyes, you prophets,
        and covered your heads, you seers.

Kaiser (1974) suggests this passage was written sometime between 742 and 722 BCE. At that time, Judah and Israel were two small vassal states lying between Egypt to the south and the Great Assyrian Empire to the north. Political survival and independence were possible only by making alliances with one or the other of these great empires and in this passage Isaiah is critical of the policy of making alliances with Egypt rather than Assyria, which at that time was in the ascendant. Some biblical scholars suggest that the cataclysmic destruction which Isaiah seems to prophesise here refers to the destruction of the Northern Kingdom of Israel in 722 BCE, but others believe it refers to the later destruction of Jerusalem, in 586 BCE.

However, the people of Jerusalem do not believe the prophet and Kaiser (pp. 270–271) continues:

> Only when the monstrous event which radically alters history comes upon them will they recognise in terror the truth of his words.... The rulers of Jerusalem now regard the prophet with extreme condescension, and so when faced with his warning and threats, they give each other the knowing looks about such political ignorance but they will soon be stupefied in horror and then will stagger around like drunk men.... It is clearly Yahweh himself who has imposed upon them the spirit of deep sleep, an unconsciousness which excludes any awareness of anyone else....

The theology concerns the powers of Yahweh, and Isaiah uses alcoholic stupor as a metaphor. Israel's leaders are oblivious of the dangers: they are in a stupor, they stagger around like drunkards and go into a deep sleep. This is *not due to wine* but the result of their political ineptness. The metaphor Isaiah uses here is similar to the previous examples (Isaiah 19[13-14] – see above) where he uses alcoholic confusion and alcoholic stupor as metaphors to criticise the political folly of the day.

*Fatal alcoholic stupor in Jeremiah 51[39] and 51[57]*
Two verses in Jeremiah, chapter 51, refer to a permanent alcoholic sleep, presumably meaning an alcoholic death:

> 51[39] I will make them drunken, that they may rejoice, and sleep a perpetual sleep, and not wake, saith the Lord.                            (King James)

> 51[57] I will make her officials and her sages drunk, also her governors, her deputies, and her warriors; they shall keep a perpetual sleep and never wake, says the king, whose name is the Lord of hosts.                            (NRSV)

The passage then goes on to describe how the Lord will punish the Babylonians. The drink (administered by the Lord) has resulted in a 'perpetual sleep', which is presumably a fatal drunken stupor. To have composed such a verse Jeremiah must have observed or at least heard of people who died following a drunken excess, and he applies this observation as a metaphor about how Yahweh will punish Babylon and its officials.

## Alcoholic coma

Coma due to alcohol is a dangerous condition and may be fatal. Blood alcohol levels above 600 mg/l are usually fatal. The clinical picture is one of a decreased respiratory rate, interrupted breathing, decreased or absent reflexes, weakened pulse, dilatation of the pupils and urinary incontinence. However, fatalities arise not only because of the alcohol but also due to associated hypoglycaemia (low sugar levels), infections, head injuries and subdural haemorrhages, epileptic fits and post-ictal confusion, and a variety of blood electrolyte disturbances. Modern management entails clarifying the cause of the unconsciousness and instituting appropriate medical treatment. In biblical times there was no such treatment and so a fatal outcome may have been more common. Jeremiah mentions the fatal outcome twice, but his purpose was to describe the punishment that the Lord could bring on the leaders of Babylon rather than provide a health warning about the consequences of heavy drinking.

## Summary of the acute effects of alcoholic intoxication

Vonghia *et al.* (2008) provide an extensive review of the clinical features of acute alcoholic intoxication and attempt to correlate particular symptoms with blood alcohol levels.

Blood alcohol levels below 50 mg/l are usually taken to be compatible with social drinking; in many countries it is permissible to drive with blood

**Table 14.1** Symptoms of alcoholic intoxication, blood alcohol levels and biblical citations

| Symptoms of acute alcoholic intoxication | Blood alcohol levels (mg/l) | Biblical citation |
|---|---|---|
| Impairment in skills-based tasks | Less than 50 | |
| Increased talkativeness and relaxation (happiness) | 50–100 | Eccl. 9[7], 10[19]; Ps. 104[15]; Zech 10[7]; Sir. 31[28] |
| Altered perception of the environment | 100–200 | Isa. 28[7] |
| Ataxia (staggering) | | Isa. 19[14], 28[7], 51[17], 29[9]; Ps. 60[3]; Jer. 25[15] |
| Impaired judgement | | Hos. 4[11]; Isa. 19[14] |
| Mood changes | | Pr. 23[29]; Jer. 1[5]; Ez. 21[33]; Sir. 31[29]; Jer. 25[16] |
| Personality changes | | Pr. 20[1]; Ps. 75[8]; Sir. 31[30]; Pr. 4[17] |
| Behavioural changes | | Lam. 4[21]; Jer. 25[15]; Ps. 60[5], 78[65] |
| Slurred speech | | |
| Amnesia | 200–400 | |
| Hypothermia | | |
| Vomiting | | Isa. 19[14], 28[8]; Jer. 15[27] |
| Nausea | | Hos. 7[5] |
| Respiratory depression | Over 400 | |
| Coma | | Gen. 9[4] (deep sleep); Is. 29[9] |
| Death | | Jer. 51[39], 51[57] (fatal stupor) |

Adapted from Vonghia *et al.* (2008).

alcohol up to this level. Above 100 mg/l, mood and behavioural changes may occur. Coma and death can occur at levels above 400 mg/l. Table 14.1, which is adapted from Vonghia *et al.* (2008), lists key symptoms of acute alcohol intoxication, approximate blood levels, and the relevant biblical citations. The numerous biblical citations of these symptoms suggests that acute intoxication, from mild to severe degrees, was quite common in ancient Israel. For some of the biblical writers, especially the prophets, this was a matter of sufficient concern to record it in their religious writings.

## Alcohol dependency

Alcohol addiction is shown by morning drinking and continued daily drinking even when it is clear that the drinking is causing harm. There are three fairly clear references to the phenomena of dependence in the Old Testament (Isa. 5[1]; Prov. 23[35]; Sirach 31[30]) and a fourth, rather more obscure reference to repeated drinking on a daily basis (Isa. $56^{9-12}$). The most direct reference to dependence, with morning drinking, is in Proverbs:

| | | |
|---|---|---|
| $23^{35}$ | 'They struck me', you will say,<br>'but I was not hurt;<br>they beat me, but I did not feel it.<br>When shall I awake?<br>I will seek another drink.' | A reference to the drunkard's<br>insensitivity to pain<br><br><br>addictive behaviour |

This is repeated in ch. 35 of Proverbs:

$35^6$    When shall I awake? I will seek another drink.

## Rabbinic and Talmudic commentary

R. Yonah writes that the drinker looks forward to growing sober so that he may drink again.

A key feature of the dependency syndrome in both DSM-5 and ICD-10 is how alcoholics can think of nothing other but seeking out their next drink. Thus item 9 of DSM-5 on alcohol dependence states: 'A great deal of time is spent drinking or trying to obtain drinks or recovering from its effects'.

A tale in the Midrash (see Ginsburg and Weinberger, 2007) describes just how strictly alcoholics confine their thoughts to drinking. Thus Midrash Tanchuma (Parasha Shemini 11) relates the story of a man whose father would drink heavily and lie in the street and get called names by children, who pelted him with stones. His son was a very pious man and so provided his father with the best wines so that the father would not have to go out to the tavern to drink. One rainy day, the son saw another drunkard lying in the street as streams of water flowed over him and children threw stones onto him and otherwise abused him. He ran home and brought his father out to show his father the depths of degradation which drinking wine can lead to. The father then bent down to the drunkard and asked him, 'Where did you get that wine from?' The son protested: 'Father I brought you here to see this man's disgrace so that you would stop drinking'. But his father replied, 'My son, in my life I have no other pleasure but this'.

## Morning drinking and tolerance

Edwards *et al.* (1997, p. 38) in their description of alcoholic dependency write about morning drinking:

> some clues to the degree of a patient's dependence are often given by the small details they provide of the circumstances and timing of the first drink of the day, and their attitude towards it. If they get up, have a bath, dress and read the paper before that drink, then dependence is not very bad. A housewife who finishes her chores before having her first drink is at a different stage of dependence from the woman who is pouring whisky into her first cup of tea.

Isaiah ($5^{11}$) also mentions morning drinking:

*All you who rise early in the morning*
*in pursuit of strong drink,*
who linger in the evening
to be inflamed by wine.

Another central feature of dependency, known as tolerance, relates to the tendency to increase the amount of alcohol consumed and this is mentioned in Sirach (31$^{30}$):

more and more wine is a snare for the fool

The pleasure of drinking on a daily basis is also alluded to in Isaiah 56, in a polemic against the fecklessness of Israel's leaders. They should be alert and watch over their people like an observant sentinel to protect them from the danger of attacks from their hostile neighbours but instead they go off drinking.

56$^{10}$ Israel's sentinels are blind,
they are without knowledge;
they are all silent dogs
that cannot bark;
dreaming, lying down,
loving to slumber.

11 The dogs have a mighty appetite;
they never have enough.
The shepherds also have no understanding;
they have all turned to their own way,
to their own gain, one and all.

12 *'Come', they say, 'let us get wine;*
*let us fill ourselves with strong drink.*
*And tomorrow will be like today,*
*great beyond measure.*

In his explanation of this passage Oswalt (1986) writes:

Isaiah has written a polemic against those who are supposed to watch over the safety of Israel and how they fail in their duties as sentinels. They represent the authority of the day, the triad of the royalty, the priesthood and the prophets. But they are asleep on the job, so there is an open invitation to the wild animals and the dogs (symbolising hostile surrounding nations) to attack them. Israel's sentinels – the shepherds – do not appreciate the dangers of the situation. The narrator in verse 12, is one of these shepherds (symbolising political/religious leaders) and he asks those around to join him in drinking wine and strong drink (*sēkēr*). Instead of watching over Israel its leaders are found to be enjoying their heavy drinking , and *'tomorrow will be like today'*. Israel's leaders are not only oblivious to the risks to the nation, but on every new day they just continue to repeat their self-indulgent but pleasurable drinking behaviours.

## Alcoholic withdrawal phenomena

Withdrawal symptoms are central to the definition of the dependence syndrome. Symptoms may occur with the abrupt cessation of drinking and result in a severe withdrawal illness known as delirium tremens ('the DTs'). This is a dangerous condition with a high mortality. More commonly, withdrawal symptoms occur during the drinking. Thus as the drinker's blood alcohol levels fall, sometimes starting in the middle of the night or early morning, they are then 'self-treated' by further drinking. The spectrum of alcohol withdrawal symptoms is wide and includes tremor, nausea, sweating, sensitivity to sound (hyperacusis), ringing in the ears (tinnitus), itching, muscle cramps, mood disturbance (most commonly acute anxiety, but also acute depression, paranoia, anger), sleep disturbance, hallucinations, and epileptic seizures. Sometimes there is a full-blown picture of delirium tremens, comprising shaking accompanied by terrifying visual hallucinations. In the Old Testament there are verses describing visual hallucinosis, fever and sleep disturbance, and there is also an account of a possible case of fatal DTs.

## Alcoholic visual hallucinosis

The essence of this condition is that the patient fleetingly and suddenly experiences any one of a variety of perceptual disturbances. The classical visual hallucinations are vivid and horrifying and typically include snakes, rats and other small animals which may appear to attack the patient as they lie in bed (Edwards, 1997, pp. 80–82).

As quoted above, Proverbs (23[33]) has the verse: 'Your eyes will see strange things / Your mind will utter perverse things', where the latter part probably refers to the incoherent ramblings of a delirious subject with the DTs.

## The death of Nabal: was this a case of fatal delirium tremens?

In I Samuel the story is told of a wealthy farmer, Nabal, who dies about 10 days after a heavy drinking bout. His story is far better known because of the intercession of his wife, Abigail, with David. Thus David, in one of his many military journeys, encamps near Nabal's estate in Carmel and makes a request that Nabal send him and his troops some provisions. David and Abigail are the central characters of this tale and Nabal himself is no more than a minor player and so barely gains a mention in any of the theological commentaries. However, from a psychiatric perspective Nabal is of great interest because he is a known drinker. The word *Nabal* literally means a wine skin, but it may also signify a boorish person, or a personality disorder. Following a bout of heavy drinking, Abigail tells him that David is about to kill him. This makes him stop drinking, but then he becomes acutely depressed and dies 10 days later, a time interval consistent with a fatal outcome of the DTs.

> I Sam 25[2] There was a man in Maon, whose property was in Carmel. The man was very rich; he had three thousand sheep and a thousand goats. He was shearing his sheep in Carmel. [3] Now the name of this man was Nabal and the name of his wife was Abigail. The woman was clever and beautiful but the man was surly and mean. He was a Calebite.

The story goes on to describe how David and his men happened to be in the vicinity of Nabal's estate. On a feast day David sent his men to seek provisions from Nabal, who became angry at this request and said to David's servants, 'Who is this David? Who is this son of Jesse?'He refuses to give David any provisions. David feels insulted and orders his men to take up their swords. Fortunately, one of David's messenger's is able to warn Abigail about how dangerous it was to offend David, who at that time was an up-and-coming military leader. When Abigail hears this she quickly gathers the required provisions, some 200 loaves of bread, two skins of wine, five ready-dressed sheep and 200 cakes of figs; she hurriedly takes them over to David and begs forgiveness:

> 25[18] 'My lord, do not take seriously this ill-natured fellow Nabal; for as is his name so is he. Nabal is his name and folly is with him, but I your servant did not see the young men of the lord you sent.

David then thanks Abigail and then a few verses of religious importance follow:

> 25[32] Blessed be the Lord, the God of Israel who sent you to me today. [33] Blessed be your good sense, and blessed be you who have kept me today from blood-guilt and from avenging myself by my own hand. [34] For as surely as the Lord the God of Israel lives, who has restrained me from hurting you, unless you had hurried and come to meet me, truly by moving there would not have been much left to Nabal as much as one male. [35] Then David received from her hand what she had brought him; he said to her 'go up to your house; see, I have granted your petition'.

P. J. Macarter (1980) in his commentary on this tale writes that the central character of this drama is now David and the theology revolves around him. Thus although David is sorely tempted to take the law into his own hands and murder Nabal for his insulting behaviour, he is diverted from this path by Abigail. Had David committed such a murder he would have been stained with blood-guilt, which would have rendered him unfit to be the King of Israel. And if David had not become King of Israel, then the later Davidic dynasty would not have come about and the history of Israel might have been very different.

It is, however, only the finale of this story that has any psychiatric significance:

> 25[36] Abigail came to Nabal; he was holding a feast in his house, like the feast of a king. Nabal's heart was merry within him for he was very drunk; so she told him nothing at all until the morning light. [37] In the morning when the wine had gone out of Nabal, his wife told him these things and his heart died within him; he became like a stone. [38] About ten days later the Lord struck Nabal and he died.

The narrator describes the time sequence of events very clearly. Nabal is a known drinker. He drinks especially heavily at the feast and becomes *merry with drink*. He *abruptly stops drinking* and is then given some bad news by his wife which makes him *acutely depressed* ('his heart died within him'; 'he became like a stone') and *ten days after his last drink he suddenly dies*.

Two significant medical phenomena occur after he stops drinking. First there is an abrupt change of mood. Thus from previously 'being merry' his heart has become like a stone and this is suggestive of an acute depressive mood. Secondly, there is his sudden unexpected death. The cause of death is unexplained (as suggested by its attribution to God). However, when a heavy drinker stops drinking he gets an alcohol withdrawal syndrome, which untreated has a mortality of around 20%.

The diagnosis here is of sudden death during alcohol withdrawal. In the days before treatment for alcohol withdrawal, 5–15% of all patients died of the DTs but nowadays, with the use of tapering benzodiazepine withdrawal regimes, the mortality is very low. In ancient Israel, death during acute withdrawal may have been much more common.

## Sudden death in alcoholism

The mortality of alcoholics is high. A survey of the problem by Lilhall and Aberry (1987) found these deaths occurred most commonly in the third to the fifth decades of life and the only finding at autopsy was a fatty liver. Blood alcohol levels measured post-mortem were generally low and it is thought that the deaths occurred mainly during an alcohol withdrawal phase as a result of a cardiac arrhythmia (a disturbance in heart rhythms). Binge drinking may cause sudden death among those with a pre-existing coronary artery disease when the alcohol triggers a fatal heart attack; more rarely, drinking can cause an arrhythmia in someone with a pre-existing cardio-myopathy, which itself can be caused by alcoholism.

The biblical phrasing 'The Lord struck Nabal' suggests his death was due to natural causes and is one of the very few general medical complications of alcoholism to gain a mention in the Bible. The narrator does not seem to make any connection between Nabal's abrupt cessation of drinking and his sudden death ten days later, indicating there was no knowledge of the effects of alcohol withdrawal at that time.

## Alcohol-related fever or body heat

> Hosea 7[5] On the day of our king the officials became sick with the heat of the wine.

Anderson and Freedman (1980, p. 458) commenting on this verse state:

> the heat of the wine may simply describe the psychological–physiological effect of wine on the body. This heat does not seem to be the same as the oven heat of the assassin's rage.

A more comprehensive account of Hosea 7[1-7] is given in further on in this chapter (see pages 527–529).

Patients who are sweating and feverish will sometimes remove their clothing and a possible example getting undressed because of drink is given in Lamentations 4[21]:

> but to you also the cup shall pass
> You shall *become drunk and strip yourself bare.*

Renkama (1998) writes:

> the image of drinking a cup of (poisoned) wine is used metaphorically in a number of pre-exilic and prophetic texts for the endurance of Yahweh's judgment, the effects of wine representing (metaphorically) the effect of Yahweh's punitive judgment. Drunkenness brings a loss of physical and mental self-control and leads a person to behave like a fool. Increased body temperature can lead a person to strip naked and expose him/herself to ridicule and ultimate vulnerability in the eyes of the enemy.

An increase of body temperature with associated sweating can occur both directly due to alcohol-induced opening up of the blood vessels (vasodilation) as well as in states of severe alcohol withdrawal (the DTs). Fevers are also more likely to occur as a result of infections such as pneumonia, which are common in alcoholism. Body temperatures could not be measured in the ancient world but 'hotness' of the body could be observed. Biblical scholars have interpreted both Hosea 7[5] and Lamentations 4[21] as suggesting the hotness is due to effects of the alcohol.

## Headache

Headache is a common symptom of withdrawal, and is most frequent on the day after a drinking bout, when it presents as a 'hangover'. There is a reference to alcohol-induced headache in the Book of Sirach:

31[29] Headache wormwood and disgrace
is wine drunk amid anger and strife.

This version is in the translation of Skehan (1987) but the NRSV translation does not mention headache. Original Hebrew versions of the book of Ben Sira are hard to come by and the oldest Hebrew version is thought to be a manuscript from the Cairo Genizah (see page 561) but it is incomplete.

## Alcohol, anger, violence and homicide in the Old Testament

There are strong associations between alcohol and anger, and also between alcohol and violence, and these are clinically important today. Almost certainly they were known during the Old Testament era and were probably troublesome at the time, as evidenced by the numerous references to alcoholic anger and violence in the Bible. Some of the references to alcoholic anger are direct and obvious but in other instances the allusion to alcoholic violence is more obscure and metaphorical.

A good example of the association between drink and violence is given in Proverbs 20[1]:

> Wine is a mocker, strong drink a brawler
> and who ever is led astray is not wise.

Waltke (2005, p. 126) writes:

> In the first line of this verse the intoxicants, which are wine and strong drink, usually signifying beer, are personified as villains. This literary mechanism is to

warn the son (who is the focus of the lecture) that the drink destroys wisdom and life. Their personification represents liquor's bad characteristics and bring to the fore its danger of transforming people into the failed types that mock at virtue and behave in a turbulent manner.

As Waltke notes, the word *Sēkār* means 'strong drink' but also means beer, and it seems as if beer-drinking brawls are not just a problem of 21st-century Britain, but may have been equally troublesome in ancient Israel.

Isaiah also describes how wine can inflame people:

5[11] All you who rise early in the morning in pursuit of strong drink who linger in the evening to be inflamed by wine.

## *Alcoholism, anger and the cup of wrath*

As well as direct references to the association between anger and drink there are important indirect, metaphorical references to this association – in particular, the 'cup of wrath'. This phrase appears in several places in the Old Testament but underlying each reference is an association between the drinking of wine, a cup and anger. Usually, it is the Lord who makes either the Israelites or their enemies drink from the 'cup of wrath', and the biblical narrators use this metaphor to show just how terrifying the anger of the Lord can be. That is, God's anger can even be as bad as the anger of a drunken alcoholic. A good example of this metaphor is given in Jeremiah, here quoted in the King James version:

25[15]  For thus saith the Lord God of Israel unto me:
        take this wine cup of this fury at my hand
        and cause all the nations to whom I said it to drink it
[16]      And they shall drink, and be moved, and be mad
        because of the sword that I will send among them.

The passage continues to list most of Israel's neighbours whose kings will become intoxicated from drinking from the cup of wrath. The anger is the Lord's, and the destruction will be violent – by the sword (after Bright, 1965). However, the purpose of this passage was not to describe alcoholism or alcoholic violence; rather, it was a theological tract about how nations destroy each other and it is God who is behind all this. Jeremiah uses the metaphor of the 'cup of wrath' to convey just how destructive and violent these events will be. Verse 16 is noteworthy as it has the phrase 'they shall drink and stagger and be mad' – with the clear implication that it is the drink that has made them go insane, indicating that a link between alcohol and madness was well understood at the time.

A further prophetic reference to the cup of wrath is given in Isaiah

51[17]  Rouse yourself, rouse yourself!
        Stand up, O Jerusalem,
        you who have drunk at the hand of the Lord
        the cup of his wrath,
        who have drunk to the dregs
        the bowl of staggering.

A very different explanation for the cup of wrath is suggested by Mackenzie (1968, pp. 123–128). He writes:

> The cup of Yahweh's anger is a fairly common prophetic image. Possibly the figure may be based on the practice of giving the condemned criminal (presumably before an execution) an intoxicating beverage as occurs in both ancient and more recent times but the figure does not suggest this. It is the cup itself which is the punishment. Intoxicating beverages of unusual strength or stronger than the tolerance of the drinker will cause reeling and staggering; these are the symptoms associated with the cup of wrath.

Mackenzie seems to be implying that the association of the cup of wrath (anger due to drink) is to the reeling and staggering (ataxia due to the drink). The phrase is also mentioned in Ezek. 23$^{32-34}$, Hab. 2$^{16}$ and Lam. 4$^{21}$, suggesting this association was commonly known at the time. Holladay (1986a, p. 673) writes 'All who drink from the cup undergo judgment'. It is possible that the image of the cup of wrath is pre-Israelite and he quotes Dahood, an expert on Phoenician-Ugaritic culture, who cites a painted vase from the Ras Shamra collection of pottery depicting the ancient Ugaritic god El with such a cup in his hand. This pottery is dated around 1400 BCE, which pre-dates Israelite society by at least 400 years, implying that knowledge of the association between alcoholic drinks and anger may have been a part of popular folklore long before biblical times.

The use of an image of the drinking vessel to convey the notion of alcoholism is still current today; for instance, a person may have 'drunk too many glasses' and being injured in an alcoholic pub brawl is sometimes called 'being glassed'. A drinker may be 'on the bottle' or be 'canned', but in the Old Testament, especially in the writings of the prophets, the cup from which the wine was drunk was also imbued with the quality of anger – the cup of wrath.

## The association between alcohol and violence

Pr. 4$^{15}$ For they eat the bread of wickedness and drink the wine of violence.

The scribes of ancient Israel, particularly the writers of Proverbs and the prophets, were troubled by the problem of alcoholic violence. Later biblical redactors over the next several hundred years had the task of editing these great works and chose to retain the verses which recorded drinking and violence, perhaps because they resonated with a truth that every later generation witness themselves, and so it may be helpful to see how the problem is viewed today.

Data from the US Department of Justice (1981) for a large prison offender population show that alcohol was a factor at the times of the offence in 39% of robberies, 57% of rapes, 61% of assaults and 53% of homicides. The prison data also showed alcohol was involved in 47% of burglaries and 46% of car thefts. Another survey based on the personal interviews of 12,000 prisoners found that drinking prior to the offence had occurred in 50% of property offences and 46% were alcohol related; of those who were drinking 60%

of the violent offenders and 68% of the property offenders reported heavy drinking prior to their offence.

Serious crimes leading to prolonged imprisonment are relatively infrequent but more minor assaults are much more common and are rather more likely to be a worry for the average citizen than single one-off major felonies. Pernanan (1991) studied the prevalence of such lesser assaults in the small Canadian town of Thunder Bay (population 112,000); he interviewed a representative sample of 933 men and women aged 20 or over. A total of 492 subjects, i.e. more than half, reported they had been victims of violence at some time since the age of 15. In around half of these episodes alcohol was involved in either the victim or the perpetrator or both. Men were more likely to be injured when their assailant had been drinking; women were at greater risk if their assailant was sober, but injury rates were higher when the assailant was judged to be drunk. Alcohol was more likely to be a factor when victim and assailant had no relationship (stranger violence), with alcohol being involved in 78% of these incidents in either the victim or the perpetrator, but in 36% of episodes of stranger violence both parties were drinking. Tavern violence, as might be expected, usually involved alcohol (80% of cases) and in these cases severe injuries were twice as frequent as in domestic violence.

We have no direct knowledge of the prevalence of either alcoholism or crime in ancient Israel, but the Old Testament provides plentiful references to both, indicating that they were common. However, repeatedly violent drunkards would have been a major challenge for the leaders of any society lacking a police force and prisons. Such a task fell to the priesthood in ancient Israel and so it should be no surprise that they also wrote about it.

While alcohol contributes to violence probably through disinhibition, the vast majority of the population do not become violent when they drink. It is thought alcohol results in violence only among those predisposed to violence or those with personality disorders. This may occur particularly in situations of conflict, where the alcohol releases the individual from normal inhibitions against violence. The notion of predisposition is discussed further on page 536 and also seems to have been recognised by Ben Sira (page 566).

## Alcohol and homicide

Alcohol plays an important role in homicide, with evidence of recent alcohol consumption often being found in either the victims or the perpetrators or both. This association was not explicitly recognised in the Old Testament, but two case histories are described which clearly document the involvement of alcohol in cases of homicide. The assassination of King Elah, who was drunk at the time, is described in I Kings 16; while the assassination of a group of unnamed judges is reported in a passage in Hosea 7, where both the victims and the perpetrators were probably intoxicated.

### The murder of King Elah

The Book of Kings records a period of great political instability in the Northern Kingdom of Israel after the reign of Jeroboam. Several kings are described, each having a relatively short reign and most meeting their end through a political assassination. Very few details are given about any of these monarchs apart from their name, who they were the son of, who they murdered to take over the throne, and finally who assassinated them. Two of these monarchs have histories that have some psychiatric interest. Elah, who was the son of King Baasha, reigned for two years and whilst he was in a vulnerable drunken state he was murdered by his servant Zimri:

> I Kings 16[8] In the twenty-sixth year of King Asa of Judah, Elah son of Baasha began to reign over Israel in Tirza: he reigned for two years. [9] But his servant Zimri, commander of half his chariots, conspired against him. When he was at Tirzah drinking himself drunk in the house of Arza ... [10] Zimri came in and struck him down and killed him, in the twenty-seventh year of King Asa of Judah, and succeeded him.

The episode describes the political assassination of a reigning monarch, who was drunk at the time, but the narrator does not link his murder to the vulnerable inebriated state of the victim. The assassin, Zimri, then ascended the throne but he had a reign of only six days and killed himself by arson in the royal palace (see Chapter 7, on suicide, page 246).

### The assassination of the court judges

A political assassination of the King and his judges, by an unidentified group of plotters, possibly from the priesthood, is described in Hosea 7. The episode involves a drunken feast, possibly including drugged or poisoned wine, culminating in an ambush and the assassination of the King and his courtiers, although the fact of the murders is never made explicit. A similar episode involving the aristocracy of Ephraim is also described in Isaiah 28, and it is thought that the same political event lies behind both passages (Anderson *et al.*, 1980, p. 448).

The historical background to this episode is described by Stuart (1987, pp. 116–117):

> Hosea chapter 7 describes the frantic, yet hopeless political intrigue of Ephraim centred around Samaria. It refers to the faithlessness of Israel, personal debauchery, and the passion for political intrigue, as well as their vulnerability in international affairs.... The setting of the passage is best related to the political instability of Samaria in the 8th century BCE. Since the fall of Jehu in 752 BCE, and with the assassination of Zechariah, three more kings, Shallum, Pekahiah and Pekah, were assassinated. In 733 BCE, Pekah was assassinated by Hosea ben Elah (not Hosea the prophet) who then reigned until 722 when the Northern Kingdom itself fell to Assyria.

The psychiatric interest in the story lies in the possibility that both the victims – the King and his courtiers as well as the perpetrators of this crime, described as 'mockers' (*lēsim*, or personality-disordered subjects) – were intoxicated by wine at the time of the offence. The King James translation of Hosea 7 is clearer than the NRSV, and so is used below. Nonetheless, the passage is tightly written and almost incomprehensible, and so as an aid to explaining its symbolism and meaning, as elsewhere I have placed some relevant biblical commentary (derived from Anderson et al., 1980) on the right-hand side of the page, opposite the relevant verse.

[7] When I would have healed Israel, then the iniquity of Ephraim was discovered, and the wickedness of Samaria: for they commit falsehood; and the thief cometh in, and the troop of robbers spoileth without.

The three states, Israel, Ephraim and Samaria, are all equally bad their falsehood, which probably refers to breaking of the covenant with Yahweh. The breaking in and banditry may be symbols for civil and social injustice.

[2] And they consider not in their hearts that I remember all their wickedness: now their own doings have beset them about; they are before my face.

A transitional verse before the next scene. Their crimes are in the open, without conscience or being hidden from God.

[3] They make the king glad with their wickedness, and the princes with their lies.

Attention shifts to the political leadership. Wickedness and lies probably refer to political intrigue, which is now commonplace.

[4] They are all adulterers, as an oven heated by the baker, who ceaseth from raising after he hath kneaded the dough, until it be leavened.

Adultery may refer to religious infidelity. The passions of the king and his plotting court officials are likened to the heat of the baker's oven. It is so hot that the baker need not tend the fire – so were Samaria's leaders. They had come to power through the heat of treachery.

[5] In the day of our king the princes have made him sick with bottles of wine; he stretched out his hand with scorners.

The king and officials are vomiting after drinking bottles of wine. Fuelled by alcohol, they entertain wickedness and drink with the scorners (Hebrew *Léşîm* denotes psychopaths). They will later be the assassins, and they drink together with the princes.

[6] For they have made ready their heart like an oven, whiles they lie in wait: their baker sleepeth all the night; in the morning it burneth as a flaming fire.

Asleep or awake they are never free from their passion for intrigue. Samaria's leaders are likened to the fire of the oven. Only when they are asleep does their frenzy abate, but as soon as they awake their murderous intentions will soon blaze up.

[7] They are all hot as an oven, and have devoured their judges; all their kings are fallen: there is none among them that calleth unto me.

The conspirators struck when they were all as hot as a furnace (i.e. angered by the wine). The word 'devoured', a continuation of the image of the fire, signals the political assassination of the unnamed judges and kings. Yahweh's comment on the event is that 'no one calleth unto me', which is taken to signify that no one protests about the palace violence or has any conscience about the killings.

The comments and explanations are after Anderson and Freedman (1980) and Stuart (1987). I have chosen to provide a detailed account of this passage because the psychiatry here is important, yet far from obvious. Essentially the passage describes the assassination of an unnamed king and his judges who were given wine by their courtiers and so are intoxicated while the perpetrators of the crime, the *léṣim*, share wine with the princes before they commit the assassination and so they too are also inflamed by drink. Hosea's aim was to highlight the depravity, political gangsterism and lack of respect for religion in Samaria immediately prior to the fall of the Northern Kingdom. It was never Hosea's purpose to draw attention to the common clinical scenario of inflamed drunken perpetrators murdering their vulnerable intoxicated victims, but crimes of this type remain common today, though more often take place in the pub rather than the royal palace. Such cases may comprise a significant portion of the workload of forensic psychiatrists and the courts.

## Alcohol and homicide: present-day understanding

Wolfgang and Strom (1956) provide a review of the pre-war literature on the topic and analysed all 621 homicides in Philadelphia between 1948 and 1952. Nearly two-thirds of the killings had taken place in the context of alcohol, usually with both parties found to be drinking. In New Jersey, Gibbens (1958) found that alcohol played a large part in crimes of homicide. In this series 30 out of the 235 perpetrators were chronic alcoholics, a figure replicated in a study of homicides in Iceland covering the period 1900–1979 (Gudjonsson and Petersson, 1982). Gillies (1976) reported from Scotland that around half of both the perpetrators and the victims had been drunk at the time of the crime, and that these drunken killers were otherwise 'psychiatrically normal'. These figures were confirmed in the National Confidential Enquiry into homicide, which found that in 1594 homicides 42% of perpetrators had a history of alcohol misuse and alcohol contributed to 39% of the homicides (Shaw *et al.*, 2006).

In the biblical examples quoted above all the murders were political assassinations but the drunkenness of the victims may have contributed to their demise. King Elah was drunk at the time of his murder and perhaps because of his drunkenness he was unable to defend himself. In the assassination at the royal court described by Hosea, both perpetrators and victims were inflamed by drink. The Bible reports on the lives and deaths only of important people of the day, but the sixth of the Ten Commandments gives a prohibition against murder, implying that death by homicide was probably also a risk for the more humble citizen as well.

## Family violence and alcohol: Jeremiah's parable of the wine jars

A parable in Jeremiah ch. 13 describes how Yahweh will make the people destroy themselves by smashing against each other while they are in a drunken state. Jeremiah says that Yahweh will do this because the people have been evil and unfaithful to him. Yahweh complains how the people never listen to him and as a consequence he will punish them by making them behave like drunken wine jars who crash into and destroy each other:

> 13[11] For as the loincloth clings to one's loins, so I made the whole house of Israel and the whole house of Judah cling to me, says the Lord, in order that they might be for me a people, a name, a praise, and a glory. But they would not listen. [12] You shall speak to them this word: Thus says the Lord, the God of Israel: Every wine jar shall be filled with wine. And they will say to you 'Do you think we do not know that every wine jar should be filled with wine?' [13] Then you shall say to them; Thus says the Lord: I am about to fill all the inhabitants of this land – the kings who sit on David's throne, the priests, the prophets, and all the inhabitants of Jerusalem – with drunkenness. [14] And I will dash them one against each other, *parents and children together*, says the Lord. I will not pity or spare or have compassion *when I destroy them*.

In verse 13 Jeremiah describes how the Lord will make the whole population become drunk; he continues in verse 14 to say they will be dashed against each other, specifically referring to parents and children, an image suggestive of aggression and violence within the family, and this will be to the point of complete destruction (?death). The Hebrew verb *nefetz* used here means 'to dash', but an even more violent meaning is given in Jeremiah 51[20-23], where *nefetz* is translated as 'to smash' and the word is repeated to describe how Yahweh will wield his war club, and will smash nations, smash men, smash women, smash children, and smash horses and farmers and so forth. The word *nefetz* thus carries connotations of uncontrolled and vindictive, highly destructive violence.

The King James version in verse 14 has 'fathers and sons' instead of 'parents and children', giving the verse a more male orientation. Holladay (1986b, p. 401) gives:

> 13[14] And I shall smash them, each against his brother, fathers and sons together, oracle of Yahweh. I shall not pity or spare them when I destroy them.

The passage alludes to the terrible force of Yahweh's anger. Many authors, from Jerome onwards, have commented that the Hebrew word for wine jars used here, *nabal* (also meaning wine skin), is sometimes used to describe a particular type of fool and, as noted (see page 398), a fool denotes someone who in modern psychiatric terminology may have a personality disorder.

The psychiatry is contained only in the last verse (14), where parents and children (fathers and sons) are all so drunk that they smash each other up; this suggests within-family or domestic violence due to alcohol. Jeremiah's purpose in these verses was religious and he wanted to convey just how angry Yahweh was because of Israel's faithlessness. He likens this anger to what seems to be domestic violence. Jeremiah may have wished to shock his readership by using the image of alcoholic domestic violence, a particularly horrific form of violence, but in so doing he must have assumed that his readers would also have been familiar with this family nightmare.

## Alcoholism and family violence

Violence within the family is a common problem, generally kept secret and until recent years attracted little attention from the caring professions. An early study of the problem in America (Strauss *et al.*, 1980) found that 16% of all married women surveyed reported violence in the previous year, and 28% reported a lifetime history of family violence. Marital violence is currently believed to affect around 4 million women annually in the USA, with around 1 million seeking emergency medical treatment in accident and emergency departments. A 1991 survey in the USA found 2.7 million children had been victims of assault, with alcohol making a significant contribution to this. The existence of alcoholic domestic violence would have been well known in such small tightly knit communities as ancient Israel. The majority of its population would have borne witness to such events, and some might also have been victims – even though they probably dared not speak about it. Jeremiah spoke of the dashing of 'fathers and sons' and so as well as parent–child violence he may also have been referring to alcoholic violence between brothers who were both drunk at the time. Hill (1992) examined a sub-group of nuclear families where at least two brothers had been hospitalised for alcoholism. Of the 29 families identified 20 (68%) of these alcoholic families had at least one or both brothers who had a diagnosis of antisocial behaviours, and in this sub-group *all the families* showed fighting behaviours between these alcoholic antisocial siblings.

Jeremiah's final phrase, 'I will not pity or spare or have compassion when I destroy them', seems to suggest a fatal outcome. Perhaps this was no more than a figure of speech to make his point, but alcoholic battery in domestic violence is commonly fatal, with two women being beaten to death every week in the UK. A Canadian study showed that 37% of all solved homicides were committed by family members. Killing between brothers (fratricide) is a rare crime but it is also known to be associated with alcoholism. Thus in the series of ten cases of fratricide reported by Bourget and Gagne (2006) six involved alcohol, with siblings being commonly 'drinking buddies', and the terminal event was usually triggered by a heated argument between the brothers. In this passage Jeremiah is writing about the magnitude of God's anger, which he compares to a case of alcoholic fratricide. Maybe he had witnessed such a case.

## Alcohol, mood changes and depression

As previously noted, alcoholism frequently occurs together with depression. The recognition of coexisting depression is important in determining the treatment and outcome of the alcoholism. There are four biblical references to depression with drinking, two of which also refer to depressed mood on alcohol withdrawal. One is in Ezekiel:

23³² You shall drink your sister's cup
deep and wide;
you shall be scorned and derided
it holds so much.
³³ You shall be *filled with drunkenness and sorrow.*
A cup of horror and desolation
is the cup of your sister Samaria.

These verses from part of Ezekiel's diatribe against the two sisters Ohalah and Oholibah. No reason is given for either the drunkenness or the sorrow: they just seem to occur together. So how did he come across the phrase 'drunkenness and sorrow'? It is unlikely that he just made it up from his imagination and there are two possible explanations: either he had encountered other drinkers who were weeping and depressed; alternatively he himself may have had personal experience of drinking and feeling miserable. We know that Ezekiel suffered from quite severe mood disorder himself, possibly a schizo-affective disorder, with both elated and mute depressive phases (see Chapter 8, page 345), and among patients of this type alcohol can sometimes bring out an underlying depression. Today patients with mood disorders will often self-medicate themselves with alcohol, to try to alleviate their depression, only to find their mood is considerably worsened by the alcohol. Did he compose this verse, basing it on his own personal experience of the effect of wine on his own mood?

A second description appears in Proverbs. The author here is the scribe lecturing his son on the harmful effects of alcohol. He places the sorrow (?depression) right at the opening of his lecture, where he says sorrow is found in 'those who linger late over wine':

23²⁹ *Who has woe? Who has sorrow*
Who has strife? Who has complaining?
Who has wounds without cause?
Who has redness of eyes?
³⁰ Those who linger late over wine.

Thirdly, the Book of Joel describes how a plague of locusts has destroyed the vineyards and so ruined the entire grape crop. This causes misery and depression to the local drunkards who will now be deprived of their regular supplies of wine:

1⁴ What the cutting locust left,
the swarming locust has eaten,
what the swarming locust has left,
the hopping locust has eaten,
and what the hopping locust has left
the destroying locust has eaten.
⁵ *Wake up, you drunkards, and weep
and wail,* all you wine-drinkers,

over the sweet wine
for it is cut off from your mouth.

The drunkards will be weeping and wailing and so probably in a low mood because the locusts have destroyed the grape crop and there will be no wine.

Finally, in 1 Samuel ($25^{36-37}$) Nabal was upset when his wife, Abigail, told him that David was about to kill him (this story is considered in more detail on pages 520–522 of this chapter). The language used in the Old Testament suggests Nabal experiences a dramatic change in mood soon before he dies. Thus 'Nabal's heart was merry within him, for he was very drunk', but later on, 'in the morning, when the wine was gone out of Nabal', 'his heart died within him: he became like a stone'. The narrator makes no link between the change in mood and the alcohol cessation, as we might do today.

## Psychiatric aspects of alcoholism and depression

In three out of these four episodes, the authors provide an understandable reason for the depression: in the case of Ezekiel it is the whoredom of Ohilobah; in the Book of Joel, it is because the locusts have destroyed the grape crop and there will be no wine; in the case of Nabal it is the bad news that his wife brings him. Only in the lecture on drink given in Proverbs is the sorrow attributed directly to the wine itself. Similarly, in the psychiatric clinic today, the vast majority of depressed alcoholic patients will attribute their depression to some quite plausible personal cause, such as a broken relationship or the loss of a job, while usually denying the role of alcohol. However, the depression associated with heavy drinking is often severe, with the patient's explanation usually insufficient to account for its severity.

A major epidemiological survey in America, the Epidemiological Catchment Area (ECA) survey, found that depression was present in 13.4% of those with an alcohol disorder, and the risk for depression was around double that for the general population (Regier, 1990). When looked at the other way round, it was found that around one in five of those with an alcohol disorder will also have depression. The rate, though, is much higher for people with bipolar disorder: around 40% of bipolars may have an associated alcohol disorder.

The miserable drunkard is a frequent visitor to the A&E department, the psychiatric clinic, the liver unit and a whole variety of other medical clinics. Diagnosing the depression separately may be important in assessing risks; for instance, the risk of suicide is far greater among alcoholics with depression and especially those with bipolar disorder. In some cases the depression itself can cause the alcoholism, which is then termed 'secondary alcoholism'. This type is more common in bipolar disorder. However, in the vast majority of cases it is the heavy drinking that has caused the depression and DSM-5 has a category called substance-induced mood disorder. The treating psychiatrist will usually need to establish which is the primary condition in order to determine the treatment plan. Although the Old Testament writers never formally recognised the association between alcohol and depression, they do at least record its presence in four separate case histories.

## Alcoholism and antisocial personality disorder (ASPD)

This is a very important association in clinical psychiatry. The ECA study in America (Regier, 1990) found that 14.3% of those with an alcohol disorder had associated antisocial personality disorder (ASPD). When the association was examined the other way, it was found that 73.6% of those diagnosed with ASPD also met criteria for alcohol abuse/dependence disorders, indicating there was a very substantial overlap between these conditions.

There are four possible references to an association between alcohol and personality disorder in the OT but, as with the depression, there is no evidence that this link was either acknowledged or understood at the time. In all four cases there is also a mention of anger and violence, which remains today the main problem of the combination of alcoholism with ASPD.

The latter part of Proverbs ch. 20, verse 1, is given slightly different meanings in the NRSV and Masoretic Text translations:

> Wine is a mocker, *strong drink a brawler.* (NRSV)
>
> Wine is a mocker, *strong drink is raging.* (Masoretic Text)

The Hebrew word for 'mocker' is *Lēs*, usually translated as a scoffer/ scorner or fool, denoting a category of personality disorder that today would correspond to a narcissistic/psychopathic type.

A second reference to the effect drink has on the fool (presumably also a personality disorder) is found in Sirach ($31^{30}$):

> Drunkenness increases the anger of a fool to his own hurt, reducing his strength and adding wounds.

The word *lēs*, for fool, is also used here. The drink seems to heighten the anger specifically for this character type. Such a pattern will be all too familiar to those working in the psychiatric services. Thus, when an already irascible type, such as those with ASPD, become disinhibited with drink they are far more likely to become aggressive, lose their temper and commit a violent offence. Most violent offences committed by people with personality disorder occur while they are under the influence of drink.

In the Book of Psalms there is mention of how wicked people drink:

$75^8$  For in the hand of the Lord there is a cup
with foaming wine, well mixed;
he will pour a draught from it,
and all the wicked of the earth
shall drain it down to the dregs.

The suggestion in this verse is that it is the 'wicked of the earth' who will drink the foaming wine. Until the more formal recognition of psychopathic and antisocial personality disorders in the 19th century, such character types were usually classed as 'wicked' and many lay people today would regard the psychopath as evil. In this verse the psalmist describes how the wicked like to drink 'foaming wine' down to the last dregs.

Finally, the word scoffers (*losesim*, plural of *lēs*) is also used in describing the alcohol fuelled assassination by the scoffers of the judges in Hosea 7[5-7] as discussed above (pages 527–529). These drunken assassins have ASPD and they commit a homicide.

Thus there are four possible references to an association between alcoholic violence and personality disorder in the OT but there is no evidence that this link was understood at the time.

## Alcoholic sleep disorder

Psalm 78 is one of the Psalms of Asaph and (after Psalm 119) is the second longest in the psalter. It describes the history of Israel not in any temporal or logical sequence, but in a series of examples and metaphors. Much of the psalm is thought to be a political and moral critique of the Northern Kingdom, which fell to the Assyrians in 722 BCE. Since there is no mention of the Babylonian exile (which took place in 586 BCE) it is thought to have been composed some time between these two catastrophes. Psalm 78 is neither about alcoholism nor sleep disorder but it has one reference to alcoholic sleep disorder. Thus verse 78[65] describes nocturnal arousal caused by alcohol withdrawal. The psalm likens the anger of God to that of a soldier who drinks wine and then wakes in the middle of the night in a disturbed state. He begins shouting and in his aroused and angry state 'puts his adversaries to rout', suggesting he may have killed someone:

78[65]   Then the Lord awoke as from sleep
         Like a warrior shouting because of wine.
[66]     He put his adversaries to rout;
         He put them to everlasting disgrace.

Weiser (1959), a German theologian, explains:

> Just as a strong man intoxicated by wine rises form sleep – a very daring picture – so God proceeds to perform new deeds. He carries on the *Heilsgeshichte* (social history) by letting it start from a different point in the course of events: as if it were a new creation.

Hossfeld and Zenger (1959) write:

> The two unusual images are applied to God: the sleeping God and the drunken warrior.... The ultimate theological message that the psalmist wishes to convey concerning God's anger is uncertain.

Soldiers in the ancient world may have been paid with free food and free wine – for example, among the provisions David seeks for his soldiers from Nabal are two skins of wine – and so drunkenness among soldiers may have been common. Traditions of paying the military with free alcohol continued right up until the early 20th century, when sailors of the English Navy received a free daily tot of rum, and so the sight of a drunken soldier may have been quite common in the ancient world.

## Violence during sleep

The phenomenon described in Psalm 78[65–66] of a drunken person waking in the middle of the night in an aroused and angry state is most likely due to the condition of alcohol-induced nocturnal confusional arousal. Alcohol has well known sleep-inducing effects. Early on in the night it reduces rapid eye movement (REM) sleep and slow-wave sleep; however, later on in the night, as the alcohol leaves the system, rebound effects occur: increased rebound REM sleep, increased dreaming and disturbing awakenings, with confusion and mood disturbance, which can occasionally result in violence. This is probably the phenomenon described here.

Mahawold and Schenck (2005, p. 961) include these phenomena among the parasomnias:

> These disorders comprise a spectrum ranging from confusional arousal (sleep drunkenness) to sleep walking and sleep talking and night terrors. Population surveys reveal a prevalence of around 3–4% for these disorders. Febrile illness, *alcohol*, prior sleep deprivation and emotional stress may trigger such arousals in susceptible individuals. Many of the medico-legal cases of sleep walking related violence have involved alcohol consumption in an individual prone to experience disorders of arousal. Automatic behaviour is sometimes seen in such arousals.

Verse 66 of this psalm describes how the soldier in his aroused state 'put his adversaries to rout', which suggests a serious act of violence during this arousal, and he has consigned them 'to everlasting disgrace', which implies that he may even have killed them. Such events can sometimes happen during nocturnal arousals, which can result in serious acts of violence, including homicides. The passage itself is about the wrath of God, which is so severe and unpredictable that the writer has likened it to the impulsive violence of a drunken soldier.

Some biblical commentators seem to have been aware that the type of violence depicted here was not of the normal pre-meditated type and so perhaps was excusable. Thus Spieckerman, quoted in Hossfeld and Zenger (1959, p. 299), writes:

> This makes the marginal theological statement sustainable, that the application of God's wrath to his whole people is only understandable *as a deed done in a destructive rage in a condition of reduced culpability.* (Emphasis added)

The status of crimes committed during nocturnal sleep arousal remains controversial but in some instances they can qualify for a legal defence of an automatism. Alcohol alone is insufficient for such a defence but usually there is a coexisting parasomnia (sleep walking, sleep talking, night terrors, etc.) and then a crime. However, violence committed during the nocturnal arousal qualifies for the defence of an automatism. This is because during an automatism subjects are unaware of their actions, and there is no pre-meditation or criminal intent; in legal terminology, there is no *mens rea*.

Whatever the ultimate meaning of these two verses, it is clear that the psalmist must have witnessed someone, possibly a soldier, who experienced a violent episode during such a nocturnal confusional arousal. Shocked by what he saw, but lacking any modern knowledge of sleep medicine, he attributed the phenomenon to God and placed his observation in his psalm.

## Alcoholism in women

Although alcoholism has always been a predominantly male disorder, in recent years there has been a growing concern about the rising rates of alcoholism among women. Biblical and earlier references suggest that alcoholism has probably always been a problem, but the vast majority of references to alcohol in the Bible concern men. There are three references to women drinking in the Old Testament: Amos 4[1], Sirach 28[8] and 1 Sam 1[14].

First, Amos:

4[1]     Hear this word, you cows of Bashan
         who are on Mount Samaria
         who oppress the poor, who crush the needy
         who say to their husbands
         *bring me something to drink.*

The verse describes an insistent demand by women that their husbands bring home something to drink – suggesting at the very least they are regular drinkers. In their explanation of this passage Anderson and Freedman (1989) write that Bashan was a very fertile part of Judah and so the cows of Bashan would have been fat and well fed. Amos uses this metaphor as a critique of the corrupt wealthy leaders of Samaria and their wives and the prophet charges them with oppressing the poor.

Secondly, ch. 26 in the book of Sirach describes all the blessings that a good wife can bring to her husband but then lists some more difficult wives, who can bring heartache and sorrow to their husbands; in this context Ben Sira lists these as the jealous wife, the one who gives her husband a tongue lashing, the unchaste wife and the drunken wife.

26[8]     A drunken wife arouses great anger, she cannot hide her shame.

Thirdly, in 1 Samuel, Hannah, in her state of mutism and depression, gives the appearance of being drunk to the high priest Eli, but denies she has had anything to drink:

> 1[13] Hannah was praying silently; only her lips moved, but her voice was not hard; therefore Eli thought she was drunk. [14] So Eli said to her, '*How long will you make a drunken spectacle of yourself? Put away your wine.*' [15] But Hannah answered 'No my lord I am a woman deeply troubled; I have drunk neither wine nor strong drink but I have been pouring out my soul before the Lord.'

In this account Hannah only gives the appearance of being drunk, when in fact she is depressed. Hannah's tale is discussed in more detail on page 466–471, but the fact that Eli confuses a depressed mute woman with a woman who was drunk suggests that he encountered drunken women during his work as a priest.

## Pre-Israelite history of female drinking

Mazzoni (1998), an Italian anthropologist, describes the very early history of female wine drinking in early dynastic Egypt and in Akkadia (northern Mesopotamia) based on archaeological evidence appertaining to the second and third millennia BCE, long before Israel existed. Seals showing women drinking in erotic poses dating from the 3rd millennium BCE have been found at the Tell Halal site and also from a 3rd millennium Syrian site. Brewing was under the patronage of the Sumerian Goddess Ninkasi, while the drunken Mother Goddess Ninmah (Ninka) creates seven imperfect humans in the 'Enki and Ninmah' tale. This is a complicated story about children born with severe congenital abnormalities whom Nimnah concedes she cannot help and in the end admits defeat and says 'I am the one driven out of my house at my own beer-pouring party' (Raglan, 1936).

These texts date at least one millennium (possibly two millennia) prior to the biblical era of Israel. Anthropologists have suggested that alcohol had a complex role in the socio-economic life of ancient Near Eastern societies. Thus in strong patriarchal societies male drinking was common but female drinking was condemned and this contributed to the political marginalisation of women in these societies (Mazzoni, 1998). The tone of the few biblical entries on drinking amongst women seems to suggest the ancient Israelites, a highly patriarchal society, also strongly disapproved of female drinking. In the modern era there has been a reversion away from the strongly patriarchal societies of Victorian England and the attitude to women who drink is a less hostile. Perhaps this is one of the societal forces underlying the current rise in female alcoholism.

## Psychiatric aspects of female drinking

Alcoholism is more common in men than women in all societies where data are available, but the sex ratio for alcoholism varies widely. In the USA this ratio is around 6:1, in Puerto Rica 4.7:1. In some Asian countries where the prevalence of alcoholism is already low the proportion of women drinkers is extremely small; thus for South Korea the sex ratio is 20:1 and for Taiwan 29:1. For modern Israel the sex ratio for alcoholism is 14:1, and in the Middle East rates for alcoholism are generally fairly low. Given the paucity of references to female drinking in the OT as opposed to the frequent mention of male drunkenness and male alcoholic violence, it seems as if there was also a substantial male predominance for alcoholism in ancient Israel as well.

Epidemiological data today suggest that women may have a later onset of more severe drinking behaviours than men, because the interval between onset and first presentation for treatment is shorter for women, indicating they may have a more severe variant and follow a more rapidly downhill path. Thus the five-year mortality of female alcoholism is double that for men. Higher rates of affective disorder (depression, anxiety, panic disorder) are found in surveys of female alcoholics and this may explain the higher rates of suicide attempts and impulsive behaviours amongst female drinkers.

Young-onset female alcoholism is probably a more strongly genetically determined condition, and is a very serious disorder. This is because it occurs during the child-bearing years. Any infant these women may be carrying will be exposed to their mother's uncontrolled drinking and therefore at risk for the foetal alcohol spectrum group of disorders (see page 548). In addition, once alcoholic women have given birth, continued drinking by the mother usually precludes safe parenting, and children of alcoholic mothers often have to be removed from their care.

There are no references to alcoholic mothers in the OT but there appears to be some recognition in the Talmud (4th–8th centuries CE) that they may harm their offspring. Thus in Kallah Rabbah 1 ch. 52a, 'children begotten during a state of inebriety are mentally deficient'. Perhaps this is a very early reference to the brain damage now termed the foetal alcohol syndrome. It also continues to say that 'the children of a drunken woman will have children who will be thought of as though they were drunk'. In an era long before there was any formal recognition of either learning difficulties or conduct disorder in children, the notion of children behaving as if they were drunk may be a reasonable approximation to what we now term children with conduct disorder. There are similar passages in Nedarin 20b which mention that children conceived during intoxication will be among those who are guilty of a transgression. The Talmud, however, does not offer a medical explanation but only a moral one. Thus 'a drunken woman is a wanton woman, one unfaithful to her husband, and her children will take after her mother'.

## Alcoholism and prostitution

Among female alcoholics, sex is sometimes sold for alcohol. An even greater problem has arisen among female drug addicts, who sell sex directly for drugs, or for money to buy drugs. There is one reference to selling sex for wine in the Old Testament, in Joel:

> 3[3] They have divided my land and cast lots for my people and traded boys for prostitutes and sold girls for wine and traded it down.

Barton (2001, p. 99) explains Joel ch. 3 as a part of the prophetic polemic against foreign nations who had ravaged Israel, and this went back to at least the time of Amos. This verse describes Yahweh's judgement on other unnamed hostile nations and how cruelly they behaved towards the conquered Israel. They divided its land and scattered and enslaved its people. Casting lots over people is a sign of contempt – their fate is trivial-ised and then decided by a mere throw of the dice, and the Babylonians are said to have cast lots over the fate of Jerusalem. Joel 3[3] specifies the exact nature of the offences of the 'other' nations. In the ancient world the sale of their captives into slavery was the norm for the victorious power, but Joel singles out the fate of captive boys and girls who are traded for trivial sums – the price of a prostitute or a bottle of wine.

Crenshaw (1995, p. 176) writes that the phrase 'gave a boy for the price of a harlot' suggests that either the boy was sold for a very cheap price or that the boy was sold into prostitution. The parallel with the girl favours the explanation that sex was exchanged for the wine; the phrase 'traded it down' suggests that it was others who benefited from the trade rather than the girl herself and then they drank the wine.

The reference is thus not to an addicted prostitute, but only to a girl who trades sex for wine, a commodity, rather than trading sex for money. Nevertheless, the reference is historically important, as it is probably the earliest written record of sex being traded for an addictive substance rather than simply for money.

## Alcohol and incest

The Book of Genesis tells the story of Lot and his daughters, who were hiding in caves and fleeing from the city of Zoar, where they had recently sought refuge. Lot's daughters were childless and the Bible explains how the family/tribe were faced with extinction as there were no other suitable and available men. In this dire situation Lot's daughters were forced to take drastic action and they decided that as their father was the only available male they would have to seduce him to become pregnant and so carry on the tribe. To facilitate this they would have to get him drunk first.

> Gen. 19[30] Now Lot went up out of Zoar and settled in the hills with his two daughters for he was afraid to stay in Zoar; so he lived in a cave with his two daughters. [31] And the first-born said to the younger, 'Our father is old, and there is not a man on earth to come into us after the manner of all the world. [32] Come, let us make our father drink wine, and we will lie with him, so that we may preserve offspring through our father.' [33] So they made their father drink wine that night; and the first-born went in and lay with her father; he did not know when she lay down or when she rose. [34] On the next day, the first-born said to the younger, 'Look, I lay last night with my father; let him drink wine tonight also; then you go in and lie with him, so that we may preserve offspring through our father. [35] So they made their father drink wine that night also; and the younger rose and lay with him; and he did not know when she lay down or when she rose. [36] Thus both the daughters of Lot became pregnant by their father. [37] The first-born bore a son, and they named him Moab; he is the ancestor of the Moabites to this day. [38] The younger also bore a son and named him Ben-Ammi; he is the ancestor of the Ammonites to this day.

Lot was one of the early Israelite patriarchs, and the facts of the incest and the key role that alcohol placed are not in dispute. Religious tradition holds that the incest was a necessary act to ensure the survival of the people and therefore should not be criticised. However, by the time of Talmud a more sceptical view appears. Thus in Genesis Rabbah the rabbis begin to suggest that the incest occurred because of Lot's lust (Neusner, 1985):

> Rabbi Yudah of Galliah and Rabbi Samuel ben Nahman both in the name of Rabbi Enema wrote 'We do not know whether Lot lusted for his daughters, or his daughters lusted for him. On the basis of what is said in the following verse, Prov. 18[1], 'He who separates himself seeks desire', it is clear that Lot lusted after his daughter....

The later academic biblical literature on the story is also divided on whether this was truly 'necessary incest' to ensure tribal survival or whether this was just an example of father–daughter incest. Von Rad (1972, p. 219) both admires and criticises the incest:

> The fact that Lot's daughters are in no way ashamed of the origin of their children, but rather proclaim it openly and fix it forever in their son's names leads to this interpretation. The sons who are born to such a bed, however, proudly proclaim the heroism of their mother and the purity of their bloods: they were not begotten from foreign seed, but from a father and daughter who are the purest thorough-breds.

However, Von Rad was also critical of Lot and his family: 'without doubt, the narrative now contains indirectly a severe judgment on the incest in Lot's house and Lot's life becomes inwardly and outwardly bankrupt'.

Bassett (1971), writing about incest in the Old Testament, says that an act of incest between father and daughter is not on a par with that between mother and son. The Book of Leviticus contains numerous injunctions about exactly which relatives can or cannot have sexual relations with each other but there are *no sex laws* in the Old Testament which specifically prohibit sexual relations between father and daughter. Apparently, the father's only loss in such a case would be the marriage price of a virgin. However, a son who has sexual relationships with his mother or a step-mother commits a rebellious sin against the father. This is because the possession of a man's wife is seen as an effort to supplant the man's wife, which in turn is viewed as an effort to supplant the man himself. This meaning of the act is especially clear in cases in which a rival is trying to supplant a royal figure. Thus, for example, Absalom sleeps publicly with his father's concubines and this becomes an important symbol of his rebellion when he seeks to supplant David and take over the Kingdom.

## Modern commentary on Lot's incest

A modern and more feminist interpretation of the story is given by I. Kutz, an Israeli liaison psychiatrist, in his article 'Revisiting the Lot of the first incestuous family: the biblical origin of shifting the blame on to the female members of the family' (Kutz, 2005). He takes the line that the story of Lot is basically a tale of family incest and child sexual abuse, as might appear in the child psychiatric clinic today. He suggests that the myth of Lot was incorporated into the biblical text by the deuteronomists as a means of dis-crediting the neighbouring idol-worshipping nations of Moab and Ammon, who were said to be descended from the sons born out of the incest, namely Moab and Ben-Ammi. Through this carefully crafted plot the biblical narrators confirm the ethnic proximity of these nations to Israel, but at the same time cast an ancient blot of shame on their origins.

He classes the story as a historical myth, rather than as recorded history, and questions the assertion that there were no men around, as there would have been plenty of men in the nearby city of Zoar. Thus in Genesis 19$^{1-9}$ Lot is portrayed as the no-good nephew of Abraham. He causes his uncle so much grief that the patriarch demands a parting of their ways: 'Pray part from me, if to the left, then I to the right, if to the right, then I to the left'.

Lot then chooses Sodom as his residence, a town infamous for its depraved sexual practices. Kutz cites additional evidence in the events which immediately precede the destruction of Sodom and Gomorrah that Lot already had a perverse relationship with his daughters. Thus two strangers arrive at his house who are said to be the angels of God but in disguise. The townsmen surround his house so that they might sodomise his guests. Lot steps outside his house to protect the two strangers, and he tries to appease the crazed mob by saying 'Look, I have two daughters, who have not known a man, let me bring them out to you and you may deal with them as you like' (Gen. 19$^8$). Kutz interprets this as Lot making an offer to submit his daughters to gang rape to placate the angry crowd. He proposes that the primary purpose of the story is to transfer the blame for the incest from the male perpetrator onto the female victim. This, he asserts, is a feature of patriarchal societies. To support his thesis he describes major works of art which portray Lot and his daughters such as Durer (1555), Francesco (1600–1646) and most strikingly Goltzius (1516–1558), which all show their roles were not reversed and Lot was obviously enjoying the company of his daughters and that it was Lot who abused his daughters.

Incest of itself is not a designated psychiatric disorder and has usually been regarded as a sexual crime. Incest is documented in the ancient Sumerian and Egyptian literature as well as in the Bible, although it is unlikely in these ancient civilisations that the connection with alcohol was made. Alcohol-related incest is a complication of alcoholism and is therefore at least in part a psychiatric problem. Incest itself is may be culturally sanctioned in some instances (as it was amongst royalty in ancient Egypt); where it is not culturally sanctioned it is held to be a crime rather than a psychiatric disorder.

Over the last 50 years there has been a growing realisation amongst both child and adult psychiatrists that father–daughter sexual relationships are common (as revealed in community surveys) but nonetheless psychologically damaging to their victims. The literature on child sexual abuse is vast. Its victims later show increased rates of anxiety disorders and depression, but most especially of borderline personality disorder. Studies of the male perpetrators of incest show they are frequently abnormal and a significant proportion may misuse alcohol. It is for this reason that the story of Lot has been included in this chapter. Bentovim *et al.* (1987) studied a large series of families (*n* = 274) referred to a sexual abuse treatment programme. Of the perpetrators, 73 (37%) had used violence and 60 (22%) had employment problems; learning difficulties were present in 14 (5%) *and 52 (19%) had abused alcohol*. Alcohol is thus one of several factors involved in child sexual abuse, contributing to around one-fifth of cases. Viewed from this perspective, the tale of Lot and his daughters is far from trivial, and the story probably derives its universal relevance from its tale of incest rather than the ostensible rationale – a lack of suitable manhood in a small area of ancient Canaan. Despite the controversial nature of the story of Lot, biblical redactors, when tasked with selecting which of the many ancient Israelite legends to include in their sacred texts, chose to retain this tale, perhaps being mindful of its allusion to a deeply disturbing aspect of family life.

## Alcoholic stupor and possible sexual abuse – the deep sleep of Noah

Noah's drunken sleep was so deep that he may have been abused by one of his sons:

> Gen. 9²⁰ Noah, a man of the soil, was the first to plant a vineyard. ²¹ He drank some wine and he became drunk and he lay uncovered in his tent. ²² And Ham, the father of Canaan, saw the nakedness of his father and told his two brothers outside. ²³ Then Shem and Japheth took a garment, laid it on both their shoulders, and walked backwards and covered the nakedness of their father; their faces were turned away, and they did not see their father's nakedness. ²⁴ When Noah awoke from his wine and knew what his youngest son had done to him, ²⁵ he said 'Cursed be Canaan; lowest of slaves shall be to his brothers.' ²⁶ He also said 'Blessed by the Lord my God be Shem; and let Canaan be his slave. ²⁷ May God make space for Japheth, and let him live in the tents of Shem; and let Canaan be his slave.'

Westerman (1984) writes:

> Drunkenness as such was not regarded as reprehensible in antiquity. If a person became drunk at a celebration, it was always good for a story but no judgment was passed on him.... The ancients were well aware of alcoholic intoxication. They knew that wine could stupefy their senses and weaken their faculties and have other dangerous consequences which could be uncovered without knowing; but this episode was something disgraceful because nakedness in the Old Testament usually refers to the notion of the loss of human and social dignity.

Thus in the Ugaritic myth 'The Tale of Aqht' the dutiful son is described as 'he who takes him by the hand when he is drunk, and carries him when he is sated with wine' (Pritchard, 1955, p. 150, 11³²⁻³³). This Ugaritic myth indicates that it was a son's duty to protect and care for a vulnerable drunken father in the same way as Ham and Japheth did for Noah.

The Talmud (Sanhedrin 70a) suggests that Noah's son wounded or castrated him. However, this seems unlikely as Noah awoke without significant injury and went on to curse Canaan. Bassett (1971) argued that the phrase 'to see a man's nakedness' refers to sexual intercourse and he cites Leviticus 20, which specifically says that if one lies with, or takes someone's wife or 'he has uncovered that man's nakedness' then the offence is incest. Bassett suggests it is Ham having intercourse with his mother – Noah's wife. H. Winkler, cited in Westerman (p. 488), suggests the offence is sodomy.

The exact nature of the offence is clearly uncertain, but the general consensus appears to be that it is sexual in nature and it took place while Noah was in a deep and drunken sleep. Perhaps it was the writer's intention only to hint at a sexual offence without being explicit. As such, it may be a very early description of a common but serious complication of alcoholism, namely the vulnerability to sexual abuse of various types during periods of intoxication. This is a far greater problem for women than for men and the risk arises during periods of drunken sleep. As the text stands, the offence is no more than an accidental case of Ham seeing his father's naked body.

## Teetotal and temperance movements in the Old Testament

Societies afflicted by alcoholism may react by legislating against its use and prohibiting the consumption of alcohol altogether, as happened in America in the 1920s during the era of prohibition; similarly, there are widespread prohibitions on the use of alcohol throughout the Arab world. In other places sects will form who vow never to drink and seek to cure those with drinking problems, such as the Methodist temperance movements of the 19th century. In recent years the Alcoholics Anonymous movement has grown hugely internationally and provides a significant component to many alcohol treatment programmes. Most temperance movements have a religious origin and so it should be no surprise that such movements also existed in ancient Israel. Two teetotal movements are described in the Old Testament: the Rechabites and the Nazirites.

### The Rechabites

The Rechabites were a small nomadic group who traced their origins back to Jonadab, who lived in northern Israel. They are thought to have originally descended from the Kenites and indeed Jethro, the father-in-law of Moses, was said to be a Kenite. Jeremiah extols their loyalty to their ancestor Jonadab and contrasts this to the fecklessness and disobedience Israel shows towards its own God Yahweh, mainly through Israelite idol worship. The Rechabites are described in Jeremiah 35:

> [5] Then I set before the Rechabites pitchers full of wine, and cups; and I said to them 'Have some wine' [6] But they answered, 'We will drink no wine, for our ancestor Jonadab son of Rechab commanded us, '*You shall never drink wine, neither you nor your children.* [7] Nor shall you ever build a house, or sow seed; nor shall you plant a vineyard, or even own one; but you shall live in tents all your days, that you may live many days in the land where you reside.' [8] We have obeyed the charge of our ancestor Jonadab son of Rechab in all that he commanded us, to drink no wine all of our days, ourselves, our wives, our sons, and our daughters [9] and not to build houses to live in. We have no vineyard or seed; [10] but we have lived in tents and have obeyed and done all that our ancestor Jonadabab commanded us.'

Lundbom (2004) explains this passage:

> Jeremiah offers the Rechabites pitchers of wine and asks them to drink wine. They refused, saying that Jonadab, the son of Rechab, commanded them not to, hence the name 'The Rechabites'. They were also forbidden to build houses, or keep vineyards, but instead they were to live in tents and live like nomads.... The Rechabite vow has all the marks of desert life, rejecting as it does agrarian and urban culture.

The Rechabites were like typical Arabs, perhaps similar to the Wahabis, a puritanical movement in Islam that began in the mid-18th century and continues to flourish today, especially in Saudi Arabia.

A comparison has also been made to the Nabetaeans, another teetotal ancient nomadic sect, recorded in the writings of Diodorus Siculus in the 1st century BCE:

They live life in the open air, claiming as native land a wilderness that has neither rivers nor abundant springs from which it is possible for a hostile army to obtain water. It is their custom to neither plant grain, set out any fruit-bearing tree, *nor to use wine* nor construct any house. (Diodurus Siculus, quoted in Lundbom, 2004)

The Rechabites are thought to have formed a small teetotal subculture living in northern Israel during the 9th century BCE. They are recorded to have witnessed Jehu's final extermination of Ahab's royal household and his decisive purge against Baal worship (2 Kings 10$^{15-27}$), held to have been an event in the 8th century BCE. There is some biblical evidence that they survived even after the exile of 586 BCE because they are recorded as helping in the rebuilding of the second Jerusalem temple (Neh. 3$^{14}$). The Mishnah Ta'an (4$^5$) also records their existence during the period of the Second Temple: 'The children of Jonadab son of Rechab, during the times of the second temple, had a fixed day for bringing in wood for the altar of the Temple, and *they were a water drinking sect*' (Milgrom, 2007). These observations suggest the Rechabites, who seem to have been a teetotal sect, may have lasted for more than four centuries, starting around the 8th or 9th century BCE through to the 5th century BCE, but there is no record of them after this.

The Rechabites appear to be the earliest recorded teetotal sect and served as an inspiration for many later teetotal movements. Such movements usually appear during eras of widespread and destructive alcoholism, as occurred in England in the early part of the 19th century, as a result of the rapid industrialisation. Methodist groups in the late 18th and 19th century founded friendly societies in northern England and Ireland, primarily to provide insurance for their members should they fall on hard times, but they also commonly adopted a religious and teetotal philosophy. Those friendly societies that were teetotal became part of the Temperance movement. The early Methodists also adopted the term Rechabite for some of these societies, a choice made by the Reverend Joseph Thomson, the minister of Mr Brotherton's chapel in Salford, a church whose members also espoused vegetarianism. A number of Rechabite societies flourished in the north of England, and in keeping with the biblical Rechabite nomadic tradition, their meetings were held in 'tents'. Further details on the friendly societies are given in *The Friendly Societies in England 1815–1875*, by Godson (1961).

## The Nazirites

The Nazirites, another ancient teetotal sect, are of particular interest to medicine today because one of the conditions of a Nazirite birth is that the mother of a Nazirite *must refrain from drinking wine during her pregnancy*. In the last 50 years this ancient taboo has, for quite different reasons, been resurrected and has assumed an important place in modern obstetric practice as it has now clear that drinking in pregnancy can harm the foetus.

The term Nazirite comes from the Hebrew *nazir*, meaning consecrated or separated, but it may also refer to hair. The biblical conditions of the Nazirite vow are described in the Book of Numbers:

6¹ The Lord spoke to Moses saying: ² Speak to the Israelites and say to them: When either men or women make a special vow, the vow of a Nazirite, to separate themselves to the Lord, ³ they shall separate themselves from wine and strong drink; *they shall drink no wine vinegar or other vinegar*, and *shall not drink any grape juice or eat grapes, fresh or dried*. ⁴ All their days as Nazirites they shall eat nothing that is produced by the grapevine, not even the seeds or the skins. ⁵ All the days of their Nazirite vow no razor shall come upon the head; until the time is completed for which they separate themselves to the Lord, they shall be holy; they shall let the locks of their hair grow long. ⁶ All the days that they separate themselves to the Lord they shall not go near a corpse. ⁷ Even if their mother, brother or sister should die, they may not defile themselves; because their consecration to God is upon the head. ⁸ All their days as Nazirites, they are holy to the Lord.

Thus the Nazirite vow essentially consisted of three elements: to abstain from wine, grapes, raisins and vinegar; to refrain from cutting the hair on one's head; and to avoid the touching of dead bodies, even of family members. Following the destruction of the Second Temple, large numbers of Jews became ascetics, vowing never to eat meat or to drink wine as they were in mourning. The Rabbis during this period discouraged taking the Nazirite vow, since 'asceticism was against the principles of Judaism' (Nedarim 76). The Rabbis were concerned about excessive mourning following this national catastrophe.

Two important Nazirites are described in the Old Testament, Samuel and Samson. They were the only children of mothers with fertility problems. Their conceptions took place only with divine intervention, after their mothers had prayed to God for help. The story of Samson's conception and his mother's pregnancy are of particular interest, since a biblical prohibition on drinking during pregnancy is described. This ban on drinking wine during pregnancy is repeated three times, suggesting that the writer must have felt quite strongly about it:

Judg. 13² There was a certain man of Zorah, of the tribe of the Danites, whose name was Manoah. His wife was barren, having borne no children. ³ And the angel of the Lord appeared to the woman and said to her, 'Although you are barren, having borne no children, you shall conceive and bear a son. ⁴ Now be careful *not to drink wine or strong drink* nor to eat anything unclean, ⁵ for you shall conceive and bear a son. No razor is to come to his head for the boy shall be a Nazirite to God from birth. It is he who will begin to deliver Israel from the hand of the Philistines.' ⁶ Then the women came and told her husband, 'A man of God came to me, and his appearance was like that of an angel of God, most awe-inspiring; I did not ask where he came from and he did not tell me his name; ⁷ but he said to me, 'You shall conceive and bear a son. *So then drink no wine or strong drink* and eat nothing unclean, for the boy shall be a nazirite to God from birth to the day of his death.

The prohibition on drinking during pregnancy is repeated twice, first spoken by the angel of the Lord and secondly when the wife of Manoah reports this visit to her husband. The story goes on to describe how the angel of the Lord visits for a second time and meets the wife of Manoah in a field but Manoah is not present at this meeting, and soon afterwards his wife conceives. Whilst the text is never explicit about who the father of this child might be, some biblical commentators have inferred that the true father is the angel of the Lord and not Manoah, and so perhaps this is also a story about male infertility. Manoah certainly makes no objection to the proceedings and he meets the angel of the Lord, who once more repeats the prohibition of drinking during pregnancy.

> 13[13] The angel of the Lord said to Manoah, 'Let the woman give heed to all that I said to her. [14] She may not eat of anything that comes from the vine. *She is not to drink wine or strong drink* or eat any unclean thing'.

Boling (1975) writes that the Book of Judges forms part of the deuteronomistic history and was probably composed in its more final form in the 7th to 9th century BCE. He dates the Samson story to somewhere between 1160 and 1100 BCE. At that time, the Israelites were probably still under Philistine domination and they resented this. The chapter starts by describing how they had been under the Philistines for 40 years, and Samson is to become their leader, a fighter who will bring down the Philistines.

Regarding verse 4, *no wine or strong drink*, Boling (1975) writes 'The strong drink referred to here is *šakar* or strong beer. The Philistines used an awesome amount of beer, as indicated by their distinctive pottery which had strainers...'. In this passage the rule of the Nazirite as set out in Numbers 6[1-8] is delightfully adapted as highly desirable pre-natal care. For example, the admonition to avoid uncleanness emanates from the Nazirite rule to avoid dead bodies and this is displaced to become an instruction to the mother to eat nothing unclean. It should be noted that rule of the Nazirite is itself rooted in the regulations for the ritual purity of the fighting man as reflected in tradition stemming from the Mosaic period. The actual verse from Deuteronomy (29[5-7]) which Boling states explains the rationale for refraining from drink to ensure victory in battle is quoted below:

> 29[5] I have led you for 40 years in the wilderness. The clothes on your back have not worn out and the sandals on your feet have not worn out; [6] you have not eaten bread, and you have not drunk wine or strong drink – so that you may know that I am the Lord your God. [7] When you came to this place King Sihon of Hesbon, and King Og of Bashan came out against us for battle but we defeated them. (Boling, 1975, pp. 219–220)

It seems as if the victory in this particular battle was in part due to the fact that the soldiers had not drunk any wine or beer, for what seems to have been 40 years. There seems to have been some knowledge that victory in a war was more likely if soldiers had not drunk either wine or beer just before a battle, and that alcohol was destructive of military prowess – probably this was the total extent of knowledge at the time.

It is important to note that Boling published his book in 1975. He was an academic biblical scholar and he would not have had any knowledge of the foetal alcohol syndrome, as this had only just recently appeared in the English medical press (Jones *et al.*, 1973). The ancients had no knowledge about the foetal alcohol syndrome or the spectrum of cognitive damage to the foetus that drinking can cause in pregnancy, but it appears that some authors, such as the scribe who wrote the Book of Judges, may have had a suspicion that an alcohol-free pregnancy might produce a better soldier than one born to a drinking mother.

## The effect of alcohol in pregnancy

Infants with foetal alcohol spectrum disorders (FAS) have a characteristic facial abnormality showing microcephaly (small head), micro-ophthalmia (small eyes), short palpeberal fissures, a thin upper lip and flattening of the maxillary area. Sometimes there is a cleft palate and poor sucking. Other developmental abnormalities may include congenital heart defects, liver and kidney problems, deafness and a variety of bone abnormalities. However, the most important abnormalities relate to the brain and result in intellectual impairment and developmental delays; for the full-blown FAS the estimated average IQ is 65.7. Prospective studies (e.g. Streissguth et al., 1980) have found similar reductions in IQ and by using a prospective method, i.e. measuring maternal alcohol consumption and hence the level of exposure in utero, they found that increasing amounts of alcohol lead to progressively lower intellectual functioning in childhood. Estimates of the prevalence of the full FAS picture vary, but one recent review gave a figure of 9 per 1,000 live births in the USA. In some countries the prevalence of FAS may be considerably higher, e.g. in South Africa, where rates of female alcoholism are very high.

The consumption of only moderate levels of as little as one or two drinks per day of alcohol during pregnancy has been found to be associated with childhood attention deficit disorders and behavioural problems. The prevalence of foetal alcohol spectrum disorders, that is, the milder degrees of cognitive deficit and behavioural problems, has been estimated to be 2–4% in European populations (Sayal, 2007). It is thought that the foetal alcohol syndrome is now the commonest preventable cause of mental retardation and so whenever the antenatal services encounter women who are still drinking they are advised about the harmful consequences of the alcohol or referred on to alcohol treatment programmes.

Scientific recognition of the foetal alcohol syndrome did not appear until the papers of Lemoine et al. (1968) and Jones and Smith (1973), but there is a lengthy history of many philosophers, physicians and others raising their concerns on the effects of drinking in pregnancy might have on the foetus and continued drinking on the way children were being reared by their alcoholic mothers (reviewed by Warner and Rossett, 1973; Abel, 1997). Burton, in his monumental work The Anatomy of Melancholy, in the 17th century, summarised much of the earlier literature and wrote. He cited Gellius:

> If a drunken man get a child, it will never likely have a good brain. Plutarch said 'one drunkard begets another', while Aristotle wrote 'Foolish, drunken or hare-brain women for the most part bring forth children like unto themselves morosos et languides. Both Carthage and Sparta had laws prohibiting the use of alcohol by newly married couples, to prevent conception whilst newly weds

might be intoxicated, and Plato recommended the same rules. (Quoted in Warner and Rossett, 1973)

Abel (1997), in his study entitled 'Was the foetal alcohol syndrome recognised in the ancient Near East', examined the older biblical, Talmudic, Egyptian and Sumerian literature. He cites Cohen (1965), who listed the dietary causes of congenital abnormalities given in the Talmud:

> Gluttonous children are born to women who eat mustard during pregnancy, ugly children to those who eat clay; while mothers who eat fish brine have children who think a lot.

Wine is not included in this list. Further, in another section of the Talmud drinking is recommended to ensure the birth of strong, healthy, good-looking children (Ketub 60b-61a).

Like the Talmud, ancient Sumerian writings mention a large number of birth defects in humans and animals (Leichty, 1970). These anomalies were reported to the king, who dispatched squads of special priests tasked with exorcising the demons thought to be responsible. In none of these cases were the abnormalities attributed to alcohol. There is, however, the famous Sumerian tale of Enki and Nimhursag (Raglan, 1936), which involves a drunken episode in pregnancy, associated with foetal abnormalities (see page 538 in this chapter).

Abel (1998) considers the ancient Egyptians to have been among the 'heaviest' drinkers in the ancient world, but they did not consider beer or wine drinking to be a health hazard (Lutz, 1992). Indeed, Hathor, the Egyptian Mother Goddess, was also the Goddess of intoxication, a combination that would make little sense if the Egyptians had thought there was any connection between drinking during pregnancy and subsequent birth defects. Abel is probably correct in his conclusion that there was no consensus or knowledge in the ancient world about the harms done by a mother who drinks during pregnancy. Nevertheless, there were occasional authors, such as the writer(s) of the Book of Judges, who seem to have had some suspicions on alcohol consumption in pregnancy and its effects on the offspring. The advice given by the Angel of the Lord to the unnamed wife of Manoah to refrain from drinking in her pregnancy and repeated three times, was then forgotten for more than 3,000 years, but is now routinely given to every pregnant woman who walks into the antenatal clinic today.

## Summary and conclusions

Psychiatrists working on the front line in adult psychiatry, child or forensic psychiatry will deal with patients suffering from alcoholism and so it is of interest to see that the harmful effects of alcohol were also matters of great concern to the writers of the Old Testament. The biblical text confirms that alcoholism must have been common in ancient Israel, at least in the earlier part of its history. The description of alcoholism and its sequelae, sometimes understood, but sometimes appearing only as an incidental to some other story, is often detailed and clinically accurate. Some passages on the dangers of excessive drinking, such as Proverbs 23 and Sirach 31, which were written as lectures from fathers to sons, show parallels with modern descriptive psychiatry, though expressed as a moral lesson. They provide an insight into how alcoholism was perceived in the ancient world, but in other passages there is no more than a glancing reference to a key symptom such as confusion, anger, depression or dependency.

There is also a second group of biblical citations, where the link between the symptoms and alcoholism is more hidden. The writer describes an event, and either wine or heavy drinking is mentioned, but no link is made between the event and the drinking; the biblical authors probably did not even realise there might have been any connection. The death of Nabal (1 Sam 25$^{37}$) is a good example of this. Here a wealthy farmer with a known history of heavy drinking ceases to drink and then dies ten days later. Modern understanding of this event would be that he might have died because of the DTs. The complications of alcoholism, alcoholic deterioration, were often used in a purely metaphorical sense or as an allegory providing a critique for some contemporary policy of state or social problem.

Anger, violence and homicide related to alcohol are frequently referred to throughout the OT. Sometimes this is directly linked to wine, but in other instances only suggestive, through metaphors such as the 'cup of wrath'. Ancient Israel was an early civilisation; there was a court and legal system, but it lacked prisons and a police force to protect its citizens. In this situation the phenomenon of random episodes of drunken violence and occasional alcoholic homicide might have been particularly feared and so it is understandable that there should be concerns about alcohol-induced violence.

Today, psychiatrists formulate their diagnoses in terms of two major standardised psychiatric glossaries, DSM-5 and ICD-10 (for further explanation see the Introduction, page 8, and pages 66–67). The DSM-5 scheme lists two main alcohol use disorders, alcohol dependence and alcohol abuse, and then goes on to describe a further 13 other conditions termed *alcohol-induced disorders*. Many of these secondary disorders also gain a brief mention in the OT. Table 14.2 lists these disorders and the biblical verses where each is mentioned.

Although almost all the neuropsychiatric complications of alcoholism are well described in the OT, the more serious physical consequences of alcoholism such as liver damage remained unrecognised for a further two millennia. Sournia (1990, p. 11) places this in the 11th century CE with the writings of Simon Seth, a physician practising in Constantinople who wrote that drinking wine to excess caused inflammation of the liver, a condition he treated with pomegranate seed. However, it was not until the 19th century and the writings of the Swedish physician Magnus Huss (1849) that a more comprehensive picture of both the somatic and psychiatric complications of alcoholism began to emerge.

Sournia also highlights the ambivalent attitude that most societies have to alcohol. On the one hand, alcohol is the lubricant to social interaction and oils the wheels of commerce; drinking forms an integral part of family festivities such as feasts and weddings as well as being a part of religious ritual and cultic festivals. In many countries, both today and in the ancient

**Table 14.2** DSM-5 alcohol-related disorders and biblical citations

| Name of syndrome | Biblical citation |
|---|---|
| Alcohol dependence | Pr. 23$^{35}$; Is. 5$^{11}$; Sir. 31$^{30}$; Amos 4$^1$ |
| Alcohol abuse | Sir. 31$^{26,30}$; Jer. 25$^{27}$; Pr. 4$^{17}$; Is. 51$^{17}$; Jer. 13$^{12-14}$ |
| Alcohol intoxication | Is. 28$^7$, 51$^{17}$; Ps. 60$^3$, 107$^{27}$; and many more |
| Alcohol withdrawal | 1 Sam. 25$^{36-38}$ |
| Alcohol-induced delirium | Pr. 23$^{33}$ |
| Alcohol withdrawal delirium | ?? 1 Sam. 25$^{37}$ |
| Alcohol-induced persisting dementia | ? Maccabees 3, ch. 12; ? Hos. 4$^{11}$; ? Isa. 28$^7$ |
| Alcohol-induced persisting amnestic disorder | ? Isa. 19$^{13-14}$ |
| Alcohol-induced psychotic disorder with delusions | Pr. 23$^{33}$; Jer. 25$^{16}$ |
| Alcohol-induced psychotic delusions with hallucination | Pr. 23$^{29}$ |
| Alcohol-induced mood disorders | Ezek. 23$^{33}$; Pr. 23$^{29}$; Joel 1$^5$; 1 Sam. 25$^{37}$ |
| Alcohol-nduced sexual dysfunction | Not described |
| Alcohol-induced sleep disorder | Ps. 78$^{65-66}$; Gen. 9$^{12-14}$ |

world, alcohol was responsible for a significant proportion of the calorific value of the diet. Alcohol always had the advantage that it could be easily stored. The size of a farmer's vineyard was taken as a measure of his wealth. The dichotomy between the beneficial and harmful effects of alcohol can be seen in the Old Testament. The author of Ecclesiastes, Qoheleth, writes only about the joy and happiness that wine can bring: 'Go eat your bread with enjoyment and drink your wine with a merry heart for God has long ago approved what you do' (Eccl. 9$^7$), or again 'Feasts are made for laughter, wine gladdens the heart' (Eccl. 10$^{19}$). By contrast, the great literary prophets Isaiah and Jeremiah are highly critical of drinking. Not only do they warn against its use, but they also draw on metaphors appertaining to alcoholic deterioration to convey their contempt for corruption in the priesthood and for the political leaders of the day, with alcoholics and politicians both being held in equal disdain. Their repeated use of such metaphors to convey a political message makes sense only if it is assumed that their audience were also quite familiar with the destructive effects of heavy drinking. Perhaps the scribes and prophets of the Bible applied their writing skills to document the harm resulting from heavy drinking to warn the people, much in the same way as the medical profession does today. References to alcoholism, wine and drunkenness become far less frequent in the later books of the OT, and seemingly alcoholism became much less of a problem later on. The puzzle of why the Israelites seemed to have given it up has been called the 'Great Jewish Drink Mystery'.

Keller (1970) suggests that the critical event in Jewish history which led to the Israelites relinquishing their drunken behaviours was their exile to Babylon in 586 BCE. Prior to this, the Hebrew people were basically just another ancient Canaanite tribe who all drank heavily, sometimes even indulging in the worship of the local Canaanite gods Baal, Aserah and Dagan, and such worship, especially during fertility rites, was often associated with drunken orgiastic behaviours. While the pre-exilic biblical literature is replete with references to drunkenness, and the numerous complications of alcoholism, these themes barely gain mention in the post-exilic literature (books such as Ezra, Nehemiah and Chronicles).

Around 40 years after the exile to Babylon, King Cyrus, the Persian monarch who conquered Babylonian, gave permission for the Jews to return to Israel, in 537 BCE. Profound changes in Jewish cultural life took place in post-exilic society. Perhaps the most important of these was the establishment of the synagogue, a small religious sanctuary present in every community, which became the centre of local worship, education and social life, which was later to become the prototype for the church and the mosque. The Hebrew nation, once just another Canaanite tribe, now became the Jewish people, worship changed in character and the drinking of wine became incorporated into religious ceremonial. These occasions included the sanctification of the Sabbath and other religious festivals such as the Passover and the various rites of passage. In addition, for the greater part of the post-exilic period the Jews lived under the hegemony of other empires, the Persians initially, then the Greeks and finally the Romans. They no longer fought wars against their neighbours, who were also part of these empires, and this absence of a need for fighting gave way to a more deeply held religious Jewish faith, eclipsing the previous militaristic and macho culture of pre-exilic Israel – and with this went its penchant for heavy drinking.

This period of comparative sobriety seems to have lasted for around 200 years, or at least until the Hellenic period and the conquest of Israel by Alexander the Great in 323 BCE. Wine bibbers are mentioned in various places in the New Testament (e.g. Matt. 11[19]). Low rates of alcoholism amongst Jews seem to have persisted into modern times for a variety of other reasons (see Keller, 1970) but this did not protect them from becoming addicted to other substances of abuse (Glatt, 1970).

Although the Old Testament is primarily a religious text, it also provides a very detailed account of the secular life of the ancient Israelites, particularly for the pre-exilic period, which dates around 2,500–3,000 years ago. Drinking wine formed an important part of daily existence, as a highly calorific foodstuff; wine was also a joy to drink, and a medicine to alleviate pain. However, alcoholism was common and so there should be no surprise to find it included in the biblical text. What is truly astonishing is the sophistication and detail of these accounts, which bear a good comparison to the modern description of alcoholism in clinical psychiatry today.

## Appendix. Alcoholism – the magnitude of the problem today

Alcohol consumption occurs on a continuum, from none at all through to a severe dependency syndrome, with no obvious demarcation between social drinking and heavy drinking, or between heavy drinking and alcoholism. Drinking behaviours become clinical disorders once they are deemed to result in a significant degree of harm and this may be social harm, such as problems within the family, legal or occupational difficulties, or harmful medical effects.

Both ICD-10 and DSM-5 (see Introduction, page 8, and pages 66–67) describe two main alcohol use disorders: alcohol dependence and alcohol abuse. The descriptions of both these syndromes is broadly similar, and so only the DSM-5 criteria for these disorders, which are fairly easy to understand, are given here.

The key features of *alcohol dependence* are tolerance to the effects of alcohol, as shown by a diminished effect of the same amount of alcohol and a need for more alcohol to achieve intoxication. Withdrawal effects will occur on cessation of drinking and these include autonomic hyperactivity, tremor, insomnia, nausea or vomiting, transient illusions or hallucinations, psychomotor agitation, anxiety, grand mal seizures within several hours of stopping or reducing prolonged heavy drinking. Alcohol-dependent subjects will spend much time thinking about drink or where the next drink will come from. There is often increased consumption and attempts to stop usually end in failure, despite physical or psychological problems resulting from the drinking

*Alcohol abuse* relates more to the consequences of drinking behaviours. There may be failure in role obligation at home or at work, risky behaviours such as drink driving, fighting, assaults as well as social and interpersonal difficulties, and even with an awareness of these difficulties subjects are still unable to reverse the pattern and stop their drinking. Because the majority of subjects with alcohol dependence will show features of an alcohol abuse syndrome as well, alcohol abuse disorder is usually not diagnosed as a separate condition because dependence is generally the main problem. However, there are a few alcoholics, such as binge drinkers, who may be alcohol free for months on end and who do not show a dependence pattern but may still cause serious damage during their drinking bouts and in these cases the diagnosis of 'alcohol abuse' alone may be helpful.

The DSM-5 scheme also lists a further 13 other conditions, termed *alcohol-induced disorders*, as listed in Table 14.2 (page 551), which confirms the breadth of the biblical description, and shows that many of the adverse neuropsychiatric and psychosocial sequelae of alcoholism were recognised in the OT. They were probably widely known in the ancient Near East at the time but nowhere else are they collected in a single volume.

### Epidemiology

Epidemiology describes the frequency with which a condition is found in the community. Grant *et al.* (2006) reported the one-year prevalence of alcohol dependence as 3.8% and alcohol abuse as 4.7% in the general population. Severe drinking behaviours which start in youth tend to ameliorate with age. The figures for alcohol dependence for those aged 18–29 was 9.2%; for 30–44-year-olds 3.8%; for 45–64-year-olds 3.8%; and for those over 65 only 0.2%. Alcohol abuse also shows a similar pattern of decline with age. The male:female ratio is 2.5:1, and in almost all societies there is a male predominance. There are also differences between ethnic minorities. Thus among young US-born male Mexican Americans rates as high as 23% are reported for alcohol dependence, and the lifetime rates for Alaskan American Indians is also high, at 6.4%. By contrast, rates of 0.45% are reported among ethnic Chinese living in Shanghai (Helzer and Cannino, 1992).

Another measure of the magnitude of an alcohol problem in a community relates is the death rate due to cirrhosis of the liver, and this appears to be highest for Mediterranean countries. Rates per 100,000 of the population were highest for Italy at 26.8, Portugal at 24.1 and France at 19.9, but somewhat lower for the USA at 10.8, the UK at 6.0 and Iceland at 1.2 (World Health Organization, 2007).

Two distinct patterns of national drinking are recognised in Europe. In the southern Mediterranean wine-producing countries (Spain, France, Portugal, Italy) wine is taken with the meal and may be a dietary supplement as well as being a stimulant and social lubricant. Drunkenness is relatively uncommon considering the very high levels of consumption. There are few legal restrictions on purchasing alcohol but death rates due to cirrhosis may be very high. By contrast, in northern Europe (Norway, Sweden, Russia, Poland) there is a greater separation of drinking from its dietary function, alcohol is more often used by a small proportion of the young male population to produce states of intoxication and there may be higher rates of neuropsychiatric complications. Ancient Israel was a Mediterranean country and there is good evidence that wine was routinely consumed with food. Even today in Jewish tradition wine is drunk with the Passover meal and taken together with bread on the Sabbath, and so a Mediterranean pattern of drinking may have prevailed in ancient Israel. Even so, the Old Testament contains numerous references to drunkenness and alcoholic complications.

## The destructiveness of alcohol

If alcohol did not have such destructive effects, it would be of little interest, to either the prophets of the Old Testament or the medical profession today. In the USA it is responsible for 5% of all deaths. Of these alcohol-related deaths, 17% were directly attributable to alcohol (mainly cirrhosis) and 45% were due to alcohol-related trauma (road traffic accidents, head injuries, work accidents, homicide and suicide) (Babor et al., 2008).

In the UK, 15–30% of male and 8–15% of female hospital admissions in urban areas are related to alcohol. Alcoholic liver disease usually starts as an acute inflammation (hepatitis) and progresses to cirrhosis, which is commonly fatal. Alcohol may also contribute to peptic ulcers, gastritis and pancreatitis, tears in the oesophagus and the vomiting of blood, gout, osteoporosis (weak bones) as well as predisposing to various cancers, including oesophageal cancer and breast cancer. Cardiovascular risks include irregularities of the heart, alcohol-induced heart muscle disease (cardiomyopathy), high blood pressure and stroke. Pregnant mothers who drink risk the foetal alcohol spectrum disorders in their babies (Babor *et al.*, 2008). None of these largely somatic complications is mentioned in the Bible; indeed, most were not recognised until the 19th century or later.

Alcohol may damage the brain, and MRI studies show a loss of brain substance in heavy drinkers. This brain damage and some neuropsychiatric complications gain mention in the OT. Alcohol has a high calorific value and alcoholics frequently neglect to eat properly, giving themselves vitamin deficiencies which may further exacerbate brain damage.

## Causes of alcoholism

Alcoholism is a complex, multifaceted disorder and, given the very large cross-cultural variation in its frequency, it is likely that social and cultural factors play a significant role. For the more severe clinical disorders, especially the alcohol dependence syndrome, genetic factors probably play an important role and it is a common clinical observation that a patient presenting with an alcohol dependence syndrome will often report one or more first-degree relatives with a similar problem. Twin studies are able to provide a quantitative estimate of how much of the cause of alcohol dependency can be attributed to genetic factors and this is known as the 'hereditability'. This has been estimated at 52–64% of the cause, with no substantial sex difference (Kendler *et al.*, 2001). No single gene has so far been identified and it is thought a large number of genes all make small contributions. Inheritance of this type is called 'polygenic'.

Certain personality factors (probably also genetically determined) may also contribute. These include childhood deviance, as indicated by hyperactivity, distractibility, sensation-seeking behaviours and impulsivity. These traits are thought to result in school failure, which in turn may lead to friendships with other equally deviant peers and so provide the social context for the onset of adolescent drinking and substance misuse.

Rates of alcoholism in the community may fluctuate over time and place. Cultural sanctions and prohibitions operate in the Arab world, with some cultures having virtual prohibition. The price of alcohol is the most important social factor and is also the most readily manipulated variable.

## Treatments

Most districts in the UK now have a dedicated alcohol specialist psychiatric team; they will also treat patients with other substance abuse disorders. Treatment programmes vary but usually involve a detoxification regime, either hospital or community based, motivational interviewing, individual or group psychotherapy, sometimes involving other family members but tailored according to the patient's needs. There is normally also a follow-up relapse prevention programme. The 'Minnesota Programme' consists of an initial residential phase lasting one to two months with a busy schedule of group therapy and work assignments, such as attending AA meetings, in order to keep therapeutic momentum going. There are many variants on this and no particular regime has been shown to be pre-eminent. There is agreement that one year after a course of treatment some 50–70% will be abstinent, but the longer-term rates for abstinence are less clear.

Alcoholics Anonymous (AA) was founded in 1935 by two recovered alcoholics (Wilson, 1994) and has proved to be both popular and effective. There are more than 3,000 groups in the UK and 88,000 worldwide. Its approach is based on the '12 steps' and the movement has a quasi-religious flavour but there is an assumption of the disease model of alcoholism. AA meetings are of central importance but anonymity and the support of fellow sufferers have made it at least as effective as the more official medical and psychiatric approaches, particularly in the realm of relapse prevention.

## References

Abel, E.L. (1997) Was the foetal alcohol syndrome recognised in the Ancient near east. *Alcohol and Alcoholism*, 32 (1): 3–7.

Albright, W.F. (1943). A votive stele erected by Benhadad I of Damascus to the God Melqart *Bulletin of the American Schools of Oriental Research*, 78, 23–29.

American Psychiatric Association (2000) *Diagnostic and Statistical Manual of Mental Disorders, 4th edition, text Revision*. Washington, DC: American Psychiatric Association.

Anderson, F.I. and Freedman, D.N. (1980) *Hosea, A New Translation with Introduction and commentary*. Anchor Bible Series New York: Doubleday and Company.

Anderson, F.I. and Freedman, D.N. (1989) *Amos. A New Translation with Introduction and Commentary*. The Anchor Bible, p. 421. New York: Doubleday.

Babor, T.F., Hernandez- Avila, C.A., Ungemack, J.A. (2008) Substance abuse: alcohol disorders. Chapter 54, pp. 971–1004 in *Psychiatry 3rd edition* Edited by Tasman, A., Kay, J., Lieberman, J.A., First, M.B., and Maj, M. John Wiley and Sons.

Barton, J. (2001) *Joel and Obadiah. A commentary*, p.99. The Old Testament Library, Louisville: Westminster: John Knox Press.

Bassett, F.W. (1971) Noah's nakedness and the curse of Canaan. A case of Incest? *Vetus Testamentum*, 21, 232–237.

Bentovim,A., Boston, P., Elburg,A.V. (1987) Child sexual abuse – children and families referred to a treatment project and the effects of intervention. *British Medical Journal*, 295: 1453–57.

Boling, R.G. (1975) *The Anchor Bible: Judges, Introduction, Translation and Commentary*. Garden City New York: Doubleday & Co. Inc.

Bourget, D. and Gagne, P. (2006) Fratricide a forensic perspective. *Journal of American Academy of Law and Psychiatry*, 34: 529–533.

Bright, J. (1965) *Jeremiah. The Anchor Bible Introduction, Translation and Notes*. pp. 162–164, New York: Doubleday.

Cohen, H. (1965) *The minor tractates of the Talmud*. Soncino Press.

Craigie, P.C., Kelly, P.H. and Drinkard, J.F. (1991) *Jeremiah*, 1–25, pp. 192–193. World Biblical Commentary: Nashville, Thomas Nelson Publishing

Crenshaw, J.L. (1995) *Joel: A new translation with introduction and commentary*. Anchor Bible Series, New York, Doubleday and Co. Inc.

Edwards, G., Marshall, E.J., Cook, C.H. (1977) *The treatment of Drinking Problems: A guide for the helping professionals*. Third edition, Cambridge, Cambridge University Press.

Encyclopaedia Judaica 2nd edition (2007), *Entry on wine* vol. 21: p. 81 Eds Skolnich F. & Berenbaum. Jerusalem: Keter Publishing.

Fox, M.V. (2000) *Proverbs 1–9. A new translation and commentary*. Anchor Bible. New York: Doubleday.

Geller, J. (1992) *Beer in Egypt in the followers of Horas: Dedication to Michael Allen Hoffman*. Ed. R. Friedman and B. Adams. Oxford: Oxbow Books.

Gibbens, T.N.C. (1958) Sane and Insane Homicide. *Journal of Criminal Law Criminology and Police Science*, 49, 110–115.

Gillies, H. (1976) Homicide in the West of Scotland. *British Journal of Psychiatry*, 128, 105 – 27

Ginsburg, E. and Weinberger, Y. (2007) *Mishlei: Proverbs. A new translation with a commentary anthologised from Talmudic, Midrashic and Rabbinic sources.* Brooklyn, New York: Mesorah Publications.

Glatt M. (1970) Alcoholism and drug dependence amongst Jews. *British Journal of Addiction*, 64: 297–304.

Godson, P.J.H. (1961) *The Friendly societies in England 1815–1875.* Manchester: University of Manchester Press.

Grant, B.F., Dawson, D.A., Stinson, F.S. *et al* (2006) The 12 month prevalence and trends in DSM.IV alcohol abuse and dependence in United States 1991 – 1992 and 2001 – 2002. *Alcohol Research and Health*, 29(2), 79–91.

Gray, J. (1963) *I and II Kings: A commentary.* London: SCM Press.

Gudgunsson, G.H. and Petersson, H. (1982) Some criminological and psychiatric aspects of homicide in Iceland. *Medicine Science and the Law*, 28, 187–194.

Harris L., and Associates Inc. (1993) *The Commonwealth Fund Survey of Women's Health.* New York: Commonwealth Fund.

Helzer, J.E. and Cannino, C.J. (1992) Comparative analysis of alcoholism in ten cultural regions. In *Alcoholism in North America, Europe and Asia.* Eds. Helzer, J.E. and Canino, C.J. (eds.) NY pp. 298 – 308 Oxford University Press, New York.

Hill, S.Y. (1992) Absence of paternal sociopathy in the aetiology of severe alcoholism: is there a type III alcoholism. *Journal of Studies on Alcohol*, 53: 161–169.

Holladay, W.L. (1986a) *Jeremiah. A commentary on the book of the Prophet Jeremiah* 1 – 25, p. 673. Philadelphia, Fortress Press.

Holladay, W.L. (1986b) *Jeremiah. A commentary on the book of the Prophet Jeremiah.* 1–25 pp. 401–406. Philadelphia: Fortress Press.

Hossfeld, F.L. and Zenger, E. (2005) *Psalms.* Volume 2, p. 299. Translated by Linda M. Moloney. Minneapolis: Fortress Press.

Huss, M. (1849) *Alcoholisms chronicus, eller chronisk alkoholsjukdom; ett bidrag till dyskrasiernes Kännedom enlight egen och andras erfarenhet:* Stockholm.

Joffe, A.H. (1998) Alcohol and social complexity in ancient Western Asia. *Current Anthropology*, 19(3): 297–322.

Jones, K.L. and Smith, D.W. (1973) Recognition of foetal alcohol syndrome in early infancy. *Lancet* 2, 999–1001.

Kaiser, O. (1974) *Isaiah 13–39 A commentary.* Translated form the German by R.A. Wilson. London: SCM Press.

Keller, M. (1970) The Great Jewish Drink Mystery. *British Journal of Addiction*, vol. 64: 287–296.

Kendler, K.S. (2001) Twin studies of psychiatric illness. *Archives of General Psychiatry*, 58, 1005–1014.

Kraus, H.J. (1989) *Psalms 60–150. A commentary.* Minneapolis: Augsburg Fortreses Press.

Kutz, I. (2005) Revisiting the Lot of the first incestuous family: the biblical origins of shifting the blame on to female members. *British Medical Journal*, 331: 1507–1508.

Leichty, E. (1970) *The Omen series Summar Izbu,* J.J. Augustin, New York: Locust Valley.

Lemoine, P., Harousseau, H., Borteyon and Menuet, J.C. (1968) Les enfants de parents alcoholiques: Anomality observes a propos de 127 cas (children of alcoholic parents: anomalies observed in 127 cases) *Question Medicine*, 21: 476–482.

Lilhall, H., Aberg, H., Selinus, I and Hedsterand, H. (1987) Alcohol intemperance and sudden death. *British Medical Journal*, 294: 1456–1458.

Lutz H. (1992) *Viticulture and Brewing in the Ancient Orient.* Heinrichs, New York.

McCarter, P.K. (1980) *I Samuel: A new translation with notes and commentaries.* Anchor Bible Series, New York: Doubleday and Co.

McKane, W. (1970) *Proverbs. A new approach.* London: SCM

Mckeating, H., (1971) *Amos Hosea and Micah,* p. 32. The Cambridge Bible Commentary. Cambridge: Cambridge University Press.

Mackenzie, J.L. (1968) *Second Isaiah. Anchor Bible Series Introduction translation and notes.* pp. 124–128. New York: Doubleday.

Mahawold, M.W. and Schenk, C.W. (2005) The parasomnias, pp. 929–930 In *The Principles and Practice of Sleep Medicine*, Eds. Krugger, M.H., Roth, T. and Dement, W.C. 4th edition. Elsevier Saunders.

Mazzoni, S. (1998) pp. 313–314, in Joffe, A.H. (1998) Alcohol and social complexity in Ancient Western Asia. *Current Anthropology*, 19(3): 217–239.

Milgrom, J. (2007) *The Rechabites* in *Encyclopaedia Judaica. 2nd edition*. Eds. Skolnik, F. and Berenbaum, M., vol. 15, pp. 46–47: Macmillan in Association with Keter Publishing House: Jerusalem

Moore, C.A. (1996) *Tobit. A New Translation with introduction and commentary*. The Anchor Bible, Doubleday. New York.

Neusner, J. (1985) *Genesis Rabbah. The Judaic commentary of the book of Genesis, vol II*.

Oswalt, J.N. (1986) *The book of Isaiah* Chapters 40–66. Grand Rapids. Michigan: William P. Eerdmans Publishing Company.

Pernanan K (1991) *Alcohol in Human Violence*. New York: Guildford Press.

Pritchard, J.B. (1955) *Ancient near Eastern texts relating to the Old Testament*. pp. 37–44, 2nd edition. Princeton N.J.: Princeton University Press.

Raglan, F.R.S. (1936) *The Hero, a study in tradition, myth and drama*. London: Methuen.

Regier, D.A., Farmer, M.E., Rae, D.S. *et al* (1990) Co-morbidity of mental disorders with alcohol and other drug abuse: Results from the Epidemiological catchment area study. *Journal of American Medical Associations*, 264, 2511–2518.

Renkama, J. (1998) *Lamentations. Historical Commentary on the Old Testament*, pp. 56–59 Pleuven: Peters Press.

Sayal, K. (2007) *Alcohol consumption in pregnancy as a risk factor for later mental health problems*. Evidence based Mental Health, 10: 98–100.

Schneider, M., Norman, R., Parry, C. *et al* (2007) Estimating the burden of disease attributable to alcohol use in South Africa in 2000. *South African Medical Journal*, 97: 664–672.

Shaw, J., Hunt, I.M., Flynn, S. *et al* (2006) The role of alcohol and drugs in homicides in England and Wales. *National confidential enquiry into suicide and homicide by people with mental illness*. Centre for Suicide Prevention, University of Manchester.

Skehan, P.W. and Di Lella (1987) *The Wisdom of Ben Sira. A new translation with notes*. Anchor Bible series, New York: Doubleday.

Strauss, M.A., Gettes, R.J. and Steinmetz, S.K. (1980) *Behind closed doors: violence in the American family*. New York, Doubleday.

Streissguth, A.P., Barn, H.M. and Sampson, P.D. *et al* (1990) Moderate pre-natal alcohol exposure: effect on child's IQ and learning problems at 7½ years. *Alcohol Clinical Experimental Research*, 14, 662–9.

Sournia, J.C. (1990) *A History of Alcoholism*. Translated by N. Hindley and G. Stanton. Oxford: Blackwell.

Stuart, D. (1987) *Hosea and Jonah*, pp. 116–117. Dallas, Texas: Word Books.

Toy, C.H. (1899) *A critical and exegetical commentary on the Book of Proverbs*. Edinburgh: T & T. Clarke.

US Department of Justice (1981) Bureau of Statistics: Survey of Inmates of State Correctional Facilities 1979 (ICSPR 7856). 2nd ICSPR Ed. Ann Arbor *International Consortium for Social and Political Research.*

Vonghia, L., Leggio, L., Ferruli, A. *et al* (2008) Acute alcohol intoxicatiion. *European Journal of Internal Medicine*. 19: 561–567.

Von Rad (1972) *Genesis. The Old Testament Library*. Translated from the German by J.H. Marks. SCM. Press: London.

Waltke, B.K. (2005) *The Book of Proverbs*, p.126. Grand Rapids: William B. Eerdmans Publishing Company.

Warner, R.H. and Rosett, H.L. (1975) The effect of drinking on offspring: An historical survey of the American and British literature. *Journal of Studies on Alcohol* 36 (ii), 1395–1420.

Weiser, A. (1959) *The Psalms. A commentary*. p542, translated from the German by Herbert Hartwell. London: SCM Press.

Westerman, C. (1994) *Genesis 1–11*. Translated from German by S.J. Scullion Minneapolis. Fortress Press.

Wilson, W. (1994) The society of alcoholics anonymous. *American Journal of Psychiatry*, 141, 259–262.

Wolfgang, M.E. and Strohm, R.B. (1956) The relationship between alcohol and criminal homicide. *Quarterly Journal of Studies in Alcohol*, 17, 411–425.

World Health Organisation (1992) *The ICD-10 classification of mental and behavioural disorders*. Geneva: World Health Organisation.

World Health Organisation (2007) *Second Report of the Expert Committee on Problems Related to Alcohol Consumption*. Geneva: World Health Organisation.

Yadin, Y. (1955) Some aspects of the strategy of Ahab and David (I Kings 20 and 2 Sam II). *Biblia* 36, pp. 332–351.

# Chapter 15

# Sirach: an observer of humanity and psychiatry

The book we now know as Sirach is also known as 'The Wisdom of Ben Sira', and 'The Wisdom of Jesus, son of Sirach', as well as by its Greek name, Ecclesiasticus, which means 'church book'. The literature on the contents of Sirach is not large and the account below draws largely on the work of Skehan and Di Lella (1987) and to a lesser extent on Coggins (1998). Ben Sira comes to us through its Greek translation made by his grandson, who tells us in the prologue why his grandfather wrote the book.

> So my grandfather Jesus, who had devoted himself especially to the reading of the Law and the Prophets and the other books of our ancestors, and had acquired considerable proficiency in them, was himself also led to write something pertaining to instruction and wisdom, so that by becoming familiar also with his book those who love learning might make even greater progress in living according to the law.

It seems as if Sirach worked as a scribe in Jerusalem and may have run some sort of school for the teaching of wisdom because there are frequent didactic passages which begin 'My son...'.

In the prologue his grandson gives some information about the dating of the work. He tells us how he came to Egypt in the 38th year of the reign of Euergetes, a monarch thought to be Ptolemy VII. He ruled conjointly with his brother between 170 and 117 BCE, which implies a date of 132 BC for the 38th year of his reign. Scholars suggest a publication of the Greek translation soon after the death of Euergetes in 117 BCE. Ben Sira is thought to have lived between 250 and 175 BCE and the original Hebrew version was thought to have been published somewhere between 190 and 180 BCE.

What is clear is that the work was written in the Hellenistic era of Judaism. During this period of Greek hegemony there was little political freedom, but the Jews of Egypt and Palestine were able to imbibe the best of Greek culture, philosophy, ideas and medicine. Indeed, the book of Sirach includes a whole chapter praising physicians and recommending consulting them in case of sickness but also to praying to God for healing.

Sirach is all in favour of the profession of a full-time scribe and writes 'The wisdom of the scribe depends on the opportunity of leisure. Thus: only one who has little business can become wise' ($38^{24}$).

He goes on to describe how the farmer can only think of ploughing the field, the smiths think about their ironwork and are deafened by the noise of the hammer, and the potter worries about his pots, and, as such, none of these can gain the understanding needed to sit on the council or be a judge. The passage seems biographical and identifies Sirach as a scribe; he seems to be an early advocate of the profession of full-time academic.

For a long time only the Greek version of Sirach was available and there was even doubt as to whether an original Hebrew version existed. However, in May 1896 two English tourists, Mrs A. S. Lewis and Mrs M. D. Dixon, took some manuscripts which they had purchased in the market in Cairo in Egypt to Solomon Schechter, then a reader in Talmudic studies in Cambridge. Schechter immediately identified them as leaves from a Hebrew version of Sirach. He was so excited by the discovery that within five months and with the help of Charles Taylor, the then Master of St John's College, he had raised sufficient funds for a journey to Egypt.

He found the source of these documents was the storeroom (*Genizah*) of the Ben Ezra Synagogue in Fustat in southern Cairo, where the Jews lived. The local community had little interest in the treasures in their storeroom and Schechter persuaded them to part with the collection. They were subsequently donated to the University of Cambridge as the Schechter-Taylor collection. There are more than 100,000 manuscripts and fragments and they continue to be studied to this day.

Further discoveries and other fragments of ancient Hebrew versions of Sirach were made among the Dead Sea scrolls, in caves 2 (2Q18) and 11 (11QPs$^a$). Finally, in 1965 Yigael Yadin discovered a section of Sirach in a Hebrew scroll found at Masada and this is thought to be the oldest Hebrew version. There are now thought to be two original Hebrew versions, two ancient Greek versions of Sirach, versions in the Syriac Peshitta, Coptic, Arabic, Latin and Ethiopic and many other languages. A substantial portion of the literature on Sirach describes the interactions between the various translations, and how one translation borrows from another.

The book is not canonical in the Jewish tradition but it was included in the LXX translation, indicating that at least early on it was held in high regard by the Alexandrian Jewish community. There are also 82 references to it in the Talmud but the Babylonian Talmud has an extensive discussion of why it is forbidden to read the book of Ben Sira (BT sanhedrin 100b). The early Church considered the work to be canonical, but with the Protestant split the work became included in the Apocrypha and for Protestants it is non-canonical, although for Catholics it remained part of their canon and is considered to be a Deutero-canonical work. In the Catholic Bible it is placed together with the other wisdom literature.

It is a lengthy work, comprising 51 chapters, and covers a very wide range of topics, including God, religion, sin and free will, character problems, poverty, human relationships, doctors, health and social justice, to mention but a few. Written in biblical verse mainly in couplets similar to the style of Proverbs, the order of its contents seems to be jumbled.

The psychiatry within it is unintended, but appears as the writer wanders almost randomly through a wide range of human problems, some of which we now place under the rubric of mental disorder. Sirach had no idea that such a concept existed. The conditions he mentions, and some only very briefly, are not properly described but are recognisable, as listed below:

- depression, grief and morbid grief
- anxiety

- the elderly
- alcoholism: temperance in wine drinking
- possible psychotic phenomena (the fantasist)
- personality disorder and bad character traits
- learning difficulties.

The remainder of this chapter concerns the verses which mention these conditions.

## Depression, grief and morbid grief

Sirach is an observer of humanity and its afflictions. His account of depression is objective but as a consequence it is somewhat insipid in comparison with the timeless verses of the Bible's great depressive sufferers, namely Job and Jeremiah.

One passage, $30^{21\text{-}24}$, describes a condition he calls sorrow:

$30^{21}$   Do not give yourself over to sorrow.
           Do not distress yourself deliberately.
$^{22}$      A joyful heart is life itself
           and rejoicing lengthens one's life span.
$^{23}$      Indulge yourself and take comfort,
           and remove sorrow far from you,
           for sorrow has destroyed many,
           and no advantage ever comes from it.

The Greek word for sorrow is *lupe*, and Sirach believes it is within a person's power to *choose* to be happy and to *choose* not to be depressed. All he needs to do is be a little more self-indulgent. He says happiness lengthens life span but perhaps the actual observation is that sorrow (depression?) shortens one's life span and this is certainly true. Thus a recent Danish study (Laursen *et al.*, 2016) found a reduction of life span of 14 years for men with depression and 10 years for women. Sirach also observes how destructive sorrow can be.

### Mourning and pathological grief

Another passage ($38^{18\text{-}21}$) describes mourning and its rituals. Sirach observes that sometimes grieving can be excessive and result in illness. He says grief can kill and take the sufferer over and can sap a person's strength. Grief in bereavement that has overstayed its welcome is now known as morbid grief.

$38^{18}$   For grief may result in death,
           and a sorrowful heart saps one's strength.
$^{19}$      When a person is taken away, sorrow is over;
           but the life of the poor weighs down the heart.
$^{20}$      Do not give your heart to grief;
           drive it away, and remember your own end.
$^{21}$      Do not forget there is no coming back;
           you do the dead no good, and you injure yourself.

*Psychiatric aspects*

Bereavement and mourning are generally held to be normal phenomena and not mental disorders; present-day thinking is that they should *not* be treated, as it is better for the long-term psychological health of the individual to work through their grief. However, sometimes, as Sirach points out, the grief can become excessive and actually harm the individual concerned.

Verse 18 begins *For grief may result in death*. There are now numerous studies on the increased mortality rate following a bereavement. Allegra *et al.* (2015) found a twofold increased mortality rate among the first-degree relatives of a large cohort of American retirees aged 50–70 years who had died between 2010 and 2012. *And a sorrowful heart saps one's strength*. The opinion expressed here is that it is the sorrow is the cause of the weakness and low energy. Today, we think of depression as an illness which incorporates the symptoms of low mood and low energy.

Verse 19 is very insightful, predicting much modern sociological research into depression and its association with poverty. Thus 19a describes how a bereavement reaction is usually short-lived: *When a person is taken away, sorrow is over*. This is contrasted with the longer-term misery of the poor, which Sirach seems to contrast to the brevity of a bereavement reaction: ¹⁹ᵇ *but the life of the poor weighs down the heart*. Sirach observes that the poor seem to be miserable but the misery seems to spare the rich. The links between poverty, social class and depression have been extensively researched in recent years. A meta-analysis of many such studies found that rates of depression were doubled among people of low socio-economic status and that this link was particularly strong among those with persistent depression (Lorant *et al.*, 2003). Elsewhere, Sirach, like the other prophets, shows some compassion to the poor, but he is the only one to pick up on the association between depression and poverty.

Finally, in verses 20 and 21 there are admonitions against grieving too much: ²⁰ᵃ *Do not give your heart to grief, drive it away,* ²¹ᵇ *you injure yourself.* Sirach would have seen people who were grieving and became quite ill and depressed in the process. Normal mourning lasts no more than three months but if it is prolonged or excessive, the term morbid grief is applied. If those grieving are depressed for more than 6–12 months then medical help is usually advised.

## Anxiety

Sirach writes quite a long stanza about anxiety, and this appears in a set of poems about the joys and miseries of life in general. There is no suggestion that anxiety is a specific affliction, but rather it is the lot of mankind in general. However, within this poem he describes many key symptoms of an anxiety disorder.

| 40¹ | Hard work was created for everyone, and a heavy yoke is laid on the children | The lot of mankind |
| | of Adam, from the day they come forth from their mother's womb until the day | From birth to death |
| | they return to the mother of all the living | ? a feminine deity |

| | | |
|---|---|---|
| 2 | Perplexities and fear of heart are theirs, and anxious thought of the day of their death. | Anxiety part of the human condition; fears of death |
| ... | | |
| 5 | There is anger and envy and trouble and unrest and fear of death and fury and strife. | Negative emotions Fears of death ? agitation |
| | And when one rests upon his bed, his sleep at night confuses his mind. | Insomnia |
| 6 | He gets little or no rest; he struggles in his sleep as he did by day. He is troubled by visions of his mind Like one who has escaped from the battlefield. | non restful quality of sleep anxiety at night ? Nightmares |
| 7 | At the moment he reaches safety he wakes up, astonished that his fears were groundless. | In an anxiety state fear without reason |

The fathers of the Church attributed the heavy yoke of human anxiety and other afflictions in this poem to original sin, with which all human beings are conceived. Sirach describes the hard lot of mankind but within this stanza he includes: perplexity, fears of death, agitation, insomnia, sleep of a non-restful quality, fears without good reason, and nightmares – all of which are frequent symptoms of anxiety disorders. Possibly because the anxiety disorders are very common (some surveys suggest up to 15% of the population) Sirach surmises these symptoms are universal afflictions.

In another passage he points out the link between anxiety and poor sleep:

31[1] Wakefulness over wealth wastes away one's flesh,
    and anxiety about it drives away sleep.
2    Wakeful anxiety prevents slumber
    and a severe illness carries off sleep.

A recent study of generalised anxiety disorder (GAD), which is the commonest type of anxiety disorder, found that rates of insomnia were raised and for the most severe cases of GAD there was a ninefold increased rate for insomnia over population base rates (Naverrette *et al.*, 2016), confirming these very early observations by Sirach.

Towards the end of his book Sirach recalls Israel's history and in ch. 48 he writes about the battle between Hezekiah and the fearsome Sennacherib, the Assyrian king. Sennacharib had invaded the country in the 8th century BCE and threatened Jerusalem but did not actually take it. Sirach writes about how terrified the people of Jerusalem were:

48[18] In his days Sennacherib invaded the country;
    he sent his commander and departed;
    he shook his fist against Zion,
    and made great boasts in his arrogance.
19   Then their hearts were shaken and their hands trembled,
    and they were in anguish, like women in labour.

The Assyrians had destroyed the Northern Kingdom in around 722 BCE and threatened Jerusalem soon after that. Sirach lived in 200 BCE, which was some 500 years after these events. Thus the terror of the people he wrote about would have all been in his imagination. Panic is also mentioned twice in Proverbs, and in both instances the verses capture its abrupt onset:

1²⁶     I will mock you when panic strikes you,
         when panic strikes like a storm.

3²⁵     Do not be afraid of sudden panic
         or the storm that strikes the wicked.

Apart from these few references, in Sirach and the Book of Proverbs, the Israelite Wisdom literature is not greatly preoccupied with the problems of depression and anxiety. Perhaps the sages who wrote about wisdom were a more sturdy group of individuals, who tended to assume the moral high ground over those less fortunate, observant of the debilitating effects of depression and panic in others, though they themselves were not sufferers.

## The elderly

For the most part, Sirach is well disposed to the elderly and says they should be venerated, perhaps because he himself is getting old:

8⁶     Do not disdain one who is old,
         for some of us are growing old.

Elsewhere he praises the wisdom of the elderly and adds:

3¹²     My child help your father in his old age,
         and do not grieve as long as he lives;
¹³     *even if his mind fails him*, be patient with him;
         because you have all your faculties do not despise him.

This is the only reference to senility (possibly even senile dementia) in the Bible. There are, however, much older and better accounts of old age in the Egyptian literature. Thus Ptahhotep, a vizier under King Isesi of the Egyptian fifth dynasty of the Middle Kingdom (*circa* 2414–2375 BC), wrote eloquently about the problems of old age long before the Hebrew Bible. The mayor of the city, the vizier Ptahhotep, said:

     My Sovereign Lord:
     Old age has arrived, infirmity has descended.
4,3    Misery has drawn nigh, and weakness increases.
     One must take a nap like a child every day,
     The eyes are blurred, the ears are deaf,
     And vigour wanes because of weariness.
     The mouth is silent and no longer speaks;
5,1    *The memory is gone and cannot recall [even] yesterday.*
     The bones ache through frailty,
     Pleasure has become repulsive, and all taste has vanished.

What old age does to men is totally despicable.
The nose becomes plugged and cannot breathe;
Even standing and sitting are a bother.
(After Simpson, 2003, p. 130)

Note that the ancients thought that all mental functions took place in the heart. The heart (mind) *recalls not the past* is perhaps the very earliest reference to senile memory failure.

## Alcoholism: temperance in wine drinking

Sirach writes about alcohol in a balanced way: it has both good and bad effects. There was a Hellenistic institution known as the symposion (which is the basis of the English word symposium), and during these gatherings a banquet was served, at which large quantities of wine were consumed and participants enjoyed a lively political and philosophical debate. Chapter 31 contains a poem about the virtues of drinking and eating in moderation, as well as the blessings and abuses of wine and the general etiquette at such banquets:

31$^{25}$    Do not try to prove your strength by wine-drinking
          for wine has destroyed many.
$^{26}$      As the furnace tests the work of the smith,
          so wine tests hearts when the insolent quarrel.
$^{27}$      Wine is very life to human beings
          if taken in moderation.
          What is life to one who is without wine?
          It has been created to make people happy.
$^{28}$      Wine drunk at the proper time and in moderation
          is rejoicing of heart and gladness of soul.
$^{29}$      Wine drunk to excess leads to bitterness of spirit,
          to quarrels and to stumbling.
$^{30}$      Drunkenness increases the anger of the fool to his own hurt,        fool = *lesim*
          reducing his strength and adding wounds.
$^{31}$      Do not reprove your neighbour at a banquet of wine,
          and do not despise him in his merrymaking;
          speak no reproach to him,
          and do not distress him by making demands of him.

The advice Sirach offers to drink only in moderation might well have come from our Department of Health, or its ancient Israelite equivalent. Sirach acknowledges that drinking wine is one of the essential pleasures of living, but it must be in moderation. However, his observations are more sophisticated than such a simple truism. Thus, in two verses he shows a degree of psychiatric insight into the problems of alcoholic anger. He writes: $^{26b}$ *So wine tests hearts when the insolent quarrel*, which means that wine may cause most damage among people who are either habitually angry or already angry. In another verse he writes $^{30}$*Drunkenness increases the anger of a fool to his own hurt*. The word for 'fool' here is *lesim* (see page 392), which corresponds to an arrogant, narcissistic psychopath, and he says when this character drinks he reduces his own strength and add to his wounds. While one cannot be certain, this seems to refer to injuries sustained during drunken brawls, a serious problem among the youth of today and seemingly also a problem in ancient Israel. The effect of alcohol on the irritable personality disorder is also noted in Proverbs (see page 434).

Finally, Sirach makes a comment on alcoholism in women, which he finds to be shameful:

26[8]    A drunken wife arouses great anger.
        She cannot hide her shame.

To the modern feminist reader, Sirach here (and in many other passages) is quite anti-women. Some scholars have suggested that he was a misogynist, although the consensus seems to be that his writings on women reflect no more than the views of the patriarchal society in which he lived, which accorded women a lowly status. His condemnation of alcohol is very much more muted than that of the warnings of the great prophets Isaiah and Jeremiah, but only Amos specifically condemns female drinking.

## Possible psychotic phenomena: the fantasist

Chapter 34 includes eight verses which advises that dreams may not be true and cautions against the folly of pursuing dreams because they are false. He mentions two character types, 'the fools' and 'the senseless people' who are prone to pursue dreams to their cost and sometimes even their lives.

34[1]   The senseless have vain and false hopes,
        and dreams give wings to fools.                    ?acting on dreams
2       As one who catches at a shadow and
        pursues the wind,
        so is anyone who believes in dreams.
3       What is seen in dreams is but a reflection,
        the likeness of a face looking at itself.
4       From an unclean thing what can be clean?
        And from something false what can be true?
5       Divinations and omens and dreams are
        unreal, and like a woman in labour,               ?delirious state in labour
        the mind has fantasies.                            ?false beliefs ?delusions
6       Unless they are sent by intervention from
        the Most High, pay no attention to them           Messages from God
7       For dreams have deceived many,
        and those who put their hope in them              Acting on dreams can
        have perished.                                    be dangerous

In the first verse he unequivocally explains his position on the futility of dreams (Skehan and Di Lella, p. 408). It is only 'the senseless' and 'fools' who take dreams seriously. Belief in the significance of dreams was widespread in antiquity, including in the OT, but Sirach says that trusting in dreams, is the mark of the fool and is the same as catching at shadows or pursuing the wind; equally, 'dreams give wings to fools', which suggests they are acting on them. The 'mind has fantasies' is more characteristic of delusions than simple nocturnal dreaming. It is interesting that Sirach lumps dreams, divination and paying attention to omens together, all of which are 'unreal'. Divination and paying attention to omens are also specifically forbidden in Leviticus ($19^{26}$) and Deuteronomy($18^{10}$).

Are the fools and senseless people he refers to here the mentally ill? Are the messages they respond to, which deliver an 'unreal' guidance, suffering from what today we might call auditory hallucinations?

## Personality disorder and bad character traits

Personality disorder, mainly of an antisocial type, is well described in Proverbs (see Chapter 10), and Sirach certainly drew from Proverbs, but most of his verses describing bad characters and their malevolent traits seem to be original and are not identical to the verses in Proverbs.

He maintains the position adopted in the earlier Wisdom literature that wisdom and fools (possibly people with personality disorders, as discussed in Chapter 10) are opposites. No single stanza describes personality disorder but isolated passages here and there, when placed together, make it clear that he is writing about characters who damage themselves and damage others – the core of the modern concept of a personality disorder.

$3^{26}$  A stubborn mind will fare badly at the end,
and whoever loves danger will perish in it.
$^{27}$  A stubborn mind will be burdened by troubles,
and the sinner add sins to sins.
$^{28}$  When calamity befalls the proud, there is no healing,
for an evil plant has taken root in him.

Several features of personality disorder are mentioned here. Stubbornness and risk-taking are both self-damaging and the risk-taker will eventually die. The calamity which befalls the proud may be a reference to capital punishment. Self-damaging behaviour is a core feature of Schneider's definition of personality disorder. The sinner who keeps on sinning and never seems to learn, however much he is punished, is nowadays termed a recidivist. It has been shown that 80% of recidivists in prison have antisocial personality disorders.

The original Hebrew for stubborn is *leb kabed*, which means heavy heart. Sirach's grandson translated this into the Greek as *Kardia sclera*, literally meaning hard-hearted (Skehan and Di Lella, 1987).

Chapter 6 of Sirach has three verses that describe a character Sirach calls 'the undisciplined' (Heb. *Hasar leb* – see Chapter 10, page 403). The undisciplined cannot inhabit the same space as wisdom and so rejects her:

$6^{20}$  She [wisdom] seems very harsh to the undisciplined;
fools cannot remain with her
$^{21}$  She will be like a heavy stone to test them
and they will not delay in casting her aside.   It is fools who reject wisdom
$^{22}$  For wisdom is like her name;
she is not readily perceived by many.   Not many notice her

These verses tell us that the character called 'the undisciplined' have rejected wisdom and cannot coexist with her. Sirach is suggesting that this character has a choice of whether to live with wisdom, by which he means to follow the law and discipline of society. The undisciplined cannot do so and so it is they who reject wisdom. From a more modern perspective, we now know that the antisocial character is the primary phenomenon and such character types exist in all societies. The passage is written assuming that the undisciplined has a choice about accepting or rejecting wisdom but we know that such characters will inevitably follow their downhill path. Wisdom is a man-made construct of the ancient world to explain the behaviours of the antisocial character by the use of opposites. If there were no antisocial characters then the central concept of wisdom would be superfluous.

Chapter 8 of Sirach provides a guide on how best to deal with angry or otherwise bad characters, suggesting they may have been a problem for the citizenry of ancient Israel.

$8^3$  Do not argue with the loud of mouth,
        and do not heap wood on their fire.
4       Do not make fun of one who is ill-bred,
        or your ancestors may be insulted....

...
10      Do not kindle the coals of sinners,
        or you may be burned in their flaming fire.
11      Do not let the insolent bring you to your feet,
        or they may lie in ambush against your words.

Sirach warns us that there are some very dangerous people out there who must be handled with caution. He uses the same word, *les*, in the same sense as it is used in Proverbs, to describe these unsavoury types.

In ch. 27 of Sirach a contrast is made between the conversations of the wise and the fool. The fool is changeable, stupid, swears and is abusive; sometimes his quarrels end in violence, perhaps suggestive of an antisocial personality type:

$27^{11}$  The conversation of the godly is always wise
          but the fool changes like the moon.      Changeable, unreliable
12        Among stupid people limit your time
          but among thoughtful people linger on.
13        The talk of fools is offensive,
          and their laughter wantonly sinful.
14        The cursing and swearing make one's      Swearing
          hair stand on end,                        Shocking
          and their quarrels make others stop       Screaming, quarrelsome
          their ears.
15        The strife of the proud leads to bloodshed  Violence linked to pride
          and their abuse is grievous to hear.        Abusiveness

The picture of the 'fool' here is of a verbally abusive, unreliable, antisocial type who swears a great deal and his anger sometimes leads to violence. It is better to avoid this type and instead to spend time with those who are thoughtful and wise.

At various points in the book he mentions particular other adverse personality traits, as in Proverbs (see Chapter 10, pages 404–417).

*Irrational anger*
1²²     Unjust anger cannot be justified
        For anger tips the scale to one's ruin.

Note here that it is the person's own anger that leads to his ruin.

*Arrogance and pride*
10⁷     Arrogance is hateful to the Lord,
        and to mortals.

10¹⁸    Pride was not created for human beings or violent anger
        for those born of women.

Note here pride is joined with violent anger, both traits commonly found in antisocial personality disorders.

*Deceitfulness*
19²⁶    There is the villain bowed down in mourning
        but inwardly he is full of deceit,
        he hides his face and pretends not to hear
        but when no one notices he takes advantage of you.

Skehan and Di Lella (1974) write: 'Even when the wicked are bowed down in grief one should be on guard because they are hypocrites and full of inner deceit'. In support of this they cite Shakespeare's *Macbeth*: 'To show unfelt sorrow is an office which the false man does easy'.

Sirach devotes many verses to condemning bad characters and bad character traits. Taken on their own these verses seem to have little meaning, but when combined together it is clear that he is writing about fairly severe antisocial personality types and antisocial traits as we understand them today. In Greek versions the word *aphron* is used for 'fools', which also sometimes means 'rogues'. In Hebrew versions some of the words he uses to describe such character types, such as *les* and *hasar leb*, are derived from Proverbs, which was probably written 400–500 BCE, whereas Sirach wrote around 200 BCE. This suggests probably from at least as early as 400 BC the ancient Israelites had both a concept and a set of words to convey the main features of an antisocial personality disorder as understood today.

## Learning difficulties: Sirach does not like stupid people

Sirach also makes occasional and disparaging references to people who are stupid. Sirach was obviously a highly intelligent person and it is not clear whether he is talking about those who are not quite as clever as him, or about the bottom 2% of the population who we now class as having learning difficulties. This group are so severely handicapped that they cannot look after themselves and are therefore vulnerable. Of course, in his day no such distinction would have been made between 'the stupid' and the 'extremely stupid'. He writes:

21$^{12}$ One who is not clever cannot be taught.
21$^{14}$ The mind of a fool is like a broken jar, it can hold no knowledge.
21$^{19}$ To a senseless person education is like fetters on his feet
and like manacles on his right hand.

Sirach's contempt for 'the stupid' continues in 22$^{9-15}$. The meaning of these verses is obvious and needs little comment:

22$^9$ Whoever teaches the fool is like one who glues pot sherds together,
or rouses a sleeper from deep slumber.
$^{10}$ Whoever tells a story to a fool tells it to a drowsy man;
and at the end he will say 'What is it?'
$^{11}$ Weep for the dead, for he has left the light behind;
and weep for the fool, for he has left intelligence behind.
Weep less bitterly for the dead, for he is at rest;
but the life of the fool is worse than death.
$^{12}$ Mourning for the dead lasts seven days,
but for the foolish or the ungodly it lasts all the days of their lives.
$^{13}$ Do not talk much with a senseless person
or visit an unintelligent person.
Stay clear of him, or you may have trouble,
and be spattered when he shakes himself off.
Avoid him and you will find rest,
and you will never be wearied by his lack of sense.
$^{14}$ What is heavier than lead?
And what is its name except 'fool'?
$^{15}$ Sand, salt, and a piece of iron
are easier to bear than a stupid person.

In this stanza Sirach elaborates on his experience of trying to teach the unintelligent; they cannot learn, it is like talking to someone who is half asleep and they don't even understand the story at the end of it. Their lack of intelligence is worse than the loss of life because it will last their whole lifetime, whereas one gets over a physical death after a brief period of mourning.

Sirach has no compassion for those born stupid; they are a heavy burden – heavier than lead. He is probably referring to those who are at the lower end of the IQ spectrum. The Book of Proverbs describes three characters who have both a personality disorder as well as learning difficulties, the *pethi* (simpleton), the *hasar leb* (empty heart) and the *ba-ar* (animal-like brute) and these are described in Chapter 10 (pages 403–404). The Book of Job also mentions those with low intelligence.

11$^{12}$ But a stupid person will get understanding
when a wild ass is born human.

The writer of this verse suggests that the condition is permanent and the subject unteachable, and this is a moral failing. By the Middle Ages, many communities looked after their weaker brethren, and they were commonly known as 'village idiots', but it was only during the 19th century that those with learning difficulties were recognised as a vulnerable special group. The rather harsh line given by Job and Sirach was probably a measure of its time.

## The modern picture of learning difficulties

Today we sequester off those with an IQ below 70 and apply the term 'learning difficulties' to these individuals. They are indeed a heavy burden. They are a vulnerable group who cannot look after themselves and need support and protection from society. Obviously this distinction was not made in ancient Israel but some of those whom Job and Sirach call stupid might have been in this group.

The essence of modern definitions of learning difficulties is that not only is there low intelligence (IQ below 70) but there is also significant functional impairment over a wide range of normal activities. DSM-5 has substituted for 'learning difficulties' the term 'intellectual disability', and its definition has three arms: first, a defect in intellect, reasoning, learning and learning from experience which can be confirmed by clinical assessment and standardised IQ testing; secondly, a defect in adaptive functioning that results in a failure to meet standards for personal independence, social responsibility and practical abilities across multiple environments such as home, school and work and community; and thirdly, onset during the developmental period.

DSM-5 has four grades of severity: mild, moderate, severe and profound. The degree of functional impairment for each of these sub-groups is laid out in the text. Males are more common among the milder cases (M:F ratio = 1.6) but less so among the severe cases (M:F ratio = 1.2). Epidemiological surveys of the population such as the Isle of Wight study (Rutter *et al.*, 1970) showed that an IQ below 70 was present in 2.5% of the population (i.e. 1 in 40) but severe learning difficulty (IQ below 50) was present in only 3 per 1,000 of the population, although more modern estimates place the overall prevalence at around 1%. People with learning difficulties have elevated rates of behavioural disorders, which, for want of a better term, are now called 'challenging behaviours'. Perhaps it was these issues that brought them to the attention of the authorities and so to the scribes of Proverbs, who seemed to accept them. Sirach seems to dislike them and is certainly contemptuous of the unintelligent.

## Concluding remarks

Sirach's teaching is said to be traditional and conservative and to reflect the teaching of Israel's sacred scriptures with its central theme being the fear of God. This meant the ability to adhere to the law and the Jewish ethical values of the day. However, in his book he meanders through his society making a vast number of observations on all manner of human behaviours, so it is no surprise that he should occasionally mention the mentally ill. They puzzle him and he cannot fit them into his Deuteronomistic 'good/bad' dichotomous picture of human nature pervasive at the time. His descriptions of anxiety, depression, alcoholism, senility, possible psychosis, personality disorders and learning difficulties are not particularly good or detailed, even by the standards of the ancient world. He also makes several very astute observations on the links between mortality, depression and poverty which modern studies have confirmed to be true. For some, such as those with learning difficulties, he has nothing but contempt, but for the elderly who are frail there is compassion. Depressives should be more self-indulgent, and he assumes they have a choice about the matter.

From the perspective of psychiatry and its history his contribution is important because he includes several different psychiatric disorders all within in a single book. He lived and wrote in Jerusalem around 2,300 years ago, a small Middle Eastern city with a population of around 40,000 at that time. Using more modern terminology, this was his 'psychiatric catchment area', which, by today's standards, is quite small, and he documents the presence of most of what we today sometimes call 'the common mental disorders'. Sirach had no concept of mental disorder and of course there are no detailed figures on their prevalence at his time, but his book suggests that perhaps the common mental disorders of yesteryear were similar to those which afflict our communities today. We shall never know how true this is, but Sirach's unique collection opens this question up.

## References

Allegra, J., Ezeamama, A., Simpson, C. and Miles, T. (2015) Population-level impact of loss on survivor mortality risk. *Quality of Life Research*, 24(12): 2959–2961. Published online 2015 June 17.

Babylonian Talmud (1938) *Tractate Sanhedrin*. Translated by I. Epstein. London: Soncino Press.

Coggins, R. J. (1998) *Sirach*. Sheffield: Sheffield Academic Press.

Laursen, T. M., Musliner, K. L., et al. (2016) Mortality and life expectancy in persons with severe unipolar depression. *Journal of Affective Disorders*, Mar 15;193:203–7.

Lorant, V., Deliege, D. D., Eaton, W., et al (2003) Socio-economic realities in depression: a meta-analysis. *American Journal of Epidemiology* 157, 98–112.

Navarrete, F., Pérez Páramo, M., et al. (2016) Prevalence of insomnia and associated factors in outpatients with generalized anxiety disorder treated in psychiatric clinics. *Behavior Sleep Medicine* 11: 1–11.

Rutter, M., Tizard, J. and Whitmore, K. (1970) *Education, Health and Behaviour*. London: Longman.

Simpson, W. K. (2003) The maxims of Ptahhotep. In *The Literature of Ancient Egypt*, p. 130. New Haven, CT: Yale University Press.

Skehan, P. W. and Di Lella, A. A. (1987) *The Anchor Bible: The Wisdom of Ben Sira: A New Translation with Notes, Introduction and Commentary* New York: Doubleday.

# Chapter 16

# Concluding remarks

The Bible is, among other things, a major textbook of psychiatry. As shown in Appendix I (page 578), around 160 psychiatric or psychiatry-related topics are mentioned in 588 verses within the Old Testament and Apocrypha. In the detail of its case histories and the magic of its verse, it far outstrips any of the other literature at the time, as well as that for many centuries thereafter.

Obviously, there is no book or chapter in the Bible entitled 'Mental health issues in ancient Israel' because such problems were poorly understood at the time, and indeed until psychiatry itself emerged as a medical speciality some 2,000 years later. But there was at least a partial understanding by the Old Testament writers that this group of topics formed an integral part of the human condition.

Most of the psychiatric disorders facing the community psychiatrist today gain a mention in the Old Testament and some of the more common problems such as depression and anxiety are extensively and repeatedly covered. Mental health issues appear under a multiplicity of different guises, dotted here and there throughout the text, but the distribution of the psychiatric entries is far from random and this distribution tells us something about the reasons why mental health issues were either included or censored out of the text. Thus there is almost no psychiatry in the Torah, the core religious text of the Jewish peoples. This section contains all the early myths and legends of the great Israelite patriarchs as well as a great deal of Jewish law. These stories are very old and even though many terrible tragedies befall its heroes, none of them seems to show any emotion or a personal reaction or depression when they experience personal catastrophe. This may explain why this section of the Bible is devoid of any psychiatry. Possibly any admission to emotional or mental disturbance might have been perceived as signs of weakness and therefore not fitting for a great hero or religious icon such as a patriarch. Emotional displays are also conspicuous by their absence from the earlier Egyptian and Mesopotamian literature from which the Hebrew literature tradition was ultimately derived. An alternative explanation might be that the later unknown biblical editors, labelled J, E, and P, who crafted the final edition of the Torah, censored out any emotional material, perhaps thinking that such signs of weakness were undermining to the authority of the text and its numerous laws, and also seemingly of no relevance to the religion which appertained to the whole cult rather than being about any individual.

The next part of the Old Testament, Judges through to the end of Kings 2, is very different. This section is known as the 'Deuteronomic History' and was edited by the Deuteronomist(s), an unknown person(s) thought to have great compassion. Apart from King David, there are no great Jewish heroes in this section; many of the characters here are quite deeply flawed, and some, like King Saul, are even frankly insane. When bad things happen, human emotion together with much psychiatric disorder flows freely from the text. Thus Hannah and Sarah are both infertile and married to men who have children by other women. Hannah (in 1 Samuel) is upset and possibly also jealous of her husband's second wife and her children, and breaks down into depression because of her own infertility; she even develops hysterical aphonia. By contrast, within the Torah, Sarah is 90 years old and childless but the text tells us nothing about how she felt about her infertility. Both Abraham and David have to take part in the potential killing of their sons. Abraham follows blindly the instructions he receives from God but fortunately does not have to carry out the act. We have no idea about how he felt about this strange command and his obedience to the instruction is taken as a sign of his great faith. By contrast, David is threatened by Absalom and eventually has to kill him. He is torn apart by the conflict and wails inconsolably, and becomes depressed and almost has a complete nervous breakdown. The Deuteronomist who edited the stories of Hannah and David seems to have retained all the emotional conflict present in these earlier tales but even here the psychiatric content is only an incidental to the main historical religious narrative.

In the next section of the Bible, the books of the great literary prophets, the psychiatry becomes much more explicit. Job, Jeremiah and Ezekiel all provide splendid accounts of their suffering, which include major psychiatric disorder. Sometimes the suffering is on behalf of their nation, Israel, as a result of its fecklessness and unfaithfulness to God, but sometimes it is purely personal and is easily recognised as psychiatric disorder. None of these prophets had any insight that they might be suffering from what today we perceive as a psychiatric condition. Job provides a truly masterful account of his depression. He ascribes his depression to God but feels very angry about it, and questions why he should have been picked out in this way. Jeremiah also blames his terrors and panics on God and perhaps this is one reason why the Old Testament God is seen as terrifying. Ezekiel provides an excellent autobiographical account of what is most probably schizo-affective disorder. The psalms of lament are also autobiographical accounts of suffering, but are much briefer and for the most part were written on behalf of the whole community of Israel but sometimes these are also deeply personal prayers.

Sometimes psychiatric disorder causes suffering to others, often through criminal behaviours, and such clients end up in the courts, with no insight into the damage that they have caused. The so-called 'fools' of Proverbs correspond closely to what modern psychiatry terms 'personality disorder', most commonly antisocial personality disorder. It is even possible to match individual DSM-5 criteria with the verses of Proverbs to show that most of the defects found in the modern 'antisocial personality disorder' can be found in the Book of Proverbs. Their dangerousness were a cause for alarm but in a society lacking a police force or prisons such types could be dealt with only by capital punishment. However, it seems that the scribes who wrote Proverbs may have worked in the courts and they became very familiar with these characters, and provide a very detailed yet poetic descriptions of the ancient Israelite psychopath.

After reaching a climax in the prophetic literature, the psychiatry in the Old Testament gradually fades away. The early post-exilic books of Chronicles, Ezra and Nehemiah have very little psychiatry. There is almost no reference to psychiatric disturbance in the remaining prophetic books, with the exception of Hosea. Most of these works were thought to have been written during the Persian period, which starts in and around 537 BCE and ends the conquest of Palestine by Alexander the Great in 323 BCE. This heralded the Greek influence and the beginnings of Hellenic Judaism. The Greeks had a different and more secular understanding of depression and insanity, and tended to include it either in their early medical literature or in their dramas, but not within their religious literature. The suffering soul of religion and the suffering psyche of the mentally ill, which were one and the same during 9th to 5th centuries BCE in Israel, seem thereafter to have followed the Greek separated pattern, and so psychiatry features much less prominently in the later Hebrew religious writing, such as the Apocrypha, the New Testament, the Koran or in any of the later religious literature.

Thus, a unique and almost magical period from the 9th to the 5th century BCE appeared in the religious literature of the small ancient Middle Eastern state of Israel, where issues of mental health entered freely into the religious writings of the Hebrew people. They neither knew that they were writing about mental disorder nor recognised it, yet they must have instinctively felt it was important enough to include this material in their account of the human condition.

Many will criticise this work for diverse reasons and I will do my best to provide a brief answer to these criticisms. First, for the deeply religious, the whole biblical text is the word of God, and so how could a late and man-made medical construction such as psychiatry find its way into these sacred texts? The short answer is that God delivers his messages through his prophets, and, like the rest of us, they are also flawed human beings, and so also subject to a variety of mental health issues, which they eloquently write about. Others will regard the Bible is far too sacred to be the focus of a mundane psychiatric excursus; but then how can one justify the many other secular books on the Bible, on its literature, history, geography, philosophy and so on, with this book being no more than another work in this genre. For some, particularly Orthodox Jews, the only commentary on the sacred texts that is permissible is that of the Talmud or some of the better-known rabbis of the Middle Ages. A more serious objection relates to the difference in cultures between modern Western civilisation and ancient Israel. It is like comparing chalk and cheese. However, the vast bulk of the comparison is between the actual symptoms recorded in the Bible and the symptoms reported by psychiatric patients today – and these do not seem to have changed very much over time. In a few instances where I have applied a modern scheme such as DSM-5, the biblical descriptions seem to stand up well to the comparison with modern diagnostic criteria. Although some would argue that the use of DSM is culturally inappropriate, a moment's reflection will reveal there is no alternative scheme with which to compare the mental illnesses of the ancient world to the modern era, or at least none that would be accepted by the vast majority of the profession today.

For some historians, psychiatry is much more than a simple description of mental disorder. It is the attempt to understand and heal mental illness. This discipline starts in the late 18th century. On the other hand, mental disorder has probably always existed and troubled humanity; this earlier phase has been termed proto-psychiatry. It comprises increasingly more sophisticated accounts of mental disorder until the realisation in the late 18th century that this was truly a branch of medicine. In this context the biblical contribution provides good and very early descriptions, and becomes the first collection of mental disorders to be housed within a single volume – hence the first textbook of psychiatry.

A further objection is that the diagnoses given here may be frankly wrong. In the Introduction it was explained that these were literary diagnoses rather than proper clinical diagnoses. Readers will need to make their own diagnoses, but the text relates how a psychiatrist nowadays might diagnose a patient presenting with the symptoms reported in the Bible. These accounts are similar to the descriptions that might be found in a novel; and in the Appendix I have placed a question mark in front of a few verses where the psychiatry appears to be uncertain.

Does this large body of part-formed psychiatry enhance or detract from the overall value of the text? Those who perceive it as detracting must presumably also perceive those who suffer from mental disorder as somehow inferior, or hold them in some sort of contempt, a position which had been widely maintained for many centuries but is now viewed as stigmatising and no longer acceptable. The inclusion of a large mass of detail on the common mental disorders must surely greatly enrich the biblical description of the human condition. It also helps to reach out to many readers, and provides a special empathy for those who are in the midst of suffering from some personal torment. My original concern that the sufferers I saw in the psychiatric clinic each week had been excluded from the sacred texts was not borne out. Mental health issues seem to have been matters of great concern to the many unknown biblical writers, even though they had no idea that some of what they were writing about was what we now call 'psychiatry'.

# Index of mental symptoms and related psychiatric phenomena in the Old Testament

A total of 160 psychiatric or psychiatry-related topics are mentioned in 588 separate verses.

Abandonment fears/separation anxiety: Psalms $88^2$, $38^{21}$; Pr $7^{19}$
Abrupt onset of mental disorder: Jer $4^{20}$, $15^8$, $6^{26}$
Acute stress reaction: 2 Sam $12^{16-18}$
Aggression (impulsive)/hot temper: Pr $14^{17}$, $14^{20}$, $17^{12}$, $20^3$, $29^{11}$, $23^{24}$, $29^{22}$, Sir $1^{22}$
Agitation: Job $3^{26}$, $20^1$, Jer $45^3$; Lam $1^3$, $3^7$; Tob $10^7$, Sir $4^5$
Alienation (feelings of): Psalms: $31^{11}$, $38^{11}$, $69^8$, $31^{11}$ $88^8$, $88^{18}$; Job $19^{15}$
Alcohol abuse: Pr 4 $^{17}$, $23^{29-35}$; Jer $13^{12-14}$, $25^{27}$; Sir $31^{26}$
Alcohol dependence: Pr 23 $^{35}$; Isa $5^{11}$; Amos $4^1$; Sir $21^{30}$
Alcohol withdrawal: I Sam $25^{36-38}$
Alcohol-induced altered perception: Isa $28^7$
Alcohol-induced behavioural changes: Lam $4^{21}$; Jer $25^{15}$; Psalms $78^{65}$
Alcohol-induced depressive mood changes: I Sam $25^{37}$; Pr $23^{29}$; Jer $1^5$, $25^{16}$, $25^{19}$; Ezek $21^{33}$; Joel $1^5$; Sir $31^{29}$
Alcohol-induced nausea: Hos $7^5$
Alcohol-induced personality changes: Pr $4^{17}$, $20^1$; Psalms $75^8$; Sir $31^{30}$
Alcohol-induced psychotic disorder: Isa $19^{13-14}$
Alcohol-induced sleep disorder: ?Gen $9^{12-14}$; Ps $78^{65}$
Alcohol-related ataxia: Isa $19^{14}$, $28^7$, $29^9$, $51^{17}$; Jer $25^{15}$; Psalms $60^3$
Alcoholic anger: Psalms $60^3$; Isa $5^{13}$, $51^{17}$; Jer $25^{16}$; Ezek $23^{32-34}$; Hab $2^{16}$; Lam $4^1$; Sir $31^{26}$, $31^{30}$
Alcoholic delirium: Pr $23^{33}$
Alcoholic deep sleep/coma: Gen $9^4$; Isa $29^9$
Alcoholic fatal coma: Jer $51^{39}$, $51^{57}$
Alcoholic fatal withdrawal: I Sam $25^{38}$
Alcoholic fever: Hos $7^5$; Lam $4^{21}$
Alcoholic impaired judgement: Hos $4^{11}$; Isa $19^{14}$; Tob $14^{15}$
Alcoholic incest: Gen $19^{30-36}$
Alcoholic memory impairment: ?Hos $4^{11}$; Isa $28^7$; 3 Macc $5^{28}$
Alcoholic violence: Jer $13^{14}$; Sir $31^{30}$
Alcoholic vomiting: Isa $19^{14}$, $28^8$; Jer $15^{27}$
Altered sense of taste: Job $6^6$
Anhedonia: Job $7^{2-3}$, $9^{25}$, $39^{25}$; Jer $8^{18}$, $16^8$, $25^{10}$, $48^{33}$; Lam $1^4$, $3^{48}$; Psalms ?$88^{10}$, ?$6^5$
Antisocial personality disorder: Pr $6^{12-19}$, 16 $^{27-30}$

Anxiety: Jer $4^{31}$, $6^{28}$; Lam $3^{14}$, $3^{65}$; Psalms, $22^1$, $38^8$, $42^{11}$, $88^3$; I Sam $2^{16}$, $28^{20}$; Pr $12^{25}$; Sir $40^7$

Anxiety and depression combined: Tob $10^{4-5}$

Aphonia (hysterical conversion): I Sam $2^{13}$

Appetite loss (due to depression): Job 6 $^7$, $33^{20}$; Jer $16^8$; I Sam $2^7$, $28^{24}$

Auditory and visual hallucinations together: Ezek $1^{28}$, $10^{13}$, $11^{1-4}$, $37^3$

Auditory experiences ?hallucinations: Job 4 $^{12}$; Ezek $1^{25}$, $1^{28}$, $2^{1-3}$, $8^{18}$–$9^1$

Auditory hallucinations commenting on thoughts or behaviours: ?Ezek $18^{18}$

Boredom (proneness to): Pr $7^{11}$

Callousness: Pr 10 $^{23}$, 19 $^{26}$

Cardiac anxiety: Job $37^1$; I Sam $28^5$

Catastrophising: Jer $4^6$, $4^{13}$, $4^{20}$, $41^3$, $42^9$, $51^{31-32}$

Catatonic stupor: Ezek $3^{24-26}$, $4^{5-6}$

Change of character: I Sam $10^6$, $10^9$, $10^{11}$

Chest pain: Jer $4^{19}$, $23^9$

Choking sensation: Job $3^{26}$, $29^{21}$, $30^{18}$

Claustrophobia: Jer $48^{42-44}$; Lam $3^7$

Command hallucination: Ezek $2^8$–$3^3$, $5^{1-2}$, $8^{7-8}$, $9^1$, $12^5$

Command hallucinations to kill: Ezek $8^{5-6}$

Compulsion to scream out: Jer $4^{19}$, $20^{8-9}$

Confusional state: 3 Macc $5^{27}$

Coprophagia: Ezek $4^{12}$

Delusional transportation: Ezek $3^{14}$, $8^3$, $11^1$, $11^{24}$

Depersonalisation: Jer $23^9$

Depersonalisation/derealisation: ?Jer $23^9$

Depressed facies: Psalms $6^8$, $31^9$, $38^{10}$, $69^3$, $88^9$

Depressed mood: Job $30^{28}$; Jer $13^6$, $20^{18}$, $49^{24}$; Lam $1^{12}$; Psalms $31^{10}$, $42^{11}$; I Sam $28^{15}$; Isa $38^{13-14}$

Depression, psychotic type: Job $19^{16-20}$; I Sam $28^{15-25}$

Depression (objective accounts): Pr 15 $^{13}$, 17 $^{22}$, $18^{14}$; Sir $30^{21-23}$

Depression (relief from): Job $8^{20-21}$, $11^{15-19}$; Jer $31^3$; Psalms $126^{5-6}$; I Sam $16^6$

Depression and poverty: Sir $38^{19}$

Depression in the morning: Job $7^{17-18}$, $24^{16-17}$; ?Psalm $88^{13}$

Depressive anergy/low energy/weakness: Job $6^{12}$, $17^7$; Jer $14^2$, $31^{12}$, $45^3$, $49^{24}$, $51^{30}$; Lam $1^6$, $1^{14}$, $3^7$; Psalms $6^2$, $77^3$, $31^{10}$; Isa $38^{14}$; Eccles $1^8$

Depressive distortion of time perception: Psalms $6^3$, $13^{1-2}$

Depressive façade: Job $9^{27}$

Depressive insomnia: Job $7^{3-4}$, $30^{17}$; Jer $9^1$, $14^{17}$; Lam $1^2$; Psalms $6^7$, $22^2$, $42^3$, $77^2$, $77^4$, $88^1$; Isa $38^{12}$, $38^{15}$

Depressive irritability: I Sam $2^6$

Depressive low self-image: Job $25^6$, $30^{19}$; Lam $1^{11}$, $3^{4-5}$; Psalms $22^6$; Tob $3^{11}$

Depressive mourning: Job $30^{31}$; Jer $4^{28}$, $6^{26}$, $8^{21}$; Lam $2^5$; Psalms $38^6$, $42^9$, $69^{11}$

Depressive mutism: Job $2^{13}$, $32^{15}$, $29^9$; Lam $1^{13}$, $2^{11}$; Psalms $38^{13}$, $38^{14}$, $77^4$

Depressive pain: Jer $45^3$; Psalms $13^2$, $38^7$, $69^{29}$

Depressive self-loathing: Job $7^8$, $10^1$, $9^{21}$

Depressive thoughts: Job, $7^3$, $7^{31}$, $30^{26}$; Lam $1^4$; Isa $38^{15}$; Psalms $22^7$, $88^{14}$

Depressive weeping: Job $2^{12}$, $16^6$, $16^{20}$; Jer $9^1$, $15^{19}$, $31^9$, $48^{31-32}$; Lam $1^{16}$, $3^{48}$, $2^{11}$; Psalms $6^7$, $69^3$, $42^3$; Isa $38^{13}$

Disgust: Jer 6$^8$
Distress (general): Psalms 13$^1$, 22$^1$, 31$^9$, 42$^5$, 69$^{17}$, 88$^2$
Dramatic behaviours (in borderline personality disorder): Pr 7$^{11}$, 9$^{13}$
Dry mouth: Psalms 22$^{15}$, 69$^3$
Ecstasy/prophetic frenzy ?hypomania: 1 Sam 10$^8$, 10$^{10}$, 10$^{12}$, 19$^{20}$, 19$^{21}$, 19$^{24}$
Epileptic fit: ? 3 Macc 2$^{22}$, ?6$^{18}$
Facial pallor: Jer 30$^6$; Nahum 2$^{10}$; Joel 2$^5$
Faint: Job 23$^{16}$; Jer 4$^{31}$; Lam 1$^{13}$; 1 Sam 28$^{20}$
Feigned insanity: 1 Sam 21$^{13-15}$
Gastric anxiety: Job 30$^{27}$; Lam 1$^{20}$, 2$^{11}$
Guilt: Job 10$^{14}$, 11$^6$, 13$^{23}$, 22$^5$; Lam 1$^{20}$; Psalms 6$^1$, ?38$^1$, 38$^4$, 38$^{18}$, 69$^5$, 69$^{27}$, 88$^7$;
 Tob 3$^{10}$
Guilty ideas of reference: Job 22$^5$
Gullibility: Pr 7$^8$, 14$^{15}$
Gustatory hallucinations: Psalms 69$^{21}$
Heightened perception: Ezek 1$^4$, 1$^{13}$, 1$^{16}$, 1$^{27}$, 10$^9$
Hissing: Jer 18$^{19}$, 19$^8$, 25$^{10}$, 27$^9$, 40$^{17}$, 50$^{13}$
Homicidal thoughts: 1 Sam 20$^{31}$
Hopelessness: Job 17$^1$, 19$^{19}$, 17$^{13-16}$, 15$^{32}$; Psalms 13$^2$, 38$^8$, 69$^{20}$, 88$^3$; Isa 38$^{18}$
Hyperacusis: Job 15 $^{21}$; Jer 4$^{19}$, 4$^{21}$, 6$^{23}$; Wisd of Sol 17$^4$
Hypersomnia; 3 Macc 5$^{12}$, 5$^{16}$
Hyperventilating, gasping: Jer 4$^{31}$
Hypnogogic phenomena: Job 4$^{12-16}$, 27$^{19}$
Ideas of reference: Lam 3$^{14}$; Psalms 69$^{12}$
Identity disturbance (in borderline personality disorder): Pr 5$^6$
Impulsivity: Pr 6$^{18}$, 14$^{29}$, 19$^2$
Increased awareness of heartbeat: Job 37$^1$; Jer 4$^{19}$
Insomnia due to anxiety: Eccl 2$^{23}$; Tob 10$^7$; Sir 30$^1$, 40$^5$
Irresponsibility (financial): Pr 21$^{27}$
Loudness of voices: Ezek 8$^{18}$, 9$^1$, 9$^5$
Low IQ/learning difficulties: Pr 1$^{22}$, 30$^2$; Psalms 73$^{22}$; Sir 21$^{12}$, 21$^{19}$, 22$^{10}$,
 22$^{9-15}$, 27$^{12}$
Mania: 3 Macc 4$^{16}$
Manipulativeness: Pr 7$^{10}$, 16$^{28}$, 18$^8$, 22$^{26}$
Memory impairment (pre-senile): 3 Macc 5$^{28}$
Mixed affective episode: 1 Sam 18$^{10}$
Mood switches: Job 11$^{15}$, 8$^{20-21}$; Psalms 6$^7$, 13$^5$, 126$^{5-6}$; Pr 14$^{13}$; Lam 5$^{15}$
Mood switches (cyclothymic): Psalms 30$^5$, 30$^{11}$
Morbid grief: Ezek 24$^{10-24}$, 24$^{27}$; Sir 38$^{18-21}$
Morbid jealousy syndrome: Ezek 16, 23; Num 5$^{14}$, 5$^{30}$
Mutism (psychotic): Ezek 3$^{15}$, 24$^{27}$, 33$^{22}$
Nihilistic delusions: ?Psalms 22$^{14}$
Non-verbal auditory hallucinations: Ezek 1$^{24}$, 2$^{13}$, 10$^5$
Olfactory hallucinations: Job 19$^{17}$; Ezek 8$^{11}$
Panic: Job 13$^{11}$, 13$^{21}$, 23$^{15-16}$, 27$^{20}$, 30$^{15}$; Jer 14$^{19}$, 17$^{17}$, 20$^3$, 20$^{10}$, 30$^5$, 49$^{24}$, 51$^{32}$;
 Lam 3$^{47}$; Psalms 6$^2$, 6$^3$, 55$^{4-6}$, 48$^{4-7}$, 88$^{15}$, 88$^{16}$; Pr 1$^{20-27}$; Wisd of Sol 17$^9$,
 17$^{10}$, 17$^{15}$, 17$^9$
Panic (nocturnal): Job 4$^{14}$, 27$^{19-20}$, 33$^{15-16}$

Panoramic visual hallucinations: Ezek 1, 8, 37

Paralysis through fear: Jer $6^{24}$

Paranoid auditory experiences: Job $19^{18}$; Lam $3^{62}$; Psalms $44^{17}$, $31^{13}$

Paranoid conspiracy beliefs: Psalms $38^{12}$, $38^{19}$, $31^{13}$, $56^6$, $69^4$; 1 Sam $22^8$, $22^{13}$

Paranoid delusions of being poisoned: Job $6^4$; Psalms $69^{21}$

Paranoid feelings of being attacked or persecuted: Job $10^{16}$, $16^{13}$, $19^{11-13}$, $30^{21}$

Paranoid feelings of being watched: Job $7^{20}$; Jer $20^{10}$, $34^9$; Psalms $69^{12}$

Paranoid plots to kill: Psalms $31^{13}$

Paranoid symptoms: Psalms $22^{13}$, $22^{16}$, $38^{12}$

Passivity phenomena: Ezek $2^2$, $2^{12}$, $2^{14}$, $8^3$, $11^1$, $11^{24}$, $22^1$

Phobia of animals: Wisd of Sol $11^{19}$, $17^9$

Phobia of heights: Eccles $12^5$

Phobia of public speaking: Jer $1^{17-18}$

Phobia of snakes: Wisd of Sol $17^9$

Psychic pain: Job $6^{10}$, $14^{23}$, $15^{20}$, $16^6$

Psychotherapy for depression: Tobit $8^{20}$; Job $16^{1-3}$; Pr $12^{25}$

Recidivism (probable): Pr $13^1$, $17^{10}$, $27^{12}$

Recklessness: Pr $14^{16}$

Restlessness: Pr $7^{11-12}$

Self-mutilation: Lev $19^{27}$; Deut $14^1$; Ezek $23^{34}$; Jer $10^6$, $41^9$, $47^3$, $48^{37}$, $49^3$; 1 Kings $41^9$

Self-mutilation (group): Jer $41^{4-7}$; 1 Kings $18^{28}$

Senility ?senile dementia: Sir $3^{13}$

Sensory inattention/poor concentration: Psalms $38^{14}$

Separation anxiety *see* Abandonment fears

Shallow affect: Pr $5^3$

Shame: Lam $1^6$; Psalms $13^1$, $30^5$, $30^{11}$

Social phobia: Jer $1^{17}$

Stripping (psychotic): 1 Sam $19^{24}$

Suicidal thoughts: Gen $27^{46}$; 1 Kings $19^4$; Job $3^{20}$; Tobit $3^3$, $3^{13}$, $3^{15}$

Suicide: Judges $9^{54}$; 1 Sam $31^{34}$

Suicide by disembowelling: 2 Macc $14^{44}$

Suicide by hanging: 2 Sam $17^{23}$

Suicide by poisoning: 2 Macc $9^{12}$

Suicide by self-immolation: 4 Macc $12^{19}$, $17^1$

Suicide planning: Tobit $3^{10}$

Tachycardia: Jer $4^{19}$

Teetotal movements: Jer $35^{5-10}$

Thirst: Job $22^7$

Thought broadcasting: ?Ezek $11^5$

Thought insertion: ?Ezek $38^{10}$

Thoughts of death: Job $3^1$, $3^{11}$, $3^{16-17}$, $3^{12}$, $3^{20}$, $17^1$, $30^{23}$; Jer $4^{19}$, $4^{29}$, $4^{31}$, $6^{23}$, $6^{25}$; Lam $1^{20}$; Psalms $13^3$, $88^4$; Tob $10^4$; Isa $38^{12-13}$; Pr $5^5$; Sir $40^2$

Thrill-seeking behaviours: Pr $26^{20}$

Tingling ?paraesthesia: Jer $19^3$

Tremor/shaking: Job $14^{14}$; Jer $4^{24}$, $23^9$, $51^{29}$, $5^{22}$; Psalms $69^{23}$; Sir $40^{19}$

Visual experience ?visual hallucination: Job $4^{15}$; Ezek $8^{10}$

Weight loss: Job $33^{21}$

# Different versions of the Bible and important Jewish religious literature referred to in this volume

## Haftarah

The *Haftarah* (Conclusion, Pl. *Haftarot*) is the reading from the Prophets which follows the reading of the Torah in synagogue religious services.

## Hehkalot

Palaces mystical literature; relates to mystical ascents to heavenly palaces.

## Jerusalem Bible

In 1943 Pope Pius XII issued an encyclical letter, *Divino afflante Spiritu*, which encouraged Roman Catholics to translate the Scriptures directly from the Hebrew and Greek texts, rather than from Jerome's Latin Vulgate. As a result, Dominicans and other scholars at the École Biblique in Jerusalem translated the scriptures into French as La Bible de Jérusalem in 1956. This French translation served as the impetus for an English translation in 1966, the Jerusalem Bible. Many translators were involved in this effort, perhaps its most famous contributor being J. R. R. Tolkien (his primary contribution was the translation of Jonah). The Jerusalem Bible was the first widely accepted Roman Catholic English translation of the Bible.

## Kabbalah

Jewish mystical literature. Historically, Kabbalah emerged, after earlier forms of Jewish mysticism, in 12th–13th-century southern France and Spain with its key text, the Zohar, and later becoming re-interpreted in the Jewish mystical renaissance of 16th-century Ottoman Palestine in Safed by Rabbi Isaac Luria (1534–1572), who is considered the father of contemporary Kabbalah.

## King James Bible (1611), the Authorised Version

In 1604 King James I of England convened the Hampton Court Conference, which proposed a new English translation in response to the criticisms of earlier translations by the Puritan faction of the Church of England. The task of translation was undertaken by 47 scholars, and the translation was mainly from Hebrew, Aramaic and Greek sources rather than from the Vulgate. It was appointed for use in all English churches, and so became known as the

'Authorised Version', although it did not displace most other versions until the mid-18th century; in the 19th and 20th century it became biggest-selling book of all time. The original printing was by Robert Barker, the King's Printer, in 1611 as a complete folio Bible. It was sold loose leaf for 10 shillings, or bound for 12 shillings. Its literary quality is unique and beautiful although the language is now thought to be somewhat archaic, but sometimes verses from the King James Bible convey the psychiatry better than the NRSV and they are quoted in a few places in this book instead of the NRSV.

## Masoretic text (MT)

The Hebrew word *masorah* is taken from the Book of Ezekiel ($20^{37}$) and originally meant 'leg cuffs'. The fixation of the text was considered to be similar in the nature of leg cuffs when first written. The Masoretes were schools of scribes and Torah scholars working between the 7th and 11th centuries CE, based primarily in Tiberias, Jerusalem and in Babylonia. Ben Asher was probably a Kairite Jew and came from a long line of distinguished Masoretes, and Ben Asher's codex became recognised as the standard text of the Bible. It is now known as the Aleppo Codex (a codex is a hand-written book as opposed to a scroll) and is written on parchment and bound in leather. The Leningrad Codex (1008 CE) was derived from the Aleppo Codex with little change. The Leningrad Codex is in extraordinarily pristine condition after a millennium of storage. In 1924, after the Russian Revolution, Petrograd (formerly Saint Petersburg) was renamed Leningrad, and, because the codex was used as the basic text for the Biblia Hebraica after 1937, it became internationally known as the Codex Leningradiensis. All later versions of the Masoretic text are taken from this manuscript.

## Midrash

Midrash ('explanation') is the rabbinic interpretation of either legal or biblical material sometimes expressed as parables.

## Midrash

Mishnah ('learning') – see Talmud entry below.

## Moffat translation

James Moffat was a Scottish academic theologian. Trained in Glasgow he became a minister for the United Free Church in Dundonald and Professor of New Testament at St Andrews. He re-translated the New Testament in 1913 and the Old Testament in 1924 and the combined version was published in 1941.

## New English Bible (1970)

C. H. Dodd, the chairman of the translation committee, summarised the translation of the New English Bible as 'free, it may be, rather than literal, but a faithful translation nevertheless'. As a result, the New English Bible is necessarily more paraphrastic at times, in order to render the thoughts of the original author into modern English. It is not widely used but is occasionally referenced in this work.

## New International Version (NIV)

This is an English-language translation of the Protestant Bible. Biblica (formerly the International Bible Society) is the worldwide publisher and copyright holder, and licenses commercial rights to Zondervan in the USA and to Hodder & Stoughton in the UK. Originally published in 1978, the NIV was updated in 1984 and 2011, and has become one of the most popular and best-selling modern translations. A 2014 survey of Americans who read the Bible found that 19% use it. A particularly useful version is the Interlinear version of John Kohlenberger III (1987), which gives a word-for-word Hebrew-into-English translation.

## New Revised Standard Version (NRSV)

This is an English-language translation of the Bible released in 1989. It is an updated revision of the Revised Standard Version, which was itself an update of the American Standard Version. The New Revised Standard Version was translated by the Division of Christian Education (now Bible Translation and Utilization) of the National Council of Churches in America. The group included scholars representing Orthodox, Catholic and Protestant Christian groups as well as Jewish representation in the group responsible for the Hebrew Scriptures or Old Testament. The mandate given to the committee was summarised in a dictum: 'As literal as possible, as free as necessary.' The RSV retained the archaic second-person familiar forms (thou/thee/thy/thine of the King James Bible) when God is addressed, but the NRSV eliminated all such archaisms. The NRSV is the version commonly preferred by biblical scholars and is used in the most influential publications in the field, and has been the main source of biblical quotations used in this work.

## Pirkei Avot (Sayings of the Fathers)

This is a collection of ethical sayings of the rabbis. It is a tractate (volume or chapter) of the Mishnah in *Seder Nezikin* (Damages).

## Qumran literature (the Dead Sea Scrolls)

Qumran is a village about 1.5 km from the north-west shore of the Dead Sea and probably inhabited by a religious community of the Essene sect. It lies adjacent to the Qumran caves, in which a set of scrolls and scroll fragments were found. These were over 2000 years old and are by far the oldest extant Hebrew literature. More than 900 scroll fragments were found and they are labelled according to the cave number they were found in.

# Peshitta

The traditional Bible of Syriac-speaking Christians (who speak several different dialects of Aramaic). Many scholars believe that its Old Testament version is based on rabbinic Targumim, although influenced by the Septuagint, and the translation of the Peshitta is usually thought to be between I and 300 CE.

# Septuagint

The Septuagint (from the Latin *septuaginta*, 'seventy', abbreviated as the LXX) is a Greek translation of the Hebrew Bible. It was primarily for the benefit of the Egyptian Jewish diaspora in Alexandria. The story is told of how King Ptolemy once gathered 72 Jewish elders and placed them in 72 separate chambers, without revealing to them why they were summoned. He entered each one's room and said: 'Write for me the *Torah* of *Moshe*, your teacher'. God put it in the heart of each one to translate identically as all the others did (Babylonian Talmud Tractate Megillah 9a–9c).

The Pentateuch section was translated in the 3rd century BCE, the remainder of the OT by 132 BCE. Because it is much older than the official Jewish Masoretic text, differences between the two versions have been used to try to elucidate exactly what the original Hebrew version might have been. Actual manuscripts are known as codices and numerous old LXX manuscripts exist. In this volume $LXX_A$ *Codex Alexandrinus* (circa 450 CE in the British Museum) and $LXX_B$ (*codex vaticanus* 350 CE in the Vatican) are mentioned but otherwise the abbreviation LXX is used throughout.

# Talmud

The Talmud ('teaching') is a vast compilation of commentaries on the Bible by the rabbis and forms the basis of rabbinical Judaism. After the destruction of the second temple by the Romans in 70 CE there was no religious site to discuss either the oral law or the written law. There was a need to codify and record Jewish religious and civil law and practice and this resulted in a set of texts known as the Mishnah (learning) and was completed by 200 CE mainly by Rabbi Judah the Prince (Judah Ha Nasi). From around 300 CE to 800 CE rabbinical commentary and discussion on each portion of the Mishnah was added on and this is known as the Gemara and the combination of both is known as the Talmud.

# Torah

The Torah is the core religious text of Judaism. It consists of the five Books of Moses: Genesis, Exodus, Leviticus, Numbers and Deuteronomy. It is also known as the Chumash and Pentateuch. It is handwritten in Hebrew on a scroll (*sefer torah*) and kept in the ark in the synagogue and a portion is read on the service on every Sabbath as well as on all the festivals. Used generically, *Torah* sometimes refers to all of Jewish law.

# Index